AIRCRAFT FINANCING

AIRCRAFT FINANCING

Third Edition

Edited by

**Andrew Littlejohns
and Stephen McGairl**

Euromoney Books

Published by
Euromoney Publications PLC
Nestor House, Playhouse Yard
London EC4V 5EX

Transferred to digital print 2003

Typeset by Euromoney Books

Printed and bound in Great Britain by
Marston Lindsay Ross International Ltd,
Oxfordshire

Contents

Appendices

Acknowledgements

The texts included in Appendices C and D are reproduced with the kind permission of Unidroit.

The text of Appendix E is reproduced from the Official Journal of the European Communities No. L 69/19 (11.3.97)

Foreword

Lasting profitability – the undiscovered country

Airlines need profits – as do the players within any industry. Is there anything different or interesting about their recent behaviour which suggests that they are *acting* on that assumption?

When it comes to our industry, the behaviour of some airlines – determined to chase growth at the expense of yields is, unfortunately, *not* different. And then of course, the recent economic crisis in Asia/Pacific is making things a great deal more interesting, in the Chinese sense, for our Members in the region.

But, whether our difficulties are entirely internal – self-inflicted if you like – or external, still too many of the world's airlines are unable to maintain a consistently profitable path. Unfortunately for our industry lasting profitability thus far *remains* 'the undiscovered country'.

Let me explain, by looking at recent history. In 1996, on their international scheduled services, the IATA airlines made US$3 billion net – a mere 2 per cent of revenue, against 4 per cent in 1995, the year of record net profit. The reason is instructive. The overall load factor rose by 0.2 points to 63.6 per cent. The passenger load factor was the highest ever, at 69.4 per cent. Net interest charges fell.

All that was good news *but* the average overall yield declined more than *six times* as fast as unit cost, 2.5 per cent against 0.4 per cent. Thus the all-important break-even load factor, after interest charges, increased by nearly a full percentage point. Airlines were, once again, succumbing to the urge to slash fares, instead of taking advantage of growth in order to increase profit.

1996 was a time of marginal cost decreases, against a background of historically high load factors, and already declining yields. There was really no need to *buy* traffic.

The time to significantly reduce yields is when large reductions in unit cost are being achieved and load factors are relatively low, such as the situation that prevailed at the start of the jet era back in the early 1960s. I concluded that, for our industry's marketing experts, price cutting continued to have a mesmerising effect. So we faced, once again, an internal self-inflicted deterioration of our profitability, resulting from our traditional lack of self-discipline.

In 1997 the airlines were closer to getting it right. Traffic, once more, increased faster than capacity – but airlines did not allow average yields to decline much faster than unit cost. They made US$5 billion net, on revenues of US$146 billion.

The success story consisted of an increase in capacity which was certainly not excessive, continued success in more than filling that capacity, another fall in average prices to the customer which was almost matched by a further reduction in the average cost of providing the capacity. The consumer was thus better-off and the industry was, in absolute terms in 1997, over 66 per cent more profitable than in the preceding year.

Are we now on the road to lasting profitability? Before you can count me among the true believers, I would mention two caveats:

- The load factor increase was a great tribute to revenue and load management techniques – but how high can load factors go, in the context of scheduled services, without incurring excessive overbooking? We seem to be breaking new ground, discovering fresh territory, every year!

- Break-even load factors also increased again, by slightly less. Which means that the dog-fight between yield and unit cost is now taking place at altitudes last seen at the beginning of the 1990s and the onset of the last recession. This cannot go on indefinitely!

What do we now think is in store for 1998? The answer is – a sharply reduced net result, of US$3.9 billion, or 2.6 per cent of net revenue. This reflects the effects of the Asian crisis and in particular, a likely inability of carriers to reduce their capacity growth in the face of softening growth of demand.

Our concerns are now focused on Asia.

The suddenness and severity of the Asian economic crisis has taken most of us by surprise – and, more particularly, the Asian carriers, which were somewhat ill-prepared for such a turn of events. It is now probable that:

- There will be a reduction in the 1997–2001 average annual growth rates for Asia/Pacific from 7.7 per cent to 4.4 per cent for passengers and 9 per cent to 6.5 per cent for cargo traffic – this would imply some 30 million fewer passengers in the year 2001 than our previous forecast, that is from 207 million down to 176 million in 2001.
- The impact of the crisis on airline profits will be in excess of US$1.5 billion in 1998 for the carriers surveyed – with an estimated US$2 billion for all carriers operating to, from and within the region.

Dealing with a crisis such as this one is always painful, but it should be regarded as an opportunity to reposition one's company and to emerge as a stronger competitor.

A crisis is an opportunity to learn, to give one courage to act, and particularly to:

- Eliminate inefficiencies in all areas of the company which were being masked by growth – for example, to critically challenge the size of overheads.
- Review the composition of the fleet – and accelerate retirement/disposition of older/less efficient aircraft.
- Take precautions to avoid over-capacity, and thus preserve yields in key markets, while maintaining market share, this being perhaps the most delicate balancing act.
- Shift capacity to take advantage of routes/markets where depressed currency is significantly increasing 'value-for-money' opportunities for leisure travel.
- Accelerate cooperation among carriers, primarily on intra-regional routes, to maintain good frequencies, avoid excess capacity and undue yield degradation. There could be more code-sharing and joint services on regional routes.
- Actively review functions which could be profitably outsourced – and where cost/effectiveness and productivity can be improved but without prejudicing safety or customer services.

IATA has played its part in all this – by getting governments to reduce taxes, request a moratorium on user charges, open up more airspace, and fostering the growth of tourism.

It is very important, particularly in Asia, not to replace endless optimism with endless anxiety. Neither view was, or is, appropriate. It is a question of applying sensible measures to specific symptoms – part of a process which the entire industry should take to heart, and part of a process that could mean, one day, that lasting profitability will no longer be an undiscovered country.

Pierre J Jeanniot
Director General
International Air Transport Association

PART I

The airlines' needs

1 Industry financing requirements approaching the 21st century

K.J. Holden

Introduction

At the time of writing, the commercial aviation industry is in its best shape since 1988–89. On the manufacturing front, aggregate production of mainstream commercial jets (those with 100 or more seats) has been successfully cut back to under 450 a year for the second year running; a comfortable 150 fewer than needed to satisfy long-term demand. At the same time, massive productivity improvements have enabled the major manufacturers to significantly reduce both the real cost of aircraft and the time required to build them, while maintaining or increasing their own profit margins. Sadly, however, this process has in the past two years brought about the collapse of one of the world's oldest and most esteemed airframe manufacturers, Fokker, and the likely merger of McDonnell Douglas and Boeing, thus potentially leaving the industry with only two manufacturers of mainstream large commercial jet aircraft.

On the airline front, there can be no better news than that the International Air Transport Association (IATA) is forecasting 6.3 per cent per annum traffic growth for the next five years following an estimated 8 per cent world air traffic growth in 1996, while the industry as a whole is heading for record US$8 billion plus profits on revenues of US$300 billion.

The decisive turning point of the industry's most recent cycle took place in 1995. The cycle began with the dramatic fall-off in traffic immediately following the Gulf War in early 1991. This was best evidenced by the fact that orders substantially exceeded deliveries (by over 40 per cent); a key turnaround indicator that when last seen in 1984 signalled the start of the late 1980s boom. Fuelled by record airline profits, orders increased to over 1,200 in 1996 making this the second highest order year ever. Included in this total were the first ever speculative orders by GE via its aircraft leasing and financing subsidiary, GE Capital Aviation Services (GECAS).

With continued strong traffic growth being widely forecast for both 1997 and 1998 on the back of a steadily improving world economy, the industry is potentially facing the prospect of a temporary shortage of aircraft in the late 1990s as traffic grows faster than new aircraft deliveries at a time when noise rules accelerate the retirement of older Stage 2 aircraft. While this is good short-term news for aircraft owners, there is growing concern that the industry could all too easily repeat the overproduction pattern of the late 1980s. Now is therefore an appropriate time to take stock and calmly assess the industry's real demand requirements and to then use this assessment as a basis for conservative forward planning, learning from past experience where appropriate, with a view to making the next cycle a less damaging one than the last.

Jet aircraft requirements

Because growth in passenger travel is the fundamental driver of every component of the air transport business, from manufacturing to airline operations and financing, it is important that all participants understand the dynamics of demand and how that demand translates into new aircraft requirements, because this is what determines the industry's long-term aircraft and financing needs. Only by doing this will we avoid the mistake of too closely focusing on short-term imbalances between supply and demand and thus exacerbating the industry's natural cyclical behaviour.

All forecasting processes involve four steps:

- the prediction of air traffic growth;
- the translation of that traffic growth into the number of seats required;
- the translation of this capacity requirement into numbers of aircraft; and
- the prediction of retirements leading, finally, to net new aircraft requirements, which are simply the sum of the net fleet increase dictated by traffic growth plus retirements.

Air traffic growth

All forecasters agree that passenger travel volume (RPMs) grows directly in response to changes in world GDP and the real cost of air travel, leading in turn to a widespread consensus that air traffic will grow at a rate of around 5 per cent annually for the next 10 to 20 years. Indeed, nearly all recent forecasts predict air traffic growth rates of between 4.5 per cent and 5.5 per cent per annum over the next 15 years (see Exhibit 1.1). This makes it more or less certain that total world air travel will be at least twice as great in 2010 as it was in 1995 *provided only that the world economy maintains an approximately three per cent per annum average growth rate between now and then*. Over the next decade or so, traffic seems likely to increase by around 5.5 per cent per annum on average.

Exhibit 1.1
TRB 1995 workshop forecast results – 20 forecasts of traffic growth through 2009

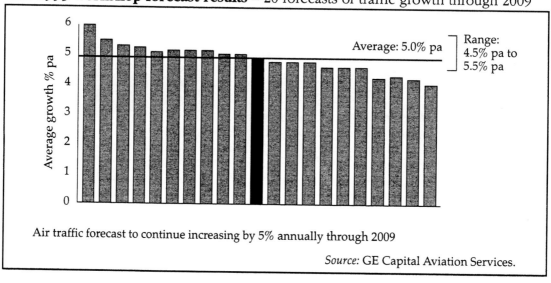

Air traffic forecast to continue increasing by 5% annually through 2009

Source: GE Capital Aviation Services.

This high rate of long-term growth is one of the key reasons why aircraft financing is so attractive, because there is no other comparably mature, large industry that offers the same degree of predictable growth.

Capacity growth

Growth in passenger demand is in practice accommodated by a combination of more seats and more efficient use of those seats. Efficiencies come from having fewer empty seats, keeping planes airborne for more hours each day and by achieving faster flying speeds. All three of these are likely to show positive trends in the years ahead, both as a result of manufacturer focus on achieving slightly increased block speeds via faster climb-out and higher cruise speeds, and airline focus on efficient fleet utilisation and ever more sophisticated yield management and scheduling systems.

In addition, and often overlooked, is the simple fact that the higher growth rate associated with long distance travel creates an automatic bias towards increased efficiency because those planes, by definition, spend less time on the ground (thus giving them higher average block speeds and utilisation) as well as which they generally operate at much higher load factors than the smaller planes used on short-haul routes.

Historically, worldwide load factors, which have risen from 55 per cent in 1970 to 62 per cent in 1980 and 70 per cent in 1996, have proven to be the main driver of increased efficiency. In contrast, during the same 25-year period, average speeds have only increased by about 3 per cent, from 388 mph in 1970 to around 400 mph today, while utilisation has, somewhat surprisingly given the rapid growth of long-haul travel, remained stuck at around 8.25 hours per day on average (most recently peaking at 8.9 hours a day in 1988 before falling back to 8.2 hours a day in 1993 and recovering to 8.5 hours a day in 1996).

On a long-term basis, it does not seem unreasonable to predict that total productivity as measured by RPMs per available seat will continue to increase by at least 1 per cent per annum on average. This would require (for example) that load factors increase by a further 4 percentage points over the next 20 years with utilisation rising to nine hours per day and average speed increasing to 420 mph over the same timeframe – none of which seem implausible targets. As a result, the most likely rate of increase for total seat capacity is around 4.5 per cent per annum in a 5.5 per cent per annum traffic growth environment.

As a practical cross-check, it is worth noting that the number of passengers carried per available seat has consistently averaged 700 since 1970, rising by up to 10 per cent in periods of above-average traffic growth and falling by a similar amount during periods of below-average traffic growth. As a result, this simple measure is a very useful barometer of industry health.

Numbers of aircraft

The total number of aircraft required is obviously related to forecast traffic growth offset by productivity gains, but it is also directly linked to the rate at which average aircraft size increases. This is in part related to the types of aircraft being built plus the already mentioned higher growth rate of long distance travel (because long-haul aircraft are on average at least twice as large as short-haul ones). It is also critically dependent on whether congestion at major airports and economies of scale accelerate the industry's long-term trend towards increased aircraft size or whether the effects of increased competition coupled with the proven passenger preference

Exhibit 1.2
TRB 1995 workshop forecast fleet increase, 1995–2009

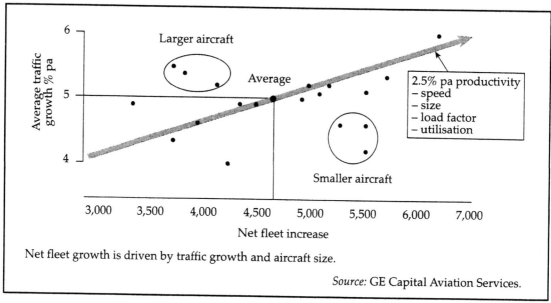

Net fleet growth is driven by traffic growth and aircraft size.

Source: GE Capital Aviation Services.

for more frequent direct point-to-point services leads to a continuation of the relatively flat trend in average aircraft size seen since the advent of US deregulation in the late 1970s. This is an area where forecasters disagree strongly.

Comparing 20 recent forecasts of traffic growth and associated increase in fleet size, it is evident that while the majority of forecasters opt for a conventional view that there will be a steady upward increase in average aircraft size at a rate of around 1.5 per cent annually as reflected by an implicit 2.5 per cent per annum total rate of productivity increase (Exhibit 1.2), smaller groups of forecasters predict either that congestion and other factors will lead to a much more rapid increase in average aircraft size or that competition will result in the addition of many more smaller aircraft.

From a financier's point of view, this does not significantly affect the total dollar financing requirement, but it does critically impact the demand for different types of aircraft and hence their likely residual values. Because this is the area of greatest uncertainty, it is the one that most merits ongoing attention as financiers are invariably more severely impacted by picking the wrong types of aircraft than by temporarily having too many of the right type.

Retirements

While there is broad agreement that aircraft retirements will average around 250 a year over the next 15 years based on the proven fact that very few aircraft play a significant role in passenger service beyond 30 years of age, forecasters differ by up to 1,000 aircraft in their estimates of retirements in any given five-year period. This is a reflection of the uncertainty as to whether individual airlines will prefer to hush-kit and life-extend older aircraft so as to achieve short-run cost savings or will instead take advantage of a buyers' market to re-equip for the longer term at favourable prices.

Exhibit 1.3
Consensus forecast of future jet aircraft demand (100 seats plus) over the next 10 to 15 years

• Passenger traffic growth (RPMs)	5–6% pa
• Capacity growth (seats)	4–5% pa
• Fleet size growth (number of aircraft)	3–4% pa
• Net fleet increase (number of aircraft)	300–400 pa
• Annual retirements (number of aircraft)	200–300 pa
• New aircraft demand	550–650 pa
Narrow body (100 seats +)	300–400 pa
Wide body	200–250 pa

Source: GE Capital Aviation Services.

New aircraft demand

Putting all of these factors together yields a strong consensus that mainstream jet aircraft demand is likely to average around 600 units a year over the next 10 years, with a possible range of 550 to 650 (see Exhibit 1.3). The importance of this to financiers is that it provides a useful benchmark against which to judge production and order rates, because it is almost certain that rates outside this range are unsustainable on any long-term basis, unless *either* GDP growth is significantly lower or higher than the 3 per cent number on which most forecasts are based *or* there is a significant change in the roughly 2:1 historic multiplier between GDP growth and air traffic growth.

In terms of dollar values, 600 aircraft a year translates into around US$37 billion worth of deliveries at today's prices and average aircraft size. Increasing aircraft size and the faster growth rate of long distance travel both lead to increasing costs *per aircraft*, because long-haul wide bodies typically cost 50 per cent more per seat than short-haul narrow bodies. As against that, manufacturer efforts to cut costs have recently resulted in net aircraft prices increasing much more slowly than general price inflation. As a result, it is likely that total new jet aircraft demand will average somewhere between US$35 billion and US$40 billion per year in today's dollars for the next five to 10 years.

Cyclicality

In practice, cyclicality has had a far greater impact on aircraft demand and aircraft values than variations in long-term forecasts of supply and demand, which have on average been reasonably accurate predictors of the future (albeit typically some 5 per cent to 10 per cent too optimistic when made in boom periods and vice versa in times of depression).

Fortunately we now have behind us three complete cycles in the jet era, beginning in 1958 when the Boeing 707 first entered service, giving us close to 40 years of history on which to base future projections. As shown in Exhibit 1.4, the degree of similarity between these cycles is remarkable; particularly between the two most recent ones. Thus in each of the last two cycles, the ratio of peak orders to deliveries in that year was 2.4:1, with orders bottoming out five to six years later at around one-quarter of the preceding orders peak and with deliveries bottom-

Exhibit 1.4
Aircraft industry cycles

	1st	2nd	3rd	4th	5th
Up cycle starts (orders > deliveries)	1958	1972	1985	1995	2002?
Boom years	7	6	4	2?	?
Up cycle ends (orders peak)	1965	1978	1989	1997?	
Orders/Deliveries	2.7	2.4	2.4		
Deliveries > Orders	1967	1980	1991		
Deliveries peak	1968	1980	1991	?	
Orders trough	1971	1982	1994		
% of peak orders	24%	28%	27%		
Deliveries trough	1972	1984	1995		
% of peak deliveries	32%	60%	59%		
Down cycle ends	1972	1985	1995	2002?	

Source: GE Capital Aviation Services.

ing out one to two years later again at 60 per cent of the preceding deliveries peak. Such consistency makes it likely (though by no means certain) that the industry will encounter the next down-cycle at some point around the turn of the century. What is frankly surprising is the fact that the amplitude of these cycles is remaining more or less constant whereas the cycle time appears to be shortening: a disappointing result given the extent to which the industry cycles are largely the self-inflicted consequence of the collective actions of the manufacturers and their customers to supply/demand pressures, making them, at least in theory, controllable.

For financiers, such vigorous and yet seemingly predictable cyclical behaviour presents both challenges and opportunities. As a minimum, it is clearly necessary to finance aircraft on a sufficiently conservative basis (including one's own balance sheet) to be able to survive the ups and downs in an industry where asset values fluctuate widely through the cycle and where

Exhibit 1.5
Worldwide airline revenues and expenditure, 1960–89

	1960s	1970s	1980s
Revenues (US$ bn)	96	383	1,204
Net income (US$ bn)	3.2	6.2	12.5
Net margin	3.3%	1.6%	1.0%
Depreciation (US$ bn)	5	19	60
Net cash flow (US$ bn)	8	25	73
Capital expenditure (US$ bn)	20	48	143
as % of revenues	21%	12.5%	12%
% financed by cash flow	40%	53%	51%

Source: The Airline Monitor.

there is a significant risk of credit failure and/or lease or debt rescheduling in the down-cycle. If this is done, then the potential exists to significantly enhance profitability by correctly timing purchases and sales in relation to the cycle.

Airline finances

World airline finances in the three decades since the beginning of the jet era are summarised in Exhibit 1.5. This shows that rapid revenue growth (quadrupling between the 1960s and 1970s and tripling again in the 1980s) was accompanied by continuous high capital expenditures and declining profit margins. Discounting the exceptional capital expenditures in the 1960s (when all airlines were forced for competitive reasons to quickly switch from piston and turbo-prop aircraft to jets), the ratio of capital expenditures to revenues has averaged 12 per cent. Somewhat surprisingly, given the airlines' lack-lustre profit record, this has consistently been financed 50 per cent out of internal cash flow even though net profit margins have declined from 3.3 per cent in the 1960s to 1.0 per cent in the 1980s.

These figures make it clear that airlines fund most of their capital expenditures from depreciation, making them less dependent on sustained high profits than might otherwise be expected.

Turning to the 1990s, the position will almost certainly be much worse thanks to the huge losses run up in the first half of the decade. Thus, as shown in Exhibit 1.6, while revenues will have doubled again, capital expenditures will have increased even faster to account for 16 per cent of revenues in this decade, and the profit margin will have shrunk even further – to around 0.5 per cent or less. When combined with the use of less conservative depreciation policies, the net result is that cash flow is likely to cover less than one-third of total capital expenditures in the 1990s creating a requirement for additional off-balance sheet financing of the order of US$90 billion. The primary cause of this shortfall was the delivery of an above-average number of aircraft (in value terms representing 17 per cent of revenues) in the first five years of the decade at a time when internal cash flow covered only 18 per cent of capital expenditures, with the second half of the decade being only slightly below the long-term trend.

Exhibit 1.6
World airline revenues and expenditure in the 1990s

	1990–94	1995–99	Decade
Revenues (US$ bn)	1,093	1,544	2,637
Net income (US$ bn)	(21)	(33)	12
Net margin	(1.9%)	2.1%	0.5%
Depreciation (US$ bn)	55	77	132
Rebuilding balance sheets (US$ bn)	–	25	25
Net available cash flow (US$ bn)	34	85	119
Aircraft acquisitions (US$ bn)	166	209	375
Total capital expenditure (US$ bn)	186	233	419
as % of revenues	17%	15%	16%
% financed by cash flow	18%	36%	28%

Source: The Airline Monitor.

Exhibit 1.7
Mid-1997 Financing Market Shares (Post 1985 Jets)

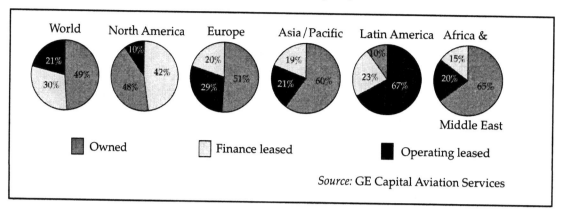

Financing shares

Airlines have traditionally financed their aircraft either on-balance sheet with the use of non-aircraft related debt finance, via finance leases or on an operating lease basis. Today roughly half of the more modern jet aircraft (those built after 1985) are owned, with 30 per cent being finance leased and 21 per cent being on operating leases (see Exhibit 1.7).

In practice, many factors other than straightforward cash flow constraints influence airlines in selecting the optimum financing mode. These include requirements for flexibility and the ability to respond to short-term changes in demand (making operating leasing particularly attractive in deregulated markets) and the availability of low-cost, tax-based funding that can

Exhibit 1.8
Aircraft values versus age in constant dollars

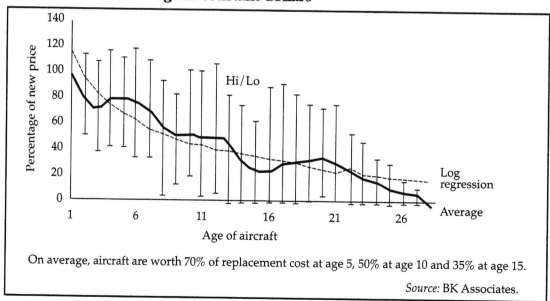

On average, aircraft are worth 70% of replacement cost at age 5, 50% at age 10 and 35% at age 15.

Source: BK Associates.

significantly lower the costs associated with certain types of finance and operating lease, to the advantage of those airlines able to make use of such products. This is reflected in the widely differing mixes of financing found in different geographic regions.

Residual value risk

No single factor is as important in determining the pricing of (and value in) an operating lease than the actual or expected residual value of the aircraft at the end of the lease. In the past, when inflation was high and when new aircraft prices typically ran ahead of inflation by 1 per cent or more annually, there was a widespread view that operating lessors made too much money at the expense of airlines, thus to some extent fostering a perception of operating leasing as the financing mode of last resort. Not only have the events of the past few years laid to rest that view as the leasing industry as a whole has suffered at least as badly as the airlines since 1991, but with new aircraft prices now rising only very slowly, if at all, residual value prediction has become a crucial part of deal evaluation on both sides; yet despite much analysis this remains in many peoples' minds something of a black art.

Notwithstanding this, historical data does permit us to reach some broad conclusions. First, modern aircraft for the most part do seem to enjoy 30-year plus useful lives, though the fate of the early wide bodies is a useful reminder that even quite technologically advanced aircraft can have relatively short useful lives where their mission is undermined by more capable aircraft offering (in this case) non-stop travel over longer distances in smaller capacity units. Within that standard, it does also seem that popular aircraft will on average be worth around 70 per cent of the price of a new one at age five, declining to 50 per cent at age 10 and 35 per cent at age 15 (see Exhibit 1.8). At any given time, however, aircraft can trade at prices that are 10 per cent to 25 per cent more or less than this 'benchmark' standard depending on their age and supply versus demand, while each new aircraft development can permanently diminish the values of preceding variants by up to 15 per cent.

Exhibit 1.9
Airline leasing versus ownership of aircraft, 1986 and 1996

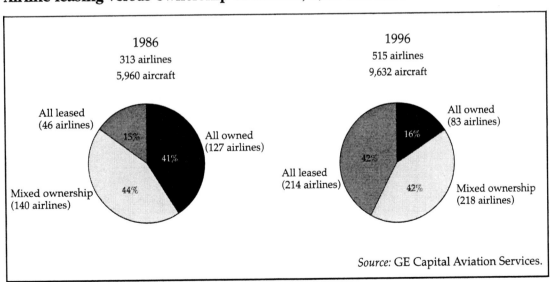

Source: GE Capital Aviation Services.

Bearing in mind the risks involved, it is scarcely surprising that, as shown in Exhibit 1.9, more and more airlines are leasing some or all of their aircraft, with many airlines now aiming to own outright one-third to one-half of their fleet (these being core aircraft for which the airline has a clearly identifiable long-term requirement) with another one-third to one-half being acquired on long-term finance leases and with a final 15 per cent to 25 per cent being acquired on operating lease. Such airlines will quickly conclude that operating lease rates (which are currently around 1 per cent per month for new aircraft with proportionately higher rates for older aircraft) represent extremely good value given their inherent flexibility and bearing in mind the limited potential for residual value upside in a low inflation environment.

The future

Notwithstanding the rapidly improving financial condition of the world's airlines, most commentators expect that around 60 per cent of all new aircraft will be financed on some form of off-balance sheet basis over the remainder of the 1990s. With capital expenditures averaging a *minimum* of US$35 billion annually during this period, it implies that there will be *at least* US$100 billion worth of new aircraft financing opportunities over the next 5 years. For the reasons outlined earlier, a significant proportion of such leased aircraft are likely to be on some form of operating lease.

Increasingly, airlines are looking to form partnership-type arrangements with one or more well-backed large financiers and lessors for the bulk of their financing, while continuing to turn to smaller players for top-up arrangements, given the importance of long-term planning and the need for guaranteed access to product. With the distinctions between straight operating leases and pure finance leases becoming increasingly blurred, those entities that have a comprehensive global reach combined with a full range of sophisticated financial products and, in particular, those companies that can combine access to a large existing portfolio with access to both money and new aircraft, will have a strong marketing edge, because they alone will be able to credibly lay claim to being a one-stop-shop for aircraft financing.

Addendum

This article was written almost a year prior to publication: in the intervening 12 months, the industry has been affected by the Asian economic crisis. While still too early to forecast its impact precisely, it is already clear that this will slow down world traffic growth and therefore result in reduced demand for aircraft in the short term, in the process confirming the tentative timing of the next cycle as shown in Exhibit 1.4. In the context of this chapter, however, it is unlikely to have a major impact on the longer term demand for aircraft and finance or on the appetite for the various modes of financing.

2 Sources of finance

Van DuBose

If the financial issues facing airlines and the markets available to them were similar to those for any other industry, this chapter would simply list the world's capital markets. But this is not the case. Due to the capital intensiveness of airlines, they have very special requirements. When you combine this large appetite for capital with the industry's cyclicality and cash flow volatility, it is no surprise that access to capital is a key concern currently confronting many airlines. The financing challenges of the sector are, of course, mitigated by the security value of modern aircraft as perceived by the financial markets.

We begin with a discussion of a typical airline's financial objectives. Because these objectives serve as a basis for assessing the airline's financial requirements and alternatives, this is followed by a description of how these financial requirements may arise. Given the trend for most airlines to be managed primarily on commercial principles and with less emphasis on 'flag-carrier' responsibilities, the assumption is that airlines are focused on shareholder value. It is against this background that we then examine the likely motivations of shareholders and airline managers as they review capital raising alternatives.

Next we review each of the major financing markets, including the equity market, debt markets, operating leasing market, tax-based leasing market, merger market and export credit programmes financing support from manufacturers. To conclude, we summarise some of the recurring themes and we attempt to predict likely future developments in sources of aircraft finance.

Financing objectives

Whether an airline's financing objectives are stated explicitly or implicitly, they will be designed to maximise the value of the business by minimising the long-term total cost of capital. Minimising cost, of course, is a meaningful objective only when taken together with an objective of keeping financial risk at tolerable levels. This is easier said than done because there is a trade-off between cost and risk. How management chooses to resolve this trade-off cannot be foreseen as there is, unfortunately, no prescribed solution. This section endeavours to identify and discuss the forms of cost and risk inherent both in the various financing alternatives and in combinations of alternatives, thus providing a guide as to the possible outcomes that make up the airline's capital structure.

Minimising the cost of capital

By definition, the optimal blend of debt and equity will serve to minimise an airline's cost of capital. Debt is effectively lower-cost financing than equity because it enables the airline's existing owners to expand the business at a fixed cost without forfeiting any value to the new capital providers. Issuing equity, on the other hand, dilutes existing shareholders, resulting in a high cost to the extent that the new shareholders receive a rate of return above the cost of debt. One would be incorrect, however to conclude that it is possible to minimise the cost of capital simply by relying on debt. This is because debt is inherently riskier for the airline than equity. Debt imposes upon a borrower an obligation to pay interest costs and to repay principal whereas equity allows the airline the option to pay dividends. Because of the higher bankruptcy risk created by debt, financial markets impose a discipline on airlines by raising the cost of both debt and equity as debt levels increase and by ultimately refusing to provide financing at all.

There is no panacea for defining the 'right mix' of debt and equity. Indeed, the mix is confused in the case of airlines by their extensive use of off-balance sheet operating leases (discussed later in this chapter) and, of course, by the existence of state-owned airlines which, until recently, did not have to abide by free market rules. In practice, each airline tends to establish its own 'comfort zone' of financial gearing, sometimes using credit ratings as a benchmark but more often looking at competitors' balance sheets for guidance.

Minimising risk

In addition to the financial risk created by debt generally, four principal risks need to be considered when establishing a financing strategy:

- access to markets;
- interest rate risk;
- currency risk; and
- aircraft values.

Access to financial markets

The desire of airlines to avoid market access risk has given rise to the old adage of 'financing when you can rather than when you have to'. Airlines wish to maintain ready access to funds on acceptable and relatively consistent terms. Thus, in order to avoid the risk of uncertain future financial market conditions airlines may fund in advance of a need and/or build up cash balances which they invest in liquid securities. These investments represent the surest form of standby facility. In addition, most airlines maintain significant, undrawn lines of credit committed by their commercial banks.

Interest rate risk

The interest rate payable on debt obligations may be either floating or fixed. By floating rate debt, we mean debt with interest payments that are reset within a given period at a margin over some appropriate index – for example one-, three- or six-month Libor. The risk involved in floating rate debt is that interest rates may continuously rise, thereby increasing the interest incurred by the borrower to unacceptable levels. Hence the ultimate costs of such debt is uncertain.

Alternatively, interest rates may be fixed from the start of periods ranging from one year to say, in the case of the US bond market, 30 years. Fixed rate debt is intrinsically less risky than floating rate debt because the borrower's payment obligations are known. However, timing is an important issue in choosing between fixed and floating rate debt markets. Borrowers will obviously be reluctant to draw down fixed rate debt when they believe interest rates are likely to fall. Interest rate swaps and other hedging devices provide some flexibility because they may be used to fix floating rate debt and vice versa. These techniques allow the borrower to separate its decision on the timing of raising debt from its decision between fixed and floating rate debt.

Currency risk

International airlines are multi-currency businesses. They sell tickets and, therefore, collect revenues in many different currencies, although the main revenue currency in most cases is that of the airline's home country. Costs are also incurred in foreign currency with respect to overseas operations, and fuel costs are payable in US dollars. The typical net currency position on an operating cash flow basis for an international airline is a surplus in all currencies except the US dollar. Certain airlines with relatively small home market revenues will, in economic terms, be short the home currency.

Airlines attempt to match their liability structure, including debt obligations as closely as possible with forecasted cash flows, taking into consideration the size, timing and predictability of such flows. Any remaining exposures are managed in the foreign exchange market. With respect to any given foreign currency exposure, the airline's treasury team may wish to make a currency bet rather than hedge perfectly. For example, management may choose to leave foreign currency profits unhedged if it feels strongly that the currency in which these profits are denominated is likely to appreciate dramatically. Alternatively, as in the case of certain currencies (notably those of developing countries), there is no available foreign exchange market. Consequently, in these markets the airline is fully exposed to currency devaluation and, therefore, may have to manage its risk through its ticket-pricing strategy.

It should be noted that airlines' principal assets, aircraft, have a cost and realisable market value denominated in dollars. To the extent that an airline is an ongoing business, the US dollar proceeds realised from any sale of aircraft are normally reinvested in new, US dollar-priced equipment. This, therefore, represents a natural currency hedge.

Aircraft values

Airlines have significant amounts of capital tied up in aircraft. Should the value of these assets deteriorate faster than the schedule set down by the airline's depreciation policy, then the airline would be obliged to absorb further write-offs. Certain aircraft financing techniques have been developed either to control or to eliminate this risk. These include various forms of asset value guarantees and operating leases. In the case of an asset value guarantee, the airline will pay a premium to minimise its downside risk, while surrendering none of the profit from upside appreciation. An operating lease effectively transfers the risks and rewards of owning aircraft to a third party, while allowing the airline lessee to operate the aircraft for a fixed monthly rent. Both asset value guarantees and operating leases are discussed further later in this chapter.

Financing needs

A financing need arises within an airline when its cash flow is in deficit. Such a deficit could be caused by any one, or a combination, of the following:

- weak internally generated operating cash flow;
- expenditure on new aircraft;
- other capital expenditure needs;
- acquisitions.

Weak internally generated operating cash flow

This may result from either a poor trading performance or a deteriorating working capital position.

With respect to profitability, the airline industry is highly cyclical. Significant swings from profit to loss occur on both an industry and an individual carrier basis. This is typically a feature of capital intensive industries with a high fixed cost base, where the trading result is very sensitive to revenue performance. It is also true that an industry that has historically included so many state-supported or state-owned participants has been able to sustain longer periods of poor profitability. The recent trend towards private sector ownership with its attendant commercial discipline has reduced the tolerance for poor financial performance.

As regards working capital, a cash flow deficiency may result from a slowdown in the collection of cash receipts from travel agents or from a squeeze put on by an airline's own creditors, such as fuel suppliers who may demand earlier payment. However, any cause of weak internal cash generation has one common characteristic: it does not represent an attractive proposition from the perspective of lenders or investors. If a cash flow deficit caused in this way is to be successfully financed, it must be clearly demonstrated as a cyclical or an extraordinary phenomenon, with a return to sustainable profitability projected as the principal means of repayment.

In order to understand whether or not an airline's financial position is healthy it is necessary to isolate trends in operating cash flow. This is not easy to do. There are sizeable elements of cash flow and profit (most notably asset disposals) that blur an airline's overall financial condition. As a result, it is easy, particularly for outsiders, to fail to recognise at an early enough stage that new capital sources are being devoted to financing operating losses.

Expenditure on new aircraft

The airline industry is highly capital intensive. New aircraft are needed to replace obsolete equipment, for growth, to meet regulatory noise requirements and to derive competitive advantage. It has occasionally been open to question as to whether the selection of expensive new equipment is always based on strict financial criteria, or whether the lure of shining new aircraft and their 'marketing' benefits are deemed to outweigh the capital cost advantages of somewhat tarnished second-hand alternatives. Either way, an enormous amount of airline capital, and therefore risk, is tied up in aircraft.

Historically, an airline's use of its capital to acquire aircraft may have resulted in a good return on investment even though acceptable operating cash flow was not achieved. This is so because of high residual values resulting from inflation and the absence of significant technical change that would have rendered existing equipment obsolete, and, therefore, of less value. There is, however, no guarantee that benign conditions for aircraft values will persist indefinitely, as the excess of supply over demand during the recession of 1990–93 amply demonstrates.

Other capital expenditure needs

These are, of course, many and varied, but of current importance are investments in information technology.

Acquisitions

The most effective method of enhancing market power is by acquisition. This was clearly illustrated in the post-deregulation US environment as the major carriers consolidated their market positions. The more regulated, flag-carrier oriented industry structure outside the US followed this pattern in the 1980s and early 1990s. To achieve strategic objectives, airlines may be prepared to pay significant premiums above stock market values to acquire other airlines. These premiums may also be justified because there are likely to be operating synergies and economies of scale from combining two airlines. Certain acquisitions have been driven by the drive to secure scarce airport slots owned by the target airline. The size and timing of an acquisition may produce financial strains, as acquisitions are often executed opportunistically when the target company becomes vulnerable. National ownership constraints have limited the activity that the open market would have dictated, and have channelled most investments into the form of minority stakes.

State-owned airlines and privatisation

As certain of the major non-US airlines are still substantially state owned despite a significant amount of privatisation during the 1990s, this important sector warrants special attention. A state-owned airline will finance in one of three ways:

1 it may be directly financed by the government;
2 it may borrow under government guarantee; or
3 it may finance independently.

Even in the third case, lenders often assume implicit government support because the flag-carrier is a symbol of national prestige and is unlikely to be allowed to go bankrupt.

Governments in all countries are currently inclined to review the possibility of accessing private markets for their more capital-hungry companies, and the most fundamental and sustainable basis for this is via privatisation. Furthermore, EU regulations seek to prevent government aid unfairly subsidising EU airlines.

There are several motivations for privatisations and a range of possible offering structures. In the cases of British Airways and Lufthansa, privatisation took place by way of flotation. The Australian government sought to privatise Qantas, first through the sale of a strategic stake and secondly through a stock market flotation.

To date, the equity flotations have involved a combination of domestic and international offerings, with preferential rights for certain investors, such as employees and domestic individuals. Claw-back mechanisms have been included to ensure that domestic demand is satisfied. In addition, partly paid features, discounts and bonus shares may be used to enhance the airline's investment appeal. Below, we briefly discuss the main considerations for both the governments and airlines concerned as they contemplate privatisation.

Government considerations

A government may review the privatisation of its flag-carrier in terms of fiscal, commercial and political objectives.

Fiscal

The proceeds from a privatisation can be used to reduce the national borrowing requirement. This assumes that the airline itself is adequately capitalised so that the proceeds flow directly to the selling shareholder. Such a transfer to non-state ownership avoids any future funding obligation for the government. Economic stimulation can be achieved through tax cuts or expenditure programmes financed by privatisation proceeds. The inclusion of international investors in the privatisation process encourages an inflow of funds to the country concerned.

Commercial

It is usually the case that business efficiency and financial performance as well as better customer service is encouraged when the airline's management is accountable to public shareholders rather than to the government.

Political

Currently, it is politically fashionable to reduce the role of government in business. Funds can be diverted to alternative investment programmes of higher social priority, while popular capitalism can be promoted through wider share ownership.

Airline considerations

An airline's approach to privatisation may be reviewed in terms of strategic objectives, its impact upon management and employees, as well as on funding and commercial benefits.

Strategic objectives

Because strategy is no longer constrained by political considerations, privatised companies can be run on an entirely commercial basis with a view to long-term profit maximisation. As a result, market strength may be enhanced and expansion facilitated.

Management and employees

Greater accountability and rewards for management encourage improved performance and efficiency. The ability to offer performance-related incentives helps to attract high-calibre personnel. Employees can be given a chance to invest in and identify with the airline.

Funding

A privatised airline obtains access to capital markets, enabling it to fund the business in a flexible manner. It similarly has the ability to use shares as an acquisition consideration which increases its strategic flexibility and competitiveness.

Commercial

The airline's image can benefit from privatisation: the move will tend to heighten its profile and create a strong marketing opportunity. Customer loyalty can also be enhanced through preferential treatment in a flotation.

Equity markets
Why raise equity?

Equity may be raised either as a primary transaction in which the new funds are raised by the airline itself, or as a secondary transaction in which existing shareholders sell shares and receive the proceeds.

Secondary offerings are not sources of capital for the airline, but facilitate the objectives of the initial owners. These may be either the entrepreneurs who developed the business and who wish to realise some capital appreciation, or, in the case of a flag-carrier, the government, whose motivations we discussed earlier. In many cases, primary and secondary offerings are combined. This is often necessary to provide for adequate capitalisation so that new investors can be persuaded to buy shares.

New equity may be considered necessary when projected future cash requirements cannot be financed entirely in the debt markets without exceeding the airline's target level of gearing. The state of the equity markets themselves will also be an important determinant of timing because equity raising is necessarily a 'lumpy' process. Consequently, many airlines may seek to raise equity opportunistically when they consider this source of financing 'cheap'.

Private versus public equity

An airline seeking to raise equity may do so in either a private or a public transaction. The disadvantage of a private transaction is that a liquid secondary market in the shares is not created. This, in theory, should limit the number of interested investors and lower the price they are prepared to pay. An airline may prefer to remain private principally for reasons of disclosure and control. Recently, several carriers have privately placed minority equity stakes with other airlines in conjunction with alliance partnerships.

Elements of an equity offering

Having broadly established the size of its equity requirement and a view on timing, an airline would have several additional elements to review prior to launching an equity offering. These may be categorised as valuation, structure and selection of markets.

Valuation

The price at which an airline issues equity is a crucial part of any offering because the price is a key determinant of the cost of the equity raised. The forces determining the valuation of a particular airline may be broken down into three types:

1 conditions in the equity market in general;
2 the expected performance of the airline sector; and
3 the carrier's rating itself within the airline sector.

In the case of an initial public offering, the airline's market value must be established. This will involve an analysis of stock market data for comparable publicly traded carriers to determine the relationship between the value that the market is currently ascribing to these airlines and their reported earnings, cash flow and asset values.

This information points to how stock is trading on a 'seasoned' basis. For new issues, investors will require evidence that investing at the issue price represents a profit opportunity. This is most often achieved via two practices. First, new offerings will be made at a discount, either to where the shares are actually trading (in the case of existing quoted companies), or to where they ought to be trading based on comparables. Secondly, the issue may be accompanied by a marketing effort from the company and its investment bankers to convey a 'story' to investors as to why this particular airline represents a good investment. If this effort is conducted successfully, it may be possible to generate sufficient demand for the shares that a sense of scarcity is created which will provide upward momentum to the post-offering share price.

Structure of the offering

A number of basic questions must be resolved in every equity offering, where the approach of the various national markets may differ. First, there will be the question of the type and amount of information to be disclosed in a prospectus. Secondly, the price may be either fixed in advance or set in a 'book-building process' under which investors place orders within an indicated price range. Thirdly, financial institutions will typically underwrite the transaction, thereby assuring completion for the issuer. Finally, there is the important consideration of existing shareholders' rights in any issue of new shares.

Domestic versus international markets

Historically, companies have tended to rely on their domestic markets to meet their equity needs. In recent years, however, there has been a trend towards the internationalisation of the equity markets. Investor interest in international equities has, in part, been fuelled by the wave of privatisations. Because of their sheer size, privatisations have of necessity been structured to tap international markets. Although the majority of publicly traded airlines are US based, and have relied on the US market, the privatisations of the major European, Asian and Latin American carriers during the 1980s and 1990s have been structured as international offerings.

There are three ways in which a major airline can attempt to access the international equity markets:

1 an investor relations programme;
2 listing on the European, US or other international stock exchanges;
3 offering ordinary shares in Europe and/or the US and/or other major markets.

With respect to both investor relations and a listing, the objective is to arouse interest in the company and to promote the purchase of existing securities. In the case of a share offering, the objective is clearly to raise new equity. These three levels of access need not be considered as alternatives, but rather as parts of an overall strategy to develop a global market for the company's stock.

Our basic conclusion is that by far the most effective way to create real investor interest is to issue equity in targeted markets. An international offering has many potential advantages over a purely domestic offering, most of which relate to the increased demand available from large foreign markets. Clearly, an international offering is particularly relevant for non-US airlines that do not have the benefits of a large domestic stock market.

The advantages of an international offering can be summarised as follows. It:

- supports the share price;
- lowers the cost of capital;
- broadens the shareholder base;
- attracts new long-term investors;
- increases international research and trading activity;
- underscores the issuer's image as a world-class company;
- aligns more closely the business base and the shareholder base; and
- enhances the company's reputation in world financial markets.

Debt markets

Debt is the most flexible and broadly available form of financing for most airlines. It can meet all the specific financing needs outlined earlier, including working capital deficits, aircraft purchases and corporate acquisitions. In the case of aircraft financing, debt is also an integral part of the leasing and manufacturer financing alternatives discussed in later sections. Certain debt markets (the commercial paper and bank markets) provide floating rate debt, whereas others (principally the longer-term bond markets) provide fixed rate debt. All the major markets provide US dollar-denominated debt, and the non-US domestic markets provide debt in the major currencies (yen, Deutschmarks, Sterling, French francs and Canadian dollars). As discussed earlier, an airline's preferred liability mix may be achieved most efficiently by borrowing in the market in which its credit is best received, and then using interest rate and currency swaps as required.

Access to debt markets

The stronger an airline's financial condition, the broader the range of debt markets it can access and the better the terms it can negotiate. Whereas many of the major airlines are able to raise funds in virtually all the debt markets, many smaller airlines tend to rely heavily on using their assets to borrow from banks on a secured basis. It is helpful to consider this borrowing capacity as a credit rating, which may either be notional or actually obtained by an airline. The two major rating agencies, Moody's and Standard & Poor's, provide ratings on both short-term obligations (such as commercial paper) and on long-term obligations (such as bond issues). Although these ratings are a prerequisite for entering the US commercial paper market and the US public bond market, they are not compulsory for other markets. However, there is a trend for investors to make decisions on the basis of rigorous credit criteria rather than name recognition. Consequently, a rating can in some cases broaden an airline's potential lender base as the rating is increasingly accepted as a standardised measure of creditworthiness (see Chapter 15).

Historically, banks have been the most important source of debt funding to airlines and are almost certain to continue to fulfil a significant role. This is so particularly because the relative complexity of airline lending requires the understanding that banks have accumulated concerning the value of aircraft as security. However, airlines, like other borrowers, may be well served to diversify their sources of finance, utilising new and often international capital markets.

The following sections review each of the debt markets, including the bank and commercial paper markets (the only short-term sources), official export credit, the Eurobond market, the US public bond market and the US private market.

The bank market

Airlines can tap a number of markets to finance temporary cash flow deficits. Traditionally, the commercial banks have met this requirement through the provision of working capital facilities, which may take the form of overdrafts, advances and bankers' acceptances.

The banks are also the most common source of committed medium-term finance, in the form of either direct corporate loans or as debt in leveraged leases for equipment purchase; these may be negotiated bilaterally or as syndicated arrangements. Availability, terms and pricing of bank debt for airlines tend to follow a cyclical pattern, becoming less favourable during periods when either or both the airline and/or banking sectors are experiencing difficulties. As a result, many airlines attempt to arrange large committed term bank facilities during periods of favourable market conditions with the aim of avoiding the need to enter the market during the next period of difficult trading.

Export credit

Because a large number of airlines' aircraft purchases represent exports, principally from the US or Europe, government-sponsored export credit programmes are widely used (see Chapter 4) and often give airlines both an alternative source of credit capacity to the bank market and attractive terms. Export credit terms for commercial jet aircraft are subject to rules coordinated among the governments of the principal aircraft and engine manufacturers.

Although direct loans are available from certain export credit agencies, most transactions involve bank loans or bond issues guaranteed by the exporter's government. Typical terms give cover of 85 per cent of the contract price with a 12-year maturity. Although credit spreads associated with export credit financing normally reflect the favourable credit ratings of the government guarantors, the export credit agencies charge guarantee fees that raise the overall cost to the airline.

The Eurobond market

The Eurobond market is extremely 'name conscious' and generally available only to household names and high-quality credits (ie AAA- and AA- rated issuers or their equivalent), although A-rated issuers can finance in the Eurobond market opportunistically.

Investors are both institutional and retail, with a substantial amount of market demand historically generated by individual investors in Switzerland, the Benelux countries, Germany and the Middle East. The US dollar is the major currency of issuance, although the Deutschmark, yen, sterling, French franc and Canadian dollar are also important. Issues normally have non-amortising maturities of 10 years or less, and an issue size typically between US$250 million and US$500 million.

The principal advantages of the Eurobond market are that it frequently offers the lowest cost of funds, it can be accessed immediately when market conditions are deemed favourable and it represents an alternative source of significant capacity to the domestic markets. The principal disadvantage of the Eurobond market is its volatility, mainly due to exchange rate movements. As a result, it is normally an opportunistic source of new funds.

The US public market

The US domestic bond market offers the broadest range of maturities, the greatest liquidity and the capacity to absorb large issues. SEC registration, US GAAP reconciliation and a rating from a credit agency are all required, and may represent an important barrier for many foreign issuers.

The US bond market is capable of rapidly absorbing large amounts of new securities in US dollars, and provides consistent access to a range of maturities from 3 to 30 years. It offers substantial call flexibility and a variety of sinking fund options. The shelf registration procedure effectively provides investment grade issuers with immediate access to the market. Unlike the Euromarket, the US bond market is not sensitive to the outlook for the US dollar. It is almost exclusively an institutional market with minimal participation by individual investors.

Most airline issuers in the US bond market use the Equipment Trust Certificate (ETC) structure under which investors receive a priority security interest in aircraft. The credit quality of these securities can be upgraded by overcollateralisation, creating Enhanced Equipment Trust Certification (EETCs), permitting non-investment grade carriers to borrow at investment grade rates of interest.

The US private market

A private debt placement in the US is a debt instrument placed with sophisticated institutional investors, the issue of which is exempt from registration requirements under the US Securities Act of 1933. A private placement is distinguished from a public offering by the number of offerees in the primary offering, the sophistication of the solicited investors and the tradeability of the security after placement. Under Rule 144A it is possible to trade these unregistered offerings, thereby encouraging the participation of certain investors who had previously bought only public issues.

Life insurance companies are the principal investors and provide stable funds for the private market. Other sources include pension funds and foreign and domestic banks through 'synthetic' floating rate loans, created by the combination of a floating rate loan and an interest rate swap.

Issuers are not required to file public statements with the US Securities and Exchange Commission. The typical size of an issue is US$100 million to US$500 million and maturities range from three to 30 years, with weighted average lives ranging from three to 20 years. Bond ratings are not required except for 144A issues because investors are sophisticated and do their own credit analysis. Lenders have recently become much more flexible on covenant issues and, with investment grade credits, covenant requirements are achieved parallel to those of existing public or Eurobond covenants. In general, there is a trend to simpler agreements.

Leasing market

Leasing is a somewhat general term but is always associated with the financing of an item of equipment. When speaking of airlines this item is predominantly aircraft. A lease can be fully defined by an analysis of how the parties involved are affected in each of the following areas:

- residual value;
- tax benefits;
- debt financing; and
- accounting treatment.

Residual value and operating leasing

The inherent value of a new or second-hand aircraft can be considered as a potential source of finance. This is most clearly the case in a sale and leaseback transaction, which in effect represents both a financing and the realisation of the airline's equity interest in its asset. In simple form, the airline sells the aircraft to a lessor at the current market price and leases it back under an operating lease for a set period. The rental charged by the lessor will reflect not only interest costs but also the residual value it is prepared to attribute to the asset at the end of the rental period. To the extent that rental payments under the leaseback are less than those of debt interest and principal repayments for a loan amount equivalent to the aircraft's purchase price in the transaction, then the saving can be attributed to the asset's residual value, which the airline has in effect sold forward to the lessor. The balance of risk and return in the aircraft's value can also be managed in other, more sophisticated ways – for example, with fixed price purchase options.

Operating leasing has during the 1980s and 1990s emerged as a major source of capital for the airline sector. In the initial stages of its growth, operating leasing was seen principally as a capital substitute for second and third-tier carriers with poor access to traditional debt and equity markets. In reality, the operating lease is a combination of debt and equity for the airline and, thus, is a legitimate capital source in its own right. In recent years major airlines have begun to embrace operating leasing as a component of their capital structure, seeing it as a low-cost source of combined debt and equity and evaluating it on a blended cost basis. This trend has, of course, required these carriers to reassess their traditional assumption that owning their aircraft residuals would always result in the lowest cost of capital.

Finally, operating leasing can sometimes offer access to certain urgently required equipment types earlier than the airline could obtain delivery from the manufacturer, because the major operating lessors often have aircraft available for early delivery.

Tax benefits and tax-based leasing

Tax benefits may similarly be analysed as a source of finance to the extent that they reduce repayment obligations. These benefits may be taken by the airline itself, and used as a deduction from taxable profits. Alternatively, tax benefits may be used by a third party lessor that will, via a lease transaction, absorb them and pass on a share of them to an airline lessee.

The tax benefit market may be broken down into two categories: domestic and cross-border. By domestic lease, we mean that lessor and lessee are resident within the same tax jurisdiction. The most active domestic tax lease markets are those of the US, the UK, Japan and Germany. By cross-border lease, we mean that the lessor is located in one jurisdiction where it claims tax deductions available from asset ownership, and the lessee is located in another jurisdiction. It is possible to structure transactions where depreciation benefits are also taken in the lessee's jurisdiction, either by the lessee itself or by another third party lessor. Usually these 'double dip' transactions are structured so that ownership is passed to the lessee in such a way as to create eligibility for depreciation on the asset in both jurisdictions.

Tax benefits and residual value are sometimes integrally related in lease transactions because in certain jurisdictions (such as the US) the availability of the former is based on the lessor retaining the latter. However, because tax-based leases are normally relatively long-term facilities of up to 25 years, retention of the residual value risks and rewards by the lessor does not significantly affect the economic impact of the transaction for either the lessee or the lessor. In recent years, the most popular source of cross-border tax benefits has been Japan, through classic Japanese leveraged leases, although proposed legislative changes may reduce the attraction of this market in the future (see Chapters 7 and 11).

Lessor debt financing

The debt portion of a lease is theoretically no different from that discussed in the section on debt markets. However, as such financings are typically long term, secured and relatively complex, they have traditionally been undertaken in the private markets. Recently, however, a trend has emerged in financial markets to achieve lower-cost funding by converting or 'securitising' complex private market transactions into public market transactions. Major aircraft leasing companies with large, diversified portfolios are typically able to follow a corporate funding strategy, accessing a variety of debt markets on an unsecured basis.

Accounting treatment

The accounting treatment of a lease transaction is important because it may affect an airline's financing capacity. A 'finance lease' or full payout lease is in reality a secured financing with tax benefits often taken by a lessor. However, significant residual value control often remains with the airline lessee, usually through the use of fixed price purchase options or provisions for sales proceeds to flow to the lessee at the maturity of the lease. Where the risk and return of ownership remains with the lessee, the finance lease will be capitalised on the airline's balance sheet. For all intents and purposes, this treatment is identical to that of owning the asset and financing it with debt. The alternative 'operating lease' does not appear on the lessee's balance sheet; there is merely a note to the accounts setting out the future rentals payable under the lease. Therefore, the attraction of operating leases is that the borrower may increase its effective borrowing capacity, and lower its cost of capital, by presenting a less geared balance sheet. As a result, considerable financial ingenuity has been directed towards the creation of financing structures that allow the airline to raise the lowest-cost funds, with the maximum possible share of the aircraft's residual value and with the minimum possible accounting impact.

From a debt perspective, lenders and credit agencies are becoming increasingly familiar with these techniques. Over time they are likely to recreate an airline's accounts, at least implicitly, to reflect a more inflated borrowing position. Similarly, international accounting standards are tending to become less tolerant of the more artificial off-balance sheet financing techniques.

From an equity market perspective, investors are unlikely to attribute significant additional value to an airline that extensively utilises operating leases. The degree to which an airline can be considered less risky because it can effectively walk away from its aircraft is counter-balanced by the fact that without permanent access to its aircraft the airline's revenue-generating capacity is materially impaired.

Merger market

By merger market, we mean the international market in which entire companies, or at least significant stakes in companies, are bought and sold. An airline will not necessarily list the merger market as a source of capital because it may, in effect, be a last resort involving the surrender of control.

Rationale

An airline may be vulnerable in the short or long term as a result of many factors – for example, its market position or its under-capitalisation. In the case of a publicly traded airline, this vulnerability may be reflected in a weak share price, which will allow a predator to launch a takeover bid. Airlines are most often acquired by other airlines because there are significant operating synergies and marketing objectives which justify their paying a relatively high price. An airline may recognise that a merger transaction represents its best strategic alternative, and this may result in either the sale of the entire company, or of a strategic stake.

In a full merger, the acquiring airline's resources are available to finance the future development of its new subsidiary. In most cases, however, the two operations will be merged into one entity. The post-deregulation consolidation within the US industry was in part the industry's structural response to the need for a smaller number of stronger, well-capitalised carriers.

In buying a strategic stake, the new airline investor may, in part, inject new capital into the investee airline by buying new shares and, in part, provide an attractive price for shares of existing owners. Partial sales have to date offered the only merger alternative in the case of cross-border transactions (except for airlines domiciled a operating within the European Union) because current foreign ownership restrictions on airlines allow only for minority, non-controlling positions to be taken by overseas investors. Alternatively, an airline may raise capital by disposing of non-core assets such as hotels or its catering business.

Valuation

Empirical analysis of the values at which companies change hands demonstrates that this merger market will typically produce different valuations to those of the equity market. This differential, which is always a premium, may reflect the value of control to the buyer or the synergy benefits available to a specific buyer. Less tangibly, the premium may represent the emotional desire of the buyer to own a particular company. A skilled investment banker representing the selling airline will be able to maximise this differential by creating a strong sense of competition among the various potential buyers.

Conclusion

The importance of the merger market as a source of capital to the airline industry is that it addresses the problem of capital shortage from a structural point of view by creating stronger, more financeable entities. Weaker airlines do not simply vanish. Unless bolstered by state support, they will reach a stage where they no longer have access to the traditional financial markets. In such cases, their last recourse may be to merge with a larger airline that perceives value in the investment, where value would not be perceived by a pure financial investor.

'Globalisation' of the airline industry is occurring even though outmoded regulations continue to restrict cross-border acquisitions and mergers in the sector. Consolidation is in fact occurring through several major airline alliance groupings, such as the Star Alliance, the KLM–Northwest–Alitalia alliance, the British Airways–American Airlines alliance and the Delta–SwissAir–Austrian–Sabena alliance. Although these alliances have begun on the basis of commercial agreements and normally without significant centralised control, it is possible that the arrangements will, when regulations permit, eventually become mergers.

Financing support from manufacturers

The airline industry relies heavily upon the suppliers of airframes and engines for financing support. This is not a traditional financing market but is, nonetheless, extremely important. In general, the support is provided to the weaker airlines that would otherwise have difficulty in obtaining finance. However, the financially strong airlines have also used their negotiating power to extract concessions from the manufacturers, particularly in the areas of 'walk away' leases or asset value guarantees.

Rationale

Manufacturers' involvement in financing their customer airlines is primarily the result of competitive pressures. On the one hand, the more attractive the potential order to the manufacturer (in terms of value and the airline's quality) and the more types of competing equipment, the greater the likelihood that financing support will be an element of the competition. On the other hand, aircraft are expensive, representing a significant capital commitment, and in the case of many airlines, can only be acquired with external financial support. This is particularly the case for under-capitalised airlines or for carriers with poor profit records. It may also be true, although difficult to demonstrate, that manufacturers prefer to dissipate the competitive pressures within the industry by providing financial support rather than by reducing equipment prices. At least initially, the former may appear to be relatively painless because the worst effect may only be to add to contingent liabilities.

The providers

Manufacturer support has traditionally been provided by the airframe producers. At the large end of the market these include Boeing and Airbus. In recent years, competition has become more intensive as Airbus, in particular, has sought to establish itself in crucial markets and to achieve its targeted market share. Given Boeing's strong market position and its strong financial position, it has been able to continue providing financing support to counter this competition. Similarly, the Airbus ownership structure has so far provided it with the financial resources to meet its strategic objectives of becoming an effective competitor to Boeing.

Another trend in recent years has been for large aircraft engine manufacturers to be drawn into the financing competition. Traditionally, the large airframe manufacturers have passed on to the engine manufacturers (General Electric, Pratt & Whitney or Rolls-Royce) a pro-rata share (typically 25 per cent) of whatever risk has been underwritten. However, particularly where there is little airframe competition in a sector, more sophisticated airlines may choose to play off the engine manufacturers. At times, airlines have sought to obtain their financing support from engine suppliers in an amount in excess of the order's engine content. (The forms of manufacturers' support are discussed in detail in Chapter 18).

Future developments

Historically, many airlines have been state owned and have looked to their shareholder for capital as of right, without the discipline of the financial markets. With a continuing trend towards privatisation, capital raising will take on an increasingly commercial perspective.

The reliance on debt or tax lease financings to meet all re-equipping needs will begin to exceed gearing tolerance. As a result, there will be much greater recourse in the coming years to operating leasing and the equity markets, particularly as the strong internal cash flow generation experienced by most carriers in the late 1990s begins to weaken cyclically.

To the extent weaker carriers are unable to access sufficient equity capital, their options may be limited to the merger market. Therefore, we can expect to witness continuing consolidation in the industry, although regulatory constraints may modify its form.

Finally, it is likely that we will see an acceleration in the trend to separate aircraft ownership from aircraft use as a means of reducing the airlines' need for capital. This may take place in a number of ways. First, operating lessors, possibly in joint ventures with manufacturers, can bridge the gap between the aircraft manufacturer and the aircraft user. Secondly, the airlines can restructure themselves into aircraft owning and aircraft operating businesses, raising capital in the markets that are best suited for each.

The airline industry is characterised by enormous capital requirements and by a tendency towards extreme cyclicality, resulting in significant profit volatility. In short, it is an extremely risky business. The continuing need to finance large-scale re-equipping, combined with increasing competition stemming from deregulation, will probably lead to fundamental structural changes in the industry, resulting ultimately in consolidation into a limited number of large airline groups, each operating on a global basis.

PART II

Financing methods

3 Commercial bank lending

Stephan Sayre and Stephen Gee

Growth of syndicated lending

The syndicated bank loan gained prominence in the early 1960s and re-emerged as a significant financing instrument in the mid to late 1970s, largely on the back of asset-hungry banks and the recycling of the petrodollar. The loans were characterised predominantly by their size and the general move towards the organisation of banks within one overall financing document, removing much of the administrative burden from the borrower.

The ensuing debt crisis among developing nations was brought to a head in the early 1980s following sharply increased oil prices and a corresponding recession. As the world's financial institutions moved away from the provision of syndicated loans to developing countries, other sectors (such as shipping and aerospace) saw renewed liquidity in the financing market, especially for first-class credits and strong, asset-backed transactions. The 1980s also saw a progression from the hybrid syndicated loan to a greater range of funding alternatives that also employed the syndicated concept. The global diversity of the market makes it difficult to substantiate this growth with figures, but the following estimates of the volume of lending illustrate the point:

1988	US$1,000 bn
1990	US$592 bn
1991	US$574 bn
1992	US$624 bn
1993	US$801 bn
1994	US$1,081 bn
1995	US$1,412 bn
1996	US$1,606 bn

The reversal in the use of the syndicated facility in the early 1990s came about largely as a result of the difficulty in forecasting future finance trends and reflects the introduction of new banking regulations (the Bank for International Settlements' convergence proposals) and the impact of a global recession. However, as the figures above illustrate, the syndicated loan is a robust concept reflecting the fundamental strength and depth of the bank market and the flexibility of the product range. Ultimately, there is no other capital market source of funds where customers can raise substantial amounts of money quickly, efficiently and with a structure adapted to suit their particular circumstances.

Growth of the aircraft market

The demand for new aircraft is driven primarily by the continuing growth of world passenger air travel which, since 1970, measured in terms of revenue passenger kilometres, has grown at an average rate of 6.3 per cent. While year-to-year variations in growth have at times been considerable, it is significant that this growth occurred over a period that encompassed two major energy crises and recessions (the mid-1970s and early 1980s) and there was only one year (1991) in which traffic failed to grow.

Historically, the growth of air travel has been driven by two main factors: (a) the growth of world income, measured by gross domestic product (GDP); and (b) a continuing reduction in the real cost of air travel.

The connection between the rate of growth of air travel and the growth of world GDP has been remarkably consistent historically, with world air travel typically growing by 2.5 per cent for each 1 per cent increase in GDP, with the remaining growth attributable, in the main, to the declining real cost of air travel.

World GDP is forecast to increase, on average, 3.2 per cent from 1996 to 2015 – nearly the same as the average for the previous two decades. From an historical perspective, such growth should yield an increase in air travel of, on average, 5.1 per cent, or, put simply, world air travel is expected to grow by 70 per cent in the next 10 years.

However, it is not expected that traffic will match the 7 per cent average growth seen in the past 20 years (1991 was the first year to record a fall in revenue passenger kilometres). It is expected that the traffic/income multiple, which historically has been over two times GDP growth, will fall to just below two. In the main, this is because real yields/air fares will only show modest falls; all airlines will want to retain more of the productivity gains that are available for profits in the mid to late 1990s, rather than cutting air fares to stimulate traffic.

Airlines fares and yields have tended to reflect trends in operating costs and changing competitive conditions:

- Air fares dropped substantially in the 1960s as efficient jet aeroplanes lowered the cost of operations.
- Between 1970 and 1981 the world economy experienced two energy crises, two major recessions, inflated labour costs and increased government regulation. Yet fares dropped an average of 2.2 per cent a year over the period.
- The 1980s were notable for free competition, automation and productivity improvements. Yields declined an average of 2.5 per cent a year between 1981 and 1990.

Yields are projected to decline only slightly through to 2000: airline costs, while continuing modestly to improve, will not support substantial yield deterioration without a loss of profitability (airline losses in 1991–92 illustrate this). The development of 'mega' carriers and consolidation among operations should ensure better control of pricing systems. Likewise, computer reservation systems (CRS) and complex yield management systems are resulting in the construction of more efficient fare structures and the optimisation of aircraft operation. Aircraft load factors, which in the early 1990s averaged around 64/65 per cent, have been increasing consistently and are expected to fluctuate around 66 per cent in the late 1990s. The more effective use of aircraft, and the trend towards the operation of larger aircraft, is such that airlines will perhaps require 14 per cent fewer aircraft by 2005 than if they had maintained the average load factors and utilisations of the late 1980s.

Between 1970 and 1995 the world's jet transport fleet has more than tripled in size to just over 11,000 aircraft. Of these, 3,600 aircraft are in the Stage 2 category and must be hush-kitted or replaced over the next few years, increasing the probability of large-scale retirement for the first time in the industry's history. Peak delivery periods in the early 1990s have also had, and will continue to have, an impact on older aircraft residual values.

Retirement of older aircraft and the imposition of stringent noise regulations mean that 1,800 aircraft may need to be retired by 2005. Against this, the industry forecasts that over 7,000 aircraft will be delivered during this period, representing around 63 per cent of the current fleet. In 1995 US dollars, this was equal to a financing requirement of over US$450 billion (or approximately US$45 billion per annum compared with the average of US$18 billion per annum required between 1970 and 1991) that airlines will need to access to fund deliveries of new aircraft up to the end of the decade.

This is the aircraft financing challenge, in a market where airline cash flows are projected to cover less than half the financing requirement and where increasingly innovative solutions will be sought both inside and outside the traditional bank finance markets.

Financing opportunities

Excluding the USA, where access to the non-bank market is providing US airlines with significant liquidity, bank finance provides the most obvious source of external funding. Poor profits and weak airline balance sheets, together with recessionary pressures in the early 1990s in contrast to the late 1980s, constrained the role of banks in providing airlines with finance for new equipment. However, bank finance has revived in recent years as airline profitability has improved. In the 1980s, banks moved the focus of their interest away from direct lending to airlines towards finance leases and asset-based financing where lenders would take comfort from the residual value of the aircraft. This trend was reversed as residual values fell in the early 1990s but rebounded sharply in the mid-1990s for the newer, fuel-efficient, high-technology aircraft. However, bank appetite for finance leases in the 12–18 year range remains limited. The question then is whether the traditional bank market is both able to finance continued expansion of the market and indeed willing to increase its direct exposure to the industry.

The latter will be determined over time, but in a market where returns are perceived as being high and risks relatively low, banks and financial institutions that have not previously participated in aerospace finance will continue to be drawn in, such is the nature of competitive markets. Only time will tell us if the recent Asian currency crisis will materially affect this appetite through the last few years of this century.

Whether the banks will be able to fund future aircraft deliveries will be determined to a much larger extent by the capital adequacy regulations imposed by the Bank for International Settlements (BIS), which agreed a minimum standard to be achieved by the end of 1992 by all banks in Belgium, Canada, France, Germany, Italy, Japan, Luxembourg, the Netherlands, Sweden, Switzerland, the UK and the USA. The regulations require that banks maintain a certain ratio of capital to risk-asset portfolios, with the aim of 'levelling the playing field'. These regulations have had a considerable impact on the pricing of products. New definitions of capital, procedures to convert certain off-balance sheet items into on-balance sheet equivalents and new categories for the weighting of assets according to their perceived credit risk have been established. This enables one to calculate the risk-asset ratio, which is derived by dividing the newly defined capital base by the total of weighted risk assets. The BIS Basle Committee (which is represented by the member countries) has set the minimum ratio of capital to weighted risk assets at 8 per cent.

In practice, this means that for every loan of US$100 million, banks must provide capital of US$8 million. If a bank agrees to lend a customer US$100 million on an 8 per cent risk-asset ratio, US$8 million of the loan will come from capital, leaving US$92 million to be raised in deposits. In pricing terms the implication is that for a bank to maintain a level of return on its equity that is consistent with its shareholders' expectations, minimum pricing levels are required. It is generally believed that further consolidation in the bank sector, coupled with a need to exact improved levels of return on equity, will materially affect (ie, push up) these minimum pricing levels through the end of the 1990s.

This is a simple example for the purposes of illustration, which does not make any allowances for additional costs and constraints that may be imposed by individual central banks (for example, the requirement in the UK that banks maintain a certain proportion of non-interest-bearing deposits). It does, however, illustrate that the BIS convergence ratios will limit the ability of the banking sector to increase its asset base purely as a direct response to demand on a marginal basis. Any increase in overall lending therefore becomes a function of the availability of capital in the banking sector.

These regulations are having a direct effect on the way in which the traditional aerospace banks are viewing the funding of future aircraft deliveries. The 1990s have seen increased emphasis on the provision and structuring of transactions where the risk-asset weightings are kept to a minimum – for example, by the use of export credit agency guarantees (discussed in the next section), where a proportion of a bank's assets lent against such guarantees carries a zero weighting for capital adequacy purposes. The scope for banks to underwrite and syndicate large transactions fluctuates depending on market appetite. When capacity is light, the banking market has tended to move away from syndicate structures and has used the 'club' bank structure, where a club of banks will typically join together to provide the aggregate financing for an airline's aircraft delivery, on mutually acceptable terms. In the mid-1990s syndicated underwritten structures have grown in importance with strong demand for assets in the banking market. As banks seek to improve their own returns, innovative forms of financing continue to be devised, broadening the investor base for aircraft-secured paper through the issuance of asset-backed securities and building upon the German leveraged lease and the other tax-driven and increasingly innovative financing structures explained elsewhere in this and other chapters.

Export credit agencies (ECAs)

One form of credit currently experiencing something of a comeback is ECA-supported finance. Traditionally an alternative contemplated only by weaker credits, the product is now being developed and adapted to serve a wider market. The inherent benefits to both airlines and financiers are such that ECA financing is losing its stigma of 'poor' credit (see Exhibit 3.1). At the same time, there have been major developments in structuring the use of the product in supporting debt-into-finance leases, leveraged leases and operating leases.

ECA-supported finance is a conduit through which a number of countries encourage the export of their goods and services. In terms of aircraft in the big-ticket market, the four major ECAs are EXIM of the US, which supports the export of Boeing and US manufactured equipment, ECGD of the UK, COFACE of France and HERMES of Germany. (In fact, the percentage of financing will be based on the contribution made to a particular aircraft: for example, if CFM engines are used in the manufacture of the A320, the French element is 49 per cent, while the German and UK elements are 31 and 20 per cent respectively; if Rolls-Royce engines are used

Exhibit 3.1
Benefits of ECA-supported facilities

Airline	Financial institution
• ECA support makes credit available where otherwise it would not have been available on a purely commercial basis. • Under the European ECA framework agreement, if an airline chooses *Large Aircraft Sector Understanding* (LASU) terms, it can enjoy a no-cost interest rate option. If the airline exercises the option and fixes at the right time, and rates subsequently rise, the airline can effectively generate sub-Libor funding when the facility is drawn. • An airline is able to take advantage of Lasu terms up to three years prior to delivery. • In view of the attractive yield which this type of financing is able to generate, the banks can pass this benefit through to the airline by aggressive pricing, particularly on the commercial element.	• Most ECA-guaranteed debt achieves a nil weighting in terms of capital. • Banks are able to transfer the airline risk into a home government major OECD government risk. • Banks are able to blend the yield on the nil-weighted ECA-guranteed debt with the 100 per cent weighted commercial debt. The resultant yield on capital weighted assets is highly attractive when compared with average yields on airline credits. • Limited commercial debt required allows transactions to be completed, which otherwise would not have been the case because of credit quality (risk) concerns.

on the same aircraft, the French element falls to 32 per cent and the German and UK elements increase to 36 and 32 per cent respectively.) There are, of course, smaller airframe manufacturers such as British Aerospace, engine makers such as Rolls-Royce, CFM, Pratt & Whitney, and simulator manufacturers such as Rediffusion that also qualify for support.

Interest rate option with no premium to pay

European ECA support takes the basic form of fixed or floating rate (pure cover) finance, guaranteed for financing periods covering 10 or 12 years. The terms and conditions of fixed rate support are determined by the Large Aircraft Sector Understanding (LASU) which came into force on 10 March 1986 and is complementary to the Arrangement on Guidelines for Officially Supported Export Credits (the 'consensus'), Annex IV of which is set out in Appendix D of this book.

The fixed rate finance provision provides for a no-cost interest rate option. Assuming an airline is 'on cover' to benefit from LASU terms, the airline is able to receive an offer from the ECA(s) to finance up to 85 per cent of an aircraft cost for up to 90 days (or 45 days in the case of tranche B finance in US dollars, on which see the next sub-section). The airline is then free to choose to accept this rate at any time within the period of the offer. This can be done for deliveries up to three years in advance. If the airline chooses not to exercise the option, the offer lapses and the airline is free to take on a further option in the future if it wishes.

If the airline exercises the option it is under an obligation to use this rate if it decides to finance the aircraft using export finance. If, however, when delivery occurs the airline has decided to utilise an alternative source of finance, it can simply walk away; in other words, the airline has no obligation to finance its deliveries using export finance support.

The particular benefit of using the fixed rate arrangement is that rates can be fixed in advance at a time when they are perceived to be low in the market. If rates rise before delivery, the airline can fix into potentially sub-Libor rates. Alternatively, if rates have fallen and cheaper alternatives are available, the airline can walk away from its obligations. In this way, the airline has the benefit of an option on interest rates without any cost or penalty.

LASU term and conditions

The LASU rates are split into two tranches – tranche A and tranche B. They also differ between 10 and 12-year commitments, the 12-year rate being 55 basis points (bp) higher than the 10-year rate. Tranche A covers the first 62.5 per cent of the aircraft purchase price and tranche B the next 22.5 per cent. This means that the export credit agencies essentially cover up to 85 per cent of the aircraft cost, with the airline arranging the finance of the residual 15 per cent. French and German support is given on a slightly different basis than that of the UK – a guarantee of 80.75 per cent (ie 95 per cent of the 85 per cent) as opposed to the full 85 per cent provision from ECGD.

Tranche A rates are based on the average long-term government bond yield (TB10) for each of the currencies to be used (at present these are US dollars, sterling, French francs, Deutschmarks and ECUs) over the preceding two-week period. Each government (plus the EU Commission for the ECU) is responsible for notifying its government bond yields on a fortnightly basis (every other Tuesday) and the rates so calculated take effect on the following day (Wednesday). Interest rates for tranche A only change if the rates differ by 10 bp or more from the rates for the previous fortnightly period. The final rates are rounded off to the nearest 5 bp.

Tranche B margins are generally more expensive than tranche A, and are calculated from the date of acceptance of the offer from the manufacturer that is eventually accepted by the airline until the intended delivery of the aircraft. It is possible for an airline to leave the fixing of the tranche B element until a few weeks before delivery.

If an airline chose to accept 85 per cent support, the blended rate would therefore be calculated as follows:

- tranche A basic interest rate plus the appropriate margin (1.2 per cent for 10 years; 1.75 per cent for 12 years) for 62.5 per cent of the aircraft cost; plus
- tranche A basic interest rate plus the appropriate tranche B margin calculated as outlined above, for 22.5 per cent of the aircraft cost. Margins for both tranches are reduced by 20 bp for ECU funding.

Although the basic LASU terms and conditions are fixed, it is possible to introduce considerable flexibility. Frequently, it is economical for the airline to take the 10-year fixed rate and for banks to massage this into a 12-year lease structure. Further, there is no reason why an attractive LASU rate fixing cannot be swapped into floating debt. If the fixing has been carried out at the right time this can create a sub-Libor floating rate for the airline.

Pure cover

The second option – the floating rate option – is through 'pure cover'. Under this option the ECAs provide insurance cover to the commercial banks. The commercial banks then lend floating rate debt to the airline backed by an 85 per cent guarantee. The price the airline attracts is simply the most competitive floating rate available from the commercial banks. Typically, an airline could expect to be quoted around 40–50 bp above 6-month floating Libor. Adjacent to this pure cover of 85 per cent is the same 15 per cent residual funding from alternative sources – usually from the same commercial banks that arrange the ECA cover. As with LASU arrangements, there is no reason why the floating debt under the pure cover cannot be fixed through an interest rate swap on the delivery date to provide fixed rate debt if this is what the airline requires.

There is no differential between pricing for a 10- and 12-year commitment under pure cover. There is, however, a premium of 50 bp which the airline has to pay on a per annum basis calculated on the outstanding amount of the guarantee. In view of this, the blended floating cost will be around 90–100 bp over six-month Libor on a floating basis.

Development of ECA support through lease structures

The ECAs now prefer to provide support through lease structures rather than direct loans. The reason for this is that the Paris Club agreements on debt rescheduling do not affect leases and, as the ECAs have historically dealt with the lesser country risks, they prefer to follow the leasing route wherever possible.

A simple ECA-supported finance lease typically would be non-tax driven, the most favoured route in recent years being a French *Groupement d'Intérêt Economique* (GIE) as lessor. Tax-neutral jurisdictions such as the Cayman Islands are also frequently used, and in many respects this option is more beneficial because it avoids potential withholding tax claims between France and, for example, the UK or Germany.

Tax leases have been added on to the simple finance lease, and transactions for numerous airlines have closed combining export credit moneys with Japanese leveraged leases or German tax leases. These structures have provided the airline with present value benefits that they would traditionally expect to see under Japanese or German leases, as well as utilising export credit moneys (without which some of the lowest ranking country credits would simply not be able to access pure commercial debt) and any beneficial interest rate available through them.

The years 1987–97 have seen enormous developments in incorporating export credit facilities in aircraft financing. However, the product still has vast potential to evolve further. We have seen, for example, the ECAs moving away to some extent from straight-line repayments, allowing some structured amortisation.

The ECAs have also moved away from their traditional position of providing support purely against country or airline risk. Now they too require a mortgage over the aircraft and look critically at the value of the asset when deciding the level of risk. The commercial banks have traditionally taken a subordinated position because of the ECAs higher percentage of financing. With only a second mortgage position, the banks are first to suffer if enforcement becomes necessary and the sale price is insufficient to pay out the ECAs and banks for their full outstanding debt. In view of this, commercial banks are now increasingly seeking a pari passu position with the ECAs – ie to share, on a pro rata basis, the first priority mortgage. This may still result in an uncovered position for the banks, but at least it is limited and certainly easier to justify in risk terms than the historic position. Some structures have resolved the issue by seeking alternative security; however, this is often not available.

A further unresolved area is that of control rights – the rights of commercial banks to act after a default by an airline. The ECAs are, to some extent, driven by political motivations and in the event of a default may sometimes not wish to accelerate matters. In that the ECAs lend the greater proportion, it is understandable that they may wish to keep absolute control in a default situation. However, the experience of Royal Jordanian and other airlines has brought recognition from all parties that a balance needs to be found, especially as, in many of the leasing structures, the commercial banks are taking a higher proportion of the financing in the later years. The response from the ECAs has been the establishment of a principle in the documentation that provides for the automatic calling of default unless all three ECAs agree not to do so. Although this is an important step forward, it still does not provide all the protection the banks require. It will be interesting to see how this issue progresses over the coming years.

Future trends

A major preoccupation at present appears to be a concern that a gap will materialise over the next few years between the investment needs of the aerospace industry and the finance available to meet those needs. With further development and more widespread acceptance, the use of export credit moneys, with the benefits of available and often attractively priced funds for airlines, and limited exposure and enhanced yields for banks, could go some way to bridging that gap.

Umbrella and standby facilities

When taking into account all the associated costs, in addition to bank interest and fees, the price of financing an aircraft acquisition can be substantial. It makes sense for an airline to minimise these costs and also to 'lock in' its interest costs by trying to finance as many aircraft as possible 'in one lot'. However, most airlines have a fleet acquisition programme spread over several years, with firm orders stretching over, perhaps, five years. Bulking aircraft together in one drawdown is not possible under these circumstances. This is where some airlines have, in the past, turned to arranging an 'umbrella' facility.

An umbrella is nothing more than a basic framework agreement setting out the essential terms and conditions under which the bank will finance a number of confirmed aircraft orders over a given period. The airline usually retains the option to choose which particular aircraft deliveries are to be financed by the umbrella. This allows the airline to take advantage of any opportunities that may arise from time to time for lower cost financing by alternative methods. Because of the option, this type of facility is also often known as a 'standby' facility. The total amount of the umbrella facility will usually be set to cover a number, but not all, of the deliveries in the airline's planned acquisition programme. The financing of a series of aircraft will, of course, run into several hundred million dollars or indeed, on occasions, billions of dollars; and the financing would usually be undertaken by a syndicate or club of major international banks.

The umbrella does not entirely do away with the need for exchange of documentation with each aircraft acquisition, but enables the various parties to avoid the often time-consuming negotiation of the basic financing terms, and to concentrate on the finer points of each acquisition. Any financing will usually be secured by a first priority mortgage or access to title to the aircraft being financed.

Given the level of the banks' commitments and the potential variation in the value of the aircraft as security – which only becomes available at future dates – this type of lending is intended for the stronger credits where it is considered that there is a low likelihood of defaulting before maturity, with the bank having to repossess and/or sell the aircraft to repay the debt. Notwithstanding the status of the airline, the banks generally only finance a set percentage, such as 85 per cent, of the net cost or independent valuation of each aircraft under the umbrella.

This gives the banks a 'cushion' in the value of their security from the outset. The airline is expected either to finance the other 15 per cent from its own resources, or to find suitable equity providers for the 15 per cent portion; these equity providers are often approached by specialist finance agents or the banks themselves.

As regards repayment, this usually takes place over a number of years – depending on the type of aircraft, typically 12–15 years – in line with expected revenues from use of the aircraft and the airline's own depreciation policy. So, for example, if the airline decides to use the umbrella at the latter end of its acquisition programme, say in year three, the banks could find themselves with a lending commitment of up to 12 years. Repayments are usually structured on a 'mortgage style' basis; that is, the amount of interest as well as reduction of the debt are taken into account in calculating an even level of repayments over the term of the loan. If the airline intends to sell the aircraft after 15 years, or if it has put the umbrella funds into a finance lease, the amortisation schedule is often structured to reduce to a percentage of the initial loan over that period. The intention is that the expected sale proceeds will be sufficient to repay this. The payment at the end of the financing is known as a 'balloon repayment'. An example is shown in Exhibit 3.2.

Security

In most cases, the banks will want to take a first priority mortgage over the aircraft being purchased. Consequently, the banks need to be satisfied with the legal jurisdiction and the aircraft registration procedures in the country in which the aircraft is to be situated, so that they can be reasonably sure of being able to access the aircraft if ever the mortgage needs to be enforced. For example, some countries do not have official aircraft mortgage registries, and the interpretation of local law makes it difficult to be sure that the interests of a mortgagee will take priority over any local charges and costs, and related liens, in the event of a default.

Exhibit 3.2
Banks' exposure under a 15-year loan

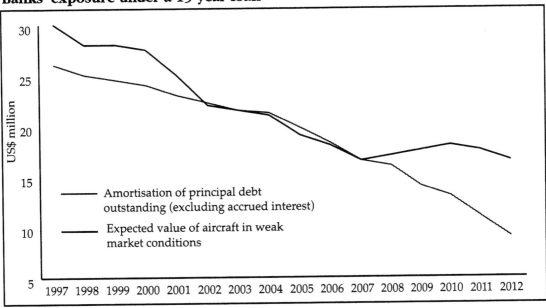

Where an airline uses the umbrella funds in a tax-driven lease structure, obtaining a first mortgage may not always be possible. Specific tax regulations may make the offering of a mortgage difficult, or proposed sub-leasing may create problems. Often in these circumstances the aircraft may have to be sold on to a separate, single purpose company (SPC) which has been set up for this transaction, usually in an offshore tax-neutral jurisdiction. This SPC, in turn, becomes the lessor. In this instance the banks would be looking to have full rights of access to the aircraft, often through being granted security (such as a mortgage or pledge) over the shares of the SPC, so that in the event of any default, the banks can take effective control over the SPC and so assume the rights of the lessor. In the event of funds being used in tax-driven lease structures, payments may need to be made through offshore financial centres. Consequently, the operation of the loan is made much easier if the banks in the syndicate have representation in the major financial centres of the world. This is one of the reasons why the syndicate in an umbrella tends to comprise the major international banks and those other banks that specialise in aerospace finance.

An airline will often want to be able to sub-lease the aircraft under the umbrella, particularly if its own route schedules are seasonal, or if it has contracts with a charter airline or if it simply wishes to maintain a high level of fleet flexibility. Consequently, the banks must consider at the outset which other airlines will be acceptable sub-lessees, and which sub-lessee countries will be acceptable. Acceptable countries will typically be those that are known to respect the governing laws binding all the parties under the documents, and which are acceptable in political risk terms.

From a security point of view, the banks have the greatest exposure during the early to middle years of the financing, when their outstanding principal is highest. Although the decision to finance only a percentage (for example, 85 per cent) of each aircraft is designed to ensure that its value does not fall below the level of the outstanding loan, the value is, of course, an estimate, and in weak market conditions collateral values may be lower than the outstanding loan principal. In the latter years, the security cover is usually greater than the outstanding loan, and the risk is concentrated more on the general performance of the airline. This is best shown by the following example (and see also Exhibit 3.2):

A new, narrow-bodied aircraft is to be financed over 15 years. It has been independently valued at US$30 million and the banks will lend 85 per cent of this figure (ie US$25.5 million). In 15 years the valuers believe the aircraft will have a worst-case value of 55 per cent (ie US$16.5 million), and the banks have agreed to amortise the loan to a 30 per cent balloon at year 15. In the initial years the loan repayments will mostly comprise interest, and the true debt outstanding to the banks will only reduce by a small (but increasing) amount each year. Conversely, the new aircraft can be expected to hold its value well in the very early years of the facility and start to depreciate more rapidly in the middle years, and then for this rate to tail off in the latter years. At some point in the early years, the estimated value of the aircraft will become less than the outstanding loan. There will be another crossover somewhere around two-thirds of the way through the loan period.

This example assumes depreciation in the value in weak market conditions throughout the 15 years. In reality, this is unlikely to occur.

As future aircraft values can only ever be an estimate, depending upon the bank's perceived status of the airline, it may seek a back-up or top-up security arrangement from the airline should the value of the aircraft fall below a predetermined level or percentage of the future value estimated at the outset. This back-up or top-up security can take a variety of forms.

The evaluation and setting up of the umbrella security structure can be time-consuming, particularly where registration is needed in foreign jurisdictions. For this reason, the umbrella agreement will usually set out a framework timetable for the airline to deal with the banks (usually through one agent bank acting for the syndicate or club). This ensures that there is a reasonable amount of time to evaluate and perfect the security structure before the airline draws the loan under the umbrella.

Insurance

The banks will also set out in the umbrella document the minimum insurance requirements that must be in place for each aircraft. In a syndicate or club deal, there will usually be a separate agreement for one of the banks to be appointed as the 'security agent' to look after all security matters. The security agent will also be designated to receive any insurance proceeds for the syndicate, and will be named as the 'first loss payee' in the event of total loss of the aircraft.

The banks will also want to have an assignment of the benefits of the various levels of hull and war-risk insurances over the aircraft, along with appropriate cut-through clauses direct to the banks for any of the insurance that has been reinsured by the primary insurers, again through the security agent if appropriate.

While these measures are taken to protect the banks, the banks also have an interest in the adequacy of the level of liability insurances taken out by the airline. After all, in the event of a major claim, if the airline's own liability insurance level is deficient in any way, the airline could have, at the least, a major cash flow problem. The banks will also be included in the liability insurance documents to cover a situation where a third party instigates action against the banks as a result of their having a security interest in the aircraft.

Personalising the umbrella

As well as the basic details discussed in the preceding sub-sections, the airline and the banks may wish to add on certain details that suit the corporate structure, operations and perceived level of risk of all the parties. These may include the following:

1 *A multi-currency option.* The airline may want to pay for the aircraft in US dollars but structure repayments in a different currency – say the currency in which it expects to obtain its ticket receipts. Depending on the currency involved, this can often be arranged by the banks through a long-term currency swap structure.
2 *A fixed rate option.* If the funds are to be put into a lease structure, the lease rentals (which in turn become the banks' source of repayment) may be on a fixed basis, whereas the banks' funding is usually based on a floating rate, generally by reference to US dollar Libor. Again, any such exposure to adverse changes may be overcome by recourse to a long-term interest swap at the start of the financing period.
3 *Guarantee or standby letter of credit financing.* An occasion may occur where the airline wants the banks to issue a guarantee or standby letter of credit to a beneficiary rather than provide funding. One example of this would be UK tax leases, where lessors typically provide their own funding but seek bank guarantees to cover the risk of airline default.

4 *Covenants.* The banks may insist on certain financial and non-financial covenants in the umbrella document that ensure the airline operates within levels which the banks and airline together believe are reasonably manageable. These are never intended to be penal covenants. The non-financial covenants are intended to ensure that the funds are used and the airline continues to operate in the way which the parties understand to be the case at the time of entering the commitment. The financial covenants may include such covenants as an annually increasing level of tangible net worth, restriction on the gearing level or a minimum interest cover covenant. These are seen by the banks as a form of early warning mechanism of any financial difficulties in the future. It follows, therefore, that the level of covenants depends on how the banks perceive the status of the airline.

What makes an airline choose to set up an umbrella facility? There is a tendency for these facilities to be set up by airlines that are considered to adopt relatively conservative policies. If the airline has concerns about the availability of the various forms of finance for major aircraft acquisitions in the future, it may decide to set up an umbrella facility as an insurance against this probability (ie as a true 'standby facility'). Alternatively, it may take the view that the banks' lending margins will increase in the future and it is worth setting up an umbrella now. Margins began to increase for airline credit facilities from the middle of 1990 and particularly during the Gulf crisis and general downturn in the airline industry in 1991. As a result, any airline that set up an umbrella early in 1990 generally came out with a favourably priced deal by 1992 standards. Low margins in 1996 are stimulating airline appetite to 'lock in' interest costs once again.

In evaluating the savings of an umbrella, the airline must take into consideration, in addition to any potential saving in bank costs:

- the savings in legal costs by agreeing just one framework document; and
- the savings on the airline's own personnel resources by having overcome the initial stage for each aircraft delivery.

An airline treasury team often puts in a considerable number of extra hours when an aircraft delivery is imminent. In terms of additional costs, however, once an umbrella facility has been set up the banks have a definite commitment to lend in the future, and therefore must maintain a certain ratio of capital reserves in accordance with the BIS convergence ratios. Consequently, banks will require a commitment fee to remunerate them for the cost of putting up this level of capital, and this cost must also be taken into account by the airline when evaluating the overall net benefit of the umbrella.

For all these reasons, the umbrella may suit the policies and requirements of only a select number of prestigious airlines. It is, however, a flexible financing method and no two deals will be identical. It is somewhat cyclical in its usage in line with the nature of the airline industry – an airline will be able to negotiate a better deal when it is itself producing favourable results and forecasts, and has a strong order book of firm aircraft orders.

Pre-delivery finance

Typically, airlines make progress payments for the purchase of new aircraft, and such payments would appear on the airline's balance sheet. In the 1980s there was considerable interest in providing pre-delivery finance based on the security of the contract with the manufacturer to deliver the aircraft and based on the perceived strong asset values. In the 1991–92 recession, interest fell as asset values weakened. Pre-delivery finance is now primarily seen in ECA-guaranteed transactions where banks are providing the balance of the cost over the 85 per cent ECA-guaranteed loans anyway. In these circumstances, there is an acceptable level of comfort that the aircraft will be delivered and post-delivery finance put in place, refinancing the pre-delivery arrangements.

Structured off-balance sheet pre-delivery financing arrangements are occasionally seen where airlines seek to reduce leverage in their balance sheet by reducing the impact of capital commitments for aircraft orders.

Bridge finance

Airlines sometimes require short-term bridging finance prior to arranging long-term debt financing for the aircraft. The time at which the airline accepts delivery of the aircraft may not be the best time to access the long-term debt market, and if the airline has a bridge facility in place, it has time to choose the best package being offered by the long-term debt market. The cost of the short-term bridging finance for the airline can, in most cases, be on better terms than can be agreed with the eventual long-term debt provider, reflecting the tenor of the loan. It is not uncommon, however, for a short term lender to build a package of measures into a bridge facility to 'incentivise' the airline to refinance. This typically takes the form of an 'exploding' pricing mechanism.

Funding operating lessors

In 1983, Tony Ryan (then chief executive) of GPA Group, the Irish mega-lessor, was quoted in *Fortune* magazine as saying, 'Airlines aren't inherently profitable, but aircraft are.' This basic premise has proved to be true, time after time, with dramatic growth in the numbers and size of organisations purchasing aircraft to lease to the operators, the airlines. The organisations that have created and, indeed, capitalised on this market are known as operating lessors. This section considers the reasons behind the emergence of this remarkable and innovative market, as well as the way in which it operates.

Background

Let us start by looking at the rationale for airlines to lease aircraft, particularly from an operating lessor. Notwithstanding credit implications, there were, traditionally, two main ways that an airline could purchase its aircraft (or any company could purchase any asset) – it could either use up internally generated reserves (cash) or it could borrow from a lender. For both of these options, there is a cost, over and above the price of the asset being purchased, and this is either the interest paid to a lender or the potential loss of return on the internally generated reserves (opportunity cost). For this latter reason, in the comparative credit freedom of the 1980s, a significant number of airlines began investigating how they could reduce the total cost of obtaining the aircraft. Furthermore, those which had borrowed from lenders were seeking ways to reduce their total debt service obligations, and those which had used internally generated funds were similarly looking to improve returns on the use of those funds.

Accordingly, the financial markets started to develop new and innovative products to meet the demands of the airline industry's more creditworthy airlines. These airlines started to use the tax-driven leveraged lease, which necessitated bank debt, corporate shareholders seeking to shelter profits and a friendly tax jurisdiction allowing tax deferrals on transport assets in which to register a special purpose leasing entity covering the aircraft being financed. On the other hand, the smaller, and arguably less creditworthy, airlines needed to find a way to minimise the debt service on capital purchases. This is where operating lessors started, and they have continued to make real inroads.

The growth in operating leasing has historically been strong, rising from an estimated 6 per cent of market share (360 aircraft) in 1981 to 13 per cent (1,000 aircraft) in 1987 and 23.5 per cent (2,975 aircraft) in 1996. The downturn in the airline industry in the early 1990s, combined with a slowdown in sale-leasebacks of used equipment by large airlines and the difficulties experienced by the GPA Group have meant only modest growth in operating leasing overall in recent years, though inter-airline leases have proved popular. Current improved market conditions and, in particular, higher operating lease rental levels and increased new equipment orders from airlines that will then need to place older aircraft from their fleets, are expected to boost the market share of operating lessors further. As of April 1997, operating lessors had a 20.6 per cent share of total outstanding aircraft orders with the manufacturers.

In its simplest form, the operating lessor will purchase an aircraft and lease it to an airline on a medium-term lease of between three and seven years. This assumes the lessor is either a more attractive risk to a lender, or that the lessor is able to negotiate a lower purchase price from the manufacturer (because of bulk purchases). Furthermore, in calculating lease payments, the lessor takes the effects of depreciation into account (as owner of the asset). The lessor is then able to offer lease payments that are more attractive to the airline than the cost of borrowing in its own name. A further advantage to the airline is that it does not carry the aircraft on its balance sheet as a fixed asset. It also provides the airline with flexibility to manage its fleet. For the operating lessor, this split between ownership and medium-term leases leads to a mismatch between long-term funding costs and short-term revenues.

Comparing an operating lessor and an airline

In the first instance, the operating lessor has minimal staff (by numbers), as staff are required solely to manage the assets (aircraft). The airline, by comparison, is responsible for the flight crews, aircraft maintenance, ticket reservations, and a host of other support activities. Accordingly, an airline's staff costs are directly proportional to the number of aircraft it operates and it has far less opportunity to take advantage of economies of scale than an operating lessor. Furthermore, operating lessors are primarily financial services companies that specialise in the buying of aircraft for lease. The overriding objective of both parties is profit maximisation, but the operating lessor will achieve this through effective management of the asset in such a way as to maximise cash flow. The airline, on the other hand, will manage the service of transporting people from A to B.

Focusing a little more on the financial structure of the airlines and operating lessors, they have one major similarity, which is the high value of fixed assets in aircraft on their balance sheets, and, in view of this, both are usually highly geared and therefore interest cover is usually low. On the asset-revenue generation side, there is a major difference, with the airline having a natural use for the aircraft over the term of the economic life of the asset. By contrast, the operating lessor is a holder of inventory aircraft that are deployed on a much shorter term than the economic life of the asset. In summary, the operating lessor is an asset value risk taker.

Cash generation and balances are also completely different: the airlines generate significant amounts of cash through ticket sales but, as tickets are usually sold in advance, there will normally be a working capital deficit as ticket purchasers will be creditors. The operating lessor's cash generation capacity comes from (a) security deposits and (b) monthly rental. With both items paid in advance, the operating lessor is cash-rich.

There is one final point that is vitally important when comparing these two operations, and that is their respective abilities to react to severe, short-term changes in the market. For example, during the Gulf War, passengers were reluctant to travel by air. This meant that there was a reduced cash inflow to the airline, but the aircraft were still flying (in the main) and needed to be both operated and maintained, which involved immediate cash outflows. Clearly, this resulted in a negative cash position that continued until passengers recommenced flying, thereby generating a cash inflow. The short-term effects of this can be seen in the dismal results that were produced by most major airlines in the financial year 1991.

Conversely, the operating lessor should not feel an immediate cash outflow as its lessees will, presumably, still be paying the rentals and therefore the cash position will be relatively unaffected. In the longer term, however, if some of the lessees are unable to make rental payments because of cash shortfalls (brought about by the longer-term effects and negative cash position mentioned above), the operating lessor can either reschedule the payments (in which case the cash flow will still be forthcoming, albeit perhaps belatedly), or it can terminate the leases and take possession of the aircraft with a view to placing them elsewhere. In this latter event, the short-term cash flow may be covered by the lease security (and even perhaps maintenance) deposits that are held by the lessee, but more likely, as the rental flow is paid six to eight weeks in advance, there is a cushion. In the longer term, the hope is that the aircraft can be re-leased, and normal cash generation resumed.

In any event, the operating lessors (especially the larger ones) will have a diversified fleet located in a number of disparate geographical locations, so individual lessee default risk is minimised.

Risk aspects of lending to an operating lessor

Unlike lending to airlines, the risk of lending to an operating lessor are largely determined by the stage in the developmental cycle at which the lessor finds itself and the markets in which it operates. There is a vast range (in both size and age) of operating lessors that were formed for a variety of reasons, concentrating on different markets with a variety of aircraft.

Notwithstanding this, however, the operating lessor needs continual liquidity and it is the ongoing provision of liquidity that is the key to success in such a cyclical market. This cyclicality means that there are going to be lean periods and therefore there needs to be sufficient 'excess capacity' in the lease income stream to carry it through those lean periods. For a lender, therefore, it is imperative that the lease income stream remains as secure as possible. Historically, lenders have tried to satisfy themselves on the creditworthiness of the lessee (notwithstanding that the primary reliance is on the operating lessor) but, as the size, and indeed range of operations of the operating lessors has increased, the underlying risk has become more diversified. This leads to lenders imposing parameters within which the operating lessor can operate to avoid the lender's nightmare of the borrower having 'all his eggs in one basket'. As the lender gains more confidence in the ability of the operating lessor to identify, negotiate and control the income stream, its need to monitor and control the activities of the operating lessor should reduce in direct proportion. Ultimately, the operating lessor is given that 'most favoured status' among lenders (particularly bankers) of 'good unsecured'.

The early 1990s were a difficult period for operating lessors with weakening lease rentals and asset values impacting on cash flows, while the loss of confidence in the industry by the lending market made raising new funding hard to achieve and increased finance costs. The much reported problems of GPA are the most public example of how operating lessors suffered in this period. Only lessors with high quality parents – eg International Lease Finance Corporation (ILFC) owned by AIG – would continue to make progress. The healthier market in 1995–96 also improved the position of operating lessors (eg GPA Aeroplanes' successful US$4 billion bond issue) with continued demand from airlines for operating leased aircraft improving rental leases and reducing off-hire periods.

Moving aside from GPA, the other major players such as ILFC, ORIX or AWAS all have different methods of financing their book. ILFC, for example, tends to finance itself largely through the capital markets, while ORIX and AWAS raise specific finance for aircraft orders. Financing costs remain all-important. All lenders will face the same considerations for each operating lessor, although the risks will differ according to the operating lessor's stage in the development cycle.

As both the operating lessors and the operating lease market grow, the operating lessors are able to be more competitive in different markets and offer increasingly attractive financing options to a greater range of lessees. They do, however, need to ensure the continual availability of finance which, in the present market, is becoming increasingly difficult. Given the finite nature of the traditional banking sources of finance (which is now nearing capacity for the time being) the operating lessors will need to be as innovative in tapping new sources of finance as they have previously been in identifying the need and structuring transactions to meet the specific requirements. In doing this it is hoped that their future will be secured (or unsecured depending upon the context).

Asset-based lending

In this chapter the different types of commercial bank lending have been discussed, but it must be recognised that in all these types of lending, varying degrees of asset risk are taken. The facilities may simply be secured on the asset, and the lending repaid in full, either under a direct loan or in a full payout finance lease, or the loan facility may have some asset risk taken by the lenders or a third party.

Secured financing

In the context of a full payout facility, the importance of the asset is in terms of the cover it provides with respect to the outstanding debt. The security has been taken because of an assessment of the credit of the borrower and the funds advanced on certain assumptions with regard to the robustness of the value of the asset. How robust that value will actually be depends to a large extent on a number of external factors, including the cyclical nature of the industry, fuel prices, leisure travel trends, communication developments and flying rights.

The asset's value as security will be dictated both by the nature of the borrower and the access that is available to the asset. For example, a narrow-bodied aircraft leased to a politically unstable jurisdiction, which is to be used wholly on a domestic basis, does not command the same value in security terms as an asset that is being used in cross-border traffic and will be maintained outside the politically unstable jurisdiction.

Because of the external nature of a number of these factors, a facility that is relying upon the security of the asset will usually provide for a formula under which the security has to be topped up to provide a certain level of cover – for example, 125 per cent of outstanding indebtedness. Additional security can be provided either by offering other aircraft assets or perhaps cash collateral or letters of credit, or, failing the provision of additional security, the outstanding indebtedness can be reduced.

Loan terms

Because of the importance of the security in the context of the facility, the loan documentation will be expected to include the following:

- full provisions relating to registration and perfection of the security (including re-registration in the event of a sub-lease);
- maintenance provisions under which the borrower is required to maintain the asset to a particular standard;
- insurance provisions under which the borrower will be required to insure the asset for a value that at least covers the outstanding indebtedness from time to time; plus
- provision for the borrower to reimburse the lenders for interest costs and expenses of enforcement, and inspection rights under which the lenders (or their security trustee or agent) can inspect the asset from time to time.

If the borrower is in a politically unstable jurisdiction, it may be possible to take out political risk insurance to mitigate the risk of sequestration or confiscation. Because the obligation of the insurers to indemnify replaces the value represented by the asset, the credit standing of the underwriters is important.

Facilities with residual risk

Some lending facilities do involve genuine residual risk being taken by the lenders or by third party asset value guarantors. This has been seen particularly in the context of option finance, where a lessee has the right to elect to terminate a lease at certain window dates, providing it with operating lease treatment for balance sheet purposes, but at the same time providing an option for a finance or full payout lease. In these circumstances, the loan provides for a balloon repayment on the relevant option date and the source of repayment will be either the sale proceeds or payment provided by the party taking the residual value risk. The residual value risk can be covered either by specialist residual value insurance or, more commonly, by an asset value guarantee syndicate. The asset value guarantee syndicate may include the borrower or lessee, banks or other financial institutions, operating lessors and, commonly, the manufacturers. For a detailed discussion of the motivations and methodology applied by the manufacturers in asset value support, see Chapter 18.

Tax-spared loans

Other chapters cover specific tax structures in greater detail. The purpose of this section is to describe briefly tax-spared loans. These are no different from a conventional loan, except that the interest element is, in effect, subsidised by the government of the borrower.

There will be a double taxation agreement between the countries of the lender and the airline, allowing credit relief to be obtained in respect of taxes that are 'spared'. Under the local laws of the airline concerned, the loan is granted full or partial exemption from the tax that would normally be deductible from interest payments, and the foreign lending bank will thus receive interest gross. However, in addition, the foreign lender will also receive an official exemption certificate that can be used to support that lender's claim for tax relief – in effect, the lender receives evidence of payment of a tax that has not been paid by the airline. The lender, therefore, benefits by receiving its interest gross *and* a certificate to use against its own tax liability. Part of this benefit is generally passed on to the airline in the form of a lower cost of borrowing.

Ordinarily, these exemptions are made available by countries that wish to encourage the development of activities and industries considered vital to improve the borrowing country's economic position, such as infrastructure improvements and supporting a national carrier. It is, therefore, the authorities in the airline's country that rule whether a financing warrants the benefits of tax sparing.

In view of the benefits available under a tax-spared loan, borrowing margins have been reduced to very low levels – considerably lower than could be justified on a pure term loan to a particular airline. However, it is usual to include a 'fall-back' margin to be used in the event that changes are made to the tax laws of the country of either the airline or lender, which reduce or negate the benefits of the tax sparing. The inclusion of a fall-back rate is also important in view of the fact that declining interest rates reduce the benefit of tax sparing and, therefore, can be called upon if declining rates diminish the lender's return to an unsustainable level.

This financing route is not used to any great extent, because although a number of double tax agreements allow for tax sparing, many countries have sought to minimise its benefits to curtail what has been seen as an abuse of the system.

Note

1 Stephan Sayre and Stephen Gee acknowledge the assistance of Ed Hansom of GPA Group plc in the preparation of this Chapter.

4 Export credit agency support

Robert Murphy

Background

Export credit agency (ECA) supported funding has been an important source of financing in the aircraft sector during the past decade. A combination of factors has contributed to this. ECA support has been important when, in times of market downturn, liquidity of the lending markets has contracted and commercial lending margins have increased. Banks also look to manage their exposure to the aircraft sector by entering into transactions with reduced or zero risk weightings for capital adequacy purposes. An ECA guarantee is one way to achieve this result. ECA support can also assist airlines to achieve the best overall cost of funds when compared with other financing alternatives then available. In addition, the growing importance of overseas and emerging markets to the aircraft manufacturers has led to an inevitable reliance upon ECA support. Commercial banks are reluctant to lend into these markets without the additional credit and/or political risk enhancement that ECA support can bring.

The use of export credit support has also been fostered by the flexibility shown by the agencies in permitting the combination of ECA support with tax-driven structures. The combination of ECA-supported debt with the Japanese leveraged lease and the German leveraged lease has been a recurring feature of transactions in recent years. Airlines have, therefore, been able to obtain the benefits of a tax-driven structure without having to give up the advantage of using export credit support for the underlying debt. In addition, Eximbank in the United States has been willing to permit debt to be financed by way of the securitisation of Eximbank-guaranteed notes, and the European agencies have also indicated some willingness to consider securitisation structures. These developments mean that ECA-backed transactions can contain enhancements that prove attractive for the airlines in terms of the overall economics of the transaction.

The purpose of this chapter is to provide an overview of the regulatory framework in which ECAs relevant to the aircraft finance sector operate, the structures that have been used in ECA transactions and some of the issues that arise in relation to such transactions.

Regulatory framework

OECD Consensus

The Berne Union (which was established in 1934 in reaction to accusations of unfair and anti-competitive conduct among countries scrambling to win exports for their domestic industries) was the first body to set parameters for the operation of export credits. The status of primary regulator now rests with the Trade Committee of the Organisation for Economic Cooperation and Development (OECD).

The OECD promotes policies designed to achieve the highest possible economic growth and employment together with a rising standard of living in member countries. At the same time, its policies are aimed at maintaining financial stability, and thus contributing in a positive way to the world economy. Further aims of the OECD are to foster sound economic expansion in both member and non-member countries in the process of economic development and to contribute to the expansion of world trade on a multilateral, non-discriminatory basis in accordance with international obligations.

To further these objectives, member states participate in the 'Arrangement on Guidelines for Officially Supported Export Credits' (referred to here as the Consensus). The main purpose of the Consensus is to provide an institutional framework for an orderly export credit market and thus to prevent an export credit race in which exporting countries compete on the basis of who grants the most favourable financing terms rather than on the basis of who provides the highest quality goods and the best service for the lowest price.

The Consensus covers officially supported export credits with a duration of two years or more in the form of guarantees, indemnities, policies of insurance or subsidies. The Consensus addresses the terms and conditions of the export credit itself, not the terms and conditions of the particular guarantee or indemnity. Primarily the Consensus deals with issues such as the percentage of the contract eligible for support, the percentage of contract payments that must be covered by a cash payment, the maximum repayment term for export credits and the parameters for setting applicable interest rates in circumstances where fixed interest rates are officially supported.

It is possible for an ECA to deviate or derogate from the terms of the Consensus provided that it notifies the other participants who are then entitled to match that deviation or derogation. However, if that deviation or derogation is significant, then it is likely to result in complaints from other OECD members.

Sector Understanding on Export Credits for Civil Aircraft

In the 'Large Aircraft' sector (which includes commercial aircraft manufactured by Boeing, including McDonnell Douglas, and Airbus) the conditions for export credit support were originally set down in the 'Large Aircraft Sector Understanding' (LASU). The conditions have now been updated by the new OECD 'Sector Understanding on Export Credits for Civil Aircraft' (the Sector Understanding - see Appendix F), although the term LASU is still used when referring to export credits for large aircraft. The Sector Understanding complements and is part of the Consensus. It sets out the particular guidelines that are applicable to officially supported export credits for the sale and lease of new and used civil aircraft – including helicopters – as well as aero engines, spares, spare engines and maintenance and service contracts.

The Sector Understanding specifies four types of aircraft:

1 *Large Aircraft:* large commercial jets manufactured by Airbus, AI(R), AVRO RJ and Boeing (including McDonnell Douglas).
2 *Category A:* turbine powered aircraft with generally between 30 and 70 seats.
3 *Category B:* other turbine powered aircraft.
4 *Category C:* all non-turbine powered aircraft.

The maximum credit period available is determined by the type of aircraft. For Large Aircraft this is 12 years; for Category A, 10 years; for Category B, seven years; and for Category C, five years.

The maximum amount that can be supported is 85 per cent of the eligible contract price. This price will generally be the 'net-net' price as determined by the relevant ECA and will typically exclude the value of all credit memoranda and other discounts provided by the manufacturer to the airline. The final eligible contract price in any transaction will be subject to the approval of the relevant ECAs who will need to be satisfied as to matters such as the price and domestic/foreign content of equipment (often by reference to invoices and other supporting information from the manufacturer). The 85 per cent applies to this net price of the airframe and installed engines.

Support at 85 per cent is also available for an initial supply of spare engines and spare parts on the following basis:

- for the first five aircraft of the type in the fleet of any one airline – 15 per cent of the aircraft price (airframe and installed engines);
- for the sixth and subsequent aircraft of that type in the fleet – 10 per cent of the aircraft price (airframe and installed engines).

The loan supported by the ECA will be required to amortise on the basis of level payments of principal semi-annually in arrears or have a repayment profile comprising equal mortgage style periodic payments (made up of principal and interest). If the transaction is structured as a loan to the airline (rather than a finance lease) then repayments will be on the basis of equal payments of principal together with interest on the declining balance of the loan.

The Sector Understanding envisages two forms of support:

1 Financing support in the form of interest support; the ECAs will 'make up' the difference between a predetermined fixed rate of interest payable by the airline and the commercial rate of return expected by the lenders.
2 'Pure cover' in the form of guarantees or insurance in respect of all or part of the airline's indebtedness to the lenders.

In a fixed rate financing the ECAs will provide both interest rate support and a guarantee or insurance covering the airline's indebtedness. In a floating rate financing the support will be by way of pure cover only.

For Large Aircraft, specific arrangements apply for determining the fixed rate of interest (referred to as the LASU rate). For other aircraft, official support at a fixed interest rate is determined on the basis of the commercial interest reference rates (CIRR) set in accordance with the Consensus.

In 'pure cover' transactions, the rate of interest is either a floating rate or a fixed rate determined by a market interest rate swap typically entered into by the lending banks.

For Large Aircraft US dollar financings, the LASU rates are linked to 10-year Treasury bond yields. For financing with a term of up to 10 years the applicable rate is the 10-year Treasury bond plus 120 basis points. For a 12-year financing, the margin is 175 basis points over the 10-year Treasury bond. Financing in Deutschmarks, French francs, sterling or ECUs is based on 10-year government bond yields for the relevant currencies plus an equivalent margin.

Revised LASU rates are released every two weeks to reflect fluctuations in government bond yields. The method of determining the LASU rate involves notionally dividing the loan into two tranches – tranche A and tranche B. Where repayments are spread over the entire life of the loan, tranche A is weighted to cover the first 62.5 per cent of the aircraft purchase price and tranche B the next 22.5 per cent, making a total of 85 per cent (ie the maximum in respect of which cover can be provided).

The tranche A rate is determined by the 10-year government bond yield for the relevant currency, together with a margin of either 1.2 per cent for up to 10-year finance or 1.75 per cent for 10- to 12-year finance. The tranche B rate is determined by using information supplied weekly by Eximbank on lending rates provided by the Private Export Funding Corporation (PEFCO) and applying average PEFCO margins to the 10-year government bond yield.

The LASU rate will include an element for the premiums due to the ECAs over the life of the export credit debt. For example, premiums of the order of 50 basis points are typically built into the rate for European ECA transactions.

The LASU rate mechanism can effectively give the airline a no-cost interest rate option which the airline is not under any obligation to use. The airline can 'lock in' to a LASU rate up to three years prior to delivery.

ECA support may also be given for used aircraft transactions. LASU fixed interest rate arrangements do not apply to used aircraft (even used large aircraft) and any fixed interest rate support will be provided at the relevant CIRR. The normal maximum repayment term depends on the age of the aircraft in question, ranging from 10 years for a large aircraft which is between one and two years old, to five years for a large aircraft which is over 10 years old.

The ECAs require advance payment of their insurance premiums or guarantee or exposure fees. These amounts will typically be financed as part of the overall transaction. It is worth noting, however, that for Airbus aircraft there is currently a premium of 50 basis points per annum on the outstanding balance of the loan payable over the life of the transaction. Eximbank's standard exposure fee for issuing a guarantee in Large Aircraft financing is 3 per cent of the amount disbursed under the Eximbank loan, payable upfront, but which may be included in the financed amount. Eximbank also applies a loan guarantee commitment fee of one eighth of 1 per cent per annum on the unutilised amount of the loan. This fee starts to accrue 60 days after Eximbank issues its final commitment.

Export credit agencies

OECD country ECAs are obliged under the Consensus to operate within the same parameters. However, there remains scope for agencies to differentiate themselves through the type of services they provide. There are also a number of structural factors that can cause ECAs to provide different types of service. For example, the ownership of the ECA can differ from country to country; it may be a government department, some form of state-owned body or company or even a private institution. Also, in some countries (eg, Germany) state-owned banks participate in the funding of a large number of export credit-backed transactions. The ECAs in these countries operate in close cooperation with the state-owned banks.

The key agencies most usually encountered in aircraft finance are the European ECAs (ECGD, COFACE and HERMES) and Eximbank in the US.

European ECAs

ECGD

In the UK, export credits are provided by the Export Credits Guarantee Department (ECGD), which is a department of the UK government reporting to the President of the Board of Trade. ECGD provides:

1 cover for commercial, political and transfer risks;
2 buyer credit or supplier credit financing;
3 insurance/guarantee support for UK suppliers or banks that fund exports by UK suppliers or for companies investing overseas.

ECGD is required by the government to trade at no net cost to public funds. Accordingly premiums, although not necessarily set at commercial rates, are charged at rates estimated to cover administrative costs and expected losses. Rates are set taking into account usual commercial factors such as country risk, the creditworthiness of the buyer, the sum insured and the duration of the exposure. For buyer credits, the ECGD guarantee covers 100 per cent of losses that may be sustained by the bank in respect of the loan. Each lending bank must be an authorised entity under UK banking legislation (the Banking Act, 1987) and acceptable to ECGD. ECGD annual reports and trading accounts show that it has supported over £4 billion of aerospace business during financial years 1991/92 to 1996/97.

COFACE

The French export agency is the Compagnie Française d'Assurance pour le Commerce Extérieur (COFACE). It is a semi-public joint stock company which is active in the provision of export credit cover, including, as is the case with aircraft, in support of financings where it acts on the instructions of the French government (acting through the Direction des Relations Economiques Exterieur - the 'DREE'). As with ECGD, COFACE maintains that it provides the broadest available range of services to exporters.

Cover for political, commercial and transfer risks is available from COFACE through buyer or supplier credits for short, medium and long terms. In limited circumstances (where, for example, the credit being supported is sufficiently strong), COFACE may offer cover for 100 per cent of losses. However, COFACE generally imposes ceilings on its cover ranging from 85 per cent to 95 per cent based on the type of risk insured and the nature of the asset exported. Typically, aircraft financing receives up to 95 per cent insurance.

COFACE gives guarantees direct to French exporters and to credit institutions (which need not be resident in France) financing French exports. In addition, it guarantees financing raised on international bond markets, and provides currency exchange risk insurance, bond insurance and cost escalation insurance, subject in each case to certain criteria being met.

Premiums are charged on the basis of an assessment of a combination of factors including buyer risk, country risk and the quantum and length of the insurance.

COFACE and ECGD have also signed a cooperation agreement that permits UK/French exporters to use a single ECA when bidding for export contracts. Under this agreement the ECA whose exporter has the major share of the contract will take the lead and offer to provide export credit terms for the whole contract on its usual terms; the other ECA provides the lead ECA with reinsurance.

HERMES

In Germany, a consortium is authorised to manage the export credit insurance business of the government. This consortium consists of Hermes Kreditversicherung Aktiengesellschaft (which is the leading party in the consortium and a private insurance corporation) and C&L Deutsche Revision. This consortium acts only in the name of and on the account of the state.

The consortium, referred to as HERMES provides short-, medium- and long-term political risk insurance and guarantees. Insurance cover cannot be obtained from HERMES for 100 per cent of a risk. Depending on the nature of the risk, the supplier is obliged to bear a proportion of the loss. In aircraft financing transactions the banks, as beneficiaries of the guarantee, are entitled to up to 95 per cent cover. Insurance can be provided either directly to the supplier or to the bank funding the buyer. To be eligible for support, it is necessary for the buyer or his guarantor to meet certain criteria, including being considered by HERMES to be a good credit risk. In addition, the supply agreements and any loan documentation must be on 'regular terms'.

HERMES also offers a limited amount of foreign exchange risk insurance, bond insurance and investment risk insurance.

Direct credits are extended through Kreditanstalt für Wiederaufbau (KfW), a corporation established under public law, and Ausfuhrkredit-Gesellschaft (AKA), a private company set up to finance export credits with funds contributed by banking syndicates. Loans are made to finance both buyer and supplier credits. Both organisations offer fixed rate funding down to Consensus minimum interest levels. KfW also funds to a limited extent in foreign currencies. Its initial foreign currency funding operations were limited to aircraft financings in US dollars and were guaranteed by HERMES. Increasingly however, KfW has financed – again mainly in US dollars – aircraft and ship sales and other transactions involving capital goods without a HERMES exchange risk guarantee.

Overall, according to *Air Finance Journal*'s survey published in March 1997, European ECA transactions accounted for financings of the order of US$5.5 billion in aggregate during the period from June 1995 to February 1997. These transactions included some US$2 billion in ECA/Japanese leveraged lease structures and US$1 billion in ECA/German leveraged lease structures.

US ECAs

The US has a number of ECAs that are either government owned or, effectively, government controlled.

The representative organisation is the Export-Import Bank of the United States (Eximbank). The other significant supporter of US exporters relevant to aircraft finance is the Private Export Funding Corporation (PEFCO). PEFCO is privately owned but Eximbank unconditionally guarantees PEFCO loans and therefore maintains a measure of control over it.

These organisations between them provide almost the whole range of services provided by the European agencies. However, percentage limits on foreign-sourced components or amount of risk coverage may differ in certain ways from those available from the European agencies. Another significant difference is that Eximbank and PEFCO may themselves provide direct loans on export credit transactions.

Eximbank's figures show the increase in its activity in the Large Aircraft sector over the past three years, with its total amount of aircraft finance transactions increasing from US$1 billion in 1995 to close to US$2.2 billion in 1997. According to data supplied to the 12th Annual Air Finance Legal Conference in November 1997, in the five-year period to 1997, public offerings (securitisations) accounted for close to 20 per cent of all Eximbank-supported transactions (in value terms) and, in the period from 1990 to 1997, Eximbank-supported Japanese leveraged leases accounted for close to 16 per cent (in value terms). The *Air Finance Journal* survey referred to above suggests that market share of Eximbank and European ECA-supported financings was split on a broadly 50/50 basis in respect of transactions covered by their survey.

Exhibit 4.1
An ECA-backed Airbus financing structure

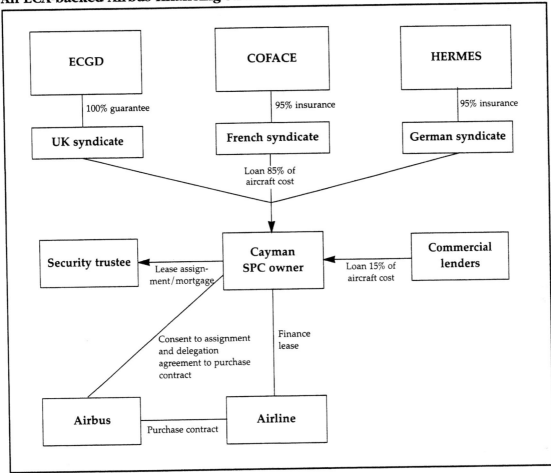

Some key issues

Structures

ECA aircraft financing will generally be structured as a finance lease. The Sector Understanding expressly contemplates this and, for various structural and security reasons, such structures tend to suit the needs of the parties to these transactions.

A fairly typical European export credit finance lease structure is illustrated in Exhibit 4.1. The exhibit shows an Airbus export credit financing provided by syndicates of lenders supported by the relevant ECAs in the three principal countries that participate in the manufacture of Airbus aircraft – France, Germany and the UK. Although there are three separate loans, they will be provided for in one loan agreement between the three syndicates of banks and the borrower (SPC).

The structure is relatively simple. The aggregate participations of each syndicate reflect the involvement of the country in which it is based in the manufacture of the aircraft in question. This varies from aircraft to aircraft. The percentages will also vary depending on the type of engine chosen by the operator.

Exhibit 4.2
An ECA-backed Airbus financing transaction with a JLL

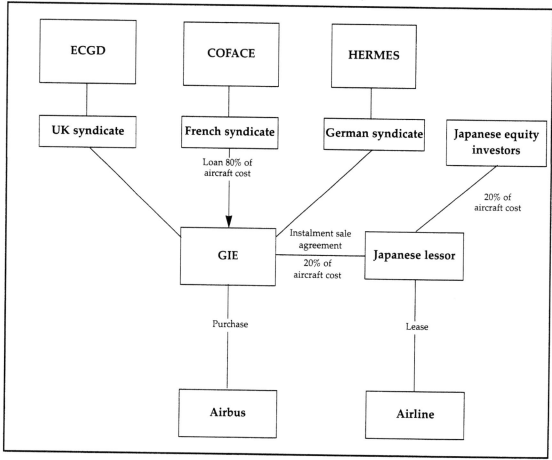

The banks in each syndicate have traditionally been British banks for the UK syndicate, French banks for the French syndicate and German banks for the German syndicate. However, it is also common in relation to the UK and French syndicates for foreign banks, acting through their London or Paris branches as appropriate, to be members of the UK or French syndicates. The German syndicates are generally made up of German banks but in some instances German branches of foreign banks have also participated. The German national export credit bank, KfW, also participates in German syndicates.

In this example, the full 85 per cent ECA support is provided and the balance of the purchase price is funded by way of a commercial loan. The aircraft will be purchased by a special purpose company (SPC) located in a tax-neutral jurisdiction or sometimes a GIE in France. This entity may be owned by the airline but will more usually be owned by one of the arrangers or lead banks and it will enter into a full payout finance lease with the airline.

The basic structure shown in Exhibit 4.1 can be enhanced to provide further benefits to the airline by combining the structure with a tax lease product such as a Japanese leveraged lease (JLL). This combined structure has been successfully used in a number of Airbus transactions and is shown in Exhibit 4.2.

To optimise the structure, the three syndicates will advance the loan to a *groupement d'intérêt économique* (GIE) based in France, which, by way of an instalment sale agreement, passes title to the aircraft to the Japanese lessor. The aircraft will then be leased by the Japanese lessor to the airline under a lease complying with the ECAs' requirements as well as the requirements of the Japanese tax authorities and the Japanese lessor. In this structure, effectively export credit support has been given in respect of the debt portion of a Japanese leveraged lease. The use of the instalment sale route reconciles the requirements of the ECAs for the lending syndicates to be comprised of banks based in the home countries and the need for the structure to be neutral from the perspective of withholding taxes that may arise in Japan.

European export credits have also been combined with German leveraged leases using various different structures. In such a transaction HERMES will not, for policy reasons, participate and thus the borrower will need to make up the funding gap with further commercial debt or other funds.

As regards Eximbank, the Eximbank/JLL product has also been devised and applied successfully in many aircraft finance transactions. The basic structure is illustrated in Exhibit 4.3. In this case, and in contrast to the European structure, the lenders are either Japanese banks or

Exhibit 4.3
An Eximbank/JLL structure

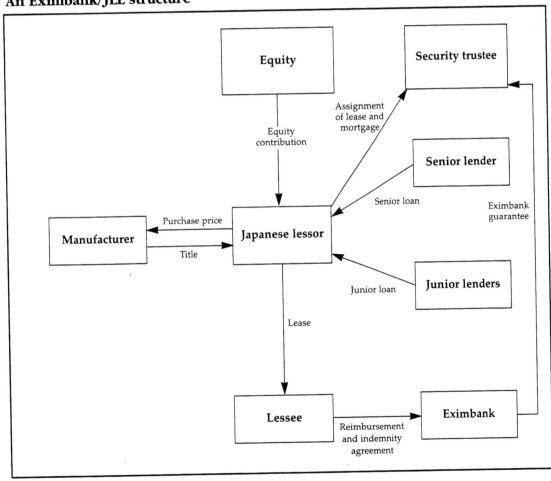

Exhibit 4.4
Eximbank/ECGD structure: Boeing aircraft with Rolls-Royce engines

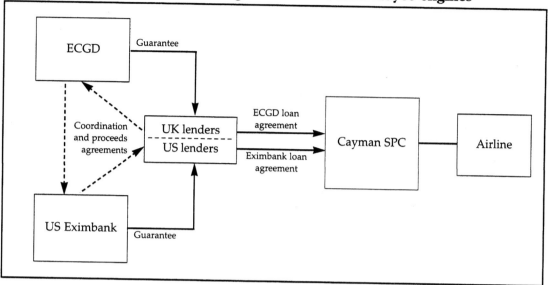

Japanese branches of foreign banks and the loans are made directly to the Japanese owner. Another feature of Eximbank transactions that differs from European ECA transactions is the reimbursement and indemnity agreement that Eximbank concludes directly with the airline. This agreement contains a range of direct agreements between Eximbank and the airline, including the amount of cover being provided, exposure and commitment fees, counter-indemnification from the airline and a range of representations and warranties from the airline.

In a non-tax-enhanced Eximbank transaction, the loans are made to a special purpose company owned by the airline and located in a tax-neutral jurisdiction.

Finally, a further structure which has been used (in cases where Boeing aircraft are fitted with Rolls-Royce engines) combines Eximbank and ECGD support (see Exhibit 4.4). These transactions are structured on the basis of separate Eximbank and ECGD loans to a special purpose owning company which then leases the Aircraft to the airline on a full payout finance lease basis. This structure enables each ECA to ensure that the loan that it supports accords with its standard terms and the relationship between the ECAs is governed by a coordination and proceeds agreement.

Other issues

In addition to compliance requirements with LASU and the Consensus, the ECAs will have much the same concerns as financiers in other types of aircraft financing transactions. Accordingly, the usual withholding tax and other tax indemnity issues, operational indemnity, insurance, maintenance, security, legal opinions and other similar issues will arise. The ECAs also have particular policy and operational requirements.

The agencies usually require as security for their commitment a duly registered first-priority aircraft mortgage. If the lessor special purpose company is owned or controlled by the airline, then a pledge of its shares will also be required. Depending upon the nature of the transaction, ECAs may also look to receive appropriate third party (including in some cases, sovereign) guarantees of the obligations of the lessee and will also seek assignment of the benefit of the lease and insurance policies in respect of the aircraft.

The ECAs will be the senior secured party and will control the exercise of rights in connection with calling defaults, accelerating and terminating the transaction and enforcing the security. The ECAs will restrict the rights of any junior commercial lenders or tax lessors in this regard. Limitations required by the ECAs include standstill periods (often up to 180 days) during which junior debt/equity parties are prohibited from proceeding against the aircraft or any other joint collateral. Limitations can also be applied to the amount of the junior debt portion that can be secured by any mortgage. Inter-creditor discussions and documents among the junior debt parties and ECAs need careful management in these transactions.

In transactions where support is given to airlines, the ECAs will limit sub-leasing rights. The agencies will generally wish their consent to be given to any sub-leasing, although some limited pre-agreed sub-leasing rights can be negotiated. In addition, restrictions apply on sub-leasing to the country of manufacture of the aircraft.

In an ECA transaction that includes a tax lease, the ECAs will want to make sure that they do not take any structural risk associated with the tax lessor's participation in the transaction. Whereas commercial lenders may be willing, depending upon the relative strength of the negotiating positions of the parties, to accept a measure of such risk, the ECAs will not generally agree to do so. So, for example, the ECAs will not accept risks associated with default by the lessor or withholding or other taxes arising in the lessor's home jurisdiction and will look to the airline or leaders to take these risks and effectively underwrite the risk of the lessor.

Overview

ECAs are set to continue to play an important role in aircraft finance transactions. Apart from comparing the relative economics of ECA transactions with other options that may be available to them, airlines considering ECA transactions need to ensure that the approval procedures and policy and documentation requirements of the relevant ECAs are fully taken into account. Experience shows that ECA transactions can proceed smoothly provided that these requirements of the ECAs are understood by all the parties to the transaction, and the ECAs are fully involved in the transaction at all the key stages (including, if appropriate, the structuring phase). This is particularly important where the proposed transaction structure is not straightforward, as is the case, for example, with combined ECA/tax structures.

5 Operating leasing

Colm Barrington

What is an operating lease?

The essence of an aircraft operating lease is that an operating lessor must arrange and manage several transactions over an aircraft's life cycle rather than look to a single lessee as the source of its income and return. Under an operating lease, a lessor does not have the credit of a single lessee to provide a return on, and to repay, the capital investment in the aircraft. Rather, it must rely on its ability to arrange several consecutive leases and to eventually sell the aircraft in order to generate its return and to repay its capital. As a result, an operating lessor receives all the benefits from achieving higher lease rates or a higher sales price and also suffers the cost of lessee defaults or lower lease rates.

In contrast, the essence of a finance lease is that the lessor looks to the credit of a single lessee rather than the value of the asset as the generator of return and the source for repayment of capital. Under a finance lease, the lessee takes most of the risks and rewards of ownership and, subject to the lessee meeting all of its obligations, the lessor's return is substantially predefined. Nevertheless, in both operating and finance leases, the lessee takes most of the operational risks and rewards from use of the aircraft.

The 'real' operating lease described briefly above differs significantly from a long-term, tax-enhanced lease that meets accounting guidelines for classification as an operating lease (resulting in the lessee not being required to reflect it on its balance sheet) but which is essentially a full or near full payout finance lease. While such leases do require the lessor to take some residual risk, this is normally negligible in relation to the expected real value of the aircraft at the end of the lease term.

In the late 1980s, several airlines, including major carriers such as British Airways and American Airlines, entered into 'walk away leases'. These were long-term leases that allowed the airlines to return the aircraft to the owners on relatively short notice and with a negligible penalty. These leases were supported by airframe and engine manufacturers (including Airbus Industrie, Boeing, General Electric and Rolls-Royce) in order to place their aircraft and engines with certain key airline customers. To meet the airlines' demands and place their products, the manufacturers took the risk that the aircraft could be returned at any time over the life of the lease.

For airlines, walk away leases provide the flexibility of operating leases. Because lessees can treat them as operating leases, they provide the ability to acquire aircraft on a long-term basis while not having to reflect the leases as balance sheet liabilities. In the case of British Airways, these arrangements, along with other structuring, had a significantly beneficial effect on its balance sheet immediately prior to privatisation. For the manufacturers these leases involve risk, but they also provide a competitive edge when it is important to win strategic airline customers.

To an extent, the business of owning aircraft on real operating leases is similar to the business of trading in commodities. The lessor's level of profit is greatly dependent on the balance of supply and demand. If demand outstrips supply, then the operating lessor can expect to see lease rates harden and sales prices rise. If supply is greater than demand, then the operating lessor will find it more difficult to find new lessees, lease rental rates will decline and the capital values of aircraft will reduce. The difference between the buoyant market conditions of the late 1980s and the depressed early 1990s is the most recent example of the two extremes of demand and supply imbalances.

An operating lessor is also a form of 'pressure valve' for the airline industry. To the extent that airlines have at least a portion of their fleets on operating leases then, if their business volumes decline, they can return aircraft to operating lessors as the lease terms end – not always at the precise time that they would like, but normally during the course of a depression in the business cycle. Similarly when business levels improve, the availability of aircraft on operating lease – normally on shorter notice than they can be acquired directly from manufacturers – allows airlines to respond to market opportunities as they arise.

So while operating lessors take the risks and rewards of aircraft ownership and airlines take the risks and rewards of aircraft operation, the fortunes of the two are closely linked. A boom in the airline business, such as was experienced in the late 1980s, will be very beneficial to operating lessors, while a depression in airline business, such as was experienced in the early 1990s, will have a negative impact on their business.

Features of operating leases

Operating leases have several characteristics that distinguish them from other types of lease. These characteristics (detailed below) are normal to operating leases, although not all operating leases include all of them:

- The term of an aircraft operating lease is normally significantly shorter than the life of the aircraft. Typically, operating leases have terms ranging from three to seven years, although there have been leases written with terms shorter than six months and longer than twelve years. With an average lease term of five years, an aircraft will therefore be leased on several occasions during its life-cycle (modern jet aircraft having lives of approximately thirty years).
- Operating lease rentals are set by market conditions rather than by reference to the purchase price of the aircraft or prevailing interest rates (although some operating lease rentals vary if interest rates change during the lease term). Unlike finance leases, which are akin to secured lending, the pricing of operating leases is closer to the pricing of a normal commercial product than to that of a financial instrument. As a very broad rule of thumb, operating lease rentals have settled at between 0.85 per cent and 1.50 per cent a month of the value of the aircraft (although 'value' may not necessarily be what the lessor paid for the aircraft). The general expectation is that monthly rental rates of modern commercial aircraft will be in the range of 0.9–1.1 per cent of the aircraft's capital value and that older aircraft will have higher rental rates.
- Operating lease rentals are normally payable monthly and in advance, although some better-credit airlines negotiate rentals monthly or quarterly in arrears.
- An operating lease will normally include a security deposit that the lessee will transfer to the

lessor prior to delivery of the aircraft under the lease. The security deposit is normally equivalent to two to three months' rental and will be in the form of cash or a letter of credit from a first-class bank. Thus the lessee's up-front contribution to the transaction (including the first month's rent) will normally be limited to about 4 per cent of the asset value. This is one of the reasons why aircraft operating leasing has become so popular among so many airlines. There are not many industries where a poor or unknown credit can acquire the use of high-value capital equipment for an up-front investment of 4 per cent.

- Operating leases normally include maintenance accruals or supplemental rents whereby the lessee pays additional amounts based on its monthly usage of the aircraft in order to build up a dedicated fund for future major maintenance expenditures. Maintenance accrual rates are usually set at the estimated hourly cost of each major maintenance event, including airframe D or equivalent checks, engine off-wing maintenance and life limited part replacement and major overhaul of landing gear and auxiliary power units.

- Operating leases generally allow the lessor to have relatively free access to the aircraft for the purpose of technical inspections. The lessor will also have approval rights over the maintenance programme and over the selection of the maintenance providers.

- An important feature of operating leases is their concentration on redelivery conditions. An operating lessor will always try to get its aircraft back at the end of a lease term in as good a technical condition as possible and with the lessee having completed major maintenance that will allow the greatest possible flexibility in remarketing the aircraft. The lessor will also want to ensure that all the maintenance value that the lessee has 'used up' during the lease term is either replaced by the completion of major maintenance, is paid for by the lessee through an end of lease maintenance adjustment (known in industry jargon as an 'upsy downsy' payment) or is held by the lessor in the form of maintenance accrual balances.

- An operating lease will also include strict insurance provisions. The lease agreement will lay down minimum insurance amounts (in the case of casualty insurance, normally at least the replacement cost of the aircraft) and the lessee will be responsible for taking out adequate insurance to cover these amounts. In the event of a casualty, all the proceeds from the insurance claim will go directly to the lessor, not merely an amount equal to a stipulated loss value or outstanding balance of financing, as in finance leases.

- An operating lease will have relatively stringent restrictions on the lessee's right to sub-lease the aircraft. In most cases sub-leasing will require the specific approval of the lessor, although in some instances certain potential sub-lessees may be pre-approved.

- Operating leases normally do not provide the lessee with any special lease renewal rights or option rights to acquire the aircraft. If the lessee has any lease renewal rights, they will normally be at a price equal to future fair market rentals and any purchase option in favour of the lessee will normally be at a price determined by future fair market value. Thus, while the lessee may have certain rights to retain use of the aircraft, it will normally be obliged to pay prevailing rates or the prevailing price on the renewal or purchase option date. An option agreement will also normally include a floor price in order to ensure that the exercise of the option by the lessee does not trigger a book loss for the lessor.

- Finally, operating leases do not generally include any financial covenants or ratios in respect of the lessee, such as one might find in a loan agreement or finance lease. On the other hand, an operating lease may include a change of control clause that triggers an event of default if the current parent of the lessee disposes of its equity interest.

Development of operating leasing

Aircraft operating leasing developed in the 1960s, mainly as a way for established airlines to pass on surplus or ageing aircraft to emerging carriers. These early days of operating leasing involved only used aircraft and only leases from one airline to another.

In the mid-1970s the business expanded and began to involve specialist lessors, such as International Lease Finance Corporation (ILFC) and Guinness Peat Aviation (GPA), who bought surplus aircraft from airlines and leased them to other airlines. In the mid-1980s these two companies, which by then had built up reasonably substantial fleets of used equipment, purchased new aircraft directly from the manufacturers. In the case of both companies this initially involved orders for new B737-300s. It was some years later before either company ordered different types from Boeing, or indeed, any aircraft from other manufacturers. In the late 1980s, ILFC, Ansett World Wide Aviation Services (AWAS) and GPA began to order large numbers of new jet aircraft from Airbus Industrie, Boeing, Fokker and McDonnell Douglas. GPA also ordered large numbers of turbo-prop aircraft from both ATR and deHavilland.

The main reason why operating leasing has developed to where it is today (with approximately 20 per cent of the world's aircraft now on operating lease) is that it has filled a real need. The airlines that use operating leases consider that the flexibility such leases provide makes up for the fact that the cash costs of the leases can be greater than the cost of acquiring the same aircraft through ownership or on long-term, tax-enhanced finance leases.

Many airlines acquire aircraft on operating lease because it is the only way that they can obtain the equipment that they need for their business. This may be because they have not made prior orders and so cannot acquire new aircraft from the manufacturers. This applies to most start-up airlines. Another reason for operating leasing is that some airlines do not have access to the capital needed to fund direct purchases, because they have poor or no credit histories or are located in jurisdictions where lenders have credit restrictions. This has applied to many South American airlines.

As a result of prior orders for new equipment or returns of aircraft from earlier leases, operating lessors normally have been able to provide aircraft on much shorter notice than manufacturers and, because of their emphasis on assets rather than credits, operating lessors have been more prepared to deal with poorer-credit airlines than have lenders.

As referred to earlier, some airlines have taken aircraft on operating lease because of their interest in improving their balance sheet ratios, particularly maintaining a low debt/equity ratio. The fact that aircraft on operating lease do not appear on airlines' balance sheets is a great advantage in this regard. If airlines were more conscious of the true costs of their entire capital structure – debt and equity – then more of them might choose the operating leasing option.

Finally, some airlines choose operating leases as a way of making a relatively short-term commitment to a particular aircraft type. This can be to take advantage of a market opportunity that may arise but which may not continue, or because the airline does not want to make a long-term commitment to further units of an aircraft type that it is planning to phase out in the foreseeable future.

Sales and operating leasebacks

Since the 1980s, many airlines have entered into sale-leaseback transactions with operating lessors or with financial investors who have had their affairs managed by companies that provide lease management services.

This business started in the United States where intermediaries arranged groups of investors who subscribed for units in income funds. The managers then used the funds to purchase large numbers of aircraft from US airlines and lease them back on operating leases. The investors expected to benefit from the rental cash flow and from residual gains when the aircraft were sold at the end of the lease terms. In some cases they also expected to receive tax benefits from their ownership of the aircraft.

Many of these early transactions were ill-conceived and the investors did not achieve their aims. The up-front cost of arranging and distributing the transactions was high (in many cases more than 10 cents in the dollar), the managers had to pay high prices to build their portfolios (the aircraft were bought at above fair market prices), the aircraft were older types that were nearing the end of their productive lives (the expected residual values were not achieved) and the credit of some of the airlines was not good (the lease cash flows ceased). In many cases the technical and maintenance condition of the aircraft at the end of the lease terms was not adequately secured.

Today, the sale-leaseback market is more mature and many of the transactions being structured make good financial sense both for the investors who are buying and leasing the aircraft and for the airlines who are selling them and leasing them back.

From the investors' perspective, the critical issue is to purchase aircraft that are relatively young in their product-cycle and that are likely to have a broad leasing market when their initial lease terms end. This will enhance the likelihood of continuing cash flows from leasing the aircraft and the probability of a secondary market for their sale. In this regard, popular narrow-body aircraft and the more widely used versions of types such as the B767 are the most popular aircraft with investors. Although many airlines with a high credit standing (such as SAS) have entered into sale–leasebacks, it is the asset quality and future residual exposure that is of greater relevance to investors. The more sophisticated investors, supported by competent and knowledgeable lease managers, are prepared to enter into sale-leaseback transactions with good quality assets but with lesser-quality credits. Because of tax regulations in Japan, such transactions have been particularly attractive to investors there, but there is also a relatively active market in other jurisdictions.

For airlines, such transactions provide all the benefits previously referred to but with the additional benefit of providing cash from the sale of the aircraft that can be used to fund operations or to acquire new equipment. For investors, they provide attractive (often tax-enhanced) returns.

Important commercial issues

For a lessor to maximise its return from an operating lease, it must focus on and successfully address several factors. This is true for both operating lessors that acquire new and used aircraft on a speculative basis, hoping that they can lease them in the future, and for investors who purchase aircraft from airlines and lease them back immediately.

An operating lease transaction cannot be shown to be profitable until the aircraft has finally been sold. This is because a significant part of the lessor's return will come from the final sales price. Operating lessors must therefore focus on the price they pay for the aircraft, on maintaining its value over the period that they own it and on maximising its value at the time they sell it. They should also be prepared to sell aircraft at times of strong market demand and hold them when market conditions are depressed. Successful operating lessors have generally been those with a continuity of capital.

Operating lessors should focus on the following issues:

1 purchase price;
2 rental rate;
3 residual value;
4 debt:equity ratio;
5 cost of debt; and
6 continuing availability of capital.

1 Purchase price

All else being equal, the purchase price of the aircraft is the single most important determinant of the lessor's return.

The major operating lessors expect to achieve low purchase prices for new aircraft as a result of making large orders with the manufacturers. Their purchasing power can give them large volume discounts on both airframes and engines – sometimes more than 20 per cent below the manufacturer's list prices. While many larger airlines can negotiate equivalent discounts, the smaller and mid-size airlines that form the major part of the operating lessors' customer base normally pay higher prices. Smaller lessors and sale-leaseback investors cannot expect prices as low as the major lessors and so must look to other features, such as tax benefits or market anomalies, in order to make satisfactory returns.

2 Rental rate

When attempting to maximise lease rental rates, the major operating lease companies should have a competitive advantage over their competitors because their broad market coverage and market intelligence should enable them to achieve the best rates available. As against this, the broad range of operating leasing industry information that is now available, both formal and informal, is significantly beneficial to potential lessees. Also, market relationships and rapid response are aspects that benefit the smaller independent and more entrepreneurial lease managers. As a result, the spread between the highest and lowest lease rates achieved during any period or cycle is not significant.

In fact, other than as a result of general market conditions, the main determinant of the level of lease rates in any particular period is the credit exposure that a lessor is prepared to take. One of the major decisions an operating lessor must take is whether to accept a relatively low rental from a good credit in a benign jurisdiction or to take a higher rental from a less good credit in a more hostile jurisdiction, or some middle position. In many cases this decision will depend on the lessor's view of its own ability to manage the asset and the lease. It may also depend on what the lessor intends to do with the aircraft over time. If the intent is to hold the aircraft, then it may be more profitable to take a higher rental and manage any problems that arise. If the lessor wishes to sell the aircraft as a financial asset to an investor that is less active in aircraft and lease management, then it may be better to accept a lower rental from a better credit that will be more recognisable and acceptable in the investor community.

3 Residual value

The third important factor in achieving a satisfactory return from an operating lease is the value actually achieved when the aircraft is sold. An operating lessor may either sell an aircraft unleased at the end of an initial or subsequent lease term or may alternatively sell the aircraft subject to an operating lease to another party that is interested in participating in the aircraft operating leasing business. This aspect of operating leasing is addressed in a later section.

In general (and simple) terms, lease rentals (at 1 per cent a month) will contribute 60 per cent of an aircraft's cost over the five-year term of an average operating lease. Allowing for moderate inflation, a lessor can expect the residual value of an aircraft after five years to be between 80 and 100 per cent of the original cost. Although lease rentals are more important on a present value basis, maximising the sales price adds significant value to an operating lease transaction.

4 Debt:equity ratio

A higher debt/equity ratio can have a significant positive input on an operating lessor's return on equity. Over the years, ILFC managed to achieve greater leverage than GPA (mainly because ILFC was active in the US capital markets and GPA relied on bank debt). As a result, ILFC's return on equity from its leasing (as distinct from aircraft sales) business was higher than GPA's. Today, the (approximate) nine-to-one leverage of GE Capital assists in achieving healthy equity returns from its aircraft operating leasing (and other) businesses.

5 Cost of debt

It is generally believed that lessors with lower borrowing costs have a significant competitive advantage over their competitors. In fact this is not the case, with the cost of debt being less important than the factors mentioned above in the overall calculation of returns.

Exhibit 5.1 summarises the issues discussed in these five sub-sections. It shows the change to an operating lessor's base case, after-tax return on equity from a 5 per cent change in each of the five variables. While a full understanding of the relationships would require a more in-depth discussion of all the assumptions in the model, the table does illustrate the relative importance of each of the factors.

Exhibit 5.1
Return on equity (ROE) elasticity for variables 1–5

Variable	Base case	Change	ROE elasticity
1 Purchase price	Fair market value	-5%	+2.3%
2 Rental rate	1% per month	+5%	+1.3%
3 Residual value	81% of purchase price	+5%	+1.0%
4 Debt:equity ratio	80:20	+5%	+0.9%
5 Cost of debt	6.5%	-5%	+0.4%

Source: Babcock & Brown

6 Continuing availability of capital

The final important factor that an operating lessor must consider, and ensure, is the continuing availability of capital. Aircraft operating leasing is a cyclical business and the debt and equity markets can be fickle. A successful operating lessor must ensure that it has continuing access to the capital that it needs to meet its commitments. It is probably not a coincidence that the only two really significant remaining operating lease companies – GECAS and ILFC – are wholly-owned subsidiaries of triple A rated companies.

Key contractual issues

The key issues that operating lessors must secure in their lease agreements relate to the preservation of the value of their aircraft. Much of an operating lease agreement will therefore deal with the conditions of the aircraft at delivery, the security for payments and the maintenance of the aircraft over the term of the lease, and the redelivery of the aircraft at the end of the lease term.

An operating lessor has several commercial and contractual tools that it can use in order to ensure that its lessees meet the obligations that they have agreed to. In summary, these are as follows:

- That all payments in lease agreements are in US dollars, the currency of international aviation. Thus the lessor takes no currency risk.
- The principal contractual provision that an operating lessor relies upon is the fact that all operating leases are 'net, net leases'. In other words, the lessee is required to operate, maintain, use and care for the aircraft as if it were its own and is also required to continue to meet its contractual and payment obligations to the lessor in all circumstances.
- Operating lessors also have certain financial protections, including security deposits, advance rentals and maintenance reserves, which provide them with certain limited protections in the event that their lessees fail to honour their contractual obligations.
- The lease provisions that lessors need to focus on are those relating to the maintenance of the aircraft during the lease term and, particularly, the condition in which the lessee is obliged to return the aircraft at the end of the term. A lessor should seek the following:
  - To have the lessee return the aircraft in a condition that allows it to be immediately leased to another airline without the need for any down time;
  - To have the aircraft in a maintenance condition that will allow at least one full year of operation before the aircraft requires any major maintenance on airframe, engines and components; and
  - To have the aircraft returned by the lessee in at least the same maintenance status as it was when delivered, or alternatively, to have the lessee pay sufficient financial compensation for the lessor to achieve this status at no cost to itself.

Operating lease rentals

Operating lease rental rates are influenced significantly by the market conditions prevailing at the time the aircraft is leased. Thus the rental rates that lessors achieve for the same aircraft type will often vary based on the time when each lease was negotiated. As a result, the date on which an aircraft is leased will, within reason, have more influence on the lease rental rate than will the date of manufacture.

Operating lease rates can be fixed or variable with interest rates. As operating lessors have developed more sophisticated treasury procedures, and in response to market demand, rentals are now generally fixed for the term of the lease.

Floating rentals are normally based off six-month LIBOR, although longer or shorter interest rate periods can be used. If based off six-month LIBOR, then every six months the monthly rental rate will be changed by an adjustment factor reflecting the difference between actual six-month LIBOR and the rate assumed in the base lease rental. A typical variable rate lease may be set up as follows:

Aircraft type	B737-300
Lease term	60 months
Base rental	US$250,000 per month
Base six-month LIBOR	5.0%
Adjustment factor	US$20,000 per 1% change in Libor
Actual six-month LIBOR	5.5% (plus 0.5%)
Adjusted monthly rental	US$260,000 (plus US$10,000)

As indicated above, the rental rates applying to different aircraft types vary over time depending on market conditions and also on such factors as aircraft specification, aircraft condition, the term of the lease and the credit of the lessee. The range of lease rentals currently applicable to good quality but used models of some popular aircraft types are set out in Exhibit 5.2.

Exhibit 5.2
Lease rental range by aircraft type (early 1998)

Aircraft type	Range of rentals
A300B4-200	US$95,000 – US$145,000
A320-200	US$300,000 – US$350,000
B737-300	US$235,000 – US$270,000
B737-400	US$260,000 – US$290,000
B737-500	US$220,000 – US$250,000
B757-200 ER	US$375,000 – US$420,000
B767-300 ER	US$625,000 – US$665,000
MD83	US$210,000 – US$240,000
	Source: Babcock & Brown

Sales of aircraft on operating lease

An operating lessor has three assets to sell–lease cash flows, residual value expectations and the tax benefits inherent in the ownership of high-value capital assets. By locating appropriate investors, a knowledgeable operating lessor can maximise its value from each of these three assets. In particular, an operating lessor can maximise the value of its aircraft and leases by sourcing investors with an appetite for tax deferral in jurisdictions where depreciation can be used to shelter profits made from other businesses. Such investors can then offer low-cost funds to the operating leasing business.

Many operating lease companies have not placed much emphasis on selling aircraft. GPA was the major exception and was a pioneer in selling aircraft on operating lease as financial assets. In 1987 it set up a special division, GPA Capital, which was responsible for selling more than US$5 billion of aircraft operating lease transactions. This was a major contributor to the US$1 billion profit that GPA made between 1988 and 1992. GPA Capital had a staff of over 30 people who concentrated entirely on the sale of aircraft and leases as financial assets and pioneered the securitisation of aircraft on operating lease.

Major buyers of modern high value aircraft on operating lease have been in Japan. There have been relatively active markets also in the United States and, to a lesser extent, in Europe and the Middle East. The breakdown of buyers of aircraft on operating lease by location is currently approximately as follows:

- Asia, 35 per cent;
- North America, 35 per cent;
- Europe, 25 per cent; and
- other, 5 per cent.

The types of investor who purchase aircraft on operating lease are varied and range from individuals to financial institutions. The breakdown by type of investor is currently approximately as follows:

- independent leasing companies, 40 per cent;
- banks, bank affiliates or insurance companies, 30 per cent;
- industrial and service companies, 25 per cent; and
- income funds, 5 per cent.

The most significant arranger of the sale of aircraft on operating lease is Babcock & Brown, which, particularly through its association with Nomura Securities, has broad distribution to investors in Japan and in other jurisdictions.

An increasingly important feature in the sale of aircraft on operating lease is asset backed securitisation, whereby a portfolio of aircraft on operating lease is sold to a special purpose company which is financed in the capital markets by the sale of several classes of bonds. So far, more than US$6 billion has been raised through such securitisations.

Operating lease management

The supervision of aircraft on operating lease is not a simple or routine task and requires ongoing and hands-on management. Just as an investor in an hotel property must employ the most qualified management to maximise the value of the investment, so too an investor in aircraft on operating lease must maximise value through ensuring that all aspects of the aircraft are managed in an optimal manner.

The tasks that full service aircraft managers undertake include purchasing, financing, leasing (and re-leasing), operational management, maintenance management and selling. As indicated in the 'important commercial issues' section earlier in this chapter, excellence in these areas is the major contributor to success at operating leasing.

Aircraft purchasing

To develop an attractive portfolio of aircraft on operating lease, a lessor must acquire the portfolio on terms as close as possible to those enjoyed by the major operating leasing companies. This is one of the more difficult but most important aspects of arranging a successful investment in aircraft on operating lease.

Financing

Depending on the credit of the lessee and the quality of the aircraft, there is often non-recourse debt financing available for aircraft on operating lease that can significantly reduce the financial commitment of an investor or can reduce the balance sheet impact of a transaction. Operating lessors must also increasingly look to the capital markets, which are becoming an important source of capital for operating lease portfolios.

Lease marketing

Responsibility for remarketing the aircraft to airlines following scheduled and unscheduled lease expiries is one of the more important tasks of a lease manager. Lease marketing includes the following primary functions:

1 planning, directing and managing marketing efforts;
2 sourcing lessees for aircraft;
3 coordinating legal, tax and accounting issues to minimise structural and tax risks; and
4 completing and executing lease contracts.

Contracts management

For aircraft on lease, the management task includes the collection of rents and other payments and monitoring the performance of lessee obligations, including maintenance and insurance covenants and compliance with insurance and other lease obligations.

At the termination of a lease the manager will arrange for a technical inspection of the aircraft to determine compliance with return conditions. In the event that an aircraft is re-leased, the manager will supervise the delivery to the new lessee. If an aircraft is not being re-leased, the manager will arrange appropriate storage, maintenance and insurance until it is re-leased or sold.

The manager will also provide reports on cash, contingent liabilities (such as airworthiness directives), aircraft utilisation, lessee financial information and insurance issues.

Aircraft sales

A manager will arrange the sale of aircraft, normally through one of the following types of structure:

• sales of unleased aircraft;
• sales with leases attached; and
• sales into tax-based leveraged and operating lease structures.

Other services
Technical

A manager will be responsible for monitoring the aircraft's technical status, including:

• managing airframe, interior and engine specification changes;
• determining maintenance accrual rates;

- monitoring airframe and engine status and shop visits;
- performing physical inspections and providing technical reports;
- monitoring airworthiness directives and service bulletin status;
- monitoring the status of technical records; and
- ensuring technical compliance when aircraft are returned at lease-end.

Accounting, budgeting and planning

A manager will assist in the owner's financial and operational reporting and budgeting processes in areas such as:

- rentals and maintenance accruals invoiced, received and outstanding;
- maintenance and other reimbursements transferred to lessees;
- lessee deposits or letters of credit received and outstanding;
- status of aircraft not on lease;
- status of aircraft undergoing maintenance; and
- other expenses, such as maintenance costs.

Legal and professional supervision

A manager will be responsible for supervising the negotiation of documentation relating to the leasing of aircraft. In addition, legal supervision will include liaising with contracts administration personnel in order to resolve contractual disputes that may arise in respect of aircraft or lease terms.

Reporting and research

From time to time, a manager will prepare industry reports, incorporating:

- market conditions for the lease and sale of aircraft generally;
- updates on sales strategy for any aircraft being marketed for sale; and
- updates on remarketing strategy for aircraft being remarketed for lease.

Annually, a manager will normally provide a review of the commercial aviation industry for the previous 12 months, together with a commentary on likely future trends. The manager will also arrange for periodic appraisals of the aircraft.

Management experience

Originally the larger operating leasing companies concentrated on the management of their own aircraft only. When GPA developed an aircraft sales business with investors in Europe, Japan and the United States, it found, in many cases, that there was a demand for its management services also. In many cases, GPA found that the market for the sale of aircraft on operating lease was greater if it provided management services to the investor.

In the late 1980s GE Capital purchased Polaris Aircraft Leasing, which was a major arranger and manager of US aircraft income funds. GE Capital (whose aircraft operating leasing division subsequently became GECAS) took over management of GPA's portfolio in 1993 as part of its agreement to assist in GPA's financial restructuring following the failure of GPA's Initial Public Offering. GECAS currently manages aircraft for GE Capital and income funds arranged by Polaris. GECAS also manages aircraft owned by GPA and several of its subsidiaries and the Airplanes Pass Through Trust, which is a US$4 billion securitised vehicle arranged to re-finance the majority of GPA's portfolio.

Until recently, ILFC had generally stayed away from third party management, concentrating instead primarily on the management of its own aircraft. However, in late 1997, ILFC sold a portfolio of aircraft to a subsidiary of Morgan Stanley, Dean Witter, Discover & Co. (which subsequently securitised it) and ILFC has entered into a long term contract to manage the 33 aircraft in the portfolio.

The most significant independent manager of aircraft on operating lease is Babcock & Brown, which has contracts to provide management services to the owners of nearly 100 aircraft valued at approximately US$3 billion, including two securitised funds.

6 Aircraft securitisation[1]

Lehman Brothers

Introduction

This chapter is devoted to a discussion of the aircraft securitisation market, with particular emphasis on the enhanced equipment trust certificate (EETC) sector. The EETC market has developed rapidly over the past four years, as a number of carriers have utilised the instrument to finance their aircraft capital requirements. Since 1994 when the first transaction was closed, over US$7 billion has been raised. As a result of this success, a liquid secondary market has developed in the securities, providing an added level of support for investors and solid total return performance for early entrants.

Still, many investors remain sceptical of the product due to the attractive pricing levels that issuers obtain relative to their stand-alone unsecured credit rating and the historical volatility of airline securities. We believe this is due to the fact that EETCs are a relatively new product and thus they have not been fully market-tested. Additionally, unlike ETCs (equipment trust certificates) and PTCs (pass-through certificates) which have essentially boilerplate structures, EETCs do have some differentiating features relating to LTVs (loan-to-value), call features, appraised values and cross-collateralisation. Consequently, a more detailed analysis is necessary. This chapter attempts to provide such an analysis, discussing EETCs, their unique structure and their value relative to other corporate securities.

Conventional ETCs

To properly analyse EETCs it is necessary to first take a look at the conventional ETC and conventional aircraft securitisations, because an EETC is essentially a hybrid of the two. ETCs first evolved in the railroad industry as equipment leasing agreements utilised to provide more attractive financing to the railroads. They were able to reduce interest costs by assigning a conditional sales contract to the lender or other third party to act as a trustee for the purchase of the equipment, thus providing the railroad rolling stock as collateral for the loan. The loan was paid at various maturities scheduled at regular intervals until fully retired, creating what became known as serial ETCs.

ETCs differed from a mortgage lien by virtue of the fact that legal title was vested with the trustee rather than the company. The trustee would lease the rolling stock back to the railroad while selling the ETCs to investors, using the lease payments to pay principal and interest on the certificates. The structure was favourable to investors because, from a legal standpoint, the railroad did not own the equipment until the certificates were fully repaid. Thus, if the railroad defaulted it would be easy for the trustee to foreclose and repossess because the railroad would not have legal title.

Airline ETC financing began as an offshoot of the rolling stock ETCs, but was for longer periods and larger amounts because an aircraft is a higher value asset. The Bankruptcy Code began to treat aircraft financing favourably in 1957, but a real boost was received in 1979 when Congress amended the Code and introduced Section 1110 protection. Section 1110 provides relief for creditors from the automatic stay imposed by the bankruptcy court in a Chapter 11 filing, assuring debt holders of either receiving scheduled principal and interest payments or being able to repossess the aircraft. The airline has 60 days following the bankruptcy filing to elect whether to cure the default and continue to make payments, failing which the aircraft can be repossessed. Requirements for Section 1110 are that:

1 the collateral must be an aircraft, aircraft engines and parts;
2 the transaction must be with a certificated US air carrier; and
3 the transaction has to be a true lease, a conditional sale or a purchase money mortgage.

Section 1110 protection

On 22 October 1994, Bankruptcy Code amendments were signed into law, which strengthened the rights of creditors by defining more clearly the terms under which Section 1110 protection is available. During the Continental, Eastern and Pan Am bankruptcies, the protection afforded creditors under the section was seriously challenged and threatened the creation of some disturbing legal precedents, mainly surrounding the ambiguity of whether or not certain ETCs and pass-throughs contained a 'true' lease of aircraft. The new amendments expanded the Code as well as strengthening the rights of creditors by more clearly defining the terms of Section 1110. The changes to the Code occurred in four primary areas:

1 For new equipment (equipment placed in service after 22 October 1994) the amendments eliminated the distinction between purchase money security interest and other security interest, so that it is clear that Section 1110 protection extends to all transactions involving qualifying aircraft and airlines whether the transaction is a lease, conditional sale, purchase money financing or a refinancing.
2 For equipment placed in service prior to the 22 October 1994 enactment date, the new amendments create a safe harbour for all leased equipment and afford the benefits of Section 1110 if the lessor and lessee have set forth in writing that the lease agreement is to be treated as a lease for US federal income tax purposes. The amendments exempt from the benefits of Section 1110, however, any aircraft placed in service prior to the enactment date which had been refinanced.
3 The new amendments extend Section 1110 protection to include nearly all operators of commercial aircraft such as commuter carriers, cargo carriers and charter operations. The section now applies to 'aircraft capable of carrying 10 or more individuals or 6,000 pounds or more of cargo' and applies to 'a debtor that is a citizen of the United States ... holding an air carrier operating certificate issued by the Secretary of Transportation pursuant to Chapter 447 or Title 49.
4 The amendments also changed the rights of the secured party so that they cannot be amended by use of Section 1129, thus precluding the debtor from 'cramming down' a secured creditor in a plan of reorganisation.

The changes in the Code increase the certainty of Section 1110 protection and lessen the potential threat of legal challenge over which aircraft are protected by the Code. Accordingly, the revisions enhanced the likelihood that investors would be made whole in the event of a Chapter 11 filing. The changes contributed to Moody's decision to revise its ratings criteria so that in circumstances where Section 1110 applies, securities issued to finance aircraft placed in service after the enactment date receive a rating up to two notches above the airline's senior unsecured rating. At the time, securities were rated just one notch above senior unsecured ratings. Additionally, for ETCs and pass-through certificates (PTCs) issued to finance equipment placed in service prior to the enactment date, Moody's upgraded by a single notch all but a few issues whose lease structures disallowed the amended protection afforded other ETCs and PTCs.

Pass-throughs

The lower level of liquidity and inefficiency for issuers with large financing needs led to the development of the pass-through certificates, which essentially pool a number of ETCs into a pass-through trust. The cash flows are then utilised to pay interest and sinking fund payments on larger, more liquid securities. The PTC spreads risk across a pool of aircraft rather than one and creates a more liquid security, containing a single maturity with principal paid via scheduled sinking fund payments, thus reducing the collateral risk over the term of the security. The added protection afforded by the pool of aircraft led to significant issuance of PTCs in the early 1990s as carriers' earnings fell and their capital needs expanded.

However, along with the additional debt and poor earnings of the 1990s came downgrades for nearly every carrier, with all but Southwest and American ETCs and PTCs ending up below investment grade with Standard & Poor's. This narrowed the investor base and resulted in significant spread widening, because ratings-constrained investors were forced to sell securities and the new cross-over buyer base (investors who were prepared to acquire downgraded securities, often in the hope that they would subsequently be upgraded) was initially reluctant to buy the ETCs and PTCs because of perceived poor liquidity. The result was a loss of the historical buyer base, a large reduction in available investors and poor performance for the ETCs and PTCs. This reduced investor base and the spread volatility that ensued provided the foundations for EETCs, because a new alternative market was needed to handle growing aircraft capital requirements, particularly in the lower credit tiers of the high yield market.

Asset-backed securities

The asset-backed securities (ABS) market became the obvious choice as a result of its growth potential, the sophistication of the dealers and investors in securitised products and growing familiarity with aircraft transactions. Initial growth in the ABS market was in the automobile loan, credit card receivables and home equity loan sectors, but growth opportunities were evident in the manufactured housing, aircraft lease, emerging markets and other sectors. The growth in the ABS market has been driven by this diversity but more importantly by the benefits that securitisation of financial assets brings to both issuers and investors. For issuers, the market has led to cheaper, more efficient funding. For investors, securitisation has provided a broader selection of fixed income alternatives, most with higher credit ratings, less downside risk and more stable cash flows. As it pertains to aircraft securitisation, by more closely reflecting the risk of the new aircraft rather than the existing corporate credit risk, the ABS market (via bankruptcy-remote structures) was expected to provide airlines and leasing companies with a new outlet to fund aircraft purchases.

Aircraft securitisation

The leasing companies such as GPA, ILFC and Ansett were expected to be primary issuers of ABS securitisations and, in fact, GPA's aircraft lease portfolio securitisation (ALPS) 1992-1 deal was a first of its kind. The performance of this deal was impaired by GPA's subsequent liquidity crisis and the inherent complexity of the deal. Analytical challenges were presented by the fact that the underlying assets were leases rather than loans, the international nature of the airlines, the relative concentration of the individual lessors in what could be termed emerging markets, and the expected residual value risk associated with the volatile aircraft market and the overall cash flow of the securities. ALPS 1992-1 was refinanced into ALPS 1996-1 in June 1996 because of the expected principal loss which the subordinated or equity tranches would have potentially suffered as a result of the lower than projected proceeds from aircraft sales.

Despite the poor performance of ALPS 1992-1, the successful ALPS 1994-1 transaction and its strong performance proved the market existed for aircraft securitisation. This paved the way for the US$4 billion Airplanes Group transaction in March 1996, which effectively restructured GPA and provided critical size to the market (which, along with the ALPS deals, now stands at over US$5 billion, with additional deals expected in the future). The involvement of the manufacturers (eg Boeing, Airbus, United Technologies) and the leading aircraft leasing company (GECAS) underscores the fact that the companies with the greatest interest in maintaining an orderly valuation market serve as a natural source of demand for refinancing alternatives and the remarketing of leases and aircraft.

Although these transactions are essentially securitisations, they are not conventional securitisations such as those involving mortgage pools, credit card receivables or auto loans. In these transactions, the performance of the underlying assets is entirely independent of the business risk of the originator/seller of the assets. However, in aircraft securitisations there is some degree of correlation between performance risk of the assets and the default risk of the originator/seller, despite the fact that the securities are backed by a large pool of aircraft and a large number of geographically diversified lessees. (Although the issuer of the securities, ALPS, is bankruptcy-remote vis-à-vis the originator, there is at least some perception that failure of the originator would reflect a general weakness in the aircraft leasing market, indirectly impacting on ALPS.)

In Exhibits 6.1–6.3 we show details of the ALPS 1996-1, ALPS 1994-1 and Airplanes Group deals, respectively. The reference is meant to provide a snapshot of the structure of each transaction: however, a better understanding is possible by looking at the methodology that the ratings agencies use in evaluating the credit risk associated with aircraft lease securitisations.

Exhibit 6.1 The ALPS 96-1 transaction

Deal:	**ALPS 96-1**
Issuer:	ALPS 92–1 Limited
Servicer:	Babcock & Brown
Offering type:	144A with registration rights
Collateral:	
Value (000s)	US$454,950
Number of aircrafts	14
Description:	Wide-bodied (42.92%) – 1 B747, 2 B767 and 1 A300
	Narrow-bodied (57.08%) – 5 B737, 1B757, 1A320, 1 F100, 2MD 83s
Stage 2/3 mix	100% Stage 3
Initial average life	6.8 years
Average age of planes at maturity	13 years
Principal payments:	
Senior debt	Lease payments
Senior debt and Class D	Lease payments and aircraft sales (re-leasing)
Number of lessees	14

Tranche	Issue size (000s)	Outstanding amount (000s)	Coupon	Step-up interest/ cap after expected maturity	Coupon cap	Expected maturity	Legal maturity	Original avg .life	Current avg. life (6/96)	Moody's	S&P	Callability	Original LTV	Current LTV (6/96)	Payment window
Class A	245,673	245,673	*Libor + 37 bp	*Libor + 87 bp/14%	13.5%	5/15/02	6/15/06	3.6	3.6	Aa2	AA	100	54%	54%	8/96–4/02
Class B	56,869	56,859	*Libor + 95 bp	*Libor + 145 bp/14.5%	14.0%	7/15/02	6/15/06	4.8	4.8	A2	A	100	66.5%	66.5%	7/99–6/02
Class C	50,045	50,045	*Libor + 135 bp	*Libor + 185 bp/15.5%	15.0%	7/15/02	6/15/06	4.8	4.8	Baa2	BBB	100	77.5%	77.5%	7/99–5/02
Class D	40,946	40,946	12.75%	13.75%		7/15/02	6/15/06	4.9	4.9	Not rated	BB–	•100+prem	86.5%	86.5%	7/99–6/02
	393,532	393,532													

* 1-month Libor.
+ All classes of notes will have to be redeemed at the same time if called.

Callability schedule
Class A, B and C   100 + accrued and unpaid interest
Class D   100+ accrued and unpaid interest + makewhole premium.
   Makewhole premium = (PV (adjusted payments) – PV(expected payments)) – premium reception amount.
   Discount rate for PV = 1% + rate interpolated from US Treasury yields for maturities closest to average life of principle adjusted payments.

Exhibit 6.2 The ALPS 94-1 transaction

Deal:	ALPS 94-1 pass-through trust
Issuer:	GPA Group
Servicer:	GECAS
Offering type:	Public issue of pass-through certificates
Collateral:	
Value (000s)	US$980,151
Number of aircraft	27
Description:	Wide-bodied – 3 B767's and 1 A 300-B4
	Narrow-bodied – 5 B737-300s, 4 B 737-500s, 3 B757-200s, 4 A320-200s, 3 Fokker 100s and 3MD 83s
Stage 3 component	100%
Initial average life	
Principal payments:	
Class A	Lease payments and aircraft sales
Other classes	Aircraft sales
Number of lessees	22

Tranche	Issue size (000s)	Outstanding amount (000s)	Coupon	Step-up interest	Coupon cap	Expected maturity	Legal maturity	Original avg. life	Current avg. life (6/96)	Moody's	S&P	FTC	Callable	Original LTV	Payment window
Class A1	172,000	143,706	*Libor + 48 bp	*Libor + 98 bp	14.5%	7/15/99	9/15/04	3.8	1.2	Aa2	AA	AA	+any time		10/94-07/99
Class A2	139,404	112,998	7.15%	9.15%		11/15/97	9/15/04	2.1	1.5	Aa2	AA	AA	+any time		10/94-11/97
Class A3	156,167	156,167	*Libor + 45 bp	*Libor + 95 bp	15.5%	12/15/99	9/15/04	5.1	3.6	Aa2	AA	AA	+any time		07/99-12/99
Class A4	140,122	140,122	7.80%	9.80%		7/15/99	9/15/04	4.2	3.8	Aa2	AA	AA	+any time	62.0%	11/97-07/97
Class B1	44,106	43,770	*Libor + 115 bp	*Libor + 165 bp	15.5%	3/15/00	9/15/04	5.0	3.1	A2	A	A	+any time		12/96-03/00
Class B2	43,994	43,994	8.20%	10.20%		12/15/00	9/15/04	4.3	2.8	A2	A	A	+any time	71.0%	12/96-12/99
Class C	86,610	86,170	9.35%	11.35		3/15/00	9/15/04	4.7		Baa2	BBB	BBB	+any time	78.0%	12/96-03/00
	782,515	726,927													
Class D	71,185		Owned by GE Capital											85.6%	
Class E	144,451		Owned by Consolidated subsidiary of GPA											100.0%	
	998.151														

* 1-month Libor.
+ All classes of notes will have to be redeemed at the same time if called.

Callability schedule
Before 9/00   100 + makewhole premium + accrued and unpaid interest
After 9/00   100+ accrued and unpaid interest

Exhibit 6.3 The 1996 Airplanes Group transaction

Deal: Airplanes pass-through certificates
Issuer: GPA
Servicer: GECAS
Offering type: Public issue of pass-through certificates
Collateral:
- Value
- Number of aircraft   2297
- Description: Wide-bodied 19, Turbo-prop 28, Narrow-bodied 182
- Stage 3 mix   93.4%
- Initial average life   6 years

Principal payments: Lease payments, aircraft sales and refinancings

Number of lessees 83

Tranche	Issue size (000s)	Outstanding amount (000s)	Coupon	Step-up interest	Coupon cap	Expected maturity	Legal maturity	Original avg. life	Current avg. life (6/96)	Moody's	S&P	Callable‡	Original LTV	Current LTV (year-end)
Class A1	850,000	850,000	*Libor + 25 bp	50 bp	NA	3/15/98	3/15/06	2.0	1.7	Aa2	AA		63.0%	59.0%
Class A2	750,000	750,000	*Libor + 32 bp	50 bp	NA	3/15/99	3/15/09	3.0	2.7	Aa2	AA		63.0%	59.0%
Class A3	500,000	500,000	*Libor + 47 bp	50 bp	NA	3/15/01	3/15/15	5.0	4.7	Aa2	AA		63.0%	59.0%
Class A4	200,000	200,000	*Libor + 62 bp	50 bp	NA	3/15/03	3/15/19	7.0	6.7	Aa2	AA		63.0%	59.0%
Class A5	598,000	598,000	*Libor + 35 bp		NA	4/15/99	3/15/19	1.6	1.4	Aa2	A		63.0%	59.0%
Class B	375,000	375,000	*Libor +110 bp		NA	3/15/09	3/15/19	7.5	7.3	A2	A		71.0%	71.0%
Class C	375,000	375,000	8,15%		NA	3/15/11	3/15/19	10.2	10.0	Baa2	BBB		79.0%	79.0%
Class D	400,000	400,000	10.875		NA	3/15/12	3/15/19	12.0	11.8	Ba2	BB		88.0%	88.0%
	4,048,000	4,048,000												

* 1-month Libor.

+ All classes of notes will have to be redeemed at the same time if called.

‡ See Exhibit 6.3a

Exhibit 6.3a
The 1996 Airplanes Group transaction: callability schedules

Callability schedule Classes A and B			Callability schedule Classes C and D		
	Premium expiration date	*Price*		*Price*	
			*Premium expiration date**	*Class C*	*Class D*
Class A1	3/15/97	102	3/15/01–3/15/02	105	107
Class A2	3/15/98	102	3/15/02–3/15/03	104	106
Class A3	3/15/98	102	3/15/03–3/15/04	103	105
Class A4	3/15/99	102	3/15/04–3/15/05	102	104
Class A5	no premium		3/15/05–3/15/06	101	103
Class B	no premium		3/15/06–3/15/07	100	102
			3/15/07–3/15/08	100	101
			on or after 3/15/08	100	100

*Date until which premium is paid. After this date the tranche is redeemed at 100%.

Ratings agency methodology for aircraft lease securitisation

Airline default or credit risk

Credit risk is primarily measured by the degree of diversification and the credit quality of the lessees.

Diversification

This is evaluated using a number of different parameters, key among which are:

- the number of lessees;
- concentration of lessees (ie the smaller the proportion of total portfolio value leased to each lessee signifies less concentration and hence less risk of default);
- breadth of types of lessees (cargo, passenger, regional carriers); and
- geographic diversity (relative to distribution of air traffic by region).

Credit quality

In most cases the lessees are not rated and so judging credit quality is a subjective process. The judgement has in the past been based on:

- financials of lessees, if available;
- rating surveillance of ILFC and GECAS, the two major aircraft operating lessors;
- kind of lessee – eg whether the lessee is a 'flag carrier' (a primary international airline) if from a less-developed country, while financially weaker airlines from developed countries have been acceptable, along with many cargo carriers;
- lessees with similar characteristics (eg same country) are more likely to default simultaneously, so correlation of default is used in analysis; and

- the lease agreement needs to be analysed for the following clauses: rent adjustments (there may be conditions that include usage thresholds); service and maintenance; insurance; level of security deposits and maintenance reserves; and default provisions.

Repossession risks

In case of default, the lessor and the security trustee for the investors should be in a position to repossess the aircraft. In some countries with less rigid legal systems, aircraft used for domestic services are hard to repossess. Often the restructuring and negotiation process is lengthy. The differences in law across jurisdictions make aircraft leases more complicated than normal securitisations (credit cards, auto loans, etc), while diversity across countries somewhat mitigates this risk.

Asset risk

Demand trends

These trends influence the value of the asset and hence need to be analysed. Some measures include:

- production (whether production of the particular aircraft model has been stopped – ie has demand for the model dried up);
- carrier trends (small to medium-sized aircraft may be more in demand and easy to remarket).

Technological risk

The aircraft in the portfolio are evaluated based on their current and likely future capabilities relative to available alternatives. A technology risk score is assigned based on:

- technology incorporated into aircraft (avionics, fuel economy, engine noise, range, etc);
- average age of the aircraft (older aircraft require more maintenance, are subject to 'airworthiness directives' and are grounded first in a recession);
- term of the lease; and
- regulation.

Diversification by aircraft type

An ideal portfolio would be one that replicates the current technology of the world fleet. The analysis is based on the variety of capabilities of aircraft models. The typical characteristics analysed are:

- narrow/wide body;
- Stage 2/Stage 3 distribution.

Diversification by manufacturer

Analysis at this stage is based on how closely the portfolio relates to the worldwide market share of the manufacturer. The analysis also weighs the competitive position of each manufacturer. Also, a financially strong manufacturer has a commitment and interest in maintaining values of its existing aircraft.

Other factors

These include considerations such as:

- engine types;
- reputation of the lessee airline for maintenance;
- geographic operating conditions (less-developed versus developed countries); and
- specialised or unusual considerations (eg hush-kitted, freighter) that could affect the resale value.

Quality of servicer

In an aircraft lease transaction, the issuer of securities is a special purpose company separate from the original owner of the aircraft. Hence the quality of the servicer is crucial to the credit-worthiness of such a transaction. By 'servicer' we mean the third party (such as GECAS or Babcock & Brown) appointed as lease manager and remarketing agent for the portfolio.

Stress tests

The credit analysis performs certain stress tests on the portfolio. Stress tests measure the sensitivity of the portfolio to changes in various variables, including:

- lessee default rates;
- market value of aircraft and lease rates in a recession;
- re-leasing of aircraft; and
- time needed to repossess and remarket aircraft.

EETCs

Like more conventional aircraft securitisations, EETCs were developed for the benefit of both the issuer and investor. For the issuer, the expansion of the EETC has led to cheaper, more efficient funding and greater balance sheet flexibility. For investors (especially ratings-constrained investors), the EETC market development has opened up a new yield-oriented asset class that allows credit quality-restrained investors sufficient yield to fund liability streams while the less risk-restrained buyer achieves higher yields than can be obtained from investments in unsecured debentures of similar credit quality. The ratings-constrained investor was the traditional investor in airline ETCs and PTCs prior to the industry downturn in the early 1990s, while the cross-over and high yield investor base became the investor of necessity after the downturn.

EETCs appeal to both investment grade and high yield investors. By structuring EETCs to appeal to both groups, the issuer markets to a larger audience, returns aircraft investment to the traditional investor base, broadens and enhances the liquidity of the securities, and achieves superior pricing and execution.

The size of the traditional investor base was the primary motivating factor behind the development of the EETC, while the structure to appeal to the market was borrowed from the ABS sector as discussed earlier in this chapter, with additional protection coming from conventional ETC/PTCs and the Section 1110 protection afforded to these securities. The early development of the market has resulted in a number of different transactions, but all contain a basic structure containing three to four tranches of senior, mezzanine and subordinated certificate holders, with the differentiation being the respective loan-to-value (LTV), cross-collateralisation of aircraft, ratings and maturity. Exhibit 6.4 (page 83–85) shows a table of selected EETC transactions and details the key differentiating points of each deal.

EETC rating methodology

The key factor underpinning the agencies' rating methodology is that the risks follow a clear and well-understood hierarchy. It is essential to realise that securitisations of lease and mortgage receivables are ultimately backed by physical capital equipment assets (ie specifically identified aircraft) that can be sold to repay investors. For both Moody's and S&P, the criteria evaluated when rating an enhanced ETC include the credit quality of the airline, the expected collateral values and amount of support for each class of the EETC, the strength of Section 1110 protection, as well as the additional support provided by the liquidity facility.

Ratings represent not only a measure of default probability, but also the severity of default as well as the timeliness of payment. While both agencies agree on the basis for evaluation, Moody's approach involves a case-by-case analysis in pinpointing ratings, while S&P has a direct formula-based approach for all EETCs. Moody's believes that for lower rated airlines it will take more enhancement to overcome a relatively higher level of corporate credit risk. Conversely, the firm maintains that the benefits of enhancement become less pronounced at the higher end of the rating scale.

An illustration of the difference in Moody's and S&P's approach is the consideration each gives to the ease of remarketing an aircraft. An aircraft with a large number in current use across a wide array of users will obviously be easier to resell or re-lease than an aircraft of limited production and usage. Conversely, S&P's analysis suggests that ratings are applied using conservative enough valuations such that a close scrutiny of each aircraft's marketability is redundant.

Because the airlines are already rated and, therefore, default risk quantified, the ratings agencies' criteria for EETCs need only to cover a narrow range of credit questions. The financings are structured either to minimise risk or reward investors accordingly. This is done by layering different tranches of debt risk into the deal.

The following requirements must be met by an EETCs in order to qualify for higher ratings:

- they must be adequately over-collateralised;
- they must qualify for protection under Section 1110 of the US Bankruptcy Code;
- they be secured by Stage 3 (reduced noise specifications) aircraft; and
- they must have a dedicated source of liquidity to cover 18 months (three payments) of interest on the 'enhanced' tranches.

It is useful to note that the exact appraisal value of aircraft involved in a securitisation is not vital because the ratings agencies recognise that the value will change from the outset of the deal. They do, however, take into consideration whether the secondary market is at a cyclical high or low. Value decline assumptions are also made from the starting point of a defined depreciation schedule that the agencies use to analyse EETC deals. This depreciation schedule is used to monitor LTVs throughout the life of the issue. Essentially, a 20 per cent residual value after 25 years is obtained via a 2 per cent annual decline for the first 15 years and a 4 per cent annual decline for the next five years, followed by a 6 per cent decline for the next 5 years. A collateral analysis reveals that all 'enhanced' tranche noteholders can be repaid after a hypothetical 25 per cent reduction in aircraft values.

The ratings agencies require an 18-month source of liquidity because this is the length of time they feel it will take to market and resell the aircraft in order to maximise value. Note that most EETC deals have no liquidity facility on the lowest rated tranche and therefore do not garner the 'enhanced' level.

S&P maintains that, given the structural requirements outlined above, EETC classes can achieve ratings above that of the airline's existing secured debt rating. The method of deriving specific EETC tranche ratings is based upon the following LTV rule: a one-notch upgrade above the airline's senior secured rating is provided for every 5 per cent of LTV below a minimum 80 per cent (required for all ETCs); there is, however, a maximum upgrade of three full categories (nine notches). For example, US Air's EETC 1996 Class A, with LTV of 32.5 per cent, achieved a rating of A+. This was nine notches above the airline's B+ senior secured rating.

Some EETCs include a cross-collateralisation provision. This means that recovery of principal will be a function of the proceeds received under all of the obligations. Excess proceeds received from the sale of some aircraft would be available to offset shortfalls that occur when other aircraft in the deal are sold. Examples of cross-collateralised EETCs include NWA Trust 1, NWA Trust 2 and US Air 1996. Additionally, JETS 1995 A and JETS 1995 B carry 'partial' cross-collateralisation.

Summary and relative value

In this chapter we have provided an overview and analysis of the aircraft securitisation market, with particular emphasis on enhanced equipment trust certificates. With EETCs structured to appeal to an expanded buyer base, investors achieve collateral protection, coupon protection through the liquidity facility and default protection, via Section 1110.

These three layers of protection as well as increased yield versus other similarly rated securities, have led to the growing popularity of the securities and solid return performance for investors. We believe investors will continue to be attracted to the market because of the broad range of risk profile investment opportunities available.

Note

1 Key sources for this chapter comprise the Handbook of Airline Economics, 1995 (Executive Editor, Darryl Jenkins), published by McGraw-Hill, New York; *Introduction to Asset-Backed Securities*, 1994, published by Lehman Brothers; *Aircraft Economics 1995 Yearbook*, and selected publications of both Standard & Poor's and Moody's.

Exhibit 6.4 Selected EETC transactions, March 1994 to present

Deal	Tranche	Coupon (%)	Expected Maturity	Current avg. life	Moody's	S&P	Callable	Makewhole premium	Original LTV (%)	Issue size (US$)	Liquidity Facility	Section 1110	Collateral	Cross-collateral	ERISA
NWA Trust 1	Class A	8.26	10/9/05	7/8/02	Baa1	AA	3/10/97	T+50	40.0	177,000	yes	yes	6 B747-200B, 4 B757-200	yes	yes
NWA Trust 1	Class B	9.36	01/9/05	6/8/02	Baa3	A	3/10/97	T+50	54.8	66,000	yes	yes	6 B747-200B, 4 B757-200	yes	yes
NWA Trust 2	Class A	9.25	21/5/07	23/5/07	A2	AA	any time	T+50	40.0	176,000	yes	yes	13 Airbus A320-200	yes	yes
NWA Trust 2	Class B	10.23	21/12/12	23/5/07	A3	A	any time	T+75	55.0	66,000	yes	yes	13 Airbus A320-200	yes	yes
NWA Trust 2	Class C	11.30	21/12/12	18/4/07	Baa2	BBB+	any time	T+100	65.0	44,000	yes	yes	13 Airbus A320-200	yes	yes
NWA Trust 2	Class D	13.87	21/6/08	21/6/08	Ba1	BB+	12/21/99 12/21/00 12/21/01 12/21/02 12/21/03 12/21/04	106.9% 105.55% 104.2% 102.78% 101.38% 100.0%	80.0	66,000	none	yes	13 Airbus A320-200	yes	yes
JETS 1994-A (UAL)	Class A-10	9.41	15/6/10	16/5/07	A2	A	8/28/99	Tsy flat	37.5	109,400	yes	yes	5 B737-300, 2 B747-400	not	yes
JETS 1994-A (UAL)	Class A-11	20.00	15/6/12	15/6/11	A2	A	8/28/99	Tsy flat	56.0	62,450	yes	yes	5 B737-300, 2 B747-400	not	yes
JETS 1994-A (UAL)	Class B-1	10.91	15/6/06	28/6/03	Baa1	BB+	8/28/99	Tsy flat	74.1	60,703	no	yes	5 B373-300, 2 B747-400	not	yes
JETS 1994-A (UAL)	Certificates	11.79	15/6/13	15/6/13	Baa2	BB+	after A&B	no	80.5	21,676	no	yes	5 B373-300, 2 B747-400	not	yes
JETS 1995-A (UAL)	Class A	8.235	1/11/12	21/12/06	A1	AA+	12/20/99	T+25	45.00	305,768	yes	yes	2 B747-400, 4 B767-300ER 3 B737-300, 3 B737-500	partial	yes
JETS 1995-A (UAL)	Class B	8.64	1/11/12	21/12/06	A1	A	12/20/99	T+25	61.00	108,717	yes	yes	2 B747-400, 4 B767-300ER 3 B747-300, 3 B737-500	partial	yes
JETS 1995-A (UAL)	Class C	10.69	1/11/13	27/3/13	Baa1	BBB-	12/20/99 5/1/10 5/1/12 5/1/13	T+25 T+100 T+150 0	71.01	68,000	yes	yes	2 B747-400, 4B767-300ER 3 B737-300, 3 B737-500	partial	yes
JETS 1995-B (UAL)	Certificates	11.44	1/11/14	1/11/14	Baa2	BB+	after A, B, C	no	77.19	42,000	none	yes	2 B747-400, 4 B767-300ER 3 B737-300, 3 B737-500	partial	yes
JETS 1995-B (UAL)	Class A	7.63	15/8/12	8/4/07	A1	AA	10/7/99	T+25	45.50	331,285	yes	yes	5 B747-400, 1 B767-300ER 1 B737-300	partial	yes
JETS 1995-B (UAL)	Class B	7.83	15/8/12	8/4/07	A3	A	10/7/99	T+25	60.00	105,575	yes	yes	5 B747-400, 1 B767-300ER 1 B737-300	partial	yes
JETS 1995-B (UAL)	Class C	9.71	1/11/13	3/4/13	Baa1	BBB	10/7/99 2/15/12 8/15/12 2/15/13	T+25 T+75 T+100 0	68.95	65,180	yes	yes	5 B747-400, 1 B767-300ER 1 B737-300	partial	yes
JETS 1995-B (UAL)	Certificates	10.91	15/8/14	15/2/14	Baa2	BB+	after A, B, C	no	74.95	43,656	none	yes	5 B747-400, 1 B767-300ER 1 B373-300	partial	yes
Continental 1996-1	Class A	6.94	15/10/13	15/2/06	A1	AA	any time	T flat	39.90	269,518	yes	yes	9 B737-500, 9 B757-200	not	yes
Continental 1996-1	Class B	7.82	15/10/13	15/2/06	A3	A	any time	T flat	53.90	94,332	yes	yes	9 B737-500, 9 B757-200	not	no
Continental 1996-1	Class C	9.50	15/10/13	15/2/06	Baa2	A-	any time	T flat	64.8	142,400	yes	yes	9 B737-500, 9 B757-200	not	no

Exhibit 6.4 continued

Deal	Tranche	Coupon (%)	Expected Maturity	Current avg. life	Moody's	S&P	Callable	Makewhole premium	Original LTV (%)	Issue size (US$)	Liquidity Facility	Section 1110	Collateral	Cross-collateral	ERISA
US Air 1996	Class A	6.76	15/4/08	18/2/06	A2	A+	any time	T flat/ par from 2/06	32.5	142,400	yes	yes	9 B757-200	yes	yes
US Air 1996	Class B	7.50	15/4/08	18/21/06	Baa1	A-	any time	T flat/ par from 2/06	45.0	54,800	yes	yes	9 B757-200	yes	yes
US Air 1996	Class C	8.93	15/4/08	18/2/06	Ba2	BBB-	any time	T flat/ par from 2/06	60.0	66,000	yes	yes	9 B757-200	yes	yes
Continental 1996-2	Class A	7.75	2/7/14	22/9/06	A1	AA	any time	T flat/ par from 9/06	35.0	82,513	yes	yes	4 B757-200, 1 B737-500	not	yes
Continental 1996-2	Class B	8.56	2/7/14	18/2/06	A3	A-	any time	T flat/ par from 9/06	50.0	35,363	yes	yes	4 B757-200, 1 B737-500	not	no
Continental 1996-2	Class C	10.22	2/7/14	22/9/06	Baa2	BBB	any time	T flat/ par from 9/06	65.0	35,363	yes	yes	4 B757-200, 1 B737-500	not	no
Continental 1996-2	Class D	11.50	2/4/08	26/6/03	Ba2	BB	any time	T flat/ par from 6/03	72.9	18,510	none	yes	4 B757-200, 1 B737-500	not	no
NWA Trust 1996-1	Class A	7.67	2/1/15	25/9/09	A2	AA	any time	Tsy flat	44.0	325,018	yes	yes	9 757-200, 2 747-400	not	yes
NWA Trust 1996-1	Class B	8.07	2/1/15	30/10/08	Baa1	A	any time	Tsy flat	58.5	106,692	yes	yes	9 757-200, 2 747-400	not	yes
NWA Trust 1996-1	Class C	8.97	2/1/15	13/5/06	Baa3	BBB-	any time	T+75	71.2	75,640	yes	yes	9 757-200, 2 747-400	not	yes
NWA Trust 1996-1	Class D	10.15	2/1/05	8/9/00	Ba1	BB+	any time	T+75	82.6	17,152	none	yes	2 747-400	not	yes
America West 1996-1A		6.850	2/7/09	27/7/05	A2	AA-	any time	tsy flat	40.0	99,522	yes	yes	8 A320, 3 V2500	no	yes
America West 1996-1B		6.930	2/1/08	3/9/02	Baa2	A-	any time	tsy flat	55.0	37,139	yes	yes	8 A320, 3 V2500	no	yes
America West 1996-1C		6.850	2/7/04	7/1/01	Ba1	BBB-	any time	tsy+75	70.0	37,747	yes	yes	8 A320, 3 V2500	no	no
America West 1996-1D		8.160	2/7/06	18/3/99	Ba3	BB	any time	tsy+75	81.0	26,618	no	yes	8 A320, 3 V2500	no	no
America West 1996-1E		10.500	2/7/06	11/9/96	B1	B+	any time	tsy+75	93.0	14,541	no	yes	8 A320, 3 V2500	no	no
America West 1997-1A		7.330	2/7/08	14/2/06	A2	AA-	any time	par w prov then tsy flat	40.0	45,936	yes	yes	4 Airbus A320-231	no	yes
America West 1997-1B		7.400	2/7/05	1/2/04	Baa2	A-	any time	par w prov then tsy flat	55.0	17,226	yes	yes	4 Airbus A320-231	no	yes
America West 1997-1C		7.530	2/1/04	8/5/02	Ba1	BBB-	any time	par w prov then tsy+75	70.0	17,226	yes	yes	4 Airbus A320-231	no	yes
America West 1997-1D		8.120	2/7/01	13/6/99	Ba3	BB	any time	par w prov then tsy+75	82.0	13,500	no	yes	4 Airbus A320-231	no	yes

Exhibit 6.4 continued

Deal	Tranche	Coupon (%)	Expected Maturity	Current avg. life	Moody's	S&P	Callable	Makewhole premium	Original LTV (%)	Issue size (US$)	Liquidity Facility	Section 1110	Collateral	Cross-collateral	ERISA
Continental 1997-1	1A	7.461	1/4/15	25/1/10	Aa3	AA+	any time	tsy flat to 4/10, then par	40.0	437,876	no	yes	8 B757-224, 18 B737-524, 4 B737-724	no	no
Continental 1997-1	1B	7.461	1/4/13	28/3/07	A2	A+	any time	tsy flat to 4/07, then par	54.0	148,333	yes	yes	8 B757-224, 18 B737-524, 4 B737-724	no	no
Continental 1997-1	1-CI	7.420	1/4/07	12/1/03	Baa1	BBB+	any time	tsy flat to 4/03, then par	60.0	111,093	yes	yes	8 B757-224, 18 B737-524, 4 B737-724	no	maybe
Continental 1997-1	1C-II	7.420	1/4/07	12/1/03	Baa1	BBB+	any time	tsy flat to 4/03, then par	61.0	10,000	yes	yes	8 B757-224, 18 B737-524, 4 B737-724	no	no
Continental 1997-2	A	7.148	30/6/07	27/6/05	Aa3	AA	any time	tsy flat to 27/6/05, then par	41.0	74,862	yes	yes	6 B737-3T0, 4 MD 82	no	yes
Continental 1997-2	B	7.149	30/6/05	6/3/04	A2	A	any time	tsy flat to 6/3/04, then par	55.0	25,563	yes	yes	6 B737-3T0, 4 MD 82	no	no
Continental 1997-2	C	7.206	30/6/04	20/7/02	Baa1	BBB-	any time	tsy flat to 20/7/02, then par	70.0	27,206	yes	yes	6 B737-3T0, 4 MD 82	no	no
Continental 1997-2	D	7.522	30/6/01	30/1/00	Ba1	BB	any time	tsy flat to 30/1/00, then par	85.0	27,369	yes	yes	6 B737-3T0, 4 MD 82	no	no
Continental 1997-3	A	7.150	24/3/13		A2	A+	any time	tsy flat to 22/8/06, then par	41.0	54,440	yes	yes	9 EMB-145 ER	no	yes
Continental 1997-3	B	7.140	24/6/07	30/4/04	Baa1	A-	any time	tsy flat to 30/4/04 then par	56.0	19,731	yes	yes	9 EMB-145 ER	no	yes
Continental 1997-3	C	7.121	24/3/05	12/2/02	Baa3	BBB	any time	tsy flat to 2/16/02 then par	68.0	14,418	yes	yes	9 EMB-145 ER	no	yes
Continental 1997-4	A	6.900	2/1/18	16/7/10	Aa3	AA+	any time	tsy flat to 16/7/01 then par	43.0	505,951	yes	yes	5 B737-524, 6 B737-724, 10 B737-824, 3 B777-200	no	yes
Continental 1997-4	B	6.900	2/1/17	1/5/09	A2	A+	any time	tsy flat to 1/5/09	55.0	134,934	yes	yes	5 B737-524, 6 B737-724, 10 B737-824, 3 B777-200	no	yes
Continental 1997-4	C	6.800	2/7/07	6/12/03	Baa1	BBB+	any time	tsy flat to 6/12/03 then par	64.0	111,112	yes	yes	5 B737-524, 6 B737-724, 10 B737-824, 3 B777-200	no	yes
Continental 1998-1	A	6.648	15/9/17	12/6/10	Aa3	AA+	any time	Tsy flat	40.0	485,605	yes	yes	4 B737-500, 6 B737-724, 7 B737-824, 5 B757-224, 2 B777-224	no	yes
Continental 1998-1	B	6.748	15/3/17	17/8/09	A2	A+	any time	Tsy flat	53.0	150,371	yes	yes	4 B737-500, 6 B737-724, 7 B737-824, 5 B757-224, 2 B777-224	no	yes
Continental 1998-1	C	6.541	15/3/08	9/5/04	Baa1	BBB+	any time	Tsy flat	64.0	136,542	yes	yes	4 B737-500, 6 B737-724, 7 B737-824, 5 B757-224, 2 B777-224	no	yes

7 A lessee's guide to structuring cross-border aircraft leases

Arthur J. Bernstein

Introduction

Simply put, cross-border aircraft leasing involves the lease of an aircraft by an airline in one country from a lessor domiciled in a second country, with the participation of a lender who might be from yet a third country. (See Exhibit 7.1 for a summary of participants.)

Exhibit 7.1
Parties to a cross-border aircraft lease

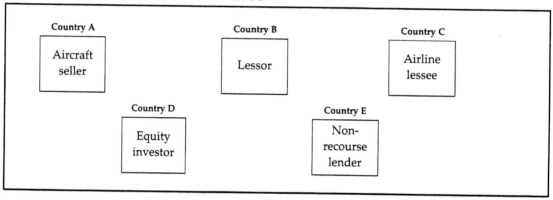

The motivation is financial. The airline, in its quest for the lowest interest cost and the longest lease term, will seek access to financing in whichever locale provides the finest terms. Usually, when such financing is arranged in the form of a lease from a lessor in a foreign jurisdiction, certain tax benefits are being exploited. Without these tax benefits, the transaction probably would have very little appeal to the airline lessee.

The frantic search by airlines, investment bankers, brokers and other professionals for the 'next' source of efficient, low-cost cross-border financing has taken on the appearance of Jason and the Argonauts searching for the Golden Fleece. Unfortunately their quest is often thwarted by governments determined to stop the loss of tax revenue. So far, nevertheless, very attractive transactions have been concluded in the US, the UK, Germany, France, Japan and elsewhere.

In order to be able to evaluate the various cross-border leasing opportunities, the airline must have a consistent frame of reference, and the purpose of this chapter is to provide a logical and rigorous method for determining the preferred cross-border leasing terms. This overlay then can be applied to the evaluation of the various transaction opportunities that may be presented to the airline.

A more aggressive stance can be taken by an airline that feels confident about its knowledge of the economics of a lease being offered. Then the prospective lessors can be presented with the 'lessee's terms' for entering into the financing. In order for an airline to be comfortable with this approach to the market, it should understand the economic motivation of the lessor. Simultaneously, the airline must have confidence in the structure that it proposes to the lessor. If the proposal to the lessor bears a close relationship to what is attainable in the lessor's market, then the lessee's credibility will be maintained. A lessor can be brought to the edge of the cliff but does not wish to be pushed off.

The basic structure

Cross-border lease financing involves the purchase of an aircraft by a taxpaying investor (the lessor) and the simultaneous contracting by an airline (the lessee) for the use of the aircraft in return for specified rental payments over a specified term. Notwithstanding the ownership of the aircraft by the lessor, the lessee wants to be able to control and operate the aircraft in the same manner as it would if it was the owner.

The leveraged cross-border lease is a variation that introduces a third party lender into the transaction. The lessor, in conjunction with the lessee, will seek to finance 50–90 per cent of the asset's cost by borrowing the funds on a non-recourse basis from banks, insurance companies, pension funds or other lenders in the private or public market who are seeking a long-term secured investment. While the lessor actually invests only 10–50 per cent of the cost of the asset, it will be entitled to 100 per cent of the tax benefits of ownership and thus can be said to have 'leveraged' its equity investment by utilising the non-recourse borrowing.

Participants

The airline lessee will be spending most of its negotiating time with the prospective equity investor who in turn may be represented by an intermediary. A community of lease brokers or 'packagers' has evolved who often develop possible sources of equity funds and bring them together with a lessee who is seeking financing proposals. Certain packagers are adept at locating unique (ie low-rate) investors who happen to be unusually aggressive in seeking leveraged lease investment for tax shelter and investment purposes.

With the equity investors providing 10–50 per cent of the funds necessary to purchase the aircraft, the other major participant in the transaction, the lender (or lenders, if the deal is large enough to require a lending syndicate), must be identified and brought into the negotiations. The lender receives a first mortgage on the aircraft and an assignment of all rentals associated with the lease agreement. In the case of a US-based foreign sales corporation (FSC) lease, the lender cannot be granted a mortgage on the aircraft. However, other security features, such as guarantees and stock pledges, provide the lender with a financeable package (see Exhibit 7.2). Most sophisticated lessees have tended to 'unbundle' the financing, that is, they seek the best terms in the secured debt market and simultaneously scour the lease-equity markets for low-cost funds.

Once all the parties to the lease financing have been identified (lessee, equity investor(s), lender(s) brokers, advisers and counsel) and various commitment letters have been executed, the documentation can be prepared.

Exhibit 7.2
A US foreign sales corporation lease

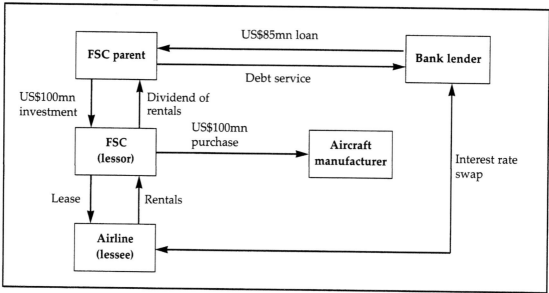

Experienced lessees will have developed a form of lease agreement that can be distributed to the parties and represents the lessee's position on key points. This aggressive approach to the leasing market can save an enormous amount of negotiating time and associated expense. The leveraged cross-border lease is a custom-crafted transaction with each party shouldering various risks on a negotiated basis. All parties should enter the process with a carefully compiled agenda and expert guidance.

The lessor's perspective

Any lease financing, whether domestic or cross-border, has its economics driven by three separate cash flow streams that are expected by the lessor. The first is the periodic net cash flow differential between rentals and debt service; this may in fact be zero if the lease is structured so that rentals are fully dedicated to debt service (see Exhibit 7.3). The second cash flow stream to the lessor results from tax benefits. This can be in the form of tax credits, as was the case in US ITC leasing, or tax deferrals resulting from accelerated depreciation schemes. Often there are additional tax effects resulting from the impact of the lease on the lessor's trade or capital tax position, for example, or the conversion of ordinary loss to capital gain. In the US-based FSC lease, the equity investor receives the benefit of a reduced rate of tax on lease rentals derived from US-manufactured aircraft operating predominantly outside the US. This export incentive is shared with the lessee in the form of reduced rentals.

The tax-deferral benefit that the lessor obtains is analogous to an interest-free loan from the government. This pool of free cash can be reinvested such that the pool grows to an amount in excess of future tax payment requirements. The primary objective of the lessor will be to generate as much of this surplus cash as possible, after quickly recouping the initial equity investment. By the end of the lease term, the lessor will want to be sitting with a cash

Exhibit 7.3
A cross-border lease of aircraft

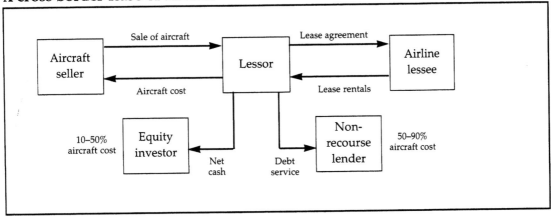

balance that is greater than that which it would have obtained by placing its equity funds in an alternative investment.

The lessee can improve the inherent benefit of the lease by cooperating with the lessor in structuring the leveraging debt. If the average life of the debt is increased, for example, most lessors will further defer the generation of taxable income. The cash flow benefit to the lessor then can be shared with the lessee as negotiated. If the lessee controls the debt placement, then a customised construction is feasible. This would allow the most favourable structure to be introduced into the lease. The lessee then could make arrangements with the lending institution to fund the debt component in a manner that maximises the specific transaction benefits.

One variation of this technique that has been utilised has been the insertion into the lease of debt denominated in a currency carrying a high coupon, such as New Zealand dollars. This drives down principal amortisation (at least on a level debt service basis), increases the average life of the debt and produces a tax-deferral benefit to the lessor. It is not clear, however, whether the costs of a currency swap and any negative balance sheet implications for lessor and/or lessee are compensated fully by this scheme. It is preferable to access debt denominated in the most appropriate currency both from a purely commercial and an accounting perspective. Then the structure of the debt can be optimised so that it fits the tax and cash flow requirements of the lessor.

The third element of the lessor's cash flow stream is the portion of the residual value of the aircraft to which the lessor will be entitled under the lease agreement. The lessee should attempt to relinquish to the lessor as little of the residual as possible. At worst, the residual participation should be capped so that the lessee can calculate the maximum cost of the financing. When a lessor requires at least a cosmetic residual value inflow, the lessee should be granted a purchase option at a fixed price. This price can be structured to equal the balloon on the leveraging debt. The purchase option in a FSC lease must be based upon the expected fair market value of the aircraft. This higher purchase option amount is offset by lower rentals throughout the lease term.

The lessee who understands the building blocks that produce the economic return to the lessor will be in a commanding position to negotiate a financing that goes to the frontier of the lessor's constraints. Ideally, the lessor's minimum requirements for cash generation and tax deferral can be accommodated within a lease structure that gives the lessee the greatest amount of pass-through benefits from the lessor's indigenous tax regime. These cross-border leases are, quite simply, financial instruments that facilitate the export of tax benefits. Once this is recognised by all parties to the lease, negotiations on the level of net cash flow or residual value participation can be brought to a speedy conclusion. Cross-border leases as discussed here are not operating leases with residual risk borne by the lessor. Therefore, the lessor's rate of return requirements should be based upon alternative tax-oriented transactions without tax risk.

Constructing the lease

The primary goal of the lessee in negotiating the structure of the cross-border lease should be to create what is effectively a low-rate loan from the lessor. This means that the lessee will be comparing the terms of this loan with alternatives available in the chosen currency. The approach recommended here requires that the lessee first determines the feasible building blocks of the lease. Each lessor domicile and capital market will influence the outcome but there are basic 'rules of the road' that can be followed in creating the lease structure which will simultaneously satisfy the lessor, the lender (if any) and the lessee.

Term of the lease

Most airlines when raising funds either through a lease or loan will be seeking the longest possible term, unless the yield curve is so positively sloped that the cost becomes prohibitive. While this is also true with the cross-border lease, the lessee will find that the relatively thin

Exhibit 7.4
Cross-border leveraged lease: Example A*

Year	Rent	Debt service	Lessor's net rent	Interest	Principal	Cumulative principal	Remaining principal
1	6.3624	3.6000	2.7624	3.6000	0.0000	0.0000	60.0000
2	6.3624	3.6000	2.7624	3.6000	0.0000	0.0000	60.0000
3	6.3624	3.6000	2.7624	3.6000	0.0000	0.0000	60.0000
4	6.3624	3.6000	2.7624	3.6000	0.0000	0.0000	60.0000
5	6.3624	3.6000	2.7624	3.6000	0.0000	0.0000	60.0000
6	6.3624	3.6000	2.7624	3.6000	0.0000	0.0000	60.0000
7	6.3624	6.3624	0.0000	3.6000	2.7624	2.7624	57.2376
8	6.3624	6.3624	0.0000	3.4343	2.9281	5.6905	54.3095
9	6.3624	6.3624	0.0000	3.2586	3.1038	8.7944	51.2056
10	12.2562	12.2562	0.0000	3.0723	9.1839	17.9782	42.0218
11	12.2562	12.2562	0.0000	2.5213	9.7349	27.7131	32.2869
12	12.2562	12.2562	0.0000	1.9372	10.3190	38.0321	21.9679
13	12.2562	3.5068	8.7494	1.3181	2.1887	40.2208	19.7792
14	12.2562	3.5068	8.7494	1.1868	2.3200	42.5408	17.4592
15	12.2562	3.5068	8.7494	1.0476	2.4592	45.0000	15.0000
Totals	130.7988	87.9762	42.8226	42.9762	45.0000		

* Percentages of aircraft cost: equity = 40; debt = 60 @ 6.00% per annum. Purchase option = 15% of aircraft cost.

Exhibit 7.5
Cross-border leveraged lease: Example B*

Year	Rent	Debt service	Lessor's net rent	Interest	Principal	Cumulative principal	Remaining principal
1	8.3481	8.3481	0.0000	4.2564	4.0917	4.0917	81.0366
2	8.3481	8.3481	0.0000	4.0518	4.2963	8.3880	76.7403
3	8.3481	8.3481	0.0000	3.8370	4.5111	12.8990	72.2293
4	8.3481	8.3481	0.0000	3.6115	4.7366	17.6359	67.4926
5	8.3481	8.3481	0.0000	3.3746	4.9735	22.6091	62.5192
6	8.3481	8.3481	0.0000	3.1260	5.2221	27.8313	57.2970
7	8.3481	8.3481	0.0000	2.8649	5.4832	33.3145	51,8138
8	8.3481	8.3481	0.0000	2.5807	5.7574	39.0719	46.0564
9	8.3481	8.3481	0.0000	2.3028	6.0453	45.1172	40.0111
10	8.3481	8.3481	0.0000	2.0006	6.3475	51.4648	33.6635
11	8.3481	8.3481	0.0000	1.6832	6.6649	58.1297	26.9986
12	8.3481	8.3481	0.0000	1.3499	6.9982	65.1279	20.004
Totals	100.1772	100.1772	0.0000	35.0494	65.1278		

* Percentages of aircraft cost: equity = 4.87; debt = 85.13 @ 5.00% per annum. Purchase option = 20% of aircraft cost.

equity markets require that the lease term bears some relationship to the tax-deferral benefit pool and certain tax rules that have developed in the lessor's domicile. For example, the minimum term of an aircraft lease in Germany will typically be nine years. This presents no problem when new aircraft are being leased. The maximum stated term outside the US will fall between 10 and 20 years. The most economic term may in fact be shorter if, for example, the lessor is utilising a depreciation scheme that allows full amortisation over a 5- to 9-year period and the lessee anticipates selling the aircraft after 10 to 12 years. By allowing the lessee to terminate the lease and purchase the aircraft for an amount equal to the balance of the leveraging loan, the lessor will incur a tax liability. The generation of this tax liability represents the repayment by the lessor of its deferred tax account. The lessee should understand that the timing of this interruption of the lease should be analysed carefully so that no penalty is being applied implicitly in the lease pricing.

Exhibit 7.4 shows the pre-tax cash flows for a lease financing designed for a true term of 15 years. Exhibit 7.5 represents the pre-tax cash flows for a 16-year lease financing designed to be terminated by the lessee at the end of the twelfth year. In both cases, the emphasis is on showing the cash flows from the lessee's perspective. When the lessee captures the residual value, as is proposed in these lease structures, term is not critical.

Leveraging debt

In a cross-border lease structure that is tax-driven, it is extremely inefficient (and costly to the lessee) for the lessor to invest more than the percentage of cost equal to the present value of the tax-deferral benefit that is being transferred to the lessee. This means that the lessee should view each cross-border lease as being composed of financings from two distinct capital markets. The first is the tax-oriented investor pool whose participants seek a rapid payback of investment followed by generation of cash through tax deferrals and reinvestment. The second is the institutional term debt market composed of lenders seeking a secured, amortising loan at a market rate of interest. We will ignore, for the purposes of this discussion, the inclusion in the lease of certain types of concessionary debt such as export credits or tax-spared loans. These debt instruments, if available, can be accessed away from the lease. In fact, lessees are advised to avoid attempting to introduce an exotic or overly complicated debt financing into the cross-border leveraged lease. If such debt is available, it should finance aircraft being purchased rather than leased.

The lessee should concentrate its efforts on negotiating the largest possible equity investment percentage from the lessor that does not require payment of rents in excess of debt service. Lessor investment money is expensive when it must be repaid by the lessee rather than by the taxpayers in the lessor's country. It should be noted, however, that there are jurisdictions or accounting rules in certain countries that require that lease rents exceed debt service and return the lessor's equity investment, even at a very low implicit rate. There are no absolute rules for structuring cross-border leveraged leases, only guidelines that determine the direction in which the lessee should travel when negotiating the structure.

In Exhibit 7.4, the debt, equal to 60 per cent of aircraft cost, has been structured such that only interest is payable for the first six years. This is followed by three different levels of debt service, resulting in a remaining debt balance equal to 15 per cent of aircraft cost at the end of the fifteenth year. This balance is extinguished by the lessee's payment of the fixed purchase price of 15 per cent of aircraft cost.

In Exhibit 7.5, debt service is level and the lessee may terminate the lease at the end of the twelfth year and purchase the aircraft for the loan balance of 20 per cent of original aircraft cost. Because there is no cash flow to the lessor in excess of debt service, the equity percentage is lower than in Exhibit 7.4 (14.87 as against 40). Both lease structures are built upon annual rent and debt service. The frequency of payment will be based upon convention in the debt market that is being accessed and the willingness of the lessor to 'carry' the lease when it begins to pay the taxes that were earlier deferred. Certain tax rules in the lessor's domicile combined with lease optimisation techniques also may influence the payment frequency. The resolution of this issue will depend upon a rate negotiation with the lender, because the lessor always can be kept whole through the rental structure.

Currency of the debt

The lessee, when not providing a custom structured loan to the lessor, will seek the least expensive source of debt for the proposed lease term. This could very well lead to a market and currency different from that of the lessor's domicile. For example, a Japanese-based lease might include debt denominated in US dollars. Then, so much of the rent as will equal debt service must be denominated in the same currency. Utilising third country debt presents two distinct problems:

1 The lessee must avoid creating a withholding tax liability arising on the payment of interest by the lessor to the lender. Very rarely, if at all, will a lessor absorb this risk or cost.
2 The lessee may be creating a balance sheet problem for a lessor in a country where accounting standards require a periodic revaluation of all debt obligations.

It is assumed that the selection of the currency by the lessee, if no tax or accounting problems are generated, has been made after analysis of all currency risk matters. This would mean that some form of hedging arrangement has been concluded. Possibilities include a swap, a rolling forward exchange agreement, or purchase of a dedicated bond portfolio designed to meet the periodic debt obligations arising out of the lease.

The lessee should preserve its right to arrange the refinancing of the debt during the lease term, if this should become advantageous while not adversely affecting the lessor. Any interest rate reduction will have to be analysed in combination with its tax effect on the lessor. Therefore, care must be taken that basis points saved on the debt component of the lease are not lost when the lease is restructured. Transaction costs of the refinancing amendments to the original documentation also have to be taken into account.

Currency of the equity

One of the key issues that must be negotiated between lessee and lessor in a cross-border lease is the currency denomination of the lessor's net rent after debt service. Both the net rent, if any, and the lessee's purchase option will be denominated in a currency designated at the inception of the lease. If the purchase option cash flow is used to amortise the balloon on the leveraging debt, then the purchase option and the debt should be denominated in the same currency in order to eliminate the lessor's currency risk.

The net rent cash flows present some room for negotiation regarding currency denomination. The lessor will have recouped its investment through the realisation of tax benefits. Therefore, the early net rent cash flows are not critical to providing the lessor with the return of its capital. In the later years, the tax payments due will be met from the deferred tax pool of cash. Again, the net rent cash flows may not be critical for the lessor's return of capital. Simply stated, the lessor will make an initial equity investment that is repaid by tax savings. The net rent cash flows, to the extent required by local tax or accounting convention, are a form of loan repayment; in this case, the loan being from the lessor to the lessee. The denomination of the cash flow stream required to amortise this lessor loan will be determined through negotiation between lessee and lessor and will be influenced strongly by current exchange rates. The lease in Exhibit 7.4, for example, could have debt denominated in Swiss francs and the lessor's net rent denominated in Deutschmarks.

The amount of lessor's net rent will be determined in part by the choice of currency because this lessor loan must relate to existing capital market conditions for loans denominated in the same currency. Thus, both the amount of tax benefits and the selected currency will drive the absolute amounts of periodic net rent that will be paid by the lessee.

Why the game is played

Given all of the structuring and negotiating required to conclude a cross-border aircraft lease, questions arise about the value of the exercise. The answer is that the lease tribulations are indeed worth the effort provided that a clear economic target is in sight.

Discussions regarding the value of a given lease structure usually include terms such as 'implicit rate' and 'front-end NPV benefit'. These are shorthand concepts for measuring certain economic characteristics of the lease. For example, the lease in Exhibit 7.4 generates a periodic cash flow to the lessor equal to the difference between rent and debt service. This differential represents the true cost to the lessee of the equity investment of 40 per cent of cost made by the lessor. Given that the only incremental financing for the lessee in the lease will, in fact, be the equity investment, the interest cost of the equity money equals 0.7 per cent per annum. This is the so-called implicit rate of the equity. Because the purchase option price of 15 per cent of cost is fully dedicated to amortising the loan, this payment by the lessee is not relevant to the analysis of the net benefit brought to the lessee by the lessor's equity investment.

Another method of analysing the lease in Exhibit 7.4 involves discounting the net rent stream at a rate that reflects the rate at which structured deposits or a bond portfolio hedge can be placed in the currency of the net rent flows. If the net rents are payable in Deutschmarks and Deutschmark-denominated government bonds can be purchased to yield 7 per cent, then the present value of the net rent stream equals 23.36 per cent of cost. By subtracting this amount from the equity infusion of 40 per cent, the front-end NPV benefit comes out at 16.64 per cent.

The appropriate method of analysis for the lessee to use will be a function of whether the net rent stream will be treated as a low-rate loan (implicit rate method) or will be defeased if it is other than zero (NPV method). In either case it would be inappropriate to include the debt service cash flows in the analysis. Because the debt component of the lease is at market rates and usually does not bring a concession to the lease, it does not generate an incremental benefit. The lessee should concentrate its analytical efforts on measuring the size of the equity infusion and its repayment pattern.

Exhibit 7.5 could represent a lease under which both the debt and equity are provided in, say, Japanese yen and the lease can be terminated (and the aircraft purchased) at the end of the twelfth year on payment of 20 per cent of cost. If the lessor has brought the complete financing package including the debt, then the lessee could compare the market rate on yen debt (with an average life equivalent to that of the lease cash flows) with the implicit rate of the lease inclusive of the 20 per cent purchase option. In this case the implicit rate equals 2.57 per cent per annum. Alternatively, the front-end NPV benefit equals 14.87 per cent of cost (the net free equity investment).

Goals for cross-border leveraged leases are easier to state than to accomplish: generate the maximum equity investment percentage at the least interest cost. The knowledgeable lessee must view the lease as a means of capturing the tax benefits of aircraft ownership in another country through the lessor's equity investment.

Operation and sub-leasing

The primary goal of the lessee when entering into a cross-border lease is a significant reduction in financing cost. The lessee should not be required to relinquish operating flexibility as a condition for concluding the lease. Because the lessor has made a favourable credit decision regarding the lessee when agreeing to enter into the lease, it would be contradictory for the lessor to attempt to restrict the lessee's use of the leased aircraft as such use contributes to the presumed credit strength.

Reality also dictates that a lessee cannot and will not allow its line operations to be disrupted by having to treat a leased aircraft differently to an owned aircraft. For example, engines must be allowed to be interchanged within the lessee's fleet. This will mean that the originally leased engines may move to a workshop in the lessee's country or elsewhere and may wind up appearing on the wings (or fuselage) of an aircraft owned (or leased) by the airline. Also, alterations to the leased aircraft may be made either to meet safety directives or to conform to the lessee's configuration as it may be updated from time to time.

As long as the lessee agrees to operate the leased aircraft in a non-discriminatory manner (ie no distinction between owned and leased aircraft), the lessor should be satisfied. Any attempt by the lessor or lender to impose operational constraints on the lessee at best will be met by hostility from the lessee and at worst will undermine the deal.

A significant exception to this rule arises in the FSC lease. Here the lessee must accept limitations on the operation of the aircraft (and engines) to the US. Major airlines that have utilised FSC leases have determined that these restrictions are manageable as regards long-range aircraft that are placed in worldwide rotation (eg MD11, 747-400) and well worth the economic benefit of the lease.

A more substantive debate involves the extent to which the lessee will be allowed to sub-lease the aircraft to another operator. The lessor's concern involves three issues:

1 continuation of ownership claim;
2 operating standards of the lessee; and
3 potential liability claims against the lessor.

The key element in reducing the lessor's general unwillingness to allow unlimited sub-leasing will be the lessee's agreement to remain primarily liable for all rent and indemnity payments arising under the lease. Therefore, the lessor must make what is ultimately a credit decision when considering the lessee's request for unlimited sub-leasing rights.

One of the extraneous arguments often raised by a lessor relates to the potential diminution in residual value that may occur when an airline other than the primary lessee is allowed to operate and maintain the aircraft. Because a key structural point in the lease should be that the lessee and not the lessor will receive the economic benefit of the aircraft residual value, the lessor's concern is unwarranted. In fact, the lessee with possession of the residual interest in the aircraft will be likely to exercise extreme caution in selecting sub-lessee airlines.

A reasonable concession to the lender is an agreement to limit sub-leases to airlines domiciled in countries with laws recognising liens such as the first mortgage and the ownership interest of the lessor. Here again, the stronger the credit of the lessee, the weaker will be the restrictions on sub-leasing imposed by the lessor and lender.

Aircraft condition at lease maturity

Cross-border lease documentation has developed as an amalgam of US, UK, German and Japanese components. For example, the use of an instalment sale agreement to effect the secured loan has often been required by Japanese lenders into the leveraged lease. While there are substantive reasons for such a construction, there are other lease elements that have made the journey from one country to another without clear justification.

The best example of this perpetuation of the unnecessary is the section of the lease governing the condition of the aircraft on its return to the lessor at the end of the lease term. In the US form of leveraged lease, the lessor may have a participation in the residual value potential. Therefore, the condition of the aircraft on its return can have a material effect on its value and the resulting economics to the US lessor. A 15-year-old wide-bodied aircraft might require a refurbishing investment of US$10 million if the airframe, landing gear and engines are close to zero time/maximum cycles. Thus, an often heavily negotiated part of a US lease is the provision specifying the standards that must be met by the airline when returning the aircraft and the reimbursement provisions if those standards are not met. This return section is a clear 'money provision'.

In the case of a cross-border lease with a reasonably low, fixed lessee purchase option (10–25 per cent) that is expected to be exercised, such a provision will never be applied because the aircraft will not be returned to the lessor. The return provision, a vestige from US leveraged leasing, should not be used to induce a negotiating battle because, if the lease is structured properly, it has no economic relevance in a cross-border lease from a domicile other than the US.

Aircraft registration

A key objective of the lessee during lease negotiation is to structure a cross-border lease in such a way that the lease effectively becomes a financing, with economic ownership (primarily residual value control) retained by the lessee. However, in order for the lessor to claim its domestic tax benefits that underpin the transaction, it generally must maintain legal title to the leased aircraft. A key determinant of ownership is the recording of the lessor as owner in the register of aircraft maintained in the lessee's country. In most countries other than the US the legal owner may register its ownership claim with the appropriate authority. (In the US the FAA will recognise the US lessee in most cross-border leases as the economic owner for registration if the lease is economically equivalent to a conditional sale agreement.) The net result is that German and Japanese owners, for example, appear in the civil aircraft registers of various European countries as owners of aircraft leased to airlines domiciled in that country.

In some countries, the trust or partnership form of ownership is not accepted for registration purposes. In these cases, each owner in a multiple ownership situation must be disclosed. This inconvenience may preclude transactions in which the equity investment is provided by a pool of investors rather than one to five institutional lessors. Even though the registered owner of a European aircraft may be a Japanese leasing company, the aircraft still will carry the European registration marking on its fuselage. Thus, there is no immediately obvious way to determine which aircraft have been the subject of cross-border leases. This is in contrast with Boeing 747 aircraft, which carry US N-registration designations but which are operated by non-US carriers. These aircraft are the relics of the cross-border ITC leasing age in the US.

Recording a mortgage

While the lessor of the aircraft wishes to have its ownership interest recorded so that domestic claims to tax benefits may be supported, the lender will require that its first mortgage lien on the aircraft be recorded and, more importantly, be recognised in the lessee's country. This first-priority claim on the aircraft will protect the lender in the event of a default by the lessee in the payment of rent. After the appropriate notice and cure periods have elapsed, the lender will want to be able to exercise its right to repossess and dispose of the aircraft.

Unless the prospective lender can be assured that the laws in the lessee's country will recognise and respect the lender's senior claim, it is highly unlikely that the loan will be forthcoming. An exception is the FSC lease, where the lender receives security other than a direct security interest in the aircraft. This issue has not created problems in those countries with well-developed law relating to mortgage claims. In fact, the cross-border leases that have been concluded have, through their own process of natural selection, involved lessees domiciled primarily in western Europe, Japan, Australia and the US. Therefore, while extreme care must be taken to ensure that the liens are recorded properly and maintained, few practical problems have arisen that would have prevented the consummation of the leases. It is extremely important that highly experienced counsel be retained by the lender in the lessee's country if the mortgage is to be recorded in that country. The US-based cross-border lease, when it involved US registration, contained a somewhat different construction. In those cases, ownership and mortgage liens were recorded with the FAA in the US, the domicile of the lessor rather than the lessee.

Default

The airline lessees that use cross-border leveraged leases are, in general, of extremely high credit quality. With the relative scarcity of equity funds available for such leasing transactions, the number of airline lessees that wish to engage in these leases exceeds the number of available 'slots'. Therefore, the selection process has resulted in a uniformly impressive list of airlines that have concluded cross-border leases. It is also generally true that the primary institutional lenders into these leases have come from among the largest banks and insurance companies in the world. The equity investors, however, may be relatively small private companies or individual investors who are seeking to purchase tax-deferral benefits. While the fronting packager or leasing company may be financially strong, the actual equity investment often will be provided through a special purpose company with minimal capitalisation.

Given these elements, along with the lessee's economic control of the aircraft, the lessee should be more concerned with the potential bankruptcy of the lessor than is often the case. In order to allay the lessee's fears of loss of the aircraft due to the bankruptcy of the lessor, the lessee should insist upon clauses in both the lease and the mortgage documents recognising the lessee's rights (a) of quiet enjoyment of the aircraft while rentals are paid according to the lease and (b) to purchase the aircraft for a fixed price. The financial demise of the equity investor must not be allowed to impair the lessee's economic position and control of the aircraft. For this reason, the lessee in a FSC lease should insist upon receiving a creditworthy guarantee of the lessor's obligation to lift liens against the aircraft.

The negotiation of the more traditional lessee events of default often leads to acrimonious debate. While the lessee will accept that rent must be paid by the end of a grace period (usually 5–10 days), most of the other events of default can create problems if not worded in a manner that reflects practical reality. Payment of amounts other than rent (eg, taxes or indemnities) should be triggered by notice from the lessor to the lessee with a reasonable response time, because these amounts usually are unpredictable, often significant, and may give rise to an opportunity for the lessee and lessor to contest the claim made by a third party. Correspondingly, if the lessor learns that a covenant (such as insurance) has been breached, the lessee should be given a reasonable period of time (often 30 days) to cure the violation. 'Hair-trigger' defaults are not in anyone's best interests.

Lessors waste an enormous amount of time at the negotiating table attempting to insert cross-default clauses. A reasonable lessee position is that, because the leveraged lease is a secured financing, default by the lessee elsewhere should not cause the subject lease to be thrown into default. This is especially true when the rent under the lease continues to be paid.

A situation could arise where the lessee is disputing a claim by a creditor in another transaction for, say, an indemnity payment. There is no valid reason why such a dispute should create an event of default under the subject lease. In the event that the lessee does default, the lessor should be required to mitigate the extent to which the remedies are used against the lessee. For example, when remedies are being exercised, the fair market value of the aircraft should be credited against the tally of economic damage to the lessor.

Early termination

The most careful and knowledgeable structuring of rentals and debt service will have been in vain if the economics of the lease are destroyed by an early termination. Most leases are concluded under the expectation that they will continue through the payment of the final rental and the exercise of the purchase option. The economics originally anticipated by the lessee will be realised if, in fact, the lease does endure for the full term.

Problems often arise, however, when the lessor and lessee turn to the negotiation of the early termination and loss mechanics and economics of the lease. In the event of a casualty or other constructive loss of the aircraft, the lessor will demand that a stipulated amount be payable pursuant to a schedule attached to the lease. This same schedule is appropriate for determining the fixed payment that the lessee must make if the lessee exercises its right to terminate the lease early. Because one of the lessee's goals will be to retain the residual value of the aircraft, the lessor will not be sacrificing residual potential in the event of a casualty loss. Therefore, both the stipulated loss value schedule and the termination value schedule will be derived using the same methodology. (A lessor may decide not to allow a voluntary early termination until some reasonable minimum period of time has elapsed.)

It is surprising that lessees often devote most of their analytical and negotiating time to rents and debt service while treating the stipulated loss and termination values (SLVs and TVs) as an afterthought. An intense and heated bidding competition will take place to select the lessor, and the winning bidder may not have submitted SLVs and TVs as part of the bidding process, but only at a later date will the lessee realise that the originally anticipated lease economics may not be preserved in the event of any early termination. The often heard lessor argument that 'insurance will pay the bill' is true only in the event of a defined casualty occurrence. (Also, this argument ignores the fact that insurance has a definite cost associated with it.) A voluntary early lease termination by the lessee may become necessary if certain operational or legal aspects of the lease become unduly burdensome. This makes careful negotiation of these values even more critical.

In the case of a dual-currency lease, the SLV schedule will have separate debt and equity components. This will provide a clear separation of the debt repayment component of SLV from the portion of SLV that will flow to the lessor in the event of an early termination.

Constructing the stipulated loss value

There are three discrete amounts that the lessor will expect to have generated by the SLV on an early termination. If the lease is terminated on the payment of SLV to the lessor by the lessee, the SLV must equal the sum of:

1 the loan balance plus accrued interest and loan prepayment penalty, if any;
2 the taxes payable by the lessor as a result of the receipt of the SLV (reduced by any remaining tax basis and any other allowable deductions); and
3 the lessor's outstanding investment.

The first two components should be determinable by both lessor and lessee without dispute when the lessee has an understanding of the tax regime in the lessor's tax domicile.

The third component of SLV, the lessor's outstanding investment, creates most of the friction in trying to agree upon an SLV schedule. Lessors will not reveal voluntarily their equity amortisation tables and reinvestment rates, which are key variables in determining the lessor's outstanding investment. Most lessees are surprised if and when they learn that the net equity position is more frequently negative rather than positive during the term of the lease.

Therefore, the lessor has a cash pool at its disposal rather than an investment that has to be financed; the lease has turned from an investment into a source of funds. This is due to the fact that the lessor's investment is recovered within the early years of the lease as a result of the rapid realisation of tax deferrals by the lessor. Thereafter, the lessor builds up a cash balance that is available to meet later tax payments or, in the event of an early termination, to contribute to reducing the SLV.

The real issue that has to be addressed by the lessor and the lessee is the extent to which the lessee will be economically penalised for an early termination. By treating the SLV as a balloon lease payment, the lessee can determine how adversely the lease economics are affected by an early termination. Most lessors are reluctant to allow the reinvestment earnings on the deferred tax account to be invaded for the purpose of reducing the SLV schedule. This should not deter an informed lessee from insisting on an equitable distribution of the deferred tax and reinvestment earnings account in the event of an early termination.

Indemnities

There is no other area of lease negotiation that carries with it the explosive capability of indemnities. More potential transactions either have broken apart or have not moved beyond a proposal stage due to the lessor's indemnity requirements. When analysing indemnity issues, it is worthwhile to separate what are termed general indemnities from tax indemnities.

The lessor and lender enter into the transaction on the basis of the lease being a totally net lease. Thus, the lessee must retain responsibility for all liabilities that may arise as a result of the possession and use of the aircraft. This is consistent with the concept of the cross-border leveraged lease as a financing vehicle with operational and economic control remaining with the lessee. Just as the lessee must provide and pay for the property and liability insurance relating to the aircraft, the lessee must protect the lessor and lender against claims brought by third parties which result from the possession and use of the aircraft.

The purpose of the general non-tax indemnity clauses is to insulate the lessor and lender from claims that are not likely to have been brought if the lease had been structured as a traditional loan. The legal ownership of the aircraft by the lessor may expose the lessor to claims that relate to control and economic ownership, but because these remain with the lessee in the properly structured cross-border lease, it is appropriate that the lessee remain primarily liable for these risks. While negotiation will produce a provision that spells out the rights of the lessee to control the contest of a claim, the lessee should be prepared to accept a reasonable net lease general indemnity package.

The tax indemnity provisions, however, present a totally different set of issues. Here, the lessee cannot be as compliant in being willing to protect the lessor. In fact, for other than certain taxes (to be discussed), the lessee should firmly resist accepting the tax risks associated with the cross-border lease. A valid description of the position that should be adopted by the lessee would be, 'We are all big boys and girls'. Therefore, the lessor must be willing to accept that the lessee will not indemnify against risks that are beyond the control of the lessee. Fear of the unknown often prevents a cross-border lease from closing if the lessor insists upon full economic protection through a tax indemnity.

Probably the greatest tax risk in the cross-border lease is the possibility that the tax authorities in the lessor's country will disallow the lessor's claim that it is entitled to ownership tax benefits. If the lessor was not allowed to claim accelerated depreciation and the resulting tax deferrals, the lease investment would become an economic disaster. In the FSC lease, the same unfortunate result would occur if the lessor could not claim the benefit of a reduced tax rate on rental income. The basic rationale for the lease – the generation of tax benefits for the lessor resulting in reduced rentals for the lessee – would have been blown away. This could occur while the lessee continues to claim ownership tax benefits in its country. (The possibility of the same asset producing ownership tax benefits in two countries simultaneously has given rise to the unflattering description of cross-border leases as 'double dip'.)

The lessee should not bear the risk of the lessor losing any or all of its ownership tax benefits (eg accelerated depreciation, interest deduction on loans). Whether the lessor's domestic tax authorities disapprove the structure of the lease or change the tax law retroactively, these risks should fall to the lessor. The lessee should take the reasonable position that:

- the lessor is better able to judge the tax climate in its own country;
- the lessor should not be jumping into the cross-border lease business if it is unsure of the validity of its claim to the tax benefits;
- the tax authorities will not be sympathetic to the pleas of the foreign lessee for any mitigation of the tax benefit loss; and
- the grossed-up payment that the lessee would have to make to the lessor in order to compensate the lessor for its loss of tax benefits would increase the lease cost beyond acceptable limits.

Therefore, the lessor should bear all tax risk in its own country. A reasonable (and required) exception to this is the lessee agreement, in the case of the FSC lease, to operate the US-manufactured aircraft (and engines) predominantly outside the US. The lessee also can bear the tax risk arising outside of the lessor's country with two main caveats:

1 The indemnity should exclude taxes that are in excess of the taxes that would have been imposed on the lessor if the cross-border lease was the sole transaction of the lessor being taxed. Thus, the fact that the lessor has other activities that are caught in a third country's tax net, and spring the tax trapdoor, should not create an indemnifiable event if the lease by itself would not have been taxed.
2 The indemnity should not cover any taxes arising in the lessee's country that are due to the actions of the lessor. For example, if the lessee's country imposes a tax on the lessor because the lessor is deemed to have created a permanent establishment in the lessee's country, the lessor should not be indemnified by the lessee.

A lessor will quite often suggest to a prospective cross-border lessee that rather than requiring a tax indemnity with a payment gross-up in the event of a loss of tax benefits, the lessor would be willing to accept an unwind of the transaction. The offer might state that the equity investment and loan would be repaid by the lessee at the time the tax benefits are disallowed, with some very low rate of interest. Unfortunately, the other side of the unwind is the fact that the lessee would have to refinance the aircraft. At best, a low-rate financing that required a time and money investment by the lessee will be lost. At worst, the lessee will have to refinance the aircraft at a substantially higher rate. Unless the lessee's full NPV benefit is protected, an unwind does not appear to be an attractive alternative for the lessee and should be resisted strongly.

Innovation: what works and what may not

It is quite clear that we are witnessing a changing of the guard with respect to the importance of various markets as sources of financing. As pressure is brought to bear on aggressive structures by less complacent tax authorities, aircraft lease practitioners have had to scramble to find new equity sources.

Because lease financing also is subject to the more general economic trends affecting currency values and interest rates, uncontrollable forces have added to the 'cyclical rotation' that seems to afflict this market. So, benefits available from Japanese leveraged leases have plummeted (and may be radically altered or eliminated if the Japanese corporate tax system is modified), while the German lease has emerged as a substantial supplier of aircraft lease funding. The market in the US has been damaged by government tax pronouncements, although a new structure, the leasehold financing, has brought a temporary respite. In fact, as a result of the most recent IRS regulations setting out the rules for rent structures, we may see a resurgence of FSC-related financings (commission and ownership).

Often the most creditworthy airlines demand that leasing transactions incorporate fully defeased debt. This eliminates most of the arbitrage loss associated with raising debt through the lease, which then is added to the corporate cash pile. Even airlines with weak credit have found an alternative to leasing – the securitisation of export credit financing. This has allowed such airlines to tap the credit markets for financing using the credit support of the export credit agencies.

Japan

The Japanese market has taken its providers on a wild ride since late 1994. The NPV benefit soared above 11 per cent only to plummet below 6 per cent by late 1995. By early 1998 the benefits were under 4 per cent. However, the low interest rates in Japan are a structural impediment to NPV benefit improvement possibilities. For example, from April 1995 to March 1998 10-year yen deposit rates dropped from 4.8 per cent to 1.8 per cent. Adding to the negatives of the Japanese leveraged lease (JLL) for many airlines is the fact that it cannot be legally defeased. Furthermore, corporate tax changes in Japan may destroy the economic basis of the JLL.

Should the JLL miraculously survive, the market will have to search for structural innovation in order to attract the most creditworthy airlines in large numbers. One technique may involve denominating the equity cash flows in a currency other than yen. For example, if the lessors would accept Deutschmark-denominated equity payments, the lessee could evaluate (and hedge) its cash flow exposure using interest rates approximately 300 basis points higher than yen rates. The resulting massive increase in NPV benefit for the lessee could be shared with the lessor by allowing the equity payment percentages to be increased. This win-win structure requires lease investors who, in this example, are comfortable with Deutschmark exposure.

United States

While we can expect extra activity in the US-based market in cross-border leases for airlines, two major impediments stand in the way. First, in 1996 the IRS issued the long-anticipated Section 467 draft regulations, to be followed in due course by the final regulations. As a result, we can expect some reduction in lease NPV benefits (and benefits associated with all highly rent-structured transactions). Also, we may expect that there will be less variation among lease bidders as pricing models of prudent lessors will tend to follow the regulation guidelines. Finally, the transaction costs of US-based defeased leases are formidable, and would deter many airline participants even without the tax sensitivity of these transactions.

The brightest spot in the US aircraft leasing market is the expected survival of FSC leases. This technique continues to bring benefits to those airlines that are taking delivery of US-manufactured aircraft to be operated predominantly outside the US. Lease financing practitioners in the US will continue to try to bring lease-equity to a market fuelled by strong sales of US-manufactured aircraft. The backlog at Boeing assures healthy demand for FSC leases into the next century.

Germany

After 15 years of sporadic activity, the German cross-border leasing market has finally developed into a reliable source of financing for certain airlines. The so-called 'three-factor test' will determine how receptive the market will be to a specific transaction involving a foreign airline: a quality airline (preferably well-known to German investors); an aircraft with German content (ie Airbus); and/or an underwriter based in Germany. Of course there will be exceptions to this rule, but the bulk of the almost US$4 billion in aircraft value financed since mid-1994 falls within at least one of these categories.

Activity has been generated by the increased participation in the business on the part of major German banks. They have gathered the necessary equity financing in the form of funds provided by hundreds of individual investors. These transactions require the creation and distribution of an elaborate prospectus and close contact with the investor base. Occasionally, private transactions can be structured under which a single investor is brought to the lease by a bank or leasing company.

Based upon the term and structure of the debt financing and purchase option amounts, airlines can obtain NPV benefits exceeding 7 per cent of aircraft cost. Furthermore, cash-rich airlines can defease the debt portion of the financing and thereby extract the equity benefits on a more efficient basis. The most unappealing aspect of German leases, limited residual sharing with the lessor, remains. However, by properly setting the sharing threshold, the airline lessee can manage this exposure.

Just as the US tax authorities have curtailed the benefits associated with outbound cross-border leases, German economic officials have been suggesting that German lease benefits should not be exported. Whether this blossoms into a serious threat to the developing aircraft leasing market remains to be seen.

Prospects

The market for cross-border aircraft leasing always has been and continues to be dynamic. Lease NPV benefit levels fluctuate as interest rates rise and fall, equity sources emerge and then withdraw, and domestic tax authorities pare down the fiscal attributes of leases. The volatility of this market will not diminish in the foreseeable future.

Conclusion

Cross-border leases that take advantage of favourable tax laws in the lessor's domicile can bring great benefits to airline lessees. Because history shows that the availability of these favourable opportunities can be short-lived, it is reasonable for those airlines in a position to take advantage of the 'current' active market to seek to do so. The costs associated with such transactions are not always explicit, however, and must be detected during rigorous lease negotiations. An informed and knowledgeable lessee will be able to meet the challenge and to emerge from the negotiations with an attractive, risk-controlled aircraft financing package.

PART III

Country and Regional Markets

8 US aircraft leasing

James V. Babcock and Mark Bewsher[1]

Introduction

The past decade has seen many changes in the US aircraft leasing market. For example:

- Whereas 10 years ago US investors focused mainly on domestic airlines, today they are just as likely to be reviewing the credit of KLM or Cathay Pacific Airways.
- 'Plain vanilla' leveraged leases have become more complex.
- The leasing structures preferred by airlines and investors have evolved through several iterations in response to changing tax rules.
- International airlines are constantly looking for the latest and most powerful cross-border enhancements.
- Manufacturers' support has played a larger role in aircraft financing in the past few years.
- Shorter-term operating leases are becoming increasingly popular for both new and used aircraft acquisition.
- Regional airlines are stronger than ever and make up an increasing percentage of the domestic leasing activity.

After the slump in the airline industry in the early 1990s, orders for new aircraft recovered strongly in 1995 and 1996, leading to a dramatic recovery in the demand for financing. In 1996 approximately US$32 billion of aircraft were financed, of which approximately US$10 billion were cross-border transactions of one kind or another. With the continuing increase in orders in 1997, the demand for financing is likely to increase further in the near to medium term.

This chapter attempts to explain the benefits leasing offers to lessees and lessors. It will also address other important aspects of US aircraft leasing. After a description of the economic and structural features of US aircraft leases, as well as some typical motivations for both lessees and lessors to enter into leases, the proposed 'Section 467' tax rules are discussed. This is followed by an examination of Pickle and FSC leases. The chapter concludes with a summary of past trends and a few predictions. Appendices 1 and 2 discuss the tax and accounting guidelines that apply to US aircraft leases.

Types of leases

Leasing terminology is sometimes confusing and we therefore start by listing the major categories of leases. For practical purposes, the vast majority of US aircraft leases undertaken at the present time fall into four categories:

1 *Operating leases.* These are for a relatively short term and the lessee's economic criterion is usually the monthly rental factor, typically in the range of 0.90 per cent to 1.20 per cent of cost.

The lessor looks primarily for its economic return in the form of the proceeds of sale of the aircraft at lease-end (the 'residual'). Any tax benefits are normally incidental.

2 *Regular domestic tax leases.* These are for a longer term and for US domestic airlines only. The lessee's objective is usually to obtain the lowest present value of rentals plus any purchase option payments. This present value is typically in the range of 82–92 per cent of cost. The lessor's primary economic benefit is tax deferral due to accelerated depreciation of the asset.

3 *MACRS C-FSC leases.* These are for US-manufactured aircraft used by US-taxpaying airlines on international service to and from the US. The lessee's all-in present value cost will typically be in the range of 80–88 per cent. The lessor enjoys domestic depreciation plus special export (FSC) tax allowances.

4 *Pickle C-FSC leases.* These are for US-manufactured aircraft used by foreign airlines. The present value cost will typically be in the range of 96–99 per cent, or, as more commonly expressed, a present value benefit of 1–4 per cent. The lessor enjoys FSC benefits but a much slower ('Pickle') rate of depreciation.

Other types of leases are:

- *Turbo C-FSC.* Virtually all MACRS C-FSCs, and many Pickle C-FSCs, use the 'turbo' enhancement.
- *Pickle leases.* These would be available for a foreign airline acquiring non-US (or US) manufactured aircraft, but generally the benefits, if any, are very small.
- *Leasehold interest structure.* This would be available for a foreign airline acquiring non-US (or US) manufactured aircraft, but generally the benefits are smaller than in other types of cross-border financing such as a Japanese or German lease.
- *O-FSC leases.* These are for US-manufactured aircraft used by a foreign airline. They are not being entered into at the present time because of uncertain tax interpretations and difficulties in securing lenders' collateral.

Economics and structuring

As indicated earlier, tax leases (sometimes called 'full-payout leases') are for terms substantially covering the useful life of the aircraft. Full-payout leases can be structured as 'single-investor leases', where the investor contributes 100 per cent of the aircraft cost, or as 'leveraged leases', where the investor's capital contribution is 'leveraged' by a substantial amount of borrowed funds.

Most airlines have preferred leveraged leasing as a source of long-term financing for new aircraft, because a leveraged lease generally offers superior economics compared with an operating lease, and it provides the airline with greater control over aircraft residual value. The focus of this chapter will be on long-term US leveraged leases.

Overview of leveraged aircraft leases

The structuring and documentation of a leveraged lease can be complicated, as a result of the subtle legal, tax and accounting issues involved: in a typical US leveraged aircraft lease the financing documents are measured more commonly in inches than by number of pages. In part, this extensive documentation is necessary given the many parties that can be involved in these transactions and their varied interests. As a simple example, both the lessor and the lender have a strong interest in assuring that the aircraft in their lease portfolios will have the highest possible residual/collateral values. All leases consequently have provisions that address the lessee's operation and maintenance of the aircraft and the 'return conditions' that the aircraft must meet at lease-end. Likewise, lessors and lenders will require the lessee to maintain certain minimum coverage at all times for hull and liability insurance.

Many of the documentation provisions in US aircraft leases are, to varying degrees, negotiable. However, with the assistance of a capable financial adviser and experienced counsel, leveraged leases can be completed smoothly and economically, as attested by the large number of transactions completed to the satisfaction of all parties.

The participants in a typical US leveraged aircraft lease include:

- a lessee, who uses the aircraft and pays rent on it;
- a lessor, also known as an equity participant, who partially funds the purchase of the aircraft;
- a lender, who provides the non-recourse debt to fund the balance of the aircraft acquisition cost; and
- an owner trustee, who performs certain administrative functions and who is technically the borrower of the debt in the lease.

The lessee also often has the option of purchasing the aircraft from the lessor at or near the end of the lease term. (The relationships of the parties in a typical US leveraged lease are shown in Exhibit 8.1.)

The owner trustee, acting on behalf of the lessor, holds title to the aircraft but confers beneficial ownership of the aircraft on the lessor. The lessor is thus entitled to all of the US tax depreciation benefits of owning the aircraft.

The debt provided by the lenders is usually long term and fixed rate. The lenders are typically institutions such as insurance companies, pension funds or commercial banks. These loans are non-recourse to the general credit of the owner trustee or the equity participant, and they are secured by (a) a lien on the aircraft and (b) an assignment of the lease, including vir-

Exhibit 8.1
Basic US leveraged lease structure

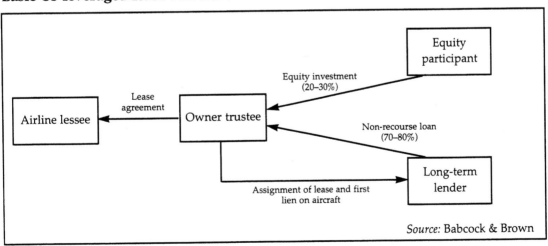

Source: Babcock & Brown

tually all payments (except lessor indemnity payments) due under the lease. The lender cannot look to the owner trustee or to the lessor for repayment in the event of lessee default. Debt service payments are usually fully funded by the rental payments from the lessee and take priority over any distributions of rent to the equity participant. The lenders are therefore subject to some credit and equipment risk, but their exposure is at a lower level than the lessor's.

There may also be an indenture trustee who represents the lenders, and handles the distribution of rental payments and other responsibilities.

The economics of US leveraged aircraft leases are driven by three principal factors:

1 the tax benefits;
2 the lease rentals; and
3 the residual value of the aircraft at the end of the lease term.

As illustrated in Exhibit 8.1, the capital structure of a leveraged lease transaction consists of an equity investment, typically equal to 20–30 per cent of the cost of the aircraft to be leased, with non-recourse debt making up the remainder. The non-recourse debt magnifies the effect of the tax benefits available to the equity participant in relation to the size of its investment. This is an important factor in explaining how leases can benefit both the equity investor and the lessee.

Exhibit 8.2
Example – rent structures

---

1 *Low-high structure:* **23 semi-annual payments at 3.7314% of cost, followed by 23 semi-annual payments at 4.5606% of cost**

Implicit rate (excluding residual)	Total undiscounted rentals	Pre-tax present value of rents discounted at an 8.00% effective rate
5.93%	190.72%	82.93%

---

2 *Level structure:* **46 semi-annual payments at 4.0084% of cost**

Implicit rate (excluding residual)	Total undiscounted rentals	Pre-tax present value of rents discounted at an 8.00% effective rate
5.92%	184.39%	83.71%

---

3 *High-low structure:* **23 semi-annual payments at 4.2675% of cost, followed by 23 semi-annual payments at 3.4916% of cost**

Implicit rate (excluding residual)	Total undiscounted rentals	Pre-tax present value of rents discounted at an 8.00% effective rate
5.91%	178.46%	84.45%

Source: Babcock & Brown

In most long-term US leveraged leases the lessor's rate of return on its equity investment depends primarily on the tax benefits, and secondarily on the free cash flow (rents in excess of debt service). The optimal debt/equity ratio varies with each transaction and is affected principally by the term of the lease, the interest rate on the debt, and the magnitude and timing of the tax benefits available. For example, a shorter tax depreciation life of the aircraft in relation to the lease term will typically result in a lower optimal debt/equity ratio, because the consequent 'acceleration' of depreciation tax benefits relative to net rental income will be able to 'service' a greater equity investment. Similarly, for any given equity investor's return, the higher the interest rate on the debt, the more likely it is that lower leverage will be advantageous.

Lessee economics and motivations

Different lessees have different financing objectives. To illustrate this, consider the three simple rent structures in Exhibit 8.2 to determine the one with the 'lowest cost' to the airline lessee. The three structures are all 'optimised' assuming a 'plain vanilla' leveraged lease and a 23-year term. For illustrative purposes, the debt portion of each lease is approximately 75 per cent of cost and has a nominal interest rate of 8.0 per cent. The aircraft under lease in each of the three examples qualifies for seven-year domestic depreciation tax benefits under the modified accelerated recovery system (MACRS).

The 'implicit rate' is the interest rate on a loan with the same cost and with debt service payments equal to the rentals. Defined another way, it is the discount rate which, when applied to all rent payments, produces a present value equal to the original cost. What is generally referred to as the present value of a rent stream, on the other hand, is the total of the discounted cash flows obtained by applying a pre-selected discount rate to all rent payments. The present value of a rent stream obviously depends upon the discount rate applied: the higher the discount rate the lower the present value cost of the rents and vice versa (exactly the relationship between bond prices and interest rate levels). The 'total undiscounted rentals' is simply the total of the rents without regard to 'the time value of money' (ie the present value at a discount rate of zero). In a real sense, therefore, all these measures of lessee cost are present value calculations with differing choices of the most appropriate discount rate.

Considering the three lease structures in Exhibit 8.2, the 'low-high' structure offers the best economics to the lessee on a present value basis, but the 'high-low' structure offers the best economics on an implicit rate basis. This simple example shows that the choice of structure depends on which economic measure of cost the lessee prefers, or, to state it another way, the lessee's discount rate.

While most of the major airline lessees evaluate leases using the present value method rather than the implicit rate, in some special situations existing business agreements or asset plans would favour structures with a higher present value cost but a lower implicit rate. Such 'implicit rate lease structures' tend to have more rapid rent amortisation – advance versus arrears payments, level or high-low payments and greater frequency of payments – than structures designed to minimise the present value rental cost.

One example in which a lessee's particular circumstances favoured an implicit rate lease structure involved a marginal credit operating lessor whose intended use of certain equipment was to sub-lease it on an operating lease basis to one of its customers. The sub-lease was structured as a six-year initial lease (with a fixed lease rate) followed by two three-year renewal terms, with the renewal rents to be negotiated at the time of each renewal. The aircraft carried substantial risk of technological obsolescence. After evaluating many different structures, the lessee finally chose a high-low lease structure for its own head lease financing that entailed higher rent payments during the early years of a 12-year head lease. From the viewpoint of the head lessor, the structure mitigated to a large extent the credit and technological risks associated with the transaction (because the high-low rent structure more rapidly amortised the head lessor's investment), and the head lessor's pricing reflected this. The transaction offered a higher present value and a lower implicit rate than alternative structures might have, but it best met the needs of all the parties.

This example illustrates that it is crucial in the lessor's pricing process to be aware of the lessee's analytical method. Many competitive lease transactions are won not because the winning lessor had the cheapest money, but because of greater sensitivity to the lessee's situation and needs. It also highlights the importance of structuring to the correct discount rate. The wrong discount rate can produce a structure that is not the best for the airline, or can even lead to the choice of a poor financing vehicle.

The discussion so far has focused exclusively on measures of pre-tax lease economics. However, some lessees will consider the financing decision on an after-tax present value basis. Among US airlines, most decide to lease (as opposed to borrow-and-buy) when they expect to be unable to consistently use the tax benefits of aircraft ownership on a current basis. US airlines that expect to be in an alternative minimum tax (AMT) situation for more than a few years generally find it more attractive economically to lease new aircraft rather than purchase them. Of course the decision to lease or buy a group of aircraft may itself alter the airline's forecasted tax scenario. Many airlines therefore engage an adviser to help develop a fleet financial plan in the context of the airline's corporate business plan, strategy and objectives.

The motivation for an airline to lease may also be strongly affected by technological/aircraft residual value considerations and by other factors such as:

- a desire to tap a diverse investor base to fund future expansion;
- a desire to match asset and liability lives;
- a desire to raise 100 per cent financing;
- a desire to keep the financing off its balance sheet or for other accounting or ratings agency considerations;
- liquidity requirements; and/or
- target capital structure plans.

It would be unwieldy to attempt to address all of these issues, but it may be useful to discuss the two principal economic factors – tax benefit utilisation and residual value risk management.

Tax-benefit utilisation

The leasing structure lets a US airline lessee use indirectly some of the tax benefits associated with aircraft ownership and lock them in for the duration of the lease, regardless of what its actual tax position turns out to be.

A lessor prices a lease based on its assumption as to how it will be able to use the tax benefits (depreciation and interest deductions) that it acquires in the transaction. The lessor shares the tax benefits with the lessee by lowering rental payments to a level that allows the lessee to enjoy lower payments under the lease than under a debt financing (ie cash flow savings).

In most US leases the lessee is assured of receiving its locked-in benefit in full because it is not required to indemnify the lessor for inability to use transferred tax benefits or for reductions in the lessor's economics resulting from tax rate changes.[2]

Residual value risk management

A 'true lease' transfers technological risk to the lessor. There are, however, some structuring techniques that leave the lessee at least some ability to participate in any residual upside. These techniques include the use of early buyout options and of capped or fixed price purchase and renewal options.

A second approach that airlines use to manage residual risks is to maintain a mix of leased and owned aircraft, thereby 'hedging' their exposure. The value of this own/lease approach, as a way to capture at least a proportion of any upside that may develop, has declined somewhat as a result of the wider availability of capped purchase and renewal options.

To some extent, these analyses may seem relatively academic. Nonetheless, they are essential and weigh heavily in the financing decisions of many passenger and freight airlines. Considerations such as these explain, at least partially, why several sophisticated US airlines have leased an otherwise seemingly disproportionate percentage of their expanding fleets.

The early buyout option (EBO)

The simple lease pricing examples quoted earlier focused on the present value or implicit rate of the rental stream as a measure of rental cost. However, this number is not comparable with

Exhibit 8.3
EBO must equal or exceed the greater of two values

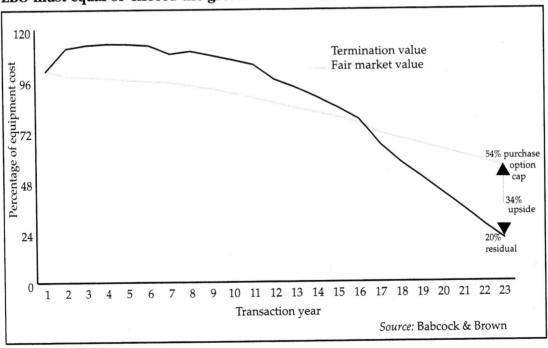

Source: Babcock & Brown

Exhibit 8.4
Year at which all-in present value cost is at a minimum

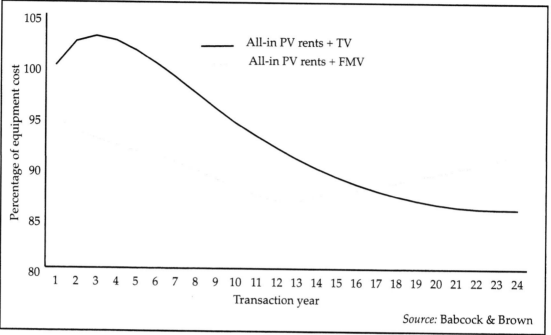

Source: Babcock & Brown

the cost of debt (100 per cent present value, if discounted at the debt rate) unless the cost of reacquiring the asset at the end of the financing term is also included.

A distinction must be made between the lessor's residual assumption and the exercise price of any purchase option that the lessor may offer the lessee at the end of the term. The lessor minimises its residual risk by assuming a residual substantially below the appraised expected fair market value (FMV). However, a purchase option with an exercise price at less than FMV would be considered a 'bargain' for tax purposes and would jeopardise the 'true lease' characterisation of the structure and hence the lessor's ability to enjoy tax ownership of the aircraft. A second test is that any purchase option should equal or exceed the inflated equivalent of the uninflated 20 per cent residual taken into account by the lessor in its pricing, as required by the IRS guidelines (see Appendix 1 to this chapter).

Because the purchase option (typically at 50 per cent of original cost, or more) will therefore be much higher than the residual assumed by the lessor in its pricing calculations (typically 25 per cent or less), the lessee may feel that, having already 'paid' the lessor for the aircraft via the rents and residual, it has to 'pay again' to reacquire it via the purchase option premium over the residual.

The use of an EBO can mitigate this problem, as indicated in Exhibits 8.3 and 8.4. As shown in Exhibit 8.3, from an economic viewpoint the EBO amount, which is set when the transaction closes, must equal or exceed the termination value (TV) at which the lessor's yield is protected. From a tax viewpoint, the EBO amount must also equal or exceed the future aircraft FMV (estimated at closing) to avoid characterisation as a 'bargain purchase option'. Exhibit 8.4 shows that, when the lessee's all-in present value cost of rents plus purchase option/EBO is calculated with the purchase option/EBO based on the higher of TV or FMV, the all-in present value cost will usually be at a minimum several years before the end of the full lease term.

114

When the EBO date (usually a single predetermined date) arrives, if the FMV at the tim[
higher than the EBO amount, the lessee will most likely exercise the EBO. If the FMV is below
the EBO, the lessee will most likely continue to pay rent through the end of the term and either
purchase the aircraft at lease-end at the (then) FMV or 'walk away' leaving the lessor to dispose
of the used aircraft.

When the EBO concept was first conceived, leases were structured to minimise full term
rental present value. The EBO amount was determined by terminating the lease at the EBO date
and calculating the EBO amount. Later, the optimisation algorithm was redesigned to focus on
minimising the all-in EBO present value.

Lessor economics and motivations

From an economic or cash flow standpoint, most lessors are motivated to invest in aircraft leases primarily by the opportunity for tax-deferral and residual value upside. In addition, from an
accounting standpoint, US lessors are allowed to front-end their overall leasing profits despite
the fact that they are simultaneously rear-ending those profits for tax purposes. This tax versus
book inconsistency contrasts with the accounting treatment of leasing in other major tax jurisdictions, such as Germany, Japan and the UK, and may in part explain the greater willingness
of certain US corporations to invest in leases as compared with their overseas counterparts.

Exhibit 8.5
Lessor's taxable income by year

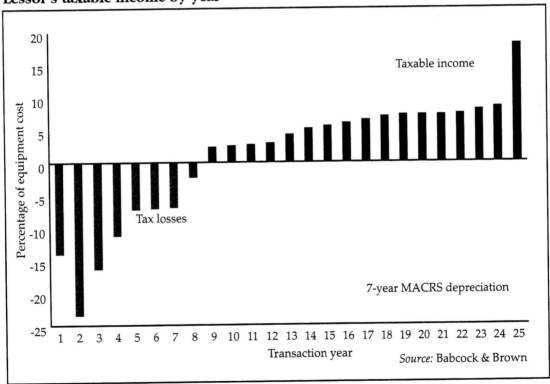

Source: Babcock & Brown

Tax deferral

The US lessor community consists primarily of companies faced with substantial current tax liabilities. Many of these investors have high marginal federal, state and local income tax rates, and consequently place a high value on tax deferral. In addition, many of these equity sources are in industries that generate large cash flows, and in some cases (such as regulated utilities) they have difficulty finding attractive alternative investment opportunities in their core businesses.

The lessor receives tax benefits in a leasing transaction as a result of deferring taxable income and accelerating deductions. Consider how a leveraged lease investment affects the lessor's taxable income:

Taxable income =	+	Accrued rent
	−	Accrued interest
	−	Depreciation
	−	Amortisation of expenses
	+	Realised residual proceeds

(at end of term or on exercise of an EBO or purchase option)

Rent usually rises through the term, while interest deductions fall as the loan is paid down. Depreciation is also high in the early years, especially when accelerated depreciation methods such as seven-year MACRS are in effect. Overall, the lease generates taxable losses in its early

Exhibit 8.6
Lessor's after-tax cash flows by year

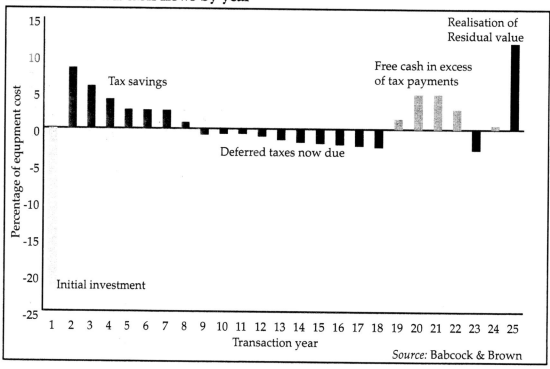

Source: Babcock & Brown

Exhibit 8.7
Lessor's investment/sinking fund balance by year

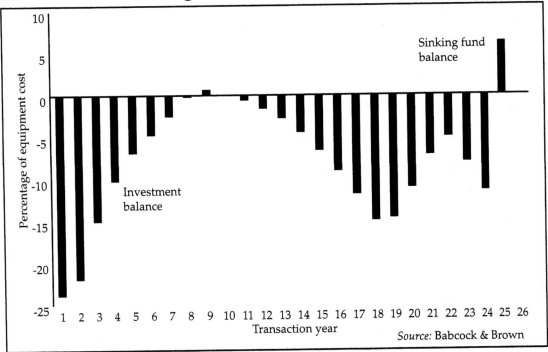

Source: Babcock & Brown

years, followed by years of positive taxable income. The early years' losses offset taxable income arising from the lessor's other activities, reducing the lessor's overall tax liability during those years. After the asset has been fully depreciated, taxable income becomes increasingly positive, as shown in Exhibit 8.5. In short, the lease defers the lessor's tax liability from the early years to the later years, which represents a significant benefit to the lessor from a 'time value of money' standpoint.

We now add the lease's pre-tax cash to the analysis and calculate the lessor's after-tax cash flow. Generally a lease begins with a large outflow for the initial investment, followed by inflows in the form of tax savings, followed by outflows representing taxes as they fall due, ending with realisation of the residual value. Exhibit 8.6 shows the after-tax cash flows for our sample aircraft lease.

The next step is to calculate the lessor's rate of return on its investment. Unlike a more traditional investment, the cash flows in a leveraged lease do not slowly pay off the original investment, with interest, over the term of the financing. Rather, the leveraged lease investment is characterised by rapid repayment of the initial investment followed by subsequent reinvestments, followed by a final repayment, as shown in Exhibit 8.7: periods of cash outflow follow periods of cash inflow. These multiple cash flow direction changes can create two problems for measuring the lessor's return in the transaction. First, the standard internal rate of return (IRR) analysis assumes that money kept in a sinking fund to cover future outflows earns at the investment interest rate – an assumption that lessors may not be willing to make. Secondly, the IRR approach can produce multiple solutions. To solve these problems, the industry has adopted a mathematical procedure called the multiple investment sinking fund (MISF) method. The MISF yield is a widely used measure of economic and accounting returns to leveraged lease lessors.

To understand the MISF method, think of the investor as a lender. Each month, the investor/lender adds interest at the yield rate on its outstanding investment balance to the investment balance. It then reduces the investment balance by any tax savings or pre-tax cash received that month. Exhibit 8.7 shows the lessor's investment being paid off during the first eight years mainly by tax savings (net of yield earnings). Once the investment balance has been reduced to zero, any further cash inflows are invested in a lower interest rate sinking fund. The lease's later cash outflows are taken first from any sinking fund, and then are supplied by the lessor as another investment. This analogy is precisely the one used in the SFAS 13 accounting rules (see Appendix 2 to this chapter): the 'interest' in this analogy is the accounting earnings the lessor recognises. An interesting and unusual effect of the MISF yield method is that leveraged lease earnings tend to be front-loaded.

Thus the MISF method deals with periods when the investor earns at the yield rate on its investment balance, and intervening periods when the investor is disinvested and takes credit for only a small interest rate, or zero, on any sinking fund balances.

Computer models can optimise leverage lease structures, producing the lowest lessee present value for a given lessor yield, or the highest lessor yield for a given present value. These models tend to create rent and debt profiles that reduce the lessor's investment balance (on which earnings at the high yield rate are charged) as quickly as possible, while minimising the use of the low-earning sinking fund. They do this in part by providing rent in excess of debt service in some of the first positive tax liability years to cover just the taxes due, deferring as long as possible the lessor's reinvestment.

In addition to MISF yield, lessors focus on other measures when evaluating leases. One such measure is the total profit, or total book income, often called simply 'cash', which equals the sum of all the cash inflows less all cash outflows. The lessor is often faced with trading between MISF yield and total book income. As a practical matter, most lessors structure leases that meet hurdles both for required MISF yield and for total cash.

Over the years, lease optimisation has become a highly specialised art. An optimisation produces the best possible structure for one party while satisfying the other parties' objectives and tax constraints on the structure. As the tax rules and interpretations have changed with time, the optimal lease structures designed to fit these rules have also evolved. The driving force is, of course, that a saving of even 10 or 20 basis points of present value benefit on a large transaction can repay considerable structuring effort. Appendix 1 to this chapter summarises the important tax constraints that leveraged leases must satisfy.

Some lessors have targets for return on assets (ROA) or return on equity (ROE). Other ways of measuring return are used in other countries; for example, in the UK the 'dual rate of return', 'merged funds' and 'actuarial return' methods are common. Although none of these other measures will be addressed here, the key point is that a given transaction may appear more or less attractive depending on the lessor's return measure. More importantly, the best structure (rent pattern, debt repayment profile and so on) for each lessor will depend on its economic measures and objectives. For example, one measure may favour a rapid payback of the initial investment while another may give more importance to the total cash profit generated over the term.

The lessee can actually obstruct lessors from providing their most competitive bids by forcing them to conform to an overly rigid lease structure. To take a trivial example, the lessee may request that rents be paid in arrears, whereas certain lessors may be able to bid a lower rental present value with an arrears-advance, or even an all-advance structure. An experienced financial adviser can help the lessee formulate its request for bids to elicit the best possible responses, and restructure transactions to meet specific lessee's needs.

Over the years, structuring techniques exploiting 'grey areas' in the IRS guidelines have been invented. The drafters of the guidelines recognised that there is an inherent tension between the premise of the modern 'triple-net' lease, in which the lessee bears essentially all of the economic burdens of possession of the asset for the duration of the lease term, and the 'benefits and burdens' analysis of case law, which requires the lessor to bear some significant risks beyond the credit risk that characterises equally a loan and a lease. Thus, the basic approach of the IRS guidelines is to ensure, by means of a set of objective criteria, that the lessor maintains a meaningful investment in the leased asset throughout the lease term, and bears the economic risk or reward of changes in the value of the leased asset at lease-end.

Structuring techniques that have been approved by US tax counsel include the following:

- 'rent holidays' when no rent is paid for a period during which the lessor makes interest and/or principal payments on the debt;
- 'sawtooth' rent structures in which rent payments are allowed to fluctuate within the year while satisfying the 90–110 test on an annual basis;
- 'flip' rent structures in which rent payments switch between arrears and advance at one or more points in the lease; and
- 'deferred equity' in which the lessor's investment is made in stages over one or more years, at points when the required debt service exceeds the rent received.

These techniques remain viable, although their use has been curtailed as discussed below.

Section 467

On 31 May 1996 the US Treasury issued proposed regulations under Section 467, which governs the treatment of rent and interest under certain rental agreements for the lease of tangible property. Although these regulations were issued in proposal form, they may be currently applicable in part to certain sale-leaseback transactions that were entered into (or substantially modified) after 3 June 1996.

Leasing transactions must be structured either with level rents or rents that do not vary from the average rent by more than 10 per cent on a calendar year basis. These regulations also specify that the 90–110 safe harbour is to be tested on an accrual calendar year basis, instead of being based on the lease year (as was previously standard). Techniques such as the 'asymmetric sawtooth' structure, which relied on the mismatch between the lease year and tax year, are no longer permissible. Reliance on the alternative 'two-thirds/one-third' safe harbour is also no longer available under the proposed regulations.

The proposals contain several references to permissible rent holidays; however, the regulations do not appear to permit rent holidays coupled with a 90–110 rent pattern. Level rent structures are still allowed a rent holiday of three months or less, or a longer rent holiday (of up to 24 months or 10 per cent of the lease term) so long as there is a substantial business purpose for the holiday.

Although final regulations have not been issued as of the time of writing, the sawtooth and flip structures as well as rent holidays can be expected to survive in some form under the final regulations.

Deferred equity has in recent years mainly been used in conjunction with the interim rent holiday. Its use going forward therefore depends mainly on the extent to which the interim rent holiday is allowed in the final 467 regulations.

In a typical domestic aircraft lease the effect of the proposed 467 rules as currently interpreted is an increase of 150–175 basis points in the rental present value cost to the lessee, using a 90–110 rental pattern with no rent holiday. Using level rents with a 3-month rent holiday would result in an increase of 200–250 basis points, compared with the pre-467 structure.

These Section 467 changes tilt a 'lease versus buy' analysis toward 'buy'. Whereas previously an airline forecasting being in AMT for three years might be economically indifferent to leasing or debt financing, now that break-even AMT period might have stretched out to four years. Thus lessors would likely see their yields decline slightly to create attractive deals for lessees under the more restrictive tax rules, or simply to compete for a slightly smaller pool of airlines wishing to lease.

Other structuring considerations

A few examples of other constraints to be considered will now be discussed briefly.

Deferred equity

This refers to the practice of letting the lessor pay some scheduled debt service, instead of structuring it to be paid from rent. Such structures can present the lessee with a credit risk in the sense that it will be financially exposed in the unlikely event that the lessor fails to make a future equity contribution, and an appropriate remedy for lessor non-performance must be carefully crafted. This deferred equity structure, if not designed correctly, can also give rise to unfavourable accounting treatment for the lessor.

Debt placement

Optimal economics are usually achieved when the debt maturity is no more than two years before the end of the lease, and when the loan balance is paid down slowly, leading to a high ratio of loan balance to asset value. But these debt requirements may conflict with the ability to find debt easily and at a competitive rate. It is important to quantify the trade-offs here before deciding upon the lease structure – for example, it may be found that debt with an average life of 15 years may lead to lower rent payments than 13-year average life debt, provided its coupon is no more than 10 basis points higher.

Refinancings

Approximately half of the aircraft financed by leveraged leases are ultimately refinanced. This may occur a few months or a year or so after the original closing, as a result (usually) of an improvement in the debt markets or the lessee's credit rating. Unless this is anticipated correctly in the original structure, debt and tax constraints (particularly given possible application of Section 467 to the refinanced transaction) may prevent the lessee gaining the expected benefit. Certain criteria must be met to allow a refinancing to avoid characterisation as a 'substantial modification' under Section 467.

State taxes

Many lessors are subjected to state, as well as federal, income taxes, which the leveraged lease can also defer, making possible a higher yield. Yet some of these lessors will price and optimise the deal ignoring state taxes, perhaps to allow them to sell down equity interests to other investors more easily. A lessee adviser will verify that termination values are not calculated at the higher level resulting from the inclusion of the state taxes, unless this issue is highlighted and negotiated at the commitment letter stage.

Foreign-source loss rules

The lease of an aircraft that will be partially or wholly used abroad can have adverse tax consequences to a US lessor. As an oversimplified summary, the Internal Revenue Code (IRC) on the one hand provides a dollar-for-dollar credit for foreign taxes paid by a US corporation but, on the other hand, limits the amount of the credit to the percentage of total taxable income that the corporation derives from foreign sources. Because taxable income and losses from leased assets are 'sourced' to the location of those assets from time to time (see Appendix 1 to this chapter) the tax losses generated in the early years of the typical leveraged lease investment reduce foreign-source taxable income and consequently the lessor's ability to use foreign tax credits.

Only a limited number of lessors will permit full foreign usage of aircraft although most will permit some. For an airline that operates both domestic and international routes, foreign-source requirements fall into two categories. With respect to the lease of intercontinental aircraft, full foreign-source usage allowances are required in order to avoid operating restrictions on the aircraft. For aircraft operated predominantly on domestic routes, some limited foreign-source allowance is necessary in order to accommodate operations to Canada, Mexico and the Caribbean. Typically, this allowance has been in the range of 5–10 per cent of the lessor's annual taxable losses as determined by the aircraft's operation.

The identification of a lessor with the capacity to tolerate foreign operation and the negotiation of the amount of foreign-source allowance is a critical component of any US leveraged lease financing. To accommodate the possibility of usage exceeding the stated allowance, leases provide for the lessee to pay indemnities to the lessor if the lessor suffers adverse tax consequences.

Aircraft residual values

As a general rule, aircraft residual value – both the assumption and the realisation – is important to the lessor's economics in any lease, and is more critical in shorter leases than in longer leases.

Lessors have historically found that aircraft maintain their values quite well, with realised residual values in many cases equalling or exceeding 50 per cent of original cost even after 20 years. For a lessor that originally assumed only a 20 per cent or 25 per cent residual value when pricing the transaction, the residual windfall can turn a normal return into a superior or even spectacular one. Aircraft are also comparatively attractive assets for a lessor because of their mobility (they are relatively easy to repossess in the event of a lessee default or bankruptcy) and because there is an active secondary market for used aircraft. However, as noted in the earlier discussion of EBOs, a good-credit airline lessee now has structuring techniques available to it to limit the residual windfall available to the lessor.

Recent yields

In 1991 (a time when the demand for equity capital greatly exceeded the supply), competitive after-tax yields for 'plain vanilla' aircraft lease transactions to US airlines were in the range of 10–15 per cent after tax. For FSC transactions, which are more complex and present a different set of risks, the yields were even higher. These yields represented the highest returns available to lessors in many years, and were even more remarkable given the low general level of interest rates. By the mid-1990s a surplus of equity capital has developed, and after-tax yields for leases to good-credit US airlines are in the range of only 6–8 per cent. Future returns to aircraft lessors will vary over time depending upon a variety of factors, including:

- the prevailing interest rate environment;
- tax legislation;
- the riskiness of the transaction (as reflected in the quality of the collateral and the credit standing of the lessee);
- the supply/demand situation in the leasing market for the tax base necessary to provide lease-equity; and
- the returns possible on alternative investments available to equity investors.

Lease portfolio management

Two final points concerning lessor economics deserve mention. First, the approach taken by many lessors in evaluating leases is to analyse and approve them as stand-alone investments. The yield analysis assumes that deferred taxes will be paid back, and that at the end of the lease investment the lessor is back to ground zero. This is a useful assumption for comparing one lease with another or for comparing a lease with alternative investment opportunities. However, it ignores a fundamental and perhaps permanent change brought about by an entry into the leveraged lease business. Over time, a lease portfolio is a net provider of quasi-capital because the reduction in income taxes during the first few years of a lease typically exceeds the cash investment in the leased assets.

Secondly, wise aircraft lessors diversify their portfolios with different lease terms, lessees and equipment types, and assure that the documentation for each lease transaction provides reasonably flexible rights to the lessor to sell, transfer or assign the leases. This last aspect has become even more important recently, as more owners of lease portfolios are looking at the prospect of selling, assigning or restructuring all or a portion of their portfolios.

Pickle leases

Prior to 1984, non-US airlines were able to enjoy the same leasing economics (based on a partial transfer of US depreciation tax benefits to the lessee) as domestic airlines. Non-US airlines were also, in many cases, able to claim depreciation tax benefits in their home jurisdiction – the traditional 'double dip' underlying most cross-border lease structures.

In 1984 Congress introduced a new rule restricting the depreciation deductions available on assets leased to entities not subject to US federal income tax. This method is referred to as Pickle depreciation (after Congressman J.J. Pickle who sponsored the legislation). Under the Pickle provisions, assets leased to a tax-exempt entity must be depreciated on a straight line basis over a period equal to the longer of the asset's alternative depreciation system (ADS) life – 12 years for aircraft – and 125 per cent of the lease term. The various depreciation systems are summarised in Exhibit 8.8.

At first it appeared that the benefit available in leases utilising Pickle depreciation would be insignificant. Then in 1991 the 'replacement lease' structure was developed, under which the lease term was divided into a basic term and a replacement term. At the end of the basic term, the lessee had the following options:

Exhibit 8.8
US depreciation systems

Lessee status	Where asset used	Depreciation system	Method		Life (years)
US taxpayer	Within or to and from US	MACRS	Declining balance/ Straight line		7
US taxpayer	Outside US	ADS	Straight line		12
Not a US taxpayer–		Pickle	Straight line	12 or 125% lease term [1]	

1 Whichever is the greater.

Source : Babcock & Brown

- exercise a fixed price purchase option; or
- locate a replacement lessee, who met certain pre-agreed credit standards, to lease the aircraft for the replacement term under substantially the same conditions as the original base-term lease; or
- pay a termination value and return the equipment to the lessor.

When the replacement lease was properly structured, most tax counsel would opine that the basic lease term, rather than the combined basic plus replacement term, could be used in calculating depreciation. In many cases an economically attractive structure for lessee and lessor could be created.

Early in 1996, however, the IRS issued final regulations that provide that any extended term during which the original lessee had any ongoing obligations under the lease in the nature of rent or in lieu of rent (such as a replacement lease obligation) had to be included when calculating the permissible Pickle depreciation. This reduced the benefit available in the Pickle lease to unattractive levels, except when combined with FSC benefits as discussed in the next section.

The lessor's economic motivations for completing Pickle leases are somewhat different than for MACRS leases. The most basic difference is that Pickle leases provide much less tax deferral than traditional leases, because of the slower tax depreciation schedule, and thus use less tax-shelter capacity. Also, these leases provide a different and in some ways more attractive accounting earnings profile for the lessor.

Leasehold interest structure

Following the demise of the replacement Pickle lease, a new structure was developed in which the US investor purchased, not an asset, but the interest as lessee of an asset. The value of this leasehold interest can then be amortised over the life of the lease creating a stream of deductions somewhat comparable with those available to a Pickle lessor. The investor then sub-leases the asset back to an affiliate of the original owner under a conventional US leveraged lease.

A number of aircraft were financed under the leasehold interest structure prior to the issue of the proposed Section 467 regulations. However, the current redesign of the structure, generally referred to as the 'lease-in-lease-out' structure, favours assets with useful lives of 40 years or more. At the present time, the alternative financing structures available to most airlines offer higher economic benefits.

Foreign sales corporation leases

Overview

Foreign sales corporation leases (FSC leases) have become an important source of financing for both US and non-US airlines. There are a number of different types of FSC leases, including:

- agency or commission FSC (C-FSC) leases;
- 'turbo FSC' leases (a variation of the C-FSC, in which the debt structure is manipulated to obtain extra benefits); and
- ownership FSC (O-FSC) leases.

All of these leases have the common feature of applying only to newly exported US-manufactured aircraft operated predominantly outside the US.

'Predominant foreign use' means use outside US territory for at least 50 per cent based on time spent or miles travelled. For depreciation purposes, however, domestic (MACRS) depreciation can be claimed if the lessee is a US taxpayer and the aircraft enters the US at least once every two weeks. Thus FSC export subsidies are available to US airlines flying US-manufactured aircraft on routes to and from the US. In contrast, non-US airlines must generally use the slower Pickle depreciation described in the previous section.

In commission FSC and turbo C-FSC transactions, a foreign sales corporation is established by the equity investor, and this entity acts as the investor's 'agent' in completing and negotiating the transaction. In an O-FSC lease, the investor establishes an offshore subsidiary which acts as the lessor. Under special rules applying to the export of 'qualifying property', a portion of the rental income under these leases can be excluded from taxation.

Since the mid-1980s, a large number of commission FSC and turbo FSC leases have been completed for US airlines – primarily for wide-bodied equipment acquired by the largest airlines for international service.

The first O-FSC leasing transaction was arranged in 1989 for KLM. Since then, over US$3 billion in O-FSC financings have been completed. However, in the past two years, uncertainty about the US tax treatment of the debt in O-FSC leases has made lessors very cautious about proceeding with new O-FSC transactions. Foreign airlines have therefore increasingly turned to the C-FSC as a vehicle for financing US-built aircraft.

In cases where the airline lessee is domiciled outside the US, these financings are typically structured so that the foreign airline is also entitled to take ownership tax benefits in its home country. For these, the FSC lease is a true 'double dip' financing.

FSCs defined

A foreign sales corporation is a special purpose corporation formed in a foreign jurisdiction with which the US maintains a tax treaty or information-sharing agreement. Bermuda and the US Virgin Islands are two of the most commonly used jurisdictions for FSCs. FSCs provide a US government-sanctioned form of tax subsidy for the export of property from the US. Income to the equity investor from 'qualified export property' generated by or through an FSC is effectively taxed at a lower rate than otherwise would be the case in a 'plain vanilla' US lease.

The requirements for qualifying a corporation as an FSC are many and technical, but can be met with relative ease by any US corporation. The tax risk of the FSC failing to qualify as such is typically borne by the lessor.

Qualified export property

The rules regarding 'qualified export property' for FSCs are, in summary, as follows:

1 *Manufactured or produced in the US.* Not more than 50 per cent of the FMV of the property may be attributable to components imported into the US.
2 *Located within the US at the commencement of the lease.* The aircraft must not have previously left the US.
3 *No use, manufacture, assembly or processing between the time of lease commencement and the delivery of the property outside the US.* In practice, this requirement means that the first use of the aircraft immediately after the lease closing should be a flight out of the US. The details of delivery of an aircraft subject to an FSC lease are critical.
4 *Predominant use outside the US.* During each taxable year in which the lessor expects to achieve FSC benefits (generally the tax-positive years of the lease), the aircraft must be used 'predominately outside of the US', which means physical location outside US territory for more than 50 per cent of the time or miles travelled.

The lessee must usually make representations with regard to at least some of these items.

Commission FSC structure

A C-FSC lease is structurally very similar to a conventional US leveraged lease incorporating MACRS depreciation, except that the equity investor can achieve above-average returns for the same use of tax base and the same credit risk.

In a C-FSC lease, as shown in Exhibit 8.9, the FSC acts as an agent of the lessor and receives a fee from the lessor for the FSC's performance of certain ministerial activities related to the lease transaction. Under the inter-company pricing rules applicable to FSCs, this fee may equal up to 23 per cent of the net taxable income generated by the lease transaction. In turn, this agency fee is deductible by the owner participant. However, 15/23 of the FSC's commission is excludable by the FSC from federal income taxation. The net effect is equivalent to a 15 per cent reduction in the federal tax rate (from 35 per cent to 29.75 per cent) applicable to the lease, but only during the lessor's tax-positive years.

The terms of the MACRS C-FSC lease are those that would normally be seen in a US leveraged lease:

- The term of the lease would depend on the lessee's credit and equipment type.
- At or prior to the end of the lease term a lessee would have the right to purchase the aircraft for a one-time only purchase option or EBO.
- The lease rentals are sufficient to cover the debt service obligations to the lender.

The terms of the Pickle C-FSC are similar to those of the Pickle lease, described in the preceding section.

The turbo FSC

The turbo FSC is a variation of the basic C-FSC lease. The C-FSC's economic benefit is enhanced by separating the interest deductions from the rental income used to compute the allowable

Exhibit 8.9
C-FSC lease structure

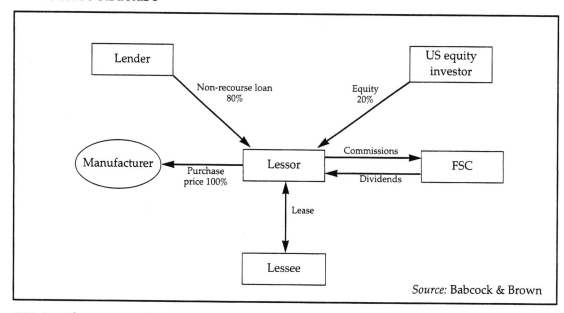

Source: Babcock & Brown

FSC fee. This is accomplished by structuring the FSC lease's debt so as to fail the requirements for non-recourse treatment under Section 861(e) of the IRC (see Appendix 1 to this chapter). Then interest expense allocated to the transaction will drop to zero when the tax basis of the equipment reaches zero (at the end of the eighth year of the lease in the case of seven-year MACRS equipment). At this point the FSC agency fees are no longer diluted by the interest deductions generated by the debt, and the FSC benefits are therefore increased.

There are several convenient ways to structure debt in a leveraged lease transaction so as to generate the turbo FSC effect. The most commonly used technique requires the lessee to close the leveraged lease financing with debt that has a shorter maturity and/or lower initial principal amount than is optimal for the lease. The interim debt is later refinanced with permanent debt that extends the maturity of the debt by more than six months and/or increases the principal amount of the debt after the initial funding by more than 5 per cent.

Other lessors have found it sufficient to fail Section 861(e) by assuming a portion of the debt on a recourse basis. The lessor assumes recourse liability for some or all of the deferred equity payments (ie debt service payments for which the lessee is not obligated to make a corresponding rental payment). This approach requires that the lender be satisfied with the creditworthiness of the lessor. In most of the turbo FSC transactions completed to date, lessors have required the use of a combination of these methods to fail Section 861(e) and effect the turbo, based on the advice of tax counsel.

The turbo effect will be greatest for assets qualifying for rapid (MACRS) depreciation, but it can still provide modest benefits for a slowly depreciating (Pickle) asset.

Ownership FSC structure

In an O-FSC structure, a US equity investor (US parent) makes a capital contribution to a US subsidiary (US sub) equal to approximately 13–15 per cent of the leased asset's cost. The US subsidiary, which is typically a special purpose corporation, borrows the balance of the cost from an unrelated party (the lender) on a recourse basis. Combining these funds, the US sub makes a capital contribution to an affiliated offshore FSC equal to 100 per cent of the asset's cost. The FSC purchases the asset from the manufacturer and leases it to the lessee (see Exhibit 8.10). Thirty per cent of the net income from the lease transaction is excluded from federal income taxation of the FSC. Dividends from the FSC to its parent are not in general subject to additional US tax.

The debt is incurred by the immediate US parent of the FSC, the US sub, which is taxable as part of the US parent's consolidated group. In effect, the lease is designed as a single-investor lease by the FSC and the US sub borrows to leverage the investment. This separation of the loan from the lease itself is referred to as the 'bifurcated debt' structure.

The bifurcated debt structure provides a particularly powerful benefit where the lessee is not a US airline and thus slower depreciation is taken at the FSC level (resulting in a higher amount of income being excluded from taxation). The key is to isolate the interest expense deductions on the debt from the deemed income of the FSC, because otherwise they would have the effect of reducing the value of the FSC's favourable tax treatment.

Because the O-FSC lease was normally used for Pickle assets, it incorporated the replacement lease structure described earlier.

Debt-related issues

The funds in an O-FSC to service the debt do not flow directly from the lessee to the lender (as would be the case in a US lease with no FSC elements) but instead flow from the foreign lessee to the FSC (in the form of rent under the lease) to the US sub (in the form of an inter-company dividend) to the lender (in the form of debt service payments). The US sub claims the interest

Exhibit 8.10
O-FSC lease structure

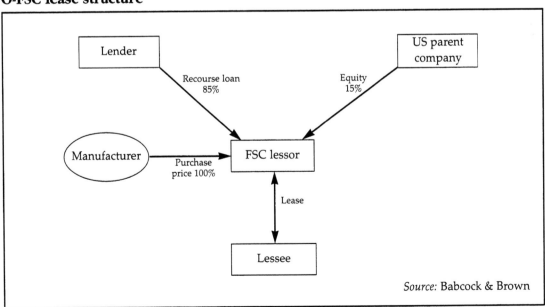

Source: Babcock & Brown

expense deduction, which is offset against the taxable portion of the dividend it receives from its FSC (ie 70 per cent of the rental income less depreciation deductions).

The bifurcated debt structure confronts lenders with a host of security concerns that distinguish an O-FSC financing from a traditional leveraged lease structure:

- The lender cannot receive a security interest in the leased asset, nor can it be assigned the lease for security purposes. Therefore, unlike the typical lease financing, the lender is lending to the US sub without a direct link to the credit of the airline lessee or the security of the aircraft; instead, the lender is lending on a recourse basis to the US sub.
- Although the structure assumes the lease rentals will ultimately flow through to the lender and be the source of debt repayment, the lender needs assurances that this flow of funds will in fact happen, given the fact that it has no recourse against the asset or the credit in the transaction (ie the foreign lessee).

The lender obtains these assurances in the forms of positive and negative covenants from both the US sub and the FSC, together with, in some scenarios, support from the equity investor by means of a guarantee or a pledge of the FSC stock, depending upon the tax concerns and preferences of counsel representing the equity investor.

Economics – airline lessee motivations

Most airlines completing Pickle-FSC transactions are domiciled in jurisdictions with tax systems that allow the airline to claim tax ownership of aircraft financed using US FSC leases. For these airlines, the FSC lease can be viewed as a debt financing that provides a favourable below-market interest rate (due to the US tax benefits).

In many instances, lessees go one step further and establish deposits (typically with a commercial bank in their home country) in order to defease economically the scheduled FSC lease payments. The result is that the FSC lease itself does not provide a source of true funding but instead can be viewed as a mechanism to reduce the cost of acquiring the aircraft. A further benefit of such defeasance is that it often enables the airline to keep the lease liability completely off-balance sheet (notwithstanding that the airline is legally obligated to make the ongoing rental payments, because under US tax rules there can be no legal release of the airline from these obligations). Defeasance also helps mitigate withholding tax concerns.

The choice between O-FSC and C-FSC

The net tax effect of a lessor investing in a turbo C-FSC compared with a vanilla lease is a reduction of 15 per cent of the taxes on the FSC income (approximately equal to rent less depreciation) in years when this quantity is positive. There is no effect during loss years.

The net tax effect of investing in an O-FSC is the loss of tax benefits in years when the FSC income is negative, but a reduction of 30 per cent of the taxes on the FSC income in years where this quantity is positive.

Thus, all other things being equal, the C-FSC is more powerful for assets qualifying for rapid (MACRS) depreciation, while the O-FSC is more powerful for assets qualifying for slower (Pickle) depreciation.

All other things are not equal, however. First, as explained earlier, the lenders in an O-FSC can only gain access to their collateral indirectly. This can make the debt more expensive, which can erase any economic advantage offered by the O-FSC over the C-FSC. An exception would be perhaps for a national bank lending in an O-FSC lease to a flag-carrying airline in the bank's home country, where comfort might be obtained on grounds other than a strict analysis of the commercial risk.

A more compelling factor, which has led to a virtual shut-down of O-FSC leases in the past two years, is an IRS challenge to the bifurcated debt structure, which, as noted earlier is designed to keep interest deductions out of the FSC income where they would dilute the FSC benefit.

Specifically, in March 1994 the IRS issued several notices regarding the characterisation of certain debt as equity. One of these, Notice 94-97, holds that non-recourse debt secured exclusively by stock of the issuer will be characterised as equity for tax purposes. In the O-FSC structure, non-recourse debt is secured exclusively by the stock not of the issuer, but of the FSC, the issuer's wholly-owned subsidiary. Some counsel feel that this could nevertheless be read as an attack on the typical debt structure in an O-FSC.

Finally, as explained previously in the 'Pickle leases' section, the inability to use the replacement lease technique as a way to shorten the aircraft's depreciable life has reduced the economic benefit obtainable from both Pickle O-FSC and Pickle C-FSC leases.

At the time of writing, therefore, the C-FSC is the only FSC structure in use, either for assets qualifying for MACRS depreciation (where it has always been the vehicle of choice) or for Pickle assets (where the benefits, though modest, can still make the effort of implementing the FSC structure worthwhile).

Trends

'Lessee's market' versus 'lessor's market'

The US leasing market has been periodically referred to as either a 'lessee's market' (ie a market in which the airline has the greater negotiating power) or a 'lessor's market'.

In the past few years, the 'lessor's market' that existed when the 1993 edition of this book was published has turned around. Lessors' yields for a given credit are at a relatively low historical level. Today's 'lessee's market' exists because of a variety of factors, including:

- The strategy of a number of former US regional banks to become major leasing players. Some have done this by taking on a large volume of competitively priced transactions.
- The return to the lessor market of some (but not all) of the lessors who had previously dropped out because their portfolios were saturated with certain aircraft types and airline credits.
- The return to financial health of some of the major domestic carriers, leading them to shelter their taxable income by owning rather than leasing an increasing proportion of their new deliveries.
- A dramatic reduction in the number of domestic aircraft being delivered, due to the slump in orders and a number of cancellations during 1993–95. Although the orders are now picking up, it will be some time before these aircraft are delivered.
- A reduction in the economic viability of Pickle and Pickle C-FSC leases for foreign carriers and the suspension of O-FSC activity, all due to a tightening of the US tax code, which has reduced the interest of foreign airlines in US-sourced cross-border leases, and hence the choices available for the would-be aircraft lessor.

This declining lessee demand has manifested itself in lower yields for lessors and more favourable terms for the airlines. However, there is a widening gap between the pricing and terms available to the top-tier airlines and their lower-rated competitors. Equity investors are much more credit-sensitive than in the past.

At the time of writing, a significant proportion of total US investor appetite is being satisfied by cross-border deals for good-credit foreign lessees, mostly outside the airline market. If changing tax rules cause this market to dry up, these investment dollars will seek a home in the domestic market, creating additional capacity and perhaps further depressing yields on leases for domestic (US) airlines.

Regional airlines

There has been increasing interest in recent years in the financing of 19 to 70-seat aircraft for regional airlines. In contrast to the major airlines who compete across the board in the national or international arena, several of the regionals are in a better position to control their niche markets, producing consistent earnings over many years. At the time of writing, a number of lessors and lenders are studying this market, including several who have previously found the general airline field too volatile.

As a result, lenders are now considering maturities of up to 16 years for regional jets of this size and 15 years for turbo-props from the better manufacturers, making total lease terms of 17–18 years possible and producing very attractive economics for both airlines and lessors.

Another aspect favouring regional financings is that these airlines place a premium on fleet flexibility. They therefore often structure the deals to restrain termination values, thus limiting the lessor's exposure as well. Extreme low-high rent structures that are optimal for the pure present value analyser are often avoided, which also limits the cost increase resulting from the new Section 467 rules.

Manufacturers' support

Support from the major airframe and engine manufacturers, in the form of back-up credit, deficiency guarantees, etc, has been strategically provided from time to time by all of the major airframe and engine manufacturers. Historically, such support was more likely to be available to weaker-credit airlines (who otherwise might not be able to finance and fulfil their orders from the manufacturer), and there was, in most cases, an explicit cost to the airline to obtain the needed support. Those manufacturers seeking to increase market share and establish relationships with US airlines have to an increasing extent been assuming significant 'asset risk'. The most extreme manifestation of this trend is the 'walk away' lease, which provides the airline with extensive rights to return the aircraft to the lessor or the manufacturer during the term, with minimal or no early-return penalties.

Other forms of manufacturer support (discussed in more detail in Chapter 18) are:

- debt guarantees;
- residual guarantees; and
- lease-in lease-out structures, where an affiliate of the manufacturer acts as the head lessee, passing some or all of the benefits of its superior credit rating down to the airline sub-lessee.

Several factors have contributed to this situation. First, the airline industry has undergone a dramatic transformation since deregulation. Today, a smaller, dominant group of major airlines is in a much stronger position to bargain with the manufacturers. Secondly, the airframe manufacturing industry is more competitive, largely because of the successes of Airbus. Thirdly, the regional airlines are becoming increasingly sophisticated, demanding the same kind of financing support previously enjoyed only by the larger airlines. And fourthly, the engine manufacturers have been persuaded to provide additional credit support over and above that provided by the airframe manufacturers.

Due to these factors, one might reasonably predict that the trend towards greater manufacturer support and involvement in US aircraft leasing will continue. Inevitably, however, there will be a limit to the extent of such support, because the manufacturers have only finite resources and balance sheet capacity.

Debt markets

There has been a noticeable increase in the diversity of debt sources and debt structures used in leveraged US aircraft leases. Today we see lenders from throughout the world participating in US lease transactions. In the 1980s, Japanese lenders participated heavily in such leases; they are less active today for a variety of reasons and European banks have filled the gap quite admirably. New lenders from South-East Asia, Europe and the Middle East have also recently increased their aircraft lending activity. Lastly, the US public debt market is currently being tapped extensively for leveraged lease debt. This ongoing search for sources of lease debt will certainly continue and will be limited only by the perceived credit and collateral risks associated with such lending and possible regulatory influences (eg, US government rules concerning the applicability of US withholding taxes).

Since 1995 several airlines have used the enhanced equipment trust certificate (EETC) as a means of gaining access to the lower-cost funds in the US public debt market, formerly available only to the best airline credits. The EETC (on which see Chapter 6) provides comfort to the lenders through a liquidity facility, typically equal to 18 months of interest on the loan, and a carefully constrained loan-to-value ratio.

Tax law changes

There have been frequent changes to the US tax laws that govern leasing. These changes have had a substantial impact on all capital intensive industries, including airlines. As the history of the investment tax credit (a special first-year tax allowance) illustrates, tax law changes seem to occur in cycles. The ITC was first introduced by Congress in 1962 as an incentive to encourage capital investment. In 1966, the ITC was suspended. It was then restored in 1967, and suspended again in 1969. In 1971, the ITC was revived, only to be eliminated by the 1986 Tax Reform Act. Likewise, there have been changes to depreciation allowances for US aircraft and to corporate tax rates.

Depending on their magnitude and timing, tax increases make recently completed and new leasing transactions more attractive to US lessors, while at the same time having a negative effect on lease investments completed several years or more prior to the tax rate increase. Conversely, a decline in tax rates reduces the value of tax benefits and thus makes leasing less attractive.

Proposed Treasury regulations issued in mid-1996 under Section 467 again disrupted the leasing industry. These regulations, described in Appendix 1 to this chapter, turned tax-based leasing as we knew it on its head by springing two novel theories on the US leasing market.

Under the first theory, the proposed regulations allow the IRS Commissioner to require rate-able accrual of rent by parties to any lease that provides for uneven accrual of rent if the Commissioner determines there is a tax avoidance motive for the uneven pattern of rental accruals. This 'rent-levelling' rule does provide a number of safe harbours, including a version of the 90–110 test. Because this part of the proposed regulations was given immediate effect, it put a chill on new leasing transactions until tax counsel reached a consensus on its application.

The second theory would provide 'deemed loan' treatment of any lease in which the pattern of cash payments does not match stated rent – that is, any lease that provides for prepaid or deferred cash rent in relation to a level or 90–110 accrual pattern. The deemed loan provisions are effective upon issuance of final regulations and, if finalised in their current form, would not significantly affect 'plain vanilla' leasing. Of course, the ultimate effect of these latest tax law changes cannot be conclusively determined until final regulations are issued.

Potentially more significant than the changes described above would be comprehensive tax reform. A variety of schemes involving a wholesale rewrite of the tax code have emerged, including flat tax and national sales tax proposals. These proposals arise out of a broad public perception that the current US tax system contains too many 'corporate welfare' provisions and political concessions, and is too complex for the average American to understand. The effects of a major reform of the US tax system on US leasing would be dramatic, but future tax changes are more likely to take the form of selective incremental changes rather than fundamental reform.

In the past two years, several pieces of legislation have been enacted specifically targeted at reducing the benefits of US leases to foreign (non-US) lessees. Whether this can be labelled a 'trend' yet is debatable, but there seems to be a clear desire on the part of the IRS to limit the 'export' of an excessive amount of US tax benefits by restricting (but not necessarily eliminating) US-sourced cross-border leasing.

In conclusion, each revision in US tax laws has generally been enacted to effect some overall governmental economic policy objective. Looking to the future, these objectives will continue to change over time (as administrations change and the perceived economic health of the US fluctuates), so it is safe to predict that there will be corresponding future tax law changes that will affect aircraft leasing. From a pure public policy standpoint, there is – one hopes – little risk that the US Treasury would promulgate regulations that are designed to eliminate lease financing entirely. After all, leveraged leasing enables capital intensive or less profitable companies to make capital investments while ensuring that they can, at least indirectly, avail themselves of the tax benefits. Thus, leasing should be viewed as a mechanism that 'levels the playing field' on which companies compete.

Pickle and FSC leases

Domestic airlines will continue to enjoy MACRS/FSC benefits in financings of aircraft intended for international service. Lessors with foreign-source tax capacity will continue to earn premium yields on these financings.

For foreign airlines, use of the replacement lease structure as a way of accelerating depreciation has been eliminated. Pickle leases without the FSC benefit are likely to prove viable only in exceptional circumstances. O-FSC leasing has been suspended due to uncertainty on several tax issues. Pickle C-FSCs should continue to be viable for many airlines, albeit with lower benefits than were available prior to the 1996 tax changes relating to replacement leases and Section 467.

A number of financial institutions (mostly banks and packagers) are working to develop new structures to accommodate the new tax rules and they are breaking new ground, both in the fields of long-term tax leasing and in operating leasing. This trend is expected to continue.

Export agency support

There has been only limited use of export credit agency (ECA) debt in US-sourced cross-border leases, because:

- EXIM practice precludes domestic 'double dipping' (ie using both EXIM and FSC subsidies on the same US-manufactured aircraft).
- The limited maturity and restricted repayment profile available on ECA debt can conflict with the requirements for optimal lease structuring. Therefore, such debt is often only utilised indirectly via a swap.
- The swap spreads, plus ECA fees, can for some airlines erode most of the economic benefit that might be derived from the use of the subsidised ECA debt.

In US domestic financings, an understanding between EXIM and the European ECAs precludes the use of ECA subsidies in financings of Airbus aircraft. Canadian and Brazilian export credits are, however, routinely utilised in the financing of Bombardier and Embraer aircraft respectively.

In practice, in today's market (in which airline borrowing margins have fallen significantly over the past few years) ECA debt is mainly used to overcome the difficulty of finding commercial lenders who would accept the airline's credit, rather than as a means to enhance the economic benefit.

Conclusion

This chapter has summarised the current US aircraft leasing market, its important economic, tax and accounting features and some of the more noteworthy trends. There are many types of leases available to US and non-US airline lessees as potential sources of financing for aircraft acquisitions, and to US lessors as potential investments. These include short-term operating leases and long-term leveraged leases and FSC leases.

For many US lessors and lessees, the long-term leveraged lease has been the preferred vehicle for investing in or financing new aircraft. There are two reasons for this. First, the leverage arising through the use of non-recourse debt in the lease structure is powerful and can simultaneously improve the economics for both lessor and lessee. Secondly, the complexity of leveraged leases and the differing motivations and economic evaluation methodologies of lessors and lessees can create opportunities for a sophisticated lease arranger to enhance the lease financing and better meet the goals of all parties.

For these reasons, the leveraged lease product is unique (compared with most other financial instruments) in that it truly can offer a win-win opportunity to both the lessee and the lessor. Leasing, moreover, has been an established and important form of financing for many years in the US, with guidelines and practices that are generally well-defined and accepted by the tax authorities and other governmental policy makers. Although changes and refinements to the leasing environment will inevitably occur in the future, US leasing should remain an important form of aircraft financing for the world's airlines.

Notes

1 Kathleen Alderfer, John Graves, Ted Niemira and Elizabeth Weir assisted in the preparation of this chapter.
2 During times when changes to tax rates or to the tax code are being considered, however, lessors may require such indemnities if they become concerned that the tax changes could reduce the future value of tax benefits that they will receive in a leasing transaction. Those indemnities usually cover only marginal income tax rate changes that occur during the then current session of Congress.

Appendix 1

Tax considerations in US leveraged leasing

The US tax constraints on leveraged leasing activity have been based on two well-established foundations. First, Revenue Procedure 75-21ª (the 'Guidelines') sets out a series of bright-line tests that must be met in order for the Internal Revenue Service to rule that a leveraged lease is a 'true lease' for US tax purposes. Second, case law provides more liberal standards than these Guidelines for true lease treatment. Upon the basis of case law, tax counsel may opine that a transaction will be treated as a true lease for US tax purposes even if not all of the Guidelines are strictly met. For economic reasons, however, aircraft leases are generally structured within these constraints except in a few, limited areas, which are described below.

This appendix examines the benefits generated by leveraged leasing and analyses the legal standards that determine whether a lease will be treated as a 'true lease' for US tax purposes. The appendix also discusses proposed regulations issued by the IRS in mid-1996 under Section 467 as they affect US aircraft leasing.

Benefits available from leveraged leasing

US leveraged leasing transactions are typically used to transfer certain tax benefits associated with asset ownership from the asset's current owner and user to a party that will derive greater economic benefits from these tax benefits. In its simplest form, a US aircraft leveraged lease involves a sale by a US airline (the 'lessee') of aircraft to a lessor that can utilise the tax deductions associated with its ownership more fully. The lessor then leases the aircraft back to the lessee and grants the lessee an option to repurchase the aircraft on a certain date.

Available tax benefits are a critical determinant of the lessor's economics and are the basis upon which the lessee's net present value benefit is calculated. For the lessor to realise its expected tax benefits, tax ownership of the aircraft must be successfully transferred from the manufacturer or the airline to the lessor and must remain with the lessor for the duration of the transaction. First, the sale of the aircraft to the lessor must be respected for tax purposes. Second, the lease of the aircraft back to the lessee must be treated as a 'true lease' – that is, the lease must in substance represent a transfer of the right to use the aircraft rather than a transfer of ownership. As tax owner of the aircraft, the lessor will be able to deduct (1) depreciation on the aircraft, which is generally taken over a seven-year recovery period on an accelerated 200 per cent declining balance method, and (2) interest on any non-recourse debt that it incurred to finance its purchase.

On the other side, the lessee will receive a net present value benefit equal to the difference between the sales price of the aircraft and the present value of the lessee's required lease payments (including the purchase option payment). The lessee will also be permitted a rental deduction that it will either offset against its current income or carry forward (or back) as a net operating loss. The pattern of rental deductions (and the lessor's corresponding rental income inclusions) is determined by Section 467 and proposed regulations under that section issued by the US Treasury in May 1996.

Because its tax benefits drive the transaction, the lessor will take the following steps to ensure that it will actually receive its expected tax benefits. First, the lessor will require an opinion of tax counsel stating that the lease is expected to be treated as a 'true lease' under current law. The criteria used by tax counsel in making this determination are set out in the next section. Secondly, the lessor will require that the lessee indemnify the lessor against the loss of the lessor's tax benefits (or their reduction) resulting from certain specified events. At a minimum, the lessor will require indemnification against the loss of tax benefits arising from certain specified acts and omissions of the lessee. Other types of indemnities that the lessor may request or demand include protection against future changes in corporate tax rates or in US tax law.

Classification of a lease as a 'true lease'

In 1975, the Internal Revenue Service published Revenue Procedure 75-21 to clarify the circumstances under which it would issue an advance ruling that a leveraged lease will be treated as a 'true lease'. At that time, lessors would not ordinarily proceed with a leasing transaction without obtaining an IRS ruling. By the early 1980s, however, lessors had begun to forego the costly and time-consuming ruling process and to rely on opinions of tax counsel that a transaction would receive 'true lease' treatment. Suitable legal opinions were only available for transactions that fell squarely within the Guidelines.

In recent years, law firms have begun to issue opinions that transactions will be respected as 'true leases' for tax purposes even though the transactions do not strictly observe certain of the Guidelines. Tax counsel base these opinions on the case law that provides more liberal rules for 'true lease' treatment than the Guidelines. This approach is appropriate considering that the Guidelines only define the circumstances under which the Service will issue a ruling and are not designed to be audit guidelines or substantive issues.

Both the Guidelines and courts generally look to the economic substance of a leasing transaction to determine which party 'owns' the leased asset for tax purposes. Formalistic criteria such as which party holds legal title to the asset or what the transaction is called in the deal documents are not considered determinative, or even indicative of tax ownership. A lessor will generally be considered the tax owner of a leased asset if the leasing transaction satisfies two general requirements. First, the lessor must maintain a substantial investment in the asset for the entire lease term. Second, the lessor must stand to benefit from increases in the asset's residual value and must take the risk of loss if the residual value is less than projected. The Guidelines formalise these two principles into a series of tests examined in the following sub-sections.

Purchase options and lessor puts

The following constraints ensure that both the upside benefit and downside risk of a change in an asset's residual value are retained by the lessor for the duration of the leasing transaction. First, the lessor cannot give the lessee a right to purchase the aircraft at the end of the lease term (or at any time prior to the end of the term) for a price below its then fair market value. Second, the lessor cannot have a right to require any entity (including the lessee) to purchase the asset at any point in the transaction.

The aircraft leasing market now accepts transactions that satisfy the spirit of these Guidelines but which go beyond their literal interpretation. For example, fixed price purchase options have become commonplace in the market. With respect to purchase options, tax counsel generally only require that the exercise price is not less than the asset's fair market value on the exercise date, as projected by an appraisal at closing which takes inflation into account.

While lessor puts are still not considered permissible, mechanisms with similar economic effects have been in the market for a number of years. For example, residual value insurance that guarantees the lessor a certain minimum residual return is widely accepted. Certain transactions have also been completed in which the equipment manufacturer has guaranteed the lessor a specified residual at the end of the lease.

A minimum unconditional 'at risk' investment

The Guidelines provide a series of constraints that ensure that the lessor maintains a minimum amount of equity at risk during the term of the transaction and that the asset has value and economic life in the hands of the lessor both during and at the end of the lease term. More specifically, the amount that the equity investor contributes directly or has borrowed on a fully recourse basis (the 'at-risk amount') must equal or exceed 20 per cent of the cost of the asset during the entire lease term. The lessor must also represent at the outset that the asset's fair market value at the end of the lease term (including all renewals at a fixed lease rate) will be at least 20 per cent of the asset's cost, without taking inflation or deflation into account. Finally, the asset's projected useful life at the end of the lease term should be at least 20 per cent of its original useful life.

In recent years, many Pickle and Pickle-FSC transactions have been completed with initial equity investments of less than 20 per cent, relying on case law rather than the Guidelines. The optimal leverage for MACRS transactions, however, is usually at or below 80 per cent. For aircraft, extending the lease term beyond 80 per cent of the aircraft's useful life is usually not practical because the useful life of aircraft is relatively long in comparison with other leased assets. The optimal aircraft lease in practice tends to fall naturally within the useful life test.

'Wintergreen' renewals may be used to extend renewal terms beyond the Guideline limits. Wintergreen renewals provide for a reappraisal of the asset at the end of the lease's base term. If the appraisal establishes that the asset's useful life is longer than was expected at closing, the lessee is permitted to renew the lease for a term that will result in an aggregate lease term of up to 80 per cent of the asset's then expected useful life. This technique basically retests the asset's useful life at the end of the base term to determine whether a renewal term can be added that will result in a longer aggregate lease term than was originally projected.

No investment by the lessee

To ensure that the lessee does not bear the benefits and burdens of ownership of the leased asset, the Guidelines prohibit the lessee or any member of the 'lessee group' from investing in the asset after it has been purchased by the lessor. An exception is provided for improvements that are 'readily removable without causing material damage to the property', normal maintenance and repairs. With respect to aircraft leases, US airlines frequently violated this test in the past without intending to do so. Airlines generally treated leased aircraft no differently from owned aircraft and thus, when modifications were commercially required, they modified their leased aircraft along with their owned aircraft.

After several years of confusion over this Guideline, the Service issued Revenue Procedure 79-48 which clarified this rule by emphasising the difference in treatment between severable improvements (in which lessees were permitted to invest) and non-severable improvements (in which lessees are not permitted to invest). Improvements that airlines routinely make are now generally considered 'severable' improvements and therefore investment in them does not violate this Guideline.

No lessee loans or guarantees

A similar constraint prevents the lessee from lending funds to the lessor to enable it to purchase the asset. The lessee is also prohibited from guaranteeing any indebtedness of the lessor that is incurred to finance the lessor's purchase of the asset.

Although the 'no loan' restriction has been almost uniformly complied with in domestic deals, the 'no guarantee' requirement has been honoured only in form. Members of the lessee group routinely guarantee lease rentals. Such guarantees (along with the rental stream) are assigned to the lender, and upon an event of default, guarantee payments are applied first to the remaining outstanding principal balance. Additionally, third party guarantees of the debt or lease obligations are often employed which, although not expressly prohibited by the Guidelines, have not been formally blessed by the IRS. There is also a concern that loan guarantees may violate the 'qualified non-recourse indebtedness' test of Section 861.

The profit requirement

The Guidelines require the lessor to represent that it will receive an overall profit from the transaction, apart from the value of the tax benefits of asset ownership.[b] This requirement was relevant in the days of ITC but now no special effort is required to pass the test. A second profit or 'cash flow' test requires a 'reasonable' pre-tax return on investment, typically two per cent per year of the term, without regard to any residual.

Uneven rent test

The tests described above bear on the 'true lease' issue (ie whether the lessor owns the asset for tax purposes). However, the Guidelines also established constraints on rent profiles. Rent structures that attempt to back-load or front-load lease rentals outside of a range of 90 per cent to 110 per cent of the average rents are subject to recharacterisation for tax accounting purposes. This constraint has been overshadowed, however, by the enactment of Section 467 of the IRC and the issuance of regulations under that section.

Section 467 developments

Section 467, which was added to the Code by the Tax Reform Act of 1984, determines the rent and interest accrual schedules for parties to rental agreements that have increasing or decreasing rents or prepaid or deferred rents. On 31 May 1996, the US Treasury issued proposed regulations that clarify (and extend) the application of this section.

The regulations are proposed only and will become fully effective only upon issuance of final regulations, except for the tax-avoidance provisions,[c] which became effective immediately, causing significant disruption to the leasing market. Certain 'plain vanilla' types of structures designed to conform with the Guidelines and generally accepted by tax counsel have been shut down, at least temporarily.

Currently effective regulations

Leases entered into after 3 June 1996 but before the final regulations are issued must be structured to avoid application of the tax-avoidance provisions of the proposed regulations, described in detail below. Few structural changes are currently required to standard US aircraft leases. Those changes that are required, however, are costly, adding as much as 250 basis points to the lessee's present value cost.

Section 467 provides generally that leases that have increasing or decreasing rents may be recharacterised to provide for rateable accrual of rentals under certain circumstances.[d] These rent-levelling provisions apply only to sale–leaseback transactions or leases that have terms (including renewals that are expected to be exercised) exceeding 5.25 years in the case of aircraft. Thus, short-term operating leases that are not sale–leasebacks will not need to rely on one of the safe harbours described below to avoid application of Section 467.

The proposed regulations provide that the Commissioner, rather than the parties to a rental agreement, will determine whether the rent agreement is subject to rent-levelling. Thus, a transaction cannot be affirmatively structured to fall within the rule if rent-levelling was for some reason considered advantageous to the taxpayer.

Rent-levelling will be imposed only in cases in which the parties structured the lease with increasing or decreasing rents for a principal purpose of tax avoidance. The regulations provide that a 'facts and circumstances' test for tax avoidance will generally apply. A special rule provides that leases of property to or from a 'tax-exempt entity' (including a foreign corporation) will be presumed to be structured for a tax avoidance purpose unless clear and convincing evidence to the contrary is provided. In almost all cases, parties will structure their transaction to fall within one of the safe harbours described below to avoid inquiry into a tax avoidance motive.

As the legislative history to Section 467 would predict, the regulations contain a number of safe harbours. The most important is the '90–110' safe harbour for leases that have allocated rents over the lease term that do not vary from average rent by more than 10 per cent (on an annual basis). The lease term examined includes (1) the base lease term, (2) renewal terms, if the renewal is expected to be exercised[e], and (3) replacement lease terms or other periods for which the lessee is required to make payments in lieu of rent.

A number of changes to the new 90–110 safe harbour make the test more difficult to meet. The safe harbour is now examined on an accrual, calendar year basis, rather than the former lease year basis. As a result, accepted structuring techniques such as the use of sawtooth rents that bridge two calendar years are no longer available. Sawtooth rents within one calendar year will probably be acceptable but generally provide only a modest benefit.

US aircraft transactions have been frequently structured with bargain renewal terms. These transactions relied on an different safe harbour, the two-thirds/one-third test, which was provided by the Guidelines[f] but is not permitted by the proposed regulations. Bargain renewals may still survive because, in many cases, rent-levelling would actually defer the lessor's taxable rental income and therefore would not be expected to be applied by the service.

Although Section 467 states that future regulations will provide a safe harbour for 'reasonable rent holidays', the proposed regulations do not appear to permit safe harbour treatment for leases that have both a rent holiday and a 90–110 rental pattern.[g] Other than this difference, the regulations preserve the safe harbours set out in the statute, including those for changes in rents based on price indices, rents constituting a fixed percentage of lessee receipts and changes attributable to payment of third party costs.

Rent-levelling in the case of a lease agreement with back-ended rents has the consequence of requiring the lessor to accrue more rental income in the early years of the transaction than the lessor actually receives in cash. If rent-levelling is imposed, the deemed loan provisions, discussed below, will be applied currently to the transaction. As a result, the lessor would be deemed to make a loan to the lessee on which the lessor would accrue interest income.

Proposed deemed loan rules

The proposed regulations also contain a provision that would treat a lease as having an embedded loan if the rents actually paid under the lease do not match the pattern of rents accrued in the lease agreement.[h] If included in the final regulations, this provision would represent a significant change from prior law.

The deemed loan provisions, however, would not ordinarily affect the treatment of 'plain vanilla' US leases except to the extent that the leases permit prepayments or deferral of rent. The deemed loan provisions provide that, to the extent the payments to a lessor exceed accrued rent, such payments would be recharacterised as loans from lessee to lessor. Conversely, to the extent that rent accruals exceed payments, the lessor would be treated as receiving the accrued income and lending cash back to the lessee.

The deemed loan provisions permit parties to stipulate in the lease agreement that prepaid or deferred rents will bear interest at a specified rate. The interest rate is considered 'adequate' if the rate is at least 110 per cent of the Applicable Federal Rate (AFR). In such case, the lessor and the lessee account for (1) the stated rent under the lease, plus or minus (depending on which party is the deemed lender) (2) the stated interest accrual. If the interest rate is not adequate, the regulations create a deemed loan (from lessor to lessee in the case of deferred amounts, or from lessee to lessor in case of prepaid amounts), bearing interest at 110 per cent of AFR.

Conclusion

In summary, although the Guidelines have strongly influenced US aircraft lease structures for over 20 years, the leasing community has continued to find creative ways to satisfy the spirit, if not always the letter, of their requirements. The proposed Section 467 regulations remind us that ingenuity will still be required of the leasing community if it is to preserve leveraged leasing economics while clearing whatever new hurdles are put in place by the US Treasury.

Other tax considerations
Alternative minimum tax

The 1986 Act for the first time made the alternative minimum tax (AMT) provisions relevant to equipment leasing by corporations. The most significant AMT provision makes the accelerated portion of depreciation an item of tax preference for corporations. The provision effectively limits the number of leasing transactions a lessor can enter: if it enters too many, it will become subject to AMT and be required to defer a large portion of the value of the depreciation deductions. Conversely, because the depreciation preference applies to property, even if it is not leased, a subtle and unanticipated consequence of the provision has been to encourage some airlines that are taxpayers, but are subject to (or expect to be subject to) AMT, to become lessees of equipment they otherwise would have owned outright.

Foreign-source loss rules

The 1986 Act also repealed Section 861(e) of the IRC, which had provided that income (and losses) derived from US-manufactured aircraft leased to a US person would be deemed 'US-source income', regardless of the location of use. In lieu of this provision, only income attributable to flights which begin and end in the US could be deemed 'US source'. All other income must be deemed at best 50 per cent US source and 50 per cent foreign source (assuming the aircraft is used 'to and from' the US).[i]

These new sourcing rules are part of an equation that determines the maximum annual amount of foreign taxes that a US taxpayer may credit against US taxes payable. This rule applies to both the operating income and expenses of the air carrier and to the lessor's income and expenses attributable to the leasing of the aircraft. Under the new provisions, the lessor's ability fully to claim foreign tax credits on a current basis (when losses are generated in the early years of the lease) may be impaired to the extent that such losses are deemed 'foreign'. As a consequence of the new provision, US airlines that fly on routes outside the US have found a more limited equity market for their transactions or, alternatively, have found that they have to indemnify against all or part of the risk of the loss by the lessor of its ability to claim foreign tax credits.

Interest allocation rules

In 1988, the Treasury issued new temporary regulations under Sections 861 and 864 of the IRC that significantly affect the allocation of interest expenses for the purposes of computing the amount of a taxpayer's allowable foreign tax credits.

Of particular interest to the leasing industry, the regulations continue the non-recourse exception to the general rule requiring that interest be allocated on a consolidated basis among the taxpayer's assets that generate US-source income and those assets that generate foreign-source income. However, the new regulations require lessors to consider, even more carefully, whether a leveraged lease will have an adverse impact on their ability to use foreign tax credits.

Under the general rules of Sections 861 and 864, a taxpayer is required to allocate interest expense as a deduction against income generated by its assets on a worldwide basis. Thus, even if an asset generates solely US-source income, such as equipment used 100 per cent domestically, any interest expense attributable to recourse debt financing of the asset will be allocated, in proportion to asset value, to the income generated by all of the taxpayer's assets, including any assets that generate only foreign-source income, thereby reducing the taxpayer's foreign tax credit limitation. Conversely, even if an asset generates foreign-source income, part of the interest attributable to its ownership will reduce US-source income, thereby increasing the taxpayer's foreign tax credit limitation.

The above analysis, however, assumes that the indebtedness generating the interest expense is recourse to the owner of the asset. A special rule applies to 'qualified non-recourse indebtedness' – QNI (as defined in the regulations). This non-recourse exception to the general rule allows interest expense generated by QNI to be deducted solely against income generated by the asset to which the non-recourse indebtedness relates. Therefore, if the asset, used 100 per cent domestically, generates US-source income and was purchased with QNI, the interest expense will not reduce the lessor's foreign-source income and thus not reduce its allowable foreign tax credit.

Under the new regulations, however, certain structures may fail to meet the non-recourse indebtedness exception. (In certain cases, such as the creation of the turbo FSC structure described earlier, where it is desirable for the lessor to generate fewer losses from a transaction, certain of these structures are used to deliberately fail the non-recourse debt exception and cause interest expense to be allocated away from the asset.) These structures include refinancings that exceed in amount (by 5 per cent) or term (by six months) the amount or term of the original financing, or that otherwise fail to meet the requirements of the regulations at the time of the refinancing.

Generally speaking, an equity investor with foreign tax credit exposure will want indebtedness used to acquire assets generating US-source income to be characterised as QNI (ie all allocated to the domestic asset). Indebtedness used to acquire assets generating foreign-source income should, if possible, fail the QNI test so that the interest expense will be (at least partially) allocated away from the foreign assets.

Notes to Appendix 1

a Rev. Proc. 75-21, 1975-1 C.B. 715, modified by Rev. Proc. 81-71, 1981-2 C.B. 731 (severable and non-severable improvements), Rev. Proc. 79-48, 1979-2 C.B. 529 (limited use property) and Rev. Proc. 76-30, 1976-2 C.B. 647 (representations required in ruling request).

b In order to submit a ruling request on a leveraged lease transaction, the parties must make the following representations concerning transaction profit. First, an analysis must be submitted that demonstrates that the lessee's payments over the lease term and the asset's residual value when taken together exceed the lessor's projected expenses in owning the asset, including its initial equity investment and financing costs. Secondly, to satisfy the cash flow requirement, an analysis must be submitted that shows that the lessee's aggregate payments over the lease term exceed the lessor's projected expenses associated in owning the asset, excluding its initial equity investment (although including direct financing costs in raising the equity investment).

c Technically, the proposed regulations provide that the final regulations will be retroactively effective on (and therefore, currently effective from) 3 June 1996 for certain tax-avoidance leasing transactions that are entered into after that date. Of course, the final regulations may in fact lay down a different effective date.

d Section 467(e)(1) provides that the constant rental amount is the amount that, if paid at the end of each rental period, would result in a present value equal to the present value of all amounts payable under the disqualified leaseback or long-term agreement.

e The regulations provide that the rent-levelling provisions will be applied only to (1) lease agreements that have fixed rentals for any rent period that exceed the fixed rent for any other period (both on an annualised basis) or (2) lease agreements that have contingent rent. Any rental payments that are not fixed as to amount and payment date are considered 'contingent rent'. The regulations provide, however, that a three-month initial rent holiday will not in itself cause an agreement to have increasing or decreasing rents and therefore to be subject to these regulations.

f A renewal option held by the lessee would generally be expected to be exercised if it is set at less than expected fair market value.

g In addition to the 90–110 safe harbour, Revenue Procedure 75-21 provides a safe harbour for rental agreements that fit within a 90–110 pattern for at least the first two-thirds of the lease term and then for the remaining one-third of the term, that have rents that do not exceed the highest annual rent paid in the initial term and that are not less than 50 per cent of average rent over the initial term.

h A separate safe harbour is provided for leases with increases and decreases in rent that are solely attributable to an initial rent holiday not in excess of 24 months or 10 per cent of the lease term, but only if the rent holiday serves a substantial business purpose.

i Internal Revenue Code, Section 863(c).

Appendix 2

Accounting treatment of US aircraft leases

Accounting for leases in the US is carried out according to methods prescribed by the Financial Accounting Standards Board in its Statement No. 13, *Accounting for Leases* (SFAS 13). Criteria used by lessees and lessors to classify leases are shown in simplified form in Exhibits 8.11 and 8.12 respectively.

Exhibit 8.11
Accounting classifications for a lease – the lessee's perspective

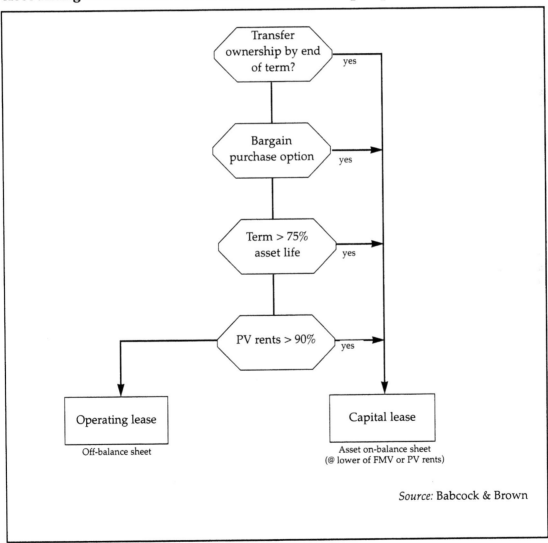

Source: Babcock & Brown

Exhibit 8.12
Accounting classifications for a lease – the lessor's perspective

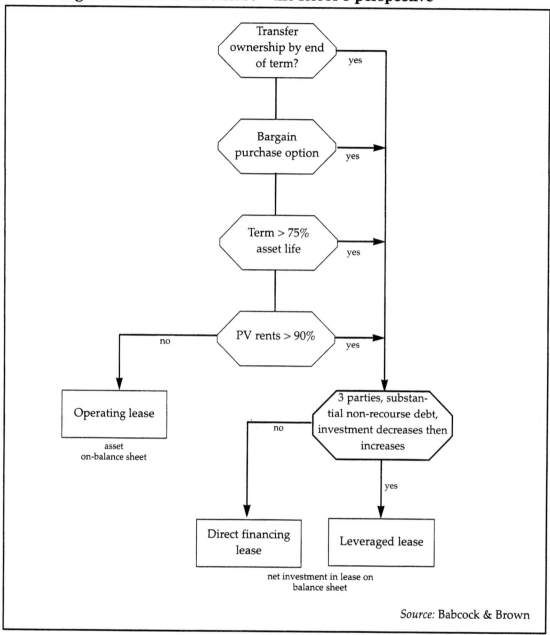

Source: Babcock & Brown

Lessee accounting

For leases, SFAS 13 draws a distinction between two different types of leases – capital leases and operating leases. In essence, a lease that transfers most or all of the risks and rewards of equipment ownership to the lessee is considered a capital lease. All other types of lease are accounted for as 'operating leases', under which the lessee is viewed as simply making rental payments on a periodic basis for the short-term use of the equipment. The mandated accounting treatment for a capital lease differs substantially from that for an operating lease.

To determine whether a particular leasing transaction should be accounted for as a capital lease or as an operating lease, the following four questions must be answered:

1 Does the lease transfer ownership of the equipment to the lessee at or before the end of the lease term?
2 Does the lease contain a bargain purchase option?
3 Does the non-cancellable lease term exceed 75 per cent of the presently anticipated economic life of the property?
4 Does the present value of the required lease payments, discounted at the lower of the lessee's incremental borrowing rate or the interest rate implicit in the lease (if determinable by the lessee), exceed 90 per cent of the cost of the equipment?

The interest rate implicit in the lease is calculated as the interest rate that discounts the minimum required lease payments and the unguaranteed portion of the lessor's residual value back to the cost of the leased equipment. Since the lessee typically does not have access to information concerning the unguaranteed portion of the lessor's residual value, most lessees are obliged to evaluate their lease accounting treatment by discounting using their incremental borrowing rate.

If the answer to any of the four questions above is yes, the transaction is accounted for by the lessee as a capital lease; otherwise it is accounted for as an operating lease.

If the transaction is a capital lease, the lessee is essentially viewed as having acquired the equipment. The aircraft is shown as an asset on the lessee's balance sheet, and the lease financing is recorded as a long-term liability. The dollar amount recorded at inception by the lessee as an asset and a liability is the smaller of (a) the FMV of the equipment, and (b) the present value, calculated as in question 4 above, of the rental and other minimum lease payments required to be made by the lessee, including any guarantee by the lessee of the residual value of the equipment at the end of the lease term. The lessee's incremental borrowing rate, for the purposes of calculating the present value described here, is the interest rate as of the inception of the lease which the lessee would have paid if it had borrowed debt funds to purchase the equipment, with repayment over a term similar to the term of the lease agreement.

Under capital lease accounting, the asset is amortised over the lease term (rather than the useful life of the asset) unless the lessee has a bargain purchase option or the lease calls for the transfer of title to the lessee at the end of the lease. The method of amortising the asset must be consistent with the depreciation policy that the lessee normally uses for its owned assets. The liability side of the balance sheet is reduced over time by the 'principal' component of the ongoing lease payments (ie the excess of the lease payment over the interest component thereof).

If the transaction is not a capital lease, it is classified as an operating lease by the lessee and no asset or liability is recorded on the lessee's balance sheet. Instead, rental payments are simply recorded, usually on a straight-line basis, as rental expense in the lessee's income statement.

Many of the lease transactions completed by the major US airline carriers, for both new and used aircraft, qualify for operating lease treatment by the lessee under SFAS 13. Airline lessees generally consider this potential off-balance sheet aspect of leasing to be a favourable benefit, because they are often trying to maintain their notional debt/equity ratios within prescribed targets.

Lessor accounting

Accounting by lessors is also prescribed in SFAS 13. Leases are classified by the lessor as direct-finance, leveraged or operating leases.

Direct-finance lease accounting presumes that the lessee owns the aircraft and that the lessor has provided long-term financing. Leases are classified as direct-finance leases if they meet any one of the four lease classification criteria (described under 'Lessee accounting' above), and meet both of the following criteria:

1 collectability of the minimum lease payments is reasonably predictable; and
2 there are no important uncertainties surrounding the amount of unreimbursable costs yet to be incurred by the lessor under the lease.

Under direct-finance lease accounting, the rents receivable and the estimated residual interest are recorded as assets. The difference between the sum of these and the cost of the equipment is unearned income, which is amortised to income using a level interest rate method over the life of the lease.

A leveraged lease is defined as one having all of the following characteristics:

1 it meets the criteria of a direct-finance lease;
2 it involves at least three parties – a lessee, a long-term creditor and a lessor (commonly called the equity participant);
3 the financing provided by the long-term creditor is non-recourse as to the general credit of the lessor; and
4 the lessor's net investment, as defined in SFAS 13, declines during the early years once the investment has been made and rises during the later years of the lease before its final elimination.

Under leveraged lease accounting, net after-tax cash flow to the lessor is projected over the life of the lease. After-tax income is allocated to periods when the lessor's after-tax investment is positive using a level interest rate method. This is the 'MISF' method described earlier in the 'lessor economics and motivations' section. The non-recourse debt is not shown on the books of the lessor.

Both direct-finance and leveraged lease accounting involve recording as an asset the value of the estimated residual interest. This estimate must be reviewed each reporting period and if a permanent impairment in value occurs, the residual interest must be written down to its new estimated value.

Leases that do not qualify as direct-finance leases or leveraged leases are classified as operating leases. The lessor will record ownership of the leased equipment in its financial statements (ie, in the plant and equipment section of the assets).

Any debt associated with an operating lease, even if non-recourse to the lessor, will appear in the liabilities section.

In the income statement, the rental revenue will be accounted for on a straight-line basis even if the payments are uneven.

The depreciation (net of booked residual value) may be expensed on a straight-line basis over the term of the lease, or on such other method as the lessor uses for other like assets in its business.

Comparison between lessee and lessor classification criteria

The airline usually wishes to keep the lease financing off its balance sheet; it does this by satisfying the accounting criteria for an operating lease. The lessor, however, usually wishes to achieve leveraged lease accounting so that it can maximise its book income in the early years. The apparent conflict between these two requirements is resolved when it is noted that the lessee does not know what residual assumption the lessor is making and can therefore use its incremental borrowing rate when calculating the present value of the rentals. Thus the lessee computes a present value below 90 per cent at its higher discount rate, and gets operating lease treatment, while the lessor computes a present value above 90 per cent at its lower discount rate, and gets leveraged lease accounting.

Prospects for future amendments to SFAS 13

From time to time, revisions to the US accounting treatment of leases have been proposed. No such proposals are under active consideration at the present time, however.

In addition, several accounting firms have published booklets giving commentary and interpretations on areas not specifically addressed in SFAS 13 or that require further explanation. These materials provide an invaluable guide to the leasing professional.

In the international arena, several countries have adopted standards similar to SFAS 13, while others have adopted standards more closely aligned with the tax treatment of leases in those countries. This discrepancy led to the creation of a working group consisting of board members and senior staff members of the standard-setting bodies of Australia, Canada, New Zealand, the UK and the US, and staff of the International Accounting Standards Committee (IASC). The working group has prepared a report entitled *Accounting for Leases: A New Approach*, which discusses the limitations of current lease accounting standards and sets out a new approach to lease accounting that has the potential to overcome the present concerns.

The proposed new approach would severely restrict the availability of operating lease accounting to US lessees and abolish leveraged lease accounting for US lessors. If adopted in its present form, therefore, it would drastically reduce the attractiveness of leasing. It is therefore likely to be vigorously opposed by lessees and lessors in the US.

It seems safe to forecast that there will be no significant changes to US lease accounting standards, or their interpretation, for at least the next few years.

9 UK leasing

Chris Boobyer

UK leasing heritage

Leasing, as a serious form of business finance, first emerged in the UK in the 1960s. However, at first, the major UK lessors (principally the subsidiaries of UK banks and finance houses) did not take readily to the leasing of aircraft, primarily due to concerns over exposure to third party liability risks.

Leasing as a product in the UK was introduced from the US where it had begun in the early 1950s and, similarly, the UK airlines became aware of aircraft lease finance from the principal US aircraft manufacturers such as Boeing and McDonnell Douglas, which used leasing as a method of product support. UK manufacturers, such as BAC, began to follow suit, offering leasing facilities to developing UK regional airlines and holiday charter operators.

It was not until the early 1970s, following the introduction of first-year allowances for expenditure on new or used aircraft, that UK aircraft leasing began to flourish, because many airlines were unable to take advantage of the available tax allowances themselves and consequently turned to leasing to obtain the benefit of tax deferral. UK tax leasing, as we know it today, became an established method of finance for UK airlines with the leasing companies purchasing the aircraft at the behest of the airline, claiming the available capital allowances and reflecting the tax benefits they received in the form of reduced rentals to the airlines. This produced effective interest rates below the equivalent cost of borrowing to finance aircraft by way of more conventional debt finance methods.

Since 1984, which saw the gradual phasing out of first-year allowances in favour of an annual writing-down allowance for tax purposes, the fiscal environment for UK leases has remained fairly stable, with a significant proportion of new aircraft acquisitions in the UK being financed by the way of domestic leasing facilities (see Exhibit 9.1). Inevitably, as lessors, lessees and arrangers became more sophisticated, increasingly complex lease structures were developed to cater for ever more demanding end-users requiring improved benefits, greater flexibility and, perhaps, off-balance sheet financing. This resulted in increased utilisation of highly structured lease financings involving cross-border leases, defeasance, option agreements, double dips and so on.

The leasing market

During the early 1990s the UK leasing industry had a roller-coaster ride to rival that of the airline industry. Following the boom years throughout most of the 1980s, the recession in the UK and the world economy hit the profitability of the major banking groups in the UK as a result of mounting bad debts and heavy provisions in respect of developing country loans. This led to the supply of tax capacity being reduced and substantial increases in lease margins among the

Exhibit 9.1
Value of aircraft financed in the UK by way of leasing, 1990–97 (£mn)

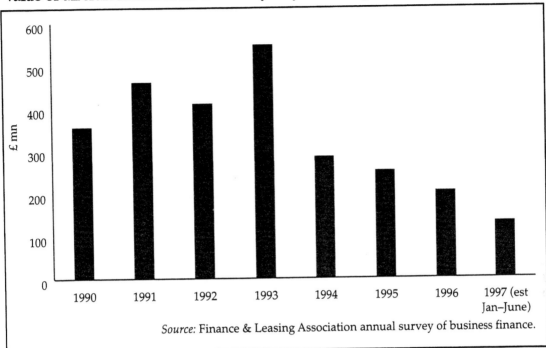

Source: Finance & Leasing Association annual survey of business finance.

bank-owned lessors that dominate the big-ticket leasing market. The combined effect of this, coupled with reduced demand for investment during the UK recession, led to a significant general decrease in UK leasing (see Exhibit 9.2).

While the tax capacity situation in the UK began to improve after 1993 due to the return of the UK clearers (joining the newest player in the market, Abbey National), growth in big-ticket leasing remained sluggish throughout 1994 as the hard-hit UK corporate sector did not have the confidence to start reinvestment programmes. Only in 1995–96 did this confidence return on the back of a slow, steady recovery in the UK economy, which led once again to a more buoyant UK leasing market. That is, until the presentation on 26 November 1996 of the Finance Bill 1997, which introduced new definitions for long-life assets that had a major impact on the aviation industry, and the Finance (No. 2) Act 1997, which introduced restrictions on sale and leaseback financing methods, along with a first-year time apportionment of the writing-down allowances available to a finance lessor.

Aircraft financing

The most recent cyclical downturn in the worldwide aviation industry was particularly severe. Following a prolonged period of significant expansion of aircraft financing worldwide in the late 1980s, the resultant slump in airline profitability, aircraft values and leasing rates led to the withdrawal from the traditional debt financing market of some major players. Given the modest levels of profitability in the airline industry generally and the common under-capitalised nature of airline balance sheets, a more cautious approach to long-term debt financing was

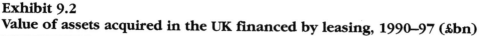

Exhibit 9.2
Value of assets acquired in the UK financed by leasing, 1990–97 (£bn)

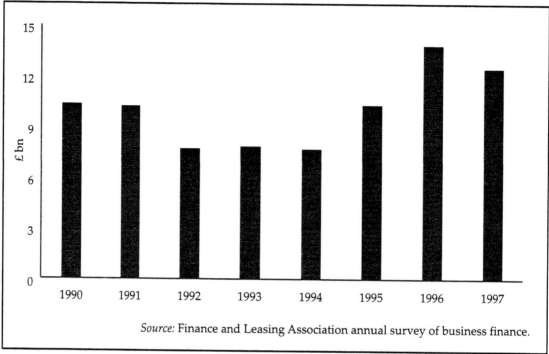

Source: Finance and Leasing Association annual survey of business finance.

adopted by many financiers. The situation was exacerbated by the capital adequacy concerns of many major banks, which retracted their lending generally or sought less volatile and less competitive markets. This led to a contraction of the global airline financing market, with lenders tending to seek higher returns for risk taking or, alternatively, requiring secured financing structures, enabling them to record lower risk-asset weightings for central bank capital adequacy purposes. This latter trend has been mirrored in the UK leasing market.

As demand for new aircraft financings continues to recover, it is clear that there is a significant role for lease finance in the expansion of the world fleet. Increasingly, this may focus more on operating leasing of aircraft as airlines require more flexibility in their fleet management policies and financiers respond to their demands and tightening fiscal regimes with more imaginative products. With financial institutions being less likely to accept substantial asset risk positions, this may leave the door open to specialist operating lessors to manage asset risk among a larger pool of airline clients.

Nonetheless, larger airlines will continue to demand a mix of financing methods for their aircraft acquisitions, and traditional finance leasing, albeit needing to adapt to using ever more complex structuring to improve the resultant tax benefits, will continue to have a role. This will be particularly so in respect of aircraft that are regarded as a core element of the operators' fleet and consequently lend themselves to a long-term commitment to tax-efficient financing.

As discussed below, the UK leasing market is not a particularly advantageous home-base for cross-border leasing to overseas airlines. The bulk of leasing business transacted in the UK is with UK-based carriers such as the national flag-carrier, other UK domiciled scheduled airlines, regional carriers and the principal charter airlines. Levels of financings in the UK are therefore strongly affected not only by the performance of the airlines but also by holiday businesses generally, which may drive fleet renewal programmes of the domestic airlines. The relative competitiveness of the UK leasing product is also influenced by the availability of tax-driven lease products from other jurisdictions.

Cross-border leasing

UK airlines have taken advantage of tax-based leasing structures emanating from overseas jurisdictions – particularly Japan and the US. While Japanese leveraged leases (JLLs) have not been suitable for combining with UK finance leases since 1990, a number of UK-based airlines have utilised JLLs themselves as an attractive financing option while continuing to benefit from domestic tax benefits.

Similarly, the US has been an active source of cross-border leasing opportunities, particularly given a stagnant home market, and US lessors have been keen to develop their business into the UK and Europe via aircraft leases. Over the years the lease structures being offered have become ever more inventive, in an attempt to squeeze the maximum benefit from the restrictive US tax legislation relating to non-US taxpayers first introduced in 1984. US leases have tended to be based around either foreign sales corporation (FSC) leases or Pickle leases, with a number of variations of the latter, including the replacement lease structure and the like-kind exchange facility.

The combination of a US lease with a UK tax lease has been achieved in the past by UK lessors capitalising on the ability of US lessors to claim depreciation benefits on financing arrangements that give the US lessee a purchase option, while the UK lessor is able to claim capital allowances on assets over which it does not yet have title but where title can be conditionally acquired under contracts stating it 'shall or may become the owner' of an asset (ie the so-called Section 60 contract). Tensions do occur between the requirements of the two jurisdictions but, where circumstances permit, these can be overcome with careful structuring allowing the interplay between the recognition of economic ownership on the one hand and legal ownership on the other to bear fruit.

Issues often arise concerning the UK lessor's need to demonstrate that it can obtain title in virtually all circumstances and dispose of the asset in a reasonably unfettered manner. In contrast, a US lessor may have concerns about whether the addition of a UK lease may result in the US lessee being economically compelled to exercise its purchase option or how US lease investors can maintain an acceptable security interest in the aircraft. More recently, the trend has been to seek UK lease benefits on assets that can be combined with tax benefits which the US corporation is able to obtain domestically within the US tax regime without involving a third party US lessor.

Such double dip transactions, utilising lease structures and their resultant tax benefits in more than one jurisdiction, can provide sufficiently attractive returns to the lessee willing to enter into a long-term financing commitment even after taking into account the high initial cost of putting such structures in place. The recent IRS proposals seeking to close certain 'loopholes' relating to US export leases currently leave an air of uncertainty as to what structures may be possible in the future and whether the benefits to be obtained from Pickle leases can be sustained at previous levels. This, combined with the indications emanating from the Japanese authorities that cross-border JLLs will not be available after September 1998, may once again lead operators to consider the benefits of UK leasing.

The 1997–98 Asian financial crisis will also have a major impact on the JLL market as investors' funds begin to evaporate and lessees question the confidence they previously held in transactions awaiting completion. Some European markets, together with US cross-border structures, may once again find favour as mainstream finance avenues for major airlines needing to fund the large fleet orders of the mid and late 1990s.

Leasing benefits

Globally leasing continues to play an important role in the field of asset financing and remains attractive to airline operators for the following reasons:

- *Cash flow:* Leasing allows acquisition of an aircraft without capital outlay on the part of the airline, because lessors typically fund the full purchase price. Rentals can be structured so as to accommodate anticipated increases in future revenues, thereby matching income to expenditure.
- *Term:* Aircraft leases are typically long term (15 years plus), more closely matching the useful life of the asset and, perhaps, providing finance on a longer-term basis than many debt facilities.
- *Alternative finance:* Leasing gives an airline an additional source of finance, perhaps keeping working capital lines free for other purposes. Most airlines finance their fleets using a mix of funding techniques, and leasing adds to this blend.
- *Balance sheet:* Certain leasing structures involving the assumption of asset risk by a party other than the lessee may be treated as operating leases for balance sheet purposes, with the consequent impact of improved gearing and return-on-asset ratios in published accounts.
- *Tax:* The principal driver behind UK lease finance is, of course, the associated tax benefits related to the 25 per cent writing-down allowances (WDAs) available to the lessor for domestic leasing (6 per cent WDAs for assets with an expected useful life of at least 25 years in the UK post the Finance Act 1997). When this benefit is reflected in the lease rentals charged to the lessee, the higher-rate allowances can result in an effective cost of finance well below other available methods. For longer-life assets, the economics are of course not so beneficial.

The tax benefits of leasing will only be relevant in circumstances where the lessee is not itself able to make sufficient use of the available capital allowances, perhaps due to an insufficiency of taxable profits against which allowances can be relieved. Alternatively there may be circumstances where the lessor is able to utilise the available allowances in a more efficient manner, possibly because the lessee is not a full-rate taxpayer. On the other hand, early termination of a long-term facility can significantly reduce the benefits available to the lessee. As such, leasing is an option usually considered by airlines for aircraft expected to remain core components of their fleet.

Some lessees may regard the conditions imposed on them in most lease agreements, designed principally to protect the interests of the lessor, to be detrimental to their operational flexibility. While such conditions are rarely onerous, they may place an obligation on the lessee to consult with the lessor in particular circumstances that would clearly not be present in respect of aircraft owned outright by the operator.

UK tax environment

The most important tax consequence to be taken into account in considering leasing is that of capital allowances (the depreciation allowed for tax purposes), which achieve a tax deferral for the lessor. In particular, it is necessary to examine the treatment of such allowances in the hands of a finance lessor following the two Finance Acts in 1997. The first Act was passed by the Conservative government and the second, in July, by the new Labour government: the legislation impacted the timing of allowances and introduced new rules on sale and leasebacks.

A lessor that acquires an aircraft for the purposes of its trade of leasing would, prior to the November 1996 Budget, have expected an entitlement to writing-down allowances at a rate of 25 per cent per annum on a reducing-balance basis. This level of capital allowances had remained largely unchanged since 1986, with the exception of a brief and temporary reintroduction of an enhanced first-year allowance (40 per cent) in 1993. Now, following new confirmed provisions within the first Finance Act 1997, capital allowances in the UK for all assets except ships and rolling stock (excluded for all expenditure incurred prior to 1 January 2011) that are expected to have a life of at least 25 years, have been reduced from 25 per cent to 6 per cent. The available capital allowances apply equally to both new and used aircraft, subject to the possible restrictions outlined below in relation to sale and leaseback arrangements. Great care is required to ensure that any aircraft that may qualify for a shorter life category, thereby attracting 25 per cent capital allowances, are properly appraised. Transitional provisions exist that enable long-life assets, where expenditure will be incurred prior to 31 December 2000 in pursuance of a contract entered into before 26 November 1996, to attract full 25 per cent capital allowances.

Capital allowances are available on the amount of capital expenditure incurred by the lessor, such expenditure generally being deemed to occur for tax purposes on the date on which the obligation to pay becomes unconditional. Anti-avoidance provisions dissuade lessors from any artificial acceleration of allowances. Furthermore, under the Finance (No. 2) Act 1997, writing-down allowances are time-apportioned according to the date they are incurred, restricting a lessor's ability to claim the full writing-down allowance on an aircraft purchased other than on the first day of its financial year. Many established lessors used to operate a portfolio of leasing companies having accounting periods spread throughout the calendar year in order to maximise the timing of the tax benefits available to them through the use of group relief.

As discussed earlier, there are occasions when a lessor may incur capital expenditure on the provision of an aircraft yet still qualify for capital allowances in circumstances where the lessor does not yet have legal ownership. To do so the lessor must enter into a contract in respect of the aircraft, such as a hire purchase or conditional sale agreement, whereby it has an option to buy the aircraft on performance of the contract. This will be a contract conforming to Section 60 of the Capital Allowances Act 1990. Generally this gives the lessor an absolute right to obtain title under the contract. By so doing the aircraft is deemed to belong to the lessor for the duration of the contract and, for tax purposes, the lessor is treated as having acquired the asset at the time of entering into the contract. This has the effect of accelerating the lessor's claim to allowances once the aircraft has been brought into use. For similar reasons, lessors are not willing to provide purchase options on leased aircraft in favour of their lessees, so as to avoid any possible recharacterisation of the lease as a hire purchase contract that could result in a consequent loss of all capital allowances.

It should be noted that while an individual lease may make the assumption, for the purposes of computing tax benefits, that each aircraft is depreciated on a stand-alone basis, in reality a lessor will 'pool' all of its assets that are eligible for writing-down allowances and will be entitled to allowances in each accounting period equal to the total value of the pool. The value of the pool is made up of the carried forward value of the pool from the previous accounting period (after taking account of any allowances claimed in such period), plus any additional qualifying capital expenditure incurred by the lessor minus the value of any disposals brought into account by the lessor, in each case in the current accounting period.

The value of the pool carried forward to the next accounting period is often referred to as the tax written-down value. It therefore follows from the operation of the capital allowance provisions that a UK domestic finance lease, where the asset was acquired on the first day of the lessor's accounting period and assuming 25 per cent WDAs, will utilise over 68 per cent of the available allowances within four years – ie it will have a tax written-down value of 31.6 per cent of its original cost to the lessor. By the end of the eight years approximately 90 per cent of the allowances will have been claimed. Where the asset is purchased midway through the lessor's accounting period, the effect of time apportionment is to increase the tax written-down values to 37 per cent at four years and 11.7 per cent at eight years.

Anti-avoidance

For sale and leaseback transactions, the value of capital allowances available to the lessor may be limited by existing anti-avoidance legislation. Generally speaking, where the vendor (and subsequent lessee) is a UK taxpayer, the lessor's entitlement to allowances is restricted to an amount no greater than the tax written-down value, notional tax written-down value, or fair market value at the time of the sale. As the amount the vendor may bring into account by way of disposal value is limited to the vendor's original acquisition cost, this effectively imposes a cap on available allowances equal to the lower of original cost or disposal value, irrespective of whether the current market value of the aircraft may of itself support a higher figure.

Further anti-avoidance provisions, introduced in 1982, relate to overseas leasing of assets and are designed to prevent UK lessors from 'exporting' capital allowances to non-UK residents. Leases that meet the requirements of the legislation in this regard qualify for a 10 per cent writing-down allowance rather than the more advantageous 25 per cent rate where the asset has an expected useful life not exceeding 25 years. The 6 per cent WDA rate will also apply to cross-border transactions where long-life assets are involved. In circumstances where the restrictive legislation is not complied with, a lessor's entitlement to capital allowances may be denied completely. In respect of aircraft, the anti-avoidance provisions do not apply where aircraft are let on a 'wet lease' basis throughout the sub-lease period (ie the lessee retains management control of the aircraft and remains principally responsible for defraying the operating costs of the aircraft) or where the leasing constitutes short-term leasing as defined in the relevant legislation. Typically, this relates to leasing offshore for periods of less than one year and no more than two years in any four, cumulatively. These exclusions allow genuine UK airline operators the flexibility of entering into short-term sub-leases on their aircraft, perhaps during the off-season, without prejudicing the availability of capital allowances. Typically, lessors would include within lease agreements provisions designed to prevent lessees sub-leasing in a manner that could prejudice the lessor's claim for capital allowances.

UK lessors have entered into a number of cross-border leases to non-UK traders, including aircraft transactions, using structures that take advantage of the export leasing provisions allowed under the current legislation. The interest of UK lessors in such transactions was sparked during a time of sluggish demand in the domestic UK leasing market, and it remains to be seen whether their appetite will be sustained when the home market is buoyant. It can be imagined that demand for such products will continue, particularly if the current uncertainty regarding the US and Japanese markets crystallises to reveal a more restrictive legislative framework and a reduced level of benefit than that to which the industry has become accustomed.

It should be noted that 'cross-border' structures can involve offshore leasing, but which, through a subsequent sub-lease, utilise an onshore operator as end-user of the aircraft who is UK-resident for tax purposes. These structures generally avoid classification as export leases and retain entitlement to full 25 per cent writing-down allowances where the expected life does not exceed 25 years.

Balance sheet treatment

There are two principal types of lease – finance leases and operating leases. Such a simplistic classification may be misleading given the plethora of leasing structures that prevail, but for the purposes of this discussion we shall ignore the type of genuine short- to medium-term aircraft operating lease finance practised by specialist operating lessors such as ILFC and GECAS, who expertly operate a global business employing skills in fleet management and aircraft trading in addition to fleet financing. We will, instead, concentrate on long-term UK lease contracts, classified as finance leases from the lessor's perspective but which may, on occasion, and with careful structuring, still enable off-balance treatment in the accounts of the lessee.

Equally, it is important to understand that contracts that allow the lessee an option to buy the aircraft, which may be classified as a 'lease' in other jurisdictions are, under English law, not leases at all. In addition to the legal ramifications, contracts containing a purchase option, such as hire purchase or conditional sale, have substantially different tax and accounting implications from those applying to leases. Most importantly, where a lessee purchase option exists, the ability to claim capital allowances may switch to the holder of the purchase option rather than the lessor. Furthermore, the capital allowances claim of the lessor could be jeopardised by the existence of a lessee purchase option if the Inland Revenue was to hold that the lessor had intended to sell the aircraft to the lessee from the outset and consequently deemed the lessor's trade to be one of buying and selling aircraft rather than leasing them. It is for these reasons that lessors will generally avoid documenting any form of purchase option in favour of a lessee in UK tax lease agreements.

The accounting treatment of lease transactions in the UK has been conducted on an established basis since the introduction of SSAP 21 in 1984. This accounting standard introduced a lease classification based on the risks and rewards of ownership, with a finance lease being classified as one that transfers substantially all the risks and rewards of ownership to the lessee. A typical aircraft finance lease is a long-term contract where the lessee remains responsible for the maintenance and insurance of the aircraft and all other operational aspects consistent with economic 'ownership' of the aircraft. Furthermore, the rentals payable by the lessee over the lease term will be sufficient to fully amortise the lessor's net-of-tax investment in the transaction, plus its profit margin. Should the lessee wish to continue leasing the aircraft beyond the originally envisaged lease term, having liquidated its primary obligation to the lessor, it may do so on payment of nominal renewal rentals. Equally, upon sale of the aircraft, the lessee usually negotiates the sale as the lessor's agent and will be entitled to receive the majority of the sales proceeds in the form of a rebate of rentals under the lease contract.

As regards the determination of a lease as either a finance lease or an operating lease, SSAP 21 also introduced an arbitrary measure by way of what is known as the '90 per cent test'. This is based on a discounting of the minimum lease payments due from the lessee under the lease agreement and comparing this to the fair market value of the aircraft. In circumstances where the present value of the minimum lease payments, discounted back at the interest rate implicit in the lease, exceeds 90 per cent of fair market value it is presumed that finance lease treatment should be adopted. All other leases are simply classified as operating leases. This single, 'pass or fail' test led to the classification of leases being open to abuse from structures developed with the aim of obtaining operating lease treatment for lessees while still inherently leaving the majority of the risks and rewards of ownership with the lessee.

Often such structures involved the use of 'walk' options, allowing the lessee to terminate the lease agreement at various times or 'windows' during the lease term without incurring further obligations under the lease. As such, there was considerable scope for creative lease structuring to enable companies to avoid capitalising assets in their balance sheets, by massaging the net present value of the minimum lease payments to qualify for the 90 per cent test, on the assumption that obligations falling due after the window date need not be included in the calculation.

Transaction substance rather than form

In 1994 FRS5 was introduced as an attempt to provide more detailed guidance on the treatment of such options by considering the commercial position of all the parties to the transaction, including their motivation for entering into the transaction and their expectations from it. In respect of leases including options, the likelihood of the option being exercised by the lessee becomes a critical factor in the evaluation process. Factors to consider here, which may affect the commerciality of the option, include:

- the cost to the airline of exercising the option (ie is it set above anticipated market value?);
- whether the conditions attached to the exercise of the option are onerous (eg for aircraft this may relate to impractical return conditions); and
- whether continued use of the aircraft would be necessary without significant disruption to the airline's operations.

It should be noted that FRS5 is not an attempt to replace SSAP 21 but an effort to more properly recognise the commercial substance of a transaction rather than its pure legal form, particularly with regard to the more complex lease transaction commonly found in the aviation market-place. By providing more detailed guidance on issues such as commerciality and economic benefit, it discourages abuse of the 90 per cent test. It is interesting to note that since its introduction a number of significant leasing transactions previously recorded as operating leases, including some aircraft leases, have been reclassified as finance leases and brought on-balance sheet by lessees. That said, FRS5 is not a panacea and, with increasingly complex aircraft lease structures being devised, issues requiring significant judgement (and fee earning capacity for aviation lawyers!) will undoubtedly remain.

In this regard, long-term tax leases involving walk away options continue to prevail under FRS5, albeit that in order to obtain operating lease treatment for the lessee they tend to include a third party (perhaps an aircraft operating lessor or residual value guarantor), which takes a commercial asset risk position within the transaction and provides the lessee with a genuine commercial basis for potentially exercising the option.

In terms of accounting treatment, aircraft acquired under a finance lease will be capitalised as an asset in the balance sheet of the airline with the obligations under the lease recorded as a liability. In the UK there is no direct mirroring of accounting depreciation and depreciation for tax purposes as exists in certain other jurisdictions. Typically the aircraft would be depreciated over the period of its useful life to the lessee, or possibly the lease term, if shorter, with the depreciation charge, together with any associated financing charge, being debited to the profit and loss account. By contrast, aircraft acquired under operating leases need not be recognised by the airline on the balance sheet as an asset, nor is the liability (other than the forthcoming 12 months rentals) disclosed as a liability. The rentals payable are charged to the profit and loss account over the lease term in accordance with UK GAAP.

For taxation purposes, rentals payable by airlines under leasing arrangements are generally deductible as a trading expense. However, the Inland Revenue may restrict the deductibility of finance lease rentals according to the guidelines introduced in its Statement of Practice issued in April 1991. This attempts to harmonise the calculation of tax depreciation with normal commercial accounting principles for the purposes of determining the deductibility of rentals. The November 1996 Budget introduced proposals to further strengthen the relationship between taxation and accounting. For all finance leases incepted from 25 November 1996 (which are not covered by the 'grandfathering' provisions contained within Part 2 of the Finance Act 1997), lessors will be taxed on the higher of the taxable profit or the accounting profit received by them, thereby negating the timing difference reflected in a hitherto commercially based escalating rental profile that matches the expected operational life and income profile of the aircraft.

The debate, tensions, ebbs and flows surrounding on or off balance sheet financing and the stability of accounting provisions as arbiters of tax treatment is set to continue. Recent proposals from the International Accounting Standards Board in the form of IAS17 and the affiliated McGregor Report have further stimulated controversy on the appropriate balance sheet treatment for lease financed equipment. The proposal that balance sheet classification should depend on whether the equipment financed is a real asset to the business or is being 'simply' rented has many of the world's lessors up in arms. There is however no risk in stating that the arguments will continue and that there will be plenty of reward for those whose professional advice is sought!

10 Leasing in other European countries

Simon Hall[1]

Introduction

This chapter examines leasing in a number of other European countries, both from the perspective of the domestic regime and the opportunities and requirements for leasing into or out of the jurisdiction. The law is stated as at March 1998 and the jurisdictions are:

- Austria;
- Denmark;
- France;
- Germany;
- Italy;
- Spain; and
- Sweden.

Jurisdictions have been selected either because of the volume of aircraft financing that has been completed in or from them, or because of the interest shown by the international financial community in them as sources of tax-based finance.

At the time of writing, the availability of finance is of more critical importance to airlines than the reduced cost of that finance through tax-advantaged financing. Tax equity has become scarcer, but it is likely that this will still be available for the better credits, or where there is a significant advantage to be gained for the jurisdiction concerned.

The harmonisation of the tax laws in Europe, and the integration of the EFTA states into the EU, is likely to give rise to significant changes in the tax laws of each of the jurisdictions considered. Substantial opportunities may also be presented for new cross-border structures or more substantial tax benefits.

In addition, the VAT regime for trade in goods (and certain supplies of services) between EU countries changed dramatically on 1 January 1993 with the establishment of the 'single market'. The eventual aim is to adopt an 'origin' system under which VAT will be charged on supplies of goods and services in the state from which the supply is made. For this system to function without distorting competition, VAT rates in the EU member states must be aligned. For the moment, the old VAT system, which taxed imports and was heavily reliant on border controls, has been replaced with a system based on the concept of acquisition: a business in one member state acquiring goods from another member state will account for VAT under the rules of its home state.

The regime has created (or highlighted) particular difficulties for certain transactions across EU state borders: it is not always easy in such cases to identify where and by whom an acquisition of goods has been made. At least until participants in the markets (and tax authorities) have become accustomed to the new regime, particular care will need to be taken in structuring and implementing cross-border leasing transactions involving more than one EU member state, not least because the EU VAT legislation has not been implemented in all member states in an identical (and therefore easily complementary) manner.

It should be noted, however, that in this chapter the focus is on leasing. The shortage of tax equity for 'traditional' leasing products has forced bankers and packagers and their lawyers to work on developing new products, transferring ideas from other markets and adapting them for aircraft financing. Energy will continue to be devoted to the development of such new products, so long as the appetite of the airlines for low-cost financing continues.

Austria

Introduction and tax background

In recent years there has been a substantial increase in leasing in general in Austria. New acquisitions of equipment for leasing in 1995 amounted to Sch26.4 billion, with the total capital investment in leased movables standing at a depreciated value of Sch54.2 billion. Cross-border aircraft leasing transactions have been finalised with, among others, Japanese, German and American lessors, and cross-border leasing from Austria has also been used for export leasing into the former Comecon states and Arab countries. Cross-border leasing primarily takes place from foreign lessors to Austrian lessees, mainly for tax reasons.

There is no specific code of law in respect of leasing arrangements and, because of the relatively short period during which leasing transactions have been carried out, many legal issues regarding lease agreements still need to be clarified (although a body of case law and administrative guidelines regarding leasing have begun to develop recently). As in Germany, lease agreements will either be characterised as rental contracts or instalment sales under the provisions of Austrian civil law (the *Allgemeines Bürgerliches Gezsetzbuch*, or ABGB).

Although a banking licence is not required, any entity (including a permanent establishment of a foreign lessor) carrying on a leasing trade in Austria must acquire a trade permit from, and register with, the Austrian Industrial Trade Authority. In addition, an Austrian-based lessor leasing an aircraft to an operator requires a special licence. Corporation tax is currently set at 34 per cent.

As in Germany, an Austrian lessee or lessor (who is subject to tax in Austria) may claim depreciation allowances only if the lessee or lessor is deemed to be the economic, as opposed to legal, owner of the aircraft. In 1984 the Austrian Department of Finance published guidelines (*Einkommensteuerrichtlinien*, or EStR) on whether the lessor or lessee would be considered the economic owner. These guidelines are updated regularly and set out the Department of Finance's views on the interpretation of the relevant tax provisions. (In certain sale and lease-back transactions, however, both the lessor and lessee are considered to be the economic owner of the leased asset and depreciation benefits are shared.)

If an Austrian lessor or lessee qualifies as the economic owner of the aircraft, the acquisition cost of the aircraft may be written off on a straight-line basis over the period of its expected useful life. This period is not set by statute or regulation but must be determined by the owner, acting reasonably and not arbitrarily. Any deviation from normal or standard depreciation terms for the industry concerned (generally 10 to 12 years in the case of aircraft) should be supportable by evidence, and care must be exercised in this regard because, in the case of full pay-out leases, a lease term of less than 40 or more than 90 per cent of the expected useful life of the aircraft will result in the aircraft being regarded as owned by the lessee for Austrian tax purposes.

In addition to the straight-line depreciation described above, an 'investment allowance' (*Investitionsfreibetrag*) may enable a lessor or lessee (whichever qualifies for depreciation allowances) to deduct 9 per cent of the cost of the aircraft from its taxable income for the year of investment, provided that the aircraft is chiefly used in Austria (this rate is 20 per cent for acquisitions prior to 31 March 1994 and 15 per cent for acquisitions prior to 30 April 1995). An investment allowance is not available where the transaction involves the sale and lease-back of a used asset, however, nor for the purchase of a used asset from an affiliated company (under Section 10 of the Austrian Income Tax Act – the *Einkommensteuergesetz*), nor for aircraft used for passenger transportation (except for aircraft of civil aeronautic schools or air transport enterprises).

Where a sufficient relationship of integration (*Organschaft*) exists, the entire profits/losses of a controlled subsidiary company may be pooled with those of a controlling parent company and taxed in the hands of the parent company. This relationship of integration exists where:

1 it can be said that a company is so dependent upon the will of another resident company that it has no will of its own (ie there must be financial, economic and organisational control by the parent); and
2 an agreement on the pooling of profits and losses has been concluded between the companies.

Financial control normally exists where a parent company owns a majority shareholding in a subsidiary.

In theory, it is not possible without shifting economic ownership for the residual value of a leased asset to be passed back to the lessee in a full payout lease (for example, by way of a nominal purchase option or a rebate of rentals). In a non-full payout lease, however, a lessee may share in the residual value of the asset to a limited extent by receiving not more than 75 per cent of any excess over the outstanding principal arising on a sale.

It is advisable to consult the Austrian revenue authorities regarding 'big-ticket' transactions prior to entering into a lease, because anti-avoidance provisions exist that may affect the accounting treatment of the transaction (although, strictly speaking, no binding tax rulings can be obtained prior to a transaction). Austria, like France, also has an abuse of law concept whereby the authorities may recharacterise a transaction, reassess tax liability and disallow tax benefits where the sole intention of a transaction is tax avoidance.

Outbound leasing

Where an Austrian lessor is considered to be the economic owner of the aircraft (which is deemed to be the case unless the EStR provides otherwise, as described below), that Austrian lessor may claim depreciation allowances as described above and possibly an investment allowance. (However, an investment allowance is not available on the sale and leaseback of a used asset, or where an aircraft is not imported into Austria and is chiefly used abroad.)

Interest on a loan taken by the lessor to fund the acquisition of the asset is tax deductible, as are payments made by the lessor under a head lease.

If an Austrian lessor is regarded as the economic owner of the leased asset, the lease payments will be treated as income of the lessor unless the payments are assigned to a third party (in which case they will be treated as attributable to the latter and not to the lessor). Such an assignment could, however, give rise to another taxable transaction (eg gift tax or stamp duty).

Where the foreign lessee is deemed to be the economic owner, however, part of the payments will be considered as non-taxable purchase price and part as taxable interest, the proportion treated as interest decreasing over the lease period.

If an Austrian lessor leasing to a foreign lessee suffers withholding tax on rental payments, the lessor may be entitled to a tax credit in respect of that foreign tax.

In Austria it is also possible to syndicate any tax benefits available in a leasing transaction by means of a general or limited partnership (OHG, KG or GmbH & Co KG) lessor. Each partner is entitled to claim a tax deduction for an appropriate share of the total depreciation available and the deduction is not necessarily limited to the amount invested by the partners (so leveraged leasing opportunities exist).

Inbound leasing

As already mentioned, to qualify for the depreciation allowances outlined earlier, an Austrian lessee under an inbound lease must be deemed to be the economic owner of the aircraft.

Broadly speaking, according to the EStR, with a full payout lease (*Amortisationsvertrag*) – in other words where the rental payments are calculated in such a way that the lessor will at least recover the cost of the aircraft, and profit as well, over the initial lease period – the lessee will be treated as the economic owner if the term of the lease is less than 40 per cent or more then 90 per cent of the expected useful life of the aircraft or if the lessee has a purchase option for nominal consideration at the end of the lease term, or the right to extend the lease period indefinitely for a less than market rate rent. (The purchase price should be considered nominal for these purposes if it is less than half the value of the asset at the time of the purchase, less straight-line depreciation over the lease period.)

If a lease is not a full payout lease (*Teilamortisationsvertrag*) – ie where the lessor does not recover the cost of the aircraft over the initial lease period – the lessee will be regarded as the economic owner of the asset only if the basic lease period coincides approximately with the expected useful life of the asset or if the lessee carries the risk of appreciation or depreciation of the value of the leased aircraft (for example, if the lessee has to indemnify the lessor against any shortfall between the proceeds of the sale of the aircraft and its outstanding principal at the time of sale, and if the lessee will receive more than 75 per cent of the proceeds of the sale exceeding the outstanding principal).

Finally, a lessee will also be considered the economic owner of the aircraft if that aircraft has been built to the particular specifications of that lessee (*Spezialleasing*) and could only be used commercially by that lessee after the lease has terminated (irrespective of the lease provisions), or where ownership of the aircraft passes automatically to the lessee at the end of the lease period.

If an Austrian lessee is not deemed to be the economic owner of the aircraft the rental payments under the lease should be fully deductible expenses for tax purposes, but where an Austrian lessee is treated as the economic owner, only part of the rental payments would be treated as a deductible expense for Austrian tax purposes (ie that part representing a notional interest cost). If an Austrian lessee does not qualify as economic owner of the aircraft, 50 per cent of lease payments may not be deductible for trade tax purposes, although this disadvantage can be avoided by means of defeasance.

Although the position is somewhat unclear, it is thought that a foreign lessor should not be subject to Austrian tax (including withholding tax) on rental payments or on any purchase price paid on exercise of an option unless the lessor has a permanent establishment in Austria.

Stamp and turnover taxes

Lease contracts are, in principle, subject to a stamp duty payable jointly by lessor and lessee at a rate of one per cent of the contract value which, if the lease is concluded for a specific term, will be the sum of *all* rentals payable. If the lease is concluded for an unlimited time period, however, the contract value will be the rental payments for three years. Careful drafting of the term of the lease can, therefore, reduce the stamp duty burden. In addition, this duty may be avoided altogether where the lease is signed and retained outside Austria (unless the parties are all Austrian) or where the lease contains a purchase option (and the agreement is then considered to be a sale agreement by the Austrian tax authorities).

Turnover tax at a rate of 20 per cent of the cost of the aircraft is payable on import of an aircraft into Austria from non-EU member states (but should be fully recoverable) and on rental payments under leases that are treated as rental contracts for Austrian tax purposes (which is the case for leases where economic ownership of the asset is not passed to the lessee). Austrian VAT (*Bestimmungstandprinzip*) applies to deliveries to an Austrian private person and, where the lessee is deemed to be the owner for tax purposes, the turnover tax base will be the sum of all rentals payable, and tax is charged on delivery of the asset. If a foreign lessor does not have a permanent establishment in Austria or within the EU, an Austrian lessee will be responsible for payment of any turnover tax on behalf of the foreign lessor.

Denmark

Introduction and tax background

According to the Danish Aviation Act, an aircraft can only be admitted to the Registry of Nationality if the owner of the aircraft is Danish. To qualify as 'a Danish owner' certain requirements are laid down in the Aviation Act. The Ministry for Transport may, however, grant an exemption making it possible for an aircraft to be registered in the Registry of Nationality even if the owner is not considered Danish under the law.

Having been granted an exemption, a foreign owner can expect the exemption to be without limitation in time in the case of a finance lease, whereas an exemption will normally expire at the latest on the date of termination of the underlying lease agreement in the case of an operating lease.

Registration of title, mortgage and other rights in respect of aircraft are included in the Registry of Rights. The Registry of Rights is governed by the Registration Act. Only rights with respect to aircraft registered in the Registry of Nationality can be entered into the Registry of Rights. Both finance and operating leases can be registered in the Registry of Rights.

There are no specific laws in Denmark governing leasing companies and leasing transactions, nor are there specific tax or commercial rules applicable to cross-border leasing. Danish exchange control restrictions have been almost entirely abolished and, therefore, no consent is required for cross-border leasing transactions to or from Denmark. No other governmental/banking consents are necessary, though certain transactions must be notified to the banking authorities.

The rate of corporate income tax is currently 34 per cent and the tax is paid on account during the financial year. Companies incorporated prior to 29 January 1992 may, however, if certain conditions are met, opt for a contribution under the old corporate tax system (a 38 per cent tax rate and assessment in November of the following year).

Consolidated taxation is permitted where one company has a 100 per cent interest in another company, either directly or via other companies with which it files a consolidated return. In cases where the subsidiary is established in a foreign country, the Danish company must hold the maximum shareholding permitted by the foreign country.

Advance binding rulings are available from the Danish revenue authorities as to the tax characterisation of particular transactions, including leasing transactions.

Special rules apply to the territories of Greenland and the Faroe Islands.

Outbound leasing

The Danish depreciation rules apply to both operating and finance leases. For a lessor to qualify for depreciation allowances it must be considered to be the legal owner of the asset. In principle, therefore, double dip transactions can be achieved in combination with states where the focus is on economic rather than legal ownership. Net present benefits have tended to be in the region of 4–5 per cent of the asset's cost. In exceptional cases, however, the lessee and not the lessor may be regarded as the legal owner if the lessee has a right to acquire the asset at the end of the lease agreement for no consideration or for a nominal consideration (including a consideration substantially below the market value of the asset). Purchasers under conditional sale agreements will normally be regarded as legal owners. Fixed price put and call options are possible, however, without prejudicing the lessor's entitlement to allowances, provided the exercise price is based on a reputable future valuation.

Tax depreciation need not coincide with the depreciation charge taken through a Danish company's statutory accounts. According to the Danish Depreciation Act, plant and machinery, including aircraft, belonging to a single enterprise are pooled and depreciation tax allowances are taken on a declining-balance basis – ie on the tax written-down value of the pool as a whole. The rate of depreciation may be selected by the taxpayer, but is subject to a maximum of 30 per cent per annum, including the year of acquisition. The place of manufacture, use of the asset and the residence of the other party to a lease are irrelevant to the tax effects for the party recognised as owner of the asset.

Under the Danish tax reform in 1993, special rules were incorporated into the Danish Depreciation Act to the effect that 'companies' are only entitled to depreciate machinery and equipment (including aircraft) that are acquired for leasing purposes, or which have already been leased at the time of acquisition, in the year following the year of acquisition. 'Companies' are defined as public limited companies (plc), private limited companies and other types of companies in which no members are personally liable for the obligations of the company and in which the company's profits are distributed according to the capital invested by the company members.

In order to compensate for the lack of right to depreciate such assets in the year of acquisition, companies may write off 60 per cent of the purchase price of the operating equipment in the income year following the year of acquisition. The tax written-down value after the purchase year is then pooled with other assets and normal depreciation allowances apply.

Individuals and other types of enterprises other than those mentioned above are covered by the general provisions of the Depreciation Act.

A special advance depreciation allowance applies to depreciable equipment having a sale price of more than Dkr700,000. In order for the advance depreciation rules to apply, the person claiming the depreciation allowance must normally have entered into a binding commitment to take delivery of the equipment. Advance depreciation can be enjoyed for a maximum of four years prior to the delivery of the equipment and cannot exceed 30 per cent of the amount by which the purchase price exceeds Dkr700,000, with a maximum of 15 per cent each year. Advance depreciation reduces the purchase price to ascertain the base for conventional tax depreciation. Special advance depreciation rules apply to ships.

In line with the regime described above, companies may at the earliest provide for advance depreciation of machinery and equipment, which is acquired for leasing purposes or which has been leased at the time of conclusion of a binding purchase agreement, in the year following the income year in which the purchase agreement was concluded.

Generally speaking, the characterisation of a lease as an operating or finance lease for accounting purposes does not bear directly on the Danish tax analysis of the transaction. If the lessor is considered legally to own the asset, the whole of the lease rentals will be considered taxable income. If, on the other hand, the lease is regarded as a purchase contract (and therefore the lessee is treated as the owner of the asset), payments under the lease will be treated as part interest and part purchase price consideration.

In a situation where the lessor is considered to be the owner, any interest paid by it to finance the acquisition of the asset for leasing, and any rent payable under a superior lease, will be tax deductible.

The lessor can credit foreign tax to which it is subject on rental income (eg by withholdings in the state of the lessee) against any Danish tax charged on that income.

Special tax rules applicable to individuals limit the advantages of the depreciation rules described if the asset is owned by one or more individuals who do not take an active part in the business.

Inbound leasing

For a Danish lessee, lease rentals are fully deductible, normally on an accruals basis, provided the assets are used for business purposes. Exceptionally, progressive or degressive rentals, or rentals fixed on a non-arm's length basis, may be challenged by the tax authorities. Also other business expenses, including insurance payments, are fully deductible by a Danish lessee. If the lessee is treated as owner, any amounts regarded as interest payable under the lease (eg by analysing the lease as an instalment sale) will be deductible for the lessee.

Despite a general (non-treaty) withholding rate of 30 per cent applicable to Danish source royalties, there is no Danish withholding tax on equipment lease rentals payable by a Danish lessee to a non-resident lessor. Denmark has accepted the OECD's recommendation that income from leasing should be excluded from the definition of royalties.

Also reflecting OECD precedent, the mere leasing of equipment to a Danish lessee will not, of itself, constitute a Danish permanent establishment of a non-resident lessor that could render the lessor subject to tax in Denmark. The position may, of course, be different if the lessor supplies personnel – for example, to operate or manage the equipment – or in some other way establishes a business presence in Denmark.

VAT, customs and stamp duties

Any supply of property in Denmark, either by way of sale or lease, is subject to Danish value-added tax at 25 per cent, this being added to the sale price or the lease rentals. However, VAT applies only to transactions regarded as taking place within Denmark, and liability will depend on the place of the utilisation of the service and the residence of the owners. Therefore, when goods located abroad are sold by a Danish enterprise to a foreign or a Danish enterprise, such a sale will be outside the scope of Danish VAT, even if the Danish or foreign enterprise has been registered for VAT purposes. The place of supply in relation to a lease of tangible movable property is deemed to be where the property is situated during the lease. In any event, no

Danish VAT or customs duties are payable in respect of the sale or leasing of aircraft for commercial purposes (ie the transportation of passengers or goods) and VAT is not added to repair works on aircraft or the supply of aircraft spare parts.

Danish VAT may be payable on the import into Denmark of goods, although again the import of aircraft for commercial purposes will not generally attract import VAT.

Although Danish stamp duty is applicable to leases of certain assets, mainly for private use, no stamp duty is payable in respect of commercial aircraft leases. The exercise of a lease purchase option may, however, attract stamp duty at 0.1 per cent of the option price payable. In practice, stamp duty is avoided on many cross-border lease documents by, for example, executing documents outside Denmark.

France

Introduction and tax background

The aircraft leasing market in France has, traditionally, been relatively narrow, and tends to be limited (although it is not technically required to be so) to equipment with a significant French content – for example, Airbus, SNECMA, Aerospatiale, ATR aircraft and, occasionally, other aircraft with CFM engines. This is mainly because of the dominant and controlling influence of major French banks.

The attraction of the French market is found in the double dip opportunities that exist, particularly in cross-border transactions with Germany and the US, and the possibility of accelerated depreciation without the requirement of a French end-user. The net present value benefit that is generally obtainable is in the range of 6–8 per cent.

Lease terms and rental structures have traditionally been flexible, although some uncertainty has been caused by rumours that the tax authorities may challenge uneven rental profiles. Corporation standard tax rate is currently 33.33 per cent. An additional contribution of 25 per cent, assessed on corporation tax paid, has to be paid by corporations having a turnover higher than Ffr 50,000,000 (with the effective rate of corporation tax being 41.66 per cent). The additional contribution is limited to 10 per cent in relation to corporations having a turnover of less than Ffr 50,000,000.

In principle, claims for depreciation made by the legal owner of an asset are recognised (except in the case of a conditional sale as described below). This means that double dip arrangements may be structured with the lessor as title holder located in France, and the lessee as economic owner situated in another jurisdiction (such as the US, the UK, The Netherlands, Belgium or Germany).

The general principle for depreciation allowances is that assets are depreciated over their 'normal useful life' (which is determined by reference to the current practice in each industry, and is generally between 12 and 15 years for aircraft) on a straight-line basis. However, the French tax authorities do not disallow depreciation allowances taken over a different period, provided the period adopted is based on specific circumstances.

In addition to straight-line depreciation, declining-balance depreciation is available for *new* aircraft (accelerated declining-balance allowances are calculated by multiplying basic straight-line allowances by 2.5 for assets with a normal useful life in excess of six years) and, at the point where the declining-balance allowances fall below the straight-line allowances, the lessor can elect to use the greater allowance. The lessor's depreciation is not limited to that percentage of the cost of the asset for which it is at risk.

In practice, French lessors take the accelerated depreciation available for new aircraft over a period of 12 years (the period of depreciation used by French airlines), which provides a depreciation rate of 20.83 per cent in the first year, although this allowance rapidly decreases (to 16.49 per cent) in the second year (2.512 (100–20.83) per cent).

Effectively, a French lessee can be passed the residual value of the leased aircraft through the exercise of a purchase option under a *crédit-bail* structure without prejudicing the lessor's tax position. (The French lessee is also entitled to remaining depreciation allowances available in relation to the asset on exercise of the purchase option.)

A group of French companies may elect to be consolidated for taxation purposes if the members of the group are connected by direct or indirect ownership links of at least 95 per cent between each company and the ultimate parent company, which itself is not 95 per cent or more owned by another French company.

Finally, it should be noted that the French tax authorities are able to recharacterise a transaction under the *abus de droit* theory, regardless of the nature of the agreement, and to refuse tax benefits for transactions that are not made for bona fide commercial reasons, but for tax avoidance only.

In addition, a draft bill to be examined by the French Parliament in April 1998 proposes to significantly reform the tax regime applicable to GIEs (or other tax transparent entities used for leasing operations). Broadly, unless a derogation is granted by the French Tax Authorities, it is proposed that depreciation allowances relating to leased assets be limited on a yearly basis to the amount of rental payments received reduced by operating expenses. Accordingly, if the proposed bill is adopted, a GIE carrying out a leasing activity would not be in a position to transfer tax losses to its members. However, if a derogation is granted (importance of the transaction and employment matters will be taken into consideration), tax advantages offered by leasing transactions will be greater due to a possible increase in depreciation allowances.

Export credit transactions

Over the past three or four years, aircraft financing in France has been dominated by export credit transactions. French banks such as Crédit Agricole Indosuez, Crédit Lyonnais, Société Générale and Banque Nationale de Paris have secured leading positions in this important market, involving in particular Airbus and ATR aircraft.

The typical 'plain vanilla' export credit financing for an Airbus aircraft involves a *groupement d'intérêt économique* (GIE). A GIE is a cross between a company and a partnership – it has separate legal personality but its profits and losses are imputed directly to its members, who are generally one or more of the banks proposing to finance the relevant transaction. It is necessary for a separate GIE to be constituted for each transaction (which generally, of course, accords with the wishes of the parties anyway).

The GIE will purchase the aircraft, generally direct from Airbus, pursuant to an assignment of the purchase agreement. It will immediately lease the aircraft down to the airline. The GIE will be financed by means of export credit supported loans from French, German and British lenders (or lenders having branches in those countries) and often by a separate 'commercial loan' (generally of 15 per cent of the total purchase price), which does not benefit from the backing of the export credit agencies, COFACE, HERMES or ECGD.

This structure has become much more common than the alternative of an export credit loan direct to the airline, and banks have grown familiar with the use of the GIE, although it is now also quite common to see a Cayman Islands special purpose company used in place of the GIE.

Until recently, the use of a GIE was thought not to pose any significant tax problem; however, in late 1995 and early 1996, two amendments were made to French tax law that threatened the continued viability of GIEs. The first change extended to GIEs the *contribution sociale de solidarités des sociétés* (CSSS), which previously had only applied to companies. The CSSS is a tax levied at the rate of 0.13 per cent on the turnover of the company or GIE; in the structure described above, the turnover broadly equates to the rentals payable by the lessee even though they are matched by an equal loan service obligation. It is hoped that GIEs used in international finance transactions will be permitted to benefit from an exemption applicable to companies only doing business abroad, but at the moment no ruling (or even guidance) has been issued.

The second tax change imposed a further levy in the form of a business licence tax. Business licence tax is at least equal to 0.35 per cent of the value added produced. It is not clear under French tax law if a French GIE leasing aircraft to a foreign lessee under a *crédit-bail* arrangement is exempt from that minimum business licence tax.

The 'plain vanilla' export credit structure is often refined so as to include other advantageous features. In particular, large numbers of aircraft have been financed using a structure blending an export credit with a Japanese leveraged lease. More recently, German tax leases have been combined with export credit structures.

Outbound leasing

Tax-based outbound leasing is almost always structured using a *crédit-bail* – essentially a lease with a purchase option – because the French lessor can continue to qualify for depreciation allowances in France as described earlier, but the existence of a purchase option permits title to be fed down the chain into the second leg of a transaction.

Law no. 66-455 of 2 July 1966 defines a *crédit-bail* as:

> the lease of equipment, goods or tools purchased for the purpose of such leasing by companies that remain the owners thereof, where such transactions, however they are qualified, provide the lessee with an option to purchase all or part of the goods so leased, upon payment of an agreed-upon purchase price that takes into account, at least in part, the rental payments.

If all of these qualifications are not met, an agreement will not be considered as a true *crédit-bail*, but as a mere lease with a purchase option. Ensuring that an agreement will be construed as a *crédit-bail* can give rise to difficult issues. Case law shows that a lease may be recharacterised as a conditional or instalment sale where the economic probability is high that the purchase option will be exercised. Further, an obligation, as opposed to an option, on the part of the lessee to purchase the asset will also destroy the character of the *crédit-bail*. If an agreement is recharacterised, the tax authorities may assert that a part of the rental payments constitute the purchase price which is, therefore, not deductible by a French lessee for tax purposes. Furthermore, the lessor could lose the right to depreciate the asset for tax purposes, and the lessee would not be able to claim the allowances because depreciation would not have been accounted for.

Nevertheless, a fairly low fixed price purchase option in the *crédit-bail* type agreement may allow a French lease to be treated as a hire purchase or equivalent in a large number of other jurisdictions and, therefore, enable the lessee to claim local tax benefits.

As the characterisation of an agreement will be crucial to the transaction, it has in the past been the practice to seek an advance clearance from the French tax authorities to the effect that an agreement would not be recharacterised. However, the authorities are currently proving unwilling to give such advance rulings.

Although there are no specific rules to the effect that a French lessor's right to depreciate a leased asset is dependent upon particular provisions being included (or not included) in the lease agreement, it is important to ensure that the normal attributes of ownership in respect of the aircraft (such as rights of inspection) are not whittled away. Otherwise there may be a risk that the lease agreement would be recharacterised as a conditional or instalment sale by the French tax authorities with the results outlined above.

If foreign withholding tax is charged on rental payments, a French lessor may be entitled to a credit against French corporation tax. However, the French tax authorities consider that the tax credit may only be offset against corporation tax due on profits of the leasing operation. As a lease often generates tax losses in the lessor's accounts during the early years of the lease period (because of the declining-balance depreciation allowances claimed), the lessor often has no tax capacity to use and the foreign tax credits are lost. Lessors are entitled to deduct interest incurred in financing the aircraft purchase.

In principle, any gain or loss arising on sale of the leased asset is subject to French standard corporation tax.

Crédit-bail activities (and indeed any leasing transactions with a purchase option) can only be carried out on a regular basis by recognised financial institutions *(établissements de crédit)* registered as such with the French banking authorities under the French Banking Act of 24 January 1984. Registration places leasing companies under the general supervision of the banking authorities and requirements as to capital adequacy (minimum capital of Ffr15 million for a *société anonyme* or *société à responsabilité limitée*), compulsory reserves, etc. This can increase operating costs and, to some extent, impair management flexibility. As registration is only necessary when a lessor regularly carries out *crédit-bail* activities, leasing companies are frequently single purpose entities, often a GIE (in order to benefit also from the favourable capital gains tax treatment outlined above) or a French partnership, a *société en nom collectif* (SNC). If *crédit-bail* activities are carried out regularly by a leasing company not registered as a financial institution, the *crédit-bail* agreements would be deemed to be void.

Inbound leasing

In order to benefit from French rules on depreciation for inbound leasing transactions, subject to one exception (the conditional sale) the lessee has to be regarded as the holder of legal title from the outset of the agreement. Therefore, the agreement has to be capable of construction in France either as a *vente à temperament* (an instalment sale where title passes immediately to the lessee) or as a *vente conditionnelle avec réservation de propriété*, which is a conditional sale where title only passes when the last instalment is paid. These types of agreement may give some scope for double dips with other jurisdictions where the lessor may still be considered to be the 'economic owner' or where the retention of legal title is sufficient.

For French law purposes, the first rule of construction is that a document is construed in accordance with its description. The agreement should not, therefore, be described as a lease if the French lessee wishes to claim depreciation allowances. Furthermore, in the case of a conditional sale, it should be possible to demonstrate that there will be an automatic transfer of title to the lessee at the end of the term of the agreement.

Where a French lessee pays rental payments to a foreign lessor, withholding tax may be incurred at a rate of 33.33 per cent on payments made for services supplied in France. This withholding is eliminated to the extent that the aircraft is operated on international routes, but tax will be withheld to the extent that the aircraft is used for domestic flights. Alternatively, France's double tax treaties may reduce the rate of withholding tax (in many cases to zero).

If an agreement is construed as an instalment or conditional sale agreement rather than as a lease, payments made under the agreement will be characterised as part payments of the purchase price and part interest on the deferred purchase consideration. Withholding tax at a rate of 15 per cent is prima facie applicable to interest paid under an instalment or conditional sale agreement, but again this may be reduced or eliminated under a double tax treaty.

A French lessee is entitled to deduct the rentals charged (whether or not assigned to a financing party under a leveraged lease), unless the agreement is considered by the French tax authorities to be a sale.

TVA, *taxe professionelle* and turnover tax

Broadly, French TVA *(taxe sur la valeur ajoutée)* at a rate of 20.6 per cent is assessable on rentals payable for aircraft to be used within the EU if the lessor is established in France for VAT purposes, or where the aircraft is used in France (or French overseas territories) and the lessor is established outside the EU (although the leasing of aircraft operated by airlines having at least 80 per cent of flights on international routes is TVA-exempt in all cases).

The acquisition in France of an aircraft brought into France will also be subject to TVA unless the airline operates chiefly (at least 80 per cent of its flights) on international routes, in which case the purchase is TVA-exempt. In addition, imports from non-EU member states may be subject to customs duties.

Taxe professionelle (or 'business licence tax') is a local tax assessed on the salaries paid and assets owned by a taxpayer carrying on a business activity (for leased assets the relevant taxpayer is considered to be the lessee, unless the lessee is exempt, in which case the assets must be included in the lessor's business licence tax base). The rate of business licence tax varies according to the taxpayer's municipality (and is typically between 11 and 20 per cent) and is assessed either on rental payments or on 16 per cent of the purchase price depending on the form of the lease (a lease without an option to purchase or *crédit-bail*). When turnover exceeds Ffr50 million, business licence tax may not, in any cases, be lower than 0.35 per cent of the value-added tax produced. There is an exemption, however, where a *crédit-bail* structure is used (as long as the agreement satisfies all the conditions of a true *crédit-bail*). The question as to whether business licence tax is applicable to assets leased abroad (other than under a *crédit-bail*) has not yet been finally determined.

Turnover tax is payable by French entities (including GIEs) with turnover in excess of Ffr5 million. The tax rate is 0.13 per cent of turnover.

Germany

Introduction and tax background

The number of leasing transactions in Germany has grown rapidly. The potential market is substantial, mainly because of the largely unused tax capacity available in Germany. Because the German tax rates for individuals are higher than those for German companies, German cross-border leveraged leases normally involve investment by German individuals who become a limited partner in a German (tax transparent) limited partnership (GmbH & Co KG, GmbH & Still). Such partnership interests are 'publicly' placed by banks or financial advisers on the basis of a more or less standardised offering prospectus.

The minimum investment by a limited partner will normally range between DM50,000 and DM100,000. As a result, a partnership may have 1,000 or more partners. On the other hand,

German companies have been reluctant to participate in cross-border leasing transactions (other than for the purpose of export financing of German equipment). Normally, the German limited partnership insists that the relevant agreements are governed by German law; this is not required by German (tax) law but is rather seen as assisting in marketing the partnership interests.

In the context of the discussions on German income tax reform (which are likely to occur after the next general election in autumn 1998), the use of German tax capacity in German leveraged leases (in particular for ships and aircraft) has been much criticised and in the future these taxation benefits may cease to be available. As is the case in France, the market tends to be almost exclusively limited to equipment with a significant German content (ie largely transactions involving Airbus aircraft), although there is no technical requirement that this be the case.

There is no specific body of German law dealing with lease arrangements, which are consequently characterised as a mix of contracts and instalment sales under the provisions of the German Civil Code.

Corporation tax in Germany is currently set at 45 per cent for undistributed profits and 30 per cent for distributed profits. In addition, German local trade taxes are levied at 15–20 per cent, depending on the municipality of the taxpayer (see further below). German individuals are subject to progressive income tax with a top marginal rate of 53 per cent. In addition, German companies and German private investors are subject to a so-called solidarity surcharge (*Solidaritätszuschlag*, raised to finance German reunification) at a rate of 5.5 per cent levied on the tax payable. Therefore, the effective surcharge (as a percentage of taxable income) for German companies ranges between 2.35 per cent (distributed earnings taking into account that the surcharge is not deductible for corporation tax purposes) and 2.475 per cent (retained earnings), while German individuals may face an additional tax burden of up to 2.92 per cent (at the highest marginal rate of 53 per cent).

The potential tax benefits available in Germany result from the fact that aircraft are, in general, depreciated over a tax useful life of 12 to 14 years, either on a straight-line basis or, alternatively, on a declining-balance basis using the lower of 30 per cent or 3 times the straight-line rate. Thus, in the case of an aircraft with a tax useful life of 12 years, a maximum annual writing-down rate of 25 per cent is available. In addition, it is possible to switch from the declining-balance to the straight-line method of depreciation, but not vice versa.

Depreciation allowances are based on the economic, and not legal, ownership of the aircraft. Economic ownership is defined in the German Tax Code (*Abgabenordnung*) as the situation where a person has the exclusive use of the asset for its normal useful life in such a way that the holder of legal title is excluded from using the asset, and the German Federal Ministry of Finance has issued guidelines on the practical aspects of this (discussed further below).

As is the case in Austria, resident companies may file consolidated returns if a sufficient relationship of integration exists (*Organschaft*). However, few company transactions have used such an *Organschaft* for corporation tax purposes because the parent company must assume unlimited liability in relation to the subsidiary activities. In addition, a subsidiary company in any *Organschaft* will not be off-balance sheet in the consolidated accounts of the German parent company. Both the limitation of liability and the off-balance sheet treatment can be achieved by using a German limited partnership, which is 'transparent' for the purposes of German corporation tax.

German double dips have, in the past, been completed with a German tax lessor claiming allowances under a Japanese lease, under a French *crédit-bail*, and sometimes with an operating lease on to a French or other third country user. Net present value benefits have tended to be in the range of 6–9 per cent of the cost of the leased asset, although generalisations are difficult given the relatively small cross-border market.

There is currently some concern in the Franco-German leasing market that the respective tax authorities may try to reduce the level of double dipping activity, even where this has been used to support Airbus transactions. In addition, the German and the Japanese tax authorities are currently in discussions about a common approach in relation to the requirements for the claiming of capital allowances. Furthermore, the German tax authorities will almost certainly look to ascertain where economic ownership truly resides in order to decide whether depreciation claims in Germany are justified.

Although (unlike in France) leasing in Germany is not covered by stringent banking regulations and no banking licence is required for a leasing company, France has tended to be more active than Germany in the cross-border market because of the complex nature of much of the relevant German law and its application in practice (particularly in relation to determining economic ownership). No exchange controls currently apply in Germany, but some reporting requirements do exist (for statistical purposes only).

Outbound leasing

Attractive cost benefits may be available if an aircraft is financed by means of a German leveraged lease and the German lessor is able to claim depreciation allowances. Typically, a German lessor (structured as a partnership) will purchase the aircraft from the airline (or take an assignment of the airline's right to purchase the aircraft from the manufacturer) and the parties will make equity contributions of between 20 per cent and 50 per cent of the acquisition cost (in order to reduce the impact of German tax restrictions on the amount of tax depreciation claimed and on the application of corresponding tax losses). The balance of the acquisition cost may be raised by a non-recourse sale of the lease receivables by the German lessor (a loan for more than 12 months would subject the German lessor to the 50 per cent restriction on the deductibility of interest for trade tax purposes).

In principle, the place of use of a leased asset and place of residence or incorporation of the lessee are irrelevant to the tax treatment of a German lessor although, as mentioned above, the German leasing market in practice tends to be limited to equipment largely manufactured in Germany or with a significant German content.

For the German lessor to be able to claim depreciation on an aircraft as the economic owner of that aircraft, the lease should have a term of not less than 40 per cent nor more than 90 per cent of the tax useful life of the aircraft. Broadly speaking, the overall effect of the lease must be to generate a pre-tax profit for the German lessor (because otherwise the leasing activity could be regarded as a 'hobby' which would have the result that the investors would not be able to claim the taxation benefits resulting from the losses of the partnership) and also to avoid the lessee being treated as economic owner under the rules outlined below. In particular, a German lessor would be treated as economic owner of the aircraft if any of the following conditions are satisfied:

- there is a full payout lease containing a purchase option in favour of the lessee for either the market value of the aircraft or not less than the tax written-down book value (determined on a straight-line basis) at the time the option is exercised; or
- there is a non-full payout lease containing a fixed price put option in favour of the lessor but no corresponding purchase option in favour of the lessee (a first right of refusal in the event that the lessor does not exercise the put option may be possible, however); or
- there is a non-full payout lease providing for the lessor to receive at least 25 per cent of any excess by which the market value of the aircraft exceeds the lessor's unamortised cost of

acquisition (even if the excess amount is derived from sales proceeds following a sale to the lessee) and which provides for the lessee to pay the difference between the unamortised cost and the sales proceeds if no excess amount is generated.

In theory, it is not possible for the residual value of a leased asset to be passed back to the lessee in a full payout lease – for example, by means of a nominal purchase option or a rebate of rentals. This follows from the general rule that tax depreciation benefits are available only to a lessor who can be regarded as the economic owner of the asset. A lessee option to extend the lease for a nominal rental secondary period would also potentially defeat the lessor's claim to tax benefits.

Investment by equity investors may be syndicated by means of a limited or general partnership (KG or GmbH & Co KG, or OHG) so that each of the partners may claim tax deductible depreciation allowances for the aircraft in proportion to the amount of their equity investment at risk (provided, of course, that the partnership/lessor is treated as having economic ownership of the aircraft).

As in Austria, trade tax may represent a significant cost for German leasing companies because 50 per cent of the interest on long-term loans is added back to calculate the taxable trade income. Trade tax is then charged on the increased income. The corresponding disadvantages in relation to German trade tax on capital are no longer in effect, since trade tax on capital was abolished in 1997. Consequently, German leasing companies (like their Austrian counterparts) avoid using long-term loans to finance assets by arranging a non-recourse sale of the lease receivables. The deferred income thus realised is not treated as a long-term liability.

If a German lessor suffers foreign withholding tax on rentals received, a credit against German tax (if any) should, in principle, be available.

Inbound leasing

As mentioned earlier, a German lessee wishing to claim depreciation on an aircraft must establish economic ownership of that aircraft and is generally likely to be treated as the economic owner of the aircraft if either the lessee has the benefit of a bargain purchase option or the option to extend the lease period indefinitely at a lower than market rate rental, or if the term of the lease exceeds 90 per cent of the useful life of the asset for German tax purposes. Depending on the type of aircraft, this generally means a period of 12 or 14 years. Where an aircraft is adapted according to the special requirements of the lessee, and on expiration of the lease term can only be economically used by the lessee, the lessee will also be considered the economic owner.

More particularly, a German lessee seeking to claim depreciation will broadly be considered the economic owner of the aircraft in the following circumstances:

- where the agreement is a full payout lease (where the lease payments during the initial lease term are at least equal to the lessor's total costs) with an initial lease period that exceeds the expected useful life of the aircraft and which contains a fixed price purchase option in favour of the lessee at the end of the initial lease term; or
- where there is a full payout lease with a basic lease period of less than 40 per cent or more than 90 per cent of the expected useful life of the aircraft; or
- where there is a full payout lease with a basic lease period of between 40 per cent and 90 per cent of the expected useful life of the aircraft and which has a purchase option in favour of the lessee for a consideration lower than both the market value and the written-down book value (determined on a straight-line basis) at the time of sale; or

- where there is a non-full payout lease with a basic lease period of between 40 per cent and 90 per cent of the expected useful life of the aircraft and which provides for the lessee to receive in excess of 75 per cent of any amount by which the market value of the aircraft exceeds the unamortised cost of acquisition to the lessor (even if such excess amount is derived from proceeds following a sale to the lessee).

German trade tax on income (*Gewerbeertragsteuer*), which is usually levied at a rate of 15–20 per cent depending on the lessee's municipality, may be a significant issue for a German lessee under a cross-border lease if the lessee does not qualify as economic owner of the aircraft, because 50 per cent of each lease payment would not be deductible for German trade tax on income purposes. It is commonly believed that a defeasance of the lessee's obligations will not be a solution to this German lessee trade tax problem. (If an agreement is not considered a true lease but rather a conditional sale agreement, payments may be partly recharacterised as interest and, to the extent so recharacterised, will be 50 per cent non-deductible.) But whether a defeasance of the lessee's obligations under such a conditional sale agreement would further reduce the German trade tax charge is likely to be contested by the German tax authorities.) Recent case law indicates that this may violate European law because such trade tax would not arise in principle where the lessor is resident in Germany.

To reduce or avoid the lessee's German trade tax problem, a foreign lessor could consider setting up a German subsidiary as the 'direct' lessor, which would either become the economic owner of the equipment under a conditional sale agreement or would act as sub-lessor. Such a structure could be tax efficient if the foreign lessor was able to use the German taxes payable by the German intermediary company as a tax credit. On the other hand, it may be possible to 'purchase' the German trade tax loss carry forward of a third party to reduce the liability.

A foreign lessor should not be liable to German corporation tax on lease payments under an inbound lease unless that foreign lessor has a permanent establishment or permanent representative in Germany which was involved in setting up the lease. Furthermore, if the lessee is treated as the economic owner of the asset, the agreement will be recharacterised as a conditional sale agreement under German law, in which case there should be no withholding tax on payments made to the foreign lessor as such payments would be treated as part purchase price and part interest (interest is not generally subject to withholding tax in Germany). Under a true lease, however, there may be a 25 per cent withholding tax on rental payments (treated as royalties) unless relief is available under a double tax treaty between Germany and the jurisdiction of the foreign lessor.

VAT (*Umsatzsteuer*)

Leases of aircraft that qualify as conditional sale agreements may only fall within the scope of German VAT if the aircraft are delivered in Germany. Leases of aircraft that qualify as rental contracts (true leases) may fall within the scope of German VAT depending upon the residence of the lessor and lessee. However, where the transaction falls within the scope of German VAT, an exemption is (broadly speaking) available in respect of the leasing or sale of aircraft where the aircraft is to be used by an airline chiefly operating on international routes, regardless of whether such routes are to, from or within the EU. If a lessee airline is resident outside Germany it is presumed to be operating on international routes. An official list is kept of German airlines that are considered to operate chiefly on international routes for German VAT purposes. If however the lessee operates any one aircraft or other means of transportation which is specifically designed to transport ill or injured persons, the exemption from German VAT will not be available.

Italy

Introduction and tax background

In the absence of specific legislation regarding leasing an interpretative framework has developed in the last few years having regard to the rules of international conventions, the practice of Italian tax or administrative authorities and by the courts' interpretation of the provisions of the Civil Code relating to contractual law as applied to leasing. In addition, Italy has ratified and is a party to the Unidroit Convention (Ottawa, May 1996) for International Finance Leasing.

In this context the more specific definitions of leasing can be traced to tax legislation and the courts' decisions, which substantially have the follwing effect:

A lease agreement will qualify as a finance lease (*locazione finanziaria*) where an asset is leased for a specified period of time and, on termination, an option to purchase the asset at a predetermined price is granted to the lessee. If the purchase option is not exercised, the lessee may either return the asset to the lessor or enter into a new lease (generally for lower rental payments based on the value of the asset at that time or on the predetermined value in the original lease). In addition, the lessee should bear the risk in relation to the asset in order for the lease to qualify as a *locazione finanziaria*.

This definition has at least served to identify the type of leasing contract to which certain Italian depreciation rules can be applied by the holder of legal title to the asset, and under which rentals may constitute a deductible cost for the lessee.

Under Italian tax law the legal owner of a leased asset (usually the lessor) has the right to depreciate the asset on a straight-line basis (until the exercise of any purchase option) over the term of the lease. If a purchase option exists, the base cost of the aircraft to be depreciated is equal to the purchase price less the purchase option price payable by the lessee at the expiry of the lease term. The standard depreciation rate for aircraft is 14 per cent per annum, but depreciation may be accelerated where the lease term is shorter than the depreciation period fixed for the asset by the relevant Ministerial Decree.

The residual value of a leased aircraft may be passed to an Italian lessee through the exercise of a purchase option without prejudicing the lessor's tax position.

Traditionally, leasing activities in Italy have been tax-driven, but the tax authorities have reduced the tax advantages to be derived from leasing transactions (by means of a requirement that the duration of a *locazione finanziaria* must be at least equal to 50 per cent of the ordinary depreciation period fixed by law for the relevant asset) and general uncertainty has made leasing companies more cautious. Furthermore, until recently the tax authorities treated sale–leaseback structures as loans by the lessor in favour of the lessee. The tax authorities indicated that a sale–leaseback agreement could not be regarded as a leasing transaction and fraud was alleged against those leasing companies that had already completed such transactions because they had taken depreciation allowances. However, the tax authorities have relented slightly, permitting a 'technical' leaseback in respect of new assets. In particular, arrangements have been allowed by the courts under which an Italian enterprise purchases an asset abroad and sells it to a leasing company, and then receives the asset back under a leasing arrangement. Although Italy's tax laws do not yet contain any general anti-avoidance provisions, efforts are being made by both the Italian tax authorities and parliament to make the legislative framework more stringent.

Finance leasing is nevertheless still carried out in Italy, and two different views have been taken by the courts as to the applicable provisions of Italian law:

1 that a *locazione finanziaria* agreement is subject to the rules governing instalment sales with reservation of title; and
2 that a leasing agreement is an atypical contract with characteristics different from those of any other contract expressly provided for by Italian law.

Despite this confusion, domestic leasing has developed in Italy – mostly because of the favourable tax rules applicable to the deduction of rental payments due under leasing contracts. Italian leasing companies have not been active in the cross-border market, however, at least partly due to uncertainties about the lessor's tax position and because of general fiscal and legal constraints. Instead, Italian leasing companies have tended to develop international business by moving into the jurisdiction required and using the laws of that jurisdiction. The availability of state subsidies for certain domestic leasing transactions (eg in the Mezzogiorno region) has also made cross-border leasing less attractive than domestic leasing. Nevertheless, some activity is evident and typical cross-border structures tend to comprise a three- to five-year lease term, semi-annual rentals in arrears, a purchase option and a 15 per cent down payment.

There are currently no Italian exchange control restrictions or consents required for leasing transactions with Italy. Law 197/1991 which, *inter alia*, regulates finance companies including leasing companies, has fixed minimum capital requirements for leasing companies of L1 billion and has given the Bank of Italy the power to control leasing companies.

Italian income tax law contains no special provisions with regard to groups of companies. Each legal entity, even when it is a member of a group, is regarded as a separate taxpayer.

Outbound leasing

The holder of legal title to a leased asset has the right to depreciate the asset on a straight-line basis until the exercise of the purchase option by the lessee at the expiry of the lease (as long as the agreement is not recharacterised as an instalment or conditional sale by the Italian tax authorities).

As outlined above, for depreciation purposes, where a purchase option exists, the base cost of the aircraft to be depreciated is equal to the purchase price less the option price payable by the lessee at the expiry of the lease term. If the lease term is less than the average economic life of the aircraft as calculated on the basis of its standard tax depreciation rate (ie 14 per cent per annum for aircraft), the lessor is allowed to depreciate the aircraft at an effective rate higher than that standard rate by depreciating the aircraft in equal instalments over the term of the lease. Double dip structures could be feasible with jurisdictions that grant tax allowances on the basis of the economic ownership of an asset, because the above treatment applies irrespective of the treatment in a non-Italian lessee's jurisdiction or the place of physical use of the asset.

Interest paid on a loan to finance the purchase of the aircraft is deductible in the same proportion as the ratio between the taxable income and total income of the Italian lessor. The lessor may also claim a tax credit for taxes paid abroad in respect of the rental payments on a basis corresponding to the ratio between the foreign income and the lessor's total income.

The new interpretation permitting a 'technical' leaseback seems certain to increase the number of outbound transactions.

Inbound leasing

As mentioned earlier, only the legal owner of an aircraft is entitled to depreciation allowances in Italy. Although as with a number of other countries (eg France and Spain), an inbound agreement could, in theory, be structured as a conditional sale or instalment sale, enabling an Italian lessee to claim depreciation on entering into the agreement (but also allowing the foreign lessor in a suitable jurisdiction to claim tax allowances), there is considerable uncertainty as to how to ensure that an agreement is treated in this way.

An Italian resident lessee is, however, entitled to deduct lease rentals due throughout the lease term, provided that the term of the lease is not less than one-half of the period over which the asset would be depreciated on a straight-line basis at the standard depreciation rate fixed by Ministerial Decree. Therefore, full deduction of lease rentals by a lessee is allowed with respect to aircraft if the term of the lease is not less than three years and seven months. In addition, on exercise of a purchase option, the lessee will be entitled to depreciate the aircraft on a straight-line basis at the standard depreciation rate (ie 14 per cent per annum for aircraft). The basis for this depreciation will be the purchase option price.

Lease rentals paid by an Italian resident lessee to a foreign resident lessor are treated as Italian source income if the leased aircraft is chiefly located and/or used in Italy – in other words, broadly speaking, not chiefly used on international routes. However, although there has been some uncertainty in the past about the withholding tax position, it now seems clear that for Italian domestic law purposes lease rentals are not subject to withholding tax. Nevertheless, rental payments may be subject to ordinary income taxation at the corporate income tax (IRPEG) rate of 37 per cent and IRAP at the rate of 4.5 per cent if the leased asset is chiefly used/located in Italy (subject to any applicable treaty reliefs).

Finally, it should be noted that after a foreign leasing company has carried out two or three inbound transactions it may be regarded as having acquired a permanent establishment in Italy. It would then have to comply with Italian accounting and other administrative procedures.

VAT, customs duties and stamp tax

VAT (at the standard rate of 20 per cent) is payable on rental payments if the lessor is a non-EU resident and the aircraft is used in Italy, or if the lessee is non-EU resident and the aircraft is used in the European Union. VAT is not payable where the aircraft is used by an airline operating chiefly in international traffic.

Customs duties may be levied on the import of aircraft under leases, except where the aircraft is produced or operated within the EU.

Lease contracts are subject to a stamp tax of L20,000 per sheet (four pages), or 100 lines, and a registration tax of L250,000. All transactions concerning Italian aircraft must be recorded in the National Aircraft Register.

Spain

Introduction and tax background

Leasing activity in Spain has increased steadily in the past three years, after being severely affected by the recession in 1991–93. In 1995, new investments in the Spanish leasing industry totalled Pta612.5 billion, compared with Pta559.4 billion invested in 1994. Profits for 1995 totalled Pta10 billion, compared with Pta2.4 billion for 1994.

As from 1 January 1994, Law 3/1994 (which implemented the Second Banking Directive) characterises a leasing company as a financial credit institution (*establecimiento financiero de crédito*) and not as a credit entity. However, Royal Decree Law 12/95 and subsequently Royal Decree 692/1996 have recharacterised the *establicimientos financiero de crédito* as credit institutions. Leasing companies are therefore subject to the regulatory authority (including registration) of the Bank of Spain. In addition a 1993 circular subjected leasing companies to the solvency ratio rules applied to credit institutions. A leasing company must have a minimum share capital of Pta850 million.

Law 26/1988 defines a contract termed an *arrendamiento financiero* as:

> a contract whose exclusive purpose is the assignment of the use of goods or assets acquired by the lessor for that purpose according to the lessee's specifications in exchange for rentals set out in the contract. The *arrendamiento financiero* contract must give the lessee a purchase option on the leased assets exercisable at the end of the leasing period. If the lessee does not exercise the purchase option, which is unlikely, the lessor may lease the asset to another lessee without fulfilling the lessee's specifications.

As a general requirement of Spanish law, a contract to lease an aircraft must have a minimum duration of two years, but successive leases of the same asset are possible if a lessee does not exercise any purchase option.

Only Spanish finance leasing companies whose articles of association state that the company's exclusive object is finance leasing business, and, since 1 January 1990, official credit entities and banks (as well as Spanish branches of any foreign entities of this type) may carry on finance leasing business in Spain. All these entities must be authorised by the Ministry of Economy and registered in a special register of the Bank of Spain.

Corporation tax is currently set at a rate of 35 per cent. Like France and Italy, Spain is a 'legal title' country for tax depreciation purposes. Consequently, a Spanish lessee under a finance lease governed by Law 26/1988 and Law 43/1995 is not able to claim depreciation on the leased equipment until it has exercised an option to purchase. Depreciation can only be claimed eventually by the lessee on the residual value of the aircraft by reference to which the purchase option has been exercised.

Depreciation allowances can be claimed on either a straight-line basis or on an accelerated basis, but it is not possible to change from one basis to another. The straight-line depreciation rate differs depending on the type of aircraft. The relevant factors that determine the rate are primarily whether it is a long-, medium- or short-range aircraft and, secondly (applicable only on medium-range aircraft), whether or not the aircraft has a jet engine. The rate ranges between 10 per cent and 15 per cent and the maximum number of years' depreciation ranges between 14 and 20 years. The accelerated depreciation rate is obtained through the *suma de digitos* (or 'rule of 78') system by reference to the cost of the asset and a period of years determined by official guidelines.

As is the case with a *crédit-bail* in France, a Spanish lessee can effectively be passed the residual value of the leased aircraft through the exercise of a purchase option without prejudicing the lessor's tax position.

A group for tax consolidation purposes consists of a controlling corporation and one or more dependent corporations. A controlling corporation must be a Spanish resident entity that owns, either directly or indirectly, more than 90 per cent of the dependent corporation(s) for a minimum period of one year prior to seeking permission to consolidate. Any losses incurred by a company prior to consolidation can only be offset against that company's profits.

Outbound leasing

Under a finance lease governed by Law 26/1988 and Law 43/1995, a Spanish lessor (having legal title to the asset) may claim depreciation. Finance lease companies should depreciate the cost of the equipment, less its residual value, during the term of the lease, which should not be less than two years. Depreciation can be claimed on a straight-line basis or, on an accelerated basis (at the lessor's choice). The rates of depreciation, both on a straight-line and an accelerated basis, are described above. It is not possible to switch from one method to the other.

If the lease agreement is structured appropriately, opportunities for double dips may exist with 'economic title' countries such as Germany, Austria and the UK.

The interest payable by a Spanish lessor under a loan taken in order to finance the purchase of an aircraft is entirely tax deductible.

Inbound leasing

For the lessee to be able to claim tax depreciation in Spain from the beginning of the lease, the document must be capable of construction for Spanish tax purposes as an instalment or conditional sale agreement. A number of aircraft leases to Spanish lessees have been structured in this way. It is not at present absolutely certain whether a non-resident lessor, not itself holding title to an aircraft (eg in a 'multi-tier' transaction), would be recognised as a conditional seller for Spanish law purposes.

Payments made under a lease governed by Law 26/1988 and Law 43/1995 are treated, with certain limitations, as a deductible expense for a Spanish lessee provided that the rental payments are specified in the lease, distinguishing in respect of each payment:

1 the lessor's recovery of the cost of the aircraft (less the option price); and
2 the finance charge.

For Spanish tax purposes, the finance charge is always fully deductible. Payments made under a conditional or instalment sale are not fully deductible. Only the annual depreciation plus the interest element paid are considered tax deductible under Spanish law.

In the case of a dry lease (a *casco desnudo*), rental payments from a Spanish resident lessee to a non-Spanish resident lessor are exempt from withholding tax, provided the lessor does not have a permanent establishment in Spain and the leased aircraft is used on international air routes. However, in the case of a wet lease, withholding tax at a rate of 25 per cent will apply, subject to relief under any applicable double tax treaty. If an agreement is structured to be a conditional or instalment sale, the payments may be treated as interest and should not be subject to withholding tax.

VAT

The structure and scope of Spanish VAT are similar to those of the other EU member states. Broadly speaking, goods and services (including leasing) are generally taxable in Spain if deemed to be supplied in Spain – in other words, if the goods are located in Spain when sold, or the supplier of services has its place of business in Spain. Therefore, where a supply is made by a non-resident to a Spanish resident, the supply is not subject to VAT in Spain. On the other hand, if the Spanish lessee exercises an option to purchase the aircraft, then the exercise of the option will be subject to VAT. An exemption is, however, available if the buyer is an airline operating chiefly on international routes transporting freight and passengers on a commercial basis.

Spanish VAT (at the standard rate of 16 per cent) is chargeable on rentals charged by a Spanish lessor to Spanish and non-Spanish resident lessees. An exemption is, however, available to a lessee which is an airline operating chiefly on international routes transporting freight and passengers on a commercial basis.

Sweden

Introduction and tax background

Since the beginning of 1990 the Swedish market has undergone considerable changes owing, inter alia, to the Swedish tax authorities' challenge to particular transactions and a review of the KB (*Kommanditbolag*) investor structure. The KB is a limited partnership vehicle established to bring together the equity investors in an asset.

The unrest in the market, together with a lack of tax capacity, severely limited the availability of equity investors and, coupled with the reduction in corporate income tax rates (now at 28 per cent), substantially reduced the attractiveness of Sweden as a source of tax-based finance for some time. However there is now a renewed and growing interest in tax-based leasing in Sweden.

Two of the challenged transactions relate to aircraft leasing, and the objections raised by the tax authorities can be summarised as follows:

1 The assets had not been duly delivered from a tax point of view.
2 If the assets had been duly delivered from a tax point of view, the transactions should nevertheless be deemed to be a credit sale and not a leasing transaction.
3 The depreciation provisions were not applicable due to the fact that the lessor did not suffer any financial risk.
4 The so-called anti-tax avoidance clause was applicable to the transactions in question.

The tax authorities' objections have not been accepted by the administrative court of appeal and the cases are now pending before the Supreme Administrative Court.

In another case a sale–leaseback transaction was questioned. The objection raised in that case was whether the purchaser/lessor acquired ownership for tax purposes if the asset was not delivered. Because, arguably, no delivery has taken place, the lessor is for tax purposes not deemed to be the owner and so depreciation allowances are not available.

In Sweden, profits or losses for tax purposes can be reallocated within an affiliated group via group contributions. The payer can deduct any paid group contribution and the recipient will include the contribution in its taxable income. In order to qualify as an affiliated group for these purposes, the parent must, throughout the whole fiscal year, hold more than 90 per cent of the shares in the relevant subsidiary companies. (There are also certain other criteria to be met.)

Outbound leasing

A key issue that arises in relation to a Swedish outbound cross-border lease is the lessor's entitlement to benefit from tax depreciation. The following must be considered:

• The lessor must acquire and retain ownership in accordance with Swedish tax law. It is necessary to conclude, on consideration of the lease and having regard to all the circumstances, that the agreement does not amount to a sale to the lessee.

- The fact that a foreign lessee obtains depreciation tax benefits in relation to the asset according to the domestic laws of its own jurisdiction does not have any impact on the Swedish lessor's right to deduct depreciation allowances in respect of the asset. However, it may be appropriate for a Swedish lessor to ascertain on what basis the foreign lessee intends to depreciate the assets, particularly if it is possible that the foreign lessee will treat the asset as though it has been purchased and is consequently owned by the lessee. This is because the right to deduct depreciation allowances in Sweden depends, to some extent, on the original intention of the contracting parties, specifically as to whether the lessee should become owner of the asset on termination of the lease. The place of manufacture and use of the asset is irrelevant to the Swedish lessor's tax position.
- To qualify for Swedish allowances the leased asset must be recorded as an asset in the lessor's balance sheet.
- The lessee may have an option to purchase but it must not be a 'bargain option'; in other words, the option should not be for a purely nominal price but must reflect the market value of the asset. This can be fixed at the outset. If the purchase option is not exercised, the lessor may have rights to require an extension of the lease.
- If the option payment obligations of the lessee are funded by a defeasance arrangement, the transaction might be viewed as a conditional sale and the lessee, not the lessor, might be considered to be the owner of the asset and consequently the lessor will not qualify for Swedish depreciation allowances.

There are two methods for calculating tax depreciation allowances in Sweden:

1 the common method is depreciation as recorded in the company's books, but subject to limits based on 20 per cent straight-line and 30 per cent declining-balance depreciation: a full-year's depreciation allowances may be taken regardless of the time of acquisition during the company's fiscal year; or
2 residual value depreciation, based on depreciation of up to 25 per cent of the asset's residual value for tax purposes.

Lease agreements normally have terms of 10 to 15 years. Most of the cross-border leases completed to date have involved defeasance agreements.

Interest payable by the lessor to finance the acquisition of an asset is deductible from its income for tax purposes.

Lease rentals are, in principle, fully taxable in the hands of a Swedish lessor. However, 'structured' rental profiles will not generally be acceptable to the Swedish tax authorities who may require the rentals to be spread evenly over the term of the lease.

Inbound leasing

If the lease is regarded as an instalment sale to the Swedish 'lessee', payments under the contract will be deductible only to the extent that they represent a financing charge. However, the lessee may, subject to certain conditions, be entitled to Swedish tax depreciation allowances. The leasing of tangible assets into Sweden could constitute a Swedish permanent establishment of the lessor. Double tax treaties might afford protection to the lessor; however, this matter has to date not been tested before the Supreme Administrative Court. In any event there are no Swedish withholding taxes on lease rental payments. In principle, lease rental payments are fully deductible for a Swedish lessee (but see the earlier comments about structured rental profiles).

VAT

Under internal tax regulations there is no VAT on lease rentals on aircraft (wet or dry lease) to be used for the purpose of transporting passengers or goods.

Conclusion

Each of the jurisdictions examined in this chapter offers opportunities for cross-border leasing, and nearly all provide the opportunity to be combined with another to provide tax benefits from both. However, where an airline is offered the opportunity to reduce the cost of finance through a tax-advantaged structure, the basic issue always remains the same. Do the cost reductions outweigh the incremental costs and risks assumed as well as the loss of operational or residual flexibility that arises as a result of the transaction? All these factors need to be identified at the outset of any transaction. Failure to do this may mean there is a risk that they only become clear during the actual negotiations. At this point, the transaction costs and the time available will dictate a result that might not, in normal circumstances, be one the airline should accept.

Note

In preparing the material for this chapter the author would like to acknowledge the assistance of the following: Murray Clayson and Rachel Couter of Freshfields' International Tax Group, together with colleagues in Frankfurt, Paris and Madrid; Maria Theresa Pflügl of Bruckhaus, Westrick, Heller, Löber (Austria); Robert Mikelsons and Gabriel Rohde of Dragsted & Helmer Nielsen Law Firm and Troels Askerud of Lunøe (Denmark); Vittorio Valieri of Studio Legale Internazionale (Italy); and Hans Wibom of Advokatfirman Vinge (Sweden).

11 The Japanese leasing market

Paul Ibbotson

The Japanese leasing market has been the dominant provider of tax-advantaged financing of aircraft for much of the past 10 years although such dominance is now threatened by regulatory changes in Japan. This chapter provides a brief historical overview of the development of leasing in Japan, a brief study of the market and the rules that govern the tax treatment of finance leases, and a look at the prospects for the future. There is also a brief discussion of the Japanese operating lease market.

Development of leasing in Japan

Cross-border financing of aircraft by the Japanese leasing industry started in the late 1970s with the so-called Samurai lease – essentially a Japanese government subsidised scheme designed partly to reduce Japan's balance of payments surplus. The Export-Import Bank of Japan provided cheap dollar funding for leasing companies that leased assets to foreign residents. It was originally intended that the acquisition of the asset be accounted for as an import while the lease out would not be treated as a re-export. Changes in the method of accounting for such imports introduced by the International Monetary Fund led to the abandonment of the scheme (and an end to the Samurai lease) within 18 months.

In 1981, the Shogun lease was developed. This was, unlike the Samurai lease, a yen-denominated financing technique created by the private sector. Shogun leases took two forms: (a) leases in the true sense; and (b) instalment sale agreements. They occasionally formed the leverage component of US and other tax-based leases.

It was from 1985, however, with the development of the Japanese leveraged lease (JLL) that Japan's big-ticket cross-border leasing industry really expanded. Official figures for the total volume of assets financed are not available, but market estimates are that in excess of US$60 billion worth of equipment has been leased on JLLs. The two years at the end of Japan's 'bubble economy' – 1989 and 1990 – saw the greatest level of activity, while annual activity since the start of the recession in Japan has grown from around US$4 billion per year to the current level of just over US$7 billion. Historically the vast majority of transactions have been aircraft financings, but the recent trend is towards the financing of other large capital assets, such as telephony and buses, for reasons explained later on this chapter. In fiscal 1996–97, it is estimated that approximately one-quarter of the total JLL market was for non-aircraft equipment.

On 16 December 1997, the ruling Liberal Democrat Party announced tax changes which will result in the end of the cross-border JLL from 1 October 1998. These tax changes are discussed below.

Exhibit 11.1
The basic JLL

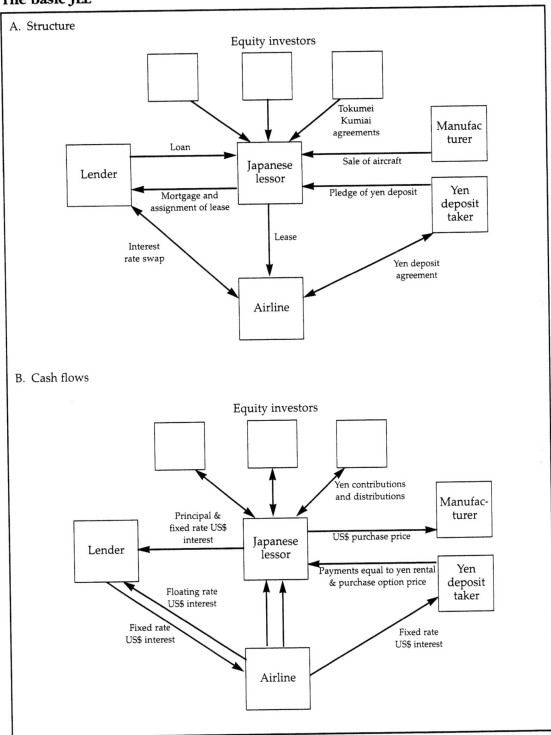

A. Structure

Equity investors

Tokumei
Kumiai
agreements

Manufac
turer

Loan

Japanese
lessor

Sale of aircraft

Lender

Mortgage and
assignment of lease

Pledge of yen deposit

Yen
deposit
taker

Interest
rate swap

Lease

Yen deposit
agreement

Airline

B. Cash flows

Equity investors

Yen contributions
and distributions

Manufac-
turer

Principal &
fixed rate US$
interest

Japanese
lessor

US$ purchase price

Lender

Floating rate
US$ interest

Payments equal to yen rental
& purchase option price

Yen
deposit
taker

Fixed rate
US$ interest

Fixed rate
US$ interest

Airline

The Japanese leveraged lease
Basic structure

The standard aircraft JLL is an extremely simple transaction (see Exhibit 11.1). Japanese equity investors contribute usually between 20 per cent and 30 per cent of the acquisition cost of the aircraft to an arrangement known as a Tokumei Kumiai. Under this arrangement, each investor makes a cash contribution to a company that becomes the lessor of the aircraft and shares in the profits and losses generated by the lease transaction in proportion to the contribution made. The Tokumei Kumiai has been likened to a partnership, but this is something of a loose description because the investors are not linked by any form of legal relationship. Although a small number of JLLs have been completed using an alternative participation arrangement called a Nin-i Kumiai, the Tokumei Kumiai has been by far the more popular structure, in part because the investment made by the investor does not appear on its balance sheet and partly because the identities of the investors are kept secret from the other participants in the transaction.

The typical investor in a JLL is a small to medium-sized privately held company that invests in order to defer corporation tax. Publicly quoted companies seldom participate in JLLs as a result of the generally applicable principle in Japan (unlike most other countries) that the accounting treatment of a transaction is the same as its tax treatment. Thus, a reduction in taxable income engineered by an investment in a JLL will be accounted for as a reduction in profits on the profit and loss account of the investor: sometimes a difficult thing to explain to an annual general meeting. The overwhelming majority of investments are tax-driven. Some companies, however, do indeed invest deliberately in order to depress book profits because the prices chargeable to large companies by small suppliers in Japan are often linked formally to the profits earned by the latter.

The lessor borrows the balance of the funds required to acquire the aircraft from banks who must, in order to avoid Japanese withholding taxes being charged on interest payments under the loan, be either (a) Japanese banks or (b) Japanese branches of foreign banks.

The aircraft is then leased to the airline over a period (almost always) of 10 years for narrow-body aircraft and 12 years for wide-bodies. The lessor is entitled to take depreciation deductions (currently on a declining-balance basis) over the statutory useful life of the aircraft (8 years and 10 years for narrow-bodies and wide-bodies respectively) and loan interest deductions. During the first half of the lease, these depreciation and interest deductions exceed rental income (which must be level throughout the lease term), generating tax losses in that period. In the latter part of the transaction – required by regulation to be no later than the mid-point of the lease term – the loan has been amortised and the asset basis been written off to such an extent that the lease becomes tax positive; that is, rental income exceeds deductions. Substantial taxable income deferral is achieved by having much of the return to the lessor in the form of a fixed price purchase option exercisable by the lessee at the end of the lease term. If the purchase option is not exercised, however, the lessee is nevertheless obliged to pay to the lessor a deficiency payment equal to the purchase option price which is rebateable out of sales proceeds, but any upside in the aircraft value is theoretically for the lessor. Thus the fiction is maintained that the JLL is a true lease; of course, in reality, whenever the aircraft is worth more than the fixed purchase option price, the lessee is always economically motivated to exercise it.

The equity contribution by the investors is made in yen, while the loan may be borrowed in any currency desired by the airline. There are two lease payment streams. One, in the loan currency, exactly matches debt service on the loan. The other, providing the return of and on equity, is in yen. An airline will usually choose the same loan currency as it would choose for a straightforward debt financing – ie a currency in which it generates substantial revenues so that hedging concerns do not arise. One gloss on this is that the higher coupon the loan currency, the greater the economic benefit of the JLL, because interest deductions are thereby increased. An airline with substantial international revenues may, therefore, choose to borrow in the weakest currency for which it has a natural hedge.

Few airlines have sufficient yen revenues to hedge their yen-denominated lease obligations. The typical hedging methods used over the years have been either:

1 a deposit made in yen, which, over time, matures in amounts and at times sufficient to match the yen lease payments; or
2 a similarly structured forward foreign exchange contract.

The deposit has the advantage that it may be pledged in favour of the lessor to secure the lessee's equity payment obligations. Indeed, for many non-flag carrier airlines in the current market, the lease arranger/equity underwriter will insist that such cash collateral is made available, because Japanese equity investors are very credit sensitive and will not usually take an unsecured risk on anything other than the very top-tier airlines. Some underwriters will additionally require, for certain airlines, an equity strip guarantee from a first-class bank supporting the lessee's yen-denominated obligations to the extent that these are not covered by the yen deposit. The yen deposit has the considerable disadvantage, however, that the need to make it deprives the airline of the benefit of 100 per cent financing. The need for complete funding of the acquisition cost is particularly great for airlines in certain developing countries, such as China. Such airlines – if they find it difficult to attract unsecured investment from the JLL equity market – will provide alternatives such as guarantees for the entirety of their lease payment obligations.

The requirement that lease rentals must be level over the term means that the loan to the lessor must be at a fixed rate. Many airlines, however, would naturally borrow at a floating rate. A common feature of JLLs today, therefore, is a swap transaction between the lessee and the banks under which the banks pay to the lessee the fixed coupon received under the loan in return for a floating rate of interest.

Rules governing the structuring of JLLs

Four principal bodies of regulation, in addition to the basic Japanese tax code, set out the guidelines under which JLLs are structured. These are:

1 *The Treatment of Corporation Tax and Income Tax With Respect to Lease Transactions* (the 1978 *Tsutatsu*, or circular).
2 *Tax Treatment of Leases Which Have a Longer Lease Term than the Statutory Depreciable Life of the Leased Property* (the 1988 *Tsutatsu*).
3 *Agreement Regarding Lease Transactions Which Have a Lease Term Not Exceeding 120 Per Cent of the Tax Useful Life of the Leased Property* (the 1988 *Moushi-awase*, or agreement).
4 *Agreement Regarding Lease Transactions Which Have a Lease Term Not Exceeding 120 Per Cent of the Useful Life of the Leased Property* (the 1990 *Moushi-awase*).

The 1978 *Tsutatsu*

This circular was issued by the National Tax Administration of Japan (NTA) to counter a perceived abuse in the domestic lease market under which leases were being written with lease terms much shorter than the statutory depreciable life of the leased asset (prescribed in each case by the Corporation Tax Law of Japan).

The 1978 *Tsutatsu* is expressed to apply to a particular type of lease transaction, defined as being one in which:

1 the lease term is fixed and the total lease payments over the lease term amount to 'almost all [generally accepted to mean greater than 90 per cent] of the acquisition cost of the [leased] property' plus interest and other expenses incurred by the lessor in acquiring and leasing the asset; and
2 the lease contains a provision prohibiting cancellation of the leasing or a requirement that, upon any such cancellation, the lessee shall be obliged to pay 'almost all' of the remaining lease payments payable over the remaining lease term.

Thus, the 1978 *Tsutatsu* applies essentially to full payout – or almost full payout - finance leases. True leases not caught by the definition are outside the ambit of the circular, but are probably still potentially subject to a general substance over form recharacterisation if the tax authorities find that 'unfair tax treatment' is accorded to such transactions by treating them as leases.

The 1978 *Tsutatsu* provides that a finance lease, as defined above, will be treated as a sale or finance transaction, rather than as a lease, if, subject to the proviso below, any of the following criteria is met:

• the lease provides for a nominal end-of-term purchase option or lease renewal for nominal rental;
• the leased asset is land or buildings;
• the leased asset is machinery of a bespoke design particular to the lessee's use, which makes it unlikely that the lessor could re-lease the asset to another user after lease expiry;
• the leased asset cannot be readily identifiable as a separately leasable asset; or
• the lease term is less than (a) 60 per cent of the statutory useful life of the leased asset (where the statutory useful life is 10 years or more, eg wide-body aircraft) or (b) 70 per cent of the statutory life (where the statutory life is under 10 years, eg narrow-body aircraft).

If any one of the above conditions is met, the lease transaction will be treated as a sale or financing *unless* it is clear from past leases of similar equipment by the lessor, the characteristics of the leased property and other circumstances that the asset will be returned to the lessor on lease expiry or scrapped. In practice, this proviso is relatively immaterial in the context of the current cross-border JLL market.

The 1978 *Tsutatsu* also contains important provisions that effectively prohibit sale and leaseback by the owner of used assets by recharacterising such transactions as financings. These provisions do not proscribe sale–leasebacks in the context of new equipment financings: thus, an airline can acquire title to a new aircraft from the manufacturer and sell it to, and lease it back from, a Japanese lessor, provided the inception of the lease is simultaneous with the acquisition by the airline. Nor does the 1978 *Tsutatsu* prevent JLLs being used to finance the acquisition of used assets in circumstances where an airline, for example, is selling a used aircraft to a third party purchaser.

The 1988 *Tsutatsu*

The substantial growth of the cross-border JLL market in 1986 and 1987 alarmed the Japanese tax authorities who, towards the end of 1987, caused a temporary shutdown in the market by announcing that they would disallow lease taxation treatment to the type of finance leases then being structured, even though they complied with the 1978 *Tsutatsu*. The target of the NTA's concern were leases with terms much greater, rather than much shorter, than the statutory useful lives of the leased assets. Such a technique, allied with inflated residual value balloons (the purchase option/deficiency payment described above), gave rise to what the authorities viewed as an excessive tax deferral-effect.

In the early part of 1988, the NTA issued the 1988 *Tsutatsu*, which became effective from 1 April of that year. It was supplemented with an 'application circular' in question and answer form that was issued on 26 April. The application of the 1988 *Tsutatsu* is, on its face, rather confusing. It provides that a transaction will be treated as a sale or a financing rather than a lease where:

(A) the lease term exceeds 120 per cent of the statutory useful life of the equipment; and either
(B) *all* of the following conditions are met:
   - the property has been acquired by the lessee and transferred to the lessor or acquired directly by the lessor but in circumstances where it is apparent (eg the lessee has selected the property or negotiated with the manufacturer) that in substance the lessee is the acquirer of the property;
   - the sum of the lease payments amounts to substantially all (again, considered to be 90 per cent or more) of the acquisition and carrying costs of the lessor;
   - there is a prohibition on cancellation of the lease or, in the event of cancellation, the lessee is obliged to pay substantially all the lease payments due over the balance of the lease term; and
   - the lease does not provide for a fair market value purchase option (and there are three subsidiary conditions which provide that, if satisfied, a lease will be deemed not to have a fair market value purchase option even if the lessee is expressed to have one); or
(C) the lease is treated by the tax authorities as an 'economically similar lease transaction' to one in which the above conditions are met.

Although, theoretically, a lease could be structured so as to fail one of the above conditions in (B) so that the 1988 *Tsutatsu* does not apply, the practical effect of the potential substance over form approach in (C) above is that leases are structured so as to comply with the bright-line test in (A). Thus, after 1988, JLLs ceased to have terms greater than 120 per cent of statutory useful life.

The 1988 *Moushi-awase*

The period following the coming into force of the 1988 *Tsutatsu* saw a redoubling of activity in the still-young JLL market. Leases were limited in term by the 1978 and 1988 *Tsutatsu*, but otherwise arrangers structured transactions very aggressively. Eventually, in December 1988, the Japan Leasing Association (JLA) issued self-regulatory guidelines to its members concerning the structuring of JLLs with lease terms not exceeding 120 per cent of statutory useful life. These guidelines are treated by the leasing industry in Japan as having regulatory force and it is clear that, on a case-by-case basis, the tax authorities would disallow a claim of ownership tax benefits by a lessor in a JLL that did not comply with the guidelines. The six guidelines are:

1 The anticipated resale value of the leased property at lease expiry must be substantial. (In practice the approval of the NTA as to the leaseability of all assets other than aircraft is sought on a case-by-case basis by Japanese leasing companies and the required level of residual value is established to the authorities' satisfaction by appraisals and other evidence.)

2 The amount of depreciation expense loss carryforward (the amount by which aggregate depreciation deductions exceed rental income) in the actual lease must not exceed 160 per cent of the equivalent amount in a specified base case that assumes (i) a lease term equal to the statutory useful life of the asset; (ii) a 10 per cent residual value; and (iii) an implicit annual lease rate of 5.5 per cent.

3 The purchase option price (a) must not exceed the estimated future fair market value at lease expiry and (b) must not exceed 45 per cent of acquisition cost (10 per cent in the case of assets other than aircraft).

4 The lease must be tax positive (that is, lease rental and other income must exceed depreciation and interest deductions for each fiscal period of the lessor) no later than 50 per cent of the way through the lease term.

5 The equity contribution by investors must not be less than 20 per cent of acquisition cost.

6 The accumulated taxable income (including sale proceeds) of the lessor/investors over the entirety of the transaction must be at least 1 per cent of acquisition cost.

These guidelines have come to be universally adopted by the industry as a safe harbour, so that finance leases structured in compliance with them and the earlier Tsutatsu will receive treatment as true leases for tax purposes, notwithstanding the residual right of the tax authorities to take a substance over form approach where a lease is deemed to have undue tax effect.

The 1990 *Moushi-awase*

Two perceived structuring abuses that rose to prominence in the late 1980s were defeasance (the assumption by a third party of the lessee's lease payment obligations in return for a cash consideration) and the 'double dipping' of tax benefits by combining JLLs with tax leases in other jurisdictions. These were finally proscribed by self-regulatory guidelines issued by the JLA in May 1990. These provide that members of the JLA will not arrange transactions in which either:

(a) a non-resident lessee that neither operates the leased property nor uses the property in an operating lease business sub-leases the property to a sub-lessee in circumstances where the lessee is entitled to claim ownership-type tax benefits in its own jurisdiction, *except* where the head lease and the sub-lease are on the same terms and conditions and the intermediary lessor does not claim ownership tax benefits; or

(b) a person assumes, directly or indirectly, all or any part of the lessee's lease payment obligations corresponding to debt service.

These rather arcane provisions have been subject to considerable scrutiny and interpretation since their adoption. Rule (a) is designed to stop two-tier double dips. It clearly does not stop an operator of an aircraft (whether an airline or an operating lease company) claiming depreciation benefits in its own jurisdiction. Indeed, one of the key attractions of the JLL for today's more profitable airlines is that in most jurisdictions a JLL lessee will be treated as having tax ownership of the aircraft, thus allowing the airline to enjoy the economic advantage of two sets of capital allowances.

It should be noted that the guideline exemption for operating leases applies only where the intermediary is an operating lessor. In other words, the sub-lessor must have an established operating lease business; it is not sufficient that the sub-lease simply be drawn as an operating lease for Japanese tax purposes. Guideline (a) also does not prohibit sub-leasing by an airline to other airlines provided the sub-lease is an operating lease not involving the transfer of tax ownership. The so-called 'back-to-back lease' exemption to the prohibition on two-tier leases allows parties to structure transactions with an intermediary inserted for reasons other than claiming foreign capital allowances. Typically, such a structure will be used to insert an intermediary in a third jurisdiction to mitigate withholding taxes that would otherwise be assessed in the airline's home jurisdiction on lease rentals paid directly to Japan. In order to qualify for the exemption, the head lease and sub-lease must be substantively identical.

The second of the May 1990 guidelines is the anti-defeasance rule. It expressly relates only to the defeasance of debt service lease payments. It should not, theoretically, affect yen deposits designed to secure the lessor's equity return, and the general view is that such deposits are inoffensive. However, the more conservative tax advisers in Japan take the view that a pledge over any other type of collateral (such as a structured note, rather than a deposit) or a pledge involving the legal release of the lessee's rental obligations is prohibited.

The concept of assumption of the lessee's obligations in the anti-defeasance rule includes guarantees of such obligations by a third party, but the payment of a simple guarantee fee by the lessee and the giving of a normal counter-indemnity to the guarantor (unless cash-collateralised or otherwise secured by the lessee) are thought not to be caught.

The end of the cross-border JLL?

On 16 December 1997 the Tax Reform Committee of the Liberal Democratic Party announced, among a series of reforms designed to stimulate tax revenue in Japan, that a leased asset which is (i) put into commercial or business service outside Japan by a non-resident or foreign corporation and (ii) subject to a lease transaction which is categorised as a 'finance lease', shall be depreciated using a straight line depreciation method over the lease term. The new rule applies to lease agreements executed on or after 1 October 1998.

The effect of replacing the declining-balance depreciation method by straight-line depreciation has a disastrous effect on the economics of JLLs. The tax effect and cash flows that could be generated by the declining-balance depreciation method in the context of the other economic parameters laid down by the various tax circulars and guidelines will make investing in cross-border JLLs a pointless exercise. However, the JLL is not completely dead. The JLL to Japanese domestic end-users (for example leases of aircraft to JAL or ANA) will survive. Nevertheless, after 1 October 1998 the cross-border JLL, to all intents and purposes, will cease to exist in the form that has dominated aircraft financing over the last ten years.

The announcement of 16 December 1997 brought to an end the rumours and conjecture over the future of the JLL market which had started in August 1996 following a report in the Nihon Keizai Shimbun financial newspaper that the Japanese Cabinet Tax Committee (Seifu Zeisei Chosa-kai) was considering the prohibition of the declining balance method of depreciation for leased assets. The uncertainty caused by what can now be seen as a statement of proposed government policy resulted in the virtual shut-down of the market between September and December 1996. Although the reforms were postponed, the continuing uncertainty regarding tax changes affected investor confidence resulting in a reduced volume of business in 1997.

JLL Market Study 1994–1998

Since the summer of 1994, long-term Japanese interest rates have fallen steadily. In August 1994 the 10-year yen swap rate was 4.95 per cent; in April 1997 it was at an all-time low of 2.7 per cent. From the lessee's perspective, a JLL is little more than a cheap yen loan for part of the aircraft cost. If yen interest rates are low anyway, the differential offered by the investor who is willing to forego yield in return for tax deferral is minimised. For their part, in order to keep JLLs competitive, investors have had to accept a reduction in their yields to little more than the minimum needed to generate the 1 per cent taxable profit over the life of the lease required by the 1988 guidelines. The economic benefits offered to the top-tier airlines by wide-body JLLs have fallen during the same period from over 12 per cent in present value terms to less than 6 per cent.

About the only investor economic parameter of significance in the current market is the so-called 'loss ratio' or 'total losses'; broadly put, this is the ratio of interest and depreciation deductions to the amount of equity contributed. As the rate of depreciation losses is constant, this parameter is most obviously affected by loan interest rate and the amount of leverage; in both cases, the higher the better. Of course, the greater the leverage, the less optimal the economic effect of the JLL for the lessee because the proportion of cheap yen in the deal is reduced.

The JLL has faced stiff competition over recent times from cross-border US products and the German leveraged lease. One of the key arguments in favour of the JLL – that it was the product of a reliable and mature market and not susceptible to regulatory threat, thus reducing execution risk – was weakened by the threatened tax changes in the autumn of 1996.

Against this rather bleak background, the JLL market probably had its best year in fiscal 1996 since the heady days of the bubble economy and defeasance deals. This is due to a number of factors. Most importantly, the Japanese economy took its first (albeit unsteady) steps out of the recession of the first half of the decade and investor confidence improved. To a certain extent – although this should probably not be overstated – a boost to appetite has come from those investors who participated in the first JLLs to be concluded after the 1988 Tsutatsu, which are now turning tax positive. For some, income will be a welcome thing, but for others the continued profitability of their businesses will mean a continued desire for further tax-deferral products.

Equity underwriters in the market have been successful at expanding the investor base. A key element in this process has been the development of shorter-term JLLs for assets other than aircraft. Equipment such as digital telephone switches, which have a statutory depreciable life in Japan of six years allowing an optimal eight-year lease term, has been subjected very successfully to JLLs in recent months. The attraction of such a deal for investors is that it only requires them to take a three to four-year view on their tax position, whereas an investment in a wide-body aircraft deal requires investors to be confident that they will have sufficient taxable profits to shelter for six years. In the economic uncertainty of the recession, the number of investors willing to take such a long-term view reduced greatly; hence the importance of shorter maturity deals in maintaining enthusiasm for the JLL as a tax-deferral product until such a time as investors feel confident and experienced enough to take a longer view.

Several deals were done where JLLs have a clear competitive edge over other cross-border tax leases. For example, over a billion dollars of JLLs combined with European export credit agency debt have been completed on Airbus aircraft. These are deals in which US FSC benefits are not available and in which the use of German tax benefits from a GLL would lead to the disallowance of the HERMES-supported debt.

Operating leases

Japanese participation in operating leasing has followed two main routes (in addition to the equity stakes taken by Japanese financial institutions in operating leasing companies such as GPA). These are, first, the underwritten, investor-oriented deals pioneered by Nomura Babcock & Brown (NBB) at the start of the decade and, secondly, the operating leasing undertaken – chiefly nowadays by trading companies – on their own account as money-on-money investments.

The investor-based deals of the first half of the 1990s were undertaken for a variety of reasons. Some were tax-based (corporate tax deferral and inheritance tax mitigation), while others were targeted mainly at achieving a capital gain. A major recipient of operating lease investment from Japan was GPA, which undertook a programme of sale–leasebacks totalling hundreds of millions of dollars in acquisition cost. The sharp fall in aircraft values in the early to mid-1990s and the financial difficulties experienced by GPA led to a considerable retrenchment in the new market.

The acquisition by Orix Corporation of Braniff Airline's order position for Airbus A320 aircraft in 1990 signalled the start of significant participation by Japanese companies in operating leasing as principals. These investment deals are not primarily tax driven; they seek to make a turn utilising the relatively low cost of funds of the participants and, ultimately, a capital gain on resale in the right market conditions. Many Japanese trading companies participate in these transactions through subsidiaries that take advantage of the favourable tax regime offered by Dublin's IFSC legislation. Something of the order of 100 to 150 aircraft have been acquired by Japanese trading and leasing companies as principals in this market in the past seven years.

The tax-based operating lease market for investors continues today, although many participants have withdrawn from this market. Those that remain, such as NBB, have needed to develop techniques for mitigating the asset risk element of the investment and ensuring that professional remarketing support is available at the end of the transaction so that investors can realise the value of their investment in a timely manner. The firming of used aircraft values in recent years has increased investor demand once more. The investor-based Japanese operating lease market has historically had an annual volume of between US$300 million and US$600 million, and is currently expected to grow.

The key distinction between the operating lease market in Japan and the much larger JLL market is the degree of risk taken by investors. The JLL investor is simply buying a yen cash flow with a virtually absolute certainty of return. Hence, JLLs are full payout finance leases with no currency exposure and the preferred lessee is a first-class flag-carrier. In addition to the asset exposure inherent in operating leases, a Japanese investor is also taking a currency exposure on a dollar asset and the typical operating lease customer tends to be a slightly less robust credit.

Future developments

The Japanese leasing market is a mature and vigorous one. There is active involvement in the aircraft leasing industry across a broad spectrum of financial institutions. The implementation of the new 1998 tax reforms will result in the end of the cross-border JLL, but it is likely that the appetite of investors nurtured so carefully over the years will remain and that alternative, derivative products will be developed to satisfy that need. Until the definitive regulations are passed it is difficult to predict the nature of such products. The consensual nature of relations between government and business in Japan will also mean that the spirit of the regulations will dictate what direction the industry moves in.

There may be something of a convergence between the purely tax-driven JLL market and the riskier operating lease deals. It is possible that the corporate tax-deferral investors who invest in JLLs would be tempted into the operating lease market, notwithstanding the attendant risks, although there would doubtless be a general move by arrangers to try to mitigate those risks.

The policy of the Japanese government to reduce direct taxation rates will also have a negative effect on the corporate tax-based leasing market, although for those fortunate investors who have invested in JLLs that are now tax positive, the reduction in corporation tax rates will mean a windfall saving.

12 The Asian perspective

Ian F. Reid

The latter part of 1997 saw considerable turmoil in the Asian markets that caught everyone by surprise. The economic miracle of the Asian economies that had dominated world growth rates seemed to trip and stumble. The transformation in economic fortunes has also changed the availability and outlook for aircraft finance, and this chapter reflects the new situation. This chapter will deal with the market for air transportation and the consequent demand for aircraft finance in the region, together with some of the commercial issues concerning aircraft financing in each of the main countries. The countries discussed are: Australia/New Zealand; China; Hong Kong; India; Indonesia; Japan; Korea; Malaysia; the Philippines; Singapore; Taiwan; Thailand; and Vietnam.

Asia – economy and growth

Despite the current economic woes in certain Asian countries that have seen their currencies severely devalued (at the time of writing, the countries most affected were South Korea, Indonesia, Thailand, Malaysia and the Philippines), Asia still represents over half the world's population and the greatest growth potential for the 21st century. China's 1.2 billion people and India's 931 million population dwarf those of the US or Europe. So far this decade, Asian countries have sustained some of the highest growth rates in the world, and are projected to continue doing so over the long term (see Exhibit 12.1).

Exhibit 12.1
Average real GDP growth per annum, 1990–97 and (projected) 1998–2005

Country	Historic 1990–97 (%)	Projected 1998–2005 (%)
China	10.4	8.4
Malaysia	8.6	7.2
Thailand	8.5	5.5
Singapore	8.4	5.8
Korea	7.5	5.8
Taiwan	6.3	5.8
Indonesia	7.7	5.0
Hong Kong	5.0	4.8
India	4.5	4.8
United States	2.1	2.0
United Kingdom	1.4	2.1

From an air transportation point of view, economic growth in the short term fuels inward investment and tourism (inbound traffic); in the long term as the countries develop the wealth to travel themselves, they create outbound traffic and domestic air transportation. It is the latter areas that are affected most by the recent economic turmoil. However, of these, the largest Asian country, China, so far has not seen significant adverse effects of the recent economic disruption.

The demand for aircraft

If we look at where commercial jet transportation in Asia stands relative to that in the West, we see there is still a big disparity and a long way to catch up. The US has a population of 264 million and over 5,000 commercial jet aircraft. That means there is one aircraft for every 51,000 people. In India there is a population of 931 million people and only 125 jet aircraft – ie one aircraft for every 7.5 million people.

Air transport is the only practical alternative for several reasons. Asia is a large continent – the distances are long and many countries are either islands or the direct journey is across water. Asia does not have the developed rail system that Europe has or the road system that the US has. Today the cost of air transportation in real terms makes it cheaper to build two airports and fly between them than invest in land infrastructure across difficult terrain.

By the end of 1996, Asia had ordered almost as many new aircraft from the manufacturers as airlines in the US (see Exhibit 12.2). In dollar terms the amount was even higher because of the larger proportion of wide-body aircraft used in Asia compared with the US and Europe. In 1997, however, the recovery of the US airlines sparked large orders that returned North America to the dominant position. There remain some 600 aircraft to be financed in Asia, which, in some of the battered economies, will be a much more difficult task in the near term than before.

Sources of finance for aircraft in Asia

Export credits

Asia is the world's largest user of export credit finance for aircraft finance and the current economic climate is likely to increase its importance. Approximately US$7.5 billion dollars

Exhibit 12.2
Airline new aircraft orders by area, end-1996 and October 1997

	31 December 1996		1 October 1997	
	Total	As a percentage	Total	As as percentage
North America	587	27.7	1,434	44.1
Asia	563	26.6	600	18.5
Europe	420	19.8	527	16.2
Latin America	30	1.4	56	1.7
Africa	24	1.1	24	0.7
Australia	19	0.9	33	1.0
Unannounced	46	2.2	34	1.1
Total	**1,689**	**79.7**	**2,708**	**83.3**
Leasing companies	431	20.3	542	16.7
	2,120	100.0	3,250	100.0

have been guaranteed by EXIM of the US and the European export credit agencies (ECAs) for aircraft in Asia in the past two-and-a-half years, representing almost 45 per cent of the financing provided. There are three main reasons why this is more important in Asia than the rest of the world:

1 The emerging nature of the market makes export financing appropriate and cost-effective in many countries.
2 The fact that Asia does not yet have any substantial aircraft manufacturing capability means that support is available to almost every country in Asia, whereas export credit support is not available to airlines in countries that manufacture large aircraft – for example the US, UK, France and Germany.
3 Export credit support will play a stronger role in the coming years than in the past due to the deterioration of the credit ratings of certain of the countries.

The ECAs had identified China, India and Indonesia as the three largest countries in Asia and the countries on which they should particularly focus. Under LASU (the Large Aircraft Sector Understanding), terms are 85 per cent finance, amortising fully over a 12-year term.

Commercial bank market

The commercial bank market has been the other main source of finance for Asia's aircraft, representing roughly the same volume as export credits. Terms are typically 10–12 years for new aircraft with banks providing 80–85 per cent of the aircraft cost but often willing to provide up to 100 per cent of the aircraft cost in the case of the better credit flag-carriers, sometimes as one loan and sometimes as a mixture of senior and subordinated debt. Bank financing may be provided by way of mortgage loans, but more often through finance leases; the past few years have seen a significant number of aircraft financed via Japanese leveraged lease (JLL) structures. Commercial loans have also been used frequently with export credits to provide 100 per cent finance (85 per cent export credit and 15 per cent commercial loan).

Japanese banks have historically provided the lion's share of the debt portion of these financings. However, recent economic difficulties have affected financial institutions as well as airlines, and problems in the Japanese banking sector have caused the cost of funds of Japanese banks to soar, impairing their ability to lend at the margins they historically used to. Their share will therefore inevitably decline in the near term and we will see a jump in the margins that commercial banks will demand for their capital.

Operating leases

Operating leases represent a significant source of aircraft financing. Purchases of new aircraft by operating lease companies account for slightly more than 20 per cent of the world's aircraft. Operating leases have been used by the major carriers in Asia to provide fleet flexibility and by smaller or less financially strong airlines to provide more advantageous cash flow financing than would be available from the bank or export credit markets. Operating leases provide for 100 per cent finance (less security deposit) and terms have typically been for five to seven years for new aircraft. In Asia, operating leases have historically accounted for slightly less than the world average (around 17–18 per cent of the aircraft fleet). This is due to the greater predominance of flag-carriers in Asia and therefore relatively fewer secondary or charter carriers as compared with elsewhere in the world. Asia's recent financial crisis is likely, however, to increase the importance of operating lessors as a source of capital for airlines.

Synthetic operating leases

Synthetic operating leases are financings structured to be off-balance sheet from the lessee's (airline's) point of view, yet to still provide the lessee with all, or a large share of, the economic residual value of the aircraft at the end of the lease. They are structured to fail the accounting tests to be recognised as a finance lease (covered elsewhere in this book) and hence can be treated by the airline as an operating lease. Most importantly, the airline does not need to show either the aircraft or any capitalised liabilities on its balance sheet. Accounting guidelines vary across different countries in Asia, although most are broadly based on US GAAP (generally accepted accounting principles).

To achieve operating lease treatment, typically these leases are not full payout and a residual risk of 10–25 per cent is taken by the financing bank. In some structures this residual risk is taken in conjunction with support from the aircraft or engine manufacturer in the form of an asset value guarantee[1] given to the lender.

Capital markets and securitisation[2]

To date, capital markets have not played a particularly big role for the Asian airlines. Classic capital market instruments such as bonds are typically issued on an unsecured basis. In an industry where most of the hard assets, namely aircraft, are already pledged to existing lenders, an unsecured bondholder to an airline is similar to a subordinated lender in other industries. Unlike the US, very few airlines in Asia have any sort of public debt rating, and rated debt issues in Asia have been confined in recent years to Australia, New Zealand and Japan. Although many of Asia's airlines are government owned, few are government guaranteed. They represent 'story paper' that is more easily sold to banks than to a wide range of public investors.

Securities issued based on the security of the aircraft, such as equipment trust certificates (ETCs) which are frequently used in aircraft financings in the US for example, are still to be completed in Asia, although at the time of writing a couple of deals were being worked on. The challenges to overcome include obtaining a public rating for the securities, which would allow them to be placed with US-based investors. Apart from the fact that, as mentioned previously, the airlines themselves are rarely rated, the main obstacle so far has been the status of bankruptcy and security laws for repossession in each country compared with the US. The fact that such laws may not have been tested yet in some countries in Asia gives a higher degree of uncertainty when assigning a public security rating based on the ability to repossess the aircraft.

The main use we have seen for securitisation so far for airlines in Asia is 12-year EXIM-guaranteed notes, which are rated triple A, registered with the US Securities and Exchange Commission and issued in the US public market in denominations as small as US$100,000. These issues have become less common recently because the aggressiveness of the commercial banks for such high-quality assets has undercut the public markets in terms of price when one takes into account that a securitisation adds additional costs in the form of legal, rating and registration fees.

The other application of securitisation in the airline industry (albeit not specifically for aircraft financing) has been that of credit card or other payment receivables to provide medium-term financing. Here the airline agrees to sell forward these receivables to a special purpose trust, which then issues notes, usually of a three- to five-year maturity. The amount of notes issued depends on the volume of the receivables that the airline generates. In the case of credit card receivables, the creditors of the trust are now the credit card companies, which are typically double A rated. Clearly the airline must remain a viable entity, continuing to sell tickets and generate receivables, although the mechanism does provide a credit enhancement, both in the short-term security of cash flow and the possible advantage, subject to applicable law, that such investors may still be able to receive payments from an airline operating in bankruptcy, while there is a moratorium on other debt.

Despite being largely overshadowed by the commercial bank market at the moment, the role of debt capital markets for airlines and aircraft finance can only become more prominent as both the airline and the investor markets mature in Asia.

Equity

The ability of airlines to secure debt financing for their aircraft is dependent on being able to demonstrate to lenders that a sufficient cushion of equity exists within the airline. As airlines grow and invest in more aircraft they need to secure more equity in proportion to their debt. This can come partly from retained earnings but also from cash calls on existing or new shareholders.

Privatisation is a key word in the industry in Asia these days as many governments try to reduce their shareholdings in their flag-carriers. This is usually accompanied by an injection of equity from the government, a conversion of debt into equity, or the donation of aircraft that were owned or financed by the government to the airline in lieu of equity. We have recently seen two mainland Chinese airlines – China Eastern and China Southern – listing on the New York Stock Exchange, while shareholders of Philippine Airlines, Malaysia Airlines and Cathay Pacific have injected new equity into their airlines, and the government of Indonesia has exchanged approximately US$750 million of debt for equity in anticipation of privatisation of the airline.

As the Asian currency crisis erodes the equity of airlines due to the predominance of US dollar debt on their balance sheets, it is clear that additional capitalisation will be required in many cases to ensure ongoing viability.

Country summaries

The following country summaries provide a generic description of aircraft financing in that country. A brief chapter such as this cannot do justice to describing the complexities involved in each country, so the summaries are designed to serve as an outline of some of the main aspects of aircraft finance from a commercial point of view. As such, it has been necessary to make broad generalisations, and the financing techniques mentioned for a particular country are generally those of the flag-carrier airline.

Australia/New Zealand

These countries represent probably the most sophisticated financial markets in the Asia–Pacific region. Australia has a well-developed domestic banking market plus a strong domestic tax leasing market with fairly well-defined tax guidelines that, like the US and UK, permit a significant level of leasing to airlines domiciled in the country but deny benefits for outbound cross-border leases.

Both Australia and New Zealand generally impose withholding taxes on interest paid to non-residents. Cross-border transactions into these countries therefore have to be carefully structured to avoid this cost, otherwise loans have to be booked by international banks in a branch in Australia. Airlines in Australia are able to structure double dip transactions via the combination of a domestic lease with certain cross-border (eg US) leases.

China

China represents the largest growing market in Asia and at the time of writing seems to have been relatively unaffected by the Asian economic crisis. Chinese airlines have exclusively financed their aircraft via leases – either true operating leases or finance leases. The finance lease structure has utilised an offshore special purpose company as lessor, but the aircraft are normally registered in China. Of the finance leases, a large proportion have in the past used the Japanese leveraged lease (JLL) structure to provide 100 per cent finance. There have been a small number of tax leases from other jurisdictions.

The rentals of the Chinese airlines under the finance leases are usually guaranteed by one of the state specialised banks – Bank of China (BOC), Industrial and Commercial Bank of China (ICBC) or China Construction Bank (CCB). Export credits both from the European ECAs and from EXIM have played a major role in the financing of Airbus and Boeing/McDonnell Douglas aircraft respectively and have been frequently integrated with JLL structures.

Approvals for the guarantee of foreign currency obligations must be obtained by the airline in advance from the State Administration of Foreign Exchange (SAFE). To date, withholding tax has not been levied by the Chinese tax authorities on rental payments made to foreign lessors under operating or finance lease. This, however, appears to be currently under review and such regulations may be modified in future to allow for specific exemptions to withholding tax.

Hong Kong

Hong Kong's status as a leading commercial centre together with its fairly liberal tax regime and low taxes has made it an important financial centre for aircraft finance in Asia. Hong Kong has no tax treaties and imposes no withholding taxes. There is a domestic tax-based leasing market available for domestic airlines – currently Cathay Pacific, Dragonair and Air Hong Kong.

Cross-border leasing from Hong Kong was effectively removed with the introduction of regulations by the Inland Revenue Department denying depreciation to Hong Kong lessors if the aircraft is leased to a foreign lessee. However, Hong Kong airlines can combine certain inbound cross-border leases with a domestic Hong Kong lease to form a double dip and the tax structured financings achieved have been among the most sophisticated in the world. The underlying source of debt finance has been primarily commercial banks, with export credit financing playing a smaller role.

In July 1997, the territory of Hong Kong reverted from Great Britain to become a Special Administrative Region (SAR) of the Peoples Republic of China. The Basic Law that came into effect provides that Hong Kong will continue to operate independently in economic matters for 50 years. To date, investment in Hong Kong and confidence in its future after the handover appear to indicate that Hong Kong will continue to play a major role as a financing centre.

India

India is a huge potential aviation market dominated by the two government-owned airlines, Air India (international) and Indian Airlines (domestic). The financing source for aircraft has been primarily the ECAs, with bank financing also a significant factor.

More recently a number of new airlines (called air taxi operators) have begun competing with Indian Airlines on domestic routes and typically procuring aircraft through operating leases. With only a few exceptions, to date most of the new airlines have not fared well and are struggling to survive financially.

As government-owned companies, Air India and Indian Airlines have a high degree of control exercised over them by the Ministry of Finance in the financings they arrange. In terms of cross-border transactions, they have historically sought, and have been able to obtain, exemptions from withholding taxes for foreign borrowings.

Indonesia

Financing aircraft in Indonesia has typically been either via pure operating leases or, more recently, synthetic operating leases, which are finance-type leases structured to be operating leases for Indonesian accounting purposes. The approvals that an airline is required to seek for offshore financing are significantly less onerous if the financing can be structured as an operating lease. To qualify as an operating lease, among other things, the airline's obligations under the lease should be less than 90 per cent of the aircraft cost. It is therefore possible to structure a quasi-operating lease with the use of a residual value guarantee that will allow the airline to have operating lease treatment while still retaining the residual value benefits.

The ECAs have been the principal providers of finance. In the past, the flag-carrier, Garuda, used to borrow with a government guarantee. However, some ECA deals have been done without a government guarantee on an asset value basis. The recent economic crisis in Indonesia will, at least for the time being, probably reverse this trend. Withholding taxes are an issue in cross-border financing and it is therefore important to structure such transactions to take advantage of certain key tax treaties.

Japan

Japan is widely associated as the largest provider of finance for aircraft in Asia as well as around the world. Japanese banks have been the most abundant lenders in the industry in recent times. Although there are no exact statistics, Japanese leasing companies and private investors appear to have financed about US$2.5 billion of new aircraft in Asia in the past two years – around one-in-five of every aircraft delivered. Being Asia's largest economy, Japan has a significant airline industry with two large international carriers. Given the scale of the Japanese banking industry, their aircraft are typically financed domestically, although there have been some cross-border leases into Japan (from the US) concluded in the past. Japan imposes withholding taxes in almost all its treaties. This is an issue for a Japanese borrower such as the lessor company in a JLL, and non-Japanese banks must book their loans in Japan (although Japanese banks can book their loans in any branch worldwide).

Korea

The growth of the Korean economy in the past 10 years and the relaxation of travel regulations have resulted in significant growth for the country's airlines. However, the recent drastic downturn in the Korean economy that precipitated the IMF rescue has had a reversal effect. The funding sources for aircraft financing in the past have been split between the ECAs, and a combination of international and Korean banks, with the latter providing subordinated loans to give 100 per cent financing. Cross-border leases, particularly JLLs, have also played a role, as have operating leases.

In future, aircraft financing will be much tougher given the difficulties with the economy and the problems experienced by local Korean banks, not to mention the high existing exposure that ECAs and commercial banks have to the country.

Malaysia

Malaysia typically finances much of the debt for its aircraft financing through the international bank market. Because of the rates charged by commercial banks in recent times, export credit supported financings have featured less. Financing techniques are quite sophisticated and Japanese or US tax leases into Malaysia have played a significant role in the past. Withholding taxes have not been an important issue for big-ticket financings because it was possible to claim exemption under the government-approved financing scheme. However, the government is now looking to encourage banks to set up an operation in Labuan (a special economic zone within Malaysia) and, as a result, is no longer giving automatic withholding tax exemption on interest to offshore lenders.

The Philippines

The Philippines' flag-carrier has typically financed its long-term aircraft acquisitions through export credit supported finance lease structures incorporating JLLs, as well as via operating leases. Financing from ECAs has been on an asset value basis without government support because the flag-carrier is privately owned. Exemptions from withholding tax can usually be obtained to facilitate cross-border transactions.

Singapore

Singapore's flag-carrier, Singapore Airlines, has the unique distinction of being so profitable that it invariably finances its aircraft purchases through internally generated cash. It is unlikely that any other airline in the world can make that claim to fame. This, together with Singapore's high credit rating, has meant that the country has become an exporter, as opposed to importer, of funds for aircraft financing and, like Hong Kong, represents a regional centre for aircraft finance professionals. Singapore has recently entered the operating lease market with Singapore Aircraft Leasing Enterprise (SALE), which was initially set up as a 50 per cent affiliate of Singapore Airlines, and looks as if it will become a major Asian-based lessor.

Taiwan

Taiwan has had a combination of withholding taxes and aircraft registration issues that have made cross-border finance for its airlines quite difficult. There is a 3.75 per cent withholding tax on rentals. As a result, most financings have been done on a local basis and only a few export credit supported financings have been completed. Some cross-border tax leases have been completed where the tax benefits gained by the lease outweigh the withholding tax costs.

Thailand

Thailand's flag-carrier is majority government owned and controlled. Historically, most international borrowings have enjoyed the direct or indirect support of the government and have attracted fine pricing from the banking community. Typical examples of financing structures have included JLLs and private placements of debt with Japanese insurance companies. More recently, however, financial pressures have resulted in synthetic operating lease structures being employed to obtain favourable balance sheet treatment. Exemptions from withholding taxes are usually obtained in aircraft financings.

Vietnam

Having only recently opened its doors to a market economy, Vietnam is very much an emerging market at a nascent stage, but one that we will see more of in the future. At the moment, aircraft financing is mainly carried out via operating leases, although the trend is towards ECA-guaranteed finance leases. The European ECAs have already supported certain financings but EXIM has not yet formally opened as at the time of writing. The flag-carrier, Vietnam Airlines, is government owned and it is expected that government support will be required to play a firm role for the medium term while the airline is in the process of modernising its jet fleet with Western aircraft.

Summary

Out of the top 14 Asian flag-carriers, half still have majority government ownership. The current government shareholdings (direct or indirect) in the various flag-carriers are set out in Exhibit 12.3.

Government support, either direct or indirect, has an impact on the creditworthiness of the national airlines of Asia and their ability and means to finance their aircraft. Tourism is an

Exhibit 12.3
Government stakes in the main Asian flag-carriers, end-1997

Country	Flag carrier	Government ownership (%)
Australia	Qantas Airways	–
China	Air China	100
Hong Kong	Cathay Pacific Airways	–
India	Air India	100
Indonesia	Garuda Indonesia	100
Japan	Japan Airlines	–
Malaysia	Malaysia Airlines	25
New Zealand	Air New Zealand	–
Philippines	Philippine Airlines	24
Singapore	Singapore Airlines	54
South Korea	Korean Air	–
Taiwan	China Airlines	71
Thailand	Thai Airways	93
Vietnam	Vietnam Airlines	100

important industry for most countries in Asia and the national flag-carrier is a key factor in that equation, as well as being a valuable source of foreign currency. Whether or not directly owned, it would be difficult to envisage any government of a major Asian country voluntarily letting its national airline fail. Many airlines in Asia are still in a controlled market and enjoy some protection internationally from bilateral traffic rights controlled by their governments. That, however, is slowly changing over time as flag-carriers are being privatised, second and third domestic competitors are being encouraged, international routes are beginning to be shared out and open-sky policies are slowly but surely coming. As this process continues, financing in future will need to rely on industry fundamentals rather than government support.

Notes

1 An asset value guarantee (AVG) typically provides that the aircraft will be worth at least a minimum amount at the end of the lease (usually equal to the unamortised amount of the loan). The AVG works on a 'window' basis only at the end of the lease, and does not provide for any particular value during the lease term.
2 Securitisation represents the conversion of more illiquid financial assets to marketable securities. A security is a much simpler instrument than a loan, and has an established transfer mechanism. The issuing banks will usually 'make a market' in these securities, so that, unlike most loans, they can be bought and sold on the secondary market. A short-term investor may buy a five-year note with the intention of selling after one year. The securities may be rated by one of the rating agencies to provide further standardisation and appeal to investors. This therefore provides a wider investor base and indeed some institutions can only invest in securities. The usual mechanism for a securitisation consists of setting up a special purpose company or trust that issues the securities.

Author's note

This article was written and updated at the end of 1997, when the economic crisis in Asia was still unfolding. As such, readers should be aware that events were evolving rapidly in some countries, and that could change some of the content of this article. The views expressed in this article are my personal views, and not necessarily those of my employer.

13 Aircraft financing in Russia

Stephen McGairl

Commercial and political background

Until the Soviet Union disintegrated in 1991, aviation in Russia meant Aeroflot. An emanation of the Ministry of Civil Aviation, Aeroflot was the airline for the entire Soviet Union, and it also ran the airports and all ancillary services for civil aviation. With the break up of the Soviet Union there was a corresponding disintegration of Aeroflot. Aircraft and other assets attached to various regional divisions of Aeroflot formed the basis for new regional airlines, but with their economic basis pulled away from under them and with no access to new sources of finance they were not viable.

Aeroflot had been able to show impressive statistics for passenger numbers on its routes, but the change to a market-based economy made these statistics meaningless. Air travel in the Soviet era was a service provided by the state with little of its revenue generated by ticket sales. The thousands of travellers reflected in Soviet passenger statistics would simply melt away in the face of the need to pay a proper price for tickets.

Emerging from the post-Soviet chaos there is a small number of airlines aiming to build services comparable with international standards and a number of 'baby flots' struggling to find a market position with ageing equipment and limited domestic markets.

The Russian government faces dilemmas both in relation to domestic airlines and domestic aircraft manufacturers. The protection of uneconomic domestic airlines and aircraft manufacturers, while satisfying a political need, is also restraining the development of the aviation sector – a sector that must develop in order to service and stimulate economic growth in the region. The government can control the awarding of route licences and hence control the extent of competition that is introduced against the scarcely viable baby flots, but protecting uneconomic domestic operators from competition is not without cost. A number of foreign airlines have already established routes to Russian provincial centres.

The aircraft factories that build Ilyushin and Tupolev designs employ thousands of people, but the market for their products is at the moment very limited. They may take some comfort from the exorbitant levels of import taxes due on Western-manufactured aircraft imported into Russia, whether purchased or on lease, although the government has granted exemptions to certain airlines to temporarily import Western aircraft without payment of those taxes.

The re-engining of Russian airframes with Western engines such as the Ilyushin Pratt & Whitney joint venture and the Tupolev Rolls-Royce project may show a way forward for Russian aircraft manufacturers to expand the market for their products and for Russian airlines to achieve Western efficiency at a more affordable cost. It appears, however, that for the moment the most dynamic of the Russian airlines continue to have an appetite for wholly Western-built equipment.

A number of deals involving Western aircraft and Russian airlines have been completed. These deals require the Western bank or lessor to confront political, economic, credit and legal issues and emerge feeling that they are manageable. In relation to all of these issues the situation has improved in the course of the past few years, although many uncertainties remain. The political landscape in Russia is a lot more settled than it was a couple of years ago, and the way in which power is exercised under the new Russian constitution is becoming clearer. Economically, the government's control of the value of the currency and the reduction in inflation have been remarkable. Assessing the credit status of Russian companies is becoming easier. A number of major Russian companies have had to confront the disciplines of foreign stock markets, and others now understand that international accounting standards have to be observed if foreign finance is to be obtained.

Impediments to doing business

The principal legal and tax issues that can impede deal making are:

- the taxes and duties payable on the import of Western aircraft; and
- the need for a Russian lessee to obtain a Central Bank of Russia (CBR) licence to pay foreign currency rentals.

Both of these issues are likely to be obscured by exemptions or opinions as to their applicability that require careful scrutiny. Beyond that, it is necessary to understand the general legal framework and to know what is and is not possible.

Import duties and import value added tax

Under Article 2 of the Law on Customs Tariffs (Law 5003-1 of 21 May 1993) (the CTL) and Article 18 of the Customs Code (adopted in the form of Law No. 5222-1 of 18 June 1993), the import of goods into Russia is subject to various import taxes, unless an exemption from import tax is applicable. The following import taxes would be payable to the customs authorities on an aircraft imported today:

- a customs clearance fee in an amount equal to 0.15 per cent of the declared value of the aircraft;
- an import duty in an amount equal to 30 per cent of the declared value of the aircraft; and
- value added tax (VAT) in an amount equal to 20 per cent of the aggregate of the declared value of the aircraft and the import duty payable in respect of the aircraft.

General

Under Articles 111 and 112 of the Customs Code, import taxes are levied on goods imported into Russia on their entry into Russian customs territory. Customs officers at the airport of entry will request that a customs clearance declaration be filed and, depending on the customs regime that applies to the aircraft, will demand payment of the applicable import taxes.

Calculation of import taxes

Import taxes are calculated as a percentage of the 'customs value' of the imported goods. The CTL defines 'customs value' as the value that the importer declares to the customs authorities in accordance with Russian law and that has been accepted by the customs authorities. The declared value is typically the value that the parties to the transaction have attributed to the property being imported. If the customs authorities believe this value to be inappropriate, however, they may use other methods to determine the value of the property.

Payment of import taxes

Import taxes may be paid either in roubles or in a foreign currency converted into roubles at the exchange rate quoted by the CBR. There are two exceptions to this general rule:

1 Article 123 of the Customs Code states that the customs authorities may require that a customs payment be made in a foreign currency to the extent that Russian law expressly authorises the customs authorities to impose this requirement. The requirement currently applies only to the 0.15 per cent customs clearance fee, one-third of which must be paid in foreign currency.
2 Paragraph 4 of the Instruction issued by the Ministry of Finance and the State Customs Committee and enacted by Order 49 of the State Customs Committee dated 30 January 1993 states that VAT may only be paid in roubles.

Import taxes are generally payable at the time the customs authorities accept a customs declaration. The customs authorities may grant an extension of up to two months (Article 121 of the Customs Code) but will require that the payment be secured by a bank guarantee or pledge during the extension period.

Exemptions relating to particular customs regimes
Free circulation

Under Article 107 of the Customs Code, 'means of transport'[1] brought into Russian customs territory must be placed under a customs regime. Goods put into free circulation are not required to be re-exported and are not eligible for general import tax relief. As discussed below, specific import tax relief may be available in certain circumstances.

Temporary import

The other type of customs regime is the 'temporary import' regime, under which aircraft imported temporarily into Russian customs territory may be fully or partially exempt from customs payments.

The length of time for which an aircraft may be imported temporarily varies depending on the position that the customs authorities take with respect to import of a particular aircraft. The Customs Code provides that the term of temporary import cannot exceed two years. Article 71 of the Customs Code, however, gives the State Customs Committee the authority to extend the temporary import period for certain categories of goods. Aircraft imported temporarily must be re-exported in their original condition, except for normal wear and tear resulting from use or storage of the aircraft.

Full exemption

A temporarily imported aircraft that is used for international transportation of passengers and goods, the equipment necessary for its normal operation and the spare parts necessary for its repair may be fully exempt from customs duties. This exemption, however, is intended to benefit foreign airlines operating in Russia. The customs authorities have specified that an aircraft and the related equipment and spare parts will only qualify for a full exemption from customs duties if the aircraft is:

- registered outside Russia;
- registered in the name of a foreign entity;
- imported by the foreign entity; and
- used on Russian territory by the foreign entity.

Partial exemption

A temporarily imported aircraft that is not eligible for a full exemption from customs duties may be eligible for a partial exemption. Partial exemption from customs duties under the temporary import customs regime results in deferral of part of the customs duties and VAT payments that would otherwise have been payable to the customs authorities if the aircraft had been put into free circulation (the free circulation amount). Under the partial exemption rules, a payment (a temporary import payment) in the amount of 3 per cent of the aggregate free circulation amount must be made in advance each month (although the importer may agree with customs to pay it quarterly). Customs payments made in respect of aircraft that are under the temporary import customs regime are not refunded on export. Payments made under the temporary import customs regime are calculated in US dollars, but are payable in roubles at the rate of exchange set by the CBR on the date on which such payment is due.

It is disadvantageous to transfer an aircraft imported under the temporary import customs regime to the free circulation customs regime. Although the aggregate payments (customs duties and VAT) made under the temporary import regime can be credited towards those due under the free circulation regime, the customs authorities will charge interest at the CBR rate from the date of import of the aircraft on the difference between the payments made under the temporary import regime and those now due under the free circulation regime.

VAT on lease rentals

Russian law also requires VAT to be paid on rental payments made in connection with leases of movable property. The Law on Value Added Tax states that VAT is payable when goods or services are 'realised' in Russia. A lease is treated as a service that is 'realised' in Russia if the lessee's place of business is in Russia. Leases to Russian airlines would therefore be treated as having been 'realised' in Russia.

A lessee is required to withhold the VAT amount from each rental payment that the lessee makes under a lease and is liable for such 'reverse charge' VAT on the full value of the lease payments. The withheld VAT amount is deemed to be the Russian lessee's input VAT and may be set off against its output VAT. Russian tax legislation does not provide for any specific liability if the lessee fails to withhold the VAT amount. The tax authorities have the right to withdraw money from a taxpayer's (and not from the tax agent's, such as the lessee's) bank account to satisfy tax debts. It is reported, however, that such withdrawals have been made from tax agents' accounts.

Power to grant exemptions from import taxes and VAT

The legal status and effectiveness of exemptions are somewhat unclear. The CTL and Russian tax laws could be construed as allowing exemptions from customs duties and import VAT, but only in respect of categories of goods or importers, not in respect of specific importers.

Under Article 34 of the CTL, the government of the Russian Federation has the exclusive power to grant exemptions from import duties. Article 34 prohibits the granting of exemptions on a case-by-case basis. In practice, however, this prohibition has been repeatedly ignored and individual exemptions have been and are still being granted.

Import VAT is not considered to be import duty and is therefore governed by Russian tax law. Russian tax law also prohibits the granting of tax exemptions on a case-by-case basis (although the relevant Article 10 of the Law on Fundamentals of the Tax System is not a model of clarity) and provides that a tax exemption is only valid if it has been adopted as a tax law. Adoption of a law requires three hearings in the state Duma, the approval of the Federation Council and execution of the law by the President. It is therefore unlikely that a particular taxpayer will be able to obtain specific relief from its import VAT obligations.

Exemptions from customs duties and import VAT obligations that are granted to a specific taxpayer in violation of the prohibitions on case-by-case relief in the CTL and the Russian tax laws may be revoked at any time. Such tax exemptions granted to importers have, in fact, previously been revoked.[2]

The granting of tax exemptions to specific entities or transactions has been a political issue in Russia for several years. The problem of individual exemptions may be seen as part of the power struggle between the Duma, which has the power to pass tax legislation, and the government, which wishes to facilitate particular transactions.

As a practical matter, the Russian approach to constitutional matters has been based more on respect for hierarchy than on respect for detailed legal analysis. An order from the Prime Minister, for example, should provide very strong comfort in practice as it is likely that the State Customs Committee would comply with it.

A decision to rely on an exemption would be as much a political judgement as a legal judgement. If an exemption was revoked or not complied with by any of the relevant taxing authorities, political action, not legal action, would probably be necessary.

Even if exemptions from customs duties and import VAT are unavailable, it may be possible to defer payment of the amounts owed. Article 24 of the Law On Fundamentals of the Tax System gives the Ministry of Finance the power to grant deferrals of tax payment obligations.

The customs authorities may grant deferrals of customs duties payments up to two months from filing the customs declaration. Under Article 121 of the Customs Code, interest is charged on the amount of the deferred payment at the then-effective CBR interest rate.

Central bank licence for foreign currency transactions

General

Russian law states that payments made in foreign currency for services provided to Russian residents and which are deferred over a period exceeding 180 days are considered 'currency transactions connected with the movement of capital'. Under Russian Federation Law 3615-1 of 9 October 1992 On Currency Regulation and Control, the Russian party to such currency transactions is required to obtain the approval of the CBR before engaging in any such transaction.

Recent CBR instructions exempt certain transactions from the requirement of CBR approval of currency operations connected with movement of capital. The CBR order of 24 April 1996 (02-94) approving the Regulations on Amendments to the Procedure for Carrying out Certain Types of Currency Operations in the Russian Federation provides, among other things, that payments by Russian residents to non-residents that are made outside Russia in connection with leases of air, sea or river vessels located outside Russia are not subject to CBR approval if the property to be leased is transferred to the lessee within 180 days of the transfer of the foreign currency lease payment.

The applicability of this exemption to foreign currency lease payments depends in part on the meaning of the phrase 'located outside Russia'. Order 02-94 does not define the concept 'located outside Russia' and no CBR interpretation of this phrase exists. Lawyers acting for Russian airlines have argued that an aircraft registered outside Russia is located outside Russia for this purpose or alternatively that location only needs to be considered at the start of the lease. However, until the CBR provides a clear interpretation of the phrase 'located outside Russia', it would be prudent to characterise all foreign currency lease rentals as payments that fall within the restrictions applicable to currency transactions involving movements of capital.

Sanctions for breach of currency legislation

The sanction prescribed for foreign currency transactions that violate the Russian foreign currency legal regime is confiscation of the transaction proceeds by the Russian government. In accordance with Article 2.4 of the Law on Currency Regulation and Control, transactions made in violation of this law are deemed to be invalid.

Russian law does not expressly prohibit the parties to a transaction that violates the Russian foreign currency legal regime from allocating among themselves the financial consequences of confiscation of the transaction proceeds. For example, the parties could include indemnity provisions in their contract requiring one party to compensate another party for any loss which that party suffers because of a violation of the Russian foreign currency legal regime, such as the absence of a valid CBR foreign currency transaction licence. If such an indemnity provision was included in a lease, a lessee might try to contest enforcement of the provision in a Russian court by arguing that the indemnity was contrary to public policy because it purported to allocate the effects of the sanction for violating the Russian foreign currency legal regime to a particular party, even though Russian law allows the budgetary authorities to seek to collect the penalty from a number of parties to the transaction.

The better view is that an indemnity against the financial consequences of a violation of the Russian foreign currency legal regime is not contrary to public policy so long as it does not purport to limit the category of persons to whom the budgetary authorities have recourse for the penalty payment. Such an indemnity would only allocate liability for the penalty payment as between the parties to a transaction and would therefore be a purely commercial matter.

Lease rentals in roubles

Roubles may only be received in Russia. Payments made to a lessor in Russia may cause it to be classified as a resident for Russian tax purposes and to lose any exemption from withholding tax on lease payments provided for by a relevant double taxation treaty.

The foreign lessor may receive lease payments in roubles only on a 'T' (current) account opened with a Russian bank and for this purpose it would need to establish an accredited representative office. T-type accounts may only be used to meet expenses of the representative office and expenses relating to a lessor's export/import operations including receipt of lease proceeds. Unlike funds held in an 'I' account, funds held in T-type accounts may not be converted into foreign currency and repatriated. So having received the lease payments on its T account, the accredited representative office would then need to transfer those payments to an I-type account and then convert the rouble payment into foreign currency and repatriate the foreign currency. There is a risk that receiving lease payments into a T account will result in the tax authorities deeming such payments attributable to the representative office, with 35 per cent corporate tax payable by the representative office.

If the lessor conducts its leasing activities in Russia through a Russian subsidiary, then that entity could enter into lease transactions with the Russian airline. It could then repatriate the lease payments as dividends after the lease payments have been converted into foreign currency. The Russian entity, however, may be required to get a CBR foreign currency licence in order to pay the dividends in foreign currency. In theory, dividend payments to foreign shareholders are free from any foreign currency transaction licensing restrictions. In practice, however, the CBR insists that Russian entities that wish to pay dividends in foreign currency to shareholders overseas obtain a licence to do so. Although there is 35 per cent corporate tax, property tax, VAT and turnover taxes, such a structure may still be tax-efficient if accomplished so that the aircraft is contributed to the charter capital of the Russian subsidiary and will therefore be exempt from import duty and import VAT.

Other aspects of the legal framework

Taxes and duties

Withholding tax

Rental payments by a Russian lessee to a non-Russian lessor are subject to a 20 per cent withholding tax. Interest payments are subject to a 15 per cent withholding tax. The withholding tax requirement is often eliminated or the withholding tax percentage reduced under the tax treaties between the former Soviet Union and other countries to which Russia has formally acceded, or under Russia's own tax treaties.

The double taxation treaty between the US and the Russian Federation should eliminate the 20 per cent withholding tax that would otherwise be applicable to rental payments payable to a US lessor. To invoke the exemption under this treaty, the lessor, not the lessee, must apply to the Russian tax authorities, who would then provide written confirmation to the lessee that it is exempt from the obligations under Russian law to withhold the 20 per cent tax from their lease payments.

Until the lessee receives a written confirmation from the Russian tax authorities that it is not required to withhold the 20 per cent tax from lease payments, the lessee must withhold the tax. If taxes have been withheld from the lease payments before the Russian tax authorities provide written confirmation of the exemption from withholding, the lessor may apply for a refund of the withheld amounts. The refund application must be submitted no more than one year after the lessor receives the lease payments from which taxes were withheld. The lessor may therefore be unable to obtain withholding tax refunds of withheld amounts that relate to lease payments that the lessor received more than a year ago.

As a practical matter, Russia does not have the resources to refund previously collected revenues and the budgetary authorities are likely to resist making refunds. Even if the lessor is successful in pressing its case for a refund, the Russian budgetary authorities are likely to issue the lessor a tax credit instead of refunding any monies.

Grossing-up clause

Article 6.5 of the Instruction of the State Tax Service of 16 June 1995, number 34, sets out the rule that one person cannot agree contractually to pay taxes on behalf of the person who actually owes the taxes. Based on this rule there is a risk that a grossing-up clause might conflict with Russian law and therefore might be unenforceable.

However, the head of the Tax Reform Department of the Ministry of Finance, Mr Ivaneev, recently stated publicly that Russian law does not prohibit grossing-up clauses. Mr Ivaneev's views are unofficial because they have not been submitted in writing to the Ministry of Justice for review and then registered with the Ministry of Justice. The tax authorities, however, would normally implement Mr Ivaneev's views immediately in their negotiations with taxpayers. Grossing-up provisions should therefore not be subject to attack by the Russian tax authorities. Russian courts, however, have not yet examined the issue of the validity of grossing-up clauses and could disagree with the interpretation given by Mr Ivaneev.

Permanent establishment

A lessor would be found to have a 'permanent establishment' in Russia if it had a fixed place of business through which it carried on business activities in Russia. The explanatory notes on the terminology of the Russia/US double taxation treaty that appear in the treaty's protocol indicate that, for the purposes of that treaty, equipment leasing is an example of an activity that does not in itself result in the creation of a 'permanent establishment'.

If a lease has been entered into through the activities of a representative office or other permanent presence in Russia of the lessor, however, there is a risk that the office or other permanent presence might be characterised as a 'permanent establishment'. If so, the profits from the lease would be subject to Russian profits tax.

Property tax

Russian property tax legislation requires foreign entities that have assets in Russia to notify the tax authorities within one month of the assets arriving in Russia. If a lessor applies to the tax authorities for relief from the withholding tax that would otherwise apply to the lease payments, however, then a lessor would not be required to provide a separate notification to the tax authorities in connection with the property tax.

If the leased aircraft do not appear on a lessee's balance sheet as assets of the lessee, then the property tax obligation would be imposed on the lessor. The lessor may be relieved of the obligation under a double tax treaty. Article 21 of the Russia/US double taxation treaty, for example, should exempt a lessor from the imposition of property taxes. Moreover, if the lessor files a request for relief from the withholding tax, the lessor will have discharged the notification obligations that Russian law imposes on the lessor in respect of the property tax and would not be required to take any further action. The burden of seeking to collect the property tax would then shift to the Russian tax authorities, who would be required to approach the lessor concerning collection of the tax. The tax authorities do not normally seek to collect property tax from companies that do not have a permanent establishment in Russia.

Sources of Russian leasing law

The second part of the Russian Civil Code, which contains detailed provisions on leasing, was enacted at the end of 1995 and is now the principal Russian law on leasing.

Most of the provisions of Russian leasing law only apply to a leasing transaction if the parties to the transaction have not entered into a detailed leasing agreement that includes provisions covering the issues that are also addressed in the law. The terms of most Western-style lease documentation would therefore supersede most of the provisions of Russian leasing law.

The following principles of Russian leasing law that appear in both the old Soviet legislation and in the new Civil Code, however, would still be applicable to leases:

- The lessor may be liable to the lessee under certain circumstances for defects in the aircraft about which the lessee did not know or could not have known at the time the lease term commenced.
- Unless a lease agreement expressly states otherwise, a lessee is presumed to have a right to renew the lease on expiration of the agreed lease term.
- The Civil Code gives a lessee the right to terminate the lease in some circumstances, such as when the condition of the aircraft renders it unusable by the lessee.
- The Civil Code states that a lessor may terminate a lease through a court procedure, but allows the parties to the lease to set out the agreed grounds for terminating the lease in the lease agreement.

Security interests

The Law on Pledge established the legal framework for security interests in Russia. This was slightly amended and supplemented by the Civil Code.

Aircraft are treated in the same way as immovable property. An aircraft mortgage, in addition to complying with certain formal requirements in the law, is not created until it has been notarised (at a cost of 1.5 per cent of the aircraft value) and registered in the state register of aircraft. However, the current state register does not provide for registration of mortgages or other legal rights in aircraft.

Choice of law and enforcement

Russian law permits a contract between a Russian party and a non-Russian party to be governed by the law of a jurisdiction chosen by the parties. Russian law, however, may still be relevant to certain matters that relate to foreign law leases to Russian airlines. First, Russian leasing law addresses matters such as the allocation to the contract parties of liability for harm caused to third parties and the judicial procedure for termination of a lease. Secondly, if a lessor wished to enforce the terms of a lease against a lessee, the enforcement action would probably be heard in a Russian court, which would apply Russian procedural and other rules in deciding the enforcement action.

Foreign court decisions, however, are enforceable in Russia only if the country in which the foreign court decision was rendered has entered into an agreement with the Russian Federation concerning mutual legal assistance. Neither the US nor the UK has entered into a mutual legal assistance agreement with the Russian Federation.

In contrast with foreign judgments, foreign arbitral awards should be enforceable in the Russian Federation. The USSR ratified the 1958 New York Convention on the Recognition and Enforcement of Foreign Arbitral Awards on 24 August 1960. The New York Convention would require a Russian court to enforce a foreign arbitral award without re-examining the substantive merits of the dispute which was arbitrated.

The Russian Federation has not yet formally acceded to the New York Convention by depositing an agreement to adhere to its terms with the Secretary General of the United Nations as required by the terms of the Convention. On 27 January 1992, however, the permanent representative of the Russian Federation brought to the attention of the Secretary General of the United Nations the text of a note from the Ministry of Foreign Affairs of the Russian Federation to the leaders of diplomatic missions in Moscow, which stated that the Russian Federation would continue to exercise the USSR's rights and honour the USSR's obligations arising under international treaties to which the USSR was a signatory. A Russian court has recently upheld the applicability of the New York Convention to a proceeding before the Russian court.

The Law on International Commercial Arbitration of 7 July 1993 also provides for the enforcement of foreign arbitral awards in the Russian Federation. The Civil Procedure Code requires an application to enforce a foreign arbitral award to be filed within three years of the effective date of the award. The Law on International Commercial Arbitration sets out a number of grounds on which a Russian court may refuse to recognise or enforce a foreign arbitral award. These grounds include, among other things, the following:

- invalidity of the agreement to arbitrate disputes;
- failure to inform the party against whom the award is rendered about the appointment of an arbitral tribunal;
- failure to give the party against whom the award is rendered an adequate opportunity to present its defence;
- the arbitral tribunal's lack of power to render the arbitral award;
- the failure of the arbitral tribunal or the arbitration proceedings to comply with the requirements of the arbitration agreement;
- Russian laws not permitting the particular matters submitted to arbitration to be decided in an arbitration proceeding;
- the arbitral award not yet being final and binding or its enforcement having been suspended in accordance with the law of the jurisdiction in which it was rendered;
- the arbitral award conflicting with Russian public policy; or
- the arbitral award being incompatible with a Russian judgment between the same parties relating to the same issues or, in some circumstances, with an earlier arbitral award or foreign judgment that satisfies the same criteria and is enforceable in the Russian Federation.

Once a dispute has been referred to foreign arbitration, a Russian court would probably refuse to grant any interim relief, such as an interim conservatory order, during the foreign arbitration proceedings.

International treaties

The USSR acceded to the 1944 Chicago Convention On International Civil Aviation on 15 October 1970. The Russian Federation agreed to be bound by the Chicago Convention as a successor state to the USSR on 24 December 1991. Russia has ratified neither the 1948 Geneva Convention on International Recognition of Rights in Aircraft nor the 1933 Convention on the Unification of Certain Rules for the Precautionary Arrest of Aircraft. On 8 February 1998 the law was passed ratifying the 1988 Ottawa Convention on International Financial Leasing (see Chapter 23).

The Air Code

Russia's Air Code was passed in March 1997. However, it does not take the foreign lessor or lender very much closer to answers to the sort of questions that are of concern. Registration of aircraft is expressed to be subject to rules that have yet to be made, while registration of ownership rights and other rights in aircraft are to be dealt with by reference to a provision of the Civil Code that concerns real property. Similarly, the state register is supposed to register mortgages but it does not yet do so.

Experience of dealing with the officials who maintain the state register is still typically a frustrating experience. It is common for officials to refuse to answer questions about the operation of the register, saying that it is secret and that only the airlines concerned can have access to it.

Future developments

Transactions completed so far have mostly been relatively short-term operating leases of aircraft registered outside Russia. The Russian registration system is clearly not yet able to provide a lender or lessor with the protections needed for a financing of a Russian-registered aircraft. The Air Code is a useful step towards this but detailed provisions on the administration of the register will be needed.

In other sectors of the Russian economy the gap between the obvious need for investment and the equally obvious inability of local companies to raise it has been bridged to a certain extent by foreign equity and finance from international financial institutions. Neither has yet happened to any significant extent in the aviation sector, despite some attempts. The development of Russian-built, Western-engined aircraft may perhaps be a stimulus for the raising of finance by Russian airlines and for legislative changes to facilitate those transactions.

Notes

1 According to Article 18 of the Customs Code, means of transport may, depending on their use, be treated as means of transport proper or as goods depending on their use.
2 The adoption of Law No. 31-FZ 'on certain matters in relation to granting exemptions to participants in foreign economic activities' on 13 March 1995 is one example of such a repeal of tax exemptions.

14 Financing national airlines in developing countries

Richard Bouma

The author specialises in aviation finance for the African market and the discussion that follows draws heavily on that experience. However, the financing needs of national airlines in all developing countries share certain similarities, even though bankers and brokers involved in negotiating aircraft packages inevitably find important local peculiarities.

Today, the preliminary issue – whether an airline is necessary at all – is debatable, as most African national airlines were established shortly after independence 35 years or more ago. There are only a few instances where economic logic has persuaded governments to participate in consortium airlines or to buy airline services from foreign carriers as needed, leaving the major investments and debts to airlines based in industrialised countries. Political motives, especially national pride, have proved stronger than economics. Indeed, many African airlines were created more for political than commercial purposes; this is a key reason why many of them lose money and will continue to do so. Once brought into being, a national airline assumes symbolic importance, placing its continued existence beyond question.

However, Africa is currently undergoing a fundamental transformation that began with the break-up of the communist bloc in Europe heralding the end of the Cold War. African countries have witnessed a dramatic reduction in activity on the part of the 'superpowers' that used to vie for influence with their respective governments. With the withdrawal of this support, more and more governments have come to the conclusion that to survive as a viable entity they need to introduce full democracy and a free market economy into their country. Unfortunately, in some states historic clan and tribal feuds have proved stronger than the democratic process and they have disintegrated into internecine strife. Nevertheless, in the majority of cases the process is working, albeit off a small base, with many countries introducing measures to attract foreign investment including the relaxation of local ownership requirements, the creation of a business-friendly tax environment and abolition of foreign exchange controls to allow the remittance of dividends and profits.

This new spirit of realism has had a positive effect on some of the national airlines in Africa in that they are installing professional management and, in some cases, working with outside consultants to privatise or partially privatise the airline. Despite this, many of the problems faced by these airlines in the past still exist, even if management now has greater flexibility to address them using market-related solutions.

Foreign exchange

The most important issue that faces airline executives and their bankers is the need for foreign exchange. Conserving foreign exchange is almost as difficult as earning it in the first place. At a typical African airline, managers confront the following difficult issues:

1 They generally have to buy their fuel and spares abroad. The airline's small fleet does not warrant bulk purchases large enough to earn discounts. Long distances and poor local rail, road and port facilities drive up transport costs.

2 They send their equipment abroad for servicing, paying in foreign currency, because the small fleet does not warrant a local maintenance shop, nor does it generate enough foreign exchange to underwrite one. Near neighbours are in the same predicament, but pooled maintenance facilities remain a goal for the future. This leaves Europe as the best alternative, regardless of the currency drain.

3 Because 'aircraft on ground' (AOG) spares can be as far as 4,000 miles from the disabled aircraft, the foreign exchange problem creates a dilemma: either spend it on inventories of large parts, or lose it as revenue during prolonged down times.

4 Aircraft insurance underwriters charge more for insurance because the fleet is small and old. Premiums are, of course, paid in foreign exchange.

5 The airline serves the domestic market, earning most of its revenues in local currency, which is subject to devaluation. The government keeps domestic fares low for political reasons. Government officials often travel free, and occasionally commandeer aircraft for official travel, disrupting commercial schedules. International flights earn foreign exchange but often their revenues subsidise the ministries of tourism and transport.

6 The central bank, avidly seeking ways to meet its debt service and other obligations, milks the airline for foreign exchange, making it hard to retain enough to pay salaries for staff abroad and other routine operational expenses.

7 Illegal local ticket sales make interlining difficult, further reducing opportunities to earn foreign exchange.

Ironically, the most common justification for keeping the national airline is its ability to earn foreign exchange for the country. However plausible this sounds on the floor of the national legislature, it rings hollow in the airline chairman's office, for foreign routes rarely earn enough to meet the airline's own foreign currency obligations. At best, selling tickets to local citizens in local currency saves foreign exchange, because otherwise they must fly with foreign airlines and pay accordingly.

Overcoming the foreign exchange handicap

Airline managers find themselves under intense pressure to earn more foreign exchange revenues and to depend less on foreign service contracts requiring foreign exchange payments.

Upgrading the fleet

The quickest solution for this problem is new equipment – it reduces operating costs and makes the airline more attractive, improving revenues:

- Generally, the newer the aircraft, the higher the fuel efficiency.
- Because they need less maintenance, newer aircraft have less down time, which saves on costs and increases availability for revenue service.
- Spare parts' inventories can be smaller, and AOG services are rarely needed.
- On a percentage of hull basis, insurance premiums are lower (although higher overall).
- Newer aircraft compete better against foreign airlines having similar or older aircraft.

The attractiveness of newer aircraft becomes part of the foreign exchange dilemma – while operating costs go down, debt service goes up. Choice of aircraft thus becomes a critical decision, embodying all the economic and political considerations alluded to above.

Choosing the right aircraft

Such considerations notwithstanding, airline management will do best to make decisions on the basis of net foreign exchange cost. Executives should bear in mind that the aircraft must be capable of non-stop service to major foreign destinations. Every landing abroad increases the cost of airport and air traffic control charges, fuel, maintenance, catering services and local employee salaries. Long, non-stop flights are more competitive with those of major foreign carriers.

The aircraft must also be the appropriate size for the routes. New aircraft with greater capacity are not a guarantee of higher ticket sales to foreigners, who tend to choose European and American airlines. The best way to capture the foreign travellers' business is not by buying the largest aircraft available on the market, but by restricting foreign airlines' access to the country's international airports.

Freight carrying capacity is important, even at the cost of some passenger seats. The national airline can compete against the major carriers for freight; to shippers, price and schedules mean more than slick marketing campaigns.

Management should use a cash basis for calculating capital cost and choosing a financing method. There is no point in trying to justify a purchase on the basis of a 20-year review of income and expenditure unless the borrower pays the debt over a similar period. Principal or lease payments should match the depreciation charge, otherwise debt service will exceed operational savings or the increased foreign exchange income.

New versus used aircraft

One area of intense political interest, and thus a focus of political interference, is the decision whether to buy new or used aircraft.

If airline management uses foreign exchange implications as a guide, it will rarely justify the purchase of a new aircraft. This is true even where there is a substantial gap in age or technology between the new aircraft and the old one it replaces. Financing is at the root of this problem: the national airline can rarely borrow enough money over a long enough period to make the new aircraft economical.

The choice thus comes down to a used aircraft for economic reasons, or a new one for political reasons. Because a new aircraft symbolises not only the nation's prestige, but also the skill of its leaders, it is easy for politicians to value these symbols far above mere business prudence. Also, this natural preference is often buttressed by unhappy past experience with used equipment. Sometimes, national airlines have unknowingly purchased overvalued aircraft. Sellers too have sometimes failed to provide adequate after-sales support.

Exporters of new aircraft do their best to make their products as attractive as possible. Governments in aircraft-exporting countries may urge governments in developing countries to buy new aircraft as offsets to increased traffic rights or even in return for economic development aid. In such cases, the manufacturers may subsidise the financing through deficiency guarantees and residual value underwriting. This relieves the airline of the need to pay deposits, and allows the financier to rely on the aircraft itself as sufficient security.

216

All these attractions of new aircraft notwithstanding, today's harsh economic and financial realities crowd in on national airlines, which have come to realise that they can only benefit the nation if they provide good service without draining foreign exchange resources from other high-priority national objectives. Economic necessity pushes the choice of used aircraft to the forefront, where management can see the wisdom of self-financing several used aircraft rather than using scarce foreign exchange to buy one or two new ones. The old adage applies here: an aircraft is new only on the day of its inaugural flight. Thereafter, it is a used aircraft like any other.

The asset-based financing package

Preoccupation with political considerations in buying aircraft for the national airline has its counterpart in the arrangement of financing. Here, however, it is foreign lenders who have been unduly swayed by political considerations, in the sense that political risk has dominated the pricing and structure of aircraft purchase transactions. Overemphasising political risk, lenders have sometimes forced airlines to accept unsuitable financing packages.

However, major banks have adapted to the developing world a technique used in financing heavy equipment sales in industrialised countries: they base their risk on the asset – the aircraft itself – rather than on the financial condition of the airline or estimates of the government's future willingness and ability to repay. Today, the banks commonly offer terms related to the life of the aircraft and its expected future value. They also offer the facility in the form of an operating lease, accepting a level of residual risk that allows the airline to keep the transaction off its balance sheet.

Within the past few years, lenders have arranged asset-based aircraft transactions in a number of African countries. Nevertheless, political risk has continued to plague the African borrower. In each of the transactions just mentioned, the documentation contained expensive and onerous restrictions. These are particularly vexing to the airlines because they have little to do with the soundness of its operation or the security value of the aircraft.

Dealing with political risk

In seeking to eliminate political risk, the banks impose the following major restrictions:

1 They require ownership outside the country, in order to avoid local mortgage registration.
2 They require foreign registration, effectively 'de-Africanising' the country risk. This poses a serious issue for government officials, who resent having a national asset under the influence, and possibly the control, of a foreign government. It complicates management for the airline's executives, who must spend foreign exchange to maintain foreign licences for pilots, comply with foreign certification requirements and make sure bilateral rights are not affected.
3 They demand comprehensive political risk or deprivation-of-use insurance, effectively eliminating any remaining country risk. (In some cases, this is an alternative to the foreign registry.) Despite its avowed purpose of eliminating country risk, the premium rate generally reflects the country's risk rating as perceived by international bankers. Airline executives consider this an unnecessary extra foreign exchange cost unrelated to their operations. Of particular concern to the airline is the inability to buy such insurance for the full term of the financing. This leaves open a small possibility that a lender will demand return of an aircraft

because political risk insurance is not available, even though the airline has fulfilled all other contractual obligations.

4 They usually insist on foreign maintenance standards and use of foreign maintenance contractors, regardless of the quality of local standards and service. This gives the lender more frequent opportunities to repossess the aircraft should the borrower default; it also helps uphold asset value, which will figure significantly in any repossession and resale. For the airline, however, it means higher foreign exchange costs.

5 They lend only to finance aircraft used in international service, again because it offers opportunities to repossess without political interference.

Lenders also believe, often mistakenly, that the aircraft will generate enough foreign exchange to service the debt. As pointed out earlier, must of the revenue on international routes is received from nationals in local currency, which saves the country foreign exchange but does not generate it. Such revenue must be presented to the central bank if it is to be converted into foreign exchange; when the central bank is short of foreign exchange, the airline must wait its turn, in some cases for months or years.

Hard currency paid by foreign passengers constitutes only a small percentage of ticket revenues. From a revenue point of view, then, an aircraft used on international routes is roughly equivalent to one in domestic service, yet lenders' requirements force fleet development in the direction of international service. In many cases, economic logic should instead dictate development of the domestic fleet, which would better serve the lender's true interest by making the company stronger and more profitable.

It is, in fact, possible to use foreign exchange savings to justify aircraft purchases for domestic routes. New aircraft have far lower fuel consumption and maintenance costs, even if the fuel and the service have to be obtained abroad. If the financing covers a long term, approximating the aircraft's useful life, these foreign exchange savings are likely to be greater than the debt service costs. Unfortunately, this argument is rarely tested today, as lenders still refuse to accept the political risk over the long term. Overemphasis of political risk can be dangerous in itself, for it obscures financial and commercial risk considerations. Where the lender evaluates the economic risks correctly, recovery of the aircraft does not become an issue, and political risk remains relatively unimportant.

Political risk in Latin America

The sensitivity of lenders to political risk in Africa is in marked contrast to their behaviour in Latin America, where many large aircraft financings have taken place recently. The lending restrictions just described rarely apply to aircraft financings in this part of the developing world.

Although lenders do use foreign ownership/leasing, they do not insist on foreign registry or maintenance. They finance aircraft for domestic routes as readily as they do those for international service. Even in Mexico and Brazil, countries with huge debts that make lenders wary of financing airlines, they are prepared to lend large sums to leasing companies, which in turn lease the aircraft without significant political risk protection.

Like African airlines, those in Latin America rarely generate net foreign exchange revenues; lenders must look to central banks for hard currency, which is a difficult proposition given the massive debt service burdens. However, Latin American airlines have proved their ability to service debt and meet lease payments. As leasing is a preferred way to finance because the financier can, if necessary, retrieve its asset and sell it for more than the payment arrears, the

Latin airlines' record on lease payments is crucial. It would appear that the larger airlines have, so far, been able to maintain their lease payments. The experience of state-owned Aeromexico's bankruptcy and Mexicana's restructuring of its debt is not regarded as being symptomatic of Latin American airlines generally.

The short history of asset-based financings in Africa has not enabled the airlines there to demonstrate a similar ability. However, African leaders take great pride in their airlines, recognise their importance to the economy, and value their aircraft as national assets. As a result, one might expect them to make strong efforts to avoid the political embarrassment, not to mention financial loss, that repossession would generate.

Dealing with financial risk

The pattern of lending in Latin America shows greater concern for financial than for political risk: successful expropriations of commercial jet aircraft are known to be few and far between. Although the implications appear to comfort lenders and lessors to Latin American airlines, the feeling has not yet spread to Africa. If African officials and airline executives were to give greater weight to economic rather than to political considerations in acquiring aircraft, perhaps concern about political risk would recede to a more sensible level. If the airlines used their more attractive assets to back financial packages, they would find it easier to finance less attractive ones, such as aircraft for domestic routes (political risk) and freight aircraft (commercial risk).

Sale–leaseback as a solution

In industrialised countries, the normal way for financiers to achieve optimal asset support is to lend against the assets to be acquired and take additional security over the airline's other aircraft. However, where developing nations are involved, this option is not attractive because it does not deal with political risk. A sale–leaseback structure will often meet the financier's needs. In selling its aircraft, the airline generates funds it can use to acquire not only replacement aircraft, but also other property not suitable for asset-based finance.

Used in Africa, the lease must be a security instrument, with equity ultimately returning to the airline. Unfortunately, so far African airlines have shown little interest in this structure, perhaps because it is similar to conventional sale–leaseback facilities used to raise cash by selling residuals. The latter is an asset trading rather than a financing facility. African airlines also make little use of operating leasing. They are particularly wary of selling valuable national assets essential to airline operations.

A long-term approach

Clearly, financial packages for airlines in developing countries can be attractive. After all, an 18-year, 100 per cent facility for British Airways, containing a number of 'walk away' options, has a far greater asset risk than a 10-year, 85 per cent package for an African airline. The essential difference between the two is political risk, but considering the excellent loss history of political risk (as compared with, say, risk of losing residual value), the developing world's airlines are an attractive market. However, if this market is to develop properly over the long term, all concerned must make greater efforts to understand one another's requirements:

- *Aircraft manufacturers* must realise that they will gain more sales if African carriers become profitable and remain profitable while they grow. Instead of pushing to sell today a few very expensive, advanced aircraft that the Africans cannot afford, they should help the airlines expand through purchases of used aircraft, providing full service support to sales of their used equipment. Manufacturers should bear in mind that every sale of a used aircraft from the industrialised countries to the developing world creates a replacement need at the selling airline.
- *Financiers* must develop their own business opportunities, not rely on manufacturers' salesmen. They must sell their skills and services directly to the airlines, providing a complete explanation of how the borrower must perform and why.
- *Airline executives* must accept the commercial realities of the aviation industry, concentrating less on what they would like to have and more on what they need.
- *Government officials and politicians* in developing countries must avoid imposing political decisions on airline executives; the more interference from government, the greater the financiers' misgivings about political risk. Good commercial judgement, allowed to operate freely, is the best guarantee of operational and financial success.
- *International airlines* disposing of used equipment must improve on their past performance, supporting future sales with maintenance training, spare parts and other services, all at realistic prices. They must bear in mind that poor support of used equipment is a powerful argument for buying new aircraft only, and if airlines in developing countries stop buying used aircraft, disposal values will fall dramatically.

Africa, like the rest of the developing world, is a market with enormous potential. That potential will become reality only if all of the stakeholders in the market accept their responsibilities and work together. At last there is finally some evidence of the responsible cooperation that the market needs, although there is still a long way to go.

PART IV

Credit and aircraft values

15 Assessing an airline's credit: The rating agency perspective

Philip A. Baggaley

Introduction

This chapter describes the methodology used by Standard & Poor's Ratings Services to assign ratings to airline bonds, commercial paper and preferred stock. The objectives of the analysis are to determine the relative likelihood of timely repayment of principal and interest (or, in the case of preferred stock, dividends) and, secondly, the prospects for recovery following a default. The result is a letter rating – the corporate credit rating – assigned to the company's inherent ability to service fixed obligations. Certain classes of securities, such as subordinated debt or some secured debt, would be assigned lower or higher ratings than the company's corporate credit rating, based on their special characteristics.

Appendices to this chapter explain how Standard & Poor's adjusts credit ratios for off-balance sheet obligations, special considerations in rating 'flag carriers' and analysis of airline equipment obligations.

Industry risk

The starting point of any rating analysis is an assessment of the airline industry, focusing on factors that affect all carriers. There are six key elements to this analysis:

1 long-term growth prospects and the effect of the economic cycle on demand for services;
2 the impact of uncontrollable economic factors, such as fuel costs and exchange rates;
3 controllable costs;
4 the effectiveness of programmes to influence supply and demand;
5 the influence of government on operations; and
6 the ability to attract capital.

Growth and economic cycles

The airline industry is often characterised as a 'growth industry', particularly outside the US and Europe. This is true to the extent that long-term traffic growth has tended to exceed the growth of GDP, and this trend is expected to continue. The growth trend of revenues, however, is more modest, because part of that traffic growth has been stimulated by declining inflation-adjusted (and sometimes nominal) ticket fares. The main impetus for traffic growth has been increasing leisure travel, the product of greater affluence and increasing awareness of foreign vacation destinations. Business travel is increasing only slowly within the mature markets of North America and Europe, with more rapid expansion on international routes. While new communication technologies, such as video-conferencing, are expected to divert some business traffic, most trips involve marketing activities where face-to-face contact is still considered necessary.

The industry has long been characterised by a high degree of sensitivity to the business cycle. Results tend to correlate strongly with changes in the level of personal disposable income, industrial production and gross national product. The industry is usually most profitable when the economy's corporate sector is strong, because business travellers pay much higher fares than leisure passengers.

In addition to being economically cyclical, the industry is highly seasonal, with the strongest earnings usually occurring in the second and third calendar quarters. This is a reflection of the fact that over half of all traffic is for leisure purposes, and summer is the predominant vacation season. Because an airline's ability to adjust capacity on a seasonal basis is very limited, the second half of September and the weeks following often see a sharp fall-off in traffic. This is typically followed, or even anticipated, by industry-wide discounts that seek to fill the empty seats.

Uncontrollable economic factors

Expenses in the airline industry, like demand, are to some extent beyond individual carriers' control. The most significant uncontrollable cost is fuel, which consumes 10–20 per cent of operating expenses. This percentage has varied with energy prices, and has sometimes been over 20 per cent. The rise and fall of fuel prices affects all carriers to some extent, but hits those with older, less fuel-efficient fleets the hardest. Airlines attempt to raise ticket prices when oil prices rise, but are able to do so only to the extent that competition and the strength of the economy allow. These limitations were painfully obvious during the Gulf War in 1990–91.

Airlines outside of the US and US carriers with significant foreign operations have another exposure – foreign currency, and especially the US dollar rates against other currencies. Aircraft purchase prices and fuel prices are generally denominated in dollars worldwide, so airlines without a large dollar source of revenue will of necessity have an unbalanced currency position. This vulnerability was highlighted for some Asian carriers (eg, Garuda, Korean Air Lines, Asiana) during the 1997-98 currency crisis in that region. In addition, ticket prices are adjusted for exchange rates only on an infrequent basis, and few US airlines have sufficient overseas expenses to balance revenues from foreign passengers.

A final uncontrollable and, unfortunately, rising burden is ticket taxes and fees. These do not appear separately on airline income statements, because revenues are reported on a net basis, but they do have the effect of dampening demand by raising the price paid by passengers. For example, US airlines were hard put to recover an ill-timed 2 per cent increase (to 10 per cent) in the federal ticket tax in December 1990, but later benefited from a lapse in the entire ticket tax for eight months in 1996 and again for two months in 1997.

Controllable costs

Labour is the prime controllable cost and most susceptible to change over time. Airline labour rates have long been among the highest in American industry. This reflects the fact that, in the regulated era, there was little incentive to control costs, because fares were based on average costs. While this situation has changed in the US, most airline employees are unionised, and a strike by any major craft, but particularly the pilots, can be financially devastating.

Labour costs involve more than wages and benefits. Work rules and productivity have a significant impact on costs, because of the complexities of scheduling a transportation network and the historical pattern of restrictive work rules. For example, Southwest Airlines, which has among the lowest costs in the industry, achieves most of its advantage through high labour productivity and asset utilisation, rather than low pay.

Travel agency commissions and other marketing expenses have grown with increasing international travel (where commissions are higher) and competition for passengers in a deregulated or liberalised environment. In the US domestic market the pattern of rising commissions reversed in 1995 when Delta announced a cap on such commissions (which are calculated as a percentage of fares). The spread of that practice and emerging use of electronic ticketing has limited somewhat the strong bargaining position of travel agencies vis-à-vis airlines. Still, with a large majority of tickets issued through travel agents, the two parties remain dependent on one another.

Supply and demand

In the deregulated environment, airlines have a theoretically unlimited ability to control supply (capacity) and demand (traffic). In the short run, demand can be affected through variations in ticket fares. One of the most striking lessons of deregulation in the airline industry is that leisure travel demand is highly elastic, and that airline seats can be filled – albeit at a cost in yield – during all but the most severe recession. The negative aspect of this is that there is a tremendous temptation to offer discounts, the product – seats on a specific flight – being highly perishable.

The use of pricing to fill empty seats reflects also the fact that airlines have little flexibility to manage capacity over the short run. The only significant expenses that vary directly with demand are commissions and in-flight services (about 20 per cent of total operating expenses). Reducing flight frequency is generally counter-productive, because cutbacks in one market will hurt traffic 'feed' to another part of the system and cede competitive advantage to other airlines. Over the long run, supply can be managed by changes to capital expenditure plans. Such cutbacks have historically been undertaken with great reluctance and only after a period of weak demand and/or lack of funding. Following the downturn of the early 1990s, more airlines (eg Air New Zealand, Alaska Airlines and America West Airlines) have been willing to pay the higher rates required to obtain some capacity on short- to medium-term leases to preserve flexibility in a downturn.

Influence of government

Although the 1978 Airline Deregulation Act removed barriers to entry and exit from markets and constraints on pricing in the US, half of the air transport system – airports and air traffic control – remains government owned. Ground infrastructure has not kept pace with the growth in air traffic, leading to crowding and delays. Four airports have federally mandated controls on takeoffs and landings, although such 'slots' can be bought and sold by airlines. One effect of this shortage is to erect barriers to entry at some airports, allowing entrenched airlines to impose higher pricing. On the other hand, congestion causes flight delays that waste fuel and use expensive assets inefficiently.

Liberalisation of aviation regimes is spreading to other regions at an increasing pace. The most far-reaching deregulation, approaching that in the US, has occurred in Canada, Australia and New Zealand. In early 1995, the signing of a liberalised US–Canadian aviation treaty opened up most transborder routes, though the three largest Canadian airports had open access phased in over several years. The Canadian domestic market had already been largely deregulated, with significant price competition among the two major airlines and various charter and start-up carriers.

The European Union's (EU) phased liberalisation proceeded to open entry for all member airlines in all EU markets in early 1997. Despite theoretically unrestricted access across borders, the changes have thus far had only a limited impact. Airport and air traffic control infrastructure constraints and the apparent willingness of regulatory authorities to use them as barriers to entry have muffled price competition in most markets. The great majority (over 80 per cent) of intra-European routes are served by only two carriers, one from each country, leading to cartel-like pricing behaviour. Yet, even with this situation, European airlines are undergoing wrenching changes. Where a third carrier has been able to enter, routes have become much more competitive and fares have fallen. With the opening up of intra-country routes, some of the highest-yielding monopoly or near-monopoly routes are now open to new entrants. Leisure traffic, especially to vacation destinations, has long been carried mostly by charter airlines, which have been largely deregulated for years. So far, few have attempted to enter scheduled service on a large scale, and the substantial separation of business routes (mostly east–west) from vacation routes (north–south), in contrast to the US case, may support continuation of this two-tier air travel industry. Even so, further opening up of European markets, plus the difficulty of the state-owned airlines in reducing their costs, will lead to increased competition over time.

The Japanese domestic market has long been heavily regulated, with only three large participants and fares set to achieve a targeted rate of return. This strict regulation is being relaxed somewhat, with much lower threshold traffic levels now needed to justify addition of a second or third carrier (routes carrying about three-quarters of total traffic are now be open to multiple carriers) on domestic routes and a wider range of permissible fares. However, infrastructure constraints, the concentrated nature of the market – there are three large airlines, and one, All Nippon Airways (ANA), carries slightly over half of domestic traffic – historical patterns of competitive behaviour, and the still substantial influence of government regulators have thus far limited the impact on price competition. However, the gradual movement toward liberalisation will likely, over time, increase pressure on the incumbents. Further, when pending and planned expansion of three major airports – Tokyo Haneda (domestic), Tokyo Narita (international), and Osaka's Kansai Airport – is completed, there will be more scope for price competition.

While regulation of route authorities and fares is diminishing, noise regulation and maintenance requirements have become an increasingly significant industry issue. Like airport congestion, they affect carriers unequally, working to the disadvantage of the financially weak and discouraging new entrants. Government controls on jet engine emissions are the next area for potentially significant regulation. One benefit of these actions is that they impose some discipline on an industry known for adding capacity aggressively, despite an historically low return earned on existing assets.

Ability to attract capital

Airline balance sheets are highly capital intensive, reflecting a heavy investment in aircraft and ground facilities. However, the income statement tells a different story. Ownership costs (interest, depreciation and rentals), while rising, account for less than 20 per cent of pre-tax expenses in most cases. This is well below labour costs, at over one-third of the total. The disparity reflects the use of long-term debt and leases to finance fixed assets, leaving annual fixed financial obligations more manageable. Accordingly, airline credit measures that compare an annual return (such as operating earnings or cash flow) with balance sheet items (such as capital or debt) will appear low relative to those of most industrial companies.

Airlines have historically enjoyed access to capital out of proportion to their usually meagre profitability. This reflects the liquidity, high value retention, and ability of creditors to repossess an airline's principal asset – its aircraft. These issues will be explored further in the discussion of financial flexibility later in this chapter.

Industry position

An airline's industry position is evaluated within the context of the industry as a whole, within specific markets and with regard to its present and planned fleet. The statistics used to measure overall market share are those common to the industry: available seat miles or available seat kilometres (one seat flown one mile or kilometre) is the basic measure of capacity; revenue passenger miles or kilometres (one revenue passenger flown one mile or kilometre) is the standard for traffic. Some carriers, particularly those with significant cargo operations, report available ton kilometres and revenue ton kilometres. This standard can be useful for examining an airline, such as KLM Royal Dutch Airlines, which derives a significant portion of its revenues from flying cargo. This information is examined primarily on a system basis but is divided, where applicable, into regional sub-sets (for US airlines, typically domestic, Atlantic, Pacific and Latin American).

From this analysis, a carrier's relative capacity and traffic shares emerge and the difference between these data are examined. From a peer group or industry perspective, the relationship between capacity and traffic is zero, because both inputs are equal to 100 per cent. An individual carrier is rarely balanced, in the sense that its share of capacity and traffic are equal. A carrier with a traffic share that exceeds its relative capacity has a premium market share. When capacity exceeds traffic, a market share deficiency exists. The size of the premium or deficiency is one measure of a carrier's overall market strength or weakness, although caution must be exercised in interpreting the results. Airlines with a short average trip length or those that dominate lightly travelled routes may find it profitable to carry fewer passengers at higher fares, and thus deliberately sacrifice overall traffic share.

An airline's market share at individual airports may be measured by its share of passenger enplanements, flight departures and boarding gates. These shares are typically high at an airline's hub airports, but those percentages are misleading because passengers connecting through a hub typically have a choice of several alternative routings on different airlines. A more relevant, though less readily available, measure of market dominance is share of local traffic – ie passengers beginning or ending their trip at that airport. US airlines earn most of their domestic profits by dominating local markets, particularly large ones with many business travellers. The leading carrier will carry a disproportionate number of such passengers because it can offer a more extensive flight schedule.

Despite theoretical free entry and exit in a deregulated environment, changes in market position are limited by practical considerations. Gate space is limited at most airports, as are take-off and landing slots at busy sites such as London's Heathrow airport. It is not economically attractive to establish a hub unless a certain threshold level of flights can be established, so even the existence of a few free gates or slots does not really ensure free entry. Because of this and the revenue implications of dominating a local market, most US airlines are focusing increasingly on their core hubs and withdrawing from markets where they are at a disadvantage. As a consequence, there are only two US airports – Chicago's O'Hare and Dallas-Forth Worth – that have hubs of two airlines, and the latter may evolve into a one-carrier hub as Delta Air Lines shrinks its operation there.

In international markets, routes are governed by treaties that may be fairly restrictive, as that between the US and UK, or relaxed, as between the Netherlands and the UK. The former establishes significant barriers to entry and, often, oligopoly profits for those with an established position. The US government has increasingly pressed for liberal 'open-skies' treaties, allowing American carriers greater access to routes into and beyond other countries in return for reciprocal rights to non-US airlines. With a large domestic market, closed to foreign competitors, and the relative cost competitiveness of large US airlines, this approach combines ideology with commercial advantage.

As airlines seek to enter restricted international markets and capture the revenue benefits of a broad route network without the large investment required to expand internally, they are increasingly turning to alliances with airlines in other countries. These range from limited marketing arrangements to cross-border ownership and closely linked joint operations. Historically, most of these arrangements were neither significant nor lasting. A combination of privatisation of state-owned airlines and liberalisation of aviation treaties has changed that pattern dramatically since the early 1990s. Privatisation created an opportunity to acquire larger positions in overseas airlines than would otherwise be possible, from large minority stakes with considerable influence to full ownership.

A second important and complementary trend has been increasing government approval to engage in joint operations, sharing revenues, costs and information on specified international routes. This approval is described as 'anti-trust immunity' in the US, and such arrangements come under the review of trade authorities in other countries, such as Australia and the UK. Interestingly, the spread of this practice, which could be considered anti-competitive in some cases, has been encouraged by the US government, with its stated policy of encouraging airline competition both domestically and on international routes. The first granting of anti-trust immunity was in 1992, when Northwest Airlines and KLM were allowed such authority in return for the signing of an 'open-skies' treaty with The Netherlands. During 1995–96, several other, larger such arrangements were approved by the US government, and the Australian authorities cleared similar cooperation between Qantas and British Airways on UK-Australian routes.

These joint venture arrangements are likely to be more significant and lasting than previous marketing or even equity exchange alliances. This is because they make possible material revenue and cost benefits beyond those available via simple 'code sharing' and joint marketing:

- Partner airlines can schedule flights and allocate capacity as a single operation, optimising the match between traffic demand and aircraft size on individual routes and in broader parts of their route systems.
- On those routes where both airlines already operate, their combination creates a more complete flight schedule (particularly important for attracting business travellers) and a more formidable competitive presence overall.
- By sharing pricing and seat inventory, the airlines can make yield management decisions with better information and are less likely to feel a need to discount tickets to pre-empt a competitor.

- Sharing of costs encourages the partner airlines to allocate ground resources in the most efficient manner (eg each airline's ground staff handle flights for both airlines at airports in their own country), maximising employee, gate, terminal and other asset utilisation.

Examination of an airline's fleet should focus on its age, proportion of planes that meet current noise regulations, the number and variety of aircraft models flown, and their suitability to the airline's markets. An ageing fleet imposes penalties in operating performance and presages heavy capital expenditure in the future. Conversely, an airline with a relatively young fleet has the flexibility to cut back on spending if the industry environment or its own financial circumstances dictate. A fleet consisting of relatively few models and engine types simplifies training and maintenance, limiting costs.

Operations analysis

This analysis considers revenue generation, cost control and the resulting operating profitability. Utilisation of capacity is measured by 'load factor' – ie revenue passenger miles divided by available seat miles. Put another way, this ratio represents the proportion of seats filled, on a distance-weighted basis. Load factor for an individual carrier can range from 40 to 80 per cent, with the average around 70 per cent. A higher load factor is, other things being equal, more desirable. However, other things, specifically pricing, rarely are equal. As noted earlier, airlines have learned how to fill seats using discounts, and some have done so quite effectively while losing money at the same time.

The standard measure of pricing is 'yield', or revenue per revenue passenger mile. This can vary widely, but major US carriers typically report figures in the 10–15 cent range, and non-US airlines often higher. Again, higher is better, but many factors can affect the reported yield. Airlines flying short stage lengths tend to have higher yields, because ticket prices are not strictly proportional to the length of trip. Carriers with low costs and spartan service may choose to compete on the basis of price, rather than amenities. The product of load factor and yield is passenger revenues per available seat mile. This is a more complete measure of revenue generation than either of its component parts, though it too is affected by factors such as average trip length.

Revenue generation

Revenue generation depends on effective management of the trade-off between pricing and utilisation. The goal of 'yield management' is to sell high-priced tickets to those who are relatively indifferent to price, such as business travellers, or to those who have few options, such as users of airports dominated by a single airline, while at the same time attracting discretionary travellers with discount prices. This objective accounts for the Byzantine structure of ticket pricing, confusing even to airline reservation agents.

Information on which to base pricing decisions comes from the computerised reservation systems, and some of the more successful practitioners of revenue management have invested considerable resources into computers and systems expertise. Revenue management has been the most effective weapon of established US carriers in their battle against low-cost discount airlines, allowing them to match advertised low fares while making such prices available only on a limited basis and to the most price-sensitive travellers.

Cost control

The standard measure of airline operating costs is operating expense per available seat mile. Like yield, this tends to be higher for airlines flying short stage (flight) lengths. This is because many costs are fixed, and can be spread out over more seat miles on longer trips. Operating cost per available seat mile typically ranges from 6 to 12 cents for US airlines and higher for those elsewhere.

The major operating cost differential among airlines is labour cost, which accounts for about one-third of total pre-tax expenses. During the mid-1980s, established, high-cost carriers responded to lower-cost new entrants (eg People Express) and bankruptcy-restructured airlines (eg Continental Airlines) with 'two-tier' wage structures in which new hires were paid at reduced rates. This strategy subsequently became a victim of its own success: the growing proportion of lower-paid 'B-scale' workers eventually created pressure for narrowing wage differentials.

In the 1990s, several US airlines have experimented with trading employee pay concessions for employee ownership. Usually, this was done out of desperation, when financial failure seemed a possibility, though the largest such case, UAL Corporation (United Air Lines), is an example of a relatively secure company taking this course. While it is likely that there will be more cases of partial employee ownership, majority employee ownership, as at UAL, appears to be the exception.

Fuel costs are the second largest expense item, but their impact, while not equal, is less uneven than that of labour expense. Aircraft lease rentals are shown as an operating expense, although they are actually a capital, rather than an operating expense. Airlines that use a high proportion of operating leases will appear to have higher operating cost per available seat mile, but lower interest expense than competitors that own their fleets. This can be an important factor in comparative analysis, and will be discussed further later on in this chapter.

Operating profitability

The product of revenue generation and cost structure is operating profitability. Transportation companies define operating margin as operating income after depreciation expense divided by revenues, in contrast to industrial companies, which typically treat depreciation as a non-operating expense. In addition to yielding a lower margin, this penalises companies that are growing rapidly, because depreciation on new assets begins immediately, but there is a delay before they can contribute to the revenue generating process. Standard & Poor's looks at operating margin both before and after depreciation expense. A further refinement is to measure profit margins before all ownership expenses (interest, depreciation and rentals). This is especially useful for cross-border comparisons.

Management

Management is particularly important in a volatile and competitive industry. Standard & Poor's assessment of a company's management generally focuses on four factors:

- managers' track record;
- innovation and industry leadership;
- skill in labour relations; and
- attitude towards financial risk.

The industry's track record has been uneven at best, with heavy losses during the early 1980s and early 1990s. Industry averages obscure a wide range of outcomes, however, with some companies performing fairly well. It should be remembered also that the period under consideration includes two recessions, fuel price fluctuations, a war and resulting fear of terrorism, and a wrenching adjustment to deregulation in the US and elsewhere.

Any judgement of management must weigh not only the results achieved, but also the obstacles faced. The privatisation and transformation of former state-owned airlines such as British Airways and Qantas is all the more impressive for the degree of change required. Likewise, the steady success of Southwest Airlines in a highly competitive environment is rare in this industry.

Labour relations are a crucially important task for management, and failure to achieve satisfactory outcomes contributed to the downfall of executives at Eastern and United. Combining good employee morale and productivity with a competitive labour cost structure is difficult, but some managements, such as that at Southwest Airlines, have managed to do so over a long period. While a satisfactory labour situation does not ensure success, its absence almost certainly means trouble.

As with all corporate rating analyses, management's financial policy is judged with respect to its impact on creditor interests. Issues considered include share repurchases, funding of acquisitions and capital expenditure, along with target capital structure and concrete steps taken to achieve it. Airlines are typically leveraged more highly than comparably rated industrials, reflecting the financeability of their assets. However, that ready access to capital has tempted airline managements to undertake ambitious growth plans and acquisitions. In the late 1980s, it even prompted several leveraged buyouts in the US. Given their industry characteristics, airlines are among the least suitable candidate for a debt-financed buyout.

Accounting quality

Standard & Poor's debt ratings are based on audited financial statements, generally for a five-year period. Analysis begins with a review of accounting quality to determine whether ratios and statistics derived from the statements accurately measure a company's relative performance. Ratings represent a scale of comparison, so it is imperative to have a common frame of reference. Accounting policies reviewed include the following:

- depreciation methods and asset lives;
- amortisation of intangibles;
- employee benefits;
- operating leases; and
- company legal structure issues.

Depreciation methods and asset lives

Most airlines depreciate new aircraft on a straight-line basis over 15 to 25 years. If a carrier uses a shorter life, as did Delta until 1986, Standard & Poor's will adjust pre-tax income and equity upward to provide comparability with competitors. The analyst must also be sensitive to the effect of changes in accounting policies. Delta's change in depreciation, as of the beginning of fiscal 1987, caused income to be overstated for some years as the small amount of remaining depreciation expense on older aircraft was spread out over longer depreciation lives. While shorter depreciation lives impact the income statement and balance sheet, there is no effect on cash flow.

Amortisation of intangibles

This includes goodwill, route rights, and pre-operating costs, particularly those associated with introducing new equipment or entering new markets. Goodwill should be evaluated on a case-by-case basis, judging whether the company has truly received value in excess of the fair market value of assets purchased.

Employee benefits

As a heavily unionised industry, most airlines have significant pension and health benefit costs. These represent an additional fixed obligation, albeit one whose exact size is subject to considerable uncertainty. Probably more important than any estimated debt equivalent amount is the cash actually paid out to fund such obligations, and its expected trend in the future.

Operating leases

Off-balance sheet aircraft and facility leases form a large and growing portion of total fixed financial obligations. Standard & Poor's uses a discounted present value model to adjust credit ratios to reflect the added financial burden (see Appendix 2 to this chapter). The debt equivalent of these leases can be substantial. It is estimated that the net present value of United Air Lines' aircraft operating leases is over US$11 billion – an amount several times greater than the company's balance sheet debt.

Issues related to a company's legal structure

The analyst should consider accounting implications of parent–subsidiary relations and the like. For example, Northwest Airlines Inc's equity is shown as considerably greater than that of its ultimate parent, Northwest Airlines Corporation (which currently has negative book equity), because purchase accounting adjustments were not applied to the subsidiary. Standard & Poor's tends to regard airline companies as an economic unit, and assumes that a parent's obligations will ultimately be serviced by cash flow from its subsidiaries. Parent and subsidiary debt ratings can differ, however, reflecting the 'structural subordination' of debt at the parent level.

Although it is not always possible to recast a company's financial statements to best reflect reality, or even to be totally comparable, it is useful to have some notion of the extent to which performance is overstated or understated. At the very least, the choice of accounting alternatives can be characterised as conservative or liberal.

Earnings protection

This category encompasses two analytical concepts – return on investment and earnings in relation to the fixed charge burden. Strong performers in one category can score poorly on the other, depending on how much debt is on the balance sheet. A company's earnings power is, in the long run, an important determinant of credit protection and a key indicator of a firm's capacity to attract capital.

The key financial ratios used in earnings analysis are pre-tax interest coverage and return on permanent capital. The former is calculated as earnings before taxes plus interest expense divided by gross interest charges. The numerator is adjusted for extraordinary items but not gain on sale of aircraft, because this represents, in essence, an adjustment of previous depreciation accounting. An operating lease model is used to capitalise off-balance sheet commitments and the imputed interest component of rentals is added to interest expense shown on the income statement (see Appendix 2 to this chapter). As noted above, Standard & Poor's will, where appropriate, calculate supplemental ratios that adjust for non-standard depreciation accounting.

A second fixed charge ratio considered is earnings before interest, taxes, depreciation and amortisation (EBITDA) interest coverage, which adds depreciation and amortisation (including the non-interest component of rentals) to the numerator of the pre-tax coverage ratio. This is particularly useful when comparing airlines across borders, where accounting practices may differ. For example, Trans World Airlines' 1995 pre-tax interest coverage (lease-adjusted) was 0.52×, while Japan Air Lines' coverage for the fiscal year ended 31 March 1996 was equivalent at 0.53×. However, JAL's more conservative depreciation accounting meant that its EBITDA coverage of 2.33× was materially above TWA's 1.18×. In this case, Standard & Poor's would focus on the EBITDA coverage as the more relevant comparison.

Return on permanent capital uses the same numerator as pre-tax coverage, but divides by average total debt (including capitalised leases), non-current deferred taxes and stockholders' equity. Erosion of equity by losses will tend to inflate returns once an airline restores profitability, because the denominator is that much smaller. Even so, airline returns on capital are low relative to those of industrials because of unsatisfactory profitability and the high cost of long-lived assets such as aircraft and airport facilities.

Historical and projected ratios are used in evaluating coverage and returns. Because debt ratings are an assessment of the likelihood of future payment of interest and principal, Standard & Poor's emphasises future performance. No attempt is made to forecast results precisely, but a range of possible scenarios is considered. Historical and projected volatility of earnings, as well as absolute levels, are taken into account in this assessment.

Cash flow adequacy

Cash flow analysis assesses a carrier's ability to generate cash from internal sources relative to the level of claims against that cash. Cash flow may be defined as funds from operations (the sum of net income, depreciation and amortisation, and the change in non-current deferred taxes) or cash from operations, which takes into account also changes in the current accounts. Current assets and current liabilities are typically a relatively small part of the balance sheet for airlines, so the difference between the two methods is not great. As with earnings measures, extraordinary items are excluded.

By far the largest component of cash flow for the industry as a whole is depreciation. This reflects both the capital intensity of airlines and the industry's mediocre profit performance. On the positive side, depreciation schedules of most airlines are often more conservative than the probable economic life of their equipment, so part of the depreciation could properly be considered deferred income. The large depreciation component means also that an airline's cash flow is considerably less variable than its earnings.

The key analytical ratio is cash flow divided by total debt. This shows, in theory at least, how quickly a carrier could repay debt if all cash flow was applied to that goal. Hence, it is akin to the concept of debt service coverage. A company that exhibits a reasonable and stable cash flow ratio can utilise greater financial leverage and is viewed more favourably than one for which cash flow coverage averages the same level but is more variable.

Cash flow to debt can be adjusted for use of operating leases by adding to the numerator the amortisation equivalent component of lease rentals and to the denominator the net present value of such rentals. Examination of the debt maturity schedule and future lease obligations is an additional and important part of this analysis. In judging potential cash flow volatility, the analyst should also consider the airline's exposure to currency fluctuations, particularly against the US dollar.

Comparison of cash flow with capital expenditure gauges a company's ability to finance capital programmes with internally generated funds. Unfortunately, reported capital spending often understates the true level of outlays, because most facilities and many aircraft are leased. If aircraft are financed using a sale–leaseback, their cost will show up in capital expenditure, but if they are leased directly no such amount appears.

Cash flow has tended to fall short of capital expenditure for most airlines, which is not surprising given the industry's expansion and the high cost of new equipment. Aircraft are long-lived assets that tend to retain value over long periods of time. Hence, lenders have accepted them as collateral, permitting carriers to pay for this asset over its useful life. Once on stream, the lender expects the asset to generate sufficient cash to allow repayment. A more reasonable test is whether internal funds cover a sufficient portion of debt repayment and capital expenditure requirements to allow maintenance of acceptable debt leverage.

Capitalisation

In many respects, the financial factor over which management has the greatest control is how the carrier is financed and, accordingly, the level of financial risk it is willing to bear. As a general rule, the greater use of debt relative to equity capital, the higher the risk for all holders of a company's obligations. Analysis, however, is not restricted to debt, because companies make wide use of off-balance sheet financings and preferred stock.

Financial leverage is the extent to which a firm uses other parties' funds or capital to finance itself. In the airline industry there are five main ingredients that make up the company capitalisation equation:

1 *Equipment financing.* The principal financing methods are secured debt and leases. Ownership of the aircraft rests with the carrier in the first two, and with an investor in the case of leases. In the case of secured debt, a security interest in the pledged asset is granted to lenders that should provide the right to repossess in the event of default; the right of a lessor to repossess is tied to its ownership of the equipment itself. In the case of a leveraged lease, creditor repossession rights tend to be indirect, arising typically from a security interest in the lease. Secured debt may be rated higher than the airline's corporate credit rating for US airlines, usually when it qualifies for special protection under Section 1110 of the US Bankruptcy Code. Section 1110 excludes purchase money secured debt, conditional sales agreements and leases from the automatic stay of creditor claims and substitution of collateral sections of the Code. (This subject is discussed in greater detail in Appendix 3 to this chapter.)

2 *Senior unsecured debt.* As a general rule, only stronger credits have the ability to finance on an

unsecured, non-convertible basis, although such debt is occasionally used by other airlines. If the use of secured obligations is extensive, particularly for speculative grade companies, Standard & Poor's may treat unsecured debt as subordinate.

3 *Subordinated debt.* Most of the airline industry's subordinated debt is issued in convertible form and is frequently regarded by the industry and commercial bankers as an equity equivalent. Standard & Poor's views such obligations as debt until converted, because holders have the same right to file a company into bankruptcy as senior creditors do. The attraction of convertible debt to the issuer is a lower borrowing rate than available on a non-convertible issue and a call on common at an above-market price. The risk is that the stock price will be consistently below the conversion price.

4 *Preferred stock.* The motivation for using preferred is generally tax-driven, both from the point of view of the issuer and the investor. Shares may be convertible or non-convertible, perpetual or subject to a sinking fund, fixed or floating rate. For the purposes of rating debt, Standard & Poor's looks at the features of the preferred stock and places it within a spectrum of instruments ranging from the most equity-like to the most debt-like. This can affect evaluation of the capital structure. For the purposes of rating preferred securities, all preferred stock is added to debt in calculating supplemental credit ratios.

5 *Common equity.* Common equity is the most permanent of all capital and bears the greatest risk. Although stock issues can fund only a very limited portion of airline capital plans, willingness to issue common shares is one measure of how management weighs the sometimes competing interests of owners and creditors.

Total debt as a percentage of debt plus equity is the key ratio reviewed to determine a company's financial leverage. Airlines' leverage is high compared with that of most industrial companies, both overall and adjusted for rating categories. This is somewhat misleading, however, because airlines often have assets worth more than their book value. Although a decline in used aircraft prices during the early 1990s largely wiped out the previous hidden value in airline fleets, international routes, takeoff and landing slots, airport gates and other assets often remain understated. To the extent that leverage ratios are intended to measure the concept of asset protection – the extent to which assets can be used to satisfy claims on the company in liquidation – consideration of such factors is appropriate.

This hidden equity is usually more than offset by the hidden debt of operating leases. As noted earlier, Standard & Poor's capitalises such leases and includes adjusted ratios in its rating determinations. Other factors that merit examination in judging leverage are goodwill, deferred gains on aircraft sale–leasebacks and deferred taxes. The composition of debt is examined to determine whether the mix of fixed and floating rate obligations and the average debt life are appropriate to the assets being financed. One positive feature of the move towards leasing, whether on or off-balance sheet, is that the repayment schedule is long and level.

Financial flexibility

Evaluation of an airline's financial flexibility begins with a review of its financing needs, plans and alternatives under stress. The major uses of cash are debt maturities, capital expenditure and acquisitions. Share repurchase and dividends tend to be rare in the airline industry. Sources of funds are more varied, and range from operating cash flow to sale of revenue assets or entire businesses. The most extreme example of the latter was the decade-long dismantling of Pan Am, which, by selling assets, held off bankruptcy longer than most observers thought possible.

Some airlines have decided to hedge against the unexpected by accumulating large holdings of cash and short-term investments. While this is common for weak airlines that cannot access bank credit, stronger airlines have also sometimes followed this course. The cash hoards can provide the wherewithal to withstand a downturn in business or a strike by unionised employees. Standard & Poor's considers such holdings to be a positive feature in financial flexibility, but recognises that the debt sometimes used to obtain them weakens earnings protection, cash flow liquidity and capitalisation.

Other airlines rely on bank lines and commercial paper to finance interim cash needs and provide back-up flexibility. This is a less expensive way of obtaining funds, but is possible only for stronger credits that can be assured of their continuing availability. Most US airline commercial paper programmes became inactive in the early 1990s, when the large airlines were downgraded to speculative grade. Beyond such formal sources of credit, Standard & Poor's will consider a company's access to public debt and equity markets.

A large pool of unencumbered assets helps assure availability of bank, equipment, and lease financing. Aircraft are readily saleable and financeable, reflecting several factors:

- Aircraft can be easily transferred from one operator to another in an active, liquid and global market.
- The value of aircraft does not decline substantially when the operating airline is in financial distress, although their price is, of course, affected by general industry conditions.
- Lessors and secured creditors can repossess aircraft financed under Section 1110 of the US Bankruptcy Code if the airline does not continue rentals or debt service in reorganisation proceedings. Legal systems outside the US tend not to have a special provision for aircraft financing, but are generally more creditor-friendly than Chapter 11 in the US.

Airlines' other major long-term asset, airport facilities, are likewise amenable to financing. Industrial revenue bonds issued by US municipal authorities but serviced by lease rentals or other payments from airlines provide tax-advantaged financing over long terms. Such financings often carry lower interest rates than the airline's credit quality would imply, because investors know that gates and terminals at crowded airports can be transferred to other airlines if the original lessee defaults. Even better, some municipalities, seeking the jobs and economic activity generated by airports, will lend their own credit strength to help a weak airline finance expansion or simply avoid shutting down.

While these inherent advantages remain significant, airlines' access to capital nevertheless changes with the industry's fortunes. A potential long-term concern is the ability and willingness of global capital markets to devote an ever-growing portion of their portfolio to aviation. The traffic growth rates projected by industry participants and observers imply a huge capital requirement over the next decade, and one that will grow faster than the world economy as a whole. Existing traditional sources of capital – retained earnings, share issuance, unsecured debt and equipment financing – may be inadequate to meet that need. Securitisation, supplier financing and subsidised financing (eg by export banks) have played a supplemental role and may become more important over time. In any case, financial condition and access to capital has already become a key factor in determining which airlines will prosper or, in some cases, which will simply survive.

Conclusion

Credit analysis is an attempt to forecast the future and, as such, is as much an art as a science. The discussion in this chapter has been designed to provide a framework for analysis and some perspective on airlines' past performance. Beyond that, the analyst must rely on his or her own experience, reasoning and judgement.

Appendix 1:
Flag carrier considerations

Almost all of the airlines outside the United States rated by Standard & Poor's can be described as 'flag carriers'. That is, they are the principal international airline of their home country. Although most have been privatised, some still retain official or unofficial links to the government. Further, most of them are important to their country's trade balance and economy.

Considerations concerning flag carrier status may be grouped into two broad categories – legal and economic. The strongest legal link is an outright government guarantee, in which case Standard & Poor's would likely assign its sovereign country rating to the airline. Full government ownership without a guarantee would be the next level of involvement. In this case, Standard & Poor's has to weigh factors such as the airline's financial viability, its importance to trade and tourism, and the role of the government in the economy as a whole. Although we do not currently rate any financially weak, 100 per cent government-owned airlines, we have assigned ratings to unprofitable national railway systems. Such railways often receive ratings close to the sovereign country rating.

Partial government ownership of its flag carrier introduces further complications. As important as the absolute level of government ownership is the 'direction' of that investment. Does the government intend to maintain its investment or privatise the airline? Thus, Qantas was until recently owned by the government of Australia, but its planned full privatisation and the stated policy of liberalising the national aviation regime were the more relevant analytical factors. Standard & Poor's thus rated Qantas BBB+ without assuming any explicit legal link to the government during this transition period.

The Qantas example illustrates also the second general category of flag carrier considerations – the economic factors. Although the Australian government has begun to award international route authorities to other airlines, Qantas is still far ahead of competitor Ansett Transport Industries Limited in this regard. Most flag carriers, even if private, have strong competitive positions. A further consideration is the role of the airline as a generator of jobs and economic activity. This is particularly important in the case of small countries dependent on tourism.

These various legal and economic considerations provide evidence to help Standard & Poor's judge how a government might react if its flag carrier was in financial trouble. Support can take many forms, such as equity contributions, loan guarantees and favourable regulatory consideration. Not all of these require that the airline be facing difficulty, and government actions often vary based mainly on the economic philosophy or tradition in that country. Thus, Japanese airlines have for years used low-cost government equipment financing. These arrangements predate the recent adverse airline environment, and reflect the prevailing approach to government involvement in aviation affairs and international trade in Japan.

One caveat should be kept in mind when evaluating the array of potential government assistance. A government's main interest is in seeing that its flag carrier (or, for that matter, any of its major airlines) continues to fly. That is not the same thing as continuing to pay its debt obligations on time. In a crisis, government support may be conditional on creditors making sacrifices, or may materialise too late to avoid a default. Canadian Airlines, while not a flag carrier, received assistance from provincial governments in Canada, and the federal government clearly favoured continued survival of two major airlines, but that did not prevent Canadian from defaulting on most of its obligations in 1994 before restructuring. Therefore, it is important to define exactly when and in what form assistance might be available before ascribing a rating benefit to it.

Appendix 2:
Adjusting for off-balance sheet leases

Airlines make heavy use of off-balance-sheet leases to finance aircraft and facilities. These leases represent a large fixed burden, although they are disclosed only in the footnotes to the financial statements. This appendix, using AMR Corporation as an example, explains how Standard & Poor's capitalises these leases to arrive at adjusted credit ratios.

Exhibit 15.1 shows the stream of future lease commitments disclosed in AMR Corporation's 1996 annual report. To derive a present value debt equivalent:

1 Split the rentals due after year five into a theoretical level stream of payments. Here, the year five amount is divided into the total, and the resulting number of years (15.4) is rounded up to 16 years. Dividing 16 into that total gives an annual payment of US$883 million for years 6 through 21.
2 Discount the entire stream of payments at a rate believed to be equal to the airline's average historical borrowing rate for senior long-term debt on the balance sheet. This requires an estimate, unless you have access to the actual rates incurred. Here, the rate used is 9.0 per cent, and the resulting present value is US$8.5 billion.

Exhibit 15.1
AMR Corporation 1996: Future minimum operating lease payments at end-1996

1997	US$992mn
1998	US$987mn
1999	US$974mn
2000	US$924mn
2001	US$919mn
Thereafter	US$14,122mn
Total	US$18,918mn

$$14,122 / 919 = 15.4 \text{ years, rounded up to 16 years}$$
$$14,122 / 16 = 883 \text{ pa in years 6–21}$$
$$PV @ 9.0\% = 8,515$$

$$\text{Debt to capital} = \frac{\text{Debt}}{\text{Debt} + \text{Equity} + \text{Deferred gains on sale–leasebacks, tax effected}}$$

$$\text{Debt to capital} = \frac{5,096}{5,096 + 5,668 + (647 - 248)} = 46\%$$

$$\text{Adjusted debt to capital} = \frac{5,096 + 8,515}{5,096 + 8,515 + 5,668 + (647 - 248)} = 69\%$$

Exhibit 15.2
AMR Corporation 1996: Adjusted interest coverage

1994 operating lease commitments as of end-1995: US$879 mn
1995 operating lease commitments as of end-1996: US$992 mn
Average = US$935 million

Proportion of PV to total lease commitments = $\dfrac{8,515}{18,918}$ = 45%

Proportion of amortisation in rentals = 935 × 0.45 = 421
Proportion of interest in rentals = 935 − 421 = 514

Pre-tax interest coverage $= \dfrac{\text{Earnings before interest and taxes}}{\text{Interest, including capitalised interest}}$

$\dfrac{1,635}{515} = 3.2 \times$

Adjusted interest coverage $= \dfrac{\text{EBIT + Interest in rentals}}{\text{Gross interest + Interest in rentals}}$

$\dfrac{1,635 + 514}{515 + 514} = 2.1 \times$

Exhibit 15.3
AMR Corporation 1996: Adjusted EBITDA interest coverage

EBITDA interest coverage $= \dfrac{\text{Earnings before interest, Taxes, Depreciation and Amortisation}}{\text{Interest, including capitalised interest}}$

$\dfrac{2,839}{515} = 5.5 \times$

Adjusted interest coverage $= \dfrac{\text{EBITDA + Average committed rentals}}{\text{Gross interest + Interest in rentals}}$

$\dfrac{2,839 + 935}{515 + 514} = 3.7 \times$

The resulting present value is the equivalent of debt and should be added to total balance sheet debt in calculating credit ratios. In Exhibit 15.1, adjusted debt to capital is calculated. Included as an equity-like component in capital are unamortised gains on sale-leaseback transactions. This account, a long-term liability, arises because US accounting principles require a company to amortise any gain or loss on an off-balance-sheet sale-leaseback of an asset over the

241

Exhibit 15.4
AMR Corporation 1996: Adjusted funds flow to debt

$$\text{Funds flow to debt} = \frac{\text{Net Income before extraordinary + Depreciation + Deferred taxes + Other non-cash expenses}}{\text{Total debt}}$$

$$\frac{1,106 + 1,204 + 218 + 115}{5,096} = 47\%$$

$$\text{Adjusted funds flow to debt} = \frac{\text{Net income before extraordinary + Depreciation + Deferred taxes + Other non-cash expenses + Amortisation in rentals}}{\text{Total debt + PV of leases}}$$

$$\frac{1,106 + 1,204 + 218 + 115 + 421}{5,096 + 8,515} = 21\%$$

life of the lease. If the analyst chooses to recognise the present value of future lease commitments by capitalising them, it is appropriate to recognise the gain on those transactions as well. This amount, US$647 million for AMR, is reduced by the associated deferred tax asset, US$248million (from the footnote on income taxes), producing an after-tax addition to equity of US$399 million.

Annual rental expense can be divided into interest and amortisation equivalents to calculate adjusted interest coverage and cash flow to debt ratios. In Exhibit 15.2, an average succeeding year committed rental expense is calculated first. This average number is used, rather than actual rental expense, because the latter includes short-term rentals that are not being capitalised. The resulting average of committed rentals (US$935 million) is then allocated to amortisation in the same proportion that the present value has to the total, undiscounted future lease commitments. In other words, if 45 per cent (US$8.5 billion divided by US$18.9 billion) of the total rentals over the life of these leases represents repayment of principal, that same 45 per cent (US$421 million of US$935 million) is used to allocate amortisation in 1996. The remaining 55 per cent represents interest equivalent (US$514 million).

This methodology differs from the standard capitalisation of leases dictated by US GAAP, in which the proportions allocated to amortisation and interest change from year to year to maintain a constant implicit interest rate. Because the actual cash obligation does not change from year to year, a constant allocation between amortisation and interest is believed to provide more useful credit information.

In Exhibit 15.2, the interest equivalent is used to calculate an adjusted pre-tax interest coverage. In Exhibit 15.3, EBITDA interest coverage is adjusted (in this case, the full amount of average committed rentals is added to the numerator of the ratio, not just the interest equivalent in rentals). In Exhibit 15.4, the amortisation equivalent in rentals is used, along with the present value derived above, to calculate adjusted funds flow to debt.

The foregoing methodology assumes that one is calculating ratios from annual financial statements with footnotes. Yet, periodic rental expense may be the only information disclosed in a quarterly report. In that case, the analyst can approximate the present value of lease commitments by using a multiple of rentals based on the prior year's annual statements. In the

Exhibit 15.5
AMR Corporation 1996: Adjusted debt to capital

Debt to capital =	$\dfrac{\text{Debt} + \text{PV leases} - \text{Cash} + \text{Pensions} + \text{Benefits}}{\text{Debt} + \text{PV leases} - \text{Cash} + \text{Pensions} + \text{Benefits} + \text{Equity} + \text{Deferred gains}}$	
(adj. for: cash, pensions, retiree benefits)		
Debt to capital = (as adj.)	$\dfrac{5{,}096 + 8{,}515 - 1{,}811 + 627 + 1{,}530}{5{,}096 + 8{,}515 - 1{,}811 + (-227) + 1{,}530 + 5{,}668 + 399}$	= 73%

example used above, the present value of US$8.5 billion is about 6.5 times (×) the actual 1995 rental expense of US$1.3 billion (the average succeeding year committed rents, calculated above, is not used because no comparable figure is available in the quarterly statements). Rental expense must be annualised, or the present value will be understated. In addition, quarterly reports often aggregate rentals and landing fees, so the prior-year annual statement should be reviewed to establish how much of the total can be considered actual rental expense.

As the exhibits make clear, inclusion of lease adjustments can have a material impact on credit ratios. This is particularly true for stronger airlines, which have relatively less balance sheet debt but have used leasing extensively to minimise tax expense.

Having calculated off-balance sheet liabilities, the analyst should further consider cash and pension liabilities, and retiree health liabilities. Adjusting for cash is easy. Cash and short-term investments (US$1.8 billion in the case of AMR) are deducted from adjusted debt to calculate adjusted net debt (US$3.3 billion for AMR; US$11.8 billion including leases).

AMR's pension plan assets total US$627 million less than projected benefit obligations, an amount that is added to debt. That amount, adjusted for taxes at 35 per cent (US$408 million), is also deducted from equity. Likewise deducted is the US$446 million prepaid pension cost, an intangible asset of dubious value. In calculating adjusted debt to capital, US$627 million is added to the numerator. For the denominator, the amounts deducted from equity (US$408 million plus US$446 million, equalling US$854 million) are larger than the liability added (US$627 million), and thus a net amount of US$227 million is subtracted.

Unlike pension liabilities, retiree health benefit liabilities have been reflected on the balance sheet since implementation of FAS 106. In the spectrum of 'debt-like' obligations, Standard & Poor's regards retiree health obligations as falling somewhere between pensions and other, non-debt accrued liabilities – ie they are the least debt-like of these balance sheet items. To reflect these obligations for AMR, the reported liability, US$1.5 billion, is added to debt. There is no reduction of equity, because that effect had already been incorporated on adoption of FAS 106 in the form of a special charge. Exhibit 15.5 shows the results of adjusting for cash, underfunded pensions and retiree health benefits.

Appendix 3:
Rating enhancement for airline equipment debt

Aircraft leases and secured debt that qualify for special protection under Section 1110 of the US Bankruptcy Code can receive ratings above the corporate credit rating of the airline issuer. Section 1110 excludes certain types of leases and secured debt from the automatic stay of creditor claims and substitution of collateral sections of the Code. Creditors may repossess collateral if the debtor does not resume debt service or lease rentals and cure any past due amounts within 60 days of filing for bankruptcy. This provides a powerful incentive for continued payment under these obligations in bankruptcy. Standard & Poor's rating enhancement is based on:

- section 1110's legal support for continuing payment of interest and principal (thus reducing default risk);
- accelerated access to collateral if payment is not made, under the provisions of Section 1110; and
- the relatively good value retention, over long periods of time, of aircraft, ease of tracking them, and the ability to realise their value by reselling aircraft to other operators in a global market.

Qualifications for rating enhancement

To qualify for Section 1110 treatment, creditors must have a security interest in the aircraft (for financings on aircraft delivered before 22 October 1994, this must be a purchase money security interest), or be a lessor, or be a conditional vendor. Collateral must be aircraft or aircraft parts, and the debtor must be an airline. In addition, Standard & Poor's accords the full rating enhancement only in those cases where an airline's size and market position make liquidation unlikely, allowing for a reasonable possibility that aircraft financing will be paid at the contracted rate. Collateral that is technologically or economically less desirable or which does not cover outstanding secured debt by a comfortable margin would also not qualify for the rating enhancement; a bankrupt airline might well allow such equipment to be repossessed rather than continue debt service.

Continental Airlines and Pan American World Airways argued in their bankruptcy proceedings during the early 1990s that Section 1110 did not apply to aircraft that had been sold and leased back to raise funds, but only to leases used to acquire new aircraft. Higher courts eventually ruled that all leases are eligible under Section 1110. However, the circuit court hearing the Continental appeal ruled that sale–leasebacks could be challenged on the grounds that the financings were secured debt in disguise and not 'true leases'. Because of this potential loophole and remaining uncertainties regarding the application of Section 1110, Congress revised that section of the Code (and its sister provision, Section 1168 for railroads) in a Bankruptcy Reform Act passed in October 1994. The revision provided that for aircraft delivered on or after enactment of the legislation, Section 1110 would apply to any financing secured by aircraft or parts, not just a purchase money secured financing. In addition, in order to limit challenges on the 'true lease' argument, any aircraft lease would be considered a true lease for the purposes of Section 1110 if both parties to the transaction expressed in writing at the time of the financing that it was intended to be a lease. The distinction between secured debt and leases, as a condition of qualifying for Section 1110 status, is moot going forward, because both forms of financing qualify.

Standard & Poor's did not revise any ratings on Section 1110 or 1168 financings as a result of this legislation because, for rated transactions, the Act only clarified that those provisions of the Code would apply as Standard & Poor's had expected they would. Rated transactions typically involve modern-technology equipment, financed by using leases. To the extent that sale–leasebacks are employed, they represent permanent financing, put in place soon after delivery of the aircraft. Therefore, these types of financings were, even prior to the bankruptcy reform, somewhat less likely to be challenged. However, there are other types of transactions, not currently rated by Standard & Poor's, that might be accorded Section 1110 treatment now which would not have been so rated earlier. One obvious example is non-purchase-money secured debt on aircraft delivered since October 1994.

The other reason why no ratings were revised is that the rating benefits of Section 1110 are limited by the economic realities of an airline bankruptcy reorganisation. Recent bankruptcies have demonstrated that airlines are often willing and able to bargain aggressively for lower rates, because lessors do not wish to repossess their equipment in a weak market. This points up the limitations of legal protection when the underlying collateral has lost value.

Degree of Enhancement

The degree of enhancement applied by Standard & Poor's depends on the above factors and the issuer's corporate credit rating. Investment grade issuers (at present, only Southwest Airlines Co) receive a 'one-notch' upgrade (eg A– to A), while speculative grade airlines would typically receive a two-notch enhancement (eg B to BB–).

When an airline is in Chapter 11 bankruptcy proceedings, ratings on Section 1110 obligations would be based on Standard & Poor's estimate of the likelihood of a successful reorganisation and the particular features of the equipment financing under consideration. Such a rating would typically be in the CCC category, but might fall into the B category if the financing in question is very well secured and/or has been affirmed by the court and the airline seems likely to reorganise successfully.

Standard & Poor's has not as yet rated aircraft equipment financings of non-US airlines, aside from multi-airline securitisations. However, ratings above the airline's corporate credit rating should be possible for obligations that are well secured with desirable equipment, and where the prevailing legal system recognises rights of secured creditors and lessors. While other legal systems rarely have provisions comparable to Section 1110, their insolvency regimes are in other respects usually more favourable to creditors than is the US Bankruptcy Code. Beyond the letter of the law, the analyst should also consider the actual track record of aircraft repossessions (if any) and treatment of creditors in the country in question.

16 Assessing an airline's credit: The lender's perspective

Klaus W. Heinemann

This chapter aims to set out a framework for the credit assessment by a bank of a secured aircraft financing transaction. There is no 'standard' approach to such credit and risk assessment because it is, by definition, a mostly subjective exercise.

Overview of risk assessment procedures

Different banks will employ various analytical procedures to make decisions about the acceptability of proposed secured aircraft transactions. But one issue that overrides such variations is the fact that secured aircraft transactions typically require an assessment of credit and risk factors stretching beyond the more customary five- to seven-year tenor of general corporate banking activity. Most secured aircraft transactions will stretch to between 10 and 18 years if one includes pre-delivery commitment periods. Although many analysts may doubt the existence of any valid method that allows for reliable judgements stretching so far into the future, a case will be made in this chapter for the existence and reasonable reliability of such a method.

It will be quite clear that such an exercise cannot be based on the analysis of historic financial data only, but must include a broader focus that includes detailed analysis of general industry trends and value fluctuations of the aircraft asset used as security. In many ways, such an analytical method is more closely related to that of an equity investor rather than a more traditional credit risk focus.

Many banks have recently introduced internal procedures for credit risk assessment of banking transactions that provide for a clear differentiation between the two key elements of lending risk management – the risk of an obligor default and the risk of loss following such a default. Sometimes this differentiation is internally expressed as 'obligor credit risk grading' as opposed to 'obligor transaction risk grading'. All asset-secured transactions of banks can show significant differentials between those two gradings. In practice, banks have experienced the significance of such a distinction between these two substantially different risk assessments following reviews of default loan recovery ratios for secured and unsecured transactions for defaulting airlines, such as Air Europe.

It is important to understand clearly that these two risk assessments – obligor credit risk and obligor transaction risk – are very different and that each require specific analytical focus. All too often credit committees are tempted to simply try and judge the 'risk of default' of, for example, an emerging market airline with marginal financial performance, for a future period of 12 years, which is clearly a futile exercise. In such a case, a more appropriate focus would be based on the 'risk of loss' of a specific transaction, analysing historic aircraft value volatilities for a given aircraft type and engine choice, initial advance rates, debt repayment profiles and the cost and timing of legal security right enforcements. The following outline is based on such an analytical differentiation.

Obligor financial credit risk

As defined above, this assessment is focusing on the possibility of an obligor default during the term of a given transaction. All defaults in the final analysis are caused by the obligor's inability to repay or prepay its financial obligations – in other words lack of sufficient cash flow to pay such obligations as they fall due. The analytical process therefore has to consider all issues that may have an impact on the obligor's ability to generate sufficient cash over time to meet all existing and future financial obligations as they fall due. In the following sub-sections we will attempt to highlight those key issues that may have a significant impact on such long-term cash flow generation ability.

Historical financial performance

This is identical to the traditional financial analysis used for most short- to medium-term bank risk products. It will therefore include the usual spreading of three years of annual financial reports and the related calculation of standard financial ratios. (It is not intended in this chapter to describe such methods in detail, because they do not differ in principle from those used for most other banking obligors.)

The most significant aspect specifically related to the airline industry with respect to historical financial data is the lack of industry standard comparisons caused by the lack of sufficient separate airline obligors within any given accounting standard outside the US. Such differences in accounting standards between countries are often related to accounting treatment of aircraft assets, representing the single most significant asset type. It is therefore important to review the different rules covering the accounting treatment of aircraft as off-balance sheet assets.

The widely used off-balance sheet treatment of aircraft, common to many airlines' financial statements, be it by way of operating lease or option lease, makes the use of traditional balance sheet ratios problematic and often almost completely meaningless. Frequently, disclosure statements with respect to related accounting principles in the obligor's annual report are insufficient to allow manual adjustment for the 'true' asset and liability position. As a minimum adjustment to be considered by every financial analyst, all disclosed future lease obligations for off-balance sheet leases need to be added to each obligor's total debt amount, before any calculation of debt-based ratios. In addition, judgements will have to be made on the true economic nature of aircraft return options, limiting such future lease rental obligations. Depending on the accounting standard used by the obligor, such options may, de facto, be of a purely cosmetic nature and not exercisable by the obligor without substantial financial penalty.

Perhaps a more useful financial ratio, replacing traditional debt/equity ratios, is based on a comparison of all aircraft-related cash outflows (such as interest, debt repayments, lease payments and maintenance cost) with operating revenue. Such a ratio might lead to meaningful comparisons among international airlines in terms of the annual operating revenue generation required to maintain their current, or proposed, aircraft fleet capacity. Another area of financial reporting that may require substantial adjustment before any meaningful comparison among international airline obligors can be attempted relates to the profit and loss account. Key areas to research here are the obligor's depreciation policy, maintenance reserve policy and treatment of sale–leaseback profits, in addition to capitalisation of certain expenses such as aircraft introduction cost and route development cost. Differences in accounting policies among obligors in these areas can dramatically alter disclosed profits and often be the critical differentiating factor between a disclosed profit or loss. It is necessary to adjust financial accounts for these issues by, for example, cleansing profit/loss figures from extraordinary gains related to sale–leaseback activities and cost capitalisations that may not lead to an asset with realistic liquidation value. Often, annual reports will provide insufficient information to make a judgement on these issues without detailed additional questioning of an obligor's management.

Cash flow analysis

This part of the financial analysis is at the very core of the analyst's judgement on the obligor's risk of default. The most common approach is to relate EBITDA (earnings before interest, taxes, depreciation and amortisation) to the obligor's total indebtedness, inclusive of off-balance sheet lease obligations. It is important to use a 'cleansed' earnings figure (as described above) for this calculation, in order to obtain a good understanding of the naked EBITDA figure produced by ordinary operations and excluding revenue of an extraordinary nature, such as book value gains from aircraft sales. As a next step, this EBITDA to total indebtedness ratio should be compared with the actual average life of the obligor's total indebtedness, as well as its contractual maturity profile, in order to determine any significant imbalances.

A thorough sensitivity analysis of the obligor's EBITDA figure should determine the possible impact of revenue/cost developments outside the obligor's direct control, such as fuel cost, air traffic control and airport charges, market yield per passenger mile and operational disruptions caused by war/strike activities. A suitable 'worst case' scenario should be defined, based on each individual bank's risk attitude and compared with existing cash positions and debt maturity profiles, in order to determine trigger levels for possible payment defaults caused by unfavourable developments in these key revenue/cost factors.

In cases of obligors raising new debt to increase existing fleet capacity, one can use this analytical method backwards by determining the necessary EBITDA level required to maintain previous coverage ratios, while increasing total indebtedness. It is then possible to determine the required RPM increases and/or investment-related operating cost reductions necessary in order to achieve the required EBITDA level. The difficult part is of course to judge how reasonable are the underlying assumptions made by the obligor in order to achieve such higher levels. RPM increases are based on assumptions of higher load factors and/or yield per passenger mile increases. Total revenue increases are based on assumptions of passenger volume growth for existing markets, increased market share, newly developed markets and any combination of these. Assumptions used by obligors for their revenue forecasts should always be reviewed in detail and with a healthy measure of common sense. For example, yield per passenger mile increases, assumed by the obligor in an environment of falling yields, or assumptions on significant market share gains against a dominant competitor, will more often than not fail to materialise.

Having reviewed the obligor's historical and forecast cash flow generation figures and its ability to cover existing and proposed debt service levels, one can start the important task of analysing the long-term stability of such cash flow generation capability. It is at this point that we move from a primarily financial review into the sphere of our obligor's general corporate, as well as regional and industrial, environment.

The airline industry

It is most important to begin reviewing this issue with a clear understanding that the global aviation industry has been in an intense transition period for the past 15 years, taking it from the status of a highly protected and regulated transportation utility expanding in a high-growth market, towards a deregulated, competitive service industry in a mature market. This transition is progressing unevenly and slowly across global markets and is far from finished. It all started with the Reagan deregulation in the US in 1981, with the US airlines being forced through a transition period that is only now reaching its conclusion (at least as far as the US domestic market segment of business is concerned). So far, air transportation between different countries remains generally under tight regulation, with the Chicago Convention governing a complex system of traffic rights for individual airlines by way of bilateral agreements between countries. These bilaterals govern every detail, such as which airline can fly where, how often, with what maximum market share and at what ticket price. They furthermore impose mostly strict controls over foreign ownership rights of airlines designated to fly under such bilaterals.

Historically, this system has protected banks remarkably well against the risk of obligor default, by shielding airlines from competition and by tending to underpin government ownership of flag-carriers, providing deep and willing pockets to refill depleted cash coffers if such airlines failed to perform financially, even under such protective conditions. This background, combined with the limited historical volatility of aircraft fair market values, has caused a remarkably modest loss experience for banks' aviation portfolios during the past 30 years of aviation banking, especially if compared with other major secured lending areas such as real estate and shipping. It is very important to understand that these cornerstones of modest loss experience are now under attack as a result of the trend towards global deregulation, privatisation and more aggressive lending structures, causing increased exposure to even modest fair market value volatilities. Any banker ignoring this change, while trying to judge credit and transaction risks over a timespan stretching to the year 2015, will suffer predictable consequences! Let's therefore examine these agents of change.

Global deregulation

As already mentioned, this trend began in 1981 with deregulation of domestic air transport in the US. Airlines were suddenly released from all regulatory restraints and could compete with each other. The result has been a very dramatic transformation of the airline business environment in the US, with many previously proud and substantial players disappearing altogether. All of this happened within a timeframe of roughly 10 years – in other words, well within the typical term of a standard aircraft term loan or finance lease.

Deregulation is currently progressing from the US to a globally applied concept. This trend manifests itself in two different forms: first, the establishment of other regionally deregulated markets, such as the European Union; and, secondly, the gradual introduction of so-called 'open-sky' bilaterals. The deregulation of the EU internal market has reached its final stage with the establishment of complete 'cabotage rights' for all airlines within the Union from 1997 onwards. This will allow, for example, British Airways to serve routes between Italy and Spain, or any other pair of EU states, if it so chooses. Already this regional deregulation is beginning to show similar results to those observed in the US. European deregulation and the resulting increased competition have already caused a visible divide between financial 'winners' and 'losers' among European airlines.

Privatisation

The only reason that this trend has not already led to the financial collapse of some European airlines, as it did in the US, is the fact that most remain in government ownership. National pride and also employment considerations have caused such governments to act as the most generous shareholders imaginable, so far! However, some European, Asian, African and Latin American airlines have already been privatised and others are lined up on the runway by their government pilots for takeoff into privatisation, as soon as the financial 'all clear' is given.

The real watershed of deregulation and privatisation of airlines in Europe, or elsewhere, has yet to be reached: what would happen if a privatised flag-carrier should run into financial trouble? Would the government of such a privatised airline continue to provide assistance? It is not easy to find a uniform answer to this question, and under certain circumstances such support might still be forthcoming, despite privatisation. In most cases, however, one would have to assume that governments would have no choice but to treat a privatised airline like any other private corporation in their respective country. Within the EU they might actually, for legal reasons, have no choice in this matter.

Future trends

There are currently no signs of further regional deregulation – US or European style. Nevertheless, deregulation is continuing its slow progress by way of the introduction of more and more open-sky bilaterals between countries, such as the US/Dutch, US/German and US/Canadian bilaterals. All have in common the almost complete abolition of competitive controls previously contained in such bilaterals. This trend, away from heavily interventionist and anti-competitive agreements, and the fact that the bilaterals have been drafted solely from the perspective of providing maximum protection for the flag-carriers concerned, continues to be fuelled by the travelling public's ever growing demand for cheaper and more efficient air travel opportunities. Open-sky bilaterals will ultimately become confined to the policing of safety and fair competition standards and may gradually replace most, if not all, existing bilaterals between all significant air travel destinations.

Shareholders of airlines, be they governments or private capital, all recognise this trend and have reacted to it by privatising and/or streamlining airline operations. They are beginning to believe that the trend to global deregulation of the industry is almost certainly unstoppable, and are trying to design strategies that ensure financial success at the end of this road. It is too early to predict the overall timeframe of this development towards mostly privatised airlines operating in a mostly deregulated global environment, but it is certain that eventually regional and global deregulation will divide airlines into winners and losers, just as it did in the US. The other certainty is the fact that aircraft funding terms of 10 to 18 years committed today will last long enough to straddle this period of change. It is for this reason that overall industry assessment is such a critical factor in each bank's risk judgement on new transactions.

Other credit risk aspects

This section aims to highlight aspects outside pure financial analysis and general industry factors that need to be investigated in order to try to assess an obligor's ability to come through the trend of industry privatisation and deregulation as a 'winner' – in other words to protect and improve its ability to produce sufficient operational cash flows to service its debt and lease obligations over time.

Ownership

This most basic issue deals with the traditional aspect of many international airline obligors enjoying 'quasi-sovereign' status, or in plain non-banker's language, the assumption that a shareholder government will, for political or whatever other reasons, not allow financial failure of the obligor. If one wishes to rely on this government ownership protection, the transaction should contain appropriate ownership maintenance clauses – ie an obligation by the government to maintain such ownership throughout the life of any given transaction. It is important that such a clause provides a government undertaking, because the obligor itself may have no control over its government's privatisation plans.

A careful assessment should also be made as to the effect of government ownership on the obligor's long-term financial performance. In many cases government ownership means political, rather than commercial, decision making with respect to senior management appointments, aircraft procurement, engine choice, route developments and employee union relations, all too often a proven recipe for future financial disaster. The cost of political, rather than commercial, decisions by airlines in this context is increasing, as deregulation increases competitive pressure. While for example, in the old, regulated world, an airline could operate a sub-optimal fleet mix, caused by 'political' aircraft ordering, this may become more difficult in the future if the airline is to compete against others that use the cost advantages of optimised fleet mixes to offer lower fare levels. In this case the financial strength of the airline's government/country, as well as its willingness to continue financial support, would require careful review. Within the EU the issue of possible illegality of such support under fair competition legislation needs to be examined.

Private ownership, on the other hand, is not entirely free from such potential pitfalls either. Majority shareholders may have their own agenda, independent from the obligor's management view on key decisions. Also, the question of access to sources of additional shareholder funds may be more restricted than in other industries as a result of remaining national ownership requirements for internationally operating airlines under the Chicago Convention.

Quality of management

This is probably the single most important aspect of long-term survival in any changing industry. The experience of an obligor's senior management, their ability to understand long-term industry trends and to react to them with appropriate strategies is an irreplaceable ingredient of future financial strength. This is where many government-owned airlines show their greatest weakness. It is only by rare chance that retired politicians, or air force marshals, become superior commercial airline managers in a changing global environment. Even if a government owner of an airline has the foresight to appoint the best commercial management available, such an appointment will not be completely successful unless it goes hand in hand with freedom from politically motivated shareholder restrictions during strategy implementation.

Another important aspect of management ability rests with their understanding of the changing regulatory framework and its overall impact on the industry and on the particular airline. As deregulation progresses, a thorough understanding of the impact of detail and timing of this process on the airline and the political process of influencing such detail and timing (ie successful lobbying) is of great importance. Frequently, commercially minded management, especially if recruited from outside the airline industry, find this particular requirement difficult to cope with, as most other globally operating industries would not be exposed to such significant regulatory issues.

Competitive environment

This requires the analysis of an airline's position in its home market and potential future developments in the light of its own strategy and that of its existing and potential future competitors, taking into account the trend towards global deregulation.

A key area for detailed investigation is the airline's current market share and to what extent this share is a result of competitive strength, as against the continued existence of protective, regulated market conditions. In most cases it will be a combination of both and one has to make a judgement as to the dominant factor. Vital here is the need to determine the existence of any residual protective market conditions following a step into more deregulated territory. Such conditions, unlikely to disappear even after deregulation, are for example found in an airline's market share dominance of significant international hub airports and its related share of airport slot positions, particularly at capacity-restricted airports. Other examples are specific niches in air transportation, which for reasons of geographical location or limited traffic potential, remain outside the interest of major airline players.

The risk of competitive pressure from other airlines has to be judged in the light of limited transferability of home base cost advantages. The high dependence of an airline on local cost environments, outside the control of the airline and its management, makes its very difficult to export home base cost advantages into a competitor's home market. Local overall employment conditions and airport/air traffic control charges are key examples and often determine 50 per cent of total costs of an airline. Also, existing reservation systems and captive travel agencies play vital roles in an airline's distribution capabilities and can represent forceful entry barriers for new competitors. The same is true of the operation of sophisticated yield management systems by airlines, where efficiency depends on the existence of expensive IT systems and reliable databases on historical passenger booking patterns. Airlines are also increasingly using alliances and franchise networks to increase commercial entry barriers against new competition.

Again we can look back to the actual experience of the deregulated market in the US, where some of the pre-deregulation airline majors successfully replaced the old regulatory barriers with these new commercial barriers in order to shield themselves from the pressure of lower-cost producers.

In the long run, as air transport moves towards a more mature and competitive market, we will observe three types of long-term winners among airlines. These three categories are low-cost airlines, niche airlines and global market dominating airlines. If one looks at the diversified trend of airline profitability during the 1990s, the emergence of this trend is apparent. Airlines that fall clearly within one of the three categories tend to perform better than those that are less focused. From an obligor credit risk perspective, it is important to understand whether an airline clearly belongs already to one of these categories, or if at least its stated strategies will lead it towards such identity over time.

Overall credit risk judgement

It is clear therefore that the judgement of an airline obligor's overall credit risk, or 'risk of default', involves the assessment of numerous factors related to past financial performance, airline industry developments and the obligor's competitive environment. Industry developments and the competitive environment play a vital role in aiding an assessment of the continuation of past financial success over a future 10–18 year horizon. Analysing these issues and their interrelationship is sometimes difficult, and conclusions may be subjective. Some credit risk analysts are therefore inclined to ignore them. Such inclination is understandable, but nevertheless indefensible. The influence of these non-financial facts and trends are too powerful in this industry to be ignored without making serious mistakes.

Obligor transaction risk

As explained at the start of this chapter, we are dividing our overall risk assessment into obligor credit risk (ie the risk of default) and obligor transaction risk (ie the risk of loss following an obligor default). The components of transaction risk assessment are examined in the following sub-sections.

The repossession risk

Once obligor default has occurred, the process of default debt recovery obviously begins with the task of gaining full control over the financed aircraft in order to generate cash by way of sale, lease, or a combination of both. The risk assessment has to focus on the legal position offered in any given transaction and needs to address the following points:

- Is the security interest established by way of title ownership over the aircraft, or by way of mortgage?
- In which jurisdiction has such security interest to be enforced?
- Are there any protective bankruptcy laws in the airline's jurisdiction that could stall enforcement procedures?
- Is there any political risk insurance cover to protect the creditor against political interference with the repossession procedure in an airline's jurisdiction, if such interference is considered possible in a given country?

The analysis of these factors should allow for an estimate of the possible duration of the repossession process and costs associated with it, such as legal fees, priority claims from mandatorily preferred creditors, re-registration and technical re-certification cost. All these costs have to be taken into account for an accurate estimate of net sales proceeds from such aircraft disposal, available for creditor claim recovery.

In more complex funding structures, such as cross-border tax leases, ECA-backed funding and structures utilising subordinate creditors, the risk of interference by such parties with the repossession process has to be reviewed. In particular, ECAs frequently maintain significant rights to suspend or postpone the repossession proceedings if they consider this necessary for political reasons.

Aircraft remarketing

This provides for the transformation of the repossessed aircraft into cash in order to satisfy outstanding creditor claims. It is a vital part of transaction risk assessment to estimate correctly the cash proceeds from this process in order to be able to calculate the most likely amount of loss in case of obligor default. It will come as no surprise that most creditors want to achieve 100 per cent recovery ratios, even in adverse market circumstances, in order to justify credit commitments to airlines, with the only possible exception being airlines with the highest obligor credit risk rating – ie high investment grade airlines. The key factors flowing into such recovery ratio calculations are as follows.

The airframe/engine combination

The historical volatility of fair market values for any given airframe/engine combination is unique and can differ significantly for different aircraft types and engine choices. Such volatilities are measured by looking at the positive and negative variations of any such combination from the base fair market value over time and during different market conditions. Each aircraft type and the obligor's engine choice has to be examined in detail to determine its unique volatility factor.

Most critical in this examination is the so-called 'user base' of any given airframe/engine combination. The more airlines using such a combination, the lower its volatility. The main reason for this is the high integration cost of new airframe/engine combinations into an airline's existing fleet. Such costs are mainly caused by pilot/maintenance training, separate spare part requirements and other fleet integration costs. This results in airlines being generally easier to persuade to add to their fleet more airframe/engine combinations identical to those they already operate. Other airframe/engine combinations, especially if offered in small numbers, will only be acceptable at significant discounts to fair market value, or if at times of market imbalances no other options exist to increase short-term capacity.

If one looks at the past fair market value performance of aircraft, or airframe/engine combinations with small user bases, such as the British Trident, the BAC 1-11 or Rolls-Royce powered Boeing 767s, one can understand the significance of this issue. Another factor influencing volatility is the size of aircraft. The largest aircraft in the short-haul and long-haul segments tend to show greater volatility than their lower capacity alternatives, as a result of airlines downsizing aircraft capacity while maintaining frequency in recessionary scenarios. Another factor historically influencing volatility has tended to be the manufacturer: in the past some airframe manufacturers have been more skillful than others in manipulating the second-hand market for their products. This factor is now rapidly losing significance with competing manufacturers learning the game of 'asset management'.

Initial advance rate and repayment profile

This determines the initial and future debt exposure profile against fair market value estimates. It is this 'cover ratio', typically measured as fair market value divided by total debt exposure at any point in time during a transaction, that is crucial for the determination of our loss recovery ratio in the case of obligor default. It will come as no surprise that the exact definition of what represents 'fair market value' is of importance in this process. Fortunately, over the past few years internationally recognised aircraft value appraisers have been working on some uniform standards. Appraisers now generally define three different variations of fair market value:

- *Base* fair market value represents the estimated market value development of a given aircraft over time in a balanced market, between a willing buyer and a willing seller without undue time pressure. It is this value that is most commonly used by airlines, banks and other investors;
- *Current* fair market value takes the actual market conditions at the time of the appraisal into account and adjusts the base value up or down accordingly; and

- *Soft* fair market value attempts to quantify the downside volatility of a given aircraft in adverse market conditions.

The most conservative calculation of the loss recovery ratio, which is at the heart of transaction risk assessment, would therefore be established by comparing an appraiser's soft fair market value estimate over the entire transaction timespan with the given debt repayment profile. The resulting ratio should exceed 100 per cent at all times in order to allow for repossession cost as detailed above, as well as other potential exposures relating to currency mismatch (non-dollar denominated funding), fixed rate funding breakage cost, etc. The extent of the required excess over 100 per cent depends of course on the individual transaction criteria and each creditor's risk appetite. Many creditors will also insist that this excess grows as the transaction moves through time, in order to cover the risk of any unforeseen adverse market or risk developments, based on the assumption that any assessment of future developments becomes more uncertain as we move through each transaction's lifespan. Again there is a close correlation between each obligor's credit risk ranking and the accuracy and error cushions required for the above recovery ratio calculation.

Other supporting factors

No transaction risk assessment is complete without due consideration of a whole host of different supporting elements that may assist any or all of the loss recovery factors. The following list gives an overview of the most commonly used supporting elements in aircraft funding transactions.

Full guarantees

Such guarantees basically shift the obligor credit risk rating from the primary obligor to the guarantor and consequently relate all other risk assessments of any given transaction to such different guarantor's credit risk rating.

Partial/deficiency guarantees

These guarantees mostly affect the calculation of total debt exposure over time, because they reduce repayment profiles by the amount of such guarantee. This in turn improves security coverage ratios and ultimately obligor transaction risk ratings, dependent of course on an independent obligor credit rating assessment of the guarantor.

Junior/mezzanine lenders

This has the same effect on transaction risk rating as under the previous sub-section, but without the requirement to assess the obligor credit risk rating of such lenders, because their investment is made at the outset and not just on default of the primary obligor.

Remarketing assistance

Sometimes transactions include remarketing assistance agreements from manufacturers, or other professional remarketing organisations. The 'monetary' value of such assistance is difficult to assess, but may nevertheless be meaningful, by reducing marketing cost or allowing for a faster remarketing success and/or better fair market value realisation. In this context, one should always assess the remarketing capabilities of guarantors or junior/mezzanine lenders. Even if no formal remarketing agreement obliges them to assist, their desire to minimise their respective exposure under such a transaction may become a powerful motivation to help the senior creditor in the remarketing process. It is important not to underestimate the value of a competent and imaginative remarketing agent. Especially in recessionary market conditions, such skill may make the difference between full and discounted/delayed fair market value realisation.

Conclusion

While the outline in this chapter of various issues worth considering in a transaction risk assessment process may look complex, it can also be stimulating because it allows aviation bankers some interesting insights into the future of their airline clients.

Possibly the most promising trend in the development of this assessment process is the clearer differentiation between credit risk and transaction risk employed within many banks' credit departments. The rating agencies have recently started to support this trend with great enthusiasm because they have developed analytical methods for the purposes of rating equipment and enhanced equipment trust certificate issues. Many elements of this analytical approach can be used, in slightly modified form, for the purpose of setting up internal procedures to determine a valid transaction risk rating and clearly distinguishing it from the more traditional credit risk rating. The proven ability of non-investment grade airlines and lessors to issue such investment grade debt instruments in the capital markets may stimulate banks to try and familiarise their credit departments with the necessary methodology. This in turn may lead to the development of a more sophisticated market for secured aircraft debt instruments.

17 Aircraft as investments

Edward Hansom

Introduction

The air transport industry recession of the early 1990s was a difficult period for investors in aircraft. The combination of a drop in air travel and record deliveries of new aircraft created an unprecedented, if temporary, surplus of aircraft. This surplus forced down aircraft values and lease rates, although the impact of the fall in lease rates on margins was mitigated for lessors (most of whom have leveraged capital structures) by the offsetting impact of falling US interest rates.

Exhibit 17.1 illustrates changes in surplus aircraft and returns on aircraft from 1987 to 1996. For aircraft lessors the negative returns of the early 1990s were as unprecedented as the 1991 drop in RPMs was for airlines. Although the previous industry recession of the early 1980s created a surplus of aircraft that reached comparable levels as a percentage of the then world fleet, this did not turn aircraft returns negative due to the impact of high inflation on the cost of new aircraft and the knock-on effect of this on the values of used aircraft.

Exhibit 17.1
Aircraft returns and world fleet surplus, 1987–96

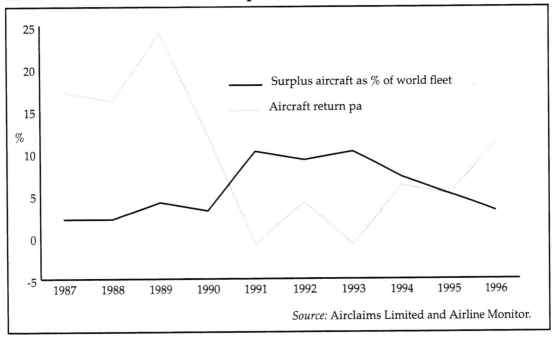

Surplus aircraft as % of world fleet

Aircraft return pa

Source: Airclaims Limited and Airline Monitor.

Despite the difficulties of recent years, the risk and reward associated with aircraft owner-ship remain, on a slightly longer view, competitive with other investments. Exhibit 17.2 com-pares returns on a diversified pool of commercial jet aircraft in the past 10 years, and the volatil-ity of those returns as measured by their standard deviation, with other asset classes available for investment in the US (aircraft leasing and sales are US dollar-denominated businesses). Although aircraft did not provide returns comparable with the equity market, represented here by the S&P 500, they had lower volatility. Aircraft returns and volatility were consistent with Treasury bonds, but these returns were inversely correlated, suggesting that aircraft can offer worthwhile diversification. Aircraft provided higher returns than US commercial real estate with very little extra volatility. (For readers who are interested, details of methodology and sources are included in Appendix 1 to this chapter.)

Aircraft investment fundamentals

In the previous edition of *Aircraft Financing* I argued that the investment fundamentals of air-craft were likely to lead to a continuation of the positive investment performance experienced by owners in the 1970s and 1980s. Of course, this argument was qualified by a cautionary acknowledgement of the cyclical nature of the air transport industry. In the light of recent expe-rience a review of those fundamentals seems useful, and must address the issue of whether there have been any fundamental changes in the nature of the industry or whether the latest turn of the cycle was just particularly sharp.

Demand

Exhibit 17.1 shows that the aircraft surplus of the early 1990s has been largely eliminated due to traffic growth and reduced new aircraft production. Typical industry forecasts now project

Exhibit 17.2
Returns on aircraft and other asset classes, 1987–96

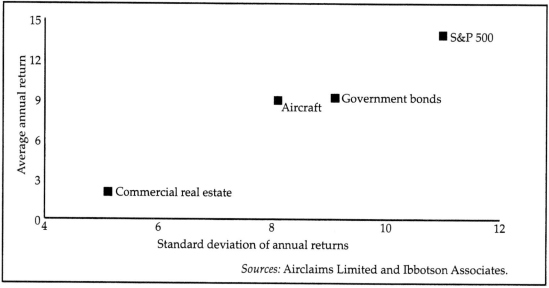

Sources: Airclaims Limited and Ibbotson Associates.

average annual deliveries for 1991–2000 inclusive of around 700 at an average annual cost of approximately US$40 billion. The volume figure is higher than was generally expected at the start of the decade (about 600) because (a) the mix of new aircraft includes fewer large wide-bodies than had been expected, and (b) air travel growth compensated for both higher increases in load factors and much lower retirals than had been anticipated. The dollar figure is as expected at the start of the decade despite higher volume due to the change in the mix of aircraft delivered and because inflation has been lower than anticipated.

Supply

The long-term trend towards concentration of new aircraft manufacturing remains intact, as Exhibit 17.3 demonstrates. The Boeing and Airbus market shares will likely increase further after the merger of the former with McDonnell Douglas and the bankruptcy of Fokker. The market position of Boeing and Airbus is based on the breadth of their product range in the market for jets with seating capacity of 100 or more. Although Bombardier and Embraer have entered the commercial jet manufacturing industry these new entrants are in fact expanding the jet market by producing smaller aircraft to compete with existing turbo-prop types, and do not appear likely to offer a material commercial threat to the big two.

Barriers to entry in commercial jet manufacturing remain formidable due to the high upfront investment involved in developing new models. The two most likely possible sources of new competition are Asia and the CIS. However, one may speculate that Asian participation may largely take the form of co-production with existing participants due to the leverage that region has as a major new aircraft purchaser, and that CIS producers will be as busy defending their existing customer base against Western-built competition as they will be in seeking new business.

Exhibit 17.3
Aircraft manufacturer market shares, 1970–96

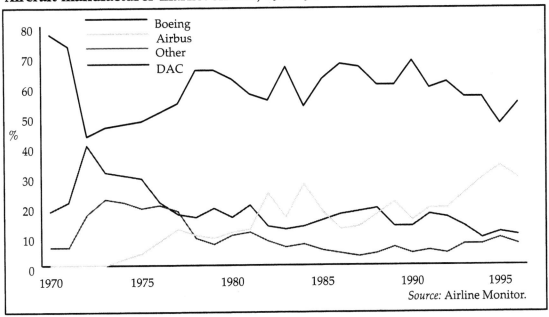

Source: Airline Monitor.

Supply versus demand/new aircraft pricing

The adjustment process that occurred in response to the aircraft surplus of the early 1990s clearly followed historical precedent by featuring a drop in new aircraft supply that allowed aircraft demand to catch up. During the recession Boeing, Airbus and McDonnell Douglas all announced initiatives to deal with this very costly volatility in production levels by addressing production lead times and production costs. Lead times prior to the 1990s were typically as much as two years and have been a very important contributing factor to the cyclical nature of the industry, best summarised as 'aircraft are ordered in good times and delivered in bad times'. Providing shorter lead times has been relatively easy to achieve in the context of declining and steady but low production, and it remains to be seen whether such aspirations will be sustainable in a more buoyant environment. However, if they are this will be of great benefit to aircraft manufacturers and owners.

If cuts in production costs are achieved, and if the resultant savings are passed on to customers, the benefits to owners are far less clear, because a reduction in inflation-adjusted new aircraft prices will almost certainly reduce used aircraft values. There were a number of competitive bidding rounds for large new aircraft orders in 1993–95 that led some industry observers to query whether a permanent reduction in new aircraft prices might be occurring. Exhibit 17.4 demonstrates what a radical change such a development would be. The cost of the average new aircraft seat has risen well ahead of inflation as long as jet aircraft have been produced, and in recessions manufacturers have cut production rather than prices. Naturally there have been improvements in technology over that period, but these have not been sufficient to render most older aircraft economically obsolete (see Exhibit 17.5), leading one to conclude that the manufacturers have retained much of the benefit of new technology in higher unit prices.

Exhibit 17.4
Indices of aircraft prices, production and US CPI, 1970–96

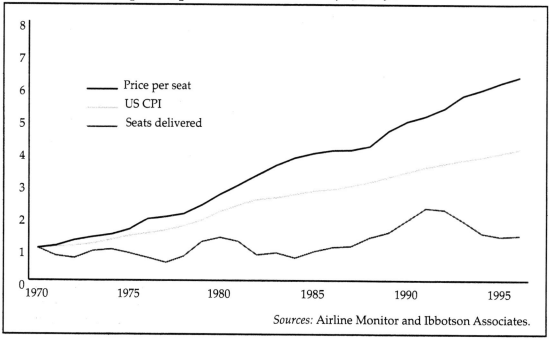

Sources: Airline Monitor and Ibbotson Associates.

It is hard to see the benefit to the major manufacturers of price reductions as well as cost reductions. In particular, Boeing and Airbus have sufficiently large market shares that they are unlikely to experience volume gains sufficient to offset the foregone margin, because aircraft ownership costs are not a sufficiently large proportion of total airline costs for a drop in the former to allow a significant drop in the overall price of air travel. In any event, it should be borne in mind that a number of the competitive bids of recent years involved competition for launch orders for new aircraft types, and such orders have traditionally involved the keenest pricing available. However, it would not be a surprise if the rate of increase in new aircraft prices relative to the US CPI slackened towards the end of the 1990s as the aircraft ordered in a recessionary environment are actually delivered, because such a change can be observed towards the end of both the previous decades, probably due to similar cycle-related factors.

Technology

From an operating cost perspective, commercial jet aircraft technology has been fundamentally mature for a long period of time. This development occurred when the first twin-engined aircraft with two cockpit crew positions were delivered in the mid to late 1960s. Although engines thereafter became more fuel-efficient and quieter and various other improvements have been made, such developments were essentially incremental and have not been sufficiently cost-effective to render previous models with such characteristics economically obsolete. In fact many aircraft not meeting this specification have had very long useful lives, and industry forecasts have typically underestimated the economic life of aircraft and overestimated future retirals.

Exhibit 17.5 shows aircraft retirals by year of manufacture (retirals include casualties, giving a minor conservative bias to the figures from an economic perspective). Based on the data in the chart, a reasonable expected economic life for an aircraft would be 30 years, and longer for successful types. There do not appear to be any impending technological developments that will change this situation, and in fact much of the focus of new aircraft development in the 1980s and 1990s has been on producing twin-engined, two cockpit crew wide-body aircraft

Exhibit 17.5
Aircraft retiral experience

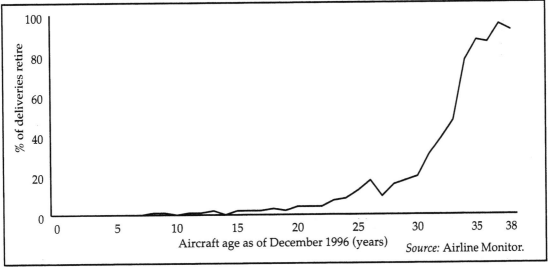

Source: Airline Monitor.

such as the B767, the B777 and the A330, so as to spread this optimal configuration over a wider proportion of the available product line. This has had a very severe and probably permanent impact on the value of older wide-body aircraft such as B747-100/200s and DC10s.

Summary

This section has revisited all the investment fundamentals that were felt to underpin the robust aircraft investment performance of the 1970s and 1980s, with the exception of airline economics, which is discussed below. Because the fundamentals appear to be intact despite the recession of the early 1990s, the recent recovery in aircraft investment performance is likely to be more than just a flash in the pan, although future downturns are inevitable.

It should be borne in mind that for more modern aircraft, owned by a typical aircraft lessor with a leveraged capital structure, margins from aircraft leasing have been more stable than lease rates or values. Exhibit 17.6 compares the average lease rate as a percentage of original cost for six different aircraft types delivered new in 1988 with medium-term US interest rates in each year from 1988 to 1996. The leasing margin seems quite robust, although market value declined by a cumulative average of 30 per cent over the eight year period.

Residual value forecasting

Both financiers and other industry participants regularly seek forecasts of the residual value of aircraft, which are normally provided by independent appraisers.

The starting point for any residual value forecast for an individual aircraft is a consideration of its current value. However, in looking at current values most appraisers factor in the industry cycle and allow for the fact that in a recession aircraft may trade below their long-

Exhibit 17.6
Aircraft rental yields and interest rates (A320, B737-300, B757-200, B767-300ER, F100 and MD83 delivered 1988)

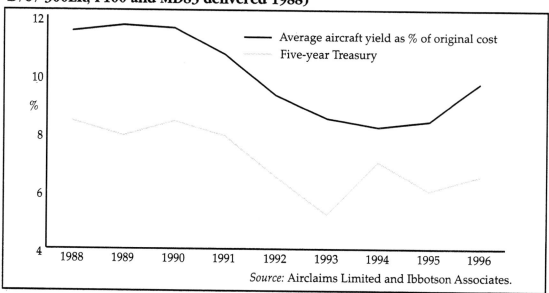

Source: Airclaims Limited and Ibbotson Associates.

run value, and vice-versa. This long-run value is typically referred to as 'base value', and is the preferred basis for forecasting.

The key model inputs for any residual value forecasts are:

- expected replacement cost;
- remaining economic life;
- future earning power;
- relative operating costs versus current and future competing aircraft types; and
- expected market conditions.

Most appraisers would be the first to admit that forecasting is more of an art than a science. As with any forecast, the user derives the greatest value by understanding the analytical framework used to derive the key inputs.

Airline economics and the role of aircraft lessors

Despite a recent recovery in profits, the world's airlines are still rebuilding their balance sheets after the heavy losses incurred during the recession. For the 1990s as a whole airlines are unlikely to be able to purchase more than 40 per cent of their new aircraft requirements from internal cash flow. According to Airclaims Limited's CASE aircraft database, the proportion of aircraft owned directly by airlines has fallen from 80 per cent in 1985 to 63 per cent in 1990 and to 56 per cent in 1995. This decline in direct aircraft ownership should not be of major concern of itself, and is not surprising given the scale of the industry's investment requirement. The role of aircraft lessors in the purchase of new aircraft declined in the early 1990s mainly due to the impact of GPA's financial difficulties on its order book, although it should be noted that ILFC's 1995 purchases of over US$3 billion amounted to well over 10 per cent of all new aircraft purchases, and that GE Capital has recently placed substantial orders with Boeing and Airbus. In August 1996 leasing companies accounted for 21 per cent of all aircraft orders, broadly in line with their share of total orders at the beginning of the decade.

The fall in aircraft values over this period has attracted a number of new entrants into the aircraft leasing market, notably the major Japanese trading companies, and a number of manufacturers have increased their leasing activity to improve their competitive position. Like ILFC and GE Capital, these new entrants bring strong balance sheets to the business and tend not to sell on their assets to the general investor market.

The general investor has been able to invest more directly in aircraft in the 1990s due to the development of aircraft securitisation through ALPS and Airplanes transactions originated by GPA and through the enhanced equipment trust certificate transactions originated by US airlines such as Northwest, Continental and USAir (see Chapter 6). Clearly these investors have for the most part bought highly rated debt securities designed to trade in line with the overall debt market rather than the aircraft market, although a number of transactions have now successfully included tranches of non-investment grade securities.

It remains to be seen whether the range of investments available to the market will expand to create widely traded securities with returns linked directly to aircraft investment performance, and a likely precondition for such a development is a sustained recovery in returns. However such an innovation is possible, as the real estate investment trust industry has demonstrated in the context of that asset class, and could have major benefits for all industry participants.

Appendix:
Methodology and sources for aircraft returns

Aircraft returns were compiled by taking estimates of aircraft historic current market values and five-year fixed operating lease rates provided by Airclaims Limited and using them to construct a time series for each aircraft type included by year of manufacture. Annual returns were calculated by dividing the annual rental income and closing value by the opening value. These returns were then weighted by value, using the number of aircraft of the given year of manufacture in service as of 1 January 1996 as recorded in Airclaims *Turbine Airliner Fleet Survey*. The aircraft types included are as follows: A300B4; A320-200; B727-200A; B737-200A; B737-300; B737-400; B737-500; B747-200B; B757-200; B767-300ER; F100; DC8-71F/CF; DC9-30; DC10-30; MD11; MD82; and MD83.

No estimates of overhead and down time costs were included, in order to meddle with the data as little as possible. In any event, the average age of the aircraft included in the survey when weighted by value is approximately five years right through the survey period, and down time for aircraft of this age during the survey period averaged below 2 per cent. Also it should be borne in mind that other investments are not overhead-free, and that aircraft lessors benefit from other sources of income not reflected in the calculated returns, such as the compounding effect of receiving rents monthly in advance, interest income on lease security deposits and certain cash flow benefits associated with aircraft maintenance payments by lessees.

Other industry data was sourced from back issues of the *Airline Monitor*, particularly the May 1996 edition including the 'World Jet Aircraft Database' and the July 1997 edition including the 'Commercial Jet Forecast'.

Data regarding other asset classes and US inflation was sourced from published and online material provided by Ibbotson Associates.

18 What to expect from manufacturers' residual value support

Colin Thaine

Introduction

Few financiers are today willing to take significant residual risks in aircraft without laying off those risks with the manufacturers or other creditworthy asset value risk takers. This is the case whether collateral is required to support the outstandings during the finance period or a balloon at the expiry. Indeed, certain used equipment can only be refinanced if, say, the sale and leaseback structure includes the grant of a put option in favour of the financier involving a third party entering into a buy-back commitment of that equipment at a future date.

Support in respect of the future value of an aircraft is on occasions provided by manufacturers to encourage a sale where it is evident that a sale and consequent financing to a particular customer would not be assured without the airframe and/or engine manufacturer's involvement.

However, it is essential that both the financier and the guarantor reach a common understanding as to the precise nature and terms of the asset value support at the term sheet stage. Failure to do so often results in neither the financier's nor the guarantor's objectives being optimised, leading sometimes to a mutation of the support device originally offered. For instance, the financier may be looking to the manufacturer to absorb certain operating risks of an airline in addition to sharing some of the asset risks. The guarantor will expect the financier to take non-repossession and other political interference risks associated with realising the equipment value.

What asset risk takers have been prepared to provide is an undertaking to a financier as to the underlying value of the aircraft – that if the aircraft is in future repossessed or returned, they will pay to the financier either (a) a scheduled (ie pre-agreed) unamortised amount of equipment cost or the outstanding loan principal ('residual value') or, as is more frequently the case, (b) all or part of the amount by which resale proceeds (less certain remarketing expenses) fall short of the residual value. Such an undertaking or 'guarantee' is, however, subject to provisos including:

- that it is limited in amount;
- that the aircraft, spare engine or other relevant item is, or is deemed to be, properly maintained and available for disposal at the time of enforcement, free of all liens other than those created by the financier; and
- that the transaction documentation is only capable of amendment with the guarantor's consent.

The terminology of such support commitments can be confusing. Where support is being provided against the need to remarket and resell an aircraft following default of the original operator, the form of guarantee is customarily described as a 'deficiency guarantee' (sometimes known as a 'first loss' deficiency guarantee or a 'limited deficiency guarantee' or a 'first loss limited deficiency guarantee'). Perhaps it would be more meaningful to describe it as a 'remarketing deficiency guarantee'.

In the case where manufacturer support is given because the airline has the right to walk away from a financing on a particular date by returning the aircraft at that date with limited recourse to it, the usual term is an 'asset value guarantee', although this might cover a 'first loss', a 'second loss', or even a 'third loss' (or a share of several slices of risk). Again, it might have been more helpful for the market to have described such a document as a 'window asset value guarantee' and so to distinguish it from guarantees triggered only after a default sale.

This chapter reviews recent trends and practices in the use of asset/residual value support and seeks to highlight the most important issues that are relevant to almost all negotiations between financiers, manufacturers (and other asset risk underwriters) and operators.

The commercial rationale for a deficiency guarantee

The purpose of a manufacturer's involvement in a customer's financing structure is to enable the financing to take place rather than assisting an airline to find the lowest cost of funds.

The airline itself will be asked to make as large an up-front cash payment as possible, so that it effectively shares in the risks and reduces the other parties' exposure. This cash payment should not be confused with the level of pre-delivery payments required from the airline, which is an entirely different matter and relates to the building of an aircraft; the concern here is with the amount of finance to be raised and secured by the asset on delivery.

A fertile source for negotiation is the level at which financiers feel comfortable in taking the risk of a remarketing loss. Manufacturers are unlikely to respond favourably to proposals that would require them to support residual value (otherwise known as asset value) risk levels, which would effectively leave them with all economic risks of the transaction and be analogous to providing a full guarantee.

The manufacturers may be prepared to issue a limited deficiency guarantee which, when aggregated with other items of collateral in a financier's security package, is intended to provide it with an adequate assurance of a full payout. A manufacturer may be prepared to 'bridge the gap' between the upper level of risk accepted by the banks and the total amount of financing being raised (the purchase price less the down payment). For example, if a bank is, at the outset, prepared to take the asset risk up to, say, 70 per cent to 75 per cent of equipment cost and the airline makes a 15 per cent to 20 per cent unrefinanced cash payment, the manufacturers should only be asked to issue a guarantee limited to a maximum amount of exposure equal to 10 per cent to 15 per cent of equipment cost in the first year of the term.

Similarly, the amount of guarantee required should decline over time as the collateral value of the aircraft begins to stabilise and fall more slowly than amortisation. A time should come during the term of the financing when the aircraft value is equal to or in excess of the outstanding loan balance or termination value. At this stage the guarantee level should reduce to zero. Consequently, a deficiency guarantee in respect of an aircraft with good residual value prospects should terminate during the term of the loan or lease (eg after, say, seven to ten years) and it should not be necessary for the guarantee to remain in force throughout such term.

While financiers are expected to take the primary credit risk of non-payment, in certain countries they are uncomfortable about taking the secondary risk of non-repossession of the equipment. Asset risk takers are most unlikely to accept the political risk of non-return of an aircraft by a foreign government or the inability to deregister an aircraft. They will argue that, if it is not available for remarketing, the aircraft's value cannot be ascertained and therefore is outside the scope of risk that an asset risk taker can be expected to assume. Accordingly, banks are expected to look beyond a deficiency guarantee to the export credit agencies and/or the commercial insurance market for political risk cover.

In recent years the combination of political risk insurance and a deficiency guarantee may well have allowed financiers, who are familiar with – but are overexposed to – countries where the assets will be based, to escape from in-house country exposure limits. By taking out political risk insurance the financier may, to a degree, remove its risk on the country. Several asset-based financings have only materialised because of the existence of these complementary support mechanisms. Recent developments in the insurance market point towards the introduction of tailored non-repossession and deprivation cover which it is expected will play a part in assisting financings to airlines where country risk is of concern to financiers. Such cover currently available from leading syndicates in the Lloyd's market is now more attractive following the underwriters' removal in 1997 of an endorsement to the Lloyd's Standard Wording 147 policy, which excluded the ability of financiers to claim under a policy consequent upon a non-renewal of the policy (which prior to such endorsement would have enabled the financier to terminate the financing and seek repossession of the aircraft with the benefit of the non-repossession cover).

Another important development in the insurance industry has seen the introduction of a new product – default termination insurance. This cover allows financiers to lay off certain airline credit risks such as:

- the non-payment of scheduled rentals following a default termination;
- the lifting of liens (Eurocontrol charges, airport charges, maintenance liens) that may attach to the aircraft following a default termination; and
- the re-creation of the technical records of the aircraft.

The availability of such cover should reduce the pressure on manufacturers to assume such risks when deficiency guarantees are being considered.

Special characteristics

The key point of a deficiency guarantee is that the manufacturer will expect the financier to look to all its other sources of recourse prior to calling on the manufacturer. Thus, after a default, all amounts received by the lessor or lenders in respect of the financing from whatsoever source (the airline, other guarantors, enforcement sale on security, etc) are applied to the outstanding financing, and only after such application and the completion of the sale may the manufacturer be required to make payment. This does not mean that the financiers must exhaust all legal remedies to collect the amounts due from the airline or such other guarantors; rather, demands must have been made on the airline and such other guarantors, and a specified period of time must have elapsed before a call is made on the manufacturer.

The financier usually expects the guarantee commitment to relate to the top slice or segment of any remarketing deficiency, often described as a 'first loss'. The airframe manufacturer and the selected engine manufacturer frequently share *pari passu* on a several basis the first loss commitment, in percentages agreed between them.

The manufacturer's guarantee commitment is often defined as the lesser of (a) the guaranteed obligations (expressed, for example, as a percentage amount of the net delivery price of the aircraft) and (b) the amount (ie deficiency or shortfall) by which the net final disposition proceeds (after taking into account the credit or debit balance of any remarketing account) falls short of the pre-agreed unamortised amount.

A notable area for keen negotiation between financiers and deficiency guarantors is whether any of the costs of holding the aircraft during the remarketing period (that is, between accelerated default and sale) can be factored into the guarantors' commitment. These considerations will be discussed later in the section dealing with the assumptions made in computing the deficiency formula in both deficiency and asset value guarantees.

What is important to appreciate is that the deficiency formula is most unlikely to reflect the actual loss sustained by the financier following an airline default and accelerated termination of the financing. Cash collateral would more often than not be needed to cover repossession and holding costs that are directly attributable to the airline's conduct and not to those costs necessarily incurred in testing the value of the aircraft in the market.

As one of the preconditions to the issue of a deficiency guarantee, the manufacturer usually requires a counter-indemnity from an appropriate party (such as the parent or holding company of the airline) and will invariably require a reimbursement agreement with the airline itself (so that in addition to any rights of subrogation, there is a direct contractual right to file a claim against the airline should the loss result from the latter's default). The financier will require the subordination of the guarantor's rights of subrogation so that any post-default monies received by the guarantor from the airline shall be paid over to the financier. The guarantor is the first loss taker and is thus to be reimbursed after the financier in respect of any cure payment or guarantee payment made by it.

Guarantors frequently seek rights to cure defaults that can be cured by the payment of money. Such cure rights are usually restricted to, say, no more than three consecutive occasions in any twelve-month period (except that no restriction is usually placed on a guarantor for curing a breach concerning the maintenance of an aircraft) and to a limited window of, say, five days following receipt of notice of default to exercise the cure right. However, a further qualification is customarily sought if the financier takes the view that its rights to repossess the aircraft or the value or integrity of the aircraft is likely to be materially prejudiced as a result of the guarantor's exercise of its cure right.

The commercial rationale for an asset value guarantee
Lease structures driven by accounting treatment

Many airline lessees have a natural preference for operating lease treatment because capitalisation of finance leases will affect the lessee's gearing, return on assets and interest cover. Thus, over recent years the terms of many leases have been such that the lessor recorded the lease as a finance lease (thus excluding the aircraft from its balance sheet and instead recording a debtor) while the lessee treats it as an operating lease (similarly excluding the asset from its balance sheet and also not recording the obligation to the lessor as a creditor).

This classification has at times been difficult to determine because of the rights to curtail or extend the lease or purchase the aircraft on terms that are arguably not a 'bargain'. In the past decade the use of extendable operating leases has increased in popularity. The lessee is permitted to exercise a put or 'walk away' option at given dates, the lessee bearing a small part of any loss on resale and the lessor, often in conjunction with a third party, bearing the majority. Alternatively, the lessee can renew the lease annually, on broadly comparable terms, or convert the lease into a finance lease. Such agreements have generally been treated under certain national accounting standards (eg the US FASB 13 and the UK SSAP 21) as operating leases by the lessee, as a consequence of which aircraft that are used in its business for a period of years, albeit much shorter than its useful life, are not included in the lessee's balance sheet, although they are disclosed in the notes. Asset value guarantees have accordingly been sought from third parties in conjunction with such lease structures.

In 1994 the UK's Accounting Standards Board re-evaluated its general asset recognition rules on off-balance sheet finance. As a result of the current financial reporting standard on asset recognition (known as 'FRS5') an entity is required to report the substance of a transaction that it may have entered into rather than the legal form. In determining the substance of a transaction into which a company has entered, the auditors will consider whether in commercial reality substantially all the risks and rewards of ownership have passed to the lessee. The use of special purpose vehicle lessors established to optimise the classification of an operating lease for a lessee will be regarded as a transparent benefit for the lessee and in substance no different from a vehicle that is a subsidiary undertaking of the lessee. Accordingly, such transactions would in future have to be included on the lessee's balance sheet.

The cognate rules in regard to leasing contracts currently set out in the UK SSAP 21 will have to be applied alongside the rules set out in FRS5. SSAP 21 determines whether the transaction is to be classified as a finance or an operating lease. There is currently a school of thought that all leases running for two years or more offered by banking-type creditors have the character of purely financial facilities, and that any elements of exposure to residual value risk by lessors or third parties are purely driven by the present rules facilitating off-balance sheet reporting by the lessee. The standard defines a finance lease as a lease that transfers substantially all the risks and rewards of ownership of an asset to the lessee but the stated guideline test for a finance lease classification (whether the present value of the minimum lease payments amounts to 90 per cent or more of the fair value of the asset) has become in practice a rule. This approach has now to be reconciled with one based on qualitative tests in considering whether or not substantially all the risks and rewards have been transferred and thus whether a lease should be capitalised. For example:

1 Are the rentals based on a market rate for use of the asset or a financing rate for use of the funds?
2 Are there put and call options? If so, are they at a predetermined rate or at the market price at the time the option is exercised?
3 Which party carries the risk of a drop in asset value and which party benefits from any capital appreciation?
4 Does the lessee have the use of the asset for a period broadly equating to the likely useful economic life of the asset?
5 Does the lessor intend to earn its total return on this transaction alone or does it intend to rely on subsequent sales or lease revenue?

Transactions that offer airlines subject to UK or similar national accounting reporting standards the best of both worlds – access to long-term financing for new equipment while treating the acquisition as an off-balance sheet item at least in the early years during which the airline has specific rights of return – will now have to bear the scrutiny of accountants applying the rules currently set out in both UK SSAP 21 and FRS5.

Operational flexibility

Walk away lease structures that are driven not by accounting considerations but by a desire for operational flexibility may prove in future to be the principal rationale for asset value guarantee support. A 'real' exposure to a residual value risk could well result from an airline electing to return an aircraft at a window date in order to eliminate surplus capacity or to take advantage of changing route structures or new technology aircraft.

However, the manufacturers' philosophy in giving asset value support to walk away leases is based on a premise that the guarantee is needed on the occasion when an aircraft is returned voluntarily because it constitutes genuine excess capacity to the operator. Accordingly, manufacturer guarantors are inclined to seek a counter-indemnity from the airline so that they are not exposed in circumstances where the lessee operator voluntarily returns the aircraft on a window date because, during a given period preceding or following return which gives rise to the manufacturer's liability, the airline has taken delivery of a replacement aircraft from a competitor manufacturer. A key point for negotiation is therefore what constitutes a 'replacement' aircraft, with discussions often focusing on comparative range and passenger seat capacity.

It should be of no surprise to anyone that manufacturers are less willing to provide this type of support (which is unconnected to the airline's ability to make lease payments), and particularly reluctant to allow an all-weather guarantee that can be triggered not only by a voluntary return on a walk away basis, but also by an airline's default prior to the window date in circumstances where limited recourse to the airline under the leasing structure enables the airline to resist giving a full counter-indemnity to the manufacturers.

Special characteristics of asset value guarantees

One might see an option lease that is fully paid out over 15 years, but with so-called window dates at, say, year three and perhaps again at year six. The airline will be required to provide a period of notice before it may exercise its option to walk away from the transaction. This period is effectively the time when the aircraft may be remarketed. Essentially, the longer the period of notice the less likelihood there is of a shortfall having to be covered.

The lessor will have recourse to the airline and possibly to the manufacturer and other risk takers, for certain agreed slices of the outstanding balances as at the window date, and may itself assume part of the residual value risk by agreeing to have no recourse at all to the airline, the manufacturer or other risk takers for one or more slices of the outstanding financing.

The way in which slices of risk are determined in an asset value guarantee will depend on the type of equipment being financed and the structure of the finance. There may be as many as five or six predetermined slices of asset value liability. Additionally, if the airline has more than one window date in which it can exercise its rights to return the aircraft, the slices of risk may be different at each window date. It is likely that the airline will be required to take a level of risk, generally the top slice, in order to give it an incentive not to return the aircraft until it is confident that the residual value is likely to be sufficient to discharge the whole of the refinancing and that there will be no shortfall.

The manufacturer will often be responsible for the second slice of potential deficiency, and in this sense its asset value guarantee is sometimes described as second loss guarantee. In such a case, the manufacturer's level of risk in the asset is likely to be over and above that with which financiers themselves feel comfortable.

Some asset value guarantee structures require payment by the asset value guarantors on the window date, whether or not the aircraft has been sold. In this case, guarantee payments are refunded to the asset value guarantors to the extent that the eventual net disposal proceeds are adequate to do so. If a guarantor makes any guarantee payment, then the net final disposition proceeds should be distributed to the guarantors and the airline in inverse order of the net asset value risk assumed (so that the party assuming the first loss position shall be paid such proceeds last, and so on – ie the 'first-in/last-out' principle).

Other structures require payment, if necessary, after sale, whether that takes place on the window dates or thereafter. In this case, the asset value guarantee will normally extend for a finite period following the return of the aircraft. Its length will be subject to negotiation; however, it is unusual for this period to extend beyond one year because the remarketing period would have commenced, say, a year before the window date at the time when notice to return the aircraft would have been given.

A recent development in this field has seen manufacturers prepared to provide asset value support to airlines as well as to financiers. This may be where the airline is leasing the aircraft from one of its affiliated companies or where the airline will be using the asset value support to assist in financing a balloon purchase option at the end of a lease term effectively by means of a sale and leaseback.

Redelivery conditions on voluntary return

It is essential that comprehensive technical return conditions should be inserted in the financing documentation to ensure that all asset value guarantors are supporting a value of the equipment at a particular window date predicated on a specified operating condition. Aircraft condition affects residual value. It is a fallacy among some lessors and financial institutions that the return of their aircraft in an airworthy condition will substantially assure the residual value. Airworthiness relates to the capability of an aircraft to perform flight operations with acceptable reliability in respect of, among other things, safety margins.

As aircraft age, the major component of their residual value simply becomes the value of the remaining service life, or conversely, the cost of maintaining them in service. The cost of pending airframe and engine overhauls and the restoration and replacement of components thus have a material influence on the residual value. There is a direct correlation between the remaining service life of components on the airframe (including landing gear) and engines, and the marketability of the aircraft.

Aircraft can remain airworthy (in that there is no imminent danger arising from their continued operation) despite postponement by stringent inspection of expensive structural repairs, with repair being undertaken only when condition becomes terminal (ie on allowable limits being exceeded). A purchaser will invariably deduct the cost of all maintenance work required from the purchase price, and thus the cost of overhaul can constitute a reduction of the realisable value of the asset.

Accordingly, loosely worded return provisions will materially dilute the residual value, and it can therefore be imagined that manufacturers will be particularly concerned with and involved in the negotiation of the maintenance and return provisions.

It is the regular practice of guarantors to require the aircraft to be in a minimum standard of return condition as a precondition to making a guarantee payment. This may be less stringent than the required return condition. Any discrepancy with the required return condition (on which is predicated the guarantors' risk level) – eg if a component's actual service life is less than that stipulated in the return criteria – may not prevent a guarantor being required to make a guarantee payment, but increasingly sophisticated adjustment formula are now being negotiated to compensate for such discrepancies.

Common features of residual/asset value support agreements

Preconditions to manufacturers' support

Assuming that the manufacturers are satisfied that (a) the transaction requires a deficiency or asset value guarantee in order to be feasible; (b) that the other relevant parties are sharing in the risks in an equitable manner (the airline itself will be asked in addition to its pre-delivery payments to make as large an up-front cash payment as possible, so that it effectively shares in their risks and reduces the other parties' exposure); and (c) that the level, profile and duration of the guarantee are justifiable in the circumstances, then there will normally be two other important preconditions to entering into either type of support agreement which the manufacturers will require to be met in order to reduce their exposure to manageable proportions:

- pro rata participation among airframe and engine manufacturers on a several basis; and
- remuneration.

Pro rata participation among airframe and engine manufacturers on a several basis

The airframe manufacturer will usually insist, as a condition to providing its own support, that the deficiency guarantee commitment is provided by both the airframe and the selected engine manufacturers, normally in percentages based on the relative price of the airframe and the price of the installed engines. An airframe manufacturer will naturally leave the requirement to support the future market value of spare engines and spare engine parts to the selected engine manufacturer.

Liability of the manufacturers under deficiency or asset value guarantee agreements is invariably expressed to be several and not joint, so that financiers cannot look to one guarantor for the failure of another to pay its agreed portion of any deficiency.

Remuneration

The airline customer will normally be required to pay a fee to the manufacturers. This remunerates the manufacturers for the risks they assume and deters an excessive or unnecessary use of any guarantee.

The fee may be expressed as a percentage of the net delivery price of the aircraft or as a percentage of the maximum exposure being assumed. A sliding scale may be introduced to encourage the airline to find a financier who is able to accept a higher level of asset exposure, which results in a corresponding reduction in the manufacturers' level of asset risk originally contemplated. In exceptional cases a manufacturer may waive an up-front fee to take a share in any up-side in asset value.

In the case of either a deficiency guarantee or an asset value guarantee, a manufacturer always takes the approach of being involved solely by way of a guarantor of the future value of its product, and will thus only assume some of the risks associated with the equipment value and none of the operating or credit risks of the airline. It is not providing a financial guarantee of the airline.

It is thus important for the financier to ensure its documentation is such that all its other rights and sources of recourse are well-documented and enforceable. Otherwise it may be the case that a residual value guarantor's obligations are reduced by virtue of a recovery that the financier is deemed to have made.

Effective redelivery and grace periods

A fundamental prerequisite common to both types of guarantee is that repossession or redelivery, as the case may be, to the owner or the remarketing agent must occur in circumstances that the owner has the immediate right and power to sell and pass good title and possession of the aircraft free from encumbrances.

In the case of an asset value guarantee where the aircraft must be available for sale on a specific window date, financiers frequently request a grace period or extension to the window date on account of events arising beyond the control of the owner or beneficiary of the guarantee. Examples could range from an aircraft at the window date being on requisition for hire by the government of the country of registration or having been hijacked (in each case for a period falling short of a total loss), or an engine failure being sustained immediately prior to the window date as a consequence of which the aircraft could not comply even with the minimum return condition stipulated by the guarantors to exist on the window date.

Computation of deficiency formulae

It is customary for the manufacturer to calculate a deficiency guarantee or asset value guarantee payment on the assumption that certain credit-risk related exposures are borne only by the financiers. These are:

1 that recourse for costs of repossession from the original debtor shall be against the airline debtor only and shall not be recouped from the sale proceeds;
2 that the aircraft has been maintained and is returned in the state of repair and condition required in the financing documents;
3 that there are no third party liens, claims or encumbrances against the aircraft; and
4 that all loss or damage is at all times fully covered by insurance.

For the purpose of calculating a deficiency, gross disposition proceeds actually received are adjusted upwards by the addition of those amounts for which the guarantors are not assuming responsibility – eg owner or operator lien costs and/or the amount of any compensation certified to be needed to put an aircraft in a condition required to satisfy the return condition stipulated by the guarantors.

Furthermore, the deficiency formula in either type of guarantee document will specifically describe what constitutes a 'final disposition'. Essentially, a sale must be negotiated on the basis of an arm's length transaction with a ready, willing and able buyer and completed on commercially reasonable terms having due regard to market conditions. While financiers will seek only a cash sale to constitute a 'final disposition', the guarantors may also wish to include a sale on a deferred basis (such as a full payout lease or instalment sale) at arm's length. The occurrence of a casualty/total insurance loss is normally treated as the automatic cessation of the guarantee obligations because the guarantors are not in the business of counter-indemnifying the primary insurance and reinsurance underwriters.

The deficiency calculation will normally describe 'final disposition proceeds' as:

1 cash (and in some instances the face amount of notes or other obligations and the present value of any deferred payments at an agreed discount rate) and the fair market value of any consideration received in respect of the aircraft (including security deposits, collateral accounts, guarantees and similar arrangements);
2 an amount equal to the amount that would be required to remove or discharge third party liens, claims and encumbrances against the aircraft;
3 the certified amount of compensation that needs to be incurred to bring the aircraft up to the state of repair and standard of maintenance required by the terms of the financing documents;
4 other receipts in the nature of interim operating lease rentals or requisition for hire compensation; and
5 any non-refundable deposit paid by a person paid under a contract or offer to purchase that has lapsed or has been terminated.

The remarketing period in a deficiency guarantee is unlikely to exceed two years from default, whereas in an asset value guarantee the period is at least coterminous with the notice period to return the aircraft.

A balance has to be struck between the financier's need to have sufficient opportunity to remarket the aircraft, and the manufacturer's concern to generate income through interim operating leases and so reduce its potential asset risk exposure and its overall need to minimise the period of its contingent liability to make a guarantee payment. A remarketing account may be opened to which will be credited such operating lease income or any other income generated by the aircraft between repossession and resale. Expenses that broadly represent holding costs of maintenance, repair, storage and insurance (including deductibles for repairable damage) during the remarketing period would be debited to the remarketing account.

The question of which party bears the responsibility of the financier's funding costs during this remarketing period is treated differently according to the circumstances prevailing in each individual case. Sometimes the manufacturer may have complete control in remarketing and the funding costs may be debited to the remarketing account. On other occasions, the manufacturer may agree to pay funding costs but these will be subtracted from the overall guarantee commitment. Alternatively, in the case of an asset value guarantee that supports an option lease, the operator may instead be required to continue to lease the aircraft for a short term beyond the return/window date at a rental equal to the funding cost, with such rental being paid direct to the financier in advance.

Financiers require to have a 'hell or high water' commitment that a final disposition will occur after repossession or redelivery of the aircraft to them. Accordingly, provision is customarily made for the financier to have the option to call for a public auction if there is no bid from a third party within, say, one month before the end of the remarketing period. The other comfort or assurance that the financiers seek relates to the receipt of the final disposition proceeds. The sale procedure frequently stipulates that the purchaser's payment obligation is supported by an irrevocable and unconditional letter of credit or cash collateral.

Control of remarketing

Manufacturers are frequently requested to provide remarketing assistance as part of their support of the financier's asset risk. Indeed, in circumstances where the outstanding balance of financing includes, for the purpose of calculating any remarketing deficiency, the financier's funding costs between repossession/return of the asset and resale, the manufacturer may require an involvement ranging from an exclusive agency to the power to direct the remarketing process. The financier frequently expresses reluctance to relinquish the governance of all remarketing activities even to an exclusive agent because, as principal, it may wish to reserve the right to solicit offers to purchase from third parties and to negotiate the terms of purchase. This can be a vexed issue between the financier and the guarantors, and the compromise ranges from an unfettered right of the owner, with mere notification to the guarantor, to an obligation to coordinate with the agent prior to embarking on such an initiative.

The manufacturer's role usually involves logistical support to the financier in its efforts to remarket the asset following a default or voluntary return (including finding intermediate operating leases before ultimate sale) on a limited recourse basis, save for wilful misconduct or gross negligence. The remarketing agent primarily agrees to use all reasonable endeavours to solicit offers to purchase on the best terms and at the best price reasonably obtainable having due regard to market conditions. Assistance in repossession, storage, reconditioning and potential modification work are areas for negotiation with the manufacturer.

It is usual for the manufacturer to qualify its assistance in terms that it will have no obligation to remarket any aircraft to a potential customer if such remarketing would interfere with or compete with another active marketing or sales activity with respect to a potential customer.

Further common manufacturer rights in both types of support agreement are:

- The right of first refusal to purchase the asset upon any proposed final disposition thereof in circumstances where an offer from a bona fide independent third party is received the terms of which would result in the risk exposure of the particular guarantor not being fully covered by the net sale proceeds of disposition. (In the case of more than one risk taker, a private auction would then ensue between those guarantors who have given notice of their desire to purchase at a price equal to or more than the price offered by the third party, with the financier being obliged to sell to the guarantor making the highest offer.)
- That the manufacturer will not assume any currency exchange risk.
- That the support commitment will lapse if the original airline debtor ceases to be the operator of the aircraft.
- That no amendments or modifications will be made to the financing documents (including giving effect to a restructuring or refinancing) without the prior consent of the manufacturer if they would materially increase the risks under the guarantee or limit the manufacturer's right of recovery under the guarantee and/or counter-indemnity.
- In the case of a deficiency guarantee, that the financier will not comprise or settle any claim for the outstanding financing if it would adversely affect the rights to which the manufacturer is or will be subrogated.

Another significant feature in any support document is the way in which gross sale proceeds and other income is to be applied and distributed among the risk takers. Manufacturers are normally agreeable to funds being allocated first to expenses of collection, second to interest (other than penalty interest) on the unamortised principal and then to the principal itself, but after that they look to sums realised for the amounts they have paid, with interest, with any additional amounts owing to the lenders or lessors coming afterwards.

Finally, where guarantee support is extended to a batch of aircraft, provision may be made to 'average' the aircraft so that any surplus net sale proceeds in respect of one aircraft may be set off against losses incurred in supporting the asset value of another.

Legal nature of manufacturer's guarantee support

As a matter of law, a contractual undertaking to make certain payments to a financier should not necessarily be treated as a guarantee. The essence of a guarantee is the assumption by the guarantor of subsidiary liability in support of the primary liability of a third party. Business people do not necessarily use terms such as guarantee, indemnity and insurance in a strict legal sense. Asset value guarantee agreements do not contain any secondary 'guarantee' obligations – each manufacturer's commitment is a primary obligation. Under a contract of indemnity, the indemnifier undertakes a first or primary liability; common law courts usually determine the nature of the contract by reference to the substance of the liability undertaken rather than from the words used by the parties to describe those obligations.

Since the proper classification of an asset value guarantee commitment in a strict legal sense is likely to be determined as a contract of indemnity, the question remains as to whether the manufacturer's support should be regarded as an underwriting or insurance commitment. If this were the case there may be difficult questions to be answered as to the validity or enforceability of such support of an asset risk – is the manufacturer authorised to carry on an insurance business?

On the face of it, the features of an asset value guarantee agreement might be said to comprise all the essential elements of a contract of insurance. By the terms of a typical asset value guarantee agreement the manufacturer undertakes a liability to the financier to pay the amount of a specified loss that the financiers may sustain in the future, if such an event occurs. As at the date of the agreement, the liability that the manufacturer undertakes is therefore contingent. The most common type of contractual undertakings given for consideration to meet the liabilities of other persons, are insurance obligations. (The consideration received by the manufacturer for providing an undertaking or indemnity to pay for the loss could be said to be the sale of its product.)

However, the legal view is that the manufacturer's indemnity is not an indemnity by way of insurance, because a contract of indemnity insurance requires the insured to have an insurable interest. The concept of insurable interest predicates loss of, or damage to, the legal and/or physical state of the thing insured which adversely affects the insured's proprietary interest in it. There must be a loss or diminution of legal rights. The value of an aircraft may be insured, for example, against the risk of loss by fire; it may not be insured against the risk of loss as a result of changes in market values or from the passing of time.

Pure economic loss resulting from the state of the market for the sale of second-hand aircraft is not such as to give the financier any insurable interest in effecting insurance against that contingency. The situation would be otherwise if the financier needed insurance against the risk of loss of earnings or profits resulting, for example, from the loss of or damage to the aircraft while in service.

It is also the widely held legal view in common law and civil law jurisdictions that both parties to an asset value guarantee have a legitimate interest in entering into such an agreement, and accordingly it would be most unlikely to be construed in a court as invalid or unenforceable as a gaming or wagering contract or on grounds that its terms are contrary to public policy.

Accordingly, asset value guarantee agreements are generally regarded as enforceable as between the parties as a contract of indemnity or undertaking to make certain payments in pre-determined circumstances, but not as contracts of insurance.

There may be occasions when it is possible to present value a periodical fee structure. In so doing, the manufacturer is able to eliminate one credit risk. The customer may only agree to this if the present value sum can be capitalised and financed as part of the original equipment cost. The financier in turn would not necessarily agree to this sum being excluded from the manufacturer's guarantee commitment.

Summary

As for the manufacturer's involvement, it is now not uncommon for the decision to select one particular airframe or engine in preference to another to depend on the particular financing support being offered by its manufacturer. The competition between engine manufacturers in particular has been very keen in recent times, and the question of asset value support has been a regular consideration.

The role of the manufacturer in asset value support will continue in a limited number of transactions on an ad hoc and selective basis. Support of resale values will normally only be considered by manufacturers if it is essential in order to enable an asset-based transaction to be successfully structured as opposed to assisting an airline to find the lowest cost of funds.

Financiers regularly encounter strenuous resistance from manufacturers to depart from underwriting only a slice of asset risk and to share additional financial losses connected with an aircraft operated by a defaulting airline. By virtue of the introduction in 1997 of a new insurance product, default termination insurance, financiers can now look to the insurance market to cover certain of those losses.

Either category of support document incorporates a complex formula for calculating a deficiency, and many hours can be spent negotiating compromise positions in the treatment of expenses and the assumption of certain credit risks. Control in remarketing the aircraft is often a hotly contested issue. It is not unusual for both the financier and the guarantors to be only partially satisfied with the outcome of the negotiations.

Some manufacturers are forming the view that a disproportionate amount of time and effort can be expended by the manufacturer in optimising what is essentially a junior lender's position for at times an inappropriate level of remuneration. Indeed, one manufacturer advocates the economic benefits of being a lender itself (or through its own intermediate vehicle) instead of assuming a sizeable exposure as a subordinated guarantor for the first 25–30 per cent loss.

A further factor that increasingly weakens the feasibility of residual value support instruments from manufacturers is the accumulation of the contingent liabilities. There is, naturally, a finite limit for each manufacturer.

Consequently there will always be a market for asset value guarantors (otherwise known colloquially as asset value underwriters) other than the manufacturers of the products.

Asset value indemnities are also provided by insurance companies either (a) in the form of contractual indemnities when governed by English law or by any one of the state laws of the Commonwealth of Australia or (b) in the form of an insurance contract when written under the laws of the United States or Bermuda (where those legal regimes recognise that there is an insurable interest in seeking protection against the fluctuation in the future market value of an asset). The advantage of the insurance approach is that an insurance company may not have to record those contingent liabilities in its financial statements in contrast with those companies that do not carry on an insurance business. However, the insurance contract is probably not as flexible a product as the current forms of indemnity contracts because any amendments to the insurance contract have to be accepted by a third party underwriter. In each case, however, the 'guarantee' fee or insurance premium is not inconsiderable.

Of course there will always be the perennial problem of whether an asset risk taker has a strong enough balance sheet to absorb not just one or two claims on one occasion but perhaps a series of claims over a very short period.

The reality will doubtless be that financiers will adopt an even more conservative attitude towards resale values and accordingly will customarily require a creditworthy partner to provide a meaningful cushion against fluctuations in market values. The challenge for the manufacturer is to assist its customers in finding a structure in which the levels of remuneration to all risk takers do not cripple the economics of an airline engaged in an increasingly competitive, low-yield market.

PART V

Legal and insurance issues

19 Legal issues in aircraft finance

Andrew Littlejohns

Every aircraft financing gives rise to a number of particular considerations. This chapter examines some of the principal issues. Many of these issues are common to both straightforward operating leases and more complex tax-based financings.

As in any transaction, the lawyer's approach is conditioned by which party he is representing – airline, financier or manufacturer. This issues discussed in this chapter primarily reflect the concerns of a financier, but they also have an impact on the interests of other parties.

In this chapter we refer to the 'state of registration' which is the country in which the particular aircraft is to be registered, and the 'habitual base' which is the country in which the aircraft is to be based.

It is convenient to categorise the issues that are most commonly encountered as follows (although clearly many issues will overlap categories):

- those relating to the structure of the transaction;
- international;
- aircraft or airline-related;
- insolvency;
- taxation;
- currency; and
- choice of law.

Structural issues

The two basic alternatives to a financier are (a) outright ownership of the aircraft as owner/lessor, or (b) a security interest as mortgagee.

In a loan/mortgage structure the financier has to be satisfied that the laws of the state of registration will recognise the proposed form of mortgage, particularly if it is governed by a different law. Some jurisdictions (such as Brazil, Chile, South Korea and the Scandinavian countries) will only recognise a mortgage if it is governed by local law and is in a particular form and language. A few countries (such as Belgium) do not recognise aircraft mortgages in any form as a valid type of security. In such countries one may have to use some different form of security interest such as a pledge.

In addition, priority of mortgages, and the procedure for perfecting and enforcing mortgages, are generally determined by local law (regardless of the governing law of the mortgage). Consequently, one also needs to check that the local procedural rules are not onerous or prejudicial (for example, in some jurisdictions, such as Spain and Brazil, a mortgaged aircraft may only be sold through the court, not by private treaty).

Even assuming that an aircraft mortgage is recognised, the financier may be concerned to know whether it can record its interest in a local aircraft mortgage register in the state of registration. Even among the Commonwealth countries, which have nationality registers similar to the UK, a number do not have aircraft mortgage registers (for example, Australia, New Zealand and Hong Kong). Generally these jurisdictions do have corporate mortgage registers, and, provided the borrower is incorporated in the host country or has a place of business there, the mortgage can be filed in that registry instead.

Nonetheless, in structures where the borrower is an offshore vehicle rather than the airline itself, the mortgage may not be eligible for registration in the state of registration. In itself this may not be serious, because a number of jurisdictions recognise unregistered mortgages and confer upon them the same priority that they enjoy under their governing law.

Leases

In a lease structure, on the other hand, the financier has to satisfy itself that the lessor's title as owner will be recognised in the state of registration, and that there is no risk that the lessee (as the person in possession) is deemed to have acquired an equity interest in the aircraft (which might mean that it could confer valid title on a third party, or that it could assert an interest in the residual value of the aircraft against the lessor). This is sometimes described as the risk of 'equity build-up' in favour of the lessee.

Some countries may not recognise a hire purchase or conditional sale agreement as giving the airline a mere possessory interest and, therefore, may give effect to it as if ownership has in fact passed to the airline.

Distinctions and consequences

Disregarding tax-related considerations, what are the legal consequences and distinctions affecting mortgage versus lease structures?

UK-registered aircraft

As a matter of English law, and in terms of a CAA-registered aircraft, the financier can be comfortable with either a loan/mortgage or a lease. If the financier takes a mortgage, this can be registered in the CAA's Aircraft Mortgage Register, conferring priority against all subsequent registered mortgages. (If the borrower is an English company or has a place of business in the UK, the mortgage should also be filed with supporting particulars at the corporate registry.)

If, on the other hand, the financier requires a title-based structure (a lease, hire purchase or conditional sale), the principle of *nemo dat quod non habet* protects the true owner, by providing that a purchaser cannot acquire good title from a non-owner (this common law principle is confirmed in the 1979 Sale of Goods Act). There are, however, certain limited exceptions to this principle. For example:

1 Where the non-owner sells under the authority of the actual owner or with his consent, or where the owner is precluded by his conduct from denying the non-owner's authority to sell.
2 Where a person who has sold equipment remains in possession of it: that person can transmit valid title to a third party who purchases in good faith without notice of the original sale. These circumstances could conceivably arise in a sale and leaseback aircraft transaction.

3 Where a purchaser buys in good faith from a person who has 'bought or agreed to buy' equipment and has possession of the equipment. This would include a purchaser under a conditional sale agreement but it does not extend to a purported sale by a hirer under a hire purchase agreement, because the hirer issues a unilateral call option and therefore has not 'agreed' to buy.

However, there is no general principle that would enable an airline (as apparent owner because it has possession) to pass title to an innocent purchaser, and therefore, in the absence of unusual circumstances, the financier can be confident in preservation of its ownership interest.

Liens

Another point to consider is whether local law provides for liens (and similar rights of detention) to hold different priority against an owner from their priority against a mortgagee. In English law there is little difference, because neither an owner nor a mortgage takes priority over possessory liens or statutory rights of detention (such as airport authority rights to detain an aircraft for unpaid navigation charges, including Eurocontrol charges).

Geneva Convention

The 1948 Geneva Convention on International Recognition of Rights in Aircraft (Appendix A) should be borne in mind. The United Kingdom (among other nations) has not ratified the Convention. This means that rights created under English law in respect of CAA-registered aircraft cannot be guaranteed the same legal effect if they have to be enforced in other jurisdictions. In the context of the present analysis, this has no influence one way or the other on choice of structure, because the Convention deals with both title interests and security interests.

The consequences of the UK not being a Convention country should not be exaggerated. In the first place, only a limited number of countries have ratified: jurisdictions that have not ratified include most of the Commonwealth nations, many African countries, all East European countries and Japan. Secondly, the Convention effectively only provides protection in a case where an aircraft is registered in one contracting state and enforcement action has to be taken in another contracting state.

Thus, for example, the ownership rights in respect of a Swedish-registered aircraft would be protected in enforcement proceedings in Italy (both countries being Convention countries), but not if those rights had to be enforced in Spain (which is not a contracting state). The financing documents will generally permit the airline to fly to any international destination unless it is a war zone or the subject of international sanctions, so it may be entirely fortuitous (and dependent on the routes flown by the particular airline) whether, in practice, the Convention provides protection. Accordingly, it should be assumed, for risk-assessment purposes when evaluating a structure, that this protection will *not* be available unless the aircraft is flying exclusively between contracting states.

Documentary taxes or filing fees

In some jurisdictions, a mortgage structure may be unattractive because local law prescribes onerous and costly procedures for creating or perfecting the mortgage (for example, a requirement that the mortgage and underlying loan documents have to be translated into the local language, notarised, consularised and filed in several central registries; alternatively, the mortgage may be subject to *ad valorem* documentary tax on the amount that it secures). One device used to avoid these difficulties is to vest title to the aircraft in a special purpose company (SPC), the shares in which are mortgaged to the financier: in other words, the financier relies on security interests in the SPC and not on collateral over the asset itself. The financier may also require to be represented on the board of directors of the SPC. In considering such a structure, the following issues should be borne in mind:

1 A charge over shares does not prevent the SPC from creating security over, or selling, the aircraft before the financier becomes aware of those acts and takes steps to exercise control over the affairs of the SPC.
2 A charge over shares is effectively subordinate to any debts or liabilities (secured or unsecured) of the SPC – that is, it is only as valuable as the net worth of the SPC. The financier should, therefore, insist on the borrower and the SPC giving covenants that the company will not incur any debts or liabilities to third parties. The financier will also want to establish some procedure for monitoring the affairs of the SPC at regular intervals. In addition, it may be desirable to enshrine the special purpose nature of the SPC in its constitutional documents, by stating that it has been incorporated for the sole purpose of owning and exploiting the particular aircraft and has no power to undertake any other activities (although such restrictions may not be binding on third parties).

In some cases, the benefits of ownership and a mortgage may be combined, by lending to an SPC that owns and leases the aircraft to the airline. The SPC then grants a mortgage over the aircraft to the financier (or agent bank). This structure is common where the credit is being provided by a syndicate of banks rather than a single lender. It confers upon the banks two alternative methods of realising this security in the event of a default.

The particular registration requirements of the aviation authority with which the aircraft is to be registered may also impose constraints on the financing structure (see the 'Registration' subsection later in this chapter). For example, a nationality requirement may dictate that the lessor is incorporated in the same jurisdiction as the lessee, which may, in turn, give rise to significant tax issues. These concerns may not arise with a loan and mortgage structure, for example.

International issues

This section examines some of the principal issues which can arise in cross-border transactions. Most of these are not peculiar to aircraft, although some are highlighted in the case of aircraft because they are mobile assets. The issues can all arise in a simple cross-border transaction where a financier in one jurisdiction is financing an aircraft to be operated in another. In transactions where the airline is a domestic carrier operating domestic routes, the financier's advisers may not need to consider any other jurisdictions. However, this is a relatively unusual luxury.

Where an aircraft is flying on international routes but is both registered and based/maintained in a single jurisdiction, for practical reasons the financier will generally not investigate the laws of the countries to which the aircraft regularly flies (for example, what laws exist in such countries as to liens and rights of detention, and what procedural difficulties might be encountered if the financier wished to enforce its security at a time when the aircraft was on the ground in one of these countries).

However, sometimes an aircraft has 'hybrid residence' – where it is registered in one country but based and/or maintained in another. In those circumstances it is prudent to obtain independent advice in both jurisdictions.

Local legal concepts

One should never underestimate the importance of full discussions with independent local counsel in the state of registration (or any other jurisdiction that is relevant). When dealing with counsel in a jurisdiction in which sophisticated financings are commonplace, particularly where the counsel is experienced in aircraft financing, this may simply consist of fine-tuning the form of opinion that has been issued in previous transactions.

However, in most other cases it is important to provide the local counsel with a clear outline of the transaction structure, the legal protections that the financier hopes to acquire and the legal issues that are commonly encountered as problem areas. That briefing, and the ensuing discussions, should take place at an early stage in the transaction (recognising, of course, that details of the transaction structure may be refined as the documents are reviewed and negotiated). It can be a little disconcerting to be advised, within days before delivery of the aircraft, that there is a local stamp duty of five per cent on all mortgages, or perhaps a usury law that prohibits a borrower from being charged interest at a rate above eight per cent.

The difficulties may be more fundamental if local law simply does not recognise some of the fundamental concepts upon which the parties have based the structure. For example, in a syndicated transaction, collateral over the aircraft may be held by one of the banks (or an affiliate of one of the banks) as trustee for the syndicate. However, the concept of a trust is a common law concept that is not generally recognised in civil law jurisdictions.

Another example is the case of a jurisdiction that has not developed sophisticated laws regarding leasing of equipment, and accordingly regards the apparent and economic owner, the airline, as the owner for legal purposes. However, this point may never actually emerge unless the local counsel is specifically asked whether there are any circumstances in which a lessee could validly pass title to a third party. Some jurisdictions (for example, Belgium) do not recognise mortgages over aircraft as creating a security interest unless there is also a transfer of possession.

Conflict of laws

In international transactions it may be necessary to consider whether there is any conflict between the different legal systems involved, for example between the governing law of the financing documents and the *lex situs* – that is, the law of the country where the aircraft is situated at the relevant time. For example, the financier will wish to satisfy itself that the lessor (in the case of a lease) or the airline (in the case of a loan) has acquired valid title to the aircraft at inception of the transaction. It is likely that the sale agreement under which title is transferred will be governed by English or New York law. However, if the aircraft is physically situated in some other jurisdiction at the time of sale, a conflict may arise. This is because under the rules of private international law, the validity of a transfer of a tangible asset such as an aircraft is governed by the law of the country where the aircraft is situated at the time of transfer. Thus, it will be necessary to check with local counsel in the country where the aircraft is situated that the laws of that country will recognise the transfer of title under the sale agreement (eg by means of the bill of sale or by physical delivery).

The same concern will arise in a loan transaction where the financier is being granted a mortgage over the aircraft under English or New York law, but the aircraft is physically situated in another jurisdiction when the mortgage is granted. The same principle as that described above governs the validity of the mortgage. So, for example, if the mortgage is taken at a time the aircraft is located in France, a French form of mortgage will be required, which will not necessarily be sufficient for the financiers, who may prefer to wait until the aircraft is outside France in international airspace before taking a more typical English law mortgage.

Political risks

In the context of an aircraft financing, political risks range from overt confiscation by the host government to covert deprivation action (an extreme example being refusal by the local immigration authorities to issue entry visas to the flight crew appointed by the financier to remove the aircraft).

It is sometimes possible to obtain some form of separate undertaking from the host government that it, and its subordinate governmental agencies, will cooperate in permitting removal of the aircraft, or its sale proceeds, at the relevant time. However, this is likely to have a moral rather than legal force, because the government is unlikely to waive sovereign immunity and, in any event, if the undertaking is breached proceedings in the courts of the host government are unlikely to be productive.

Accordingly, in transactions where political risks are considered significant by the financier, it is common for some form of independent protection to be required. Typically, this takes the form of a separate, political risk insurance policy. The policies currently available in the London market cover a broad range of covert and overt political actions. However, like any insurance contract, they are subject to exclusions, conditions and warranties. A proposed policy form can be viewed from either the broad commercial perspective or the more analytical (some might say pedantic) legal perspective.

As there is little experience in the banking community of claims (whether settled or contested) under aircraft political risk policies, financiers and their advisers tend to be cautious in reviewing proposed policies. In the absence of actual claims that would 'test' the policy wording, detailed analysis and refinement of such policies is a somewhat speculative exercise. Nonetheless, it is worth summarising the following inherent limitations in the policies currently available:

- Cover is not generally available for a period in excess of three years (although see Chapter 21 for recent developments), and consequently if the financing period exceeds this period, the financier will remain exposed to the risk that the insurers refuse to renew, and political risks mature after the policy expires.
- There is commonly a six-month waiting period between the claim arising and the insurers becoming liable to settle a claim. This is intended to enable both the assured and the insurer to investigate possible methods of overcoming the particular obstruction in the host country. However, the financier is exposed if (during this period) a physical loss of the aircraft occurs, because physical destruction is not covered by the political risks policy and may not be covered by the fleet policies (if these have expired or been cancelled in the meantime).
- In cases that do not consist of overt confiscation by the host government, there may be difficulties in proving causation (the insurers may claim that the assured's loss was caused by one of the excluded risks, not by covert political action).
- The typical Lloyd's policy provides coverage against confiscatory action by 'the foreign government'. This is defined as the present or any succeeding government or governmental authority.

Difficulties of proof may arise if it is the airline that withholds the aircraft, and the assured claims that the airline is acting under the instructions of the government while the insurers claim that the airline is acting independently. Even if the assured's argument is sustained, the insurers may still have a basis for disclaiming liability on the grounds that the policy only extends to actions by the government, not to actions of the airline under governmental instruction (this ground may be weaker if the airline is a state-owned body as opposed to a private enterprise).

- A political risk policy does not cover mere delays and difficulties in repossession – for example, delays in obtaining a local court order where there is no governmental interference.
- There is always a risk of breach of the numerous conditions or warranties (although in the absence of claims experience, this risk is impossible to quantify).
- In financing structures involving both loans and leases, the policy protects against losses suffered by the lessor, not by the lender / mortgagee: accordingly, in these structures the lender is not protected against breaches of the policy by the lessor, nor against political risks that mature after the lender's security has become exercisable.

These are issues that financiers should bear in mind when considering the extent to which this type of protection really allays their concerns. However, for as long as these types of policies are the only form of independent hedge that can generally be obtained for this perceived risk, they will doubtless continue to be written in substantial numbers.

Flag-carriers and debt rescheduling

In providing credit to a state-owned airline in a country that has incurred substantial foreign debt, and has experienced difficulties in servicing and repaying that debt, the financier may incur some degree of risk that the financing will be rescheduled. To date, rescheduling agreements executed by debtor nations with the foreign banks have *excluded* aircraft financings from the ambit of rescheduled foreign debt, and it is to be hoped that this will remain the case.

Refinancing agreements commonly contain a negative pledge covenant by the debtor government prohibiting the creation of security, as regards both the government itself and public entities (which may include the national airline). One of the common exclusions from the negative pledge is collateral that secures external debt incurred for the purpose of acquiring tangible property: this exclusion permits charges over the aircraft itself and revenues arising *directly* out of the operation of the aircraft. If a financier's collateral package includes an assignment by the airline of revenues generated by the aircraft, it may be necessary to require the airline to demonstrate that a specific proportion of its overall fleet revenues are attributable to the particular financed aircraft. A general assignment of all revenues would probably infringe the negative pledge.

Sovereign immunity

In transactions where the airline is government owned, legal issues arising from potential sovereign immunity need to be carefully considered. These issues also arise in cases where some form of contractual obligation is assumed by the government itself (for example, by way of guarantee).

Under public international law, foreign states were historically accorded absolute immunity from jurisdiction or enforcement in relation to all their activities, whether governmental or commercial. However, as governments and governmental bodies became increasingly involved in normal commercial activities, this traditional theory has been progressively restricted so that it applies only to public and governmental acts. This restrictive theory is encoded in English law by the 1979 State Immunity Act and in the US by the 1976 Foreign Sovereign Immunities Act.

The UK Act provides that a state is *not* immune from proceedings in respect of which it has submitted to the jurisdiction of the UK courts; nor as respects proceedings relating to (a) a commercial transaction entered into by the state, or (b) an obligation of the state, which, by virtue of a contract (whether a commercial transaction or not), falls to be performed wholly or partly in the UK.

Subject to these restrictions, the Act provides that a state is immune from the jurisdiction of the UK courts. 'State' is defined to include any governmental department, but does *not* include any 'separate entity' – an entity that is distinct from the executive organs of the government and is separately capable of suing or being sued. A separate entity is immune from UK jurisdiction only if the proceedings relate to anything done by it in the exercise of sovereign authority and the circumstances are such that a state itself would have been immune.

Unlike the corresponding US statute, the UK Act expressly states that loans and guarantees, as well as the supply of goods or services, constitute commercial activities and therefore are not subject to sovereign immunity.

In order to obtain the full benefits of the UK Act, the loan or lease should include an appointment by the airline of an agent for service of process within England, together with a consent for giving of any relief in connection with proceedings on the agreement, a general consent to the issue of any process and the manner of service of process, and a submission to the jurisdiction of the English courts. If such a submission is included, technically no express waiver of immunity is necessary, but such a waiver is normally included to avoid any doubt.

Issues related to the aircraft or airline

Liabilities of the financier

Under the 1982 UK Civil Aviation Act, strict liability (ie liability irrespective of fault) is imposed on the owner of an aircraft for loss or damage (including death or personal injury) caused to persons or property on the ground by the aircraft or things falling from it. However, where the aircraft has been bona fide demised, let or hired out for any period exceeding 14 days and the crew are not employees of the owner (ie a dry lease), this strict liability is transferred to the lessee. Thus, this provision will not in practice apply to an aircraft financier, whether the financing is lease-based or mortgage-based.

If the financier is not liable to third parties by virtue of a statutory provision, and if there is no connection by way of contract between the financier and an injured third party, the financier may still be at risk of liability if the third party can establish that the financier owes it a 'duty of care' *and* has been negligent in failing properly to discharge that duty (as under English law). It is generally thought to be extremely unlikely that a successful negligence claim in the English courts could be pursued against an aircraft mortgagee, and the same can probably also be said for a finance lessor (in the absence of unusual circumstances, such as if the financier actually knew that the aircraft was being improperly operated and failed to take action).

However, in the international context, it should be borne in mind that the conventions on liability generally provide protection to operators rather than financiers, or have received limited international support. Because liability for an accident may be determined in the country in which the accident occurs, it is impossible to predetermine in the abstract which country's rules might apply.

More and more consumer protection legislation is being enacted, particularly in the European Union. The 1985 EU Directive imposed a requirement on all member states to enact a system of strict liability for loss, damage and injury caused by defective products. 'Products' are defined by reference to 'goods' and would include an aircraft.

In the UK the Directive has been implemented by the 1987 Consumer Protection Act (CPA), which is based on the general principle that where any damage is caused wholly or partly by defects in a product, every relevant person shall be strictly liable unless certain specified defences apply. It is worth examining the effect of this Act briefly, because it deals with the principles contained in the Directive which are applicable throughout the EU. Those who may be liable under the CPA include:

- producers of the products;
- any persons who have imported the product into the EU from a place outside the EU in order, in the course of any business, to supply it to another (in other words, the persons who have imported the asset into the EU for the first time); and
- if the plaintiff is not able to find out who the above people are, it can sue its 'supplier' provided it has asked the supplier who supplied him and has not been told. This means in effect that the 'forgetful' supplier may be liable.

However, it is a complete defence if the defendant can show that it did not at any time 'supply' the product to another. Supply is defined to include selling, hiring out or lending the goods. In relation to aircraft, the CPA specifically provides that:

> ... aircraft ... shall not be treated... as supplied to any person by reason only that services consisting in the carriage of goods or passengers in that ... aircraft ... or in its use for any other purpose are provided to that person in pursuance of an agreement relating to the use of the ... aircraft ... for a particular period or for particular ... flights.

So the passengers of an aircraft cannot sue the carrier under the CPA unless the carrier has supplied to someone else (for example, by way of sub-lease).

The CPA provides that if a person (the 'ostensible supplier') supplies goods to another person (the 'customer') under a hire purchase agreement, conditional sale agreement or credit sale agreement or under an agreement for hire of goods (other than a hire purchase agreement) and:

1. the ostensible supplier carries on the business of financing the provision of goods for others by means of such agreement; and
2. in the course of that business acquired its interest in the goods supplied to the customer as a means of financing the provision of them for the customer by a further person (the 'effective supplier'), then the effective supplier, not the ostensible supplier, will be treated as supplying the goods to the customer.

This helps the 'straightforward' finance lessor. There may, however, be more of a problem for the operating lessor. The fact that at the end of many leases the aircraft is sold on may also cause problems for the financier, since in selling the aircraft the financier will not fall within the 'hiring of goods' exemption described above. However, there is a specific exemption in the CPA for the lessor who sells to its lessee.

If a financier is caught by the provisions of the CPA, can it simply name its supplier and escape liability? This depends on it being able to name any of the producer, the own brander or the first importer into the EU or (failing that) to name its immediate supplier. If the aircraft was produced outside the EU but the financier is within the EU, it is the financier who will be the first to import into the EU. In those circumstances, the CPA liability falls on the financier and cannot be passed outside the boundaries of the EU.

The financier may try to obtain protection by joining the producer or supplier of the aircraft into the action. This would be done by seeking an indemnity by way of third party proceedings. However, such proceedings would have to be brought in contract or in tort: while the financier would be liable to the person originally damaged by the aircraft without that person having to prove negligence, the financier itself would have to show a breach of contract or negligence on the part of the producer.

There are other defences available under the CPA, one of which entails proving that the defect in the aircraft did not exist at the 'relevant time', which is the date of supply by an importer and the date of sale by the manufacturer.

Nevertheless, there is a strong incentive for financiers when acting as sellers to make sure that there are no defects in the aircraft that could subsequently cause personal injury or damage to private property, or that they are at least adequately protected for such injury or damage.

The risks of such liability need therefore to be covered in the transaction. (The financier should always include a comprehensive disclaimer with regard to the condition of the aircraft.) The lease or mortgage should also contain an extensive general indemnity to cover such risks (from whatever cause and even if arising out of defects present at the time of the sale) and, in addition, the lessee/borrower will be required to effect third-party liability insurance for the benefit of the lessor/mortgagee (see Chapter 20).

Possessory liens

Liens are potentially a significant thorn in the side of the financier, because they may be exerted against the aircraft by repairers or workmen in any jurisdiction to which the aircraft flies. Whether or not a lien arises, and how it can be exercised and enforced, depends of course on the law of the place where the aircraft is located.

Under English law, a repairer's lien can only be exercised against the asset to which the unpaid charges for work carried out relate (and not against other assets that happen to be in the possession of the repairer). The lien only arises if the work has been completed and has improved the asset (so a lien will not arise in respect of mere maintenance). It is a question of fact in each case whether there has been improvement. On the other hand, a repairer's lien can be exercised against the aircraft (or part of the aircraft, such as an engine) even if the repairs were commissioned by the airline – ie the lien can also be upheld against an 'innocent' owner or mortgagee.

The financing documents will commonly prohibit the airline from permitting liens to arise, but unless the repairer has notice of this prohibition it will be entitled to assume that it will have a lien for unpaid charges.

Other rights of detention

In English law there are certain statutory provisions that permit the relevant authorities to detain and sell aircraft (and other jurisdictions have similar rules). These relate to airport and navigation charges.

Airport charges

Under the 1982 Civil Aviation Act, any UK airport authority is authorised to detain an aircraft located in the UK which has accrued unpaid airport charges, whether or not the charges were incurred by the current operator of the aircraft, and also to detain any other aircraft operated by the defaulting operator. If the charges are not paid within 56 days after the detention date, the authority can obtain a court order to sell the aircraft and use the proceeds to satisfy the unpaid charges. (The airport authority has a statutory duty to ensure that the aircraft is sold for the best price that can reasonably be obtained: accordingly, if the financier suffers loss as a consequence of a sale at an undervalue, it has a statutory action for breach of duty against the authority.)

The broad scope of this provision means that a financer's aircraft could be detained to satisfy charges incurred not by its own lessee/borrower, but by a previous operator, or charges that do not relate to the financed aircraft at all, but have been incurred in respect of other aircraft in the fleet.

It is some comfort that if the airport authority proposes to sell an aircraft, it must take steps to notify the court application to any persons whose interests may be affected, and to give them an opportunity of becoming a party to the proceedings.

Navigation charges

There is a similar statutory right of detention under the UK Civil Aviation Act for unpaid charges in respect of air navigation services supplied by the CAA, Eurocontrol or the Government of Canada (in the case of the latter two authorities, the CAA will effectively detain the aircraft on behalf of the relevant authority). In a 1987 case, the High Court confirmed that this right of detention extends to aircraft that at the time of detention are being operated by a new, non-delinquent operator. Thus the CAA was empowered to seize seven aircraft belonging to Emery Air Freight even though it was the previous operator, not Emery, which had failed to pay navigation service charges.

Financiers sometimes require the airline to authorise Eurocontrol to provide periodic statements to the financiers of the outstanding Eurocontrol charges. This information will be historical and generally is as much as 30 days out of date. However, it does enable the financier to police the level of charges and the timeliness with which the outstanding charges are settled.

It is prudent, when acquiring a used aircraft (whether from an airline, a financier or a liquidator or similar officer) to insist on an indemnity in respect of any liabilities or security interests imposed on the aircraft in respect of any pre-purchase period. However, as in any transaction the value of such an indemnity depends on the creditworthiness of the indemnifier; in addition, a significant period may elapse between the acquisition date and the date when the CAA or other authority acquires an opportunity to seize the aircraft.

Registration

To some extent, the financing structure will be dictated by the registration requirements of the aviation authority that is responsible for the operator. Generally speaking, there is no 'flag of convenience' in terms of aircraft registration. Virtually every nation's rules on registration require either the owner or the operator to have a connection with the particular nation. Some registers operate on the basis of title only, and others on the basis of both ownership and operation. Even title registers such as the FAA register in the US permit registration in the name of the economic owner – eg a lessee under a full-payout finance lease or a purchaser under a conditional sale agreement.

Early investigation of the particular register's requirements is essential. By way of example, the UK Air Navigation (No. 2) Order 1995 contains a miscellaneous list of the classes of persons who are 'qualified' to be the owner of a CAA-registered aircraft, with the principal category being any Commonwealth company. However, whether or not a qualified person is the owner, the aircraft may be registered by the CAA if it is 'chartered by demise' to a qualified person.

Nevertheless, the Order also provides that an aircraft shall not be registered in the UK if (among other things) it could 'more suitably be registered' in some other Commonwealth country, or it would be 'inexpedient in the public interest' for the aircraft to be registered in the UK. The practical effect of these rules is as follows:

1 If the aircraft is owned by a UK airline or leased to a UK airline, it will be eligible for registration on the basis of the operator's identity, regardless of the identity/nationality of the owner or mortgagee.

2 Conversely, where an aircraft is being operated by a non-UK airline, the CAA will generally refuse registration, on the grounds of either suitability of some other Commonwealth state, or general inexpediency. (An exception is made in practice for short-term – 12 months or less – wet-leases or winter leases.) The CAA considers that it is not appropriate for an aircraft to be subject to CAA airworthiness standards in circumstances where the aircraft is based offshore and supervision of those standards is impracticable. This means that the CAA is clearly not a 'register of convenience' for financiers.

3 If the operator of the aircraft is an English company, the Order does not look behind the corporate veil. In other words there is no requirement that the shareholders or officers of the company must be UK nationals or residents. This contrasts with the nationality tests in the US prescribed by the Federal Aviation Act and in other jurisdictions such as Italy.

Maintenance

The financier will wish to be satisfied that proper maintenance and repair facilities have been arranged for the aircraft, either by reviewing the facilities of the operator itself if it has such facilities, or (in the case of a smaller airline) where there is a maintenance agreement in force between the operator and a third party airline possessing the proper facilities, by reviewing the agreement. It is unlikely that the financier will be a contractual party to these arrangements, but it may wish to review the maintenance agreement to satisfy itself that there are no unduly onerous provisions, or provisions that may operate to the detriment of the aircraft as collateral: for example, some maintenance agreements provide that the maintaining airline acquires title to any parts removed by it in the course of maintenance or repair, which may be at odds with the provisions of the financing documents. In addition, the financier may require notification to it of any disputes between the operator and the maintaining airline.

Finally, the financier may require some form of 'step-up' arrangement under which the maintenance performer agrees that if the operator defaults under the financing, the financier may (pending a distress sale) continue to have the benefit of the maintenance agreement itself.

Pooling of engines and components

'Pooling' is a broad term that embraces (1) interchange of large and small items of equipment between different aircraft in one airline's fleet, and (2) interchange of equipment between different airlines.

Financing documents commonly permit pooling of components and small items of equipment, both within the fleet and with other airlines, subject to certain protections: for example, requiring that (a) the pool has computerised central records; (b) the pool manager agrees with the financier to inform it on request of the location of any particular item; and (c) any item that is pooled because it requires repair is returned to the original operator as soon as practicable (ie without impeding the normal operation of the relevant fleet or fleets).

Pooling of complete engines or complete engine modules tends to cause more serious problems, because a single engine constitutes a substantial proportion of the total aircraft value. In the first place, the financier should determine with the airline whether the governing principle is to be 'title preservation', also known as title tracking (the principle that a detached engine will remain vested in the original financier irrespective of its location), or 'title exchange' (the principle that if substitution of an engine takes place, the financier will acquire title to the substituted engine, at least while it is on the financier's airframe). Airlines would ideally prefer maximum flexibility, having the right either to exchange title or to preserve title under such arrangements. Title exchange also has attractions for the financier in the sense that, if title exchange can be legally achieved, the financier can be reasonably confident that (notwithstanding intervening engine interchanges) it will be able to repossess its aircraft with engines that are owned by it, or mortgaged to it.

However, there are both commercial and legal difficulties inherent in the title exchange concept. Even if the financing documents state that the airline may only exchange the original engines for engines of the same age and condition, there is a risk that, on repossession, the installed engine will differ (in one aspect or another) from the original engines and will consequently possess a different residual value. That value may of course be greater or less than the value of the original engines, but nonetheless the financier is dependent on whether the airline complies with its covenants.

Title exchange provisions do impose a legally binding obligation on the airline as lessee or mortgagor. Accordingly, if a lessee airline substitutes an engine owned by the airline itself, such provisions may constitute an agreement for exchange of title between the financier and the airline (the consideration on each side being receipt of title to the substituted engine). There may be an implied agreement that title shall pass on delivery, and that the airline is authorised to effect such delivery (by physical exchange of engines) as agent for the financier. In the case of a mortgage transaction, the borrower airline can create a valid security interest over subsequently installed engines that it (the airline) owns, although (at least under English law) this may operate as an equitable charge rather than a legal mortgage if the future engines are not specifically identified in the financing documents. Alternatively, such a charge might be construed by the courts as a 'floating' charge if the financing documents authorise the airline to deal freely with the 'charged' assets: in English law, a floating charge may be subordinate to fixed charges even if they are created after the floating charge.

However, these comments apply solely to substitute engines owned by the airline itself. If the airline installs an engine owned by a third party, then unless the third party can be shown to have acquiesced in the arrangements, it is very unlikely that title exchange provisions can be binding on it, so as to effect a valid transfer of title from the third party to the financier. Although English law possesses general principles of annexation of goods to land, and of assets becoming merged with one another, there is no direct authority to suggest that either of these principles applies to aircraft – that is, there is no recognised concept of an engine automatically becoming merged with ownership of the airframe on which it is installed.

It should be noted at this point, however, that one or two countries *do* regard an airframe owner as acquiring title to any installed engine: The Netherlands is the main case, and new legislation on mortgages in Indonesia will apparently have the same effect there.

If an airline defaults or becomes insolvent, it may be very difficult to disentangle the ownership of each engine in the fleet, and the security interests applicable to each engine. One possible method of avoiding this confusion is for the airline and all its financiers to enter into a global agreement that sets out parameters for title exchange or title preservation and creates a framework binding on all the parties. Such an agreement is becoming quite common in the case of some UK airlines. However, it is only likely to be feasible in the case of smaller airlines, or where the airline has only a limited number of engines of the particular model, or where there are only a limited number of financiers.

Where the airline has pooling arrangements with other airlines, the complexity and potential for confusion is even more aggravated. Such agreements fall into two categories:

1 short-term emergency 'loans' of engines, under which it is commonly stated that title remains vested in the existing owner; and
2 maintenance pooling agreements where there is commonly a provision for title exchange.

Such provisions may be effective in respect of engines owned by the pool airlines themselves, but it is very doubtful whether they have any effect in relation to engines owned by third party financiers.

Insurance

Strictly speaking, the financier will generally have full recourse to the airline for the outstanding balance of the financing if the aircraft suffers a total loss. However, in practice the financier is unlikely to rely on the airline's credit alone, and consequently the financier and its advisers will insist on reviewing the airline's fleet insurances thoroughly in order to satisfy themselves that the financier has a good prospect of recovering sufficient insurance proceeds to discharge the financing in full. In addition to reviewing the hull and war policies, the financier will also insist on being a named additional assured under the airline's fleet liability policies so as to protect it (as well as the airline) against potential 'deep pocket' claims by passengers, dependants or other affected third parties in the event of a crash or other incident.

Airline insurances give rise to a whole series of detailed legal concerns from the financier's perspective, which it is beyond the scope of this chapter to examine. However, the key point to note is that the introduction a few years ago of a standard form of policy endorsement (known as AVN67B) in the London insurance market to record the interests of the financier has greatly simplified the lawyer's task in this area.

Manufacturer's warranties

A purchase contract for new aircraft is generally entered into between the manufacturer and the airline at a time before the airline has arranged (or finalised) its financing for the acquisition. In the contract (or in ancillary documents such as the product assurance document and customer support document) the manufacturer provides various product warranties to the airline together with additional support facilities (eg maintenance training, flight training, service support).

In a lease structure, the purchase contract is usually novated or assigned (by an agreement between manufacturer, airline and financier) so that the financier assumes the right and obligation to purchase the aircraft. It therefore becomes important to determine how the original warranties will be allocated between airline and financier. One common method is for the three parties to agree (often in a separate agreement) that for as long as the airline remains the lessee of the aircraft, the airline, rather than the financier as purchaser, will be entitled to the benefit of the warranties and other support items; however, if the lease is terminated following an airline default/insolvency the financier will, on notifying the manufacturer, be substituted as the beneficiary.

In loan structures, the aircraft mortgage will typically include a security assignment to the financier of the benefit of the manufacturer's warranties: however, it should be made clear that this assignment may only be exercised in the event of the airline's default/insolvency, and in the meantime the airline continues to be entitled to exercise the warranties. The manufacturer should consent to any such assignments.

Quiet enjoyment

'Quiet enjoyment' means the right of the airline to use the aircraft in its business throughout the period of the financing, without interference from the financier or other parties in the transaction. In a two-party structure (whether by way of loan or lease) this is a straightforward issue, as the documents will contain an express covenant to this effect from the lender or lessor. The covenant should include an undertaking by the financier to discharge any 'lessor's liens' that might arise – ie liens or other security interests over the aircraft that arise as a result of the financier's own business activities (such as financings for other end-users) and not as a result of the airline's operation of the financed aircraft or other aircraft in its fleet.

In transactions involving more than two parties (such as multi-tiered lease structures, or structures combining a loan with a lease) the airline should be advised to obtain an express quiet enjoyment undertaking from the other parties, because (a) the airline otherwise has no direct contractual relationship with those parties, and (b) in the absence of an express undertaking, it may be uncertain as a matter of law whether the airline would acquire any implied quiet enjoyment right. In return for this direct quiet enjoyment undertaking, the 'unconnected' third party will typically insist on certain reciprocal undertakings from the airline (eg an undertaking to enter into a direct lease with the third party if the airline's direct contracting counterparty defaults or becomes insolvent).

However, in some multi-tier transactions such arrangements may be inappropriate. For example, an airline may acquire the use of an aircraft under a long-term finance lease and then agree to sub-lease it on a short-term basis (eg under a winter lease) to a second airline. In those circumstances the owner/lessor would normally insist on the original lessee providing it with an assignment of the lessee's rights as sub-lessor under the sub-lease: however, alternatively the owner/lessor might agree to waive such a requirement if the sub-lessee expressly agrees with the owner/lessor that its rights as sub-lessee are subordinate to those of the owner/lessor, and accordingly the sub-lessee will relinquish possession of the aircraft to the owner if the intermediate airline defaults under the headlease.

Return condition

In lease financings, the return condition of the aircraft at the end of the lease may be important. This depends on whether the lease is a finance lease or an operating lease. A finance lease will usually not contain detailed stipulations regarding the physical condition of the aircraft on redelivery at the end of the lease term: instead, it will simply provide in general terms that the aircraft must be in 'good condition', subject to 'fair wear and tear' from normal commercial operation. Nonetheless, the lease will oblige the airline to store the aircraft at its expense pending resale if it is not sold on the return date.

In an operating lease, on the other hand, the return condition of the aircraft will have a critical effect on the residual value possessed by it on redelivery, and consequently very detailed stipulations are commonplace.

Such stipulations also appear in hybrid 'walk away' leases, ie finance leases where the lessee has an option to return the aircraft at a pre-agreed date or dates (often called 'window dates') during the lease term, without the lessor having recourse to the lessee for the unamortised cost.

Insolvency issues

This section examines some of the insolvency issues and related issues that arise concerning collateral and the enforcement of collateral. 'Collateral' in this context includes ownership rights in a lease financing.

Validity of collateral

In a title-based financing such as a lease, the financier needs to satisfy itself that it has acquired valid title to the aircraft from the seller. In the case of a used aircraft, ideally (although often not commercially feasible) the financier's lawyers should check the entire chain of title back to the manufacturer (for example by insisting on production of the complete series of bills of sale). This alone will not provide certainty, because the bill of sale alone will not necessarily be effective to pass title in the jurisdiction in which the asset was located at the time of sale.

In a security-based financing, the financier needs to satisfy itself that the airline has validly acquired title, and that the financier itself has acquired a valid first priority security interest. English law (unlike certain civil law jurisdictions) is relatively flexible as regards the form of documentation required to create a mortgage. If the validity of a mortgage is challenged, it is likely to be not on the grounds of improper form, but rather on the basis that the mortgagor lacked the necessary corporate capacity, or on the basis of certain provisions of insolvency law. As regards corporate capacity, it will be necessary to check the company's constitutional documents as well as requiring properly worded board resolutions. Lenders will generally require a legal opinion on those aspects.

Insolvency laws generally provide a mechanism for challenging security created within a fixed 'jeopardy' period by reason of the security being deemed to be a preference or fraudulent conveyance in favour of the secured creditor. English law is no exception.

In the event of insolvency of an English company, the main grounds on which a prior transaction (including a mortgage) might be set aside are 'transactions at an undervalue' and 'preferences'. A transaction at an undervalue is one entered into by a company for a consideration of lesser value than the value provided by the insolvent company. In such circumstances the court has power to make an order restoring the position to that which it would have been if the company had not entered into the transaction. However, the court will not make an order if the insolvent company had entered into the transaction in good faith for the purpose of carrying on its business, and there were reasonable grounds at that time for believing that the transaction would benefit the company.

A preference is given if the company does or permits anything that puts a creditor (or a guarantor) of the insolvent company in a better position in liquidation than that in which the creditor/guarantor would otherwise have been. Again, the court has power to restore the position so as to cancel the preference. This provision only applies if the insolvent company was influenced by a desire to produce the preference in favour of the relevant third party.

In relation to both transactions at an undervalue and preferences, the provisions only apply if the company was at that time unable to pay its debts as they fell due (or became unable to pay them as a result of the transaction). In addition, a transaction at an undervalue may only be challenged if it has taken place in the two years prior to the commencement of insolvency proceedings. The equivalent period for preferences is only six months. However, where the transaction at an undervalue or the preference is between connected parties (for example, a company and its director) there are some important modifications to these rules. The challenge period for preferences is extended to two years and there is presumed to be the requisite desire to prefer unless the contrary is shown. In relation to undervalue transactions, the challenge period remains at two years, but the company is presumed to be insolvent at the time of the transaction – thus making any challenge easier from an evidential standpoint.

However, in practice, where a mortgage is given to secure the amount of the loan advanced to finance the acquisition of an asset, it is unlikely that either of these provisions would operate to upset the mortgage.

One of the issues to be considered in an aircraft financing, as in any other transaction, is whether any of the financing documents (apart from the express collateral documents such as the aircraft mortgage) create a security interest that should be registered, particularly if registration is necessary in order to perfect the security. This is an important issue under English law, because an unregistered charge is void against a liquidator or administrator, and against any creditor of the company (although not against the company itself).

The types of provision that *may* be thought to require registration are:

1 undertakings by the company to create security in future (this may constitute an equitable charge);
2 provisions constituting assignment (by way of security); and
3 rights by way of set-off that are broader in scope than common law rights.

If a lease or loan agreement contains such a security interest, there is also a confidentiality issue because each English company (and each foreign company having a place of business in the UK) is required to keep a copy of every document creating a charge at its registered office (or principal UK place of business in the case of a foreign company), and these copies are open to inspection by any creditor or shareholder. Accordingly, as there are likely to be confidential provisions in the loan agreement (such as the interest rate and facility fees), which neither the company nor the financier wish to be disclosed to other creditors, a common solution is to 'hive off' any provisions that may constitute registrable charges into separate documents that can be separately filed.

Priority of collateral

Different countries employ different systems and rules to determine priority of security interests. Priority might be determined by the time of creation of the security interests, or by the time of registration or the date of action. In England, the priority of security interests is generally determined by the time of creation. But aircraft have a separate register under the 1972 Mortgaging of Aircraft Order, which provides a statutory system for priorities of mortgages over CAA-registered aircraft. However, registration is not evidence of validity, so does not relieve the financier from the requirement to satisfy itself that the mortgage is valid in the first place. It is also possible to preserve priority in advance through the use of priority notices, which give the mortgage priority from the date of the priority notice provided the mortgage is valid in the first place and is filed within 14 business days after the filing of the priority notice.

Enforcement of collateral

The financier will wish to be satisfied that, in the event of default or insolvency of the airline, it has ready access to the aircraft. If the lessee or borrower is an English company, the key statute is the 1986 Insolvency Act. The Act preserved (subject to certain amendments) the traditional concept of liquidation, and created a separate new procedure called 'administration', which applies to insolvent companies and is designed to assist in either the preservation of profitable parts of the business as a going concern or the orderly realisation of the company's assets.

Administration can provide the company with a breathing space, either prior to liquidation or in some cases as an alternative. It involves the appointment of an insolvency practitioner known as an administrator who carries out the administration proposals. The Act does not override the power of a secured creditor to appoint its own receiver in respect of the property financed (in the case of a creditor under a floating charge over all the company's property, such a receiver is now known as an 'administrative receiver'): however, the Act includes some provisions that have a major impact on such creditors.

First, the Act provides that once a petition for an administration order has been presented to the court, no steps may be taken to enforce any security over the company's property, or to repossess goods in the company's possession under any 'hire purchase agreement' except with the leave of the court (and subject to such terms as the court may impose). The expression 'hire purchase agreement' is defined much more widely than in the normal sense, as it includes conditional sale agreements, 'chattel leasing agreements' and retention of title agreements. (A chattel leasing agreement is defined as an agreement for the bailment of goods which is 'capable of subsisting' for more than three months.) No distinction is made between operating leases and finance leases. This provision means that a lessor or mortgagee should be advised to apply to the court for a repossession order as soon as it becomes aware of an administration petition being presented.

These provisions of the Insolvency Act restricting repossession of leased or mortgaged assets do *not* contain any exclusions for the benefit of aircraft financiers that would correspond to Section 1110 of the United States Bankruptcy Code (discussed in Chapter 6).

Secondly, the administrator is given power to sell leased and mortgaged property as if he were the owner (and as if there were no mortgage): a court order is required for such a sale, and the administrator has to satisfy the court that the sale will be likely to promote the purpose of the administration order. The administrator is then required to apply the net sale proceeds in discharging the sums due under the mortgage or lease. It is not clear what is to happen to the balance of the sale proceeds – it appears they *may* be retained in the administration, which for an operating lessor would be seriously prejudicial. In order to protect the financier, the Act also provides that if the sale price realised by the administrator is less than open market value, the administrator is required to make good any shortfall. Commentary on this provision of the Act is fairly speculative until relevant case law has accumulated. However, it is worth pointing out that, in relation to leased property, the wording of the relevant provisions is expressed in terms that are readily applicable in the case of a single-tier lease structure, but are difficult to construe in the case of a multi-tiered structure. It is possible that the court would hold the provision to be inapplicable in a head lease / sub-lease structure.

The Insolvency Act, and accompanying rules, do not make it clear who has status to appear before the court on an application to sell. For example, it is not clear whether an interested third party such as an asset value guarantor would have status. The rules merely state that the administrator must give notice of the venue for hearing the application to the holder of the security or the owner under the lease. In any event, in the case of big-ticket equipment such as aircraft, there may be scope for the financier to argue before the court that in a specialised market he is likely to be more skilled than the administrator in arranging a sale at the best price available.

There are legitimate ways of avoiding the dangers of the Insolvency Act. In particular, the holder of a floating charge over all the company's assets is entitled to veto the appointment of an administrator if he has previously appointed his own administrative receiver. In asset financing, it is unlikely that the airline will be prepared to give a floating charge to any single financier (although some financiers in other areas take floating charges without negative pledges, on the basis that the borrower could execute a series of qualifying floating charges in favour of each of his financiers) but there may be scope for the provision of finance to a special purpose subsidiary which can more readily give a floating charge. However, in practice financiers take the view that the pitfalls of the Act are simply an inherent risk that must be accepted in providing finance to an English company.

Cross-default and cross-collateral

In multi-aircraft financings, it is essential to ensure that the documents contain adequate trigger provisions to ensure that (a) a default by the airline in respect of any one aircraft will entitle the financier to terminate the financing of the other aircraft too, and (b) each aircraft stands as collateral not only for the loan or lease debt attributable to it but also for the debt attributable to the other aircraft.

Sale arrangements

In a security-based structure, once the financier has succeeded in taking possession of the aircraft following a default, it will probably exercise its right under the mortgage to appoint a receiver. In English law, a mortgagee, when exercising its power of sale, owes a duty to the mortgagor to take reasonable care to obtain a proper price (and one way of satisfying this duty may be to accept the highest bid at a properly publicised auction, or to arrange a private sale on the basis of more than one valuation). However, the mortgage will invariably state that any receiver appointed by the financier is deemed to be the agent of the airline, and accordingly it is the airline that is responsible for any negligence or misconduct by the receiver.

Penalties

In a lease financing, the lease will provide that on the occurrence of any one of a number of specified events of default, the lessor will be entitled to (a) terminate the lessee's right to possession of the aircraft, and (b) require the lessee to pay to the lessor an amount equal to the outstanding balance of finance (either by reference to a specific table of termination values, or by reference to an amount representing the aggregate of all future lease rentals, discounted to present value).

In English law, the enforceability of such provisions is not always as straightforward as one might expect. As a general principle of English contract law, where the parties to a contract agree that, in the event of a breach, one will pay to the other a specified amount, that amount may be classified by the courts either as a penalty (which is irrecoverable) or as liquidated damages (which are recoverable).

A penalty is a contractual provision, the true purpose of which is not to facilitate recovery of damages suffered by the lessor (without the difficulty and expense of proving actual damage) but rather to ensure that the contract is not broken by requiring payment of an amount which is extravagant in comparison with the greatest loss that the lessor might have suffered. The case law also establishes that if the lessee commits a breach of the lease that is not sufficiently serious to amount to repudiation by the lessee of its commitment, a provision in the lease that purports to make the lessee pay for breaches occurring after the date of termination (regardless of the seriousness or triviality of the breach that led to the termination) is unenforceable as a penalty.

At a first review, these principles appear to undermine the fundamental business arrangement from the lessor's perspective. However, in practice the pitfalls of the penalty concept can be largely avoided by making it clear in the lease that the time for performance by the lessee of each of its obligations (including rental payments) is 'of the essence'. If such a provision is included, the court is much more likely to be persuaded that, for example, a failure to make a single rental payment constitutes repudiation of the contract, thus justifying the lessor in demanding payment of the full outstanding balance instead of merely the unpaid rental. It will also be helpful if the lease requires the lessor to give the lessee credit for any resale or re-lease proceeds received by the lessor after the date of termination.

Generally, the penalty concern does not arise in a loan transaction, where the outstanding balance of the loan represents a *debt* already owing by the airline to the financier, so that the legal proceedings by the financier in the event of a default will be for recovery of that debt, and not for damages (the penalty principle only applies to actions for damages, not for debt).

Asset value guarantees

A type of collateral that is common in aircraft financing is the asset value guarantee (AVG), discussed further in Chapter 18. This is an undertaking by a third party to the financier that if the financed aircraft is resold on termination of the financing, and the resale proceeds fall short of a pre-agreed amount, the third party will pay to the financier all or part of the shortfall.

The AVG first emerged in aircraft financings as a form of support by the manufacturer (generally known as a 'deficiency guarantee') under which the manufacturer agreed that if the airline defaulted under the financing, and there was a 'deficiency' of resale proceeds, the manufacturer would make good to the financier all or part of that deficiency. As these traditional deficiency guarantees were predicated on a default by the airline, the manufacturer would typically insist on receiving a counter-indemnity from the airline in respect of any payments made under the deficiency guarantee.

AVGs have now evolved into financing instruments that support leases to the airline with 'walk away' or 'option' rights (that is, the airline has an option to redeliver the aircraft at pre-agreed dates, with either no obligation or a limited obligation to pay off the balance of financing at those dates), as well as (or instead of) situations where the airline defaults or becomes insolvent.

Negotiations on AVGs of all kinds tend to focus on specific contractual provisions, particularly the rights of the guarantor (for example, the right to 'cure' payment or other defaults by the airline; remarketing rights; rights of pre-emption; and the right to approve any future amendments to the other financing documents).

The guarantor will also insist on the AVG provisions ensuring that it is not exposed to certain related risks – in particular, the guarantor expressly disclaims responsibility for the presence or absence of liens on the aircraft, for any defect in the return condition of the aircraft, for any damage that is (or should be) covered by insurance, and for exchange rate risks (for example, if the financing is denominated in a currency other than US dollars).

Interesting legal issues also arise in connection with AVGs. For example, it may be important to determine the legal character of an AVG as a contract. Generally, an asset value guarantee is not a guarantee (or contract of suretyship) in the legal sense of that word. It is a contract of indemnity – an undertaking to keep a third party (the beneficiary of the AVG) harmless from loss and represents a primary obligation of the 'guarantor'. By contrast, a contract of guarantee is an undertaking to answer for the debt or default of another person and to see to it that the other person performs *its* primary obligations. Nevertheless, AVGs do possess certain characteristics of genuine guarantees: for example, the traditional manufacturer's deficiency guarantee provides that the obligation to make a payment is conditional on a default by the airline; the benchmark against which the resale proceeds are measured to determine the deficiency is, broadly, the unamortised balance of financing, *not* a table of projected residual values for the aircraft; and the manufacturer may be expressly entitled to certain subrogation rights that are not dissimilar to those available to a guarantor.

A second question is whether an AVG constitutes a contract of insurance. If it does, and the asset value guarantor was held to be carrying on an insurance business, the guarantor might require authorisation from the relevant regulatory authority.

Tax issues

Tax is a very important aspect in any financing transaction, even if the transaction is not 'tax-leveraged'. Specialist tax advice is a necessity in most financings. This section outlines some of the principal tax issues that need to be addressed.

General tax indemnities

Both finance leases and operating leases will usually include some form of general indemnity by the lessee in favour of the lessor in respect of taxes. This indemnity will cover taxes associated with the document itself (for example, stamp duty or other documentary taxes); taxes associated with the sale or transfer of possession of the aircraft; value-added taxes; and taxes incurred as a result of the operation of the aircraft. However, the well-advised lessee will usually insist on excluding from this indemnity taxes on the overall income or capital gains of the lessor (except in tax-leveraged leases, as described below).

Tax-leveraged financings

In financings that are based on the availability of tax benefits to one or more parties in one or more jurisdictions, the tax indemnity provisions may extend to income taxes. In some transactions these provisions are expressed not as indemnities but as provisions entitling the lessor to adjust rentals and/or termination payments if the assumed tax benefits are refused or disputed by the tax authorities, or are not available at the time, or to the extent anticipated. The latter approach is generally that adopted in the case of UK tax leases (ie leases predicated on the availability of UK writing-down allowances to the lessor) but is not found in US or Japanese tax-based leases, for example.

Withholding taxes

The parties and their advisers will usually satisfy themselves before closing that the financier and the airline are based in jurisdictions such that no withholding tax will have to be deducted by the airline from payments (whether of rental in a lease structure, or of interest in a loan structure) to the financier. Nonetheless, there is always the risk of a future change of law, and it is the airline that is typically expected to assume this risk, by way of a requirement for rentals or interest payments to be grossed up if withholding tax is imposed in future. In this case, the well-advised lessee will usually request undertakings by the financier (1) to pass back to the airline any tax credit or similar benefits realised by the financier as a result of the withholding, and (2) to cooperate with the airline (albeit at the airline's cost) in seeking to restructure the transaction so as to circumvent the withholding tax.

Currency issues

Dollar assets

In the world market, aircraft are generally regarded as 'dollar assets' – that is the underlying value of a particular aircraft at any particular time is generally expressed in US dollars rather than in any other currency. Consequently, as the financier will generally have based its financial assumptions on future dollar values, aircraft financings are most commonly denominated in US dollars. However, there are exceptions to this general principle. For example, UK tax lessors are generally English companies with sterling balance sheets, and consequently possess sterling taxable profits and tax capacity; expenditure for depreciation purposes is converted into sterling. This does not of itself usually present any great problem, because the dollar purchase price of the asset can simply be converted into dollars at the spot exchange rate on the delivery date. However, the fact that during the lease term the principal balance outstanding will be denominated in sterling can, of course, lead to a mismatch between the sterling balance at any particular time and the dollar residual value at that time, if there have been currency fluctuations since the original delivery date calculation. Accordingly the lessor may require the lessee to provide cash collateral (or equivalent cover, such as a standby letter of credit) periodically to ensure that the financier's net exposure does not exceed the dollar exposure that it originally assumed in structuring the financing.

In many cross-border transactions, currency risks are inevitable, but can be mitigated or avoided altogether by forward exchange contracts or swap contracts. However, the tax treatment of such arrangements (eg the treatment of actual or notional currency gains or losses in the hands of a particular party) needs to be carefully considered.

Exchange control

Airlines in many jurisdictions are, like other entities, subjected to exchange control regulations. The financier will naturally wish to satisfy itself, as one of the conditions precedent to closing, that all necessary exchange control consents from the airline's central bank have been obtained. In some transactions the financier may seek a direct undertaking from the central bank to ensure that the necessary foreign currency is made available to the airline to enable it to service its obligations throughout the financing, and that the airline will be permitted to remit that currency to the financier without restriction. Little can be done to guard against the subsequent imposition of exchange control, other than to provide for the loan to be accelerated or the lease to be terminated in those circumstances – if it can be done in time.

Judgment currency

Notwithstanding these initial checks, there is always an inherent risk that the financier may at some stage recover payments from the airline in a currency other than the stated currency of obligation. For that reason, the financing document should include an undertaking by the airline to indemnify the financier for any losses that the financier suffers as a result of payment being made in such other currency. In a cross-border financing, this problem may arise because of legal restrictions in the airline's country regarding recoverability of judgments in foreign currencies. For example, although the lease or loan agreement will probably be denominated in US dollars, if the airline defaults or becomes insolvent the financier will probably have to take legal proceedings in the local courts to recover outstandings, and local law may provide that judgments can only be given in the local currency, perhaps converted from the currency of obligation (dollars) at some arbitrary rate, or by reference to exchange rates on some date other than the date when the judgment award or payment is made.

So far as English law is concerned, if a contract provides expressly (or impliedly) for a particular currency in which a debt is to be paid, or damages are to be calculated, judgment will be given in that currency (ie judgments of English courts can be given in currencies other than sterling). However, in a cross-border transaction the financier's advisers will wish to consult with local counsel in the airline's country to establish the procedural rules governing this aspect.

Choice of law

Any cross-border financing transaction involves more than one nation and therefore, potentially, more than one body of law. As regards equipment leasing generally, the international community has made some efforts to impose uniform rules on leasing contracts. However, it is unusual to find any form of standardised documentation of this kind in use in aircraft financings.

A fundamental question to be determined in analysing any financing is the proper law of the document. Generally, the financing document will contain an express choice of law. It is important for the parties to be confident that this choice will be upheld in the event of a subsequent dispute. As far as English law is concerned, the English courts will uphold the parties' choice of governing law provided that the choice was made in good faith and there is no reason for avoiding that choice on the grounds of public policy (for example, where a particular country's law was chosen to govern the contract in order to avoid mandatory provisions under some other legal system that would otherwise naturally have prevailed). However, on the other hand the English courts will uphold the choice of English law as the governing law of a contract even in cases where neither the parties nor the subject matter have any connection with England. To that extent, the English courts respect the right of foreign entities to choose English law as an objective body of law to govern their contracts.

A problem encountered in some cross-border financings is that the laws of the airline's own country may insist on the financing document (particularly if it is a lease or mortgage) being governed by those laws. In these cases it becomes particularly important to obtain the advice of local counsel regarding the effect of those laws on the enforceability of the contract terms.

Conclusion

In this chapter, the principal legal issues commonly encountered in aircraft financing have been outlined. Most of these issues will arise in some form in any cross-border transaction, whether the structure chosen is simple or complex. Innovation will continue to be required from the lawyer in providing the financier with security and certainty, while at the same time preserving operational flexibility for the airline.

20 Insurance considerations

Peter J.C. Viccars

Before discussing the insurance implications of aviation financing transactions it is probably helpful to identify and describe the principal aviation insurance markets and the cover that is available from them – in particular identifying the insurances that an airline is likely to arrange in respect of aircraft it operates.

Markets worldwide

The markets can be divided into three major categories: (a) the London market, (b) the overseas markets, and (c) the US market.

The London insurance market, based around Lloyd's, is still probably the largest single centre for aviation insurance. Lloyd's itself, of course, is not a single entity but a collection of individual risk takers. The other constituent members of the insurance market in London are various companies with underwriting rooms located within close proximity to Lloyd's. For our purposes, these companies can be divided into two categories:

1 Specialist companies set up to underwrite aviation business, like the Westminster Aviation Insurance Group and the British Aviation Insurance Group (BAIG). This latter company underwrites on behalf of Royal and Sun Alliance Insurance, Commercial Union Assurance, and General Accident Fire and Life Assurance Corporation.
2 Aviation departments of the other insurance companies (both UK and overseas based companies).

The London market probably has the premier position as lead underwriter of the majority of the world's aviation business outside the US, particularly in respect of airline risks, which is where the greater capacity requirement exists.

Throughout the rest of the world there are national markets established in various countries. The relative size and strength of each largely reflects the level of aviation activity within each country, with the US being the largest single national market-place. Major players in the US market include Associated Aviation Underwriters (AAU), American International Group (AIG), Insurance Company of North America (CIGNA), Southeastern Aviation Underwriters (SEAU), Southern Marine and Aviation Underwriters (SMAU) and United States Aviation Underwriters (USAIG). These insurers can provide substantial airline hull and liability capacity. At least a part (and probably most) of major US airline placements are made in the US market (which will also lead the placing), with the London and other aviation insurance centres worldwide acting as co-insurers. The US market can and does participate in non-US business but to a much smaller extent and as co-insurers rather than as a leader.

Looking at the global insurance market, what must be appreciated is that by insurance industry standards the aviation market operates at two extremes. On the one hand, the industry by its very nature has some of the highest potential catastrophe exposures, measurable in hundreds of millions of dollars, but on the other hand one of the smallest premium bases in the insurance industry. Despite this, there is over-capacity in airline business for the attractive risk. If each and every insurer were to subscribe their full capacity to any one risk there would be an oversubscription. However, even in a market with a surplus of capacity the less attractive risk (such as that with a very bad loss record or other unattractive features) may still be difficult to place. These days most airline business is placed on a 'verticalised' basis, which ensures that the lowest possible pricing (overall) is achieved. The placement is built up from the bottom with the first slice being placed at the lowest price. Further slices are added according to the rates and capacities that are available. This methodology, pioneered by the leading insurance brokers, is now widely used to ensure that the total placement is achieved at the most cost-effective price.

At the same time what has been happening in recent years is that the number of individual underwriting units has reduced, while the total volume of capacity has increased slightly. As costs of operation continue to rise some underwriters have withdrawn, while others have either pooled their capacity or alternatively have assigned their capacity to another underwriter or supported others through reinsurance arrangements.

Reinsurance is another influence on market capacity. Nearly all direct insurers arrange reinsurance protection either to increase their capacity to write business or to mitigate their loss in the event of a serious accident – or a combination of these factors. A high incidence of very expensive losses will have the reinsurers looking harder and longer at aviation business with the result that the direct insurers may have to pay more for their reinsurance protection or buy less reinsurance or, again, some combination of the two.

Reinsurance is of three main types – fac, treaty and excess of loss:

- *Fac*, or facultative, is reinsurance of a single risk either on an identical basis to the original risk or perhaps selecting a part of that risk (for example, total loss only being selected from a hull all risks policy, or excess liability being selected from a policy covering liability from the first dollar).
- *Treaty* is usually a whole account arrangement. A reinsurer or group of reinsurers agree to take a proportion of an original insurer's portfolio on a given basis for a given period. Under this arrangement they will take a share of every piece of business the original insurer writes within the category of risk covered by that treaty. In a hard market, placing of treaties becomes more difficult and as a result some reinsurance capacity may be lost, leaving the original insurer a choice of either writing a smaller line or retaining more of the risk itself.
- *Excess of loss* is a method of limiting how much an original insurer can lose in respect of any one accident. In times following poor experience in the aviation market, the cost of buying excess of loss, not surprisingly, increases.

Insurances the operator will effect

The typical wide-bodied aircraft operator will be insuring hulls for sums up to US$200 million each aircraft and liabilities up to a limit as high as US$1.5 billion any one occurrence. To the insurance market this adds up to a potential maximum exposure of US$1.7 billion for just one loss against a world picture which, during the recent past, has generated between US$350 million and US$2.2 billion per annum from airline business, depending on market conditions, growth and other factors. No single insurer has the financial resources to retain risk of this magnitude or even a substantial proportion of such a risk. As I have already indicated, each airline's insurances have therefore to be effected with a number of insurers each taking a share or, alternatively, they are sometimes placed with a single insurer with the risk being spread by way of reinsurance participations. In either case the markets I have identified will be involved.

Most airlines arrange 'fleet' policies to cover any and all aircraft they own, operate or are otherwise responsible for. Let us first look at cover and, as an example, examine a typical Boeing 747 jumbo jet aircraft in airline service internationally and the sort of insurance cover its operator will normally arrange. (It should be added that while the comments are made in this context, they will equally apply to any other aircraft, although obviously, the size of the machine and the purpose of its use are very relevant.)

Hull 'all risks'

The hull 'all risks' policy will usually refer to something like 'all risks of physical loss or damage to the aircraft from any cause except as hereinafter excluded'. The standard exclusions are:

- *Wear, tear and gradual deterioration.* In common with most non-marine policies, these perils are thought to be a trading expense and not a peril to be insured. If any improvement is made to the condition of the aircraft as a result of effecting repairs (eg new replacing old) then a contribution for this 'betterment' will normally be required from the assured.
- *Ingestion damage.* Caused by stones, grit, dust, sand, ice, etc, and resulting in progressive engine deterioration, this is also regarded as 'wear and tear and gradual deterioration', and as such excluded. Ingestion damage caused by a single recorded incident (such as ingestion of a flock of birds) where the engine or engines concerned have to shut down is not regarded as wear and tear and is covered, subject to the applicable policy deductible.
- *Mechanical breakdown.* Similarly, aviation insurers consider this to be an operating expense, but subsequent damage outside the unit concerned is usually covered. However, it is possible to obtain insurance cover against mechanical breakdown of engines by way of a separate policy, but this cover has a high degree of exposure and as a result is relatively expensive. The majority of airlines do not purchase it, probably viewing such exposure as a part of the 'engineering' budget.
- *War and allied perils.* These are largely insured separately under a hull 'war risks' policy, discussed later.

Airline hull 'all risks' policies are subject to a standard level of deductible, applicable in the event of partial (non-total) loss of the aircraft. This deductible is dependent on the type and size of the aircraft concerned. Deductibles too can be reduced by means of a separately placed 'deductible insurance' policy. The level of deductible applied to aircraft in commercial or airline use is currently as set out in Exhibit 20.1 in respect of all types of partial losses (flight, taxiing, ingestion or ground), while for non-jet aircraft the deductible is dependent on weight.

In the event of an incident arising involving the application of more than one deductible, only one deductible shall apply, being the highest deductible applicable to the incident. This deductible is applied as an aggregate deductible for all losses arising out of that incident. Deductibles are reviewed from time to time (the last revision took place in July 1984).

'All risks of physical loss or damage' does not include loss of use, delay, grounding or any other consequential loss. What the policy will cover is the reinstatement of the aircraft to its 'pre-loss' condition, if repairable damage is involved, or some other form of settlement in the event that more substantial damage is sustained. Exactly what form of settlement will depend on the policy conditions.

Exhibit 20.1
Deductible applied to aircraft in commercial or airline use

Aircraft	Deductible
Jets	
1 Wide-bodied aircraft	US$1,000,000
(including Boeing 757s and Concorde)	
2 Narrow-bodied aircraft	US$500,000
3 Hybrid aircraft	US$750,000
(Boeing 737-300/400/500 series, DC 8–70 and DC 9–80)	
Non-jets	
1 Group A aircraft	US$200,000
(includes Britannia, Vanguard, Belfast)	
2 Group B aircraft	US$100,000
(includes ATR 42/72, HS748, BAe ATP, Viscount, DHC-7, DHC-8, F27	
Convair 580/640, Dart Herald, YS 11, SF340, Shorts SD 30,	
Shorts SD360, Transall)	
3 Group C aircraft	US$50,000
(includes Jetstream, Beech 99, Beech Kingair, DHC6-Twin Otter,	
Casa 212, Embraer Bandeirante, Piper Cheyenne III,	
Rockwell Commander, Swearingen Metro)	

If the aircraft concerned is insured on an 'insured value' basis, insurers have the option to offer the airline a replacement for the aircraft that has been lost or to pay to the assured an amount not exceeding the insured value. In the event of the insurers electing to pay a sum of money, they would normally pay the market value of the aircraft, but never more than the insured value; however, the market value could of course be lower than the insured value.

Despite these possibilities, today the vast majority of airline hull 'all risks' policies are arranged on an 'agreed value basis'. This provides that the insurers agree with the assured, for the policy period, the value of the aircraft and as such, in the event of total loss of the aircraft, this agreed value is payable in full. Under an agreed value policy the replacement option is deleted.

It should be noted that an aircraft can be insured in any currency and for any amount, although obviously as far as the amount is concerned, insurers may ask for justification of an agreed value requested. Aircraft can even be insured in more than one currency, the only requirement being that the premium is paid in the currency or currencies in which the aircraft is insured.

Hull 'war risks'

The hull 'all risks' policy will contain the exclusion of 'war and allied perils'. The hull 'war risks' policy will usually refer to something like 'cover for loss of or damage to the aircraft against claims excluded from the assured's hull 'all risks' policy as caused by ...', followed by a listing of the so-called 'war and allied perils'.

Generally, throughout the aviation insurance world, 'war and allied perils' have a defined meaning. In the London aviation insurance market there is a standard exclusion clause entitled the 'War, Hijacking and Other Perils Exclusion Clause' (known as AVN48B). This lists and defines these so-called allied perils.[1]

WAR, HIJACKING AND OTHER PERILS EXCLUSION CLAUSE (AVIATION) – AVN48B

This Policy does not cover claims caused by:

a) War, invasion, acts of foreign enemies, hostilities (whether war be declared or not), civil war, rebellion, revolution, insurrection, martial law, military or usurped power or attempts at usurpation of power.

b) Any hostile detonation of any weapon of war employing atomic or nuclear fission and/or fusion or other like reaction or radioactive force or matter.

c) Strikes, riots, civil commotions or labour disturbances.

d) Any act of one or more persons, whether or not agents of a sovereign power, for political or terrorist purposes and whether the loss or damage resulting therefrom is accidental or intentional.

e) Any malicious act or act of sabotage.

f) Confiscation, nationalisation, seizure, restraint, detention, appropriation, requisition for title or use by or under the order of any Government (whether civil, military or *de facto*) or public or local authority.

g) Hijacking or any unlawful seizure or wrongful exercise of control of the Aircraft or crew in flight (including any attempt at such seizure or control) made by any person or persons on board the aircraft acting without the consent of the Insured.

Furthermore this Policy does not cover claims arising while the Aircraft is outside the control of the Insured by reason of any of the above perils. The Aircraft shall be deemed to have been restored to the control of the Insured on the safe return of the Aircraft to the Insured at an airfield not excluded by the geographical limits of this Policy, and entirely suitable for the operation of the Aircraft (such safe return shall require that the Aircraft be parked with engines shut down and under no duress).

The US market uses a similar clause entitled the 'Common North American Airlines War Exclusion Clause'.

COMMON NORTH AMERICAN AIRLINES WAR EXCLUSION CLAUSE

This Policy does not apply to all loss or damage directly or indirectly arising from or occasioned by or happening through or in consequence of:

A) (i) War – invasion – acts of any independent unit or individual engaged in activities in furtherance of a program of irregular warfare or acts of belligerents or foreign enemies (whether accorded diplomatic recognition or not) – civil war, revolution, rebellion or insurrection, or any attempt thereat or civil strife arising therefrom – warlike operations or hostilities – martial law, exercise of military or usurped power, or any attempt at usurpation of power (any of the foregoing applying whether war be declared or not).

(ii) Capture, seizure, arrest, restraint, detainment, confiscation, nationalisation, requisition, wilful damage or destruction, or any attempt at any of the foregoing, whether by any independent unit or individual engaged in activities in furtherance of a program of irregular warfare or by any Government or by any public or local authority.

Any or all of the above applying howsoever and wheresoever occurring.

B) Any hostile detonation of any weapon of war employing atomic or nuclear fission and/or fusion or other like reaction or radioactive force or matter.

C) Other than as excluded in paragraph (A) herein above, any unlawful seizure, diversion, or exercise of control of the aircraft, or attempt, by force or threat thereof or by any other form of intimidation by any person or persons whether on board the aircraft or otherwise.

D) Other than as excluded in paragraph (A) herein above, strikes, lockouts, labour disturbances, riots, civil commotion.

E) Other than as excluded in paragraph (A) herein above, vandalism, sabotage, malicious act or other act intended to cause loss or damage.

The final paragraph of AVN48B also applies the exclusion to any loss or damage occurring while the aircraft is outside the control of the operator by reason of any of these 'war' perils.

The majority of the excluded 'war and allied perils', other than the detonation of a nuclear weapon and a war between the great powers (the aviation insurance world identifies these as the USA, the Russian Federation, China, France and the UK), are covered under a hull 'war and allied perils' policy. Once again this policy will cover 'all risks of physical loss or damage' and does not include loss of use, delay, grounding or any other consequential loss. No deductibles are normally applicable in respect of losses arising out of 'war and allied perils'. There are, however, specific cancellation provisions as follows:

1 Underwriters may give notice effective on the expiry of seven days to review the rate of premium and/or the geographical limits.

2 The insurance may be cancelled by the underwriters or the insured giving notice not less than seven days prior to the end of each period of three months from inception. (This is to give effect to a recommendation that 'war' policies should only be placed for three months at a time, but this is a rarely invoked provision.)

3 An automatic right to review the rate and/or geographical limit seven days after any hostile detonation of any nuclear weapon of war.

4 Automatic termination on the outbreak of war between any of the 'five great powers'.

All airline war policies are subject to a aggregate limit. That is to say there is a specified maximum sum that will be payable in respect of any or all claims made occurring during the policy period. This limit is usually expressed as a dollar amount and will usually be around the sum of the top three valued aircraft. Some larger carriers will have a limit in excess of this, but all airline war policies will have a specified maximum sum payable.

In addition to excluding war between the five great powers and nuclear war, insurers will also usually exclude:

- confiscation etc by the 'state' of registration (this exclusion can often be deleted in respect of financial interests – albeit in some instances at an additional premium charge);
- any debt, failure to provide bond or security or any other financial cause under court order or otherwise;
- the repossession or attempted repossession of the aircraft either by any title holder or arising out of any contractual agreement to which any assured protected under the policy may be party;
- delay and loss of use (although there is often an extension to the policy for a limited amount for extra expenses necessarily incurred following confiscation or hijacking).

The aircraft hull 'war and allied perils' policy must not be confused with 'political risks' insurance. The principal difference between the two is that whereas the hull 'war and allied perils' policy, which is normally effected by the aircraft operator, insures against physical loss or damage arising from the perils insured, the political risks insurance, which is usually effected by the aircraft owner or lessor (it is usually not permissible for it to be effected by the operator) insures against financial loss arising from the (different) perils insured under that policy.

The prime difficulty in the case of the hull 'war and allied perils' policy, and particularly the 'confiscation' peril, is that of proof of loss. If an aircraft crashes it is very easy to obtain proof of loss. If, on the other hand, an aircraft is parked without obvious sign of either damage or restraining influence, the situation is somewhat more difficult. If the aircraft is registered in the same state as its operator is based the task of proving loss is even more difficult, especially if the airline operating the aircraft is state owned.

If an aircraft is confiscated, seized, etc, there is usually no predetermined date in the insurance policy at which the aircraft is deemed to be 'lost'. The policy is to cover physical loss or damage. In the event of the operator or owner being deprived of the aircraft, the issue will be to demonstrate that all reasonable steps have been and are being taken to effect recovery of the aircraft. The other important thing will be to demonstrate that there is no likelihood of the return of the aircraft in the near future and therefore that it is 'lost'.

The aircraft hull 'war and allied perils' policy will cover the aircraft on an 'agreed value' basis against physical loss or damage to the aircraft.

Spares

Under most 'hull' policies the word 'aircraft' means hulls, machinery, instruments and the entire equipment of the aircraft – including parts removed but not replaced. Once a part is replaced it is no longer, from an insurance viewpoint, part of the aircraft. Conversely, once a spare part is attached to an aircraft as a part of that aircraft (not in the hold as cargo or on the wing as an extra pod) it is no longer a 'spare'.

Having established when a spare is a spare, how is it insured as such? Usually in one of two ways. Either under a 'spares' section of a hull policy or by a separate spares policy. In either case the scope of coverage will probably be similar: 'all risks' while on the ground and in transit for a limit of any one item and/or any one sending and/or any one location.

War risks can also be covered (in respect of international transits). Strikes, riots and civil commotions are covered in accordance with Institute Strikes Clauses. Spares coverage is usually subject to a small deductible except, however, in respect of ground running of spare engines when the deductible applied is the one that would be applied if the engine was installed in the type of aircraft to which it is normally fitted. Spares are normally covered for an agreed value – usually replacement cost.

Liabilities

An airline operating aircraft between major cities internationally is exposed to potential liability claims of enormous amounts. The 'classic' imagery often used to identify this is the two jumbos colliding over Manhattan. However, it is probably the ground accumulation of aircraft and other property and people in addition to the loaded aircraft flying in and out that can make the airport location the ultimate in potential exposure. Aircraft liability exposures, for insurance purposes, are normally divided into the following:

- passengers liability (including baggage);
- cargo liability;
- mail liability; and
- aircraft third party liability.

The last category would provide coverage in respect of damage caused by the aircraft to third party persons and property, whereas the first three refer to persons or goods carried on board the aircraft itself. Policies covering all of these liabilities will normally exclude damage caused to the assured's own property and liability to its employees in the course of their employment.

The remaining liabilities are often referred to as 'airline general third party'. These are the liabilities arising from the 'ground operations' of the airline. The operator of a fleet of aircraft will often develop a substantial 'back-up' service and support organisation and will often sell its surplus capacity to others. These are services such as ground handling, maintenance, overhaul and so on. The risks involved are described as premises, hangarkeepers and products liability.

All these ground liability risks must arise from what are described as 'aviation occurrences', being those involving aircraft or parts relating thereto, or arising at airport locations or arising at other locations in connection with the airline's business of transporting passengers/cargo or arising out of the sale of goods or services to others involved in the air transport industry.

Airlines arrange insurance for all their liability exposures, often in a single liability policy. Most policies are placed on a combined single limit basis. This means bodily injury and property damage combined. In the past, personal injury was included but now this has been separated. It should be mentioned, however, that these days the term 'bodily injury', in addition to bodily injury, sickness and death resulting at any time, will include shock and mental anguish. 'Personal injury', on the other hand, is defined as 'offences against the person', such as false arrest, malicious prosecution, invasion, libel or slander and the like. In respect of personal injury, the full policy limit, whatever that may be, is not available. A standard limitation on this coverage is applied to all assureds of US$25 million for any one offence and in the aggregate during the policy period.

Cover for 'personal injury' is provided for the 'named assured' only in accordance with a standard endorsement that reads, as follows:

PERSONAL INJURY EXTENSION – AVN60

The insurance provided by this policy extends to include the Named Insured's legal liability for damages sustained by any person arising out of one or more of the following offences committed during the policy period.

1 False arrest, restraint, detention or imprisonment.
2 Malicious prosecution.
3 Wrongful entry, eviction or other invasion of the right of private occupancy.
4 Inadvertent discrimination with respect to withholding or refusal of transportation except with respect to overbooking.
5 The publication or utterance of a libel or slander or of other defamatory or disparaging material in violation of an individual's right of privacy except publication or utterance in the course of or related to advertising, broadcasting or telecasting activities conducted by or on behalf of the Name Insured.
6 Incidental medical malpractice error or mistake by a physician, surgeon, nurse, medical technician or other person performing medical services but only for or on behalf of the insured in the provision of emergency medical relief.

The following additional exclusions shall apply to the Insurance provided by this extension:

(a) liability assumed by the Named Insured under any contract or agreement
(b) personal injury arising out of the wilful violation of penal statute or ordinance committed by or with the knowledge or consent of the Named Insured
(c) personal injury arising out of offence 5 above,
   (i) if the first injurious publication or utterance of the same or similar material was made prior to the effective date of this insurance
   (ii) if such publication or utterance was made by or at the direction of the Insured with the knowledge of the false nature thereof
(d) liability for personal injury sustained by any person directly or indirectly related to the past, present or potential employment of such person by the Insured.

Financing and insurance

Having reviewed the principal types of insurance that an airline is likely to arrange in respect of aircraft it operates we now turn our attention to the insurance implications involved in the financing of an aircraft.

When financing or leasing an aircraft, a bank or other financial institution must concern itself with the insurance protection arranged because after the aircraft itself, the insurance is a secondary 'collateral'. As already explained, the majority of operators arrange 'fleet policies' covering all aircraft that they operate or are responsible for. Any aircraft being financed will therefore, most probably, be insured under such arrangements, rather than under separate (individual) insurance(s). The financier should obviously ensure it is protected under the insurances of the operator, but what protections should be sought and what is available in the insurance market? Clearly this will depend on the structure and nature of the individual transaction. Also, what is available from the insurance market will be influenced by current trading conditions in that market and by the size and standing of the operator concerned.

To give a detailed set of guidelines for insurance suitable for every style and type of transaction imaginable is difficult if not impossible. Individual transactions will involve different circumstances requiring varying treatment. Insurance is an important, not to say vital issue and as such one that should be given attention early in the life of the transaction, not as an afterthought. It is a subject worthy of careful and serious consideration, every bit as important as drafting the documentation itself. The market does change and there will be issues in individual cases that merit professional advice.

The aircraft itself

We have already identified the type and scope of cover usually arranged. The amount of insurance cover to be procured is obviously a very important question. There are varying methods of calculating the value to be insured, ranging from the historic purchase price to the current second-hand market value or the aircraft replacement cost, or a combination of these or other factors. The financial package arranged in acquiring the aircraft plays an increasing role in determining the amount of insurance cover required. It is obviously desirable that the physical loss or damage insurance is arranged on an 'agreed value' basis so there is certainty about what is payable.

The value of the aircraft would normally be specified by the owner or lessor of the aircraft and tied to the termination sum payable under the lease or the amount of the loan outstanding at any given time. Although there is obviously considerable freedom in specifying the value required, the insurers will be required to agree to this value. A specified amount that is out of line with the current cost of a new machine or the second-hand market value of a similar machine might cause the required value to be queried.

The protection that might be sought under the hull insurance (and similarly under the hull 'war and allied perils' insurance) is the inclusion of the financier as an additional assured for its respective rights and interests.

Additional assured

It is desirable for the lessor/mortgagee to be an additional named assured rather than taking an assignment of the insurances or simply having its interest noted. Joint insurance ensures:

- that there is a direct contractual relationship with the insurers;
- any claim would have to be negotiated with the lessor/mortgagee as well as the operator; and
- as the interest of the lessor/mortgagee in the insurance is original and not derivative (ie through the operator), the interest is not liable to prejudice to the same extent (eg on a breach of warranty by the operator).

Assignment

An assignment of insurance is required in order to give binding legal effect to the 'loss payee' clause in all circumstances by giving notice to the insurers. Effectively therefore what is assigned is not the policy of insurance but rather the benefit of that policy – ie claims monies due. Obviously, if the aircraft concerned are to be covered within the context of a fleet policy (or policies), assignment can only be made in so far as the insurances relate to the aircraft concerned. Assignment of liability insurances is not practicable because the beneficiary under any liability insurance would be the third party making a claim rather the airline.

Loss payable clause

The form of the loss payable clause will be pre-agreed by the insurers and the lessor/mortgagee. It would normally specify that all payments on a total loss will be made direct to the lessor/mortgagee, that all payments above an agreed financial limit will also be paid to the lessor/mortgagee and that amounts below that limit can be paid direct to the lessee/borrower unless and until the insurers have been notified that an event of default has occurred.

Breach of warranty cover

Most airline policies contain warranties, reading something like the following:

The assured shall take all reasonable precautions to ensure that:

- At the commencement of each flight, the aircraft shall have a current and valid certificate of airworthiness or other permit to fly issued by a competent authority and shall be airworthy and in every way fit to fly.
- All government regulations and instructions for civil aviation are complied with.
- The aircraft shall operate in accordance with the weight restriction imposed by such aircraft's certificate of airworthiness.

Failure to comply with these warranties could cause invalidation of the insurance, but while they are onerous, they are also common sense and a part of the airline's own business requirements. However, there are in addition a number of other provisions in the policy, a breach of which by the insured could invalidate the cover. For example, inaccuracies in the policy declaration or failure to comply with notification requirements could give rise to this result.

Protection can be obtained by financiers, up to the amount of their interest, under a device known as 'breach of warranty' cover. Very often the requirement for this is set out in the lease/finance contract in precise terms. Historically, insurers used to insist on providing this coverage only in accordance with a standard market endorsement (known as AVN28) which has now been withdrawn from use in respect of airline business.

The financier's main concern is that it is entitled to receive the insurance proceeds (the 'loss payable' clause deals with that) and to ensure that it still gets paid even though the airline is not entitled to payment because they have not complied with the policy warranties (which is what breach of warranty cover is designed to take care of).

Contribution rights

Insurers are entitled to claim a contribution from any other valid insurances available for the same loss. Any usual policy will limit the liability of the insurers to the proportion of the loss or liability that the limit of cover under that policy bears to the aggregate of the limit of cover under all valid and collectible insurances in respect of such loss or liability. In these circumstances, the total amount recoverable could be less than anticipated or required under the financing. For this reason the financing documents will prohibit the lessee/borrower from effecting other insurance cover without consent, and the insurers might be requested to waive any rights of contribution, although for the reasons outlined above, they may well refuse in the case of a hull policy.

Waiver of subrogation

The insurers will be entitled to be subrogated to the rights of the lessor/mortgagee under the loan or lease and in respect of any other security held against the lessee/borrower, unless such rights are specifically waived. Such waivers are generally available. However, insurers will be very interested in retaining their rights of subrogation against the manufacturer, supplier or overhauler of the aircraft.

Notice of cancellation or change

Because of risks the lessor/mortgagee runs as a result of the failure of the insurances, or the insurances not complying with the specified requirements of the financing transaction, there will usually be a specific requirement endorsed on the policy that 30 days (7 days or such lesser period as may be customarily available in the case of war risks and allied perils) notice of cancellation must be given to the additional assureds before the cancellation of the policy is effective as regards them. Equally the additional assured will be interested to receive notice of any material change to the policy terms and conditions that affects their interest. Again, a notification requirement on the part of the insurers will usually be requested. It should be emphasised that all such notices are effected from the time that they are given by insurers, not when they are received. In addition, an obligation in the broker's undertaking (see below) can be included, requiring any such notices to be promptly reported.

Set-off rights

Insurers would normally have a right to set off unpaid premiums against any claim. On a fleet policy this would clearly be of particular concern to a lessor/mortgagee. Insurers will generally accept a requirement to waive any rights of set-off or counterclaim in respect of unpaid premiums for all aircraft other than the aircraft in question. In addition, there may be an express statement to the effect that the additional assureds have no legal liability to pay premiums, although they might endeavour to reserve the right so to do, at their option.

Liabilities

Under the liability insurance there are more complicated issues. The airline has a liability as operator of the aircraft, but the financier may have a (separate) liability as owner, lessor or lender. However, from the insurance perspective the risk position is little different in any of these situations. A financier is most likely to become involved in litigation because of the perception that the financier has more money than any other party involved. The financier is not in the business of operating, using or maintaining aircraft, so it has no 'operational' interest in any aircraft and could only have a real exposure for liability on the basis of some duty of care or direct interference with the aircraft – eg a failure to adequately control the maintenance of the aircraft by the operator. There is, in addition, an obvious exposure to legal costs.

It is for this reason that the financier requires to be added as an additional assured to the operator's liability insurance. Just who should be named? Is the position different for a lessor or owner as opposed to a mortgagee? In practice, there is no difference. So long as the non-operational party has a financial interest it needs protection. The assureds should therefore include the owner, the lessor or the mortgagee as appropriate, but also their respective directors, officers, employees, agents and so on. The inclusion of parties should be qualified 'for their respective rights and interests, warranted no operational interests'. It is desirable to warrant no operational interest to help overcome any resistance the insurers may have to providing both protection as an additional assured and breach of warranty coverage.

Cross-liability claims

A 'cross-liability' or 'severability of interest' clause can be helpful. The purpose of these clauses is similar; to separate the interests of the various assureds, so that the insurance operates as a separate policy for each assured. There are two types of cross-liability clause – a one-way and a two-way. The one-way cross-liability clause provides that even if a party has been added to a policy as an additional assured this will not prevent recovery of claims under the policy by the (original) named assured in respect of claims made against them by the additional assured or its employees. The two-way cross liability clause, on the other hand, states that each of the assureds shall be considered as a third party to the others.

Severability of interests

A 'severability of interest' clause provides expressly that the insurance shall operate in all respects, except in respect of the 'limit of liability', as if each party insured was the subject of a separate policy. There is some resistance in the markets to providing this in addition to a breach of warranty clause, but it must be recognised that this puts the matter beyond doubt for the financier.

Indemnities

Any usual policy will specifically exclude the insurer's liability in respect of liabilities that are assumed by the insured only under an agreement and would not have otherwise attached to the insured – eg the general indemnity provisions of a lease/mortgage. Accordingly, financiers find it desirable to cover the indemnities given, not least because they feel it will provide additional security for the obligation. Historically, a specific endorsement to this effect was often requested of insurers. However, the value of such an endorsement was always questionable. Insurers were only ever prepared to provide coverage in this respect to the extent of the risks covered by the policy (as, for example, a policy will not cover penalties, taxes, fines or patent infringement) and the financier, as an additional assured will enjoy the full benefit of the same scope of coverage as is provided by the policy to the operator. Industry practice is now that insurers will no longer agree to any such specific endorsement.

Liability limits

A question frequently asked is what limit of liability coverage should be required. As has already been stated, the size of the aircraft concerned (and its potential for causing damage) is a very relevant factor. Equally the area into which it will operate is also a major consideration. A small aircraft operating only in remote regions and using small airstrips incurs considerably less potential exposure than an aircraft flying between major airports where wide-body jets such as Boeing 747s are in frequent use. When looking at commercial airline operations, obviously the number of passengers carried and the basis of carriage are also relevant factors.

There are various regimes under which aircraft airline operators are entitled to limit their liability, but these are numerous and the impact of the regimes is difficult to quantify in advance. Really, the best advice that can be given is to require as much liability insurance as the operator can reasonably and commercially afford to ensure adequate protection for the most disastrous accident. Airlines will resist effecting insurance cover above normal fleet limits or limits effected by comparable operators. Claims experience over the past few years has demonstrated that the maximum paid out on any liability claim for any aircraft type has been US$500 million, but it would not be prudent to assume that limits will not be exceeded in the future.

Mortgagee's interest/owner's interest insurance

An alternative that, these days, is hardly ever utilised by financiers is to effect a special owner's interest or mortgagee's interest policy. This policy provides the cover afforded by the primary insurances but only operates in the event of the exhaustion or invalidation of the primary insurances. It does not, however, cover insolvency of the primary insurers. It gives rise to an additional cost that will be resisted by the lessee/borrower, and should be unnecessary if the lessor/mortgagee becomes an additional assured and if the endorsements to the policy discussed above are effected.

Reinsurance

Where the insurance is not effected on a direct basis with insurers of recognised responsibility who normally participate in such aviation insurances in the major recognised insurance markets, but by law or regulation or as a requirement of the lessee/borrower, the primary insurance is placed with a single insurer or group of insurers who will not retain the risk but will effect substantial reinsurance, the financiers will often insist on specifying the level of reinsurance arranged and the markets with which such reinsurance is arranged. The financiers will also require that the reinsurers are advised of the finance/lease transaction and confirm that the reinsurance policy will be endorsed in a similar manner to the primary policy. A requirement for a 'cut-through' clause may also be included. This clause requires that payment be made by the reinsurers directly to the loss payee nominated in the original policy instead of paying the primary insurer. There will still, however, be a need to provide satisfactory proof of loss and the reinsurers will also require a proviso to the effect that any payment made under such a 'cut-through' arrangement shall not contravene any law, statute or decree of the home state of the lessee/borrower. In a reinsurance situation, financiers sometimes seek an assignment of the reinsurance policy. This is not practicable. The reinsurance policy is a contract between the primary insurer and its reinsurers, and the lessee/borrower is not a party to this contract. However, reinsurers will on occasions acknowledge or 'note' the assignment of the original policy.

Insurers

Financiers may well be concerned about the 'risk takers' with whom the insurance is placed, more especially if the risk is placed with a single insurer or a small group of insurers. Increasingly, 'captive' insurance companies are becoming involved in airline insurance. (A 'captive' is an insurance company established by a company to assist in that company's insurance needs.) In such circumstances, reinsurance assumes greater significance. Whether talking about insurance or reinsurance, the requirement is essentially likely to be the same, namely that coverage has been placed with reputable insurers of recognised responsibility who normally participate in airline insurance programmes. It is not unusual for financiers to insist on retaining a discretion as to the acceptability of the insurers.

Insurance protection

While each finance or lease agreement will be different, the likely insurance requirements should be fundamentally similar. The main issues that are likely to arise have been discussed in this chapter and, in summary, the requirements that may be anticipated will probably look something like this:

1 Under the 'physical damage' insurances (hull 'all risks', hull 'war risks' and spares):
   - *Agreed value:* In the case of an aircraft, for it to be insured for a specified amount on an agreed value basis. In the case of an engine or spare (not fitted to and forming part of an aircraft), for it to be insured on an 'agreed value' basis for either a specified amount (in the case of an engine) or perhaps the replacement cost in the case of a spare part or a spare parts inventory.
   - *Additional assured:* The financier/lessor will wish to be nominated as an additional assured in respect of their property.
   - *Loss payee:* The financier/lessor will wish to be nominated as loss payee (to receive any money to be paid out under the policy) in respect of their property.
   - *Waiver of insurers' rights of subrogation:* Against the financier/lessor.
   - *A 50 per cent/50 per cent provision:* Confirmation thereof.

2 Under the liabilities insurances:
- *Scope/limits:* To prescribe the type and level of coverage.
- *Additional assureds:* The financier/lessor (and their respective directors, officers, employees, servants and agents) will wish to be nominated.
- *Severability of interest:* Clause to be included.
- *Primary to and non-contributory:* Provision to be included in favour of the financier/lessor.
3 Under all the insurances:
- *Specific reference:* To the agreement.
- *Worldwide cover:* Subject to such exclusions as the financier/lessor may agree.
- *'Breach of warranty cover'.*
- *No responsibility for premium/waiver of set-off.*
- *Notice of cancellation or material change.*
- *No operational interest:* Acknowledgement that the financier/lessor has none.

The good news is that the insurance industry has recognised that the requirements under these agreements show such a high degree of consistency that it has been able to respond by producing a standard endorsement. The 'Airline Finance/Lease Contract Endorsement' was first published (under the reference AVN67) for use after 1 February 1991. This first edition was not well received and, as a result, was extensively revised by a special working party of underwriting and broking representatives. Much time and effort was spent in collecting comments and criticisms about the clause, reviewing and debating them. The worrying thing that came out in the comments made was the number of misconceptions and misunderstandings that appeared to exist about how aviation insurance works.

A revised edition of the Endorsement, AVN67A, was published in May 1993. This was not fundamentally different from the original, but what it did do was attempt to recognise some of the concerns that had been expressed and make certain aspects of the language used more 'friendly' without changing the underlying concepts.

In October 1994 a further revision, AVN67B, was published. This latest version has been modified very slightly so as to make it appropriate for entire aircraft or equipment (be it an engine or a spare part or a consignment of parts). There are two versions of AVN67B – one for hull 'all risks'/liabilities/spares, and the other for hull 'war risks'.

THE TEXT OF AVN67B

AIRLINE FINANCE/LEASE CONTRACT ENDORSEMENT — AVN67B

It is noted that the **Contract Party(ies)** have an interest in respect of the **Equipment** under the **Contract(s)**. Accordingly, with respect to losses occurring during the period from the **Effective Date** until the expiry of the Insurance or until the expiry or agreed termination of the **Contract(s)** or until the obligations under the **Contract(s)** are terminated by any action of the Insured or the **Contract Party(ies)**, whichever shall first occur, in respect of the said interest of the **Contract Party(ies)** and in consideration of the **Additional Premium** it is confirmed that the Insurance afforded by the Policy is in full force and effect and it is further agreed that the following provisions are specifically endorsed to the Policy:

1 Under the Hull and Aircraft Spares Insurances

1.1 In respect of any claim on Equipment that becomes payable on the basis of a Total Loss, settlement (net of any relevant **Policy Deductible**) shall be made to, or to the order of the **Contract Party(ies)**. In respect of any other claim, settlement (net of any relevant **Policy Deductible**) shall be made with such party(ies) as may be necessary to repair the **Equipment** unless otherwise agreed after consultation between the Insurers and the Insured and, where necessary under the terms of the **Contract(s)**, the **Contract Party(ies)**. Such payments shall only be made provided they are in compliance with all applicable laws and regulations.

1.2 Insurers shall be entitled to the benefit of salvage in respect of any property for which a claims settlement has been made.

2 Under the Legal Liability Insurance

2.1 Subject to the provisions of this Endorsement, the Insurance shall operate in all respects as if a separate policy had been issued covering each party insured hereunder, but this provision shall not operate to include any claim howsoever arising in respect of loss or damage to the **Equipment** insured under the Hull or Spares Insurance of the Insured. Notwithstanding the foregoing the total liability of Insurers in respect of any and all Insureds shall not exceed the limits of liability stated in the Policy.

2.2 The Insurance provided hereunder shall be primary and without right of contribution from any other insurance which may be available to the **Contract Party(ies)**.

2.3 This Endorsement does not provide coverage for the **Contract Party(ies)** with respect to claims arising out of their legal liability as manufacturer, repairer, or servicing agent of the **Equipment**.

3 Under ALL Insurances

3.1 The **Contract Party(ies)** are included as Additional Insured(s).

3.2 The cover afforded to each **Contract Party** by the Policy in accordance with this Endorsement shall not be invalidated by any act or omission (including misrepresentation and non-disclosure) of any other person or party which results in a breach of any term, condition or warranty of the Policy PROVIDED THAT the **Contract Party** so protected has not caused, contributed to or knowingly condoned the said act or omission.

3.3 The provisions of this Endorsement apply to the **Contract Party(ies)** solely in their capacity as financier(s)/lessor(s) in the identified **Contract(s)** and not in any other capacity. Knowledge that any **Contract Party** may have or acquire of actions that it may take or fail to take in that other capacity (pursuant to any other contract or otherwise) shall not be considered as invalidating the cover afforded by this Endorsement.

3.4 The **Contract Party(ies)** shall have no responsibility for premium and Insurers shall waive any right of set-off or counterclaim against the **Contract Party(ies)**, except in respect of outstanding premium in respect of the **Equipment**.

3.5 Upon payment of any loss or claim to or on behalf of any **Contract Party(ies)**, Insurers shall to the extent and in respect of such payment be thereupon subrogated to all legal and equitable rights of the **Contract Party(ies)** indemnified hereby (but not against any Contract Party). Insurers shall not exercise such rights without the consent of those indemnified, such consent not to be unreasonably withheld. At the expense of Insurers, such **Contract Party(ies)** shall do all things reasonably necessary to assist the Insurers to exercise said rights.

3.6 Except in respect of any provision for Cancellation or Automatic Termination specified in the Policy or any endorsement thereof, cover provided by this Endorsement may only be cancelled or materially altered in a manner adverse to the **Contract Party(ies)** by the giving of not less than Thirty (30) days notice in writing to the **Appointed Broker**. Notice shall be deemed to commence from the date such notice is given by the Insurers. Such notice will NOT, however, be given at normal expiry date of the Policy or any endorsement.

EXCEPT AS SPECIFICALLY VARIED OR PROVIDED BY THE TERMS OF THIS ENDORSEMENT:

1 THE CONTRACT PARTY(IES) ARE COVERED BY THE POLICY SUBJECT TO ALL TERMS, CONDITIONS, LIMITATIONS, WARRANTIES, EXCLUSIONS AND CANCELLATION PROVISIONS THEREOF.

2 THE POLICY SHALL NOT BE VARIED BY ANY PROVISIONS CONTAINED IN THE CONTRACT(S) WHICH PURPORT TO SERVE AS AN ENDORSEMENT OR AMENDMENT TO THE POLICY.

SCHEDULE IDENTIFYING TERMS USED IN THIS ENDORSEMENT

1 **Equipment** (specify details of any aircraft, engines or spares to be covered):

2 **Policy Deductible** applicable to physical damage to the **Equipment** (insert all applicable Policy deductibles):

3 (a) **Contract Party(ies)**:
   AND (b), in addition, in respect of Legal Liability Insurances:

4 **Contract(s)**:

5 **Effective Date** (being the date that the **Equipment** attaches to the Policy or a specific date thereafter):

6 **Additional Premium**:

7 **Appointed Broker**:

AIRLINE FINANCE/LEASE CONTRACT ENDORSEMENT — AVN67B (HULL WAR)

It is noted that the **Contract Party(ies)** have an interest in respect of the **Equipment** under the **Contract(s)**. Accordingly, with respect to losses occurring during the period from the **Effective Date** until the expiry of the Insurance or until the expiry or agreed termination of the **Contract(s)** or until the obligations under the **Contract(s)** are terminated by any action of the Assured or the **Contract Party(ies)**, whichever shall first occur, in respect of the said interest of the **Contract Party(ies)** and in consideration of the **Additional Premium** it is confirmed that the Insurance afforded by the Policy is in full force and effect and it is further agreed that the following provisions are specifically endorsed to the Policy:

1 In respect of any claim on **Equipment** that becomes payable on the basis of a Total Loss, settlement (net of any relevant **Policy Deductible**) shall be made to, or to the order of the **Contract Party(ies)**. In respect of any other claim, settlement (net of any relevant **Policy Deductible**) shall be made with such party(ies) as may be necessary to repair the **Equipment** unless otherwise agreed after consultation between the Insurers and the Assured and, where necessary under the terms of the **Contract(s)**, the **Contract Party(ies)**.
Such payments shall only be made provided the same are in compliance with all applicable laws and regulations.

2 Insurers shall be entitled to the benefit of salvage in respect of any property for which a claims settlement has been made.

3 The **Contract Party(ies)** are included as Additional Assured(s).

4 The provisions of this Endorsement apply to the **Contract Party(ies)** solely in their capacity as financier(s)/lessor(s) in the identified **Contract(s)** and not in any other capacity. Knowledge that any **Contract Party** may have or acquire or actions that it may take or fail to take in that other capacity (pursuant to any other contract or otherwise) shall not be considered as invalidating the cover afforded by this Endorsement.

5 The cover afforded to each **Contract Party** by the Policy in accordance with this Endorsement shall not be invalidated by any act or omission (including misrepresentation and non-disclosure) of any other person or party which results in a breach of any term, condition or warranty of the Policy PROVIDED THAT the **Contract Party** so protected has not caused, contributed to or knowingly condoned the said act or omission.

6 The **Contract Party(ies)** shall have no responsibility for premium and Insurers shall waive any right of set-off or counterclaim against the **Contract Party(ies)**, except in respect of outstanding premium in respect of the **Equipment**.

7 Upon payment of any loss or claim to or on behalf of any **Contract Party(ies)**, Insurers shall to the extent and in respect of such payment be thereupon subrogated to all legal and equitable rights of the **Contract Party(ies)** indemnified hereby (but not against any Contract Party). Insurers shall not exercise such rights without the consent of those indemnified, such consent not to be unreasonably withheld. At the expense of Insurers, such **Contract Party(ies)** shall do all things reasonably necessary to assist the Insurers to exercise said rights.

8 Except in respect of any provision for Cancellation or Automatic Termination specified in the Policy or any endorsement thereof, cover provided by this Endorsement may only be cancelled or materially altered in a manner adverse to the **Contract Party(ies)** by the giving of Seven (7) days (or such lesser period as may be customarily available) notice in writing to the **Appointed Broker**. Notice shall be deemed to commence from the date such notice is given by the Insurers. Such notice will NOT however be given at normal expiration date of the Policy or any endorsement.

EXCEPT AS SPECIFICALLY VARIED OR PROVIDED BY THE TERMS OF THIS ENDORSEMENT:

1 THE CONTRACT PARTY(IES) ARE COVERED BY THE POLICY, SUBJECT TO ALL TERMS, CONDITIONS, LIMITATIONS, WARRANTIES, EXCLUSIONS AND CANCELLATION PROVISIONS THEREOF.

2 THIS POLICY SHALL NOT BE VARIED BY ANY PROVISIONS CONTAINED IN THE CONTRACT(S) WHICH PURPORT TO SERVE AS AN ENDORSEMENT OR AMENDMENT TO THE POLICY.

1 **Equipment** (specify details of any aircraft, engines or spares to be covered):
2 **Policy Deductible** applicable to physical damage to the **Equipment** (insert all applicable Policy deductibles):
3 **Contract Party(ies)**:
4 **Contract(s)**:
5 **Effective Date** (being the date that the **Equipment** attaches to the Policy or a specific date thereafter):
6 **Additional Premium**:
7 **Appointed Broker**:

AVN67B: A section-by-section commentary

As will be readily appreciated, these two versions of AVN67B are virtually identical and have only been drawn up differently to reflect the cover provided by the respective insurances. There follows a commentary on each section of the Airline Finance/Lease Contact Endorsement.

The preamble

The preamble introduces certain defined terms (in bold type in the Endorsement) that are identified in the schedule at the end of the clause.

The Endorsement extends protection to the Contract Party(ies). It is important how Contract Party(ies) are identified in the schedule. Provision is made for extra parties to be nominated in respect of liability insurance. While the 'body corporate' will advance the money or own the Equipment and be entitled to protection under the physical loss and damage insurances, their directors, officers, employees, servants and agents may well also need to be protected for liability risks. It is also important (not least in the context of what is referred to as 'breach of warranty' protection, as afforded by Clause 3.2 of the Endorsement) that Contract Parties are identified separately if several as well as joint protection is a requirement.

The terms Equipment and Contract(s) are self evident, but it is important that the proper details are given to insurers.

The actual period of insurance coverage is precisely defined in the preamble as running from the Effective Date until the expiry of the insurance or the expiry or agreed termination of the Contract(s). In addition the preamble to the Endorsement recognises that other events may terminate the insurance coverage. It cannot be certain that this language works in every situation, but the Working Group spent a great deal of time on this issue trying to identify most if not all of the things that can cause termination of the insurance cover. I am aware, however, that this is one area that still gives some lessors concern. AVN67B is not the correct vehicle to provide ongoing coverage after the termination of the Contract(s). Once the Equipment has been returned or the finance or lease arrangement terminated, the coverage required by the Contract Parties is different!

There is a provision to charge an additional premium, as there is in every standard endorsement providing additional coverage. What has come to light is that, legally, if an Additional Premium is not charged, there is no 'consideration' for providing the coverage to the Contract Party(ies). On a practical basis underwriters have been identifying a notional Additional Premium which means there is no actual extra cost to the airline.

The preamble also contains a statement that '... the Policy is in full force and effect ...'. These words are, in my opinion, vitally important as they confirm that coverage is in force, but more importantly that insurers cannot subsequently claim that some act or event had voided the policy before the endorsement was effected.

Provisions applicable to the hull and spares insurances (Clause 1)

In the event that a claim becomes payable as a Total Loss it shall be paid to or to the order of the Contract Party(ies). In all other events Insurers must retain the ability to fulfil their obligation, under the policy, to put the Assured back into the position he was in prior to the accident either by paying for or causing the repair of the Equipment, especially in the case of an entire aircraft.

While many lease and finance contracts prescribe what is to happen to the physical damage insurance policy proceeds in all circumstances, this really is not practicable if underwriters are to be able to fulfil their obligations in the event of repairable damage. AVN67B does, however, acknowledge the need to consult, where required by the Contract(s), with the Contract Party(ies).

Also, newly introduced into AVN67B, is a statement that underwriters are entitled to the benefit of salvage in respect of any property for which they have paid a claim. This language has been included to take care of an increasingly common situation, where, following the installation of a leased engine on a leased aircraft, the value of the aircraft is increased. If underwriters are therefore in effect paying for the aircraft (including a leased engine) and have had to agree to a higher value (notwithstanding the removal of the engine that has been replaced) they will expect to receive the benefit of salvage for everything they pay for – even if one engine (the replaced one) was not even on the aircraft at the time of loss.

Provisions applicable to the Liability Insurances (Clause 2)

The first paragraph (2.1) confirms the separation of the interests of each party from a cover point of view, although of course this does not increase the overall policy limit. Insurers have also included language to prevent a Contract Party attempting to recover a deductible or any other loss that relates to the physical damage of the Equipment the subject of the Contract.

It is confirmed that the liability insurance shall be primary and without right of contribution from any other insurance which the Contract Party(ies) might have available to it/them. This is another area that continues to provoke comment. The main question that has arisen is 'why isn't this provision applicable to the physical damage policies too?' The fact of the matter is that the position is different. In the case of liability there can be many different exposures – the owners', the lessors', the operators', the maintenance contractors' and so on. It is therefore both logical and sensible to prescribe the order in which any insurance that has been arranged protecting these liabilities should respond.

In respect of physical loss or damage to the Equipment there is however a different position. The Equipment can only be paid for *once*. If the Contract Party(ies) have contractually obligated the Insured to insure the Equipment and have received evidence of that insurance having been arranged, to then arrange another insurance covering the same equipment in the same way would create 'double insurance', which is not allowable.

It is the principle of insurance that the parties should be put back in the position they were in before the loss. To collect the same loss twice would therefore breach this intention. If other insurances are arranged covering the Equipment but on a different basis (such as 'total loss only' or contingent, etc) it is these policies that should contain a qualification that they will only pay *after* the 'prime' policy has paid and/or to the extent that the policyholder has not been made 'whole' by the prime insurance.

The other issue that has been raised is: why shouldn't the Contract Party(ies) be protected if the Insured has taken out another liability insurance, so that 2.2 would refer to any other insurance available to the Contract Party(ies) *and the Insured?* The fact is that by the language, as drafted, it is already confirmed that as far as the Contract Party(ies) are concerned the insurance to which the (AVN67B) Endorsement is attached will respond first – that is what 'primary' means. The liability insurance requirement of the Contract(s) is therefore satisfied and no further qualification is necessary.

The statement contained at 2.3 regarding manufacturers, repairers and servicing agents, I believe, is equally clear. While such organisations are protected in their capacity as Contract Party(ies) they will not be afforded 'products liability' coverage for their other capacity.

Provisions applicable to all insurances (Clause 3)

The inclusion of the Contract Party(ies) as additional assureds is confirmed by 3.1.

It is 3.2 that provides what is referred to as 'breach of warranty' coverage. It states that 'The cover afforded to each Contract Party by the Policy in accordance with this Endorsement shall not be invalidated by any act or omission (including misrepresentation and non-disclosure) of any other person or party which results in a breach of any term, condition or warranty of the Policy PROVIDED THAT the Contract Party so protected has not caused, contributed to or knowingly condoned the said act or omission'.

Insurers have publicly accepted that the onus of proof, as respects this proviso, clearly lies with insurers and this view is certainly backed up by the textbooks on insurance law. The inclusion of reference to act or omission including misrepresentation and non-disclosure is undoubtedly a major concession on the part of insurers and one that has very much been welcomed by the financiers, lessors and their lawyers.

Paragraph 3.3 was newly included in AVN67B and it replaces the 'Other Interests' Endorsement (AVN70) which was introduced to deal with the situation where any Contract Party(ies) may have another relationship with the Operator of the Equipment, other than that assumed under the Contract(s) acknowledged under the Endorsement. This language says that the only contractual relationship which will be taken into account as far as concerns the coverage provided by the Endorsement, and 3.2 ('breach of warranty') in particular, is that of the Contract Party(ies) as such. For example, any information that any Contract Party(ies) has as a result of any other relationship with the Operator will not be considered in the context of identifying whether the Contract Party has 'knowledge' of an event giving rise to a breach of warranty (as described in 3.2).

Item 3.4 confirms that the financier/lessor is not responsible for premium and confirms that underwriters waive any right of set-off or counterclaim against them, 'except in respect of outstanding premium in respect of the Equipment'.

Item 3.5 restates a matter of insurance practice. If any underwriter pays a claim, be it a marine, non-marine or aviation policy, it is a principle that, to the extent of any such payment, the insurers have a right to take over the subrogation rights of the party to whom they have paid against any third party, from whom they may be able to recover some or all of the payment they have made because that party has an involvement, in some way, in the causation of that loss.

The language does confirm that underwriters will not seek to exercise rights of recourse against any Contract Party(ies). The Contract Party(ies) are required to 'do all things reasonably necessary to assist' underwriters in exercising their subrogation rights.

Item 3.6. confirms that 'Except in respect of any provision for Cancellation or Automatic Termination' the cover provided by the endorsement cannot be cancelled or materially adversely altered without giving 30 days (or such lesser period customarily available in respect of war and allied perils) notice in writing to the appointed broker. This makes clear that underwriters do not send out notices to the parties who ask to be advised of cancellation or material change in the insurances. They never have done so! The 'real world' situation is formally confirmed – namely that underwriters give notices to the appointed broker who is then obliged to relay that notice to the Insured and all the other interested parties, including any Contract Parties. The other important thing that is confirmed is that notices are effective from the time that they are given by insurers, not the time that they are received. This has always been the case, although many contracts and certificates of insurance may have said otherwise.

The capitalised words, 'except as specifically varied or provided by the terms of this endorsement the contract party(ies) are covered by the policy subject to all terms, conditions, limitations, warranties, exclusions and cancellation provisions thereof' that appear just above the schedule are very important. These words confirm that AVN67B does override the policy to the extent specified in the Endorsement. This removes the uncertainty, expressed in the past, that the 'Subject to the policy terms, conditions, limitations, exclusions and cancellation provisions' that appeared at the end of virtually every certificate of insurance left in doubt whether what was shown overrides the basic policy or not. This language in AVN67B makes the position clear.

Insurance of indemnity provisions is something you will not find mentioned in AVN67B. This matter was reviewed in much detail by the working group. First, it should be remembered that the physical damage policies (hull, hull war and spares) will cover just that and only that. The Contract Party(ies), by being added to the Operator's liability insurance, enjoy the full protection of that policy – to the same extent that the Operator does. The addition to the liability insurance of a statement that the policy will 'insure the indemnity provisions, *but only to the extent of the risks covered by the policy*' will therefore provide nothing extra. In the past insurers had been prepared to include this statement, but are now taking the view that it has no value and are therefore discontinuing this previous practice.

In conclusion, AVN67B does offer a consistency of approach, and while it is too much to hope that it will be the *total* solution to every finance or lease agreement, it should make life easier for everyone involved in the insurance aspects of financing and leasing.

Certificates of insurance

In most financing, it is a requirement that, prior to drawdown and on each renewal anniversary, a certificate of insurance is provided evidencing compliance of the cover with the underlying requirements of the lease/finance contract.

As previously mentioned, most of the world airlines' risks are of such size that no single insurer can retain 100 per cent of such risk. Therefore, the risk is spread among many insurers. It is obviously not practical to obtain from each participating insurer evidence of its agreement to the requirements of any particular contract. Equally for reasons of confidentiality or practicability, it may not be feasible for the lessor/mortgagee to review the terms of the policy in advance of closing a transaction. Accordingly, it has become a practice that the firm of brokers effecting the insurance placement are mandated by the whole body of the insurers subscribing to a risk to issue evidence of the insurance arranged – both its general terms and conditions and the specific agreements given with respect to individual contracts. Style and layout of certificates of insurance varies from broking house to broking house, although the introduction of

AVN67B should ensure a greater degree of consistency at least in that part of the certificate confirming what has been agreed in respect of the particular finance or lease agreement. The brokers are solely authorised to evidence what has been agreed by the requisite underwriters.

The financier, in the absence of seeing the policy, is wholly dependent on the accuracy of the certificate to verify that the insurance provisions of the financing documents have been complied with. At insurers' insistence, all certificates are normally qualified 'subject to the policy terms, conditions, limitations and exclusions'. This is to indicate that all other general terms and conditions of the policy have not been varied. If there is concern as to the protection provided, insurance advisers can be commissioned to review and report on the insurance arranged.

Letter of undertaking

This is a letter, given by the insurance broker in its capacity as broker to the airline, in which certain things are undertaken by the broker as principal vis-à-vis an aircraft lessor or mortgagee. Normally it will encompass such things as holding the benefit of insurance contracts to the order of the aircraft owner (or lessor or mortgagee, etc), giving advice of any notices of cancellation or material change given by the insurers or advice in the event that the airline does not pay premiums due under the policy. Finally, the broker is often required to undertake to advise in the event that it ceases to be broker to the airline concerned.

Note

1 The author gratefully acknowledges the kind permission of Lloyd's Aviation Underwriters Association to reproduce the text of standard market clauses quoted in this chapter.

21 Aircraft repossession insurance

David Maule[1]

Aircraft repossession insurance started to be underwritten by Lloyd's of London in the early 1980s. The cover is purchased by banks and leasing companies financing the sale of aircraft to Third World airlines. (The rationale for the purchase of the cover is explained in Chapter 20.)

The principal drawback with the cover has been the fact that whereas leases of aircraft are often concluded for periods of 10 years or more, the maximum duration of the cover has traditionally been limited to three years. In the early years of the cover certain financiers of aircraft sought to solve this problem by inserting a clause in the lease contract whereby the non-renewal of the insurance policy was deemed to be an event of default, whereby the lessor would be entitled to repossess the aircraft. The idea behind this was that if the lessee subsequently blocked the repossession, this would be covered by the existing insurance policy.

The leading Lloyd's underwriters soon responded with a measure to counter this by inserting the following additional exclusion into the standard policy wording: 'Excluding any loss arising out of any provision of the lease agreement that permits or purports to permit the assured to exercise rights of repossession in circumstances where underwriters hereon decline to renew or extend this policy'. This exclusion is still included. However, the situation has recently improved in that Lloyd's has become more relaxed about offering periods of cover in excess of three years. Seven-year periods are now available and longer periods are envisaged. Furthermore, competition from other insurers is accelerating this trend (see the 'Insurers' section later in this chapter).

The aircraft repossession market remains extremely profitable for insurers. Annual premium income to Lloyd's is estimated at US$50 million. To the author's knowledge there has been only one paid claim to date – US$11 million for a risk in Yugoslavia. There have also been some relatively small contributions made by insurers to pay for unforeseen costs in removing aircraft blocked in countries in order to prevent claims occurring. Potential claims have also arisen in recent years in Brazil, the Dominican Republic, Venezuela, Yemen and Zambia. The general softness of the insurance market in traditional fields such as standard marine and aviation insurance means that the capacity available for aircraft repossession insurance has risen substantially. In today's market it would be possible to place a sum insured of US$500 million in most countries of the world. There are, however, currently four countries in which there are capacity limitations. The country that has traditionally presented insurers with capacity difficulties, Brazil, has more recently been joined by three others – Mexico, China and Russia – in which insurers have underwritten significant sums of aircraft repossession insurance. Ethiopia and the Philippines have also seen large amounts of cover purchased.

The insurance policy wording that has now been adopted as standard by the London market is called 'LSW 147 amended'. This incorporates the exclusion highlighted above and other variants from the initial LSW 147 wording introduced in the late 1980s. The previous market wording (RJM R.L.A.I) has largely been discarded.

The text of this policy wording will now be examined in detail and some areas in which improvements can be made to the standard wording on a case-by-case basis will be reviewed. The insurers like to restrict such improvements to regular purchasers of the cover and a new entrant to the field might encounter some resistance from insurers if the best wording with all of the 'trimmings' was insisted upon.

Definitions

The policies start with definitions that include:

- insured peril;
- foreign government; and
- waiting period.

Insured peril

According to the policy, an insured peril means an action taken by the foreign government, being:

(a) Confiscation, seizure, appropriation, expropriation, nationalisation, restraint, detention or requisition for title or use of the insured aircraft by the foreign government.
(b) Refusal or failure of the foreign government to allow the assured to exercise their rights to repossess the insured aircraft in accordance with the terms and conditions of the lease agreement.
(c) Refusal or failure of the foreign government to allow the assured to remove the insured aircraft from the foreign country following the assured's exercise of their rights to repossess the insured aircraft in accordance with the terms and conditions of the lease agreement.
(d) Refusal or failure of the foreign government to allow the assured to deregister the insured aircraft from the aviation registration authorities of the foreign country following the assured's exercise of their rights to repossess the insured aircraft in accordance with the terms and conditions of the lease agreement.
(e) Refusal or failure of the foreign government, following a compulsory sale or other compulsory disposal for divestiture of the insured aircraft in the foreign country, to allow the assured to obtain the proceeds of sale, disposal or divestiture in United States dollars or another currency which is freely convertible into US dollars in the international exchange markets, following perils as per (a), (b), (c) and (d) above.

In all cases there has to be an action or inaction of the foreign government – ie the government of the lessee's country. It has been recognised that this could be caused by a supranational body such as the United Nations and thus one of the improvements that can be obtained is the following addition: 'It is understood and agreed that actions taken by, or refusal or failure by, the foreign government directly caused by or at the express instruction of the United Nations, or any future supranational authority embodied with similar powers, are covered by this policy, subject to such actions, refusal or failure being otherwise covered under the terms and conditions of this policy.'

Foreign government

Just precisely what constitutes the foreign government is often the subject of some debate between the assured and insurers. The standard definition is that it means 'the present or any succeeding governing authority of the foreign country, or any definable region thereof, provided that such governing authority exercises effective legislative, executive and judicial control therein, and without having regard to the manner of its accession'.

However, in the event that the lessee, as is often the case, is the state-owned national flag-carrier of the foreign country then the definition of foreign government can be extended to include the lessee. Hence there is no discussion with insurers as to whether the defaulting lessee is acting independently of the government. Note this is only possible with state-owned airlines. If the airline is private then in order to start the process of repossessing an aircraft following an event of default under the lease agreement, the lessor would normally seek recourse to the judicial system in place in the lessee's country. Only once a judgment is obtained in the lessor's favour and the foreign government fails to allow the judgment to be exercised is there a basis for a claim.

Insurers also recognise that obtaining such a judgment can be fraught with difficulty and can take considerable time. It is therefore possible to extend the definition of foreign government to include obstruction by the foreign judiciary, defined as 'any court, tribunal, authority or other agency acting under the authority or instructions of such government or governmental authority'.

Waiting period

In all cases there is a waiting period – ie the period between the event that starts the ball rolling towards a claim (normally an event of default under a lease agreement) and the claim payment itself. This is defined as 'the period specified in the schedule hereto and prior to the expiry of which underwriters hereon shall not be liable for any loss or damage to the insured aircraft. The waiting period shall commence from the date of advice to underwriters of an event likely to give rise to a claim under this policy.

However, if the assured satisfies underwriters that there is no reasonable prospect of the action of the foreign government being reversed or cancelled during the waiting period, underwriters will pay the agreed value to the assured on being so satisfied, notwithstanding that the waiting period has not expired.'

The actual waiting period is negotiable on a case-by-case basis. Frequently, two different waiting periods may be offered by underwriters:

- a waiting period for the events covered under insured peril (a), which tends to be very short or non-existent; and
- a waiting period for insured perils (b), (c), (d) and (e), which is usually between 90 and 180 days, with 180 days being perhaps most common.

To some extent, the length of the latter period will depend on the advice received in the legal opinion (the importance of which is discussed under 'Warranties' below).

The waiting period is a standard feature of all types of political risk insurance, be it for contract frustration, confiscation or unfair calling of guarantees, and is applied for the good reason that problems can frequently be resolved within a certain period after an incident. The existence of the waiting period also gives underwriters and assureds the opportunity to consider how best they should act to tackle a particular situation. The distinction between the waiting period under (a) on the one hand, and (b), (c), (d) and (e) on the other, is that under (a) there is a positive act that is not likely to be reversed within a reasonable length of time.

It is possible to negotiate a guaranteed maximum payout period of say 45 days following insurers' agreement to indemnification.

Exclusions

The policies then list the exclusions as follows:

1 *Material default by the assured:* 'Excluding any loss arising from material default by the assured (or any agent, sub- or co-contractor of the assured) in the performance of their obligations under the lease agreement'.
2 *Loss or damage during waiting period:* 'Excluding loss or damage to the insured equipment arising from any cause whatsoever prior to the expiry of the waiting period'.
3 *War:* 'Excluding any loss arising from destruction or physical damage directly or indirectly occasioned by, happening through or in consequence of war, invasion, acts of foreign enemies, hostilities (whether war be declared or not), civil war, rebellion, revolution, insurrection, military or usurped power'.
4 *Non-compliance with laws:* 'Excluding any loss arising from any failure of the assured to obtain all permits and authorisations necessary at inception of this policy and/or make every endeavour reasonably practicable to keep such permits and authorisations in force during the currency of this policy and/or make every endeavour reasonably practicable to obtain such new permits and authorisations as may be stipulated by the foreign government during the currency of this policy'.

Two further exclusions now appear as standard in the LSW 147 amended wording. The first (mentioned above) is the non-renewal/extension exclusion, which remains standard. The second is the 'rights of repossession in the event of non-payment of premium under this policy' exclusion, which states: 'Excluding any loss arising out of any provision contained in the lease agreement that permits, or purports to permit, the assured to exercise rights of repossession due to any failure of the lessee to pay or reimburse the assured the cost of insurance premiums due under this policy'.

Two of the above exclusions deserve further comment. First, the war exclusion is currently a topic of some debate at Lloyd's. At the beginning of 1997 Lloyd's withdrew from the so called 'War Risks Agreement', whereby no insurer who has signed the agreement covers the risk of war on land-based assets. This exclusion could now be deleted. However, the perils embraced by this exclusion should be covered by the hull war risks policy taken out by the airline and, as a back-stop for the lessor, there exists the possibility of taking out a contingent hull war policy, of which more below.

Secondly, the 'loss or damage during the waiting period' exclusion also causes some problems for financiers, but again there is a solution. Aircraft repossession insurers feel that damage to the aircraft during the waiting period should be covered by the airline's hull or hull war policy, not by the aircraft repossession policy. This is disliked by financiers because they have no control over the existence or worth of such policies. There have been attempts made to transfer the liability for such damage during the waiting period from the airline's aviation policies to the financier's non-repossession policy. For a time this was successful but latterly the non-repossession insurers have taken a tougher stance and the current view prevails as above. The solution for the financier again lies in the purchase of the additional contingent hull war policy, as described below.

Conditions

The conditions in an aircraft repossession insurance policy are, in the context of insurance generally, of a routine nature and many are negotiable in the circumstances of particular cases. It is not worth listing all of these but three, where alterations are possible, are worth highlighting:

1 *Due diligence:* The standard reads, 'The assured shall use due diligence and do and concur in doing all things reasonably practicable to avoid or diminish any loss herein insured'. As a broker one is often asked to define what is meant by 'due diligence'. The standard response is to say that the assured must at all times act as if uninsured and this holds good here. However, financiers like to be given clear directives in the event of a potential loss so the following additional clause can be added: 'The assured shall be deemed to have complied with this condition including but not limited to if the assured shall have acted in accordance with the express written directions of the underwriters during the waiting period'.
2 *Immediate notice of loss:* The standard reads, 'Upon the discovery of any event likely to give rise to a claim under this policy, the assured shall immediately give notice thereof to the underwriters hereon.' This is considered too onerous by some financiers, particularly as it is sometimes difficult to define at what point an event is likely to give rise to the claim. Hence this condition can be watered down to the following clause entitled simply 'Notice of loss': 'Upon the discovery of any event likely to give rise to a claim under this policy, the assured shall within a reasonable period thereafter give notice thereof to the underwriters hereon'.
3 *No cancellation and no return of premium for short interest, unless specifically agreed at inception:* Even though this is not popular the insurers are prepared to consider return of premium paid when this is pre-agreed and to allow for certain foreseeable events. One of the most common is in the event of early termination of the lease agreement by mutual consent. Hence the following addition can be included without difficulty: 'However, in the event that the lessee exercises its option as provided for in the lease agreement to terminate the lease agreement, underwriters hereon agree to return the unused portion of the premium on a pro rata basis, subject to no claim having been submitted under the policy and the assured granting to underwriters a full release from liability under the policy'.

Warranties

The warranties in an aircraft repossession insurance policy include the important 'legal opinion' warranty which reads as follows:

Warranted that a written independent legal opinion of a qualified lawyer in the foreign country shall be supplied by the assured to underwriters confirming that the laws of the foreign country in effect at the date it is submitted do not prevent or hinder the assured's exercise of its rights under the lease agreement. Underwriters confirm that the opinion provided by the assured satisfies the warranty set forth herein and the underwriters agree to endorse a copy of such opinion and attach it to the policy.

In all cases therefore, insurers will require such a legal opinion to be obtained and endorsed on to the policy. The standard practice is for the leading insurer or insurers to initial the legal opinion provided by the assured and for this to be submitted to the Lloyd's policy signing office to be attached to the policy when issued.

Cost

At the beginning of the 1990s the premium rates for this class of business had started to harden, but with the excellent claims record, the large amounts of capacity available and the softness of the general insurance and reinsurance markets, the rates for aircraft repossession insurance have decreased of late.

In this class of business, unlike all other sectors of political risk insurance, the country of risk is not the most important factor. More important is the identity of the aircraft being leased and on which routes it is being flown. The point is that the more international these are, the easier it is for the lessor to exercise repossession rights in the event of default by the lessee under the lease agreement. Under the insurance of export contracts the risk on a sale to India, for example, presents a better risk than a sale to Zambia. However, paradoxically, in aircraft repossession insurance, a Zambia risk could be perceived as a better risk than India – eg a wide-bodied Boeing used on the Lusaka–New York route is a more attractive risk than a small commuter aircraft flying on internal routes in India only, because the latter would be more difficult to repossess in the event of default by the lessee.

Rates therefore cannot so easily be classified into country categories as in other forms of political risk insurance. However, the standard per annum rates currently range from 0.2 per cent per annum for the best risks to 1.5 per cent per annum for the worst.

Insurers

Lloyd's is by far and away the dominant player in this market. The only other insurer prepared to consider aircraft repossession insurance in a leading role and with significant capacity is the American International Group (AIG). The latter, based in New York but with political risk insurance headquartered in London for all non-American business, is able to offer up to US$150 million of capacity per risk. Significant also is that it has begun to entertain periods of risk of up to 10 years. If Lloyd's sees itself as in danger of losing business to AIG because of the longer periods of cover available from the latter, this will surely accelerate Lloyd's drive into offering equally long periods of cover.

Contingent hull war covers

The problem of the 'loss or damage during waiting period' exclusion in an aircraft repossession policy has been mentioned above. Under normal circumstances, such loss or damage if this occurred would be covered by the airline's hull or hull war policies. There is potential danger in the event of a deterioration in the political situation.

All hull war policies contain provisions allowing the insurers to impose increased rates in the event that they consider the political situation to have deteriorated such that an increased rate is justified. In the event that the airline refuses to pay such an increased rate the policy can be cancelled. Additionally, under certain circumstances (eg the outbreak of war) the insurers are entitled to cancel or not renew the airline's hull war policy. Lastly, most hull war covers contain an aggregate limit that may be used up in paying claims on other losses. This last problem was highlighted during the Gulf War when the losses sustained by Kuwait Airways breached their aggregate limit.

The 'contingent hull war policy' is taken out by the financier or lessor to provide up to 180 days of actual war cover in the event of any of the above occurrences. Such an occurrence would be deemed to be an event of default under the lease agreement and would entitle the lessor or financier to institute proceedings to repossess the aircraft. If it was not for the existence of the contingent hull war policy, the aircraft would not be covered against war risks during the waiting period under the repossession policy.

Such situations are of concern to the financier but thankfully have remained in the realms of theory to date, as there have not been any claims made under any such contingent hull war policies (to the best of the author's knowledge). Consequently, the rates are very low. The premium consists of two parts – a commitment fee paid at inception which guarantees the second part, the war risk cover at a fixed rate. The commitment fee is around 0.1 per cent to 0.2 per cent per annum. The fixed war risk rate obviously varies depending on the locality of the airline. In this class of business, unlike aircraft repossession insurance, the political situation in the country of the lessee is very much the overriding factor in determining the rate.

Export credit agencies

The previous edition of this book examined the possibility that there would be increased cooperation between export credit agencies and the private market. The example was taken whereby the UK's Export Credit Guarantee Department (ECGD) in 1989 provided aircraft repossession cover to Banque Indosuez in respect of the UK portion of an Airbus A310 being leased to Somali Airlines. The policy covered the full period of the lease of 12 years and was 95 per cent reinsured at Lloyd's for an initial period of three years. (The German and French portions were insured by HERMES and COFACE, respectively, without reinsurance.)

In practice this has remained to date an isolated case. The principle objection to further cooperation by the export credit agencies with the private market, either in the form of co-insurance or reinsurance, is that the latter has hitherto been unable to match the former in terms of the period of cover offered. Indeed this is why HERMES and COFACE were disinclined to follow ECGD's example in the Somali Airlines case described above.

The fact that the private market is now able to offer longer periods of cover opens up greater possibilities of cooperation between the two sides.

Conclusion

The appetite of private market insurers for aircraft repossession insurance remains healthy and the capacity available for individual transactions has never been better. The fact that the principal objection to its use by financiers – the maximum three-year timeframe – is also being undermined, means that the market should continue to grow.

Note

1 The author would like to acknowledge the help given in the preparation of this chapter by Barnabas Hurst-Bannister of Janson Green syndicates at Lloyd's.

22 The regulatory framework for airline operations

Neil D. Lewis

The international framework

The regulation of international air transport has become increasingly important in the context of aircraft financing during the 1990s. There has been a strong move towards deregulation or liberalisation of the skies, emanating particularly from the US and Europe, which has freed airlines in each of those markets from the constraints of the highly regulated environment set down by the Chicago Convention of 1944. However, there is an ongoing debate on 'open skies' between Europe and the USA. This has resulted in a patchwork of bilateral treaties between European Union (EU) member states and the USA rather than deregulation of air transport between those markets. In Asia and other markets around the globe 'open-skies' policies are being debated on a country-by-country basis without significant changes being announced, although there has been some deregulation in the Japanese domestic market.

Nevertheless, it appears that liberalisation will continue and in such a changing environment the extent to which an airline will profit or lose from such liberalisation is an important credit issue for financiers. This Chapter seeks to explain the background to the liberalisation or open-skies developments and the main areas of regulation that will interest financiers and airlines alike.

The Chicago Convention

Notwithstanding the deregulation of the US and EU aviation markets, the principles laid down in the Chicago Convention of 1944 still govern international air travel. States that are parties to the Chicago Convention agreed that they should have the power to grant each other certain rights to fly over each other's territories and also the ability to place certain restrictions on the exercise of such rights. The actual rights granted and restrictions imposed are either contained in a multilateral agreement between several states, such as the Five Freedoms Agreement of 1944, or have been individually negotiated in separate bilateral treaties.

The Final Act of the Chicago Convention was signed in 1944 by 51 states. The Convention laid down various obligations concerning the flight and manoeuvre of aircraft, and established the International Civil Aviation Organisation (ICAO) which subsequently became a specialised agency of the United Nations. ICAO's functions cover a wide range of areas such as aircraft design, airport design and management, the provision of air navigation services, the maintenance of fair competition between carriers and the general oversight of inter-state relationships in civil aviation.

The Chicago Convention established the general principle that each state should have the absolute right to control the operation of scheduled international air services over or into its territory. This principle has underpinned the international aviation system (sometimes referred to as the 'Chicago system') that has developed from the Chicago Convention itself, the Five Freedoms Agreement and a web of bilateral treaties.

The Five Freedoms Agreement

Following signature of the Chicago Convention, approximately 20 states signed the International Air Transport Agreement, otherwise known as the Five Freedoms Agreement, which was intended to establish general and universal ground rules for international air transport. Among other things, the Five Freedoms Agreement defined the five different air navigation rights that have frequently been used in subsequent agreements:

- *First* – The privilege for aircraft of one state to fly across another state's territory without landing;
- *Second* – The privilege for aircraft of one state to land in another state for non-traffic purposes (for example for refuelling);
- *Third* – The privilege for aircraft of one state to bring passengers, mail and cargo from its home state to another state;
- *Fourth* – The privilege to take on board passengers, mail and cargo in another state for carriage to an aircraft's home state; and
- *Fifth* – The privilege to take on board passengers, mail and cargo in another state for carriage to a third state and to put down passengers, mail and cargo from the third state in the other state.

Sixth, Seventh and Eighth Freedom rights have also been informally recognised, along with true cabotage:

- *Sixth* – The privilege to take on board passengers, mail and cargo between two countries by an airline of a third on two routes connecting in its home country;
- *Seventh* – The privilege to take on board passengers, mail and cargo between two countries by an airline of a third on a route outside its home country;
- *Eighth* – The privilege to take on board passengers, mail and cargo within a country by an airline of another country on a route with origin/destination in its home country (also known as consecutive cabotage); and
- *True cabotage* – The privilege to take on board passengers, mail and cargo within a country by an airline of another country (ie a true domestic service).

Bilateral treaties

The Chicago Convention contemplated that parties who had not signed the Five Freedoms Agreement should regulate air services between them as they saw fit with the use of bilateral treaties negotiated between individual states. The US–UK bilateral treaty signed in Bermuda in 1946 (and updated by 'Bermuda 2' in 1977) set a precedent that has been followed and adapted in many subsequent bilateral treaties.

The principal rights granted under Bermuda 2 are:

1 the grant of the first two freedoms to each party;
2 the designation of particular carriers for carriage between the US and the UK;

3 the designation of specified routes, gateway airports and intermediate airports on which and at which aircraft of designated carriers from the other contracting state can fly and land;
4 the exclusion of rights of cabotage except in specified circumstances;
5 the grant of rights to maintain commercial support operations in the other state, such as the provision of ground handling services at specified airports;
6 the establishment of a permanent Tariff Working Group and filing requirements for tariff changes;
7 the grant of rights to operate international charter services between any point in the US and the UK; and
8 the designation of specific cargo operations.

Since 1993, the British and US governments have been negotiating the replacement of Bermuda 2 with a more liberal regime providing greater competition and more consumer choice. This replacement would be more in line with the open-skies agreement that the US signed with The Netherlands in August 1992. Negotiations towards a 'Bermuda 3' have been very slow and are still continuing despite a 'mini-deal' announced in 1995.

Negotiations have been complicated and politicised by the proposed alliance between British Airways and American Airlines. The main contentious issues in relation to Bermuda 3 are the rights of US airlines to use London, Heathrow and the rights of British airlines to access non-hub airports in the US.

The Netherlands, Germany, Belgium, Luxembourg, Austria, Finland, Sweden and Denmark have all signed bilateral US open-skies arrangements in the face of opposition from the European Commission.

To date, the EU has not had much impact on the air transport links between EU member states and non-EU countries, which are regulated by a web of bilateral treaties. However, the EU Council of Ministers decided in principle in March 1993 that negotiations with third countries may be conducted at the EU level, on a case-by-case basis, if the Council has agreed that there is a 'clearly defined common interest among EU member states' and it is apparent that a better result can be achieved for EU member states if they negotiate at the EU level rather than pursue separate bilateral negotiations. The Council reiterated its view that the European Commission's external aviation policy should be developed by the Council under Article 84(2) of the EEC Treaty, which is part of the Transport title. The Commission's view that external aviation policy recommendations and negotiations with third countries fell within its sphere under Article 113, part of the Economic Policy title, was overruled by the European Court of Justice in November 1994. Nevertheless, on 4 April 1995 the European Commission approved a draft mandate to negotiate an open-skies agreement with the US. It is not clear whether this will progress in the face of Council opposition.

The European Commission and Mr Kinnock, the current Transport Commissioner in particular, have become increasingly insistent that an EU-wide aviation agreement with the US would produce better results for individual EU member states than those that could be achieved by simple pursuit of a bilateral approach. The US has also said that it would prefer an open-skies deal with the EU, but in the absence of a single negotiating authority has approached individual EU member states.

Problems facing airlines in a Chicago system market

A major problem for the big European carriers was and continues to be that the major US airlines, after 10 years of deregulation, are generally much more efficient than they are. It is estimated that the operating costs of Europe's airlines are approximately one-and-a-half times those of America. Labour costs of the big European carriers per passenger mile are substantially more than those of the major US airlines. Airport and navigation charges are extremely high and the air traffic control system is inadequate, being currently run from 52 different centres. Add to this the inefficiencies of state-owned carriers, which may be forced by their governments to fly unprofitable routes or to retain surplus labour, and it is easy to see why the US airlines have the edge. Although the European carriers are catching up, the impediments to creating an environment in which European carriers can compete effectively were identified by a 'Committee of Wise Men' which was established in June 1993 to address these general concerns about the future of the European airline industry. The committee conducted an in-depth analysis of the situation facing the aviation industry and made recommendations to improve its competitiveness. The committee published its final report in February 1994, and its principal recommendations are as follows:

1 The European Community (EC) internal market must be made to work by enforcing its rules (eg the 'Third Package' of liberalisation measures described in the next section) and effectively addressing sensitive issues like slots, state aids, mergers and alliances.
2 As a matter of urgency, infrastructure bottlenecks must be removed, and new provisions of the Maastricht Treaty should be activated to provide EC funds needed to establish an efficient single air traffic management system and a truly European airport network.
3 Future efforts to harmonise national regulations must be linked to a clearly demonstrated cost-saving effect.
4 Innovative forms of financing investments must be facilitated by updated rules on taxation and ownership in order to help air carriers overcome their current financial problems.
5 A genuine EC approach to external aviation relations must be quickly established as this is vital for realising the economic potential of the single aviation market within the EC and for the mutual interest of the EC and its external partners.

The committee report is not a legally binding document for the EU institutions. It is, however, expected that the European Commission will consult the report in drawing up legislative proposals or applying EC law affecting air transport in the future.

The Clinton administration convened a commission with a similar remit to look into problems affecting the US airline industry and ensure its competitiveness. The commission's final report was accepted in August 1993. Its key recommendations included:

1 A move away from the bilateral regime towards negotiating multinational agreements.
2 The level of foreign shareholders' voting rights in US carriers should be raised from 25 to 49 per cent, provided that reciprocal ownership and market access rights are granted and that the investor is not state owned.
3 Permission for airlines in distress to continue using Chapter 11 bankruptcy protection, but bankruptcy court judges should be forced to impose an 'absolute limit' of one year for a bankrupt carrier to have the exclusive right to file a plan of reorganisation.
4 Airline fuel should be exempted from transportation tax; passenger ticket tax should be reduced from 10 to 8 per cent and the waybill tariff from 7 to 5 per cent.
5 The air traffic control system should be reformed and spun off to an independent body with revenue-raising powers. Policy control would, however, remain with the government.
6 Steps should be taken to remove capacity constraints – eg by federal spending on airports.

In response to the commission's report, US Transportation Secretary, Federico Pena, unveiled proposals reflecting some of its recommendations (eg 2, 3 and 5 above), but rejecting the plans for tax relief.

With regard to arrangements between the EC and other states on air transport matters, the EC entered into an agreement which came into effect in August 1993 between the EC and Norway (and also Sweden which has subsequently joined the EU) which applies the Third Package to Norway.

The EEA Agreement that came into effect at the beginning of 1994 extended EC aviation legislation (up to and including the Second Package) to the remaining EFTA states, excluding Switzerland, which, as a result of a referendum in December 1992, chose not to be a part of the EEA.

The European Commission is currently negotiating extension of the single European aviation market to 10 further Central and Eastern European countries (Poland, Czech Republic, Slovak Republic, Hungary, Bulgaria, Romania, Latvia, Lithuania, Estonia and Slovenia).

Summary

The Chicago system was founded in the context of the general belief that efficient air transport services could only be provided in an environment where carriers could operate extensive services for the public good, free from 'wasteful' competition or duplication. As the system developed, individual states were able to introduce elements of competition through the negotiation of bilateral treaties. However, the Chicago system's recognition of each state's sovereignty to its airspace enables states to exercise extensive control over the use of their airspace and the provision of air services in that airspace. This allows them to impose their own regulatory policies on significant portions of the international air transport sector, resulting (in the eyes of many commentators) in the development of an uneven playing field for airline competition.

In particular, the Chicago system encourages the development of 'flag-carriers' – usually state-owned concerns with interests that are often closely linked with those of their parent governments. The ability of states to designate particular carriers to operate specified routes allowed states to continue to protect their flag-carriers from domestic and international competition. Many states have also been prepared to subsidise heavily the operations of unprofitable and uncompetitive carriers, apparently for political or nationalistic rather than economic or consumer-driven reasons.

The Chicago system therefore erected substantial regulatory barriers to entry to new markets or expansion in existing markets. These regulatory restrictions have been compounded in recent years by restrictions on airport and airspace capacity. To date, this combination has been most restrictive in Europe, where some states have operated highly regulated markets and where air traffic congestion is at its worst. It is to be hoped that the gradual removal of regulatory restrictions within the EC following the Third Package of liberalisation measures (described in the next section) and the recommendations of the Committee of Wise Men will enable existing carriers to compete more directly with each other, and to allow new or small competitors to join the fray.

Following the US committee's recommendations to move towards multilateral air transport agreements, and the EC committee's comments on the subject, a gradual shift away from the system of bilateral agreements that has prevailed since the Chicago Convention might be engendered. Certainly, so long as national bilateral deals are prevalent, political lobbying will determine who flies where with a resulting impact on trade and business.

The EC regulatory framework
Introduction

How has the EC liberalisation been achieved so far? Articles 74 to 84 of the EEC Treaty set out the basic objectives of the European Community (EC) regarding the adoption of a common transport policy. However, as a result of the Chicago Convention and the nature of the industry that derived from this, for many years air transport was largely excluded from the normal EC competition rules (Articles 85 and 86 of the EEC Treaty, and see Council Regulation 141/62 and the decision of the ECJ in the Nouvelles Frontières case1). However, various developments over recent years have brought the EC air transport sector within the sphere of the regime for competition regulation, which in turn has led to an uneasy relationship between the increasingly different regulatory systems governing air transport within and outside the EC.

First, the Single European Act of 1986 (the SEA) made important amendments to the EEC Treaty, with effect from 1 July 1987. These amendments included a provision for the adoption of measures to create a single internal market by the end of 1992, being 'an area without frontiers in which the free movement of goods, persons, services and capital is ensured ...'. This provided fresh impetus for the inclusion of air transport in the EC competition regime. A further provision of the SEA (Article 16) amended the EEC Treaty (Article 84(2)) to allow many EC Council decisions on air transport policy to be taken by qualified majority rather than by unanimity. This alteration was considered necessary to enable the EC to extend the scope of its regulatory authority over the air transport sector in the face of anticipated opposition to reforms from certain EU member states.

Secondly, the European Commission was given power to enforce Articles 85 and 86 of the EEC Treaty in the field of international air transport services between EC airports (Council Regulation 3975/87). Air transport between the EC and non-EC countries remains outside the direct scope of Articles 85 and 86, but is within the ambit of Articles 88 and 89, meaning that either EU member states (Article 88) or the European Commission (Article 89) have certain powers to review transactions and apply the principles of Articles 85 and 86 to them. In effect, this means that EC carriers are subject to EC competition-based regulation as well as that provided by the Chicago system.

Karel van Miert, the current EU Competition Commissioner, has asserted the European Commission's power under Article 89 to investigate the proposed British Airways/American Airlines alliance, as well as retrospectively reviewing the other transatlantic alliances between Northwest/KLM, United/Lufthansa/SAS and Delta/Sabena/Swissair/Austrian. It is not clear under EU law that this approach is correct. There is a strong argument, currently being used by the UK, that each EU member state has sole jurisdiction to review proposed alliances that affect routes to non-EU countries. Indeed the UK has passed legislation enabling the UK authorities to deal with EC competition rule cases where the Commission has no power of enforcement – ie principally relating to services to non-EU states.[2]

Thirdly, Council Regulation 4064/89 (the Merger Regulation) gives the European Commission jurisdiction to review concentrations between undertakings in two circumstances, providing the applicable criteria are satisfied. The first is where aggregate worldwide turnover of the undertakings is more than ECU5 billion and where at least two undertakings have EC-wide turnover exceeding ECU250 million, unless each party achieves more than two-thirds of its EC turnover within the same EU member state. In addition, as from 1 March 1998[3], a concentration must be notified to the European Commission where:

- the combined aggregate worldwide turnover of the undertakings concerned exceeds ECU 2.5 billion;
- in each of at least three Member States, the combined aggregate turnover of all of the undertakings concerned exceeds ECU 100 million;
- in each of those same three Member States, the aggregate turnover of at least two of the undertakings concerned exceeds ECU 25 million;
- the aggregate Community-wide turnover of each of at least two undertakings concerned is more than ECU 100 million; and
- the undertakings concerned do not achieve more than two thirds of their Community-wide turnover within one and the same Member State.

The Merger Regulation has already had an impact on the air transport sector, and will become increasingly significant as carriers forge alliances to meet the demands of a more liberal and competitive EC environment.

Each area of EC competition regulation is examined in more detail in the following sub-sections.

Article 85

Article 85(1) sets out the fundamental principles prohibiting anti-competitive behaviour by two or more undertakings. For this prohibition to apply, there must exist:

1 some form of agreement or concerted action between two or more undertakings;
2 which has as its object or effect the prevention, restriction or distortion of competition within the EC; and
3 which may have some effect on trade between EU member states.

Article 85(3) authorises the European Commission to exempt practices falling within Article 85(1) if they fulfil certain criteria relating to the preservation of competition and the grant of benefits to consumers. Such exemptions may be given to entire categories of agreements by so-called 'block exemptions' issued by the European Commission, or failing which, on individual application by the parties concerned. (An example of an individual exemption was the European Commission's decision in January 1996 to exempt the Lufthansa/SAS alliance.)

Between 1987 and 1990 the initial moves towards reconciling existing regulations and practices in the air transport sector with Articles 85 and 86 were made with the adoption and implementation of the so-called first and second air transport liberalisation packages. The main elements of the first two packages and the related measures adopted at that time were as follows:

- Various EC directives and regulations under Article 84 opened up existing restrictive bilateral arrangements relating to fares, capacity-sharing, access to routes and air cargo services.
- The European Commission was given powers to enforce Articles 85 and 86 in the area of international air transport within the EC.
- Block exemptions from the effects of Article 85 were issued covering a wide range of agreements relating to air transport, including joint planning and coordination of capacity for scheduled services, sharing of revenue from scheduled services, consultations on fares and conditions for scheduled services, slot allocation and scheduling procedures at airports, cooperation on computer reservation systems, ground technical and operational handling services, in-flight catering services and consultations on cargo rates.

As a general rule, the purpose of the first two packages of liberalisation measures was to adapt existing market practices over a period of time to permit more open competition along the lines of the EC regime for regulating competition in other markets. While not rejecting the principle that each state should have some control over the operation of its air routes, the European Commission was gradually extending its authority over how that control should be exercised. The European Commission has made further proposals to obtain authority to extend its rights to apply EU competition rules to the provision of air transport services on routes to non-EU countries.

The Third Package

The Third Package of liberalisation proposals was adopted by the EC Council of Ministers in June 1992. The principal terms adopted under the Third Package were as follows:

- *Fares:* Under the Fares and Rates Regulation (2409/92), as from 1 January 1993 carriers can set their own fares on services within the EC. This is subject to safeguards against predatory (ie unreasonably low) pricing or unreasonable price rises, which will allow EU member states on either end of the relevant route to have the proposed fare change suspended while the European Commission investigates the fare structure. Charter fares can be freely set by the airlines and national authorities are no longer able to impose other restrictions (eg seat only sales) on charter services.
- *International routes:* Restrictions on international services within the EC have been lifted.
- *Consecutive cabotage:* Under the Market Access Regulation (2408/92), from 1 January 1993 until 1 April 1997, any EC carrier was able to operate domestic services in another EU member state so long as the domestic route follows on from a flight from the carrier's licensing EU member state and the passengers on the domestic route do not exceed 50 per cent of the carrier's seasonal capacity on the relevant international route.
- *Domestic routes:* EU member states were able to continue to regulate access to domestic services for their own carriers until 1 April 1997, though this had to be done on a non-discriminatory basis.
- *Full cabotage:* Full cabotage rights, whereby EC carriers can operate any domestic routes in any EU member state, were introduced from 1 April 1997.
- *Licensing rules:* Under the Licensing Regulation (2407/92), existing national rules governing the grant of operating licences to carriers were superseded from 1 January 1993 by provisions for the grant of a common EC operating licence. (This is dealt with in more detail below.)

A common feature of the regulations comprising the Third Package is that they all apply to scheduled, non-scheduled and cargo services and to both international and domestic operations within the EC.

The Third Package does not affect air transport between EU member states and non-EC countries, which continues to be regulated by the relevant bilateral treaties.

EC regulations associated with the Third Package have narrowed the scope of the original block exemptions under the First and Second Packages referred to above. Regulation 1617/93, which came into effect on 1 July 1993 and applies until 30 June 1998, exempts various categories of agreements from Article 85 only in connection with joint planning and coordination of schedules, joint operations, consultations on passenger and cargo tariffs on scheduled air services and slot allocation at airports. Regulation 3652/93, containing a revised block exemption for computerised reservation systems (CRSs), came into effect on 1 January 1994, following the adoption of a revised Code of Conduct for CRSs (Regulation 3089/93) in December 1993. The revised code reduces the advantages to airlines of owning CRSs by requiring them to create a legal and technical division between their internal reservation system and the computerised systems they offer to travel agents. The code of conduct also requires CRSs to be operated without discrimination as to access and fees between owners' flights and those of other air carriers. As CRSs are now heavily regulated and externally audited, it is not anticipated that there will be much more anti-trust activity in this area.

The European Commission has issued a number of decisions on the application of the access provisions in the Third Package:

1 In the Viva Air case,[3] the French authorities tried to stop the Spanish airline Viva Air from operating a Madrid–Paris Charles de Gaulle service on the grounds that Iberia, its parent company, already ran a Madrid–Orly service and the traffic distribution rules for the Paris airports did not allow an airline group to serve both Paris airports. The European Commission held that Viva Air had its own operating licence and should be treated separately from Iberia. It also noted that, as the Paris traffic distribution rules had not been published, the French authorities could not use them to justify traffic distribution arrangements that would otherwise be prohibited under the Market Access Regulation.

2 By the time of the TAT decision[5] (relating to Orly–London) the French government had published traffic distribution rules for the Paris airport system, which did not permit services between Orly and London. TAT (a French airline at that time 49.9 per cent owned by British Airways) complained to the European Commission that it was being prevented from operating three routes from Orly to London Gatwick, Toulouse and Marseilles, in contravention of the Third Package legislation. The French government's restrictions had also prevented a number of other British airlines from providing services from the UK to Orly airport. The European Commission's decision of 27 April 1994 upheld TAT's complaints, finding that the action of the French authorities on the domestic services constituted discriminatory practice to the advantage of Air Inter, the Air France-owned monopoly operator on the routes. On the Orly–Gatwick route, the European Commission found that the practice of restricting most intra-community flights to Paris Charles de Gaulle was contrary to the Third Package and was discriminatory. The decision came into effect immediately on the Gatwick–Orly route and after six months on domestic routes.

3 In the second TAT case, TAT applied to operate on routes from Orly to Marseilles and Toulouse, and was refused by the French authorities on the basis of Articles 3(iv) and 5 of Regulation 2408/92. Article 3(iv) permits EU member states to refuse access to domestic routes to domestic licensed carriers without discrimination where (Article 5) an exclusive concession had already been granted as at 1 January 1992. The court decided that (i) the alleged concession was discriminatory in breach of Article 8(i); (ii) the alleged concession was invalid under Article 5, as it related only to Orly (and not Paris generally). Accordingly it could not be said that there was no other transport available (Article 5), as TAT already had Paris CDG routes to Toulouse and Marseilles; (iii) the concession (to Air Inter) should have been terminated in 1990 as part of Air France's undertakings to take over UTA/Air Inter. Accordingly, any French licensed carrier could apply for such route authorities. The decision also limits the scope of the Article 5 exclusive concession defence, by bringing into the equation other airports in the same airport system, as well as road and rail links, all of which can constitute 'other transport available' for the purposes of the Article. The decision was subsequently upheld by the ECJ on appeal by Air France.[6]

4 One condition of approval for Air France's restructuring plan and related state aid was that Orly be open to EC competitors.

5 In November 1994 KLM, Lufthansa and Lauda Air lodged complaints for lack of access to Orly Airport. The French authorities brought forward the date for access to 1 January 1995, subject to capacity restraints regarding a number of flights and size of aircraft. This allowed Lauda Air, Lufthansa and KLM to operate routes from Orly.

6 On 14 March 1995 the European Commission ruled on a complaint by the United Kingdom regarding French traffic distribution rules/access to Orly as applied by Article 8.1 of Regulation 2408/92. The decision stated that (i) rules restricting number of flights and aircraft capacity were not discriminatory; (ii) the rules were disproportionate to the aim of redirecting traffic to Charles de Gaulle and should be amended for the 1996 Summer season.

7 In relation to the Orly–Bordeaux routes, it was reported that TAT and Air Liberté had been permitted to compete.

8 For an account of a further complaint, by the French independent airline AOM, in relation to Orly, see the 'Article 86' sub-section below.

Impact of the Third Package

When the Third Package was announced the provisions were perceived as a series of compromises rather than bold departures. In October 1996 the European Commission produced a report to the European Parliament evaluating the impact of the Third Package. The report notes that the effect of the liberalisation measures has been slow although satisfactory. Unlike the US experience, liberalisation in the EU has happened in a progressive way without major upsets. Although there has been no spectacular reduction in fares or any dramatic disappearance of large carriers, the number of routes has increased from 492 to 520 and there has been an increase in the level of competition on a significant number of domestic routes. Air fare reduction has only happened on routes where there are at least three operators. In particular, fares have fallen significantly on routes such as Barcelona–Madrid and London–Paris. On the other hand, most of the fully flexible fares continue to increase and some could be described as excessive.

The physical factor obstructing the aims of the Third Package is that the infrastructure necessary to cope with liberalisation, in the air and on the ground, is inadequate. However, major investment in new air traffic control systems and airport capacity is finally taking place. The more fundamental obstacle is the lack of political will among EU member state governments.

The European Commission has estimated that infrastructure charges account for 25 per cent of operational costs. These are believed to be 40 per cent higher than in the United States. These costs mainly concern ground handling, airport fees and air traffic control, and a number of steps have been taken to attempt to reduce the gap.

Ground handling

The EU adopted a directive on access to the ground handling market in the EU. The directive aims to lower costs and raise standards and also to allow airlines to self-handle if they wish. Liberalisation will take place in the following main steps (and subject to certain limited postponement and service restriction rights of EU member states):

1 From 1 January 1998 airlines will have the freedom to self-handle the following services: passenger handling, ground administration and supervision, flight operations and crew administration, aircraft maintenance, catering services, aircraft services (such as cleaning) and surface transport on any airport regardless of volume of traffic; and also the freedom to self-handle baggage handling, ramp handling, fuel and oil handling and freight and mail handling at airports with an annual traffic of at least one million passengers.
2 From 1 January 1999 airlines will have the freedom to contract-in third party handling services at airports that have annual traffic of at least three million passengers. EU member states may limit the number of suppliers with regard to certain services (but not limited to just one supplier).
3 From 1 January 2001 airlines will have full ground handling freedom at airports with at least two million passengers. Also at least one of the limited number of third party suppliers authorised with regard to certain services must be independent of the airport operator and airlines having more than 25 per cent of the traffic at that airport.

Airport fees

The European Commission has proposed a framework for airport charges in the EU based on the principles of cost-effectiveness, transparency and non-discrimination. A draft directive is awaited.

Air traffic control

On 6 March 1996 the European Commission published a White Paper on the management of air traffic, which called for a single, coherent and uniform system to be set in place throughout Europe. This proposes that the regulation and management of traffic flows be divided from other operational tasks. Supplanting existing inter-governmental structures, responsibility in the first area would be conferred to a reinvented Eurocontrol cooperating closely with a new European Air Safety Authority endowed with genuine political legitimacy. Control over operational activities such as navigation, surveillance and commercial services would be retained by EU member states.

Until the EC air network can handle significantly larger volumes of traffic, the scarcity of slots at major airports and delays due to air traffic control will constitute a formidable barrier to entry into and expansion in the EC air transport sector, whatever rights and opportunities are granted in Brussels.

Article 86

Article 86 prohibits any abuse of a dominant position in the EC or a substantial part of it, insofar as it may affect trade between EU member states. Article 86, therefore, is primarily concerned with preventing unilateral anti-competitive behaviour by a single carrier, although such behaviour by two or more dominant carriers may also fall within the ambit of the prohibition. It was held in the Ahmed Saeed case[7] that Article 86 had direct effect in EU member states in the air transport sector even before the implementation of Council Regulation 3975/87 (see above).

Article 86 can be a useful instrument for the extension of EC competition policy over existing practices in the air transport sector. For example, Aer Lingus[8] was fined ECU750,000 in 1992 for refusing to provide interlining facilities to British Midland on the London-Dublin route, and was also ordered to cooperate with British Midland on that route for two years so that interlining facilities would be guaranteed, at least until British Midland was firmly established on the route.

The application of Article 86 clearly depends heavily on the definition of the relevant geographical or product market on which the carrier may be dominant. The Aer Lingus case illustrates that a single route can, in certain circumstances, constitute a relevant market when determining whether or not a carrier has a dominant position under Article 86. The European Commission has adopted a similar approach when investigating dominant positions under the Merger Regulation.

This is likely to have significant implications for a sector that has developed on the basis of the protected markets and privileged positions deriving from the Chicago system. By definition, where only two airlines have been historically designated by their parent states to operate a particular route, they might well be considered to occupy a position of dominance for the purposes of Article 86 (depending on the availability of alternative routes). Furthermore, it is no defence to argue that alleged dominance derives from the grant of rights by an EU member state, as Article 90 of the EEC Treaty provides that EU member states granting special or exclusive rights to particular undertakings may not maintain in force any measures that are contrary to (among other things) Articles 85 and 86.

In March 1996, the French independent airline AOM submitted a complaint to the European Commission regarding a contravention of Article 86 by the French government and the Paris airports in favour of Air France. The dispute arose in January 1996 when AOM tried to reverse an agreement of December 1994 to transfer all its activities from Orly West to Orly South by the end of March 1996, a move that would allow exclusive use of the Orly West terminal for Air France. The allegations were that, in moving AOM to make room for Air France, the state-owned carrier would hold a monopoly of the West terminal, and this constituted an abuse of a dominant position in breach of Article 86.

Article 86 is relevant not only to the provision of air transport itself but also to the provision of ancillary services such as CRSs and ground handling.

Carriers may also be vulnerable because the scarcity of slots at congested airports presents a formidable obstacle to potential competitors. It is quite possible that, in certain circumstances, the use of slots to maintain a privileged position at a home base would constitute an abuse of a dominant position under Article 86. Problems of congestion and limited resources are likely to preserve many of the strong positions of larger carriers even after the regulatory system that created those positions has changed. Accordingly, Article 86 is likely to continue to play an important role in the implementation of the European Commission's philosophy.

This means that larger airlines, flag-carriers and their respective advisers must be cautious when reviewing commercial proposals that entail elements of exclusivity or discrimination. Not only does the European Commission appear keen to intervene on its own behalf, but there have also been several instances of complaints filed with the UK Civil Aviation Authority (CAA) and/or the European Commission and/or the European Court of Justice by smaller or newer airlines looking to gain ground against their larger or longer established rivals, or larger carriers looking to preserve their positions against new competitors. In the Aer Lingus decision, Sir Leon Brittan (the then head of the competition directorate at the European Commission) warned:

> This decision is evidence of the Commission's determination to act against airlines holding dominant positions, if they attempt to prevent the development or maintenance of competition. At a time when the European air transport industry is being liberalised, airlines making use of the new opportunities for competition should be given a fair chance to develop and sustain their challenge to established carriers.

The Merger Regulation (Regulation 4064/89)

Airline mergers are subject to prior notification to and clearance by the European Commission if they meet the turnover thresholds of the Merger Regulation.

Mergers falling within the Merger Regulation must be notified to the European Commission within one week of the first to occur of:

- the conclusion of the merger agreement;
- the announcement of a public bid; or
- the acquisition of a controlling interest in the target.

Failure to notify can give rise to substantial fines. The merger must be suspended for four weeks from signing and the European Commission must complete its preliminary review of the proposals within one month of notification.

Cases that give rise to serious doubts as to their compatibility with the common market (in the view of the European Commission) are subject to a further review by the European Commission of up to four months. The European Commission will block transactions that it considers would create or strengthen a dominant position that would significantly impede effective competition in the common market. Few transactions have been blocked to date,[9] although many have been investigated in depth and several have required modification in order to obtain clearance, some with conditions attached.

The first Merger Regulation decision directly involving the air transport sector was the acquisition by Delta of PanAm's Frankfurt operations in 1991.[10] Two significant factors came out of this case. The first was in relation to calculating turnover for the purpose of the Merger Regulation's thresholds and the second was in relation to definition of the relevant markets.

Article 5(1) of the Merger Regulation provides that turnover in the EC or in an EU member state shall comprise products sold or services provided in the EU or in an EU member state. This, according to the European Commission, creates three possibilities in the case of an airline merger:

- to calculate operating revenues in terms of country of destination;
- to allocate operating revenues in a 50/50 ratio between the country of origin and the country of destination; or
- to treat revenues as arising in the EU member state in which the relevant ticket sale occurred.

As the turnover thresholds for Delta/PanAm were met in all three cases, the European Commission declined to offer advice as to the circumstances in which each option should be adopted. In the more recent case of Swissair/Sabena (Case No. IV/M616), the geographic allocation of turnover was made on the basis of the 'point of sale' criterion, although the decision mentions that the 50/50 test is equally met.

The choice of methods for calculating turnover also arose in Air France/Sabena[11] and British Airways/TAT.[12] In neither case did the European Commission resolve the issue; in Air France/Sabena the 50/50 option was suggested as the preferable option, but this was not followed in BA/TAT. In its draft notice on the calculation of turnover, the European Commission suggested that airlines' turnover should be calculated by reference to the place of ticket sale. However, this reference was eventually withdrawn from the final version of the Notice.[13] The issue therefore remains unresolved, but the place of ticket sale approach probably comes closest to the general principles for calculating turnover, as set out in the Notice.

In the Delta/PanAm decision, the European Commission gave its views on market definition, and these views were further amplified in its decision in the Air France/Sabena decision. The European Commission found that the main principles of market definition in the context of scheduled air transport were as follows:

- the relevant market will be either a particular route or a bundle of routes if they are substitutable from the consumer's point of view;
- substitutability is affected by various factors, including the length of the routes, the distance between the different airports at the end of the routes forming the bundle and the number of frequencies on each route;
- it is not necessary, when looking at substitutability, to distinguish between business class, tourist class or other classes; and
- alternative methods of transport (eg charter flights, trains) generally constitute distinct markets.

In the British Airways/TAT decision, the European Commission adopted a similar approach in finding that the relevant market was for London–Paris and London–Lyons services, because the city pairs were not substitutable by other routes. This approach was subsequently upheld by the European Court of First Instance.[14]

In Swissair/Sabena,[15] the European Commission distinguished between certain routes that were treated as a market when bundled together (eg between EU departure points and various destinations in Africa) and other routes that individually constitute separate markets (such as the individual routes between Switzerland and Belgium).

So the application of a competition regime to a market developed under a previously restrictive (and therefore exclusionary) regulatory system carries dangers for many operators. As previous cases indicate that a market share of 25 per cent may be sufficient to constitute a dominant position that could be incompatible with the common market, larger carriers might encounter serious difficulties in obtaining clearance for mergers with carriers operating similar route structures.

In practice, the European Commission does appear to adopt a pragmatic, case-by-case approach to decisions under the Merger Regulation, often securing undertakings from the parties to remedy anti-competitive aspects of mergers. For example, the European Commission decided that the Air France/Sabena combination would have a monopoly or a dominant position on various routes and at Brussels airport, but nevertheless cleared the transaction when the airlines and their sponsor governments had given adequate undertakings to promote the interests of new entrants on the routes in question and at Brussels Zaventem airport.

Undertakings of a similar nature were given by British Airways to secure clearance of the British Airways/TAT transaction, in particular in relation to route access and slots (discussed later in this chapter). It may be seen from these decisions that the European Commission's chief concern is to protect the access of new entrants to routes dominated by existing carriers and also to slots at congested airports, in keeping with the policy of liberalisation underlying the Third Package.

State aids

The last area of EC competition law to be considered is that concerning state aid, which is regulated by Articles 92 to 94 of the Treaty of Rome. State aid has been one of the most controversial areas of EU aviation policy and would be again if any of the carriers that have had state aid packages approved by the European Commission were to require further aid or breached conditions regarding existing aid.

State aid is the provision of resources or other advantages, *in any form whatsoever*, by an EU member state to an undertaking. It is for the European Commission to decide whether particular aid is compatible with the EC Treaty. If the aid distorts or threatens competition then, pursuant to Article 92(1), it is likely, insofar as it affects trade between EU member states, to be regarded as incompatible with the EC Treaty.

EU member states are required to notify the European Commission before putting into effect any plans to grant or alter aid, so that the European Commission can decide whether the proposed aid is compatible with the EC, and if not, can issue proceedings. If aid is not notified until after it is put into effect, then even if it is later found to be compatible, that does not remedy the illegality. If the European Commission finds that the aid is incompatible then it can declare it incompatible with the common market, and order repayment of any sums already paid, together with interest.

The European Commission's position on state aid has gradually been clarified since early 1984 (i) by the recommendations of the Committee of Wise Men; (ii) under a communication from the European Commission dated 15 November 1994; and (iii) as a result of various decisions of the European Commission in relation to applications for approval of state aid through state-owned airlines such as Air France, Sabena, Olympic, TAP, Aer Lingus and Iberia.

The Committee of Wise Men considered the issue of state aids in its report in 1994.[16] The committee recognised that the most effective way to phase out privileged treatment of state-owned carriers would be to privatise all air carriers. It therefore exhorted governments to work towards privatisation, but recognised that privatisation normally requires prior restructuring. The committee concluded that financial support to airlines should be banned if it violates the rules of the EC Treaty by exceeding normal commercial conditions. For a brief transitional period, however, the committee agreed that there would be a need for some state-owned airlines to be given a genuine 'one time, last time' opportunity to receive state aid to set them on a sound commercial footing. The conditions of such approvals should include the following:

(a) a clear and genuine 'one time, last time' condition;
(b) the submission of a restructuring plan leading to economic and commercial viability within a specified timeframe, proven by access to commercial capital markets. The plan must attract significant interest from the private sector and ultimately lead to privatisation;
(c) the validity of such a plan and its chances of success being assessed by independent professionals, hired by the European Commission to take part in the European Commission's assessment procedure;
(d) an undertaking on the part of the government concerned to refrain from interfering, financially or otherwise, in commercial decision making by the carrier concerned;
(e) the prohibition of the airline using public money to buy or take over another air carrier or to extend its own capacities beyond overall market development. Instead, reduction of capacity should be envisaged;
(f) acceptable proof that the competitive interests of other airlines are not negatively affected; and
(g) careful monitoring, assisted by independent professional experts, of the implementation of the restructuring plan.

The 'Communication from the European Commission of 15 November 1994[17] gave guidelines for the application of Article 92 and 93 of the EC Treaty to state aids in the aviation sector. The main provisions of the guidelines are as follows:

(a) Direct aids aimed at covering operating losses on air routes are only acceptable if the aid relates to public service obligations or aid of a social character (provided it is granted without discrimination).

(b) Capital injections will not be aid if they meet the market economy investor test. This test will normally be satisfied where the structure and future prospects for the company are such that a normal return (by way of dividend payments etc) can be expected within a reasonable period.

(c) The European Commission will apply the market economy investor test to assess whether any loan financing provided by the state or by a state-controlled bank to a state-owned entity is made on normal commercial terms and whether such loans would have been available from a commercial bank. If this is not the case, the loan will constitute aid.

(d) The European Commission requires that state guarantees be contractually linked to specific conditions before it will accept them. The amount of aid that the guarantee represents is the difference between interest rates obtainable by the borrower with and without the state guarantee. If the relevant financing would not have been available at all without such a guarantee, then the entire amount of the borrowing will be considered aid.

(e) Regional aid for companies established in a disadvantaged region may be authorised pursuant to Articles 92 and 93.

(f) Aid to promote certain economic activities may be authorised pursuant to Articles 92 and 93 of the EC Treaty. Accordingly, the European Commission will be prepared to allow in certain cases state aid given in connection with a restructuring programme for an airline. Once such aid has been received, further aid will not be permitted except where this is necessitated by exceptional circumstances, unforeseeable and external to the airline in question.

(g) The privatisation of an airline may not involve aid if the disposal is made by way of an unconditional public invitation to tender on transparent and non-discriminatory terms, and certain other conditions are fulfilled. However, privatisations that do not fulfil these conditions may involve aid that will be assessed by the European Commission in the usual way.

(h) The grant of exclusive rights for activities that are accessory to air transport (such as duty-free sales) will not generally involve aid where the grantee is selected in circumstances that would be acceptable to a concession grant or operating under normal market economy conditions. In other circumstances, the grant of such exclusive rights may involve an aid element.

(i) Aid below ECU1 million over three years will qualify for an accelerated clearance procedure so long as such aid is linked to a specific investment objective. Operating aids are excluded.

Exhibit 22.1
Examples of European Commission-approved aid injections since 1990

Airline	Aid (US$ bn)
Air France	3.70
Olympic	2.30
Iberia	1.89
Alitalia	1.60
TAP	1.10
Aer Lingus	0.25
	Source: EC published data

Capital injections and state aids have certainly contributed to over-capacity and uneconomic pricing in the European aviation market. Non-aided privately owned carriers such as British Airways argue that there is distortion of competition between them and the state-owned/aided carriers.

The European Commission has approved injections of more than US$10 billion since 1990 (see Exhibit 22.1). However, it has attached some fairly stringent conditions to its approvals. For example:

Sabena (1991)
- no preferential treatment from state;
- Sabena's preference shares to be converted to ordinary shares; and
- adherence to the restructuring plan as notified to the EC.

Iberia (1992 and 1996)
- implementation of restructuring plan including:
  - salary freeze in 1995 and 1996;
  - reduction of 3,500 employees between 1996 and 1997;
  - an overall reduction in fleet size; and
  - an upgrade of software systems to improve seat capacity;
- sale of Latin American interests, (principally Aerolineas Argentinas, Austral and one third of its 38 per cent holding in Ladeco SA of Chile); and
- aid to be used to fund redundancy payments and reduce gearing.

Aer Lingus (December 1993)
- legal separation of European and transatlantic routes;
- authorisation of further equity injection subject to conditions;
- cap on UK–Ireland and Dublin–LHR route capacity to 1993 levels;
- no management interference from state;
- no acquisition of shareholdings in other carriers;
- no increase in size of fleet;
- second and third tranches of aid provisional on independent verification of implementation of proposed cost reductions; and
- no further aid.

TAP (1994)
- implementation of a restructuring plan;
- authorisation of further equity injection subject to conditions;
- tax exemption to end by end of restructuring period;
- no increases to EC market share;
- annual report to EC;
- no acquisitions of shareholdings in other carriers; and
- no further aid.

Air France (1994)
- implementation of three-year restructuring plan;
- no management interference from state;
- formal separation between Air Inter and Air France;
- capacity cap on EEA routes;

- sale of hotel chain;
- open Orly airport to competitors;
- limit on traffic growth;
- no further aid; and
- third tranche of aid conditional upon European Commission clearing Air France of accusations made by SAS of using aid to reduce fare prices (a practice expressly prohibited when the original aid was granted in 1994).

Alitalia (1997)
- Implementation of a three year restructuring plan which includes:
  - reduction by 10 per cent of Alitalia's operations (27,000 flights per year);
  - no increase in the size of the fleet;
  - selling non-core businesses (eg, 35 per cent of Hungarian airline Malev);
  - reduction in workforce by 1,200;
- not to be price leader in current markets;
- no preferential treatment from state;
- no interference in management of airline from state shareholder;
- aid to be used for restructuring not for purchasing holdings in other operators; and
- no further aid.

State aids: Olympic

The European Commission has only once refused to approve aid to an airline. On 1 May 1996 the Commission blocked a £34 million state aid package for the Greek airline Olympic following evidence that the Greek parliament had included an additional write-off for the airline without permission from the European Commission and was continuing to interfere in the airline's business. This package was to have been the second tranche of a £417 million recapitalisation plan agreed 18 months previously. The European Commission has insisted that:

- the additional write-off is deducted from the 1996 payout; and
- a written guarantee is given that the Greek government will stop interfering in the day-to-day running of the airline.

State aids: Iberia

On 31 January 1996, the European Commission approved an immediate injection of Pta87 billion (£460 million) for Iberia and left the door open for a further Pta20 billion (£106 million) in 1997, provided that certain cost savings and productivity improvements were met. It also required Iberia to sell Aerolineas Argentinas, Austral and a third of its holding in Ladeco SA (Chile). The payments were to be allowed under the market investor principle and were not classified as state aid.

State aids: VLM

The English airline Cityflyer Express, operating in Belgium with a flight from London Gatwick to Antwerp, challenged before the Court of First Instance the European Commission's decision of 26 July 1995 regarding aid granted by the Flemish Region of Belgium to the Belgian airline Vlaamse Luchttransportmaatschappij (VLM) in the form of an interest-free loan of Bfr20 million. In its decision, the European Commission had condemned the aid because it involved no interest payments and required VLM to pay interest. But Cityflyer alleged that the loan itself amounted to state aid and not just the interest-free factor, which the European Commission had failed to recognise. At the time of writing, the court's decision has not yet been issued.

State aids: Conclusion

The refusal of further aid to Olympic together with the conditions that the European Commission has attached to these approvals of state aid demonstrate the Commission's aim to enforce a tougher state aid regime. This is further highlighted by the fact that in approving second and third tranches of aid for both TAP and Aer Lingus, the European Commission employed independent auditors to ensure that both airlines had adhered to their previously submitted restructuring plans.

On the other hand, since the start of EC liberalisation in 1987, national flag-carriers still account for approximately 80 per cent of EC air traffic, and all but 10 per cent of domestic routes in the EC are operated by a single airline. Among other things this shows that, despite EC policy, the European Commission often bows to intense political pressure to allow unprofitable flag-carrying airlines to survive.

Liberalisation – conclusion

To date liberalisation has produced a relatively small increase in competition on European air routes with little effect on most fares. Any downward pressure on fares has usually been caused by a new entrant on a particular route.

In addition, the European Commission has frequently stated that it does not wish to oversee a repeat of the US form of deregulation that has led to the development of a small number of 'mega-carriers', and has drawn a distinction between 'deregulation' (as in the US) and controlled 'liberalisation' in the EC. Nevertheless, alliances between European airlines are being made at a rate that suggests that by the end of the decade European air travel may be dominated by only five or so major airlines.

For their part, EC carriers have been quick to invoke the EC competition rules as a means of reviewing the transactions of their competitors. For example:

- Air France, British Midland, Virgin and the Belgian authorities sought to prevent British Airways acquiring Dan-Air[18] by means of actions brought in the European Court of First Instance and the English Court of Appeal.
- Air France has also sought to attack the BA–TAT merger in the European Court of First Instance.
- British Airways and the UK government challenged the grant of state aid to Air France.

The cooperation agreement between SAS and Lufthansa also attracted the attention of the European Commission and other carriers. The agreement was exempted by the European Commission (decision of 16 January 1996) provided that several conditions were complied with. These included:

- Giving up slots at Frankfurt, Düsseldorf, Stockholm and Oslo airports to enable other airlines to operate competing services.

- Freezing for a defined period the number of daily frequencies on certain routes when a new entrant decided to serve one of those routes.
- Dropping agreements with other airlines. In the case of SAS this involved terminating its agreement with Swiss Air and Austrian Airlines. In the case of Lufthansa it involved terminating its agreements with Transwede and Finnair.

Finally, the aviation industry is awaiting with some anticipation the European Commission's recommendation to the Council of Ministers relating to the American Airlines/British Airways alliance. This includes a comparison with the Star and Atlantic Excellence alliances.

Slot allocation

Introduction

Slot allocation procedures are crucial for an airline's overall business for two reasons. First, certain slots have acquired significant rarity value and so might be viewed as some form of 'asset' or resource of the airline, albeit one that may not appear on the airline's balance sheet. Secondly, the unavailability of slots at congested airports plays a dominant part in shaping the competitive environment in which the airline operates. For airlines with numerous slots at important international hubs, the present system of slot allocation guarantees a significant position in certain markets and affords a degree of protection against competitors. For airlines without such slots, airport capacity restrictions can strangle attempts to develop new route systems and will nullify any attempts by the regulators to open up inter-carrier competition. The importance which regulators now place on slot allocation can be seen by the demand for British Airways to give up slots at London Heathrow as a condition for approval of its alliance with American Airlines.

Accordingly, the availability of slots has a great impact on an airline's operations and ultimately on its profitability and creditworthiness. From a financier's perspective this is not reflected in an airline's balance sheet. In most jurisdictions the relevant authorities, at least in the EC, are unwilling officially to recognise any property rights in slots, which means that they are only as secure as the administrative system allocating them allows. For example, the EC Slot Allocation Regulation provides that 'grandfather rights' will not apply to a slot used less than 80 per cent of the time it was available. Furthermore, the pool system under the EC regulation is intended to favour new entrants at the expense of other carriers. Factors such as these make it difficult on a prudent basis to attribute value to an airline in respect of its slots. However, the European Commission has indicated that it is willing to recognise that a market exists for selling airport slots, and it will be interesting to see the effect of that on airlines' financial statements.

To deal with the problem of excess demand for slots, many airports around the world use guidelines issued by IATA to allocate slots. Under the IATA guidelines, slot allocation is overseen by a scheduling committee, which will generally be comprised of representatives of the airlines using the airport. An airline wanting to land or take off at such an airport must apply to the scheduling committee for a slot, which is generally granted for a six-month season (ie summer or winter). The scheduling committee allocates slots according to the following IATA rules, which must be applied without favouritism:

1 A slot operated by an airline for scheduled services should entitle the airline to the same slot in the following season ('grandfather rights').
2 If an airline had a slot in the previous season, but used it less than a specified proportion of

the time, the slot will be allocated to another airline in the next season ('use it or lose it').

3 After slots have been allocated in accordance with grandfather rights, 50 per cent of the remaining slots should be given to airlines who qualify as 'new entrants'.

4 If two airlines compete for the same slot, the schedule that involves the most use of the slot will take priority.

5 If the procedures described above do not resolve competing demands for slots, then the scheduling committee will come to a decision reflecting the following factors:

(a) extending a schedule to operate for consecutive seasons;
(b) accommodating larger aircraft;
(c) taking account of different daylight hours in different time zones; and
(d) arranging a more practical schedule.

The EC Slot Allocation Regulation

The EC has long been concerned about the restrictions on free and open competition that result from limitations of airport and airspace capacity. While one solution would clearly be to increase capacity by developing bigger airports and more technologically advanced air transport systems, the expense and environmental obstacles to such developments have tended to concentrate efforts on the reallocation of existing resources – ie slots.

In January 1993, the EC Council of Ministers finally adopted a new regulation (Regulation 95/93) governing the allocation of slots, after many months of preparation and negotiation by the European Commission. The Slot Allocation Regulation follows many of the principles adopted by IATA, but with some variations, summarised in the following sub-sections.

Coordinated airports

The Slot Allocation Regulation requires EU member states to carry out a capacity analysis at an airport when air carriers representing more than half of the operations at the airport and/or the airport authority consider that capacity is insufficient for actual or planned operations at certain periods or when new entrants encounter serious problems in securing slots or when an EU member state considers it necessary. If the analysis does not indicate that the problems can be resolved in the short term, the airport must be designated a 'fully coordinated airport' for the periods during which capacity problems occur. Slots at fully coordinated airports must be allocated, and their use monitored, by an independent airport coordinator appointed by the relevant EU member state. The airport coordinator should be assisted by a coordination committee drawn from representatives of the participating airlines, the airport authorities and the air traffic control authorities. EU member states may provide for any airport to be designated a 'coordinated airport', provided certain principles are adhered to in its management. Most of the provisions described below in respect of fully coordinated airports apply also to coordinated airports.

Grandfather rights

Where a carrier has operated a slot that has been cleared by the coordinator, it will be entitled to operate the same slot in the next equivalent season (though see the 'Slot pools' section below).

Slot transfers

Slots may be exchanged between carriers or used by the same carrier for different routes, subject to prescribed safeguards covering the requirements of regional services and the maintenance of undistorted competition between carriers. However, slots allocated to new entrants operating an intra-EC service may not be exchanged for the first two years.

Regional services

EU member states may reserve certain slots for regional services where the route is to a peripheral or development region and is considered vital for the economic development of the region, or in order to meet EC-imposed public service obligations.

Slot pools

coordinated airports must set up slot pools for all newly created slots, unused slots and slots relinquished by other carriers. This provision is backed up by the power to withdraw slots from carriers if existing slots are not used. Furthermore, a carrier must demonstrate that it has used a series of slots for at least 80 per cent of the time during the period for which they have been allocated in order to claim grandfather rights in the next season. New entrants must be allocated at least 50 per cent of the slots available in slot pools, unless requests by new entrants amount to less than 50 per cent.

New entrants

New entrants are defined as carriers requesting slots at an airport and holding, or having been allocated, fewer than four slots at that airport on that day, or carriers requesting slots for a non-stop intra-EC service where no more than two other carriers operate a direct service on the same route on the same day and holding, or having been allocated, fewer than four slots at that airport on that day for that service. However, a carrier holding more than 3 per cent of the slots at the airport on the relevant day, or more than 2 per cent of the slots available on that day in the airport system of which that airport forms part, will not qualify as a new entrant. There is no qualification as to the applicant's size or resources in determining new entrant status.

Reciprocity

The Slot Allocation Regulation contains provisions enabling the European Commission to withdraw the benefits of the regulation from carriers from non-EC states that discriminate against EC carriers.

Review

The EC Slot Allocation Regulation contains an inbuilt review mechanism. The Department of Transport in the UK circularised UK airlines and other interested parties seeking their views, and a number of concerns were raised with the Department, including:

- the intended composition and nature of coordination committees;
- what constraints apply to the exchange or transfer of slots by air carriers;
- the procedures to be followed by air carriers with complaints about allocations, particularly in relation to what constitutes a 'new entrant';
- what constitutes the non-utilisation of a slot, triggering its return to the pool;
- whether an offer of slots within two hours of requested timing is generally to be regarded as an acceptable slot allocation.

On 25 October 1995 the Department published a paper setting out those aspects of the regulation it thought should be taken into account by the European Commission as part of its review. It deals in particular with the implementation of the regulation and proposed several modifications to the text. The concerns about the implementation of the regulation in other parts of the EC include:

- the independence of the coordinator at each airport, especially its independence from major home-based carriers;
- the right of all carriers including foreign carriers using an airport regularly to participate in the process of determining the capacity available for slot allocation at that airport;
- the establishment at each fully coordinated airport of a properly constituted coordination committee; and
- the right of all carriers including foreign carriers using an airport regularly to participate directly in the coordination committee of that airport.

Slot allocation in the UK

The EC Slot Allocation Regulation came into effect on 21 February 1993 and the measures necessary to implement it fully in the UK were contained in the Airports Slot Allocation Regulations 1993 which came into force on 12 May 1993. For the purposes of the EC Slot Allocation Regulation, Heathrow, Gatwick and Manchester are fully coordinated airports while Birmingham, Glasgow and Stansted are coordinated airports.

Although slot allocation in the UK is performed by an independent company, Airport Co-ordination Limited, the overall supervision of air traffic control and airport regulation at UK airports is the responsibility of the CAA under the Civil Aviation Act 1982. The CAA also regulates the UK airline industry and is the statutory adviser to the government on airline industry affairs.

One of the CAA's functions is to grant public use licences to airport operators under the Air Navigation Order 1985, pursuant to such conditions as it thinks fit, so long as such conditions are consistent with the CAA's statutory duties. For example, the three London airports (Heathrow, Gatwick and Stansted) are owned and operated by BAA plc, the independent company that is the privatised successor to the former British Airports Authority. BAA holds a public use licence for those airports granted by the CAA under the Air Navigation Order 1985.

Slot allocation in the US

The EC slot allocation system may be compared with that in operation in the US. In the US, the effect of wide-ranging anti-trust legislation is that air carriers cannot meet to discuss services, fares, routes or schedules. One of the results of this is that there are few restrictions at US airports limiting the allocation of landing and takeoff slots.

The most significant restriction in the US is the slot allocation mechanism run by the Federal Aviation Authority at four airports where demand for slots is particularly strong. The airports are Kennedy and LaGuardia at New York, O'Hare International at Chicago and Washington National.

The High Density Traffic Airports Rule was instituted in 1969 and provides for slots at the four airports to be divided between various types of user, covering both national and international flights. The rule itself did not provide a method for allocation of slots between airlines. Since 1986, slots have been allocated between airlines under the so-called 'buy-sell' rule introduced the previous year. The main elements of the buy-sell rule are as follows:

1 Carriers that held slots on 16 December 1985 were entitled to retain those slots without payment.
2 Any slot that is not used 65 per cent of the time in any two-month period must be returned to the FAA.
3 The separation of slot pools between various types of user established under the rule is preserved.
4 Carriers can purchase, sell, swap or lease most slots, except international slots.
5 International slots are allocated under special procedures and transfer of these slots is restricted.
6 Slots that become available are allocated by means of a lottery, and 25 per cent of available slots are reserved for 'new entrants'.

The buy-sell rule specifically provides that carriers are to have no proprietary rights in the slots held by them.

The system is widely regarded as being fairly efficient in practice, although it has been criticised for making it too difficult for new entrants to obtain slots. An easy way for an incumbent airline to prevent competition from start-up airlines at its hubs is to refuse to sell slots or price them out of the market. The commission set up by President Clinton in 1994 (see above) recommended that the FAA should 'review the rule that limits operations at 'high density' airports with the aim of either removing these artificial limits or raising them to the highest practicable level consistent with safety requirements'. However, the resulting study, published in mid-1995, recommended that the rule remain unchanged but be reviewed in the future with a view to optimising airport capacity.

Similar factors to those affecting the allocation and transfer of takeoff and landing slots affect the allocation and transfer by the US authorities of the right to fly international routes. The US International Air Transportation Policy Statement, published in April 1996, did not deal with the issue of whether it should continue to allow airlines to treat international routes allocated by the government as assets and buy and sell them for large sums.

Impact for airlines

As slots are merely permissions to land and take off at airports at specified times they could, in theory, be granted and revoked at will by the scheduling committee, although the grandfather principle has traditionally offered security of tenure for slots operated in the previous corresponding season. The introduction of a limited 'use it or lose it' principle in the EC Slot Allocation Regulation emphasises that a slot is not an asset to which a carrier has a proprietary right, although in practice it may have some rights as the 'carrier in possession'. This is in contrast to the position at certain US airports described above, where slots can be revoked by airport authorities but carriers also have the right to sell and lease slots to other carriers (but again expressly no proprietary interest). The current European Transport Commissioner has made it clear that he favours the introduction of the tradeable slot in the EU.

Financial implications

The agreements in 1990/1991 between PanAm and United Airlines and TWA and American Airlines in respect of routes to and from London Heathrow give an indication of the value attributed to regular access to a major international hub; in these cases, substantial sums were paid for intangible assets that did not appear on the seller's balance sheet. For example, American paid US$445 million for three former TWA routes to London. More recently, large sums were offered for the three transatlantic routes that USAir was forced to divest itself of in order to gain approval in the US for its tie-up with BA (see below). It seems inevitable, therefore, that any evaluation of an airline's credit or prospects must take some account of its route structure and slot portfolio. Furthermore, such a review must also examine the carrier's ability to acquire and retain slots at important hubs, because without these the airline obviously cannot maintain and expand its route network. It is no coincidence that the most congested airports lie at the ends of the most popular and profitable routes.

Airline licensing

Following the Chicago system, most countries operate a nationality qualification for the licensing of airlines. In the EU, however, it was always uncertain whether national systems for granting operating licences contravened fundamental provisions of the Treaty of Rome. Certainly, Articles 7 (non-discrimination on grounds of nationality), 52 (freedom of establishment throughout the EC) and 221 (equal treatment of nationals of other EU member states) did not sit comfortably with individual nationality requirements in respect of ownership and control of airlines, particularly after the decision in one of the Factortame cases.[19] Nevertheless, until the Third Package EU member states continued to operate licensing systems based, to a greater or lesser extent, on the nationality of the aircraft operator or owner.

The Third Package provided for common licensing requirements for air transport undertakings and obliges EU member states to grant operating licences to any undertaking that is majority owned and effectively controlled by nationals of any EU member state, provided the undertaking satisfies the common standards. Clearly, the adoption of this proposal has radically affected the policies of some EU member states and is likely to open up the air transport sector, both in terms of inter-airline competition and in terms of operators' abilities to obtain financing on aircraft registered throughout the EC.

This section reviews the EC Air Carrier Licensing Regulation and goes on to consider the licensing systems in the UK and the US.

The EC Air Carrier Licensing Regulation

The Air Carrier Licensing Regulation provides as follows:

1 EU member states shall only grant operating licences or maintain them in force where the regulation is complied with, and must do so in the case of a carrier meeting the requirements of the regulation. No carrier established in the EC can operate without an operating licence. The possession of an operating licence does not confer in itself any rights of access to specific routes or markets. The EC Market Access Regulation provides specific rights of access to intra-EC routes, while each EU member state's existing national arrangements, including

bilateral agreements, will continue for routes to non-EC countries.

2 The principal qualifications for being granted an operating licence by an EU member state include the requirements that a carrier should have its registered office and principal place of business in that EU member state, that it should be owned and continue to be owned 'directly or through majority ownership' by EU member states and/or nationals of EU member states, and that it should at all times be 'effectively controlled' by such states or persons. 'Effective control' is defined by reference to the exercise, directly or indirectly, of 'decisive influence' over the carrier in question. This means that a carrier established in an EU member state will be entitled to an operating licence from that EU member state provided it is majority-owned and controlled in any EU member state.[20]

3 New applicants for a licence must supply detailed financial information. Once a carrier has a licence, it need only notify to its licensing authority major changes in ownership (10 per cent or more) and changes in fleet size and other substantial changes in operations.

4 A carrier must supply its licensing authority annually with its audited accounts. The licensing authority may at any time require further financial and other information, in particular if there are clear indications that the carrier has run into financial problems.

5 The requirements described above in connection with the provision of information to licensing authorities do not apply to carriers operating only aircraft of less than 10 tonnes maximum takeoff weight and/or less than 20 seats. Such carriers need only satisfy a minimum capital test and be able to demonstrate their financial viability when required to do so.

6 A carrier must have at least one aircraft at its disposal, whether through ownership or lease, to qualify for a licence. Furthermore, the EU member state issuing the operating licence must require that the aircraft used by the carrier are registered, at the EU member state's option, either in its own national register or otherwise within the EC. If the EU member state takes the former course, it must allow the transfer on to its register of aircraft registered in other EU member states and aircraft owned by nationals of other EU member states, subject to airworthiness certification but without any delay or discriminatory fee.

7 The registration requirements described above can be waived by EU member states in the case of 'short-term' leases to meet temporary needs of carriers or otherwise in exceptional circumstances. It is believed that 'short-term' would normally mean a single traffic season.

8 A carrier must have a valid Air Operator's Certificate (AOC) in order to obtain an operating licence. National regulations regarding AOCs will apply until such time as the appropriate harmonised measures, which are currently being developed by the Joint Aviation Authorities, become EC law. A carrier must also be insured to cover liability in case of accidents.

9 Air carriers leasing aircraft from or to other carriers must obtain the prior approval of their licensing authorities. An EU member state may not approve a wet lease to a carrier licensed by it unless standards equivalent to those imposed by the relevant AOC are met.

The effect of the Air Carrier Licensing Regulation is that the holder of an EC operating licence (and a valid AOC issued by an EU member state) will, under the EC Market Access Regulation, have extensive access (subject, of course, to capacity constraints) to intra-EC routes. Secondly, the regulation expressly refers to the ability of EC carriers to lease aircraft registered anywhere in the EC, which will have implications for lessors and operators alike and should open up new opportunities for both.

A number of airlines are now taking advantage of fifth, sixth, seventh or eighth freedom rights available under the Third Package. For example:

- Fifth freedom: BA – Heathrow–Turin–Thessaloniki;
- Sixth freedom: BA – Oslo–Gatwick–Athens;
- Seventh freedom: TAT (BA) – Paris–Copenhagen;
- Eighth freedom: BA – Heathrow–Hanover–Leipzig.

The UK airline licensing system

The EC Air Carrier Licensing Regulation came into effect on 1 January 1993. The changes to UK law necessitated by it were made in the Licensing of Air Carriers Regulations 1992, which also came into effect on 1 January 1993 (the 1992 regulations). The 1992 regulations provide that the CAA shall be the authority in the UK whose function is to issue Operating Licences under the EC Air Carrier Licensing Regulation. The 1992 regulations also make the necessary changes to the Civil Aviation Act 1982 (the 1982 Act), the statute under which all air carriers were licensed in the UK prior to 1 January 1993.

Licences will continue to be issued by the CAA under the 1982 Act in two situations:

1 where the licence relates to a route not covered by the EC Market Access Regulation (eg routes to non-EC countries), in which case it is called a Route Licence; and
2 where the carrier is based in the Channel Islands or the Isle of Man (which are, for these purposes, outside the EC), in which case the licence is called an Air Transport Licence.

In considering an application for a Route Licence or an Air Transport Licence under the 1982 Act, the CAA must be satisfied that the applicant is controlled by EC nationals or persons who are for the time being approved by the Secretary of State.

The CAA will only grant an Operating Licence, a Route Licence or an Air Transport Licence to an applicant with a valid AOC. The CAA must grant an AOC if it is satisfied that the applicant is competent to secure the safe operation of aircraft of the types specified in the certificate, on flights of the description and for the purposes specified in the certificate. The CAA may grant the certificate subject to such conditions and for such period as it thinks fit. The CAA may also suspend or revoke the certificate and take appropriate measures to prevent the aircraft from flying if it is dissatisfied with the manner in which the aircraft is being operated.

The US airline licensing requirements

Ever since the Air Commerce Act of 1926, US policy has held that strategic reasons, both commercial and military, demand that only airlines owned and controlled by US citizens should be licensed to operate in the US. The relevant ownership restrictions are now set out in the Federal Aviation Act of 1958 (the 1958 Act). Under the 1958 Act, a US airline may only be owned by a 'citizen of the United States', who is defined as:

1 an individual who is a citizen of the United States or one of its possessions; or
2 a partnership of which each member is such an individual; or
3 a corporation or association created or organised under the laws of the United States ... of which the president and two-thirds or more of the board of directors and other managing officers thereof are such individuals and in which at least 75 per cent of the voting interest is owned or controlled by persons who are citizens of the United States or of one of its possessions.

It should be noted that the requirement is only that 75 per cent of the voting interest should be US-held, not that 75 per cent of the stock of the corporation should be US-held. This means that a foreign investor might, in theory, be able to hold more than 25 per cent of the stock of a US airline corporation, provided its share of the voting stock was no more than 25 per cent and the other conditions were also satisfied.

However, it appears that in practice the US authorities feel justified in taking a restrictive view of what constitutes foreign control. This can be seen from Secretary Skinner's comments at his confirmation hearing in 1989:

> I understand that the Federal Aviation Act already contains safeguards to prevent unwarranted foreign ownership of US carriers. The Act requires that any US air carrier be both 75 per cent owned and entirely controlled by citizens of the US. Thus, I am told that even where the numerical requirement regarding stock ownership is met, the Department examines a prospective owner carefully to ensure that no foreign entity will be in a position to exert control over a US air carrier.

Nevertheless, foreign airlines have over the years successfully acquired stakes in US airlines. For example, Ansett Airlines of Australia acquired 20 per cent of the voting stock in America West Airlines in 1987, and in 1989 KLM was allowed to take a 25 per cent stake in Northwest Airlines, carrying 5 per cent of the votes (although KLM had originally wanted to take a 57 per cent stake).

A conspicuous example of the effect of the 1958 Act was the prolonged, and ultimately successful, attempt by British Airways to take a stake in USAir. Under the original scheme announced in July 1992, British Airways would have invested US$750 million for a 44 per cent equity stake carrying 21 per cent of the votes in USAir. However, the other major US carriers lobbied vigorously against the link-up, and when it became clear to the US government that it was not going to extract from the UK the hoped-for concessions on access to the UK for US carriers, the deal was abandoned. The more modest version of the scheme eventually signed provided for British Airways to invest US$300 million for a 24.6 per cent share of the equity of USAir with 19.9 per cent of the voting stock. British Airways has subsequently sold this holding in the wake of its proposed link-up with American Airlines.

Aircraft registration

The Chicago Convention

The Chicago Convention lays down the following in relation to the nationality of aircraft:

1 that aircraft have the nationality of the state in which they are registered (Article 17);
2 that an aircraft cannot be validly registered in more than one state, but that its registration may be changed from one state to another (Article 18); and
3 that each contracting state is to adopt measures to ensure that every aircraft carrying its nationality mark, wherever such aircraft may be, shall comply with the rules and regulations relating to the manoeuvre of aircraft there in force (Article 12).

The Chicago Convention does not, however, stipulate that contracting states must adopt a common approach regarding the requirements that must be satisfied before an aircraft is entitled to be entered on their registers, nor does it require that there be any 'genuine link' between the ownership of an aircraft and its nationality. Indeed, the Chicago Convention expressly provides that each contracting state is free to regulate the registration and the transfer of registration of aircraft in accordance with its own national laws and regulations (Article 19).

Most countries' laws provide that an air carrier licensed by them can only operate using aircraft entered on their national register. The EC Third Package introduced some exceptions to this general rule.

Nationality requirements

The varying requirements of the aircraft registries of different states illustrate that there is no common approach to registration. Certain states only permit aircraft that are owned by nationals of that state to be entered on their register, while other states permit the entry on their register of aircraft that are foreign-owned but which are operated under a lease or similar arrangement by an operator who is a national of that state. Other states permit aircraft that are leased to nationals of that state to be entered on their register, even though the aircraft are sub-leased to operators established outside the state in question. In the case of owners or operators that are corporations, the nationality requirements of certain states will be satisfied if the owner or operator is simply incorporated in the state in question, while other states impose additional requirements as to the nationality of the management and/or shareholders of the owner or operator. The result of this divergence of approach is that an aircraft may, at first sight, be eligible for registration in more than one state, which means that the parties to an aircraft financing transaction may have a choice of countries in which the aircraft in question may be registered.

Registration and the EC Third Package

Aircraft registration was not addressed as a separate issue by the Third Package of air transport liberalisation measures. However, measures adopted under the Third Package have significant implications for the registration of aircraft in the EC. The relevant measures are contained in the EC Air Carrier Licensing Regulation referred to earlier, which states in its recitals that 'within the internal market, air carriers should be able to use aircraft owned anywhere in the Community, without prejudice to the responsibilities of the licensing EU member state with respect to the technical fitness of the carrier'. Articles 8 and 10 of the EC Air Carrier Licensing Regulation contain the specific provisions, the effect of which is as follows:

1 The basic rule is that aircraft operated by an EC licensed air carrier should be registered, at the option of the EU member state issuing the licence, in its national register or within the EC.
2 The first exception to the rule in 1 above is that an EU member state may not require an aircraft that is leased to be registered on its own register if:
   (a) the aircraft is registered within the EC;
   (b) the lease has been approved by the appropriate licensing authority; and
   (c) the registration of the aircraft would necessitate structural changes to it.
3 An EU member state may grant a waiver of the rule in 1 above in the case of 'short-term lease agreements to meet temporary needs of the air carrier or otherwise in exceptional circumstances'.
4 When applying the rule in 1 above, EU member states must accept on their national registers aircraft owned by nationals of other EU member states and transfers from registers of other EU member states without any discriminatory fee and without delay (subject to airworthiness certification).

Most EU member states have required the owners (or operators) of aircraft registered in their territory to satisfy a local nationality requirement. The rules under the Third Package effectively overrule any such requirement to the extent described above, although it seems fairly clear (after the decision in Factortame) that, as regards nationals of EU member states, such requirements are anyway inconsistent with EC law.

Code-sharing

Introduction

Airlines have realised that given the scarcity of slots, regulatory constraints and imperfect load factors, it would make sense to 'share flights' with other operators. Code-sharing can take several forms. The essence is that two or more carriers, each under its own (or their combined) designator code(s) and/or flight number(s), sell seats on a single flight provided by the operating partner. Usually, the code-shared flight connects to a flight operated by the code-sharing partner. By attaching its designator code (and same flight number) to both flights, the code-sharing partner is able to market and sell both flights as if the connection would be on-line (connecting to a flight of the same air carrier) instead of inter-line (connecting to a flight of another air carrier). Code-sharing is sometimes described as interlining under the airline's own code and is generally considered to bring advantages to consumers (in terms of check-in procedures, flight connections and extended frequent flier benefits) so long as the details of the airlines involved are clearly published. Code-sharing is also argued to be pro-competitive in that it enables carriers to market their services on routes that they are unable to operate themselves, on account of either capacity or regulatory constraints.

As code-sharing has become more common, it has begun to attract attention from competition/anti-trust authorities. The concern has been that the ability to enter new markets by partnership rather than by competition might reinforce the position of incumbent carriers on lucrative routes, permit carriers to divide such routes between them and raise barriers to entry to potential competitors.

Concern has also been voiced that unless fare-paying passengers are kept fully aware of the code-sharing arrangements they may be paying for a service they did not choose.

Almost every major airline now has a web of code-sharing agreements with other airlines, which range from simple block-seating arrangements to full strategic alliances. The most powerful of the latter is the 'Star' alliance between Lufthansa, United Airlines, Air Canada, SAS, Thai Airways International and Varig. Others include Northwest and KLM; British Airways and Qantas; and Swissair, Sabena, Austrian Airlines and Delta Airlines (known as 'Atlantic Excellence'). Such partnerships stem from the belief that the competitive airlines of the future will be those that can offer the most extensive full-service global network. In search of 'global reach', these airlines are building cooperative networks to tap into worldwide traffic flows, especially between the 'triad' markets of North America, Western Europe and the Far East. All of these alliances are subject to current speculation or announcements that new members will be invited to join.

Smaller regional airlines can also use code-sharing arrangements to increase potential on short-haul routes. For example the UK's British Midland has used its extensive domestic route network and slot allocations at Heathrow to attract partners who can then offer passengers a variety of destinations in the UK.

EC competition law

Code-sharing agreements may fall within the ambit of Article 85(1) as agreements that affect trade between EU member states, if their object or effect is to restrain competition. Where one of the two participating carriers ceases to operate a route that both formerly served, this would appear to reduce/restrain competition.

Code-sharing may also amount to an infringement of Article 86 where the effect is to establish dominance in the relevant market (eg the route between two cities) and where there is evidence of abusive conduct, such as an attempt to eliminate other competition from the route or restrict competitors' access to the route.

Authorisation in the UK

In the UK, it is generally the responsibility of the foreign party to a proposed code-share to apply to the UK Department of Transport (UK DOT) under its operating permit if it is intending to operate code-share agreements with a UK airline through any point in the UK. The procedure would be to notify the UK DOT of the agreement. The UK DOT is particularly interested in checking flight schedules to ensure that the timing of flights link up.

As regards the US and UK, the whole process is now simpler since the 'mini-deal' between the US and the UK has been signed and the code-sharing arrangements restrictions have been appreciably liberalised.

An authorisation is in the form of a reissued operating permit that will clearly state the code-sharing agreement. No notification is necessary to the CAA because the operating permit will be copied to them from the UK DOT.

It is also a condition for an operating permit that the airline undertakes responsibility to make clear to customers exactly who will be operating the aircraft they are travelling on.

If any flight is into other countries (regardless of whether within the EC) the authorisation is a separate issue for each country, and depends upon the bilateral agreement with that country.

The process of authorisation only takes a few days and in practice the UK DOT is notified some months in advance of code-sharing agreements coming into operation.

Conclusions

The air transport industry is going through a period of considerable change which, to an extent, has been disguised by the current generally strong financial performance of airlines in almost every sector. Three factors can be seen to be underlying this change: deregulation in the US and the development of a liberalised regime in the EC, the growth of global carriers and predicted long-term increases in demand putting pressure on existing capacity worldwide, but particularly in the EC. Liberalisation in the Asian and other markets is moving at a slower pace.

These factors will undoubtedly alter the landscape for operators in the air transport sector, although changes will continue to arise only after they have been thoroughly debated and the necessary political will is present. Large carriers will have to be more careful to avoid falling foul of the competition regulators in the way they operate. We have already seen the delays and uncertainty surrounding the British Airways/American Airlines alliance caused by regulatory issues. Nevertheless, the scramble by large carriers to forge alliances with carriers in other lucrative markets will continue and it will be interesting to observe who the winners and losers will be. Medium-sized carriers may be faced with a choice – to grow to compete with the large carriers, or to concentrate on niche markets and risk competition with smaller carriers. For new and niche carriers there will be opportunities for expansion and development, but the costs of operation and competition are likely to rise, along with the risks of making the attempt. The new wave of low-cost carriers in the EC is adding to the size of the market (ie creating more passengers) rather than taking business away from existing operators. However, established carriers will act to protect their markets and, ironically, this may lead to re-regulation to protect new entrants. All carriers should be keeping a watchful eye on the possibility of a downturn in the aviation market and how liberalisation measures would affect them then.

In the EC, liberalisation measures that have been implemented or proposed will tend to favour the more efficient operators, and a consolidation of air carriers is already under way. However, infrastructure limitations will continue to restrict progress to open competition. Gradual moves towards bringing relations with third countries under the control of the EC are likely to reinforce this trend in the long term.

It will be important for all those connected with the air transport sector to keep up with the changes taking place. These will have direct consequences for the businesses of operators and financiers and also for the travelling public.

Notes

1. *Ministère Public v Asjes* [1986] 3 CMLR 173.
2. EC Competition Law (Articles 88 and 89) Enforcement Regulations 1996, SI 1996, 2199.
3. This second threshold test was introduced by Council Regulation No 1310/97
4. *Viva Air,* Case No. VII/AMA/I/93.
5. *TAT,* Case Nos. VII/AMA/II/93 and VII/AMA/IV/93.
6. Case No. VII/AMA/IV/1993 (OJ 1994 Air 127, page 32).
7. *Ahmed Saeed Flugreisen v Zentrale zur Bekämpfung unlauteren Wettbewerbs* [1990] 4 CMLR 102.
8. *British Midland v Aer Lingus* [1992] 4 CMLR 337.
9. *Aérospatiale-Alenia/De Havilland,* Case No. IV/M053; *MSG Media Service,* Case No. IV/M969; *Nordic Satellite Distribution,* Case No. IV/M490; *RTL/Veronica/Endemol,* Case No. IV/M322; and *Gencor/Lonrho.*
10. *Delta Air Lines/Pan Am,* Case No. IV/M130.
11. *Air France/Sabena,* Case No. IV/M157.
12. *British Airways/TAT,* Case no. IV/259.
13. Commission Notice 94/C 385/04.
14. *Air France v Commission,* CFI ICH 19 May 1994.
15. *Swissair/Sabena,* Case No. IV/M616.
16. *Expanding Horizons.* A report by the Comité des Sages for Air Transport to the European Commission, January 1994.
17. VII/C/2 – 88/1/94 Rev 2.
18. *British Airways/Dan Air,* Case No. IV/M278 and Case No. C-274/94.
19. *Commission v UK* [1991] 3 CMLR 706.
20. For an examination of how nationality issues arise, see Commission decision 95/404 [1995] OJ L239/19 relating to the Swissair equity participation in Sabena.

23 International conventions affecting aircraft financing transactions

Stephen McGairl

The role of international law

Aircraft financing is essentially an international activity. The funding can come from anywhere. The tax structuring may straddle several countries and the asset is constantly on the move. And yet the legal structures that are available to put together a financing, and the legal remedies available when it goes wrong, are largely structures and remedies of one or more national legal systems and most of the relevant law was developed in the context of domestic consumer transactions. The role of international law in these international transactions is very small. It is worth examining the reasons why there is not more international law and the reason why the situation may need to change.

Governments have, to a certain extent, protected financiers from many of the difficult issues arising from aircraft financing. They have been sovereign borrowers where the national airline was being financed. They have been lenders and risk takers, through export credit agency support, where the objective of extending a manufacturer's markets was sufficient reason for accepting legal risks arising in those countries.

The process of creating international law through conventions is long and difficult. Typically, much of the preparatory work is undertaken by academic and government lawyers with relatively low levels of involvement of practitioners. The final form of any convention emerges from a diplomatic conference at which governments negotiate compromises and the outcome can be soft and unspecific language designed to accommodate different national views. The results, not surprisingly, disappoint practitioners and provide material for many years of debate among practitioners and academics as to what the convention actually means.[1]

For a convention to have any impact on the way international transactions are carried out it needs to achieve wide enough support to be ratified by a large number of countries. Those preparing conventions have to face the dilemma that a bold convention, the terms of which would provide a real solution to a problem, may be unpalatable to enough countries to mean that it only actually applies in a small number of cases. Conversely, a convention that is universally acceptable may be so because it does not achieve anything very radical and therefore is of little real value.

The extent of anticipated demand for new aircraft, the emergence of substantial new markets, the gradual disengagement of governments from airline ownership and pressure on government funds for export support all mean that new sources of funding and a different approach to risk taking may be needed in future. This throws into focus the deficiencies of national legal systems and current international law to deal adequately with the issues that affect international aircraft finance. Pure asset-based finance depends on eliminating the uncertainties of a financier's repossession rights. This will be essential to attracting sufficient funds to meet the demand for new aircraft that manufacturers currently anticipate. International law could achieve this, leaving the financiers to price their product on the basis of credit risk and asset value risk without a further premium for legal uncertainty.

If an aircraft financier drew up a list of the sort of legal issues that might impede an aircraft financing transaction in a particular country and which merit international solutions, the list might include the following:

- non-recognition of the lessor's title or interest;
- unreliable or slow judicial repossession remedies;
- non-recognition of security interests;
- volatile local laws and taxation system;
- deregistration concerns;
- bankruptcy laws that impede repossession of leased assets;
- confiscation, requisition and detention risks;
- non-acceptance of the parties' own choice of law and allocation of risks and responsibilities;
- non-recognition of a judgment obtained in the forum chosen by the parties for dispute resolution.

This chapter describes some existing conventions and one proposed convention to examine how useful international law is, or could become, in dealing with these issues of concern for aircraft financing.

Existing international conventions

Matters already the subject of international conventions include arrest of aircraft, choice of law, choice of jurisdiction, enforcement of judgments and arbitral awards, the recognition of proprietary rights and international leasing.

Arrest of aircraft

The Rome Convention on Precautionary Arrest 1933

A number of countries have provisions in their laws protecting from arrest or seizure aircraft used for public transport. Such laws are relevant where enforcement is sought in the airline's home country.

Internationally, some protection is available to airlines in the 28 countries that are parties to the 1933 Rome Convention on Precautionary Arrest, which aims to protect an aircraft registered in a contracting state from arrest or detention in another contracting state in the following circumstances:

1 the arrest must be a form of pre-trial or interim relief, rather than enforcement of a judgment debt;
2 the aircraft must be (a) appropriated to a state service, including postal service; (b) actually being used for public transport; or (c) appropriated to public transport, unless the debt being enforced relates to the journey the aircraft is about to make;
3 the arrest must not relate to insolvency proceedings or the enforcement of customs or criminal laws.

The protection is immunity from arrest, or if that does not work, a liability for damages on the arresting creditor. Where arrest is permitted, it can always be lifted by the deposit of an appropriate bond for the disputed amount.

Choice of law

The Rome Convention on the Law Applicable to Contractual Obligations 1980 and the Inter-American Convention on the Law Applicable to International Contracts 1994

In international transactions there is a tendency to choose a governing law for reasons of familiarity and certainty rather than necessarily on the basis of the closest connection with the contracting parties. Indeed, the choice may be made precisely so as not to have a connection with the airline and to give the lessor or lender some protection against adverse changes in the law of the airline's country. In each case the legal basis for the choice must be examined and, if necessary, tested against the mandatory rules of the legal system that has been displaced by the choice.

Is an airline from country X allowed, under the laws of country X, to choose English law to govern its obligations? It is generally only in the courts of country X that this is going to be an issue. The answer may be:

- the national airline cannot be subject to a foreign law – an argument sometimes raised but usually not sustained when challenged;
- a foreign law can be chosen provided that one of the parties is a non-resident of the country whose law would otherwise have applied;
- a foreign law can be freely chosen provided that it was a bona fide choice not made to avoid mandatory rules that would otherwise have applied.

International law provides an answer in the case of matters heard by courts in European Union countries. The Rome Convention of 1980, now adopted by most countries within the EU, codifies the liberal view of choices of law.

Having excluded from its scope certain types of legal questions (such as legal capacity, family matters, negotiable instruments, arbitration and jurisdiction agreements, corporate law issues, agency, trusts and procedural matters), the Rome Convention states its principal rule: 'A contract shall be governed by the law chosen by the parties'.

The Rome Convention applies to the contractual relations of the parties. It does not displace the rules applying to transfers of title or the creation of security interests, as to which the applicable provision of the *lex situs* of the aircraft may need to be observed. Nor does the Rome Convention affect the applicability of any bankruptcy law.

The Rome Convention applies even where a transaction is wholly domestic (ie where all parties are in the same country), subject to the continued application of any mandatory rules of that country. As it applies in England, the Rome Convention rule would be the basis for the validity of a choice of any foreign law. There need be no other EU connection.

In an international transaction the rule is subject to two qualifications:

1 Effect may be given to mandatory rules of the law of a country with which the transaction has a close connection if under that law those rules are to apply irrespective of the law applicable to the contract, the court having considered the nature, purpose and consequences of those rules. (This is perhaps one of the most unsatisfactory parts of the Rome Convention

leading to uncertainty and a risk of the parties' intentions being overridden. This qualification does not apply to actions brought in the English courts.)

2 Mandatory rules of the law of the country in whose court the contract is being litigated may override the chosen law if that is the effect of those rules. (This would allow an English court to apply its rule that it will not enforce a contract that would be illegal in the place where it is to be performed, notwithstanding the parties' choice of law.)

The Inter-American Convention on the Law Applicable to International Contracts of 1994 is in very similar terms to the Rome Convention, with the courts of contracting states applying the chosen law even if the chosen law is not that of a contracting state. It contains similar qualifications of the parties' choice by reference to the mandatory rules of the forum displacing the chosen law and the possible application of the mandatory rules of the country with which the contract has 'close ties'.

Jurisdiction, enforcement of judgments and arbitral awards

The Brussels Convention on Jurisdiction and the Enforcement of Judgments in Civil and Commercial Matters 1968 and the New York Convention on the Recognition and Enforcement of Foreign Arbitral Awards 1958

Each country has its own rules as to whether its courts:

1 will accept jurisdiction in any particular case;
2 will accept that the courts of another country have jurisdiction in any particular case; or
3 will enforce judgments issued by a court of another country.

In aircraft financing transactions where the parties and their assets are often spread worldwide, these are important questions. The defendant in an enforcement action may have assets in lots of places or the aircraft may be the only relevant asset. Plaintiffs will want to balance the likelihood of succeeding in their action in a jurisdiction in whose courts they have confidence with the need to obtain a speedy right of attachment on assets that may be located somewhere else. These decisions are frequently difficult and rely on an assessment of the likelihood of a challenge to jurisdiction or of a challenge to the enforceability of a resulting judgment.

There are many bilateral treaties on the enforcement of judgments, but a more ambitious piece of international law is the Brussels Convention of 1968, which operates between most EU member states, and the Lugano Convention of 1988 which is in the same form but extends its provisions to EFTA members.

The Brussels Convention has been much discussed in legal textbooks and its detailed technical provisions are beyond the scope of this work. Essentially it establishes a set of rules that determine which European country has jurisdiction for civil and commercial matters. The basic rule is that, where the defendant is domiciled in a contracting state, jurisdiction should be in the courts of the defendant's domicile.

A choice of jurisdiction in a court of a contracting state given by contract (even though the parties may not be domiciled in a contracting state) will, however, be recognised under the Brussels Convention by the courts of contracting states and the courts of other contracting states will refuse jurisdiction.

A judgment of a court of a contracting state will be directly enforceable in the courts of other contracting states without any re-examination of the merits of the case. While this is subject to the usual qualifications relating to procedural compliance and the public policy of the contracting state where enforcement is sought, the refusal to enforce on such grounds would be subject to review by the European Court of Justice. Outside the scope of the Brussels Convention, enforcement of judgments without a re-examination of the merits would depend on there being a relevant bilateral treaty in place.

For many parts of the world a more effective international regime is that applicable to arbitral awards. The New York Convention on the Recognition and Enforcement of Foreign Arbitral Awards of 1958 has been ratified by 114 countries and is actually applied in some that have not formally ratified it – for example, in some of the countries of the former Soviet Union.

It provides for arbitral awards to be enforced in contracting states without a re-examination of the merits of the case, subject to the qualifications of procedural compliance and public policy. The coverage of the New York Convention makes arbitration a useful option for dispute resolution in many emerging markets.

Recognition of proprietary interests

The Geneva Convention 1948

Ownership, leases and mortgages are created under the rules of a national legal system. There is no international legal regime relating to property rights. Because of the mobility of aircraft, issues arising from ownership, leases and security interests may well have to be decided in a different country, which has different legal concepts, and, in particular, different rules about the priority of those legal rights, from that where the rights were created.

The Geneva Convention was an attempt to deal with this problem by displacing existing conflict of laws rules and allowing aircraft to carry with them the legal attributes of their country of registration.

The Geneva Convention regime did not require any contracting state to make changes to its own laws on property rights, but required it to accept that any aircraft arriving on its territory under the flag of another Geneva Convention country carried with it the legal rights and property interests created and duly registered under the law of that country.

Basic principle of recognition

Each contracting state undertakes to recognise property rights in aircraft that have been created in accordance with the law of another contracting state, that is the country of registration of the aircraft, and which rights are recorded in a public register in that country. The rights so recognised are:

1 rights of property;
2 rights to acquire coupled with possession;
3 rights to possession under leases of six months or more;
4 security interests.

Registration

The aircraft's certificate of registration shows where the public register of property rights is to be found. The particulars recorded must be available to any person in the form of a certified copy or extract, and all matters recorded must appear in the same record.

Priority rule

While any contracting state may recognise rights in aircraft other than those specified in the Geneva Convention, the rights specified in the Geneva Convention should have priority. The priority of the rights specified in the Geneva Convention is determined in accordance with the law of the country of registration.

Special priority is accorded to salvage compensation and extraordinary expenses indispensable for the preservation of the aircraft incurred in a contracting state (not necessarily the state of registration). This priority lasts for three months and thereafter only if the claim is noted on the register.

Enforcement by sale

While the existence and priority of rights in aircraft are to be determined in accordance with the law of the state of registration, the procedure for enforcement by sale is determined by the Geneva Convention and by the law of the place where the execution sale takes place.

The Geneva Convention prescribes periods of notice, protection for superior creditors and protection for purchasers where the Geneva Convention's procedures have been observed.

Transfers between contracting states' registers

An aircraft registered in a contracting state will not be transferred to the register of another contracting state without the consent or discharge of all holders of recorded rights.

What happens where the Geneva Convention does not apply?

If enforcement of a property right such as a security interest takes place in a non-Convention state, the court in the jurisdiction of enforcement would first need to consider its own conflict of laws rules to decide what law governs the question of validity. Many countries use as their starting point for this question the *lex situs* – that is the law of the place where the aircraft was at the time that the security interest was created. If this rule was applied universally and consistently it would in fact achieve substantially the same sort of result as the Geneva Convention.

However, the *lex situs* rule does not always solve the problems of mobile assets such as aircraft. Some countries will only apply the law of the place where the aircraft was at the time of creation of the security if the security interest is analogous to a security interest of a type found in the law of the place of enforcement. If this place of enforcement is a civil law country having a precisely defined list of security interests that can be created there, a foreign security interest created in a common law country and not corresponding to any security interest known in the law of the place of enforcement may be held to be invalid. As a general principle, civil law does not accept security interests in mobile equipment where the debtor remains in possession, although this principle is modified to different degrees in civil law countries.

If validity is established, the priority of the creditor holding the foreign security interest is likely to be determined in accordance with the priority rules of the jurisdiction of enforcement, taking account of local creditors and any locally created competing securities.

Problems with the Geneva Convention

The difficulties for countries considering ratifying the Geneva Convention were that:

1 They might be obliged to give effect to property rights, particularly security interests, of a type that could not exist under their own legal system.

2 They would have to accept rules of priority of security interests that significantly reduced the rights of government agencies to attach aircraft for unpaid taxes, landing charges and such like.

The Geneva Convention has been signed by 79 countries; 69 have ratified it, but significant areas of the world have not. Canada, Australia, Japan and the United Kingdom, for example, have presumably decided that they can get their aircraft financed without having to sacrifice their rights of detention and attachment. Because the Geneva Convention can only work where an aircraft registered in one contracting state is the subject of legal proceedings in another contracting state, financiers of aircraft involved in international traffic have to discount the Geneva Convention benefit because of the real risk of proceedings taking place in a non-contracting state.

International leasing

The Ottawa Convention 1988

The Ottawa Convention describes its objectives as being to:

1 remove legal impediments to the international financial leasing of equipment;
2 maintain a fair balance of interests between the different parties to the transaction;
3 make international financial leasing more available;
4 adapt the rules of law governing the traditional contract of hire to the 'distinctive triangular relationship' of the financial leasing transaction; and
5 formulate certain uniform rules relating primarily to the civil and commercial law aspects of international financial leasing.

This list of objectives immediately raises questions as to whether all of the items on the list were appropriate in the context of the sort of high-value transactions that are structured as international leases.

Much of the Ottawa Convention prescribes rules for the contractual relationship between the lessor, the lessee and the supplier. For aircraft finance transactions these are largely irrelevant because the parties will invariably write their own, much more detailed, provisions making their own allocation of risks and responsibilities.

The Ottawa Convention also deals with the issues of the recognition of a lessor's rights as against third parties and a lessor's liability for damage caused by an aircraft. These are clearly matters that merit an international law approach, although the Ottawa Convention does not in any way dispose of them.

The lessor's real rights

Article 7.1 declares that the lessor's 'real rights' in the equipment shall be valid against the lessee's trustee in bankruptcy and creditors.

This is an important statement of principle. The courts of a small number of countries have been too inclined to ignore the legal structure of transactions chosen by the parties and to deal with competing creditors as if a leasing transaction was really a loan. In the case of aircraft, the recognition of the lessor's real rights is subject to compliance with any public notice requirements – for example, registration in the country where the aircraft is registered.

It is not easy, however, to decide where the limits of this provision lie. Which lessors have 'real rights'? Which country's legal system is to answer the question? If the lessor is the owner then its rights would probably be considered 'real' (in the sense of being capable of being defended against third parties) in most countries. Whether an intermediate lessor's rights are real is much more problematical.

If a lessor has real rights it is not normally because it is a lessor, but because it has rights in another capacity – eg as owner. An intermediate lessor in a chain of leases will probably have rights only as lessee under a superior lease. In the absence of guidance in the Ottawa Convention it will probably be the court being asked to enforce the rights (for example the bankruptcy court of the airline's home country), and the court would apply its own legal principles to answer the question. In other words, the result would be unpredictable.

A lessor who also had a mortgage granted to it by a superior lessor or owner would also presumably be able to invoke the Ottawa Convention to assert the validity of its mortgage rights in the aircraft of which it is lessor.

In a complex multi-party transaction it may be that only one of the parties (the legal owner at the top of the chain for example) is able to benefit from the Ottawa Convention. No protection is given to operating lessors, although, as is always the case with attempts to define the difference between finance and operating leases, the boundaries are imprecise.

Third party liability

Article 8, paragraph 1.b provides that: 'The lessor shall not, in its capacity as lessor, be liable to third parties for death, personal injury or damage to property caused by the equipment'. Again this is an important statement of principle, although its practical effect will be very limited.

The protection does not apply to liability arising from any other capacity that the lessor has in relation to the aircraft. If the other capacity was manufacturer this would be a sensible distinction to make. A manufacturer's product liability is wholly different in nature from the liability of a finance company in a leasing transaction. However, if the lessor is also the owner the Ottawa Convention gives no protection for liabilities arising in the capacity of owner.

It is the strict (ie no fault) liability that is most of concern to finance companies. In the UK, for example, there is strict liability on owners of aircraft, not on lessors, so the Ottawa Convention does not help. Perhaps here the intermediate lessor is better off than the owner/lessor at the top of the lease chain, although the intermediate lessor might conceivably have some liability arising from its capacity as lessee under its head lease.

Any convention limiting third party liability is of value if a sufficient number of countries ratifies it so that it is more likely than not that the limitation will apply to any particular incident. The Ottawa Convention has so far been ratified by only five countries.

Prospective international law

The Unidroit Convention on International Interests in Mobile Equipment

Unidroit has been working for a number of years on a convention to provide an international legal regime for leases, conditional sales and security interests in high-value mobile equipment. The proposed convention is ambitious as it prescribes rules of enforcement and priority that would override relevant national laws. The expectation is that this would be acceptable because of the extremely narrow scope of the convention. Special enforcement and priority rules that only applied to aircraft and certain other high-value equipment would not mean that a contracting state's laws were fundamentally undermined.

Types of equipment

The draft convention contains a list of types of equipment to which the convention might apply, but in relation to each type of equipment the convention would come into force only when there was also a protocol relating to the specific equipment concerned. An aircraft protocol is at an advanced stage of preparation, having been considered by many industry representatives and having received support in particular from leading manufacturers and from IATA and ICAO. The function of the protocol is to adapt the basic principles of the convention to the particular circumstances of the equipment concerned, as further described below.

Remedies

The draft convention sets out the default remedies that the holder of an international interest would be allowed to exercise in the relevant contracting state. It is in the exercise of remedies by a lessor or secured creditor that there is the greatest divergence between civil law and common law legal systems. While in common law countries a creditor may typically exercise self-help remedies subject to an obligation to do so in a manner that does not disregard the interests of other parties, civil law countries typically protect the interests of other parties by requiring enforcement action to be taken through judicial proceedings only. The draft convention addresses this issue by providing for a range of remedies that the creditor can exercise, subject to a duty to exercise them 'in a commercially reasonable manner'. It then provides that a contracting state may, in its instrument of ratification of the convention, declare that those remedies can only be exercised in that country with the leave of the court.

In view of the fact that the proposed convention would only apply to high-value equipment, the draft convention provides that the test of what is 'a commercially reasonably manner' for the purposes of enforcement action, and the determination of the events that can give rise to an entitlement to exercise remedies under the convention, should be left primarily to the agreement of the parties.

The provision of effective and speedy remedies for creditors is one of the objectives of the convention and the draft lists a number of types of interim judicial relief that a creditor should be entitled to when the asset is in a contracting state, whether or not any substantive dispute is being dealt with in the courts of that country.

The remedies provided include taking possession, control, custody or management of the equipment and selling or leasing it. This is an important aspect of asset finance protection. Without it, lenders and lessors need to add other layers of security to cover a period when the lessee has defaulted but the principal security – the equipment – is simply not available.

International registry

The international interest created pursuant to the proposed convention would be registered in an international registry especially established for the purpose. The registry would contain entries of the international interests themselves, prospective international interests (to assist in closing transactions), assignments and prospective assignments of international interests and subordination of interests. Much of the detail of registration would be dealt with in the equipment-specific protocols.

One of the guiding principles of those preparing the convention has been to try to construct a system that has the highest possible degree of certainty in its effects. For this purpose the priority rules are, compared with some rules of domestic law, strict, or even brutal. The convention is only designed for high-value transactions between sophisticated parties and for that purpose total reliance on, and confidence in, the information shown in the register at any time is the most satisfactory approach.

The register is therefore conclusive as to the priority of competing interests. This may either be a question of the time of registration of interests or a reflection of the terms of a subordination agreement that has itself been entered on the register.

Assignments

In order to permit lease security assignments, portfolio sales, securitisations and such like transactions to benefit from the provisions of the convention, assignments of international interests are dealt with extensively to provide substantially the same level of protection to the assignee of an interest as to the original grantee.

Optional provisions

One of the issues that caused governments to be reluctant to ratify the Geneva Convention was the strict rule of that convention that subordinated non-consensual liens such as tax liens to the rights recognised under the convention. In order to try to avoid the fate of the proposed convention depending on whether a particular government is or is not prepared to give up its tax liens, the draft of the convention envisages that contracting states will be able to choose the position they take in relation to such non-consensual rights and interests. In this way, although the convention will not be quite as kind to secured creditors in those countries that have made that reservation, it will at least provide most of the benefits of the convention and secured creditors will have to take account of the tax lien risk in that country.

The aircraft protocol

At the time of writing, work on the preparation of the aircraft protocol is proceeding with the enthusiastic participation of representatives of the aviation industry. This is driven by the desire to lower the risk premium attached to financing in many countries of the world and to enable finance to be provided from a broader range of sources, including those that depend on the availability of investment ratings.

Being equipment-specific, the protocol is able to address a number of the principles set out in the draft convention and propose even more rigorous application of those principles to the specific context of aircraft financing. It envisages a time limit on enforcement action, a special insolvency rule to enable leased aircraft to be freed from lengthy insolvency proceedings, remedies to include de-registration and export, a choice of law recognition provision stricter in its terms than that of the Rome or Inter-American Convention and provisions for the International Registry of International Interests in Aircraft.

At this stage more work remains to be done, but the intention is that the aircraft protocol should be submitted to a diplomatic conference for signature at the same time as the convention itself. The convention is of no effect unless an equipment-specific protocol is entered into to give effect to its principles for that equipment. It is likely that the aircraft protocol will be the first equipment-specific protocol to be produced for this purpose.

Note

1 For further discussion of the process of international law making and its limitations see 'Rethinking the Notion of Uniformity in the Drafting of International Commercial Law' by Jeffrey Wool, *Uniform Law Review* 1997-1, at pp 46–57.

APPENDICES

Appendix A

Convention on the International Recognition
of Rights in Aircraft

Geneva, 19 June 1948

Whereas the International Civil Aviation Conference, held at Chicago in November–December 1944[1], recommended the early adoption of a Convention dealing with the transfer of title to aircraft,

Whereas it is highly desirable in the interest of the future expansion of international civil aviation that rights in aircraft be recognised internationally,

THE UNDERSIGNED, duly authorised, HAVE AGREED, on behalf of their respective Governments, AS FOLLOWS:

ARTICLE 1

(1) The Contracting States undertake to recognise:

(a) rights of property in aircraft;
(b) rights to acquire aircraft by purchase coupled with possession of the aircraft;
(c) rights to possession of aircraft under leases of six months or more;
(d) mortgages, hypotheques and similar rights in aircraft which are contractually created as security for payment of an indebtedness;
provided that such rights:
  (i) have been constituted in accordance with the law of the Contracting State in which the aircraft was registered as to nationality at the time of their constitution, and
  (ii) are regularly recorded in a public record of the Contracting State in which the aircraft is registered as to nationality.
    The regularity of successive recordings in different Contracting States shall be determined in accordance with the law of the State where the aircraft was registered as to nationality at the time of each recording.

(2) Nothing in this Convention shall prevent the recognition of any rights in aircraft under the law of any Contracting State; but Contracting States shall not admit or recognise any right as taking priority over the rights mentioned in paragraph (1) of this Article.

ARTICLE 2

(1) All recordings relating to a given aircraft must appear in the same record.
(2) Except as otherwise provided in this Convention, the effects of the recording of any right mentioned in Article 1, paragraph (1), with regard to third parties shall be determined according to the law of the Contracting State where it is recorded.
(3) A Contracting State may prohibit the recording of any right which cannot validly be constituted according to its national law.

ARTICLE 3

(1) The address of the authority responsible for maintaining the record must be shown on every aircraft's certificate of registration as to nationality.
(2) Any person shall be entitled to receive from the authority duly certified copies or extracts of the particulars recorded. Such copies or extracts shall constitute *prima facie* evidence of the contents of the record.
(3) If the law of a Contracting State provides that the filing of a document for recording shall have the same effect as the recording, it shall have the same effect for the purposes of this Convention. In that case, adequate provision shall be made to ensure that such document is open to the public.
(4) Reasonable charges may be made for services performed by the authority maintaining the record.

---

(1) 'Miscellaneous No. 6 (1945)', Cmd. 6614.
In these Appendices * indicates that a party has made a reservation to a treaty which is recorded by the depositary. Details are correct as at 31 December 1992.

Article 4

(1) In the event that any claims in respect of:

(a) compensation due for salvage of the aircraft; or
(b) extraordinary expenses indispensable for the preservation of the aircraft,

give rise, under the law of the Contracting State where the operations of salvage or preservation were terminated, to a right conferring a charge against the aircraft, such right shall be recognised by Contracting States and shall take priority over all other rights in the aircraft.

(2) The rights enumerated in paragraph (1) shall be satisfied in the inverse order of the dates of the incidents in connexion with which they have arisen.

(3) Any of the said rights may, within three months from the date of the termination of the salvage or preservation operations, be noted on the record.

(4) The said rights shall not be recognised in other Contracting States after expiration of the three months mentioned in paragraph (3) unless, within this period:

(a) the right has been noted on the record in conformity with paragraph (3); and
(b) the amount has been agreed upon or judicial action on the right has been commenced. As far as judicial action is concerned, the law of the forum shall determine the contingencies upon which the three months' period may be interrupted or suspended.

(5) This Article shall apply notwithstanding the provisions of Article I, paragraph (2).

Article 5

The priority of a right mentioned in Article I, paragraph (1) (d), extends to all sums thereby secured. However, the amount of interest included shall not exceed that accrued during the three years prior to the execution proceedings together with that accrued during the execution proceedings.

Article 6

In case of attachment or sale of an aircraft in execution, or of any right therein, the Contracting States shall not be obliged to recognise, as against the attaching or executing creditor or against the purchaser, any right mentioned in Article I, paragraph (1), or the transfer of any such right, if constituted or effected with knowledge of the sale or execution proceedings by the person against whom the proceedings are directed.

Article 7

(1) The proceedings of a sale of an aircraft in execution shall be determined by the law of the Contracting State where the sale takes place.

(2) The following provisions shall, however, be observed:

(a) The date and place of the sale shall be fixed at least six weeks in advance.
(b) The executing creditor shall supply to the Court or other competent authority a certified extract of the recordings concerning the aircraft. He shall give public notice of the sale at the place where the aircraft is registered as to nationality, in accordance with the law there applicable, at least one month before the day fixed, and shall concurrently notify by registered letter, if possible by air mail, the recorded owner and the holders of recorded rights in the aircraft and of rights noted on the record under Article 4, paragraph (3), according to their addresses as shown on the record.

(3) The consequences of failure to observe the requirements of paragraph (2) shall be as provided by the law of the Contracting State where the sale takes place. However, any sale taking place in contravention of the requirements of that paragraph may be annulled upon demand made within six months from the date of the sale by any person suffering damage as the result of such contravention.

(4) No sale in execution can be effected unless all rights having priority over the claim of the executing creditor in accordance with this Convention which are established before the competent authority, are covered by the proceeds of sale or assumed by the purchaser.

(5) When injury or damage is caused to persons or property on the surface of the Contracting State where the execution sale takes place, by any aircraft subject to any right referred to in Article I held as security for an indebtedness, unless adequate and effective insurance by a State or an insurance undertaking in any State has been provided by or on behalf of the operator to cover such injury or damage, the national law of such Contracting State may provide in case of the seizure of such aircraft or any other aircraft owned by the same person and encumbered with any similar right held by the same creditor:

(a) that the provisions of paragraph (4) above shall have no effect with regard to the person suffering such injury or damage or his representative if he is an executing creditor;

(b) that any right referred to in Article I held as security for an indebtedness encumbering the aircraft may not be set up against any person suffering such injury or damage or his representative in excess of an amount equal to 80 per cent of the sale price.

In the absence of other limit established by the law of the Contracting State where the execution sale takes place, the insurance shall be considered adequate within the meaning of the present paragraph if the amount of the insurance corresponds to the value when new of the aircraft seized in execution.

(6) Costs legally chargeable under the law of the Contracting State where the sale takes place, which are incurred in the common interest of creditors in the course of execution proceedings leading to sale, shall be paid out of the proceeds of the sale before any claims, including those given preference by Article 4.

ARTICLE 8

Sale of an aircraft in execution in conformity with the provisions of Article VII shall effect the transfer of the property in such aircraft free from all rights which are not assumed by the purchaser.

ARTICLE 9

Except in the case of a sale in execution in conformity with the provisions of Article 7, no transfer of an aircraft from the nationality register or the record of a Contracting State to that of another Contracting State shall be made, unless all holders of recorded rights have been satisfied or consent to the transfer.

ARTICLE 10

(1) If a recorded right in an aircraft of the nature specified in Article I, and held as security for the payment of an indebtedness, extends, in conformity with the law of the Contracting State where the aircraft is registered, to spare parts stored in a specified place or places, such right shall be recognised by all Contracting States, as long as the spare parts remain in the place or places specified, provided that an appropriate public notice, specifying the description of the right, the name and address of the holder of this right and the record in which such right is recorded, is exhibited at the place where the spare parts are located, so as to give due notification to third parties that such spare parts are encumbered.

(2) A statement indicating the character and the approximate number of such spare parts shall be annexed to or included in the recorded document. Such parts may be replaced by similar parts without affecting the right of the creditor.

(3) The provisions of Article 7, paragraphs (1) and (4), and of Article 8 shall apply to a sale of spare parts in execution. However, where the executing creditor is an unsecured creditor, paragraph (4) of Article 7 in its application to such a sale shall be construed so as to permit the sale to take place if a bid is received in an amount not less than two-thirds of the value of the spare parts as determined by experts appointed by the authority responsible for the sale. Further, in the distribution of the proceeds of sale, the competent authority may, in order to provide for the claim of the executing creditor, limit the amount payable to holders of prior rights to two-thirds of such proceeds of sale after payment of the costs referred to in Article 7, paragraph (6).

(4) For the purpose of this Article the term 'spare parts' means parts of aircraft, engines, propellers, radio apparatus, instruments, appliances, furnishings, parts of any of the foregoing, and generally any other articles of whatever description maintained for installation in aircraft in substitution for parts or articles removed.

ARTICLE 11

(1) The provisions of this Convention shall in each Contracting State apply to all aircraft registered as to nationality in another Contracting State.

(2) Each Contracting State shall also apply to aircraft there registered as to nationality:

(a) the provisions of Articles 2, 3, 9; and
(b) the provisions of Article 4, unless the salvage or preservation operations have been terminated within its own territory.

ARTICLE 12

Nothing in this Convention shall prejudice the right of any Contracting State to enforce against an aircraft its national laws relating to immigration, customs or air navigation.

ARTICLE 13

This Convention shall not apply to aircraft used in military, customs or police services.

ARTICLE 14

For the purpose of this Convention, the competent judicial and administrative authorities of the Contracting States may, subject to any contrary provision in their national law, correspond directly with each other.

ARTICLE 15

The Contracting States shall take such measures as are necessary for the fulfilment of the provisions of this Convention and shall forthwith inform the Secretary-General of the International Civil Aviation Organisation of these measures.

ARTICLE 16

For the purposes of this Convention the term 'aircraft' shall include the airframe, engines, propellers, radio apparatus, and all other articles intended for use in the aircraft whether installed therein or temporarily separated therefrom.

ARTICLE 17

If a separate register of aircraft for purposes of nationality is maintained in any territory for whose foreign relations a Contracting State is responsible, references in this Convention to the law of the Contracting State shall be construed as references to the law of that territory.

ARTICLE 18

This Convention shall remain open for signature until it comes into force in accordance with the provisions of Article 20.

ARTICLE 19

(1) This Convention shall be subject to ratification by the signatory States.

(2) The instruments of ratification shall be deposited in the archives of the International Civil Aviation Organisation, which shall give notice of the date of deposit to each of the signatory and adhering States.

ARTICLE 20

(1) As soon as two of the signatory States have deposited their instruments of ratification of this Convention, it shall come into force between them on the ninetieth day after the date of the deposit of the second instrument of ratification. It shall come into force, for each State which deposits its instrument of ratification after that date, on the ninetieth day after the deposit of its instrument of ratification.

(2) The International Civil Aviation Organisation shall give notice to each signatory State of the date on which this Convention comes into force.

(3) As soon as this Convention comes into force, it shall be registered with the United Nations by the Secretary-General of the International Civil Aviation Organisation.

ARTICLE 21

(1) This Convention shall, after it has come into force, be open for adherence by non-signatory States.

(2) Adherence shall be effected by the deposit of an instrument of adherence in the archives of the International Civil Aviation Organisation, which shall give notice of the date of the deposit to each signatory and adhering State.

(3) Adherence shall take effect as from the ninetieth day after the date of the deposit of the instrument of adherence in the archives of the International Civil Aviation Organisation.

ARTICLE 22

(1) Any Contracting State may denounce this Convention by notification of denunciation to the International Civil Aviation Organisation, which shall give notice of the date of receipt of such notification to each signatory and adhering State.

(2) Denunciation shall take effect six months after the date of receipt by the International Civil Aviation Organisation of the notification of denunciation.

ARTICLE 23

(1) Any State may, at the time of deposit of its instrument of ratification or adherence, declare that its acceptance of this Convention does not apply to any one or more of the territories for the foreign relations of which such State is responsible.

(2) The International Civil Aviation Organisation shall give notice of any such declaration to each signatory and adhering State.

(3) With the exception of territories in respect of which a declaration has been made in accordance with paragraph (1) of this Article, this Convention shall apply to all territories for the foreign relations of which a Contracting State is responsible.

(4) Any State may adhere to this Convention separately on behalf of all or any of the territories regarding which it has made a declaration in accordance with paragraph (1) of this Article and the provisions of paragraphs (2) and (3) of Article 21 shall apply to such adherence.

(5) Any Contracting State may denounce this Convention, in accordance with the provisions of Article 22, separately for all or any of the territories for the foreign relations of which such State is responsible.

IN WITNESS WHEREOF the undersigned Plenipotentiaries, having been duly authorised, have signed this Convention.

DONE at Geneva, on the nineteenth day of the month of June in the year one thousand nine hundred and forty-eight in the English, French and Spanish languages, each text being of equal authenticity.

This Convention shall be deposited in the archives of the International Civil Aviation Organisation where, in accordance with Article 18, it shall remain open for signature.

CONCLUDED

19 Jun 1948, Geneva

ENTRY INTO FORCE

17 Sept 53. Later acceptances effective 90 days after deposit: Arts 20,21.

PARTIES

ALGERIA 10 Aug 64; ARGENTINA 31 Jan 58; BAHRAIN 3 Mar 97; BANGLADESH 6 Jan 88; BELGIUM 22 Oct 93; BOSNIA & HERZEGOVINA 7 Mar 95; BRAZIL 3 Jul 53; CAMEROON 23 Jul 69; CENTRAL AFRICAN REPUBLIC 2 June 69; CHAD 14 Feb 74; CHILE 19 Dec 55; CONGO, PEOPLE'S REPUBLIC OF 3 May 82; CÔTE D'IVOIRE 23 Aug 65; CROATIA 5 Oct 93; CUBA 20 Jun 61; DENMARK 18 Jan 63; ECUADOR 14 Jul 58; EGYPT 10 Sep 69; EL SALVADOR 14 Aug 58; ESTONIA 31 Dec 93; ETHIOPIA 7 Jun 79; FRANCE 27 Feb 64; GABON 14 Jan 70; GERMANY 7 Jul 59; GHANA 15 Jul 97; GREECE 23 Feb 71; GRENADA 28 Aug 85; GUATEMALA 9 Aug 88; GUINEA 13 Aug 80; HAITI 24 Mar 61; HUNGARY 21 May 93; ICELAND 6 Feb 67; IRAQ 12 Jan 81; ITALY 6 Dec 60; KENYA 15 Jan 97; KUWAIT* 27 Nov 79; LAO PEOPLE'S DEMOCRATIC REPUBLIC 4 Jun 56; LEBANON 11 Apr 69; LIBYAN ARAB JAMAHIRIYA 5 Mar 73; LUXEMBOURG 16 Dec 75; MACEDONIA, FORMER YUGOSLAV REPUBLIC OF 30 Aug 94; MADAGASCAR 9 Jan 79; MALDIVES 5 Sep 95; MALI 28 Dec 61; MAURITANIA 23 Jul 62; MAURITIUS 17 Apr 91; MEXICO* 5 Apr 50; MONACO 14 Dec 94; MOROCCO 13 Dec 93; NETHERLANDS,* KINGDOM OF 1 Sep 59; NIGER 27 Dec 62; NORWAY 5 Mar 54; OMAN 19 Mar 92; PAKISTAN 19 Jun 53; PARAGUAY 26 Sep 69; PHILIPPINES 22 Feb 78; PORTUGAL 12 Dec 85; ROMANIA 26 Oct 94; RWANDA 17 May 71; SEYCHELLES 16 Jan 79; SLOVENIA 9 Apr 97; SRI LANKA 24 Jan 94; SWEDEN* 16 Nov 55; SWITZERLAND 3 Oct 60; THAILAND 10 Oct 67; TOGO 2 Jul 80; TUNISIA 4 May 66; TURKMENISTAN 16 Sep 93; UNITED STATES OF AMERICA* 6 Sep 49; URUGUAY 21 Aug 85; UZBEKISTAN 8 May 97; YUGOSLAVIA 16 Oct 91; ZIMBABWE 6 Feb 87

(Dates shown are those of deposit of instruments of ratification or adherence by the State.)

SIGNATORIES

AUSTRALIA 9.6.50; BELGIUM 19.6.48; CHINA 19.6.48; COLOMBIA 19.6.48; DOMINICAN REPUBLIC 19.6.48; IRAN 18.3.50; IRELAND 30.11.48; PERU 19.6.48; UK 19.6.48; VENEZUELA 19.6.48.

Appendix B

Convention on International Civil Aviation
International Air Services Transit Agreement
International Air Transport Agreement

Chicago, 7 December 1944

PREAMBLE

WHEREAS the future development of international civil aviation can greatly help to create and preserve friendship and understanding among the nations and peoples of the world, yet its abuse can become a threat to the general security, and

WHEREAS it is desirable to avoid friction and to promote that cooperation between nations and peoples upon which the peace of the world depends,

THEREFORE, the undersigned Governments having agreed on certain principles and arrangements in order that international civil aviation may be developed in a safe and orderly manner and that international air transport services may be established on the basis of equality of opportunity and operated soundly and economically,

Have accordingly concluded this Convention to that end.

PART I. – AIR NAVIGATION

Chapter I. – General Principles and Application of the Convention

ARTICLE 1

Sovereignty

The contracting States recognise that every State has complete and exclusive sovereignty over the airspace above its territory.

ARTICLE 2

Territory

For the purposes of this Convention the territory of a State shall be deemed to be the land areas and territorial waters adjacent thereto under the sovereignty, suzerainty, protection or mandate of such State.

ARTICLE 3

Civil and State aircraft

(a) This Convention shall be applicable only to civil aircraft, and shall not be applicable to state aircraft.

(b) Aircraft used in military, customs and police services shall be deemed to be state aircraft.

(c) No state aircraft of a contracting State shall fly over the territory of another State or land thereon without authorisation by special agreement or otherwise, and in accordance with the terms thereof.

(d) The contracting States undertake, when issuing regulations for their state aircraft, that they will have due regard for the safety of navigation of civil aircraft.

ARTICLE 4

Misuse of civil aviation

Each contracting State agrees not to use civil aviation for any purpose inconsistent with the aims of this Convention.

Chapter II. – Flight over Territory of Contracting States

ARTICLE 5

Right of non-scheduled flight

Each contracting State agrees that all aircraft of the other contracting States, being aircraft not engaged in scheduled international air services, shall have the right, subject to the observance of the terms of this Convention, to make flights into or in transit non-stop across its territory and to make stops for non-traffic purposes without the necessity of obtaining prior permission, and subject to the right of the State flown over to require landing. Each contracting State nevertheless reserves the right, for reasons of safety of flight, to require aircraft desiring to proceed over regions which are inaccessible or without adequate air navigation facilities to follow prescribed routes, or to obtain special permission for such flights.

Such aircraft, if engaged in the carriage of passengers, cargo, or mail for remuneration or hire on other than scheduled international air services, shall also, subject to the provisions of Article 7, have the privilege of taking on or discharging passengers, cargo, or mail, subject to the right of any State where such embarkation or discharge takes place to impose such regulations, conditions or limitations as it may consider desirable.

ARTICLE 6

Scheduled air services

No scheduled international air service may be operated over or into the territory of a contracting State, except with the special permission or other authorisation of that State, and in accordance with the terms of such permission or authorisation.

ARTICLE 7

Cabotage

Each contracting State shall have the right to refuse permission to the aircraft of other contracting States to take on in its territory passengers, mail and cargo carried for remuneration or hire and destined for another point within its territory. Each contracting State undertakes not to enter into any arrangements which specifically grant any such privilege on an exclusive basis to any other State or an airline of any other State, and not to obtain any such exclusive privilege from any other State.

ARTICLE 8

Pilotless aircraft

No aircraft capable of being flown without a pilot shall be flown without a pilot over the territory of a contracting State without special authorisation by that State and in accordance with the terms of such authorisation. Each contracting State undertakes to ensure that the flight of such aircraft without a pilot in regions open to civil aircraft shall be so controlled as to obviate danger to civil aircraft.

ARTICLE 9

Prohibited areas

(a) Each contracting State may, for reasons of military necessity or public safety, restrict or prohibit uniformly the aircraft of other States from flying over certain areas of its territory, provided that no distinction in this respect is made between the aircraft of the State whose territory is involved, engaged in international scheduled airline services, and the aircraft of the other contracting States likewise engaged. Such prohibited areas shall be of reasonable extent and location so as not to interfere unnecessarily with air navigation. Descriptions of such prohibited areas in the territory of a contracting State, as well as any subsequent alterations therein, shall be communicated as soon as possible to the other contracting States and to the International Civil Aviation Organisation.

(b) Each contracting State reserves also the right, in exceptional circumstances or during a period of emergency, or in the interest of public safety, and with immediate effect, temporarily to restrict or prohibit flying over the whole or any part of its territory, on condition that such restriction or prohibition shall be applicable without distinction of nationality to aircraft of all other States.

(c) Each contracting State, under such regulations as it may prescribe, may require any aircraft entering the areas contemplated in sub-paragraphs (a) or (b) above to effect a landing as soon as practicable thereafter at some designated airport within its territory.

ARTICLE 10

Landing at customs airport

Except in the case where, under the terms of this Convention or a special authorisation, aircraft are permitted to cross the territory of a contracting State without landing, every aircraft which enters the territory of a Contracting State shall, if the regulations of that State so require, land at an airport designated by that State for the purpose of customs and other examination. On departure from the territory of a contracting State, such aircraft shall depart from a similarly designated customs airport. Particulars of all designated customs airports shall be published by the State and transmitted to the International Civil Aviation Organisation established under Part II of this Convention for communication to all other Contracting States.

ARTICLE 11

Applicability of air regulations

Subject to the provisions of this Convention, the laws and regulations of a contracting State relating to the admission to or departure from its territory of aircraft engaged in international air navigation, or to the operation and navigation of such aircraft while within its territory, shall be applied to the aircraft of all contracting States without distinction as to nationality, and shall be complied with by such aircraft upon entering or departing from or while within the territory of that State.

ARTICLE 12

Rules of the air

Each contracting State undertakes to adopt measures to ensure that every aircraft flying over or manoeuvring within its territory and that every aircraft carrying its nationality mark, wherever such aircraft may be, shall comply with the rules and regulations relating to the flight and manoeuvre of aircraft there in force. Each contracting State undertakes to keep its own regulations in these respects uniform, to the greatest possible extent, with those established from time to time under this Convention. Over the high seas, the rules in force shall be those established under this Convention. Each contracting State undertakes to ensure the prosecution of all persons violating the regulations applicable.

ARTICLE 13

Entry and clearance regulations

The laws and regulations of a contracting State as to the admission to or departure from its territory of passengers, crew, or cargo of aircraft, such as regulations relating to entry, clearance, immigration, passports, customs, and quarantine shall be complied with by or on behalf of such passengers, crew or cargo upon entrance into or departure from, or while within the territory of that State.

ARTICLE 14

Prevention of spread of disease

Each contracting State agrees to take effective measures to prevent the spread by means of air navigation of cholera, typhus (epidemic), smallpox, yellow fever, plague, and such other communicable diseases as the contracting States shall from time to time decide to designate, and to that end contracting States will keep in close consultation with the agencies concerned with international regulations relating to sanitary measures applicable to aircraft. Such consultation shall be without prejudice to the application of any existing international convention on this subject to which the contracting States may be parties.

ARTICLE 15

Airport and similar charges

Every airport in a contracting State which is open to public use by its national aircraft shall likewise, subject to the provisions of Article 68, be open under uniform conditions to the aircraft of all the other contracting States. The like uniform conditions shall apply to the use, by aircraft of every contracting State, of all air navigation facilities, including radio and meteorological services, which may be provided for public use for the safety and expedition of air navigation.

Any charges that may be imposed or permitted to be imposed by a contracting State for the use of such airports and air navigation facilities by the aircraft of any other contracting State shall not be higher,

(a) as to aircraft not engaged in scheduled international air services, than those that would be paid by its national aircraft of the same class engaged in similar operations, and

(b) as to aircraft engaged in scheduled international air services, than those that would be paid by its national aircraft engaged in similar international air services.

All such charges shall be published and communicated to the International Civil Aviation Organisation: provided that, upon representation by an interested contracting State, the charges imposed for the use of airports and other facilities shall be subject to review by the Council, which shall report and make recommendations thereon for the consideration of the State or States concerned. No fees, dues or other charges shall be imposed by any contracting State in respect solely of the right of transit over or entry into or exit from its territory of any aircraft of a contracting State or persons or property thereon.

ARTICLE 16

Search of aircraft

The appropriate authorities of each of the contracting States shall have the right, without unreasonable delay, to search aircraft of the other contracting States on landing or departure, and to inspect the certificates and other documents prescribed by this Convention.

Chapter III. – Nationality of Aircraft

ARTICLE 17

Nationality of aircraft

Aircraft have the nationality of the State in which they are registered.

ARTICLE 18

Dual registration

An aircraft cannot be validly registered in more than one State, but its registration may be changed from one State to another.

ARTICLE 19

National laws governing registration

The registration or transfer of registration of aircraft in any contracting State shall be made in accordance with its laws and regulations.

ARTICLE 20

Display of marks

Every aircraft engaged in international air navigation shall bear its appropriate nationality and registration marks.

ARTICLE 21

Report of registrations

Each contracting State undertakes to supply to any other contracting State or to the International Civil Aviation Organisation, on demand, information concerning the registration and ownership of any particular aircraft registered in that State. In addition, each contracting State shall furnish reports to the International Civil Aviation Organisation, under such regulations as the latter may prescribe, giving such pertinent data as can be made available concerning the ownership and control of aircraft registered in that State and habitually engaged in international air navigation. The data thus obtained by the International Civil Aviation Organisation shall be made available by it on request to the other contracting States.

Chapter IV. – Measures to facilitate Air Navigation

ARTICLE 22

Facilitation of formalities

Each contracting State agrees to adopt all practicable measures, through the issuance of special regulations or otherwise, to facilitate and expedite navigation by aircraft between the territories of contracting States, and to prevent unnecessary delays to aircraft, crews, passengers and cargo, especially in the administration of the laws relating to immigration, quarantine, customs and clearance.

ARTICLE 23

Customs and immigration procedures

Each contracting State undertakes, so far as it may find practicable, to establish customs and immigration procedures affecting international air navigation in accordance with the practices which may be established or recommended from time to time, pursuant to this Convention. Nothing in this Convention shall be construed as preventing the establishment of customs-free airports.

ARTICLE 24

Customs duty

. (a) Aircraft on a flight to, from, or across the territory of another contracting State shall be admitted temporarily free of duty, subject to the customs regulations of the State. Fuel, lubricating oils, spare parts, regular equipment and aircraft stores on board an aircraft of a contracting State, on arrival in the territory of another contracting State and retained on board on leaving the territory of that State shall be exempt from customs duty, inspection fees or similar national or local duties and charges. This exemption shall not apply to any quantities or articles unloaded except in accordance with the customs regulations of the State, which may require that they shall be kept under customs supervision.

(b) Spare parts and equipment imported into the territory of a contracting State for incorporation in or use on aircraft of another contracting State engaged in international air navigation shall be admitted free of customs duty, subject to compliance with the regulations of the State concerned, which may provide that the articles shall be kept under customs supervision and control.

ARTICLE 25

Aircraft in distress

Each contracting State undertakes to provide such measures of assistance to aircraft in distress in its territory as it may find practicable, and to permit, subject to control by its own authorities, the owners of the aircraft or authorities of the State in which the aircraft is registered to provide such measures of assistance as may be necessitated by the circumstances. Each contracting State, when undertaking search for missing aircraft, will collaborate in coordinated measures which may be recommended from time to time pursuant to this Convention.

ARTICLE 26

Investigation of accidents

In the event of an accident to an aircraft of a contracting State occurring in the territory of another contracting State, and involving death or serious injury, or indicating serious technical defect in the aircraft or air navigation facilities, the State in which the accident occurs will institute an enquiry into the circumstances of the accident, in accordance, so far as its laws permit with the procedure which may be recommended by the International Civil Aviation Organisation. The State in which the aircraft is registered shall be given the opportunity to appoint observers to be present at the inquiry and the State holding the inquiry shall communicate the report and findings in the matter to that State.

ARTICLE 27

Exemption from seizure on patent claims

(a) While engaged in international air navigation, any authorised entry of aircraft of a contracting State into the territory of another contracting State or authorised transit across the territory of such State with or without landings shall not entail any seizure or detention of the aircraft or any claim against the owner or operator thereof or any other interference therewith by or on behalf of such State or any person therein, on the ground that the construction, mechanism, parts, accessories or operation of the aircraft is an infringement of any patent, design, or model duly granted or registered in the State whose territory is entered by the aircraft, it being agreed that no deposit of security in connection with the foregoing exemption from seizure or detention of the aircraft shall in any case be required in the State entered by such an aircraft.

(b) The provisions of paragraph (a) of this Article shall also be applicable to the storage of spare parts and spare equipment for the aircraft and the right to use and install the same in the repair of an aircraft of a contracting State in the territory of any other contracting State, provided that any patented part or equipment so stored shall not be sold or distributed internally in or exported commercially from the contracting State entered by the aircraft.

(c) The benefits of this Article shall apply only to such States, parties to this Convention, as either (1) are parties to the International Convention for the Protection of Industrial Property[1] and to any amendments thereof; or (2) have enacted patent laws which recognise and give adequate protection to inventions made by the nationals of the other States parties to this Convention.

ARTICLE 28

Air navigation facilities and standard systems

Each contracting State undertakes, so far as it may find practicable to:

(a) Provide, in its territory, airports, radio services, meteorological services and other air navigation facilities to facilitate international air navigation, in accordance with the standards and practices recommended or established from time to time, pursuant to this Convention;

(b) Adopt and put into operation the appropriate standard systems of communications procedure, codes, markings, signals, lighting and other operational practices and rules which may be recommended or established from time to time, pursuant to this Convention;

(c) Collaborate in international measures to secure the publication of aeronautical maps and charts in accordance with standards which may be recommended or established from time to time, pursuant to this Convention.

Chapter V. – Conditions to be fulfilled with respect to Aircraft

ARTICLE 29
Documents carried in aircraft

Every aircraft of a contracting State, engaged in international navigation, shall carry the following documents in conformity with the conditions prescribed in this Convention:

(a) Its certificate of registration;
(b) Its certificate of airworthiness;
(c) The appropriate licences for each member of the crew;
(d) Its journey log book;
(e) If it is equipped with radio apparatus, the aircraft radio station licence;
(f) If it carries passengers, a list of their names and places of embarkation and destination;
(g) If it carries cargo, a manifest and detailed declarations of the cargo.

ARTICLE 30
Aircraft radio equipment

(a) Aircraft of each contracting State may, in or over the territory of other contracting States, carry radio transmitting apparatus only if a licence to install and operate such apparatus has been issued by the appropriate authorities in the State in which the aircraft is registered. The use of radio transmitting apparatus in the territory of the contracting State whose territory is flown over shall be in accordance with the regulations prescribed by that State.

(b) Radio transmitting apparatus may be used only by members of the flight crew who are provided with a special licence for the purpose, issued by the appropriate authorities of the State in which the aircraft is registered.

ARTICLE 31
Certificates of airworthiness

Every aircraft engaged in international navigation shall be provided with a certificate of airworthiness issued or rendered valid by the State in which it is registered.

ARTICLE 32
Licences of personnel

(a) The pilot of every aircraft and the other members of the operating crew of every aircraft engaged in international navigation shall be provided with certificates of competency and licences issued or rendered valid by the State in which the aircraft is registered.

(b) Each contracting State reserves the right to refuse to recognise, for the purpose of flight above its own territory, certificates of competency and licences granted to any of its nationals by another contracting State.

ARTICLE 33
Recognition of certificates and licences

Certificates of airworthiness and certificates of competency and licences issued or rendered valid by the contracting State in which the aircraft is registered, shall be recognised as valid by the other contracting States, provided that the requirements under which such certificates or licences were issued or rendered valid are equal to or above the minimum standards which may be established from time to time pursuant to this Convention.

ARTICLE 34
Journey log books

There shall be maintained in respect of every aircraft engaged in international navigation a journey log book in which shall be entered particulars of the aircraft, its crew and of each journey, in such form as may be prescribed from time to time pursuant to this Convention.

ARTICLE 35

Cargo restrictions

(a) No munitions of war or implements of war may be carried in or above the territory of a State in aircraft engaged in international navigation, except by permission of such State. Each State shall determine by regulations what constitutes munitions of war or implements of war for the purposes of this Article, giving due consideration, for the purposes of uniformity, to such recommendations as the International Civil Aviation Organisation may from time to time make.

(b) Each contracting State reserves the right, for reasons of public order and safety, to regulate or prohibit the carriage in or above its territory of articles other than those enumerated in paragraph (a): provided that no distinction is made in this respect between its national aircraft engaged in international navigation and the aircraft of the other States so engaged; and provided further that no restriction shall be imposed which may interfere with the carriage and use on aircraft of apparatus necessary for the operation or navigation of the aircraft or the safety of the personnel or passengers.

ARTICLE 36

Photographic apparatus

Each contracting State may prohibit or regulate the use of photographic apparatus in aircraft over its territory.

Chapter VI. – International Standards and Recommended Practices

ARTICLE 37

Adoption of international standards and procedures

Each contracting State undertakes to collaborate in securing the highest practicable degree of uniformity in regulations, standards, procedures, and organisation in relation to aircraft, personnel, airways and auxiliary services in all matters in which such uniformity will facilitate and improve air navigation.

To this end the International Civil Aviation Organisation shall adopt and amend from time to time, as may be necessary, international standards and recommended practices and procedures dealing with:

(a) Communication systems and air navigation aids, including ground marking;
(b) Characteristics of airports and landing areas;
(c) Rules of the air and air traffic control practices;
(d) Licensing of operating and mechanical personnel;
(e) Airworthiness of aircraft;
(f) Registration and identification of aircraft;
(g) Collection and exchange of meteorological information;
(h) Log books;
(i) Aeronautical maps and charts;
(j) Customs and immigration procedures;
(k) Aircraft in distress and investigation of accidents;

and such other matters concerned with the safety, regularity, and efficiency of air navigation as may from time to time appear appropriate.

ARTICLE 38

Departures from international standards and procedures

Any State which finds it impracticable to comply in all respects with any such international standard or procedure, or to bring its own regulations or practices into full accord with any international standard or procedure after amendment of the latter, or which deems it necessary to adopt regulations or practices differing in any particular respect from those established by an international standard, shall give immediate notification to the International Civil Aviation Organisation of the differences between its own practice and that established by the international standard. In the case of amendments to international standards, any State which does not make the appropriate amendments to its own regulations or practices shall give notice to the Council within 60 days of the adoption of the amendment to the international standard, or indicate the action which it proposes to take. In any such case, the Council shall make immediate notification to all other States of the difference which exists between one or more features of an international standard and the corresponding national practice of that State.

ARTICLE 39

Endorsement of certificates and licences

(a) Any aircraft or part thereof with respect to which there exists an international standard of airworthiness or performance, and which failed in any respect to satisfy that standard at the time of its certification, shall have endorsed on or attached to its airworthiness certificate a complete enumeration of the details in respect of which it so failed.

(b) Any person holding a licence who does not satisfy in full the conditions laid down in the international standard relating to the class of licence or certificate which he holds shall have endorsed on or attached to his licence a complete enumeration of the particulars in which he does not satisfy such conditions.

ARTICLE 40

Validity of endorsed certificates and licences

No aircraft or personnel having certificates or licences so endorsed shall participate in international navigation except with the permission of the State or States whose territory is entered. The registration or use of any such aircraft, or of any certificated aircraft part, in any State other than that in which it was originally certificated shall be at the discretion of the State into which the aircraft or part is imported.

ARTICLE 41

Recognition of existing standards of airworthiness

The provisions of this Chapter shall not apply to aircraft and aircraft equipment of types of which the prototype is submitted to the appropriate national authorities for certification prior to the date three years after the date of adoption of an international standard of airworthiness for such equipment.

ARTICLE 42

Recognition of existing standards of competency of personnel

The provisions of this Chapter shall not apply to personnel whose licences are originally issued prior to a date one year after initial adoption of an international standard of qualification for such personnel; but they shall in any case apply to all personnel whose licences remain valid five years after the date of adoption of such standard.

PART II. – THE INTERNATIONAL CIVIL AVIATION ORGANISATION

Chapter VII. – The Organisation

ARTICLE 43

Name and composition

An organisation to be named the International Civil Aviation Organisation is formed by the Convention. It is made up of an Assembly, a Council and such other bodies as may be necessary.

ARTICLE 44

Objectives

The aims and objectives of the Organisation are to develop the principles and techniques of international air navigation and to foster the planning and development of international air transport so as to:

(a) Ensure the safe and orderly growth of international civil aviation throughout the world;
(b) Encourage the arts of aircraft design and operation for peaceful purposes;
(c) Encourage the development of airways, airports, and air navigation facilities for international civil aviation;
(d) Meet the needs of the peoples of the world for safe, regular, efficient and economical air transport;
(e) Prevent economic waste caused by unreasonable competition;
(f) Ensure that the rights of contracting States are fully respected and that every contracting State has a fair opportunity to operate international airlines;
(g) Avoid discrimination between contracting States;
(h) Promote safety of flight in international air navigation;
(i) Promote generally the development of all aspects of international civil aeronautics.

ARTICLE 45

Permanent seat

The permanent seat of the Organisation shall be at such place as shall be determined at the final meeting of the Interim Assembly of the Provisional International Civil Aviation Organisation set up by the Interim Agreement on International Civil Aviation signed at Chicago on 7th December, 1944. The seat may be temporarily transferred elsewhere by decision of the Council.

ARTICLE 46

First meeting of Assembly

The first meeting of the Assembly shall be summoned by the Interim Council of the above-mentioned Provisional Organisation as soon as the Convention has come into force, to meet at a time and place to be decided by the Interim Council.

ARTICLE 47

Legal capacity

The Organisation shall enjoy in the territory of each contracting State such legal capacity as may be necessary for the performance of its functions. Full juridical personality shall be granted wherever compatible with the constitution and laws of the State concerned.

Chapter VIII. – The Assembly

ARTICLE 48

Meetings of Assembly and voting

(a) The Assembly shall meet annually and shall be convened by the Council at a suitable time and place. Extraordinary meetings of the Assembly may be held at any time upon the call of the Council or at the request of any 10 contracting States addressed to the Secretary General.

(b) All contracting States shall have an equal right to be represented at the meetings of the Assembly and each contracting State shall be entitled to one vote. Delegates representing contracting States may be assisted by technical advisers who may participate in the meetings but shall have no vote.

(c) A majority of the contracting States is required to constitute a quorum for the meetings of the Assembly. Unless otherwise provided in this Convention, decisions of the Assembly shall be taken by a majority of the votes cast.

ARTICLE 49

Powers and duties of Assembly

The powers and duties of the Assembly shall be to:

(a) elect at each meeting its President and other officers;

(b) Elect the contracting States to be represented on the Council, in accordance with the provisions of Chapter IX;

(c) Examine and take appropriate action on the reports of the Council and decide on any matter referred to it by the Council;

(d) Determine its own rules of procedure and establish such subsidiary commissions as it may consider to be necessary or desirable;

(e) Vote an annual budget and determine the financial arrangements of the Organisation, in accordance with the provisions of Chapter XII;

(f) Review expenditures and approve the accounts of the Organisation;

(g) Refer, at its discretion, to the Council, to subsidiary commissions, or to any other body any matter within its sphere of action;

(h) Delegate to the Council the powers and authority necessary or desirable for the discharge of the duties of the Organisation and revoke or modify the delegations of authority at any time;

(i) Carry out the appropriate provisions of Chapter XIII;

(j) Consider proposals for the modification or amendment of the provisions of this Convention and, if it approves of the proposals recommend them to the contracting States in accordance with the provisions of Chapter XXI;

(k) Deal with any matter within the sphere of action of the Organisation not specifically assigned to the Council.

Chapter IX. – The Council

ARTICLE 50

Composition and election of Council

(a) The Council shall be a permanent body responsible to the Assembly. It shall be composed of 21 contracting States elected by the Assembly. An election shall be held at the first meeting of the Assembly and thereafter every three years, and the members of the Council so elected shall hold office until the next following election.

(b) In electing the members of the Council, the Assembly shall give adequate representation to (1) the States of chief importance in air transport; (2) the States not otherwise included which make the largest contribution to the provision of facilities for international civil air navigation; and (3) the States not otherwise included whose designation will ensure that all the major geographic areas of the world are represented on the Council. Any vacancy on the Council shall be filled by the Assembly as soon as possible; any contracting State so elected to the Council shall hold office for the unexpired portion of its predecessor's term of office.

(c) No representative of a contracting State on the Council shall be actively associated with the operation of an international air service or financially interested in such a service.

ARTICLE 51

President of Council

The Council shall elect its President for a term of three years. He may be re-elected. He shall have no vote. The Council shall elect from among its members one or more Vice-Presidents who shall retain their right to vote when serving as acting President. The President need not be selected from among the representatives of the members of the Council but, if a representative is elected, his seat shall be deemed vacant and it shall be filled by the State which he represented. The duties of the President shall be to:

(a) Convene meetings of the Council, the Air Transport Committee, and the Air Navigation Commission;
(b) Serve as representative of the Council; and
(c) Carry out on behalf of the Council the functions which the Council assigns to him.

ARTICLE 52

Voting in Council

Decisions by the Council shall require approval by a majority of its members. The Council may delegate authority with respect to any particular matter to a committee of its members. Decisions of any committee of the Council may be appealed to the Council by any interested contracting State.

ARTICLE 53

Participation without a vote

Any contracting State may participate, without a vote, in the consideration by the Council and by its committees and commissions of any question which especially affects its interests. No member of the Council shall vote in the consideration by the Council of a dispute to which it is a party.

ARTICLE 54

Mandatory functions of Council

The Council shall:

(a) Submit annual reports to the Assembly;
(b) Carry out the directions of the Assembly and discharge the duties and obligations which are laid on it by this Convention;
(c) Determine its organisation and rules of procedure;
(d) Appoint and define the duties of an Air Transport Committee, which shall be chosen from among the representatives of the members of the Council, and which shall be responsible to it;
(e) Establish an Air Navigation Commission, in accordance with the provisions of Chapter X;
(f) Administer the finances of the Organisation in accordance with the provisions of Chapters XII and XV;
(g) Determine the emoluments of the President of the Council;
(h) Appoint a chief executive officer who shall be called the Secretary General, and make provision for the appointment of such other personnel as may be necessary, in accordance with the provisions of Chapter XI;
(i) Request, collect, examine and publish information relating to the advancement of air navigation and the operation of international air services, including information about the costs of operation and particulars of subsidies paid to airlines from public funds;
(j) Report to contracting States any infraction of this Convention, as well as any failure to carry out recommendations or determinations of the Council;
(k) Report to the Assembly any infraction of this Convention where a contracting State has failed to take appropriate action within a reasonable time after notices of the infraction;
(l) Adopt, in accordance with the provisions of Chapter VI of this Convention, international standards and recommended practices; for convenience designate them as Annexes to this Convention; and notify all contracting States of the action taken;
(m) Consider recommendations of the Air Navigation Commission for amendment of the Annexes and take action in accordance with the provisions of Chapter XX;
(n) Consider any matter relating to the Convention which any contracting State refers to it.

ARTICLE 55

Permissive functions of Council

The Council may:

(a) Where appropriate and as experience may show to be desirable, create subordinate air transport commissions on a regional or other basis and define groups of States or airlines with or through which it may deal to facilitate the carrying out of the aims of this Convention;

(b) Delegate to the Air Navigation Commission duties additional to those set forth in the Convention and revoke or modify such delegations of authority at any time;

(c) Conduct research into all aspects of air transport and air navigation which are of international importance, communicate the results of its research to the contracting States, and facilitate the exchange of information between contracting States on air transport and air navigation matters;

(d) Study any matters affecting the organisation and operation of international air transport, including the international ownership and operation of international air services on trunk routes, and submit to the Assembly plans in relation thereto;

(e) Investigate, at the request of any contracting State, any situation which may appear to present avoidable obstacles to the development of international air navigation; and, after such investigation, issue such reports as may appear to it desirable.

Chapter X. – The Air Navigation Commission

ARTICLE 56

Nomination and appointment of Commission

The Air Navigation Commission shall be composed of twelve members appointed by the Council from among persons nominated by contracting States. These persons shall have suitable qualifications and experience in the science and practice of aeronautics. The Council shall request all contracting States to submit nominations. The President of the Air Navigation Commission shall be appointed by the Council.

ARTICLE 57

Duties of Commission

The Air Navigation Commission shall:

(a) Consider, and recommend to the Council for adoption, modifications of the Annexes to this Convention;

(b) Establish technical sub-commissions on which any contracting State may be represented, if it so desires;

(c) Advise the Council concerning the collection and communication to the contracting States of all information which it considers necessary and useful for the advancement of air navigation.

Chapter XI. – Personnel

ARTICLE 58

Appointment of personnel

Subject to any rules laid down by the Assembly and to the provisions of this Convention, the Council shall determine the method of appointment and of termination of appointment, the training, and the salaries, allowances, and conditions of service of the Secretary General and other personnel of the Organisation, and may employ or make use of the services of nationals of any contracting State.

ARTICLE 59

International character of personnel

The President of the Council, the Secretary General and other personnel shall not seek or receive instructions in regard to the discharge of their responsibilities from any authority external to the Organisation. Each contracting State undertakes fully to respect the international character of the responsibilities of the personnel and not to seek to influence any of its nationals in the discharge of their responsibilities.

ARTICLE 60

Immunities and privileges of personnel

Each contracting State undertakes, so far as possible under its constitutional procedure, to accord to the President of the Council, the Secretary General, and the other personnel of the Organisation, the immunities and privileges which are accorded to corresponding personnel of other public international organisations. If a general international agreement on the immunities and privileges of international civil servants is arrived at, the immunities and privileges accorded to the President, the Secretary General, and the other personnel of the Organisation shall be the immunities and privileges accorded under that general international agreement.

Chapter XII. – Finance

ARTICLE 61

Budget and apportionment of expenses

The Council shall submit to the Assembly an annual budget, annual statements of accounts and estimates of all receipts and expenditures. The Assembly shall vote the budget with whatever modification it sees fit to prescribe, and, with the exception of assessments under Chapter XV to States consenting thereto, shall apportion the expenses of the Organisation among the contracting States on the basis which it shall from time to time determine.

ARTICLE 62

Suspension of voting power.

The Assembly may suspend the voting power in the Assembly and in the Council of any contracting State that fails to discharge within a reasonable period its financial obligations to the Organisation.

ARTICLE 63

Expenses of delegations and other representatives

Each contracting State shall bear the expenses of its own delegation to the Assembly and the remuneration, travel, and other expenses of any person whom it appoints to serve on the Council, and of its nominees or representatives on any subsidiary committees or commissions of the Organisation.

Chapter XIII. – Other International Arrangements

ARTICLE 64

Security arrangements

The Organisation may, with respect to air matters within its competence directly affecting world security, by vote of the Assembly enter into appropriate arrangements with any general organisation set up by the nations of the world to preserve peace.

ARTICLE 65

Arrangements with other international bodies

The Council, on behalf of the Organisation, may enter into agreements with other international bodies for the maintenance of common services and for common arrangements concerning personnel and, with the approval of the Assembly, may enter into such other arrangements as may facilitate the work of the Organisation.

ARTICLE 66

Functions relating to other agreements

(a) The Organisation shall also carry out the functions placed upon it by the International Air Services Transit Agreement[2] and by the International Air Transport Agreement[3] drawn up at Chicago on 7th December, 1944, in accordance with the terms and conditions therein set forth.

(b) Members of the Assembly and the Council who have not accepted the International Air Services Transit Agreement or the International Air Transport Agreement drawn up at Chicago on 7th December, 1944, shall not have the right to vote on any questions referred to the Assembly or Council under the provisions of the relevant Agreement.

PART III.- INTERNATIONAL AIR TRANSPORT

Chapter XIV. – Information and Reports

ARTICLE 67

File reports with Council

Each contracting State undertakes that its international airlines shall, in accordance with requirements laid down by the Council, file with the Council traffic reports, cost statistics and financial statements showing among other things all receipts and the sources thereof.

Chapter XV. – Airport and other Air Navigation Facilities

Article 68

Designation of routes and airports

Each contracting State may, subject to the provisions of this Convention, designate the route to be followed within its territory by any international air service and the airports which any such service may use.

Article 69

Improvement of air navigation facilities

If the Council is of the opinion that the airports or other air navigation facilities, including radio and meteorological services, of a contracting State are not reasonably adequate for the safe, regular, efficient, and economical operation of international air services, present or contemplated, the Council shall consult with the State directly concerned, and other States affected, with a view to finding means by which the situation may be remedied, and may make recommendations for that purpose. No contracting State shall be guilty of an infraction of this Convention if it fails to carry out these recommendations.

Article 70

Financing of air navigation facilities

A contracting State, in the circumstances arising under the provisions of Article 69, may conclude an arrangement with the Council for giving effect to such recommendations. The State may elect to bear all of the costs involved in any such arrangement. If the State does not so elect, the Council may agree, at the request of the State, to provide for all or a portion of the costs.

Article 71

Provision and maintenance of facilities by Council

If a contracting State so requests, the Council may agree to provide, man, maintain, and administer any or all of the airports and other air navigation facilities, including radio and meteorological services, required in its territory for the safe, regular, efficient and economical operation of the international air services of the other contracting States, and may specify just and reasonable charges for the use of the facilities provided.

Article 72

Acquisition or use of land

Where land is needed for facilities financed in whole or in part by the Council at the request of a contracting State, that State shall either provide the land itself, retaining title if it wishes, or facilitate the use of the land by the Council on just and reasonable terms and in accordance with the laws of the State concerned.

Article 73

Expenditure and assessment of funds

Within the limit of the funds which may be made available to it by the Assembly under Chapter XII, the Council may make current expenditures for the purposes of this Chapter from the general funds of the Organisation. The Council shall assess the capital funds required for the purposes of this Chapter in previously agreed proportions over a reasonable period of time to the contracting States consenting thereto whose airlines use the facilities. The Council may also assess the States that consent any working funds that are required.

Article 74

Technical assistance and utilisation of revenues

When the Council, at the request of a contracting State, advances funds or provides airports or other facilities in whole or in part, the arrangement may provide, with the consent of that State, for technical assistance in the supervision and operation of the airports and other facilities, and for the payment, from the revenues derived from the operation of the airports and other facilities, of the operating expenses of the airports and the other facilities, and of interest and amortisation charges.

Article 75

Taking over of facilities from Council

A contracting State may at any time discharge any obligation into which it has entered under Article 70, and take over airports and other facilities which the Council has provided in its territory pursuant to the provisions of Articles 71 and

72, by paying to the Council an amount which in the opinion of the Council is reasonable in the circumstances. If the State considers that the amount fixed by the Council is unreasonable it may appeal to the Assembly against the decision of the Council and the Assembly may confirm or amend the decision of the Council.

ARTICLE 76
Return of funds

Funds obtained by the Council through reimbursement under Article 75 and from receipts of interest and amortisation payments under Article 74 shall, in the case of advances originally financed by States under Article 73, be returned to the States which were originally assessed in the proportion of their assessments, as determined by the Council.

Chapter XVI. – Joint Operating Organisations and Pooled Services

ARTICLE 77
Joint operating organisations permitted

Nothing in this Convention shall prevent two or more contracting States from constituting joint air transport operating organisations or international operating agencies and from pooling their air services on any routes or in any regions, but such organisations or agencies and such pooled services shall be subject to all the provisions of this Convention, including those relating to the registration of agreements with the Council. The Council shall determine in what manner the provisions of this Convention relating to nationality of aircraft shall apply to aircraft operated by international operating agencies.

ARTICLE 78
Function of Council

The Council may suggest to contracting States concerned that they form joint organisations to operate air services on any routes or in any regions.

ARTICLE 79
Participation in operating organisations

A State may participate in joint operating organisations or in pooling arrangements, either through its Government or through an airline company or companies designated by its Government. The companies may, at the sole discretion of the State concerned, be State-owned or partly State-owned or privately-owned.

PART IV. – FINAL PROVISIONS

Chapter XVII. – Other Aeronautical Agreements and Arrangements

ARTICLE 80
Paris and Havana Conventions

Each contracting State undertakes, immediately upon the coming into force of this Convention, to give notice of denunciation of the Convention relating to the Regulation of Aerial Navigation signed at Paris on 13th October, 1919,[4] or the Convention on Commercial Aviation signed at Havana on 20th February, 1928,[5] if it is a party to either. As between contracting States, this Convention supersedes the Conventions of Paris and Havana previously referred to.

ARTICLE 81
Registration of existing agreements

All aeronautical agreements which are in existence on the coming into force of this Convention, and which are between a contracting State and any other State or between an airline of a contracting State and any other State or the airline of any other State, shall be forthwith registered with the Council.

ARTICLE 82
Abrogation of inconsistent arrangements

The contracting States accept this Convention as abrogating all obligations and understandings between them which are inconsistent with its terms, and undertake not to enter into any such obligations and understandings. A contracting State which, before becoming a member of the Organisation has undertaken any obligations toward a non-contracting State or a national of a contracting State or of a non-contracting State inconsistent with the terms of this Convention, shall take immediate steps to procure its release from the obligations. If an airline of any contracting State has entered into any such inconsistent obligations, the State of which it is a national shall use its best efforts to secure their termination forthwith and shall in any event cause them to be terminated as soon as such action can lawfully be taken after the coming into force of this Convention.

ARTICLE 83

Registration of new arrangements

Subject to the provisions of the preceding Article, any contracting State may make arrangements not inconsistent with the provisions of this Convention. Any such arrangement shall be forthwith registered with the Council, which shall make it public as soon as possible.

Chapter XVIII. – Disputes and Default

ARTICLE 84

Settlement of disputes

If any disagreement between two or more contracting States relating to the interpretation or application of this Convention and its annexes cannot be settled by negotiation, it shall, on the application of any State concerned in the disagreement, be decided by the Council. No member of the Council shall vote in the consideration by the Council of any dispute to which it is a party. Any contracting State may, subject to Article 85, appeal from the decision of the Council to an ad hoc arbitral tribunal agreed upon with the other parties to the dispute or to the Permanent Court of International Justice. Any such appeal shall be notified to the Council within sixty days of receipt of notification of the decision of the Council.

ARTICLE 85

Arbitration procedure

If any contracting State party to a dispute in which the decision of the Council is under appeal has not accepted the Statute of the Permanent Court of International Justice[6] and the contracting States parties to the dispute cannot agree on the choice of the arbitral tribunal, each of the contracting States parties to the dispute shall name a single arbitrator who shall name an umpire. If either contracting State party to the dispute fails to name an arbitrator within a period of three months from the date of the appeal, an arbitrator shall be named on behalf of that State by the President of the Council from a list of qualified and available persons maintained by the Council. If, within 30 days, the arbitrators cannot agree on an umpire, the President of the Council shall designate an umpire from the list previously referred to. The arbitrators and the umpire shall then jointly constitute an arbitral tribunal. Any arbitral tribunal established under this or the preceding Article shall settle its own procedure and give its decisions by majority vote, provided that the Council may determine procedural questions in the event of any delay which in the opinion of the Council is excessive.

ARTICLE 86

Appeals

Unless the Council decides otherwise, any decision by the Council on whether an international airline is operating in conformity with the provisions of this Convention shall remain in effect unless reversed on appeal. On any other matter, decisions of the Council shall, if appealed from, be suspended until the appeal is decided. The decisions of the Permanent Court of International Justice and of an arbitral tribunal shall be final and binding.

ARTICLE 87

Penalty for non-conformity of airline

Each contracting State undertakes not to allow the operation of an airline of a contracting State through the air space above its territory if the Council has decided that the airline concerned is not conforming to a final decision rendered in accordance with the previous Article.

ARTICLE 88

Penalty for non-conformity by State

The Assembly shall suspend the voting power in the Assembly and in the Council of any contracting State that is found in default under the provisions of this Chapter.

ARTICLE 89

War and emergency conditions

In case of war, the provisions of this Convention shall not affect the freedom of action of any of the contracting States affected, whether as belligerents or as neutrals. The same principle shall apply in the case of any contracting State which declares a state of national emergency and notifies the fact to the Council.

Chapter XX. – Annexes

ARTICLE 90

Adoption and amendment of Annexes

(a) The adoption by the Council of the Annexes described in Article 54, sub-paragraph (1), shall require the vote of two-thirds of the Council at a meeting called for that purpose and shall then be submitted by the Council to each contracting State. Any such Annex or any amendment of an Annex shall become effective within three months after its submission to the contracting States or at the end of such longer period of time as the Council may prescribe, unless in the mean time a majority of the contracting States register their disapproval with the Council.

(b) The Council shall immediately notify all contracting States of the coming into force of any Annex or amendment thereto.

Chapter XXI. – Ratifications, Adherences, Amendments and Denunciations

ARTICLE 91

Ratification of Convention

(a) This Convention shall be subject to ratification by the signatory States. The instruments of ratification shall be deposited in the archives of the Government of the United States of America, which shall give notice of the date of the deposit to each of the Signatory and adhering States.

(b) As soon as this Convention has been ratified or adhered to by twenty-six States it shall come into force[7] between them on the thirtieth day after deposit of the twenty-sixth instrument. It shall come into force for each State ratifying thereafter on the thirtieth day after the deposit of its instrument of ratification.

(c) It shall be the duty of the Government of the United States of America to notify the Government of each of the Signatory and adhering States of the date on which this Convention comes into force.

ARTICLE 92

Adherence to Convention

(a) This Convention shall be open for adherence by members of the United Nations and States associated with them, and States which remained neutral during the present world conflict.

(b) Adherence shall be effected by a notification addressed to the Government of the United States of America and shall take effect as from the thirtieth day from the receipt of the notification by the Government of the United States of America, which shall notify all the contracting States.

ARTICLE 93

Admission of other States

States other than those provided for in Articles 91 and 92 (a) may, subject to approval by any general international organisation set up by the nations of the world to preserve peace, be admitted to participation in this Convention by means of a four-fifths vote of the Assembly and on such conditions as the Assembly may prescribe: provided that in each case the assent of any State invaded or attacked during the present war by the State seeking admission shall be necessary.

ARTICLE 94

Amendment of Convention

(a) Any proposed amendment to this Convention must be approved by a two-thirds vote of the Assembly and shall then come into force in respect of States which have ratified such amendment when ratified by the number of contracting States specified by the Assembly. The number so specified shall not be less than two-thirds of the total number of contracting States.

(b) If in its opinion the amendment is of such a nature as to justify this course, the Assembly in its resolution recommending adoption may provide that any State which has not ratified within a specified period after the amendment has come into force shall thereupon cease to be a member of the Organisation and a party to the Convention.

ARTICLE 95

Denunciation of Convention

(a) Any contracting State may give notice of denunciation of this Convention three years after its coming into effect by notification addressed to the Government of the United States of America, which shall at once inform each of the contracting States.

(b) Denunciation shall take effect one year from the date of the receipt of the notification and shall operate only as regards the State effecting the denunciation.

Chapter XXII. – Definitions

ARTICLE 96

For the purpose of this Convention the expression:

(a) 'Air Service' means any scheduled air service performed by aircraft for the public transport of passengers, mail or cargo.

(b) 'International air service' means an air service which passes through the air space over the territory of more than one State.

(c) 'Airline' means any air transport enterprise offering or operating an international air service.

(d) 'Stop for non-traffic purposes' means a landing for any purpose other than taking on or discharging passengers, cargo or mail.

SIGNATURE OF CONVENTION

In witness whereof, the undersigned Plenipotentiaries, having been duly authorised, sign this Convention on behalf of their respective Governments on the dates appearing opposite their signatures.

DONE at Chicago the seventh day of December, 1944, in the English language. A text drawn up in the English, French, and Spanish languages,[*] each of which shall be of equal authenticity, shall be opened for signature at Washington, DC. Both texts shall be deposited in the archives of the Government of the United States of America, and certified copies shall be transmitted by that Government to the Governments of all the States which may sign or adhere to this Convention.

CONCLUDED
7 Dec 1944, Chicago

ENTRY INTO FORCE

4 April 1947. Later acceptances effective 30 days after deposit: Arts 91,92.

PARTIES

AFGHANISTAN 4 Apr 47; ALBANIA 28 Mar 91; ALGERIA 7 May 63; ANGOLA 11 Mar 77; ANTIGUA AND BARBUDA 10 Nov 81; ARGENTINA 4 Jun 46; ARMENIA 18 Jun 92; AUSTRALIA 1 Mar 47; AUSTRIA 27 Aug 48; AZERBAIJAN 9 Oct 92; BAHAMAS 27 May 75; BAHRAIN 28 Aug 71; BANGLADESH 22 Dec 72; BARBADOS 21 Mar 67; BELARUS 4 Jun 93; BELGIUM 5 May 47; BELIZE 7 Dec 90; BENIN 29 May 61; BHUTAN 17 May 89; BOLIVIA 4 Apr 47; BOSNIA & HERZEGOVINA 13 Jan 93; BOTSWANA 28 Dec 78; BRAZIL 8 Jul 46; BRUNEI DARUSSALAM 4 Dec 84; BULGARIA 8 Jun 67; BURKINA FASO 21 Mar 62; BURUNDI 19 Jan 68; CAMBODIA 16 Jan 56; CAMEROON 15 Jan 60; CANADA 13 Feb 46; CAPE VERDE 19 Aug 76; CENTRAL AFRICAN REPUBLIC 28 Jun 61; CHAD 3 Jul 62; CHILE 11 Mar 47; CHINA 20 Feb 46; COLOMBIA 31 Oct 47; COMOROS 15 Jan 85; CONGO 26 Apr 62; COOK ISLANDS 20 Aug 86; COSTA RICA 1 May 58; COTE D'IVOIRE 31 Oct 60; CROATIA 9 Apr 92; CUBA 11 May 49; CYPRUS 17 Jan 61; CZECH REPUBLIC 4 Mar 93; DENMARK 28 Feb 47; DJIBOUTI 30 Jun 78; DOMINICAN REPUBLIC 25 Jan 46; ECUADOR 20 Aug 54; EGYPT 13 Mar 47; EL SALVADOR 11 Jun 47; EQUATORIAL GUINEA 22 Feb 72; ERITREA 17 Sep 93; ESTONIA 24 Jan 92; ETHIOPIA 1 Mar 47; FIJI 5 Mar 73; FINLAND 30 Mar 49; FRANCE 25 Mar 47; GABON 18 Jan 62; GAMBIA 14 May 77; GEORGIA 21 Jan 94; GERMANY 9 May 56; GHANA 9 May 57; GREECE 13 Mar 47; GRENADA 31 Aug 81; GUATEMALA 28 Apr 47; GUINEA 27 Mar 59; GUINEA-BISSAU 15 Dec 77; GUYANA 3 Feb 67; HAITI 2 Mar 48; HONDURAS 7 May 53; HUNGARY 30 Sep 69; ICELAND 21 Mar 47; INDIA 1 Mar 47; INDONESIA 27 Apr 50; IRAN, ISLAMIC REPUBLIC OF 19 Apr 50; IRAQ 2 Jun 47; IRELAND 31 Oct 46; ISRAEL 25 May 49; ITALY 31 Oct 47; JAMAICA 26 Mar 63; JAPAN 8 Sep 53; JORDAN 18 Mar 47; KAZAKHSTAN 21 Aug 92; KENYA 1 May 64; KIRIBATI 14 May 81; KOREA, DEMOCRATIC PEOPLE'S REPUBLIC 16 Aug 77; KOREA, REPUBLIC OF 11 Nov 52; KUWAIT 18 May 60; KYRGYSTAN 25 Feb 93; LAO PEOPLE'S DEMOCRATIC REPUBLIC 13 Jun 55; LATVIA 13 Jul 92; LEBANON 19 Sep 49; LESOTHO 19 May 75; LIBERIA 11 Feb 47; LIBYAN ARAB JAMAHIRIYA 29 Jan 53; LITHUANIA 8 Jan 92; LUXEMBOURG 28 Apr 48; MACEDONIA, FORMER YUGOSLAV REPUBLIC OF 10 Dec 92; MADAGASCAR 14 Apr 62 ; MALAWI 11 Sep 64; MALAYSIA 7 Apr 58; MALDIVES 12 Mar 74 ; MALI 8 Nov 60;

MALTA 5 Jan 65; MARSHALL ISLANDS 18 Mar 88; MAURITANIA 13 Jan 62; MAURITIUS 30 Jan 70; MEXICO 25 Jun 46; MICRONESIA, FEDERATED STATES OF 27 Sep 88; MOLDOVA 1 Jun 92; MONACO 4 Jan 80; MONGOLIA 7 Sep 89; MOROCCO 13 Nov 56; MOZAMBIQUE 5 Jan 77; MYANMAR 8 Jul 48; NAMIBIA 30 Apr 91; NAURU 25 Aug 75; NEPAL 29 Jun 60; NETHERLANDS 26 Mar 47; NEW ZEALAND 7 Mar 47; NICARAGUA 28 Dec 45; NIGER 29 May 61; NIGERIA 14 Nov 60; NORWAY 5 May 47; OMAN 24 Jan 73; PAKISTAN 6 Nov 47; PALAU 3 Nov 95; PANAMA* 18 Jan 60; PAPUA NEW GUINEA 15 Dec 75; PARAGUAY 21 Jan 46; PERU 8 Apr 46; PHILIPPINES 1 Mar 47; POLAND 6 Apr 45; PORTUGAL 27 Feb 47; QATAR 5 Sep 71; ROMANIA 30 Apr 65; RUSSIAN FEDERATION 15 Oct 70; RWANDA 3 Feb 64; SAINT LUCIA 20 Nov 79; SAINT VINCENT AND THE GRENADINES 15 Nov 83; SAN MARINO 13 May 88; SAO TOME AND PRINCIPE 28 Feb 77; SAUDI ARABIA 19 Feb 62; SENEGAL 11 Nov 60; SEYCHELLES 25 Apr 77; SIERRA LEONE 22 Nov 61; SINGAPORE 20 May 66; SLOVAKIA 15 Mar 93; SLOVENIA 13 May 92; SOLOMON ISLANDS 11 Apr 85; SOMALIA 2 Mar 64; SOUTH AFRICA 1 Mar 47; SPAIN 5 Mar 47; SRI LANKA 1 Jun 48; SUDAN 29 Jun 56; SURINAME 5 Mar 76; SWAZILAND 14 Feb 73; SWEDEN 7 Nov 46; SWITZERLAND 6 Feb 47; SYRIAN ARAB REPUBLIC 21 Dec 49; TAJIKISTAN 3 Sep 93; TANZANIA, UNITED REPUBLIC OF 23 Apr 62; THAILAND 4 Apr 47; TOGO 24 Jun 48; TONGA 2 Nov 84; TRINIDAD AND TOBAGO 14 Mar 63; TUNISIA 18 Nov 57; TURKEY 20 Dec 45; TURKMENISTAN 15 Mar 93; UGANDA 10 Apr 67; UKRAINE 10 Aug 92; UNITED ARAB EMIRATES 25 April 72; UNITED KINGDOM 1 Mar 47; UNITED STATES OF AMERICA 9 Aug 46; URUGUAY 14 Jan 54; UZBEKISTAN 13 Oct 92; VANUATU 17 Aug 83; VENEZUELA 1 Apr 47; VIETNAM 13 Mar 80; WESTERN SAMOA 21 Nov 96; YEMEN 17 Apr 64; ZAIRE 27 Jul 61; ZAMBIA 30 Oct 64; ZIMBABWE 11 Feb 81;

(Dates shown are those of deposit of instruments of ratification or adherence by the State.)

AMENDMENTS

1947	Amending Protocol (Art 93 bis). In force 20 March 1961.
1954	Amending Protocol (Art 45). In force 16 May 1958.
1954	Amending Protocol (Arts 48a, 49e and 61). In force 12 December 1956.
1961	Amending Protocol (Art 50a). In force 17 July 1962.
1962	Amending Protocol (Art 48a). In force 11 September 1975.
1971	Amending Protocol (Art 50a). In force 16 January 1973.
1971	Amending Protocol (Art 56). In force 19 December 1974.
1974	Amending Protocol (Art 50a). In force 15 February 1980.
1977	Amending Protocol (Final Clause). Not yet in force.
1980	Amending Protocol (Art 83 bis). Not yet in force.
1984	Amending Protocol (Art 83 bis). Not yet in force.
1989	Amending Protocol (Art 56). Not yet in force.
1990	Amending Protocol (Art 50a). Not yet in force.

Notes

(1) 'Treaty Series No.55 (1938)', Cmd. 5833
(2) 'Treaty Series No. 8 (1953)', Cmd. 8742.
(3) 'Miscellaneous No. 6 (1945)', Cmd. 6614.
(4) 'Treaty Series No. 2 (1922)', Cmd. 1609.
(5) State Papers, Vol. 128, page 505.
(6) 'Treaty Series No. 67 (1946)', Cmd. 7015.
(7) 4 April 1947.
(8) It was not found possible to draw up a text in the French and Spanish languages for signature. An authentic trilingual text was provided by the Buenos Aires Protocol of 1968.

Protocol relating to an Amendment to the Convention on International Civil Aviation signed at Chicago on 7 December 1944

Montreal, 27 May 1947

The Assembly of the International Civil Aviation Organisation,

Having been convened at Montreal by the Interim Council of the Provisional International Civil Aviation Organisation, and having met in its First Session on May 6th 1947, and

Having considered it advisable to amend the Convention on International Civil Aviation done at Chicago on December 7th 1944[1],

Approved on the thirteenth day of May of the year one thousand nine hundred and forty-seven, in accordance with the provisions of Article 94(a) of the Convention on International Civil Aviation done at Chicago on December 7th 1944, the following proposed amendment to the said Convention which shall be numbered as 'Article 93 bis':

'ARTICLE 93 BIS

(A) Notwithstanding the provisions of Articles 91, 92 and 93 above,

(1) A State whose government the General Assembly of the United Nations has recommended be debarred from membership in international agencies established by or brought into relationship with the United Nations shall automatically cease to be a member of the International Civil Aviation Organisation;

(2) A State which has been expelled from membership in the United Nations shall automatically cease to be a member of the International Civil Aviation Organisation unless the General Assembly of the United Nations attaches to its act of expulsion a recommendation to the contrary.

(B) A State which ceases to be a member of the International Civil Aviation Organisation as a result of the provisions of paragraph (A) above may, after approval by the General Assembly of the United Nations, be readmitted to the International Civil Aviation Organisation upon application and upon approval by a majority of the Council.

(C) Members of the Organisation which are suspended from the exercise of the rights and privileges of membership of the United Nations shall, upon the request of the latter, be suspended from the rights and privileges of membership in this Organisation',

Specified on the sixteenth day of May of the year one thousand nine hundred and forty-seven, pursuant to the provisions of the said Article 94(a) of the said Convention, that the above mentioned amendment shall come into force when ratified by twenty-eight Contracting States, and

Instructed at the same date the Secretary General of the International Civil Aviation Organisation to draw up a Protocol embodying this proposed amendment and to the following effect, which Protocol shall be signed by the President and the Secretary General of the First Assembly.

Consequently, pursuant to the aforesaid action of the Assembly,

The present Protocol shall be subject to ratification by any State which has ratified or adhered to the said Convention. The instruments of ratification shall be transmitted to the Secretary General of the International Civil Aviation Organisation for deposit in the archives of the Organisation; the Secretary General of the Organisation shall immediately notify all Contracting States of the date of deposit of each ratification;

The aforesaid proposed amendment of the Convention shall come into force, in respect of the States which have ratified this Protocol, on the date on which the twenty-eighth instrument of ratification is deposited[2]. The Secretary General of the Organisation shall immediately notify all the States parties to or signatories of the said Convention of the date on which the proposed amendment comes into force;

The aforesaid proposed amendment shall come into force in respect of each State ratifying after that date upon deposit of its instrument of ratification in the archives of the Organisation.

State	Date of Deposit	State	Date of Deposit
Afghanistan	March 2, 1948	Malawi	November 30, 1964
Algeria	November 29, 1965	Malaysia	October 1, 1962
Angola	April 10, 1977	Mali	January 10, 1961
Antigua and Barbuda	October 17, 1988	Malta	May 25, 1965
Argentina	November 19, 1963	Mauritania	April 2, 1962
Austria	April 25, 1983	Mauritius	September 1, 1970
Bahamas	July 25, 1975	Mexico	September 12, 1949
Bahrain	November 1, 1971	Morocco	June 21, 1957
Brazil	October 14, 1949	Myanmar	October 25, 1951
Bulgaria	December 16, 1969	Netherlands	February 24, 1955
Burkina Faso	February 1, 1971	New Zealand	September 22, 1947
Canada	August 22, 1947	Nicaragua	July 9, 1962
Central African		Niger	April 8, 1988
Republic	May 22, 1962	Norway	July 18, 1962
Chad	August 28, 1964	Pakistan	July 19, 1948
Chile	March 18, 1968	Panama	September 24, 1963
China	March 24, 1948	Papua New Guinea	October 5, 1992
Congo	May 26, 1962	Philippines	November 17, 1952
Costa Rica	July 5, 1960	Poland	February 21, 1969
Cuba	September 30, 1963	Romania	May 31, 1966
Cyprus	July 5, 1989	Rwanda	November 15, 1965
Czechoslovakia	April 21, 1948	Sao Tome and	
Dominican Republic	November 10, 1947	Principe	September 18, 1980
Ecuador	January 11, 1965	Saudi Arabia	February 25, 1966
Egypt	November 24, 1949	Senegal	February 28, 1961
El Salvador	January 22, 1963	Seychelles	January 22, 1981
Fiji	April 4, 1973	Singapore	January 4, 1967
Gambia	January 25, 1978	Somalia	September 30, 1964
Guinea	June 26, 1959	Sri Lanka	December 9, 1948
Guyana	December 14, 1988	Sudan	April 8, 1960
Hungary	October 30, 1970	Swaziland	January 31, 1974
India	December 15, 1947	Syria	January 23, 1953
Indonesia	July 17, 1961	Tanzania	April 10, 1963
Iran	April 27, 1950	Thailand	December 3, 1957
Iraq	December 9, 1950	Tunisia	May 23, 1961
Italy	October 8, 1952	Turkey	September 28, 1965
Ivory Coast	March 20, 1961	Uganda	September 16, 1976
Jamaica	October 18, 1963	United Kingdom	January 19, 1948
Kenya	May 31, 1964	Uruguay	March 20, 1979
Lebanon	August 20, 1973	Vanuatu	January 31, 1989
Lesotho	September 11, 1975	Venezuela	February 3, 1978
Luxembourg	July 11, 1972	Zambia	October 12, 1965
Madagascar	December 7, 1962		

Notes

(1) 'Treaty Series No. 8 (1953)', Cmd. 8742.

(2) The Protocol of Amendment entered into force on March 20, 1961.

Protocol relating to an Amendment to the Convention of 7 December 1944 on International Civil Aviation

Montreal, 14 June 1954

The Assembly of the International Civil Aviation Organisation,

Having met in its Eighth Session, at Montreal, on the first day of June, 1954, and

Having considered it desirable to amend the Convention on International Civil Aviation done at Chicago on the seventh day of December, 1944[1],

Approved, on the fourteenth day of June of the year one thousand nine hundred and fifty-four, in accordance with the provisions of Article 94(a) of the Convention aforesaid, the following proposed amendment to the said Convention:–

> At the end of Article 45 of the Convention, the full stop shall be substituted by a comma, and the following shall be added, namely:
> 'and otherwise than temporarily by decision of the Assembly, such decision to be taken by the number of votes specified by the Assembly. The number of votes so specified will not be less than three-fifths of the total number of contracting States.',

Specified, pursuant to the provisions of the said Article 94(a) of the said Convention, forty-two as the number of contracting States upon whose ratification the proposed amendment aforesaid shall come into force, and

Resolved that the Secretary General of the International Civil Aviation Organisation draw up a Protocol in the English, French and Spanish languages, each of which shall be of equal authenticity, embodying the proposed amendment above-mentioned and the matters hereinafter appearing,

Consequently, pursuant to the aforesaid action of the Assembly,

This Protocol shall be signed by the President of the Assembly and its Secretary General;

This Protocol shall be open to ratification by any State which has ratified or adhered to the said Convention on International Civil Aviation;

The instruments of ratification shall be deposited with the International Civil Aviation Organisation;

This Protocol shall come into force among the States which have ratified it on the date on which the forty-second instrument of ratification is so deposited[2];

The Secretary General shall immediately notify all contracting States of the deposit of each ratification of this Protocol;

The Secretary General shall immediately notify all States parties or signatories to the said Convention of the date on which this Protocol comes into force;

With respect to any contracting State ratifying this Protocol after the date aforesaid, the Protocol shall come into force upon deposit of its instrument of ratification with the International Civil Aviation Organisation.

State	Date of Deposit	State	Date of Deposit
Afghanistan	March 15, 1956	Korea, Democratic	
Algeria	November 29, 1965	People's Republic	June 27, 1978
Angola	April 10, 1977	Korea, Republic of	May 23, 1957
Antigua and Barbuda	October 17, 1988	Laos	June 4, 1956
Argentina	September 21, 1956	Lebanon	August 20, 1973
Australia	August 23, 1957	Lesotho	September 11, 1975
Austria	April 13, 1956	Libya	December 6, 1956
Bahamas	July 25, 1975	Luxembourg	March 17, 1955
Bahrain	November 1, 1971	Madagascar	December 7, 1962
Belgium	January 28, 1955	Malawi	November 30, 1964
Bolivia	May 23, 1956	Malaysia	March 28, 1961
Brazil	June 17, 1959	Mali	January 10, 1961

Bulgaria	December 16, 1969	Malta	May 25, 1965
Burkina Faso	February 1, 1971	Mauritania	April 2, 1962
Cameroon	November 14, 1961	Mauritius	September 1, 1970
Canada	September 2, 1958	Mexico	May 13, 1955
Central African		Morocco	June 21, 1957
Republic	May 22, 1962	Nauru	September 3, 1975
Chad	August 28, 1964	Netherlands	December 14, 1955
Chile	March 18, 1968	New Zealand	May 8, 1958
China	February 28, 1974	Nicaragua	July 9, 1962
Congo	May 26, 1962	Niger	April 8, 1988
Costa Rica	July 5, 1960	Norway	April 18, 1956
Cuba	August 12, 1963	Pakistan	October 21, 1955
Cyprus	July 5, 1989	Panama	September 24, 1963
Czechoslovakia	February 21, 1957	Papua New Guinea	July 25, 1979
Denmark	June 4, 1955	Peru	May 16, 1958
Dominican Republic	December 28, 1954	Philippines	August 13, 1956
Ecuador	January 11, 1965	Poland	May 23, 1962
Egypt	March 15, 1955	Portugal	September 20, 1955
El Salvador	May 26, 1980	Romania	May 31, 1966
Estonia	August 21, 1992	Russian Federation	May 4, 1971
Ethiopia	October 25, 1954	Rwanda	November 15, 1965
Fiji	April 4, 1973	Sao Tome and Principe	September 18, 1980
Finland	December 30, 1954	Saudi Arabia	February 25, 1966
France	September 21, 1964	Senegal	February 28, 1961
Gambia	January 25, 1978	Seychelles	January 22, 1981
Germany	April 27, 1959	Singapore	January 4, 1967
Ghana	August 15, 1961	Somalia	September 30, 1964
Greece	December 12, 1956	South Africa	May 24, 1956
Guatemala	October 6, 1959	Spain	June 6, 1955
Guinea	June 26, 1959	Sri Lanka	January 6, 1955
Haiti	September 13, 1957	Sudan	April 8, 1960
Honduras	June 1, 1955	Swaziland	January 31, 1974
Hungary	October 30, 1970	Sweden	July 8, 1955
Iceland	July 5, 1955	Switzerland	April 17, 1956
India	January 19, 1955	Syria	March 8, 1956
Indonesia	November 24, 1959	Tanzania	April 10, 1963
Iran	February 19, 1973	Thailand	January 18, 1960
Iraq	March 25, 1955	Tunisia	May 23, 1961
Ireland	January 4, 1955	Turkey	December 23, 1955
Italy	March 24, 1958	Uganda	September 16, 1976
Ivory Coast	March 20, 1961	United Kingdom	February 17, 1955
Jamaica	October 18, 1963	Vanuatu	January 31, 1989
Japan	June 21, 1956	Venezuela	February 3, 1978
Kenya	May 31, 1964	Zaire	August 23, 1962
		Zambia	October 12, 1965

Notes

(1) 'Treaty Series No. 8 (1953)', Cmd. 8742

(2) 16 May 1958.

Protocol relating to certain Amendments to the Convention of 7 December 1944 on International Civil Aviation

Montreal, 14 June 1954

The Assembly of the International Civil Aviation Organisation,

Having met in its Eighth Session, at Montreal, on the first day of June 1954, and

Having considered it desirable to amend the Convention on International Civil Aviation done at Chicago on the seventh day of December, 1944[1],

Approved, on the fourteenth day of June of the year one thousand nine hundred and fifty-four, in accordance with the provisions of Article 94(a) of the Convention aforesaid, the following proposed amendments to the said Convention:-

In Article 48(a), substitute for the word 'annually' the expression 'not less than once in three years';
In Article 49(e), substitute for the expression 'an annual budget' the expression 'annual budgets'; and
In Article 61, substitute for the expressions 'an annual budget' and 'vote the budget' the expressions 'annual budgets' and 'vote the budgets',

Specified, pursuant to the provisions of the said Article 94(a) of the said Convention, forty-two as the number of contracting States upon whose ratification the proposed amendments aforesaid shall come into force, and

Resolved that the Secretary General of the International Civil Aviation Organisation draw up a Protocol, in the English, French and Spanish languages, each of which shall be of equal authenticity, embodying the proposed amendments above-mentioned and the matters hereinafter appearing.

Consequently, pursuant to the aforesaid action of the Assembly,

This Protocol shall be signed by the President of the Assembly and its Secretary General;

This Protocol shall be open to ratification by any State which has ratified or adhered to the said Convention on International Civil Aviation;

The instruments of ratification shall be deposited with the International Civil Aviation Organisation;

This Protocol shall come into force among the States which have ratified it on the date on which the forty-second instrument of ratification is so deposited[2];

The Secretary General shall immediately notify all contracting States of the deposit of each ratification of this Protocol;

The Secretary General shall immediately notify all States parties or signatories to the said Convention of the date on which this Protocol comes into force;

With respect to any contracting State ratifying this Protocol after the date aforesaid, the Protocol shall come into force upon deposit of its instrument of ratification with the International Civil Aviation Organisation.

State	Date of Deposit	State	Date of Deposit
Afghanistan	March 15, 1956	Bahamas	July 25, 1975
Algeria	November 29, 1965	Bahrain	November 1, 1971
Angola	April 10, 1977	Belgium	January 28, 1955
Antigua and Barbuda	October 17, 1988	Bolivia	May 23, 1956
Argentina	September 21, 1956	Brazil	June 17, 1959
Australia	April 22, 1955	Bulgaria	December 16, 1969
Austria	April 13, 1956	Burkina Faso	February 1, 1971
Cameroon	November 14, 1961	Malaysia	March 28, 1961
Canada	November 4, 1954	Mali	January 10, 1961
Central African		Malta	May 25, 1965
Republic	May 22, 1962	Mauritania	April 2, 1962
Chad	August 28, 1964	Mauritius	September 1, 1970
Chile	December 20, 1967	Mexico	May 13, 1955
China	February 28, 1974	Morocco	June 21, 1957
Congo	May 26, 1962	Myanmar	August 16, 1957

Costa Rica	July 5, 1960	Nauru	September 3, 1975
Cuba	October 29, 1962	Netherlands	May 31, 1955
Cyprus	July 5, 1989	New Zealand	June 8, 1956
Czechoslovakia	February 21, 1957	Nicaragua	July 9, 1962
Denmark	June 4, 1955	Niger	April 8, 1988
Dominican Republic	December 28, 1954	Norway	April 18, 1956
Ecuador	January 11, 1965	Pakistan	October 21, 1955
Egypt	March 15, 1955	Panama	September 24, 1963
El Salvador	February 13, 1980	Papua New Guinea	July 25, 1979
Estonia	August 21, 1992	Peru	September 25, 1957
Ethiopia	October 25, 1954	Philippines	July 27, 1955
Fiji	April 4, 1973	Poland	May 23, 1962
Finland	December 30, 1954	Portugal	September 20, 1955
France	September 21, 1964	Romania	May 31, 1966
Gambia	January 25, 1978	Russian Federation	May 4, 1971
Germany	April 27, 1959	Rwanda	November 15, 1965
Ghana	August 15, 1961	Sao Tome and	
Greece	December 12, 1956	Principe	September 18, 1980
Guatemala	October 6, 1959	Saudi Arabia	February 25, 1966
Guinea	June 26, 1959	Senegal	February 28, 1961
Honduras	June 1, 1955	Seychelles	January 22, 1981
Hungary	October 30, 1970	Singapore	January 4, 1967
Iceland	July 5, 1955	Somalia	September 30, 1964
India	January 19, 1955	South Africa	May 24, 1956
Indonesia	October 18, 1955	Spain	June 6, 1955
Iran	February 19, 1973	Sri Lanka	January 6, 1955
Iraq	March 25, 1955	Sudan	April 8, 1960
Ireland	January 4, 1955	Swaziland	January 31, a974
Israel	May 13, 1957	Sweden	July 8, 1955
Italy	March 24, 1958	Switzerland	April 17, 1956
Ivory Coast	March 20, 1961	Syria	March 8, 1956
Jamaica	October 18, 1963	Tanzania	April 10, 1963
Japan	June 21, 1956	Thailand	July 18, 1956
Kenya	May 31, 1964	Tunisia	January 16, 1961
Korea, Democratic		Turkey	December 23, 1955
People's Republic	June 27, 1978	Uganda	September 16, 1976
Korea, Republic of	May 23, 1957	United Kingdom	February 17, 1955
Laos	June 4, 1956	Uruguay	March 20, 1979
Lebanon	August 20, 1973	USA	May 22, 1956
Lesotho	September 11, 1975	Vanuatu	January 31, 1989
Libya	December 6, 1956	Venezuela	July 6, 1956
Luxembourg	March 17, 1955	Zaire	August 23, 1962
Madagascar	December 7, 1962	Zambia	October 12, 1965
Malawi	November 30, 1964		

Notes

(1) 'Treaty Series No. 8 (1953)', Cmd. 8742.

(2) 12 December 1956.

Protocol relating to an Amendment to the Convention on International Civil Aviation signed at Chicago on 7 December 1944
Montreal, 21 June 1961

The Assembly of the International Civil Aviation Organisation,

Having met in its Thirteenth (Extraordinary) Session, at Montreal, on the nineteenth day of June 1961,

Having noted that it is the general desire of Contracting States to enlarge the membership of the Council,

Having considered it proper to provide for six additional seats in the Council and, accordingly, to increase the membership from twenty-one to twenty-seven,

and having considered it necessary to amend for the purpose aforesaid the Convention on International Civil Aviation done at Chicago on the seventh day of December 1944[1],

Approved, on the twenty-first day of June of the year one thousand nine hundred and sixty-one, in accordance with the provisions of Article 94(a) of the Convention aforesaid, the following proposed amendment to the said Convention:
In Article 50(a) of the Convention the expression 'twenty-one' shall be deleted and substituted by 'twenty-seven',

Specified, pursuant to the provisions of the said Article 94(a) of the said Convention, fifty-six as the number of Contracting States upon whose ratification the proposed amendment aforesaid shall come into force, and

Resolved that the Secretary General of the International Civil Aviation Organisation draw up a protocol, in the English, French and Spanish languages, each of which shall be of equal authenticity, embodying the proposed amendment above-mentioned and the matter hereinafter appearing.

Consequently, pursuant to the aforesaid action of the Assembly,

This Protocol has been drawn up by the Secretary General of the Organisation;

This Protocol shall be open to ratification by any State which has ratified or adhered to the said Convention on International Civil Aviation;

The instruments of ratification shall be deposited with the International Civil Aviation Organisation;

This Protocol shall come into force in respect of the States which have ratified it on the date on which the fifty-sixth instrument of ratification is so deposited[2];

The Secretary General shall immediately notify all Contracting States of the date of deposit of each ratification of this Protocol;

The Secretary General shall immediately notify all States parties or signatories to the said Convention of the date on which this Protocol comes into force;

With respect to any Contracting State ratifying this Protocol after the date aforesaid, the Protocol shall come into force upon deposit of its instrument of ratification with the International Civil Aviation Organisation.

State	Date of Deposit	State	Date of Deposit
Algeria	November 29, 1965	Kuwait	July 3, 1962
Angola	April 10, 1977	Laos	March 7, 1962
Antigua and Barbuda	October 17, 1988	Lebanon	June 18, 1962
Argentina	November 19, 1963	Lesotho	September 11, 1975
Australia	January 19, 1962	Libya	August 17, 1962
Austria	July 17, 1962	Luxembourg	October 3, 1963
Bahamas	July 25, 1975	Madagascar	December 7, 1962
Bahrain	November 1, 1971	Malawi	November 30, 1964
Belgium	February 15, 1962	Malaysia	October 3, 1961
Benin	March 30, 1962	Mali	July 12, 1961
Brazil	March 6, 1969	Malta	May 25, 1965
Bulgaria	December 16, 1969	Mauritania	April 2, 1962

Burkina Faso	September 8, 1965	Mauritius	September 1, 1970
Cameroon	November 14, 1961	Mexico	April 9, 1962
Canada	October 17, 1961	Morocco	December 8, 1964
Central African		Netherlands	May 8, 1962
Republic	May 22, 1962	New Zealand	May 14, 1962
Chad	August 28, 1964	Nicaragua	November 17, 1961
Chile	December 20, 1967	Niger	September 14, 1961
China	February 28, 1974	Nigeria	March 7, 1962
Congo	May 26, 1962	Norway	October 10, 1961
Costa Rica	January 9, 1964	Pakistan	April 30, 1962
Cuba	October 29, 1962	Panama	July 9, 1962
Cyprus	July 31, 1962	Papua New Guinea	July 25, 1979
Czechoslovakia	March 9, 1962	Paraguay	May 26, 1969
Denmark	May 15, 1962	Peru	March 12, 1964
Dominican Republic	October 24, 1961	Philippines	November 12, 1962
Ecuador	January 11, 1965	Poland	May 23, 1962
Egypt	February 27, 1962	Portugal	May 29, 1962
El Salvador	January 22, 1963	Romania	May 31, 1966
Estonia	August 21, 1992	Russian Federation	May 4, 1971
Ethiopia	January 23, 1963	Rwanda	November 15, 1965
Fiji	April 4, 1973	Sao Tome and Principe	September 18, 1980
Finland	September 18, 1961	Saudi Arabia	February 25, 1966
France	November 20, 1962	Senegal	March 5, 1962
Gambia	January 25, 1978	Seychelles	January 22, 1981
Germany	August 16, 1962	Sierra Leone	May 15, 1962
Ghana	April 16, 1962 ·	Singapore	January 4, 1967
Greece	May 26, 1965	Somalia	September 30, 1964
Guinea	August 21, 1961	South Africa	February 13, 1962
Honduras	December 20, 1962	Spain	April 2, 1962
Hungary	October 30, 1970	Sri Lanka	May 28, 1962
India	December 18, 1961	Sudan	May 31, 1962
Indonesia	July 28, 1961	Swaziland	January 31, 1974
Iraq	October 3, 1973	Sweden	December 28, 1961
Ireland	April 9, 1962	Switzerland	May 22, 1962
Israel	February 12, 1962	Syria	July 16, 1962
Italy	May 17, 1963	Tanzania	April 10, 1963
Ivory Coast	November 14, 1961	Thailand	January 17, 1962
Jamaica	October 18, 1963	Tunisia	December 27, 1961
Japan	June 4, 1962	Turkey	September 28, 1965
Jordan	July 27, 1961	Uganda	September 16, 1976
Kenya	May 31, 1964	United Kingdom	January 4, 1962
Korea, Democratic		USA	March 23, 1962
People's Republic	June 27, 1978	Venezuela	February 6, 1962
Korea, Republic of	February 16, 1962	Zambia	October 12, 1965

Notes

(1) 'Treaty Series No. 8 (1953)', Cmd. 8742.

(2) The amendment entered into force on 17 July 1962.

Protocol relating to an Amendment to Article 48(a) of the Convention on International Civil Aviation signed at Chicago on 7 December 1944

Rome, 15 September 1962

The Assembly of the International Civil Aviation Organisation,

Having met in its Fourteenth Session, at Rome, on the twenty-first day of August, 1962,

Having noted that it is the general desire of contracting States that the minimum number of contracting States which may request the holding of an extraordinary meeting of the Assembly should be increased from the present figure of ten,

Having considered it proper to increase the said number to one-fifth of the total number of contracting States,

And having considered it necessary to amend for the purpose aforesaid the Convention on International Civil Aviation done at Chicago on the seventh day of December, 1944[1],

Approved, on the fourteenth day of September in the year one thousand nine hundred and sixty-two, in accordance with the provisions of Article 94(a) of the Convention aforesaid, the following proposed amendment to the said Convention:

In Article 48(a) of the Convention, the second sentence be deleted and substituted by 'An extraordinary meeting of the Assembly may be held at any time upon the call of the Council or at the request of not less than one-fifth of the total number of contracting States addressed to the Secretary General.

Specified, pursuant to the provisions of the said Article 94(a) of the said Convention, sixty-six as the number of contracting States upon whose ratification the proposed amendment aforesaid shall come into force, and

Resolved that the Secretary General of the International Civil Aviation Organisation draw up a protocol, in the English, French and Spanish languages, each of which shall be of equal authenticity, embodying the proposed amendment above-mentioned and the matter hereinafter appearing.

Consequently, pursuant to the aforesaid action of the Assembly,

This Protocol has been drawn up by the Secretary General of the Organisation;

This Protocol shall be open to ratification by any State which has ratified or adhered to the said Convention on International Civil Aviation;

The instruments of ratification shall be deposited with the International Civil Aviation Organisation;

This Protocol shall come into force in respect of the States which have ratified it on the date on which the sixty-sixth instrument of ratification is so deposited[2];

The Secretary General shall immediately notify all Contracting States of the date of deposit of each ratification of this Protocol;

The Secretary General shall immediately notify all States parties or signatories to the said Convention of the date on which this Protocol comes into force;

With respect to any contracting State ratifying this Protocol after the date aforesaid, the Protocol shall come into force upon deposit of its instrument of ratification with the International Civil Aviation Organisation.

In faith whereof, the President and the Secretary General of the Fourteenth Session of the Assembly of the International Civil Aviation Organisation, being authorised thereto by the Assembly, sign this Protocol.

Done at Rome on the fifteenth day of September of the year one thousand nine hundred and sixty-two in a single document in the English, French and Spanish languages, each of which shall be of equal authenticity. This Protocol shall remain deposited in the archives of the International Civil Aviation Organisation; and certified copies thereof shall be transmitted by the Secretary General of the Organisation to all States parties or signatories to the Convention on International Civil Aviation aforementioned.

State	Date of Deposit	State	Date of Deposit
Algeria	November 29, 1965	Lebanon	July 20, 1977
Angola	April 10, 1977	Lesotho	September 11, 1975
Antigua and Barbuda	October 17, 1988	Luxembourg	September 2, 1965
Argentina	June 10, 1986	Madagascar	April 24, 1967
Australia	August 1, 1963	Malawi	November 30, 1964
Austria	May 12, 1964	Malaysia	January 20, 1964
Bahrain	November 1, 1971	Malta	May 25, 1965
Barbados	November 23, 1984	Mauritius	September 1, 1970
Brazil	March 6, 1969	Mexico	February 9, 1979
Bulgaria	December 16, 1969	Netherlands	August 26, 1964
Burkina Faso	July 12, 1963	New Zealand	August 24, 1964
Cameroon	July 2, 1969	Niger	December 17, 1962
Canada	January 22, 1965	Norway	February 26, 1963
Chad	August 28, 1964	Pakistan	November 27, 1963
Chile	December 20, 1967	Papua New Guinea	October 5, 1992
China	February 28, 1974	Philippines	November 12, 1963
Cuba	June 15, 1964	Poland	February 21, 1969
Cyprus	July 7, 1989	Portugal	May 23, 1963
Czechoslovakia	June 8, 1964	Romania	May 31, 1966
Denmark	October 30, 1963	Russian Federation	September 4, 1975
Ecuador	January 11, 1965	Rwanda	November 15, 1965
El Salvador	February 13, 1980	Sao Tome and	
Estonia	August 21, 1992	Principe	September 18, 1980
Finland	February 4, 1963	Saudi Arabia	February 25, 1966
France	December 3, 1964	Senegal	August 15, 1974
Gambia	January 25, 1978	Seychelles	January 22, 1981
Germany	July 27, 1964	Singapore	January 4, 1967
Greece	May 26, 1965	Somalia	September 30, 1964
Guatemala	April 29, 1980	South Africa	September 17, 1963
Guinea	August 19, 1976	Swaziland	January 31, 1974
Hungary	October 30, 1970	Sweden	May 10, 1963
Iceland	May 9, 1990	Switzerland	February 3, 1964
India	October 6, 1970	Syria	May 14, 1964
Indonesia	December 9, 1963	Tanzania	April 10, 1963
Iran	February 19, 1973	Thailand	February 28, 1963
Iraq	April 26, 1977	Tunisia	September 30, 1965
Ireland	February 14, 1963	Turkey	September 14, 1977
Israel	March 21, 1978	Uganda	September 16, 1976
Italy	February 13, 1969	United Kingdom	September 18, 1963
Ivory Coast	January 14, 1963	Uruguay	March 20, 1979
Jamaica	September 28, 1964	USA	November 8, 1963
Japan	June 14, 1972	Vanuatu	January 31, 1989
Kenya	July 22, 1964	Venezuela	March 11, 1964
Korea, Democratic		Zambia	October 12, 1965
People's Republic	June 27, 1978		
Korea, Republic of	July 2, 1965		

Notes

(1) 'Treaty Series No. 8 (1953)', Cmd. 8742.
(2) The Protocol entered into force on 11 September 1975.

Protocol relating to an Amendment to Article 50(a) of the Convention on International Civil Aviation signed at Chicago on 7 December 1944

New York, 12 March 1971

The Assembly of the International Civil Aviation Organisation,

Having met in Extraordinary Session, at New York, on the eleventh day of March 1971,

Having noted that it is the general desire of contracting States to enlarge the membership of the Council,

Having considered it proper to provide for three seats in the Council additional to the six seats which were provided for by the amendment adopted on the twenty-first day of June 1961[1] to the Convention on International Civil Aviation (Chicago, 1944)[2] and, accordingly, to increase the membership of the Council to thirty,

And having considered it necessary to amend for the purpose aforesaid the Convention on International Civil Aviation done at Chicago on the seventh day of December, 1944,

Approved, on the twelfth day of March 1971, in accordance with the provisions of paragraph (a) of Article 94 of the Convention aforesaid, the following proposed amendment to the said Convention:

In paragraph (a) of Article 50 of the Convention, the second sentence shall be deleted and replaced by:

'It shall be composed of thirty contracting States elected by the Assembly.'

Specified, pursuant to the provisions of paragraph (a) of Article 94 of the said Convention, eighty as the number of contracting States upon whose ratification the proposed amendment aforesaid shall come into force, and

Resolved that the Secretary General of the International Civil Aviation Organisation draw up a protocol, in the English, French and Spanish languages, each of which shall be of equal authenticity, embodying the proposed amendment above-mentioned and the matters hereinafter appearing.

Consequently, pursuant to the aforesaid action of the Assembly,

This Protocol has been drawn up by the Secretary General of the Organisation;

This Protocol shall be open to ratification by any State which has ratified or adhered to the said Convention on International Civil Aviation;

The instruments of ratification shall be deposited with the International Civil Aviation Organisation;

This Protocol shall come into force in respect of the States which have ratified it on the date on which the eightieth instrument of ratification is so deposited[3];

The Secretary General shall immediately notify all Contracting States of the date of deposit of each ratification of this Protocol;

The Secretary General shall immediately notify all States parties to the said Convention of the date on which this Protocol comes into force;

With respect to any contracting State ratifying this Protocol after the date aforesaid, the Protocol shall come into force upon deposit of its instrument of ratification with the International Civil Aviation Organisation.

In witness whereof, the President and the Secretary General of the aforesaid Extraordinary Session of the Assembly of the International Civil Aviation Organisation, being authorised thereto by the Assembly, sign this Protocol.

Done at New York on the twelfth day of March of the year one thousand nine hundred and seventy-one, in a single document in the English, French and Spanish languages, each of which shall be of equal authenticity. This Protocol shall remain deposited in the archives of the International Civil Aviation Organisation; and certified copies thereof shall be transmitted by the Secretary General of the Organisation to all States parties to the Convention on International Civil Aviation done at Chicago on the seventh day of December 1944.

State	Date of Deposit	State	Date of Deposit
Algeria	February 1, 1972	Luxembourg	July 11, 1972
Angola	April 10, 1977	Madagascar	January 16, 1973
Antigua and Barbuda	October 17, 1988	Sudan	November 21, 1973
Argentina	June 7, 1971	Swaziland	January 31, 1974
Australia	December 15, 1971	Sweden	June 11, 1971
Austria	September 10, 1973	Switzerland	September 28, 1972
Bahrain	November 1, 1971	Syria	March 26, 1973
Barbados	June 14, 1971	Tanzania	June 25, 1971
Belgium	May 21, 1971	Thailand	September 14, 1971
Benin	August 15, 1972	Togo	January 12, 1973
Brazil	June 15, 1971	Trinidad and Tobago	July 10, 1972
Bulgaria	June 4, 1971	Malawi	April 29, 1971
Burkina Faso	June 15, 1992	Malaysia	June 15, 1971
Canada	May 12, 1971	Mali	November 1, 1971
Chile	October 10, 1972	Malta	June 10, 1971
China	February 28, 1974	Mauritania	January 28, 1977
Costa Rica	November 14, 1973	Mauritius	June 9, 1971
Cuba	June 18, 1971	Mexico	September 4, 1973
Cyprus	July 7, 1989	Morocco	June 17, 1971
Czechoslovakia	June 15, 1971	Myanmar	October 28, 1971
Denmark	June 4, 1971	Nauru	September 3, 1975
Ecuador	June 11, 1971	Netherlands	June 29, 1971
Egypt	July 17, 1972	New Zealand	June 9, 1971
Estonia	August 21, 1992	Nicaragua	August 24, 1973
Ethiopia	June 16, 1971	Niger	October 12, 1971
Finland	May 13, 1971	Nigeria	August 23, 1971
France	September 13, 1972	Norway	June 17, 1971
Gambia	January 25, 1978	Pakistan	August 20, 1971
Germany	August 25, 1972	Panama	June 11, 1971
Ghana	October 18, 1972	Papua New Guinea	July 25, 1979
Greece	June 21, 1971	Philippines	June 9, 1971
Guinea	August 19, 1976	Poland	June 15, 1971
Guyana	December 20, 1972	Portugal	July 26, 1971
Hungary	July 6, 1972	Romania	November 10, 1971
Iceland	May 17, 1971	Russian Federation	June 15, 1971
India	June 15, 1971	Rwanda	March 17, 1972
Indonesia	June 14, 1971	Sao Tome and	
Iran	January 24, 1972	Principe	September 18, 1980
Iraq	February 10, 1976	Saudi Arabia	September 20, 1971
Ireland	June 15, 1971	Senegal	February 16, 1972
Israel	March 21, 1978	Seychelles	January 22, 1981
Italy	July 3, 1974	Singapore	May 31, 1971
Jamaica	June 15, 1971	South Africa	June 15, 1971
Japan	June 14, 1972	Spain	August 27, 1971
Jordan	April 19, 1972	Sri Lanka	December 29, 1971
Kenya	February 10, 1972	Tunisia	October 25, 1971
Korea, Democratic		Turkey	September 14, 1977
People's Republic	June 27, 1978	Uganda	May 25, 1971
Korea, Republic of	June 18, 1971	United Kingdom	June 11, 1971
Kuwait	June 15, 1971	Uruguay	September 19, 1975
Laos	June 14, 1971	USA	March 27, 1972
Lebanon	May 4, 1972	Yemen	May 31, 1971
Lesotho	September 11, 1975	Zaire	September 7, 1971
Libya	April 27, 1972	Zambia	April 20, 1972

Notes

(1) 'Treaty Series No. 59 (1962)', Cmd. 1826.
(2) 'Treaty Series No. 8 (1953)', Cmd. 8742.
(3) The Protocol entered into force on 16 January, 1973.

Protocol relating to an Amendment to Article 56 of the Convention on International Civil Aviation

Vienna, 7 July 1971

The Assembly of the International Civil Aviation Organisation,

Having met in its Eighteenth Session, at Vienna, on the fifth day of July 1971,

Having noted that it is the general desire of Contracting States to enlarge the membership of the Air Navigation Commission,

Having considered it proper to increase the membership of that body from twelve to fifteen, and

Having considered it necessary to amend for the purpose aforesaid the Convention on International Civil Aviation done at Chicago on the seventh day of December 1944[1]

(1) Approved, in accordance with the provisions of Article 94(a) of the Convention aforesaid, the following proposed amendment to the said Convention:

'In Article 56 of the Convention the expression 'twelve members' shall be replace by 'fifteen members',

(2) Specified, pursuant to the provisions of the said Article 94(a) of the said Convention, eighty as the number of contracting States upon whose ratification the aforesaid amendment aforesaid shall come into force, and

(3) Resolved that the Secretary General of the International Civil Aviation Organisation draw up a protocol, in the English, French and Spanish languages, each of which shall be of equal authenticity, embodying the proposed amendment above mentioned an the matters hereinafter appearing:

(a)The Protocol shall be signed by the President of the Assembly and its Secretary General.
(b)The Protocol shall be open to ratification by any State which has ratified or adhered to the said Convention on International Civil Aviation.

Consequently, pursuant to the aforesaid action of the Assembly,

This Protocol has been drawn up by the Secretary General of the Organisation;

This Protocol shall be open to ratification by any State which has ratified or adhered to the said Convention on International Civil Aviation;

The instruments of ratification shall be deposited with the International Civil Aviation Organisation;

This Protocol shall come into force in respect of the States which have ratified it on the date on which the eightieth instrument of ratification is so deposited;

The Secretary General shall immediately notify all Contracting States of the date of deposit of each ratification of this Protocol;

The Secretary General shall immediately notify all States parties to the said Convention of the date on which this Protocol comes into force[2];

With respect to any Contracting State ratifying this Protocol after the date aforesaid, the Protocol shall come into force upon deposit of its instrument of ratification with the International Civil Aviation Organisation.

In witness whereof, the President and the Secretary General of the Eighteenth Session of the Assembly of the International Civil Aviation Organisation, being authorised thereto by the Assembly, sign this Protocol.

Done at Vienna on the seventh day of July of the year one thousand nine hundred and seventy-one, in a single document in the English, French and Spanish languages, each of which shall be of equal authenticity. This Protocol shall remain deposited in the archives of the International Civil Aviation Organisation, and certified copies thereof shall be transmitted by the Secretary General of the Organisation to all States parties to the Convention on International Civil Aviation done at Chicago on the seventh day of December 1944.

State	Date of Deposit	State	Date of Deposit
Algeria	February 2, 1977	Laos	September 27, 1971
Angola	April 10, 1977	Lebanon	August 17, 1972
Antigua and Barbuda	October 17, 1988	Lesotho	September 11, 1975
Argentina	August 18, 1972	Libya	September 20, 1972
Australia	March 4, 1974	Luxembourg	July 11, 1972
Austria	September 10, 1973	Madagascar	January 16, 1973
Bahrain	November 1, 1971	Malawi	September 20, 1971
Barbados	January 6, 1972	Mali	July 11, 1972
Belgium	February 16, 1972	Malta	November 14, 1971
Bolivia	December 30, 1974	Mauritania	December 20, 1976
Brazil	December 17, 1971	Mauritius	November 15, 1971
Bulgaria	April 12, 1972	Mexico	July 7, 1972
Burkina Faso	June 15, 1992	Morocco	November 10, 1971
Cameroon	August 8, 1972	Myanmar	October 28, 1971
Canada	December 3, 1971	Netherlands	June 29, 1972
Chad	March 2, 1973	New Zealand	December 1, 1971
Chile	September 6, 1972	Nicaragua	October 31, 1973
China	February 28, 1974	Niger	April 8, 1988
Congo	November 13, 1978	Norway	January 10, 1972
Cuba	January 3, 1975	Oman	July 4, 1974
Cyprus	July 5, 1989	Pakistan	October 25, 1973
Czechoslovakia	November 13, 1972	Panama	April 5, 1972
Denmark	September 10, 1971	Papua New Guinea	July 25, 1979
Dominican Republic	May 30, 1972	Philippines	February 1, 1972
Ecuador	May 2, 1975	Poland	May 17, 1976
Egypt	July 17, 1972	Qatar	January 20, 1972
El Salvador	February 13, 1980	Romania	September 6, 1974
Estonia	August 21, 1992	Russian Federation	February 9, 1972
Ethiopia	September 9, 1971	Rwanda	March 17, 1972
Finland	October 7, 1971	Sao Tome and	
France	September 13, 1972	Principe	September 18, 1980
Gabon	January 10, 1973	Saudi Arabia	September 20, 1971
Gambia	January 25, 1978	Senegal	March 10, 1972
Germany	September 16, 1977	Seychelles	January 22, 1981
Greece	November 15, 1971	Singapore	September 24, 1971
Guatemala	February 11, 1974	Spain	July 3, 1974
Guinea	August 19, 1976	Sri Lanka	June 8, 1972
Guyana	December 20, 1972	Swaziland	January 31, 1974
Hungary	July 6, 1972	Sweden	December 16, 1971
Iceland	September 27, 1971	Switzerland	September 28, 1972
India	December 21, 1971	Syria	March 26, 1973
Indonesia	May 10, 1972	Tanzania	June 15, 1978
Iran	February 19, 1973	Thailand	September 14, 1972
Iraq	August 10, 1972	Trinidad and Tobago	October 22, 1974
Ireland	July 11, 1972	Tunisia	July 10, 1974
Israel	March 21, 1978	Turkey	September 14, 1977
Italy	July 3, 1974	Uganda	December 19, 1974
Jamaica	September 9, 1977	United Kingdom	December 7, 1971
Japan	June 14, 1972	Uruguay	September 19, 1975
Jordan	May 15, 1972	USA	February 25, 1974
Kenya	February 10, 1972	Vanuatu	January 31, 1989
Korea, Democratic		Venezuela	February 3, 1978
People's Republic	June 27, 1978	Zaire	January 22, 1973
Korea, Republic of	February 25, 1972	Zambia	September 14, 1972
Kuwait	October 12, 1971		

Notes

(1) 'Treaty Series No. 8 (1953)', Cmd. 8742.
(2) The Protocol entered into force on 19 December 1974.

Protocol relating to an Amendment to Article 50(a) of the Convention on International Civil Aviation

Montreal, 16 October 1974

The Assembly of the International Civil Aviation Organisation,

Having met in its Twenty-first Session, at Montreal on 14 October 1974,

Having noted that it is the general desire of contracting States to enlarge the membership of the Council,

Having considered it proper to provide for three additional seats in the Council, and accordingly to increase the membership from thirty to thirty-three, in order to permit an increase in the representation of States elected in the second, and particularly the third, part of the election, and

Having considered it necessary to amend for the purpose aforesaid the Convention on International Civil Aviation done at Chicago on the seventh day of December, 1944[1],

(1) Approved, in accordance with the provisions of Article 94(a) of the Convention aforesaid, the following proposed amendment to the said Convention:

In Article 50(a) of the Convention, the second sentence shall be amended by replacing 'thirty' by 'thirty-three'.

(2) Specified, pursuant to the provisions of the said Article 94(a) of the said Convention, eighty-six as the number of contracting States upon whose ratification the proposed amendment aforesaid shall come into force, and

(3) Resolved that the Secretary General of the International Civil Aviation Organisation draw up a Protocol, in the English, French and Spanish languages, each of which shall be of equal authenticity, embodying the proposed amendment above-mentioned and the matter hereinafter appearing.

(a) The Protocol shall be signed by the President of the Assembly and its Secretary General.
(b) The Protocol shall be open to ratification by any State which has ratified or adhered to the said Convention on International Civil Aviation.
(c) The instruments of ratification shall be deposited with the International Civil Aviation Organisation.
(d) The Protocol shall come into force in respect of the States which have ratified it on the date on which the eighty-sixth instrument of ratification is so deposited[2].
(e) The Secretary General shall immediately notify all Contracting States of the date of deposit of each ratification of the Protocol.
(f) The Secretary General shall immediately notify all States parties to the said Convention of the date on which the Protocol comes into force.
(g) With respect to any Contracting State ratifying the Protocol after the date aforesaid, the Protocol shall come into force upon deposit of its instrument of ratification with the International Civil Aviation Organisation.

Consequently, pursuant to the aforesaid action of the Assembly,

This Protocol has been drawn up by the Secretary General of the Organisation;

In witness whereof, the President and the Secretary General of the Twenty-first Session of the Assembly of the International Civil Aviation Organisation, being authorised thereto by the Assembly, sign this Protocol.

Done at Montreal on the sixteenth day of October of the year one thousand nine hundred and seventy-four, in a single document in the English, French and Spanish languages, each of which shall be of equal authenticity. This Protocol shall remain deposited in the archives of the International Civil Aviation Organisation, and certified copies thereof shall be transmitted by the Secretary General of the Organisation to all States parties to the Convention on International Civil Aviation done at Chicago on the seventh day of December 1944.

State	Date of Deposit	State	Date of Deposit
Algeria	April 22, 1975	Lebanon	February 26, 1979
Angola	April 10, 1977	Lesotho	September 7, 1977
Antigua and Barbuda	October 17, 1988	Libya	October 1, 1976
Argentina	February 1, 1978	Luxembourg	November 2, 1976
Australia	April 18, 1978	Madagascar	January 11, 1978
Austria	August 5, 1976	Malawi	October 15, 1975
Bahrain	April 3, 1975	Maldives	January 31, 1975
Barbados	June 25, 1975	Mali	July 27, 1978
Belgium	February 19, 1976	Malta	March 19, 1975
Brazil	February 16, 1979	Mauritania	March 6, 1979
Bulgaria	August 19, 1975	Mauritius	June 25, 1975
Burkina Faso	June 15, 1992	Mexico	March 18, 1976
Canada	April 26, 1978	Morocco	March 8, 1977
Cape Verde	April 18, 1980	Netherlands	November 20, 1975
Chile	May 28, 1975	New Zealand	September 20, 1977
China	July 21, 1975	Nicaragua	February 13, 1980
Colombia	February 15, 1980	Niger	September 7, 1976
Cuba	November 25, 1977	Norway	March 11, 1975
Cyprus	July 5, 1989	Oman	April 8, 1975
Czechoslovakia	April 25, 1979	Pakistan	November 2, 1976
Denmark	March 27, 1975	Panama	August 28, 1980
Dominican Republic	February 10, 1976	Papua New Guinea	October 5, 1992
Ecuador	October 25, 1977	Peru	July 19, 1978
Egypt	July 22, 1975	Philippines	May 4, 1981
El Salvador	February 13, 1980	Poland	May 17, 1976
Estonia	August 21, 1991	Qatar	July 27, 1976
Ethiopia	April 22, 1975	Romania	August 19, 1975
Fiji	May 15, 1975	Russian Federation	August 2, 1977
Finland	March 6, 1975	Sao Tome and	
France	August 22, 1977	Principe	September 18, 1980
Gambia	January 25, 1978	Saudi Arabia	December 12, 1983
Germany	September 16, 1977	Senegal	August 4, 1980
Ghana	September 2, 1977	Seychelles	January 22, 1981
Greece	January 18, 1977	Singapore	October 4, 1977
Guatemala	August 15, 1981	Spain	February 11, 1975
Guyana	January 13, 1976	Sudan	May 23, 1979
Hungary	December 19, 1977	Swaziland	December 30, 1974
Iceland	August 19, 1975	Sweden	May 28, 1975
India	May 27, 1975	Switzerland	February 26, 1976
Indonesia	November 18, 1977	Syria	July 11, 1975
Iran	August 25, 1975	Tanzania	June 15, 1978
Iraq	February 10, 1976	Thailand	March 6, 1981
Ireland	January 19, 1976	Togo	December 15, 1975
Italy	June 18, 1982	Tunisia	April 14, 1976
Jamaica	September 9, 1977	Turkey	September 14, 1977
Japan	September 3, 1981	Uganda	September 16, 1976
Jordan	May 16, 1975	United Kingdom	February 29, 1980
Kenya	February 11, 1977	Uruguay	July 14, 1977
Korea, Democratic		USA	October 20, 1977
People's Republic	June 27, 1978	Vanuatu	January 31, 1989
Korea, Republic of	February 17, 1975	Venezuela	February 3, 1978
Kuwait	February 21, 1975	Yemen	April 30, 1976

Notes

(1) 'Treaty Series No. 8 (1953)', Cmd. 8742.
(2) The Protocol entered into force on 15 February, 1980.

Protocol relating to an Amendment to the Convention on International Civil Aviation
Montreal, 30 September 1977

The Assembly of the International Civil Aviation Organisation,

Having met in its Twenty-second Session at Montreal on 30 September 1977,

Having noted Resolution A21-13 on the authentic Russian text of the Convention on International Civil Aviation,

Having noted that it is the general desire of Contracting States to make a provision that the Convention aforesaid exist in authentic Russian text,

Having considered it necessary to amend, for the purpose aforesaid, the Convention on International Civil Aviation done at Chicago on the seventh day of December 1944[1],

(1) Approves, in accordance with the provisions of Article 94(a) of the Convention aforesaid, the following proposed amendment to the said Convention:

Replace the present text of the final paragraph of the Convention by:

'Done at Chicago the seventh day of December 1944 in the English language. The texts of this Convention drawn up in the English, French, Russian and Spanish languages are of equal authenticity. These texts shall be deposited in the archives of the Government of the United States of America, and certified copies shall be transmitted by that Government to the Governments of all the States which may sign or adhere to this Convention. This Convention shall be open for signature at Washington, DC.',

(2) Specifies, pursuant to the provisions of the said Article 94(a) of the said Convention, ninety-four as the number of Contracting States upon whose ratification the proposed amendment aforesaid shall come into force, and

(3) Resolves that the Secretary General of the International Civil Aviation Organisation draw up a Protocol, in the English, French, Russian and Spanish languages each of which shall be of equal authenticity embodying the proposed amendment above-mentioned and the matter hereinafter appearing.

Consequently, pursuant to the aforesaid action of the Assembly,

This Protocol has been drawn up by the Secretary General of the Organisation.

The Protocol shall be open to ratification by any State which has ratified or adhered to the said Convention on International Civil Aviation.

The instruments of ratification shall be deposited with the International Civil Aviation Organisation.

The Protocol shall come into force in respect of the States which have ratified it on the date on which the ninety-fourth instrument of ratification is so deposited[2].

The Secretary General shall immediately notify all Contracting States of the date of deposit of each ratification of the Protocol.

The Secretary General shall immediately notify all States parties to the said Convention of the date on which the Protocol comes into force.

With respect to any Contracting State ratifying the Protocol after the date aforesaid, the Protocol shall come into force upon deposit of its instrument of ratification with the International Civil Aviation Organisation.

In witness whereof, the President and the Secretary General of the aforesaid Twenty-second Session of the Assembly of the International Civil Aviation Organisation, being authorised thereto by the Assembly, sign this Protocol.

Done at Montreal on the thirtieth day of September of the year one thousand nine hundred and seventy-seven, in a single document in the English, French, Russian and Spanish languages, each of which shall be of equal authenticity. This Protocol shall remain deposited in the archives of the International Civil Aviation Organisation, and certified copies thereof shall be transmitted by the Secretary General of the Organisation to all States parties to the Convention on International Civil Aviation done at Chicago on the seventh day of December 1944.

State	Date of Deposit	State	Date of Deposit
Afghanistan	September 28, 1983	Lesotho	October 26, 1978
Algeria	January 16, 1984	Luxembourg	October 18, 1979
Antigua and Barbuda	October 17, 1988	Malawi	February 27, 1978
Argentina	November 14, 1979	Malaysia	May 15, 1978
Australia	December 7, 1979	Mauritius	July 5, 1979
Austria	April 25, 1983	Mexico	June 1, 1987
Bahrain	February 7, 1990	Netherlands	May 17, 1979
Barbados	December 5, 1978	New Zealand	May 30, 1990
Belgium	September 20, 1985	Niger	April 8, 1988
Bulgaria	December 11, 1978	Norway	April 24, 1978
Burundi	October 10, 1991	Oman	May 1, 1991
Canada	April 26, 1978	Pakistan	August 29, 1978
China	April 26, 1984	Papua New Guinea	October 5, 1992
Cuba	December 22, 1978	Poland	May 7, 1979
Cyprus	July 5, 1989	Romania	August 24, 1978
Czechoslovakia	December 18, 1978	Russian Federation	March 23, 1978
Denmark	August 9, 1982	Saudi Arabia	June 25, 1991
Ecuador	April 22, 1988	Senegal	November 27, 1981
Estonia	August 21, 1992	Seychelles	September 23, 1983
Ethiopia	September 6, 1979	Singapore	September 22, 1986
Finland	January 8, 1979	Spain	September 25, 1979
France	August 14, 1979	Sri Lanka	January 30, 1984
Germany	February 15, 1984	Sweden	March 2, 1979
Greece	October 23, 1980	Switzerland	March 4, 1980
Guatemala	May 12, 1980	Syria	July 18, 1989
Guyana	November 21, 1986	Thailand	January 13, 1987
Haiti	September 21, 1984	Togo	April 24, 1987
Hungary	July 6, 1978	Turkey	November 13, 1992
Iceland	June 11, 1979	UAE	January 22, 1987
India	January 31, 1985	Uganda	February 3, 1992
Indonesia	November 20, 1990	United Kingdom	October 6, 1978
Iraq	August 31, 1978	Uruguay	November 10, 1981
Italy	October 13, 1983	USA	March 8, 1982
Jordan	November 2, 1979	Vanuatu	January 31, 1989
Korea, Democratic		Vietnam	September 20, 1983
People's Republic	April 17, 1979	Yemen	January 9, 1980
Kuwait	April 21, 1978	Zambia	May 15, 1990
Lebanon	September 15, 1980		

Notes

(1) 'Treaty Series No. 8 (1953)', Cmd. 8742.
(2) The Protocol is not yet in force.

Protocol relating to an Amendment to the Convention on International Civil Aviation

Montreal, 6 October 1980

The Assembly of the International Civil Aviation Organisation having met in its Twenty-third Session at Montreal on 6 October 1980,

Having noted Resolution A21-22 and A22-28 on lease, charter and interchange of aircraft in international operations,

Having noted the draft amendment to the Convention on International Civil Aviation prepared by the 23rd Session of the Legal Committee,

Having noted that it is the general desire of Contracting States to make a provision for the transfer of certain functions and duties from the State of registry to the State of the operator of the aircraft in the case of lease, charter or interchange or any similar arrangements with respect to such aircraft,

Having considered it necessary to amend, for the purpose aforesaid, the Convention on International Civil Aviation done at Chicago on the seventh day of December 1944[1],

(1) Approves, in accordance with the provisions of Article 94(a) of the Convention aforesaid, the following proposed amendment to the said Convention:

Insert after Article 83 the following new Article 83 bis:

'ARTICLE 83 BIS

Transfer of certain functions and duties

(a)Notwithstanding the provisions of Articles 12, 30, 31 and 32(a), when an aircraft registered in a contracting State is operated pursuant to an agreement for the lease, charter or interchange of the aircraft or any similar arrangement by an operator who has his principal place of business or, if he has no such place of business, his permanent residence in another contracting State, the State of registry may, by agreement with such other State, transfer to it all or part of its functions and duties as State of registry in respect of that Aircraft under Articles 12, 30, 31 and 32(a). The State of registry shall be relieved of responsibility in respect of the functions and duties transferred.

(b)The transfer shall not have effect in respect of other contracting States before either the agreement between States in which it is embodied has been registered with the Council and made public pursuant to Article 83 or the existence and scope of the agreement have been directly communicated to the authorities of the other contracting State or States concerned by a State party to the agreement.

(c)The provisions of paragraphs (a) and (b) above shall also be applicable to cases covered by Article 77.',

(2) Specifies, pursuant to the provisions of the said Article 94(a) of the said Convention, ninety-eight as the number of Contracting States upon whose ratification the proposed amendment aforesaid shall come into force and

(3) Resolves that the Secretary General of the International Civil Aviation Organisation draw up a Protocol, in the English, French, Russian and Spanish languages, each of which shall be of equal authenticity, embodying the proposed amendment above-mentioned and the matter hereinafter appearing:

(a) The Protocol shall be signed by the President of the Assembly and its Secretary General.
(b) The Protocol shall be open to ratification by any State which has ratified or adhered to the said Convention in International Civil Aviation.
(c) The instruments of ratification shall be deposited with the International Civil Aviation Organisation.
(d) The Protocol shall come into force in respect of the States which have ratified it on the date on which the ninety-eighth instrument of ratification is so deposited(2).
(e) The Secretary General shall immediately notify all Contracting States of the date of deposit of each ratification of the Protocol.
(f)The Secretary General shall immediately notify all States parties to the said Convention of the date on which the Protocol comes into force.
(g) With respect to any Contracting State ratifying the Protocol after the date aforesaid, the Protocol shall come into force upon deposit of its instrument of ratification with the International Civil Aviation Organisation.
Consequently, pursuant to the aforesaid action of the Assembly,

This Protocol has been drawn up by the Secretary General of the Organisation.

In witness whereof, the President and the Secretary General of the aforesaid Twenty-third Session of the Assembly of the International Civil Aviation Organisation, being authorised thereto by the Assembly, sign this Protocol.

Done at Montreal on the sixth day of October of the year one thousand nine hundred and eighty, in a single document in the English, French, Russian and Spanish languages, each of which shall be of equal authenticity. This Protocol shall remain deposited in the archives of the International Civil Aviation Organisation, and certified copies thereof shall be transmitted by the Secretary General of the Organisation to all States parties to the Convention on International Civil Aviation done at Chicago on the seventh day of December 1944.

State	Date of Deposit	State	Date of Deposit
Antigua and Barbuda	October 17, 1988	Italy	November 29, 1985
Argentina	August 12, 1987	Kenya	October 13, 1982
Austria	April 25, 1983	Korea, Republic of	April 23, 1981
Bahrain	February 7, 1990	Lebanon	April 14, 1983
Bangladesh	September 2, 1988	Luxembourg	October 1, 1986
Barbados	October 5, 1981	Malawi	December 13, 1990
Belgium	September 23, 1983	Mali	January 11, 1984
Brazil	October 30, 1990	Mauritius	August 6, 1990
Bulgaria	July 7, 1981	Mexico	June 20, 1990
Burkina Faso	June 15, 1992	Monaco	May 9, 1991
Burundi	October 10, 1991	Morocco	January 29, 1987
Canada	October 23, 1985	Netherlands	November 5, 1981
Chile	June 28, 1982	Niger	April 8, 1988
Cuba	May 17, 1984	Oman	March 11, 1981
Cyprus	July 5, 1989	Pakistan	May 27, 1987
Czechoslovakia	February 25, 1983	Panama	August 3, 1982
Denmark	December 22, 1983	Papua New Guinea	October 5, 1992
Ecuador	June 20, 1991	Philippines	January 31, 1984
Egypt	September 11, 1981	Qatar	March 8, 1990
Estonia	August 21, 1992	Russian Federation	February 3, 1988
Ethiopia	June 25, 1981	Saudi Arabia	June 25, 1991
Fiji	September 21, 1992	Seychelles	September 23, 1983
Finland	December 18, 1991	Singapore	May 7, 1991
France	August 27, 1982	Spain	July 11, 1983
Germany	October 19, 1983	Sweden	July 13, 1987
Greece	September 25, 1984	Switzerland	February 21, 1985
Grenada	November 8, 1990	Togo	April 24, 1987
Guatemala	April 26, 1983	Trinidad and Tobago	January 31, 1991
Guyana	May 2, 1988	Tunisia	April 29, 1985
Haiti	September 21, 1984	Turkey	November 13, 1992
Hungary	May 27, 1981	UAE	February 18, 1987
Iceland	May 9, 1990	Uganda	March 10, 1982
Indonesia	July 29, 1987	United Kingdom	March 16, 1981
Iraq	March 4, 1982	Uruguay	January 7, 1982
Ireland	March 29, 1990	USA	February 15, 1982
Israel	February 25, 1983	Vanuatu	January 31, 1989

Notes

(1) 'Treaty Series No. 8 (1953)', Cmd. 8742.
(2) The Protocol is not yet in force.

Protocol relating to an Amendment to the Convention on International Civil Aviation
Montreal, 10 May 1984

The Assembly of the International Civil Aviation Organisation

Having met in its Twenty-fifth Session (Extraordinary) at Montreal on 10 May 1984,

Having noted that international civil aviation can greatly help to create and preserve friendship and understanding among the nations and peoples of the world, yet its abuse can become a threat to general security,

Having noted that it is desirable to avoid friction and to promote that cooperation between nations and peoples upon which the peace of the world depends,

Having noted that it is necessary that international civil aviation may be developed in a safe and orderly manner,

Having noted that in keeping with elementary considerations of humanity the safety and the lives of persons on board civil aircraft must be assured,

Having noted that in the Convention on International Civil Aviation done at Chicago on the seventh day of December 1944[1] the contracting States

- recognise that every State has complete and exclusive sovereignty over the airspace above its territory.
- undertake, when issuing regulations for their state aircraft, that they will have due regard for the safety of navigation of civil aircraft, and
- agree not to use civil aviation for any purpose inconsistent with the aims of the Convention,

Having noted the resolve of the contracting States to take appropriate measures designed to prevent the violation of other States' airspace and the use of civil aviation for purposes inconsistent with the aims of the Convention and to enhance further the safety of international civil aviation.

Having noted the general desire of contracting States to reaffirm the principle of non-use of weapons against civil aircraft in flight,

(1) Decides that it is desirable therefore to amend the Convention on International Civil Aviation done at Chicago on the seventh day of December 1944,

(2) Approves, in accordance with the provision of Article 94(a) of the Convention aforesaid, the following proposed amendment to the said Convention:

Insert, after Article 3, a new 'Article 3 bis':

'ARTICLE 3 BIS'

(a) The contracting States recognise that every State must refrain from resorting to the use of weapons against civil aircraft in flight and that, in case of interception, the lives of persons on board and the safety of aircraft must not be endangered. This provision shall not be interpreted as modifying in any way the rights and obligations of States set forth in the Charter of the United Nations.

(b) The contracting States recognise that every State, in the exercise of its sovereignty, is entitled to require the landing at some designated airport of a civil aircraft flying above its territory without authority or if there are reasonable grounds to conclude that it is being used for any purpose inconsistent with the aims of this Convention; it may also give such aircraft any other instructions to put an end to such violations. For this purpose, the contracting States may resort to any appropriate means consistent with relevant rules of international law, including the relevant provisions of this Convention, specifically paragraph (a) of this Article. Each contracting State agrees to publish its regulations in force regarding the interception of civil aircraft.

(c) Every civil aircraft shall comply with an order given in conformity with paragraph (b) of this Article. To this end each contracting State shall establish all necessary provisions in its national laws or regulations to make such compliance mandatory for any civil aircraft registered in that State or operated by an operator who has his principal place of business or permanent residence in that State. Each contracting State shall make any violation of such applicable laws or regulations punishable by severe penalties and shall submit the case to its competent authorities in accordance with its laws or regulations.

(d) Each contracting State shall take appropriate measures to prohibit the deliberate use of any civil aircraft registered in that State or operated by an operator who has his principal place of business or permanent residence in that State for any purpose inconsistent with the aims of this Convention. This provision shall not affect paragraph (a) or derogate from paragraphs (b) and (c) of this Article',

(3) Specifies, pursuant to the provision of the said Article 94(a) of the said Convention, one hundred and two as the number of contracting States upon whose ratification the proposed amendment aforesaid shall come into force(2), and

(4) Resolves that the Secretary General of the International Civil Aviation Organisation draw up a Protocol, in the English, French, Russian and Spanish languages each of which shall be of equal authenticity, embodying the proposed amendment above-mentioned and the matter hereinafter appearing.

(a) The Protocol shall be signed by the President of the Assembly and its Secretary General.
(b) The Protocol shall be open to ratification by any State which has ratified or adhered to the said Convention on International Civil Aviation.
(c) The instruments of ratification shall be deposited with the International Civil Aviation Organisation.
(d) The Protocol shall come into force in respect of the States which have ratified it on the date on which the one hundred and second instrument of ratification is so deposited[2].
(e) The Secretary General shall immediately notify all contracting States of the date of deposit of each ratification of the Protocol.
(f) The Secretary General shall immediately notify all States parties to the said Convention of the date on which the Protocol comes into force.
(g) With respect to any Contracting State ratifying the Protocol after the date aforesaid, the Protocol shall come into force upon deposit of its instrument of ratification with the International Civil Aviation Organisation.

Consequently, pursuant to the aforesaid action of the Assembly,

This Protocol has been drawn up by the Secretary General of the Organisation.

In witness whereof, the President and the Secretary General of the aforesaid Twenty-fifth Session (Extraordinary) of the Assembly of the International Civil Aviation Organisation, being authorised thereto by the Assembly, sign this Protocol.

Done at Montreal on the tenth day of May of the year one thousand nine hundred and eighty-four, in a single document in the English, French, Russian and Spanish languages, each text being equally authentic. This Protocol shall remain deposited in the archives of the International Civil Aviation Organisation, and certified copies thereof shall be transmitted by the Secretary General of the Organisation to all States parties to the Convention on International Civil Aviation done at Chicago on the seventh day of December 1944.

State	Date of Deposit	State	Date of Deposit
Antigua and Barbuda	October 17, 1988	Kuwait	July 18, 1986
Argentina	December 1, 1986	Lesotho	March 17, 1988
Australia	September 10, 1986	Luxembourg	May 10, 1985
Austria	January 11, 1985	Madagascar	September 10, 1986
Barbados	November 23, 1984	Malawi	December 13, 1990
Bahrain	February 7, 1990	Mali	March 4, 1987
Bangladesh	June 3, 1986	Mauritius	November 7, 1989
Belgium	September 20, 1985	Mexico	June 20, 1990
Brazil	January 21, 1987	Morocco	July 19, 1990
Burundi	October 10, 1991	Nepal	October 26, 1987
Cameroon	January 28, 1988	Netherlands	December 18, 1986
Canada	September 23, 1986	Niger	April 8, 1988
Chile	November 26, 1984	Nigeria	July 8, 1985
Colombia	March 10, 1989	Norway	October 16, 1985
Cyprus	July 5, 1989	Oman	February 21, 1985
Czechoslovakia	September 28, 1992	Pakistan	June 10, 1985
Denmark	October 16, 1985	Panama	May 22, 1987
Ecuador	April 22, 1988	Papua New Guinea	October 5, 1992
Egypt	August 1, 1985	Portugal	June 17, 1991
Estonia	August 21, 1992	Qatar	October 23, 1990
Ethiopia	May 22, 1985	Russian Federation	August 24, 1990
Fiji	September 21, 1992	Saudi Arabia	July 21, 1986
Finland	December 18, 1991	Senegal	May 2, 1985
France	August 19, 1985	Seychelles	August 8, 1985
Gabon	November 1, 1988	South Africa	June 28, 1985
Greece	October 16, 1987	Spain	October 24, 1985
Guatemala	September 18, 1987	Sweden	October 16, 1985
Guyana	May 2, 1988	Switzerland	February 24, 1986
Hungary	May 24, 1990	Thailand	July 12, 1985
Ireland	September 19, 1990	Togo	July 5, 1985
Italy	June 12, 1986	Tunisia	April 29, 1985
Ivory Coast	June 5, 1987	UAE	February 18, 1987
Jordan	October 8, 1986	United Kingdom	August 21, 1987
Korea, Republic of	February 27, 1985	Uruguay	September 1, 1987

Notes

(1) 'Treaty Series No. 8 (1953)', Cmd. 8742.
(2) The Protocol is not yet in force.

Protocol relating to an Amendment to Article 56 of the Convention on International Civil Aviation

Montreal, 6 October 1989

The Assembly of the International Civil Aviation Organisation

Having met in its Twenty-seventh Session at Montreal on 6 October 1989,

Having noted that it is the general desire of Contracting States to enlarge the membership of the Air Navigation Commission,

Having considered it proper to increase the membership of that body from fifteen to nineteen, and

Having considered it necessary to amend, for the purpose aforesaid, the Convention on International Civil Aviation done at Chicago on the seventh day of December 1944[1],

(1) Approves, in accordance with the provisions of Article 94(a) of the Convention aforesaid, the following proposed amendment to the said Convention:

'In Article 56 of the Convention the expression 'fifteen members' shall be replaced by 'nineteen members',

(2) Specifies, pursuant to the provisions of the said Article 94(a) of the said Convention, one hundred and eight as the number of contracting States upon whose ratification the aforesaid amendment shall come into force[2], and

(3) Resolves that the Secretary General of the International Civil Aviation Organisation shall draw up a Protocol, in the English, French, Russian and Spanish languages each of which shall be of equal authenticity, embodying the amendment above-mentioned and the matter hereinafter appearing.

(a) The Protocol shall be signed by the President of the Assembly and its Secretary General.
(b) The Protocol shall be open to ratification by any State which has ratified or adhered to the said Convention on International Civil Aviation.
(c) The instruments of ratification shall be deposited with the International Civil Aviation Organisation.
(d) The Protocol shall come into force in respect of the States which have ratified it on the date on which the one hundred and eighth instrument of ratification is so deposited[2].
(e) The Secretary General shall immediately notify all contracting States of the date of deposit of each ratification of the Protocol
(f) The Secretary General shall immediately notify all States parties to the said Convention of the date on which the Protocol comes into force.
(g) With respect to any Contracting State ratifying the Protocol after the date aforesaid, the Protocol shall come into force upon deposit of its instrument of ratification with the International Civil Aviation Organisation.

Consequently, pursuant to the aforesaid action of the assembly,

This Protocol has been drawn up by the Secretary General of the Organisation.

In witness whereof, the President and the Secretary General of the aforesaid Twenty-seventh Session of the Assembly of the International Civil Aviation Organisation, being authorised thereto by the Assembly, sign this Protocol.

Done at Montreal on the sixth day of October of the year one thousand nine hundred and eighty-nine, in a single document in the English, French, Russian and Spanish languages, each text being equally authentic. This Protocol shall remain deposited in the archives of the International Civil Aviation Organisation, and certified copies thereof shall be transmitted by the Secretary General of the Organisation to all States parties to the Convention on International Civil Aviation done at Chicago on the seventh day of December 1944.

State	Date of Deposit	State	Date of Deposit
Austria	April 22, 1991	Malawi	December 13, 1990
Brazil	July 22, 1992	Mali	May 13, 1991
Burkina Faso	June 15, 1992	Mauritius	August 6, 1990
Canada	September 14, 1992	Mexico	October 11, 1990
Czechoslovakia	January 24, 1992	Netherlands	August 14, 1990
Denmark	September 24, 1990	Norway	November 7, 1990
Ecuador	May 4, 1990	Papua New Guinea	October 5, 1992
Estonia	August 21, 1992	Saudi Arabia	June 25, 1991
Finland	April 11, 1990	Spain	November 28, 1991
France	July 24, 1990	Sweden	June 1, 1990
Greece	March 10, 1992	Switzerland	November 15, 1990
Grenada	May 31, 1991	Togo	February 19, 1991
Hungary	May 24, 1990	Turkey	November 13, 1992
Iceland	May 9, 1990	UAE	July 9, 1990
India	September 1, 1992	Uruguay	September 30, 1992
Kuwait	November 18, 1992	USA	January 13, 1992
Lesotho	December 17, 1990	Vanuatu	February 27, 1991

Notes

(1) 'Treaty Series No. 8 (1953)', Cmd. 8742
(2) The Protocol is not yet in force.

Protocol relating to an Amendment to Article 50(a) of the Convention on International Civil Aviation
Montreal, 26 October 1990

The Assembly of the International Civil Aviation Organisation

Having met in its Twenty-eighth Session (Extraordinary) at Montreal on 25 October 1990;

Having noted that it is the desire of a large number of Contracting States to enlarge the membership of the Council in order to ensure better balance by means of an increased representation of Contracting States;

Having considered it appropriate to increase the membership of that body from thirty-three to thirty-six;

Having considered it necessary to amend, for the purpose aforesaid, the Convention on International Civil Aviation done at Chicago on the seventh day of December 1944[1],

(1) Approves, in accordance with the provisions of Article 94(a) of the Convention aforesaid, the following proposed amendment to the said Convention:

'In Article 50(a) of the Convention the second sentence shall be amended by replacing 'thirty-three' by 'thirty-six'.';

(2) Specifies, pursuant to the provisions of the said Article 94(a) of the said Convention, one hundred and eight as the number of contracting States upon whose ratification the proposed amendment aforesaid shall come into force[2];

(3) Resolves that the Secretary General of the International Civil Aviation Organisation draw up a Protocol, in the English, French, Russian and Spanish languages each of which shall be of equal authenticity, embodying the amendment above-mentioned and the matter hereinafter appearing:

(a) The Protocol shall be signed by the President of the Assembly and its Secretary General.

(b) The Protocol shall be open to ratification by any State which has ratified or adhered to the said Convention on International Civil Aviation.

(c) The instruments of ratification shall be deposited with the International Civil Aviation Organisation.

(d) The Protocol shall come into force in respect of the States which have ratified it on the date on which the one hundred and eighth instrument of ratification is so deposited [2]

(e) The Secretary General shall immediately notify all contracting States of the date of deposit of each ratification of the Protocol

(f) The Secretary General shall immediately notify all States parties to the said Convention of the date on which the Protocol comes into force.

(g) With respect to any Contracting State ratifying the Protocol after the date aforesaid, the Protocol shall come into force upon deposit of its instrument of ratification with the International Civil Aviation Organisation.

Consequently, pursuant to the aforesaid action of the Assembly,

This Protocol has been drawn up by the Secretary General of the Organisation.

In witness whereof, the President and the Secretary General of the aforesaid Twenty-eighth Session (Extraordinary) of the Assembly of the International Civil Aviation Organisation, being authorised thereto by the Assembly, sign this Protocol.

Done at Montreal on the twenty-sixth day of October of the year one thousand nine hundred and ninety, in a single document in the English, French, Russian and Spanish languages, each text being equally authentic. This Protocol shall remain deposited in the archives of the International Civil Aviation Organisation, and certified copies thereof shall be transmitted by the Secretary General of the Organisation to all States parties to the Convention on International Civil Aviation done at Chicago on the seventh day of December 1944.

State	Date of Deposit	State	Date of Deposit
Burkina Faso	June 15, 1992	Korea, Republic of	January 21, 1991
Canada	April 19, 1991	Mauritius	April 17, 1991
Denmark	April 28, 1992	Netherlands	October 22, 1991
Estonia	August 21, 1992	Norway	September 23, 1991
Finland	December 18, 1991	South Africa	October 8, 1991
Iceland	November 4, 1992	Spain	September 29, 1992
India	July 9, 1992	Sri Lanka	December 24, 1991
Kenya	October 30, 1991	Sweden	February 7, 1992
Korea, Democratic People's Republic	March 1, 1991	UAE	November 18, 1991

Notes

(1) 'Treaty Series No. 8 (1953)', Cmd. 8742.
(2) The Protocol is not yet in force.

INTERNATIONAL AIR SERVICES TRANSIT AGREEMENT

Chicago, 7 December 1944

The States which sign and accept this International Air Services Transit Agreement, being members of the International Civil Aviation Organisation, declare as follows:-

ARTICLE I

Section 1

Each contracting State grants to the other contracting States the following freedoms of the air in respect of scheduled international air services:–

(1) The privilege to fly across its territory without landing;
(2) The privilege to land for non-traffic purposes.

The privileges of this section shall not be applicable with respect to airports utilised for military purposes to the exclusion of any scheduled international air services. In areas of active hostilities or of military occupation, and in time of war along the supply routes leading to such areas, the exercise of such privileges shall be subject to the approval of the competent military authorities.

Section 2

The exercise of the foregoing privileges shall be in accordance with the provisions of the Interim Agreement on International Civil Aviation[1] and, when it comes into force, with the provisions of the Convention on International Civil Aviation[1], both drawn up at Chicago on 7th December, 1944.

Section 3

A contracting State granting to the airlines of another contracting State the privilege to stop for non-traffic purposes may require such airlines to offer reasonable commercial service at the points at which such stops are made.

Such requirement shall not involve any discrimination between airlines operating on the same route, shall take into account the capacity of the aircraft, and shall be exercised in such a manner as not to prejudice the normal operations of the international air services concerned or the rights and obligations of a contracting State.

Section 4

Each contracting State may, subject to the provisions of this Agreement–

(1) Designate the route to be followed within its territory by any international air service and the airports which any such service may use;
(2) Impose or permit to be imposed on any such service just and reasonable charges for the use of such airports and other facilities; these charges shall not be higher than would be paid for the use of such airports and facilities by its national aircraft engaged in similar international services: provided that, upon representation by an interested contracting State, the charges imposed for the use of airports and other facilities shall be subject to review by the Council of the International Civil Aviation Organisation established under the above-mentioned Convention, which shall report and make recommendations thereon for the consideration of the State or States concerned.

Section 5

Each contracting State reserves the right to withhold or revoke a certificate or permit to an air transport enterprise of another State in any case where it is not satisfied that substantial ownership and effective control are vested in nationals of a contracting State, or in case of failure of such air transport enterprise to comply with the laws of the State over which it operates, or to perform its obligations under this Agreement.

ARTICLE II

Section 1

A contracting State which deems that action by another contracting State under this Agreement is causing injustice or hardship to it, may request the Council to examine the situation. The Council shall thereupon inquire into the matter, and shall call the States concerned into consultation. Should such consultation fail to resolve the difficulty, the Council may make appropriate findings and recommendations to the contracting States concerned. If thereafter a contracting State concerned shall in the opinion of the Council unreasonably fail to take suitable corrective action, the Council may recommend to the Assembly of the above-mentioned Organisation that such contracting State be suspended from its rights and privileges under this Agreement until such action has been taken. The Assembly by a two-thirds vote may so suspend such contracting State for such period of time as it may deem proper or until the Council shall find that corrective action has been taken by such State.

Section 2

If any disagreement between two or more contracting States relating to the interpretation or application of this Agreement cannot be settled by negotiation, the provisions of Chapter XVIII of the above-mentioned Convention shall be applicable in the same manner as provided therein with reference to any disagreement relating to the interpretation or application of the above-mentioned Convention.

ARTICLE III

This Agreement shall remain in force as long as the above-mentioned Convention; provided, however, that any contracting State, a party to the present Agreement, may denounce it on one year's notice given by it to the Government of the United States of America, which shall at once inform all other contracting States of such notice and withdrawal.

ARTICLE IV

Pending the coming into force of the above-mentioned Convention, all references to it herein, other than those contained in Article II, Section 2, and Article V, shall be deemed to be references to the Interim Agreement on International Civil Aviation drawn up at Chicago on 7th December, 1944; and references to the International Civil Aviation Organisation, the Assembly, and the Council shall be deemed to be references to the Provisional International Civil Aviation Organisation, the Interim Assembly, and Interim Council, respectively.

ARTICLE V

For the purposes of this Agreement, 'territory' shall be defined as in Article 2 of the above-mentioned Convention.

ARTICLE VI

Signatures and Acceptances of Agreement

The undersigned delegates to the International Civil Aviation Conference, convened in Chicago on 1st November, 1944, have affixed their signatures to this Agreement with the understanding that the Government of the United States of America shall be informed at the earliest possible date by each of the Governments on whose behalf the Agreement has been signed whether signature on its behalf shall constitute an acceptance of the Agreement by that Government and an obligation binding upon it.

Any State a member of the International Civil Aviation Organisation may accept the present Agreement as an obligation binding upon it by notification of its acceptance to the Government of the United States, and such acceptance shall become effective upon the date of the receipt of such notification by that Government.

This Agreement shall come into force as between contracting States upon its acceptance by each of them. Thereafter it shall become binding as to each other State indicating its acceptance to the Government of the United States on the date of the receipt of the acceptance by that Government. The Government of the United States shall inform all signatory and accepting States of the date of all acceptances of the Agreement, and of the date on which it comes into force for each accepting State.

In WITNESS WHEREOF, the undersigned, having been duly authorised, sign this Agreement on behalf of their respective Governments on the dates appearing opposite their respective signatures.

DONE at Chicago the seventh day of December, 1944, in the English language. A text drawn up in the English, French and Spanish languages[2], each of which shall be of equal authenticity, shall be opened for signature at Washington, DC. Both texts shall be deposited in the archives of the Government of the United States of America, and certified copies shall be transmitted by that Government to the Governments of all the States which may sign or accept this Agreement.

CONCLUDED
7 Dec 44, Chicago

30 Jan 45. Later acceptances effective upon deposit: Art 6

PARTIES

AFGHANISTAN 17 May 45; ALGERIA 16 April 64; ARGENTINA 4 Jun 46; AUSTRALIA 28 Aug. 45; AUSTRIA 10 Dec 58; BAHAMAS 27 May 75; BAHRAIN 12 Oct 71; BANGLADESH 9 Feb 79; BARBADOS 10 Jul 70; BELGIUM 19 Jul 45; BENIN 23 Apr 63; BOLIVIA 4 Apr 47; BRUNEI 4 Dec 84; BULGARIA 21 Sep 70; BURKINA FASO 25 Sep 1992; BURUNDI 19 Jan 68; CAMEROON 30 Mar 60; CHILE 24 Apr 74; COSTA RICA 1 May 58; CUBA 20 Jun 47; CYPRUS 12 Oct 61; CZECHOSLOVAKIA 18 Apr 45; DENMARK 1 Dc 48; ECUADOR 28 Jul 83; EGYPT 13 Mar 47; EL SALVADOR 1 Jun 45; ETHIOPIA 22 Mar 45; FIJI 14 Feb 73; FINLAND 9 Apr 57; FRANCE 24 Jun 48; GABON 15 Jan 70; GERMANY 9 May 56; GREECE 21 Sep 45; GUATEMALA 28 Apr 47; GUYANA* 28 Apr 86; HONDURAS 13 Nov 45; HUNGARY 15 Jan 73; ICELAND 21 Mar 47; INDIA 2 May 45; IRAN 19 Apr 50; IRAQ 15 Jun 45; IRELAND 15 Nov 57; ISRAEL 16 Jun 54; ITALY 27 Jun 84; IVORY COAST 20 Mar 61; JAMAICA 18 Oct 63; JAPAN 20 Oct 53; JORDAN 18 Mar 47; KOREA (REPUBLIC OF) 22 Jun 60; KUWAIT 18 May 60; LEBANON 5 Jun 74; LESOTHO 2 Oct 75; LIBERIA 19 Mar 45; LUXEMBOURG 28 Apr 48; MADAGASCAR 14 May 62; MALAWI 27 Mar 75; MALAYSIA 31 May 45; MALI 27 May 70; MALTA 4 Jun 65; MAURITANIA 11 May 79; MAURITIUS 13 Sep 71; MEXICO 25 Jun 46; MOROCCO 26 Aug. 57; NAURU 25 Aug. 75; NEPAL 23 Nov 65; NETHERLANDS 12 Jan 45; NEW ZEALAND 19 Apr 45; NICARAGUA 28 Dec 45; NIGER 16 Mar 62; NIGERIA 25 Jan 61; NORWAY 30 Jan 45; OMAN 23 Feb 73; PAKISTAN 15 Aug 47; PANAMA 8 Oct 82; PARAGUAY 27 Jul 45; PHILIPPINES* 22 Mar 46; POLAND 6 Apr 45; PORTUGAL 1 Sep 59; RWANDA 6 Jul 64; SENEGAL 8 Mar 61; SEYCHELLES 16 Oct 79; SINGAPORE 22 Aug 66; SOMALIA 10 Jun 64; SOUTH AFRICA 30 Nov 45; SPAIN 30 Jul 45; SRI LANKA 31 May 45; SWAZILAND 30 Apr 73; SWEDEN 19 Nov 45; SWITZERLAND 6 Jul 45; THAILAND 6 Mar 47; TOGO 24 Jun 48; TRINIDAD 14 Mar 63; TUNISIA 26 Apr 62; TURKEY 6 Jun 45; UAE 25 Apr 72; UK 31 May 45; USA* 8 Feb 45; VANUATU 14 Jan 88; VENEZUELA 28 Mar 46; ZAMBIA 13 Oct 65.

Notes

(1) 'Treaty Series No. 8 (1953)', Cmd. 8742.
(2) A French translation of this Agreement was to be made by the United Nations Organisation but no Spanish translation is now contemplated.

INTERNATIONAL AIR TRANSPORT AGREEMENT

The States which sign and accept this International Air Transport Agreement being members of the International Civil Aviation Organisation declare as follows:

ARTICLE I

(1) Each contracting State grants to the other contracting States the following freedoms of the air in respect of scheduled international air services:

(1) The privilege to fly across its territory without landing;

(2) The privilege to land for non-traffic purposes;

(3) The privilege to put down passengers, mail and cargo taken on in the territory of the State whose nationality the aircraft possesses;

(4) The privilege to take on passengers, mail and cargo destined for the territory of the state whose nationality the aircraft possesses;

(5) The privilege to take on passengers, mail and cargo destined for the territory of any other contracting State and the privilege to put down passengers, mail and cargo coming from any such territory.

With respect to the privileges specified under paragraphs (3), (4) and (5) of this Section, the undertaking of each contracting State relates only to through services on a route constituting a reasonably direct line out from and back to the homeland of the State whose nationality the aircraft possesses.

The privileges of this Section shall not be applicable with respect to airports utilised for military purposes to the exclusion of any scheduled international air services. In areas of active hostilities or of military occupation, and in time of war along the supply routes leading to such areas, the exercise of such privileges shall be subject to the approval of the competent military authorities.

(2) The exercise of the foregoing privileges shall be in accordance with the provisions of the Interim Agreement on International Civil Aviation[1] and, when it comes into force, with the provisions of the Convention on International Civil Aviation[1], both drawn up at Chicago on December 7, 1944.

(3) A contracting State granting to the airlines of another contracting State the privilege to stop for non-traffic purposes may require such airlines to offer reasonable commercial service at the points at which such stops are made.

Such requirement shall not involve any discrimination between airlines operating on the same route, shall take into account the capacity of the aircraft, and shall be exercised in such a manner as not to prejudice the normal operations of the international air services concerned or the rights and obligations of any contracting State.

(4) Each contracting State shall have the right to refuse permission to the aircraft of other contracting States to take on in its territory passengers, mail and cargo carried for remuneration or hire and destined for another point within its territory. Each contracting State undertakes not to enter into any arrangements which specifically grant any such privilege on an exclusive basis to any other State or an airline of any other State, and not to obtain any such exclusive privilege from any other State.

(5) Each contracting State may, subject to the provisions of this Agreement,

(1) Designate the route to be followed within its territory by any international air service and the airports which any such service may use;

(2) Impose or permit to be imposed on any such service just and reasonable charges for the use of such airports and other facilities; these charges shall not be higher than would be paid for the use of such airports and facilities by its national aircraft engaged in similar international services: provided that, upon representation by an interested contracting State, the charges imposed for the use of airports and other facilities shall be subject to review by the Council of the International Civil Aviation Organisation established under the above-mentioned Convention, which shall report and make recommendations thereon for the consideration of the State or States concerned.

(6) Each contracting State reserves the right to withhold or revoke a certificate or permit to an air transport enterprise of another State in any case where it is not satisfied that substantial ownership and effective control are vested in nationals of a contracting State, or in case of failure of such air transport enterprise to comply with the laws of the State over which it operates, or to perform its obligations under this Agreement.

ARTICLE II

(1) The contracting States accept this Agreement as abrogating all obligations and understandings between them which are inconsistent with its terms, and undertake not to enter into any such obligations and understandings. A contracting State which has undertaken any other obligations inconsistent with this Agreement shall take immediate steps

to procure its release from the obligations. If an airline of any contracting State has entered into any such inconsistent obligations, the State of which it is a national shall use its best efforts to secure their termination forthwith and shall in any event cause them to be terminated as soon as such action can lawfully be taken after the coming into force of this Agreement.

(2) Subject to the provisions of the preceding Section, any contracting State may make arrangements concerning international air services not inconsistent with this Agreement. Any such arrangement shall be forthwith registered with the Council, which shall make it public as soon as possible.

ARTICLE III

Each contracting State undertakes that in the establishment and operation of through services due consideration shall be given to the interests of the other contracting States so as not to interfere unduly with their regional services or to hamper the development of their through services.

ARTICLE IV

(1) Any contracting State may by reservation attached to this Agreement at the time of signature or acceptance elect no to grant and receive the rights and obligations of Article I, Section 1, paragraph (5), and may at any time after acceptance, on six months' notice given by it to the Council, withdraw itself from such rights and obligations. Such contracting State may on six months' notice to the Council assume or resume, as the case may be, such rights and obligations. No contracting State shall be obliged to grant any right under the said paragraph to any contracting State not bound thereby.

(2) A contracting State which deems that action by another contracting State under this Agreement is causing injustice or hardship to it may request the Council to examine the situation. The Council shall thereupon inquire into the matter, and shall call the States concerned into consultation. Should such consultation fail to resolve the difficulty, the Council may make appropriate findings and recommendations to the contracting States concerned. If thereafter a contracting State concerned shall in the opinion of the Council unreasonably fail to take suitable corrective action, the Council may recommend to the Assembly of the above-mentioned Organisation that such contracting State be suspended from its rights and privileges under this Agreement until such action has been taken. The Assembly by a two-thirds vote may so suspend such contracting State for such period of time as it may deem proper or until the Council shall find that corrective action has been taken by such State.

(3) If any disagreement between two or more contracting States relating to the interpretation or application of this Agreement cannot be settled by negotiation, the provisions of Chapter XVIII of the above-mentioned Convention shall be applicable in the same manner as provided therein with reference to any disagreement relating to the interpretation or application of the above-mentioned Convention.

ARTICLE V

This Agreement shall remain in force as long as the above-mentioned Convention; provided, however, that any contracting State, a party to the present Agreement, may denounce it on one year's notice given by it to the Government of the United States of America, which shall at once inform all other contracting States of such notice and withdrawal.

ARTICLE VI

Pending the coming into force of the above-mentioned Convention, all references to it herein other than those contained in Article IV, Section 3, and Article VII shall be deemed to be references to the Interim Agreement on International Civil Aviation drawn up at Chicago on December 7, 1944; and references to the International Civil Aviation Organisation, the Assembly, and the Council shall be deemed to be references to the Provisional International Civil Aviation Organisation, the Interim Assembly, and the Interim Council, respectively.

ARTICLE VII

For the purposes of this Agreement, 'territory' shall be defined as in Article 2 of the above-mentioned Convention.

ARTICLE VIII

Signatures and Acceptances of Agreement

The undersigned delegates to the International Civil Aviation Conference, convened in Chicago on November 1, 1944, have affixed their signatures to this Agreement with the understanding that the Government of the United States of America shall be informed at the earliest possible date by each of the governments on whose behalf the Agreement has been signed whether signature on its behalf shall constitute an acceptance of the Agreement by that government and an obligation binding upon it.

Any State a member of the International Civil Aviation Organisation may accept the present Agreement as an obligation binding upon it by notification of its acceptance to the Government of the United States, and such acceptance shall become effective upon the date of the receipt of such notification by that Government.

This Agreement shall come into force as between contracting States upon its acceptance by each of them. Thereafter it shall become binding as to each other State indicating its acceptance to the Government of the United States on the date of the receipt of the acceptance by that Government. The Government of the United States shall inform all signatory and accepting States of the date of all acceptances of the Agreement, and of the date on which it comes into force for each accepting State.

IN WITNESS WHEREOF, the undersigned, having been duly authorised, sign this Agreement on behalf of their respective governments on the date appearing opposite their respective signatures.

DONE at Chicago the seventh day of December, 1944, in the English language. A text drawn up in the English, French and Spanish languages, each of which shall be of equal authenticity, shall be opened for signature at Washington, DC. Both texts shall be deposited in the archives of the Government of the United States of America, and certified copies shall be transmitted by that Government to the governments of all the States which may sign or accept this Agreement.

CONCLUDED
7 Dec 44, Chicago

ENTRY INTO FORCE

8 Feb 45. Later acceptances effective upon deposit: Art 8

PARTIES

BOLIVIA 4 Apr 47; BURUNDI 19 Jan 68; COSTA RICA 1 May 58; EL SALVADOR 1 Jun 45; ETHIOPIA 22 Mar 45; GREECE* 28 Feb 46; HONDURAS 13 Nov 45; LIBERIA 19 Mar 45; NETHERLANDS 12 Jan 45; PARAGUAY 27 Jul 45; TURKEY* 6 Jun 45.

Notes

(1) 'Treaty Series No. 8 (1953),' Cmd. 8742.

436

Appendix C

Unidroit Convention on international financial leasing
Ottawa, 28 May 1988

The States parties to this convention,

RECOGNISING the importance of removing certain legal impediments to the international financial leasing of equipment, while maintaining a fair balance of interests between the different parties to the transaction,

AWARE of the need to make international financial leasing more available,

CONSCIOUS of the fact that the rules of law governing the traditional contract of hire need to be adapted to the distinctive triangular relationship created by the financial leasing transaction,

RECOGNISING therefore the desirability of formulating certain uniform rules relating primarily to the civil and commercial law aspects of international financial leasing,

HAVE AGREED as follows:

Chapter I – Sphere of application and general provisions

ARTICLE 1

1 This Convention governs a financial leasing transaction as described in paragraph 2 in which one party (the lessor),

(a) on the specifications of another party (the lessee), enters into an agreement (the supply agreement) with a third party (the supplier) under which the lessor acquires plant, capital goods or other equipment (the equipment) on terms approved by the lessee so far as they concern its interests; and
(b) enters into an agreement (the leasing agreement) with the lessee, granting to the lessee the right to use the equipment in return for the payment of rentals.

2 The financial leasing transaction referred to in the previous paragraph is a transaction which includes the following characteristics:

(a) the lessee specifies the equipment and selects the supplier without relying primarily on the skill and judgment of the lessor;
(b) the equipment is acquired by the lessor in connection with a leasing agreement which, to the knowledge of the supplier, either has been made or is to be made between the lessor and the lessee; and
(c) the rentals payable under the leasing agreement are calculated so as to take into account in particular the amortisation of the whole or a substantial part of the cost of the equipment.

3 This Convention applies whether or not the lessee has or subsequently acquires the option to buy the equipment or to hold it on lease for a further period, and whether or not for a nominal price or rental.

4 This Convention applies to financial leasing transactions in relation to all equipment save that which is to be used primarily for the lessee's personal, family or household purposes.

ARTICLE 2

In the case of one or more sub-leasing transactions involving the same equipment, this Convention applies to each transaction which is a financial leasing transaction and is otherwise subject to this Convention as if the person from whom the first lessor (as defined in paragraph 1 of the previous article) acquired the equipment were the supplier and as if the agreement under which the equipment was so acquired were the supply agreement.

ARTICLE 3

1 This Convention applies when the lessor and the lessee have their places of business in different States and:

(a) those States and the State in which the supplier has its place of business are Contracting States; or
(b) both the supply agreement and the leasing agreement are governed by the law of a Contracting State.

2   A reference in this Convention to a party's place of business shall, if it has more than one place of business, mean the place of business which has the closest relationship to the relevant agreement and its performance, having regard to the circumstances known to or contemplated by the parties at any time before or at the conclusion of that agreement.

1 The provisions of this Convention shall not cease to apply merely because the equipment has become a fixture to or incorporated in land.

2 Any question whether or not the equipment has become a fixture to or incorporated in land, and if so the effect on the rights *inter se* of the lessor and a person having real rights in the land, shall be determined by the law of the State where the land is situated.

ARTICLE 5

1 The application of this Convention may be excluded only if each of the parties to the supply agreement and each of the parties to the leasing agreement agree to exclude it.

2 Where the application of this Convention has not been excluded in accordance with the previous paragraph, the parties may, in their relations with each other, derogate from or vary the effect of any of its provisions except as stated in Articles 8(3) and 13(3)(b) and (4).

ARTICLE 6

1 In the interpretation of this Convention, regard is to be had to its object and purpose as set forth in the preamble, to its international character and to the need to promote uniformity in its application and the observance of good faith in international trade.

2 Questions concerning matters governed by this Convention which are not expressly settled in it are to be settled in conformity with the general principles on which it is based or, in the absence of such principles, in conformity with the law applicable by virtue of the rules of private international law.

Chapter II – Rights and duties of the parties

ARTICLE 7

1 (a) The lessor's real rights in the equipment shall be valid against the lessee's trustee in bankruptcy and creditors, including creditors who have obtained an attachment or execution.

(b) For the purposes of this paragraph 'trustee in bankruptcy' includes a liquidator, administrator or other person appointed to administer the lessee's estate for the benefit of the general body of creditors.

2 Where by the applicable law the lessor's real rights in the equipment are valid against a person referred to in the previous paragraph only on compliance with rules as to public notice, those rights shall be valid against that person only if there has been compliance with such rules.

3 For the purposes of the previous paragraph the applicable law is the law of the State which, at the time when a person referred to in paragraph 1 becomes entitled to invoke the rules referred to in the previous paragraph, is :

(a) in the case of a registered ship, the State in which it is registered in the name of the owner (for the purposes of this sub-paragraph a bareboat charterer is deemed not to be the owner);
(b) in the case of an aircraft which is registered pursuant to the Convention on International Civil Aviation done at Chicago on 7 December 1944, the State in which it is so registered;
(c) in the case of other equipment of a kind normally moved from one State to another, including an aircraft engine, the State in which the lessee has its principal place of business;
(d in the case of all other equipment, the State in which the equipment is situated.

4 Paragraph 2 shall not affect the provisions of any other treaty under which the lessor's real rights in the equipment are required to be recognised.

5 This article shall not affect the priority of any creditor having:

(a) a consensual or non-consensual lien or security interest in the equipment arising otherwise than by virtue of an attachment or execution, or
(b) any right of arrest, detention or disposition conferred specifically in relation to ships or aircraft under the law applicable by virtue of the rules of private international law.

ARTICLE 8

1 (a) Except as otherwise provided by this Convention or stated in the leasing agreement, the lessor shall not incur any liability to the lessee in respect of the equipment save to the extent that the lessee has suffered loss as the result of its reliance on the lessor's skill and judgment and of the lessor's intervention in the selection of the supplier or the specifications of the equipment.
(b) The lessor shall not, in its capacity of lessor, be liable to third parties for death, personal injury or damage to property caused by the equipment.
(c) The above provisions of this paragraph shall not govern any liability of the lessor in any other capacity, for example as owner.

2 The lessor warrants that the lessee's quiet possession will not be disturbed by a person who has a superior title or right, or who claims a superior title or right and acts under the authority of a court, where such title, right or claim is not derived from an act or omission of the lessee.

3 The parties may not derogate from or vary the effect of the provisions of the previous paragraph in so far as the superior title, right or claim is derived from an intentional or grossly negligent act or omission of the lessor.

4 The provisions of paragraphs 2 and 3 shall not affect any broader warranty of quiet possession by the lessor which is mandatory under the law applicable by virtue of the rules of private international law.

ARTICLE 9

1 The lessee shall take proper care of the equipment, use it in a reasonable manner and keep it in the condition in which it was delivered, subject to fair wear and tear and to any modification of the equipment agreed by the parties.

2 When the leasing agreement comes to an end the lessee, unless exercising a right to buy the equipment or to hold the equipment on lease for a further period, shall return the equipment to the lessor in the condition specified in the previous paragraph.

ARTICLE 10

1 The duties of the supplier under the supply agreement shall also be owed to the lessee as if it were a party to that agreement and as if the equipment were to be supplied directly to the lessee. However, the supplier shall not be liable to both the lessor and the lessee in respect of the same damage.

2 Nothing in this article shall entitle the lessee to terminate or rescind the supply agreement without the consent of the lessor.

ARTICLE 11

The lessee's rights derived from the supply agreement under this Convention shall not be affected by a variation of any term of the supply agreement previously approved by the lessee unless it consented to that variation.

ARTICLE 12

1 Where the equipment is not delivered or is delivered late or fails to conform to the supply agreement:

(a) the lessee has the right as against the lessor to reject the equipment or to terminate the leasing agreement; and
(b) the lessor has the right to remedy its failure to tender equipment in conformity with the supply agreement,

as if the lessee had agreed to buy the equipment from the lessor under the same terms as those of the supply agreement.

2 A right conferred by the previous paragraph shall be exercisable in the same manner and shall be lost in the same circumstances as if the lessee had agreed to buy the equipment from the lessor under the same terms as those of the supply agreement.

3 The lessee shall be entitled to withhold rentals payable under the leasing agreement until the lessor has remedied its failure to tender equipment in conformity with the supply agreement or the lessee has lost the right to reject the equipment.

4 Where the lessee has exercised a right to terminate the leasing agreement, the lessee shall be entitled to recover any rentals and other sums paid in advance, less a reasonable sum for any benefit the lessee has derived from the equipment.

5 The lessee shall have no other claim against the lessor for non-delivery, delay in delivery or delivery of non-conforming equipment except to the extent to which this results from the act or omission of the lessor.

6 Nothing in this article shall affect the lessee's rights against the supplier under Article 10.

Article 13

1 In the event of default by the lessee, the lessor may recover accrued unpaid rentals, together with interest and damages.

2 Where the lessee's default is substantial, then subject to paragraph 5 the lessor may also require accelerated payment of the value of the future rentals, where the leasing agreement so provides, or may terminate the leasing agreement and after such termination:

(a) recover possession of the equipment; and
(b) recover such damages as will place the lessor in the position in which it would have been had the lessee performed the leasing agreement in accordance with its terms.

3 (a) The leasing agreement may provide for the manner in which the damages recoverable under paragraph 2(b) are to be computed.

(b) Such provision shall be enforceable between the parties unless it would result in damages substantially in excess of those provided for under paragraph 2(b). The parties may not derogate from or vary the effect of the provisions of the present sub-paragraph.

4 Where the lessor has terminated the leasing agreement, it shall not be entitled to enforce a term of that agreement providing for acceleration of payment of future rentals, but the value of such rentals may be taken into account in computing damages under paragraphs 2(b) and 3. The parties may not derogate from or vary the effect of the provisions of the present paragraph.

5 The lessor shall not be entitled to exercise its right of acceleration or its right of termination under paragraph 2 unless it has by notice given the lessee a reasonable opportunity of remedying the default so far as the same may be remedied.

6 The lessor shall not be entitled to recover damages to the extent that it has failed to take all reasonable steps to mitigate its loss.

Article 14

1 The lessor may transfer or otherwise deal with all or any of its rights in the equipment or under the leasing agreement. Such a transfer shall not relieve the lessor of any of its duties under the leasing agreement or alter either the nature of the leasing agreement or its legal treatment as provided in this Convention.

2 The lessee may transfer the right to the use of the equipment or any other rights under the leasing agreement only with the consent of the lessor and subject to the rights of third parties.

Chapter III - Final provisions

Article 15

1 This Convention is open for signature at the concluding meeting of the Diplomatic Conference for the Adoption of the Draft Unidroit Conventions on International Factoring and International Financial Leasing and will remain open for signature by all States at Ottawa until 31 December 1990.

2 This Convention is subject to ratification, acceptance or approval by States which have signed it.

3 This Convention is open for accession by all States which are not signatory States as from the date it is open for signature.

4 Ratification, acceptance, approval or accession is effected by the deposit of a formal instrument to that effect with the depositary.

Article 16

1 This Convention enters into force on the first day of the month following the expiration of six months after the date of deposit of the third instrument of ratification, acceptance, approval or accession.

2 For each State that ratifies, accepts, approves, or accedes to this Convention after the deposit of the third instrument of ratification, acceptance, approval or accession, this Convention enters into force in respect of that State on the first day of the month following the expiration of six months after the date of the deposit of its instrument of ratification, acceptance, approval or accession.

ARTICLE 17

This Convention does not prevail over any treaty which has already been or may be entered into; in particular it shall not affect any liability imposed on any person by existing or future treaties.

ARTICLE 18

1 If a Contracting State has two or more territorial units in which different systems of law are applicable in relation to the matters dealt with in this Convention, it may, at the time of signature, ratification, acceptance, approval or accession, declare that this Convention is to extend to all its territorial units or only to one or more of them, and may substitute its declaration by another declaration at any time.

2 These declarations are to be notified to the depositary and are to state expressly the territorial units to which the Convention extends.

3 If, by virtue of a declaration under this article, this Convention extends to one or more but not all of the territorial units of a Contracting State, and if the place of business of a party is located in that State, this place of business, for the purposes of this Convention, is considered not to be in a Contracting State, unless it is in a territorial unit to which the Convention extends.

4 If a Contracting State makes no declaration under paragraph 1, the Convention is to extend to all territorial units of that State.

ARTICLE 19

1 Two or more Contracting States which have the same or closely related legal rules on matters governed by this Convention may at any time declare that the Convention is not to apply where the supplier, the lessor and the lessee have their places of business in those States. Such declarations may be made jointly or by reciprocal unilateral declarations.

2 A Contracting State which has the same or closely related legal rules on matters governed by this Convention as one or more non-Contracting States may at any time declare that the Convention is not to apply where the supplier, the lessor and the lessee have their places of business in those States.

3 If a State which is the object of a declaration under the previous paragraph subsequently becomes a Contracting State, the declaration made will, as from the date on which the Convention enters into force in respect of the new Contracting State, have the effect of a declaration made under paragraph 1, provided that the new Contracting State joins in such declaration or makes a reciprocal unilateral declaration.

ARTICLE 20

A Contracting State may declare at the time of signature, ratification, acceptance, approval or accession that it will substitute its domestic law for Article 8(3) if its domestic law does not permit the lessor to exclude its liability for its default or negligence.

ARTICLE 21

1 Declarations made under this Convention at the time of signature are subject to confirmation upon ratification, acceptance or approval.

2 Declarations and confirmations of declarations are to be in writing and to be formally notified to the depositary.

3 A declaration takes effect simultaneously with the entry into force of this Convention in respect of the State concerned. However, a declaration of which the depositary receives formal notification after such entry into force takes effect on the first day of the month following the expiration of six months after the date of its receipt by the depositary. Reciprocal unilateral declarations under Article 19 take effect on the first day of the month following the expiration of six months after the receipt of the latest declaration by the depositary.

4 Any State which makes a declaration under this Convention may withdraw it at any time by a formal notification in writing addressed to the depositary. Such withdrawal is to take effect on the first day of the month following the expiration of six months after the date of the receipt of the notification by the depositary.

5 A withdrawal of a declaration made under Article 19 renders inoperative in relation to the withdrawing State, as from the date on which the withdrawal takes effect, any joint or reciprocal unilateral declaration made by another State under that article.

ARTICLE 22

No reservations are permitted except those expressly authorised in this Convention.

ARTICLE 23

This Convention applies to a financial leasing transaction when the leasing agreement and the supply agreement are both concluded on or after the date on which the Convention enters into force in respect of the Contracting States referred to in Article 3(1)(a), or of the Contracting State or States referred to in paragraph 1 (b) of that article.

ARTICLE 24

1 This Convention may be denounced by any Contracting State at any time after the date on which it enters into force for that State.

2 Denunciation is effected by the deposit of an instrument to that effect with the depositary.

3 A denunciation takes effect on the first day of the month following the expiration of six months after the deposit of the instrument of denunciation with the depositary. Where a longer period for the denunciation to take effect is specified in the instrument of denunciation it takes effect upon the expiration of such longer period after its deposit with the depositary.

ARTICLE 25

1 This Convention shall be deposited with the Government of Canada.

2 The Government of Canada shall:

(a) inform all States which have signed or acceded to this Convention and the President of the International Institute for the Unification of Private Law (Unidroit) of:
(i) each new signature or deposit of an instrument of ratification, acceptance, approval or accession, together with the date thereof;
(ii) each declaration made under Articles 18, 19 and 20;
(iii) the withdrawal of any declaration made under Article 21(4);
(iv) the date of entry into force of this Convention;
(v) the deposit of an instrument of denunciation of this Convention together with the date of its deposit and the date on which it takes effect;
(b) transmit certified true copies of this Convention to all signatory States, to all States acceding to the Convention and to the President of the International Institute for the Unification of Private Law (Unidroit).

IN WITNESS WHEREOF the undersigned plenipotentiaries, being duly authorised by their respective Governments, have signed this Convention.

DONE at Ottawa, this twenty-eighth day of May, one thousand nine hundred and eighty-eight, in a single original, of which the English and French texts are equally authentic.

PARTIES TO THE OTTAWA CONVENTION

FRANCE, 23.4.91; ITALY, 29.11.93; NIGERIA, 25.10.94; PANAMA, 26.3.97; HUNGARY, 7.5.96

Appendix D

Preliminary draft Unidroit Convention on international interests in mobile equipment[1]

Chapter I – Sphere of application and general provisions

ARTICLE 1

In this Convention the following words are employed with the meanings set out below:

(a) 'agreement' means a security agreement, a title reservation agreement or a leasing agreement;
(b) 'applicable law' means the law applicable by virtue of the rules of private international law;
(c) 'associated rights' means:
  (i) rights relating to ownership, possession, use or control of an object as defined in the Protocol; and
  (ii) all rights to payment or other performance secured by or associated with the object;
(d) 'chargee' means the grantee of an interest in an object under a security agreement;
(e) 'chargor' means the grantor of an interest in an object under a security agreement;
(f) 'court' means a court of law or an administrative or arbitral tribunal established by a Contracting State;
(g) 'Intergovernmental Regulator' means the intergovernmental regulator referred to in Article 17(1);
(h) 'international interest' means an interest to which Article 2 applies;
(i) 'leasing agreement' means an agreement by which one person ('the lessor') grants a lease or sub-lease of an object (with or without an option to purchase) to another person ('the lessee');
(j) 'object' means a mobile object of a category listed in Article 3;
(k) 'obligee' means the chargee under a security agreement, the conditional seller under a title reservation agreement or the lessor under a leasing agreement;
(l) 'obligor' means the chargor under a security agreement, the conditional buyer under a title reservation agreement, the lessee under a leasing agreement [or the person whose interest in an object is burdened by a registrable non-consensual right or interest];
(m) 'prospective assignment' means an assignment that is intended to be made in the future;
(n) 'prospective international interest' means an interest that is intended to be created or provided for as an international interest in the future;
(o) 'Protocol' means, in respect of any category of object and associated rights to which this Convention applies, the Protocol in force in respect of that category of object and associated rights;
(p) 'registered' means registered in the International Registry pursuant to Chapter V;
(q) 'registered interest' means an international interest [or a registrable non-consensual right or interest registered pursuant to Chapter V;
(r) [registrable non-consensual right or interest' means a right or interest registrable pursuant to a declaration made under Article 38(1);
(s)] 'Registrar' means, in respect of any category of object and associated rights to which this Convention applies, the person designated under Article 17(3)
[(t)] 'Regulations' means regulations made by the Intergovernmental Regulator under Article 17(3);
[(u)] 'secured obligation' means an obligation secured by a security interest;
[(v)] 'security agreement' means an agreement by which a chargor grants or agrees to grant to a chargee an interest ('security interest') in or over an object to secure the performance of an existing or future obligation of the chargor or a third person;
[(w)] 'title reservation agreement' means an agreement by which one person ('the conditional seller') agrees to sell an object to another person ('the conditional buyer') on terms that ownership does not pass until fulfilment of the condition or conditions stated in the agreement;
[(x)] 'unregistered interest' means a consensual [or non-consensual right or] interest [(other than an interest to which Article 38(2) applies)] which has not been registered;
[(y)] 'writing' means an authenticated record of information (including information sent by teletransmission) which is in tangible form or is capable of being reproduced in tangible form.

ARTICLE 2

1 This Convention provides for the constitution and effects of an international interest in mobile equipment and associated rights.

2 For the purposes of this Convention an international interest in mobile equipment is an interest in an object of a category listed in Article 3:

    (a) granted by the chargor under a security agreement;

    (b) vested in a person who is the conditional seller under a title reservation agreement; or

    (c) vested in a person who is the lessor under a leasing agreement.

3 Whether an interest to which the preceding paragraph applies falls within sub-paragraph (a), (b) or (c) of that paragraph is to be determined by the applicable law.

ARTICLE 3

This Convention applies in relation to a mobile object, and associated rights relating to a mobile object, of any of the following categories:

    (a) airframes;

    (b) aircraft engines;

    (c) helicopters;

    (d) [registered ships;

    (e)] oil rigs;

    [(f)] containers;

    [(g)] railway rolling stock;

    [(h)] space property;

    [(i)] objects of any other category each member of which is uniquely identifiable.

ARTICLE 4

This Convention shall apply when at the time of conclusion of the agreement creating or providing for the international interest:

    (a) the obligor is located in a Contracting State; or

    (b) the object to which the international interest relates has been registered in a nationality register [or a State-authorised asset register,] in a Contracting State or otherwise has a close connection, as specified in the Protocol, to a Contracting State.

ARTICLE 5

For the purposes of this Convention, a party is located in the State in which it is incorporated or registered or in which it has its principal place of business or, if it has more than one such place, its principal executive office.

ARTICLE 6

In their relations with each other the parties may, by agreement in writing, derogate from or vary the effect of any of the provisions of Chapter III, except as stated in Articles 9(2)-(6), 10(2) and (3), 13(1) and 14, or of Article 34(2).

ARTICLE 7

1 In the interpretation of this Convention, regard is to be had to its purposes as set forth in the preamble[2], to its international character and to the need to promote uniformity and predictability in its application.

2 Questions concerning matters governed by this Convention which are not expressly settled in it are to be settled in conformity with the general principles on which it is based or, in the absence of such principles, in conformity with the applicable law.

Chapter II – Constitution of an international interest

ARTICLE 8

An interest is constituted as an international interest under this Convention where the agreement creating or providing for the interest:

    (a) is in writing;

    (b) relates to an object in respect of which the chargor, seller or lessor has power to enter into the agreement;

    (c) enables the object to be identified in conformity with the applicable Protocol; and

    (d) in the case of a security agreement, enables the secured obligations to be identified.

Chapter III – Default remedies

ARTICLE 9

1 In the event of default in the performance of a secured obligation, the chargee may exercise any one or more of the following remedies:
    (a) take possession or control of any object charged to it;
    (b) sell or grant a lease of any such object;
    (c) collect or receive any income or profits arising from the management or use of any such object;
    (d) apply for a court order authorising or directing any of the above acts.

2 Any remedy given by sub-paragraph (a), (b) or (c) of the preceding paragraph shall be exercised in a commercially reasonable manner. A remedy shall be deemed to be exercised in a commercially reasonable manner where it is exercised in conformity with a provision of the security agreement except where the court determines that such a provision is manifestly unreasonable.

3 A chargee proposing to sell or grant a lease of an object under paragraph 1 otherwise than pursuant to a court order shall give reasonable prior notice in writing of the proposed sale or lease to interested persons.

4 Any sum collected or received by the chargee as a result of exercise of any of the remedies set out under paragraph 1 shall be applied towards discharge of the amount of the secured obligations.

5 Where the sums collected or received by the chargee as a result of the exercise of any remedy given in paragraph 1 exceed the amount secured by the security interest and any reasonable costs incurred in the exercise of any such remedy, then unless otherwise ordered by the court the chargee shall pay the excess to the holder of the international interest registered immediately after its own or, if there is none, to the chargor.

6 In this Article and in Article 10 'interested persons' means:
    (a) the chargor;
    (b) any guarantor or surety under a guarantee (including a demand guarantee or standby letter of credit) given to the chargee;
    (c) any person entitled to the benefit of any international interest which is registered after that of the chargee;
    (d) any other person having rights subordinate to those of the chargee in or over the object of which notice in writing has been given to the chargee within a reasonable time before exercise of the remedy given by paragraph 1(b) or vesting of the object in the chargee under Article 10(1), as the case may be.

ARTICLE 10

1 At any time after default in the performance of a secured obligation, all the interested persons may agree, or the court may on the application of the chargee order, that ownership of (or any other interest of the chargor in) any object covered by the security interest shall vest in the chargee in or towards satisfaction of the secured obligations.

2 The court shall grant an application under the preceding paragraph only if the amount of the secured obligations to be satisfied by such vesting is reasonably commensurate with the value of the object after taking account of any payment to be made by the chargee to any of the interested persons.

3 At any time after default in the performance of a secured obligation and before sale of the charged object or the making of an order under paragraph 1, the chargor or any interested person may discharge the security interest by paying the amount secured, subject to any lease granted by the chargee under Article 9(1). Where, after such default, the payment is in full made by an interested person, that person is subrogated to the rights of the chargee.

4 Ownership or any other interest of the chargor passing on a sale under Article 9(1) or passing under paragraph 1 of this Article is free from any other interest over which the chargee's security interest has priority under the provisions of Article 28.

ARTICLE 11

In the event of default by the conditional buyer under a title reservation agreement or by the lessee under a leasing agreement, the conditional seller or lessor, as the case may be, may terminate the agreement and take possession or control of any object to which the agreement relates. The conditional seller or lessor may also apply for a court order authorising or directing either of these acts.

ARTICLE 12

1 The parties may provide in their agreement for any kind of default, or any event other than default, as giving rise to the rights and remedies specified in Articles 9 to 11 or 15.

2 In the absence of such an agreement, 'default' for the purposes of Articles 9 to 11 and 15 means a substantial default.

ARTICLE 13

1 Subject to paragraph 2, any remedy provided by this Chapter shall be exercised in conformity with the procedural law of the place where the remedy is to be exercised.

2 Any remedy available to the obligee under Articles 9 to 11 which is not there expressed to require application to the court may be exercised without leave of the court except to the extent that the Contracting State where the remedy is to be exercised has made a declaration under Article Y or in the Protocol.

ARTICLE 14

Any additional remedies permitted by the applicable law, including any remedies agreed upon by the parties, may be exercised to the extent that they are not inconsistent with the mandatory provisions of this Chapter.

ARTICLE 15

1 A Contracting State shall ensure that an obligee who adduces *prima facie* evidence of default by the obligor may, pending final determination of its claim, obtain speedy judicial relief in the form of one or more of the following orders:
  (a) preservation of the object and its value;
  (b) possession, control, custody or management of the object;
  (c) sale or lease of the object;
  (d) application of the proceeds or income of the object;
  (e) immobilisation of the object.
2 Ownership or any other interest of the obligor passing on a sale under the preceding paragraph is free from any other interest over which the chargee's security interest has priority under the provisions of Article 28.
3 A court of a Contracting State has jurisdiction to grant judicial relief under paragraph 1 where:
  (a) the object is within the territory of that State;
  (b) one of the parties is located within that territory; or
  (c) the parties have agreed to submit to the jurisdiction of that court.
4 A court may exercise jurisdiction under paragraph 1 even if the trial of the claim referred to in that paragraph will or may take place in a court of another State or in an arbitral tribunal.
5 Nothing in this Article shall limit the availability of any form of interim judicial relief under the applicable law.

Chapter IV- The international registration system

ARTICLE 16

1 An International Registry shall be established for registrations of:
  (a) international interests, prospective international interests [and registrable non-consensual rights and interests];
  (b) assignments and prospective assignments of international interests; and
  (c) subordinations of interests referred to in sub-paragraph (a) of this paragraph.
2 Different registries may be established for different categories of object and associated rights. For the purposes of this Convention, 'International Registry' means the relevant international registry.
3 For the purposes of this Chapter and Chapter V, the term 'registration' includes, where appropriate, an amendment, extension or discharge of a registration.

[ARTICLE 17

1 The Protocol shall designate an Intergovernmental Regulator to exercise the functions assigned to it by this Chapter, Chapter V and the Protocol.
2 The Protocol may provide for Contracting States to designate operators of registration facilities in their respective territories. Such operators shall be transmitters of the information required for registration and, in such capacity, shall constitute an integral part of the registration system of this Convention. The Protocol may specify the extent to which the designation of such an operator shall preclude alternative access to the International Registry.
3 The Intergovernmental Regulator shall establish the International Registry and designate the Registrar. The Intergovernmental Regulator shall oversee the International Registry and the operation and administration thereof. The manner in which such oversight is conducted and the responsibilities of the Registrar and the operators of registration facilities shall be prescribed in the Protocol and in regulations ('the Regulations') from time to time made by the Intergovernmental Regulator[3].
4 In the exercise of their respective functions under this Convention and the Protocol, the Registrar, the operators of registration facilities and the International Registry shall be deemed to be an international Organisation and, in the carrying out of the functions set out in this Convention and the Protocol, shall not be subject to the law or jurisdiction of the courts of the States in which they are situated.
5 The Protocol [shall] [may] provide procedures for the review of acts or missions of the Registrar or operators of registration facilities alleged to be in contravention of this Convention, the Protocol or the Regulations and for any remedial action.
6 The Protocol may prescribe the procedures pursuant to which the Registrar and the operators of registration facilities may request advice from the Intergovernmental Regulator regarding the exercise of their respective functions under this Convention, the Protocol and the Regulations.]

Chapter V – Modalities of registration

ARTICLE 18

The Protocol and Regulations may contain conditions and requirements, including the criterion or criteria for the identification of the object, which must be fulfilled in order to effect a registration.

ARTICLE 19

The information required for a registration shall be transmitted, by any medium prescribed by the Protocol or Regulations, to the International Registry or registration facility prescribed therein.

ARTICLE 20

1 A registration shall take effect upon entry of the required information into the International Registry database so as to be searchable.

2 If an interest first registered as a prospective international interest becomes an international interest, the international interest shall be treated as registered from the time of registration of the prospective international interest.

3 Paragraph 2 applies with necessary modifications to the registration of a prospective assignment of an international interest.

4 The International Registry shall record the date and time a registration takes effect.

5 A registration shall be searchable in the International Registry database according to the criterion or criteria prescribed in the Protocol.

ARTICLE 21

1 By the transmission of the required information to the International Registry in conformity with the Protocol and Regulations:

    (a) an international interest may be registered by the holder thereof if the agreement relating to it conforms to the provisions of Article 8 and, in the case of a security agreement, the chargor has, therein or elsewhere, consented in writing to the registration;

    (b) a prospective international interest or a prospective assignment of an international interest may be registered by the intended grantee or assignee respectively if the intending grantor or assignor has consented in writing to the registration;

    (c) [a registrable non-consensual right or interest in relation to which a declaration has been made pursuant to Article 38(1) may be registered by the holder thereof;

    (d)] the registration of a registered interest may be amended by the holder but the holder may do so only if the chargor has consented in writing thereto;

    [(e)] the assignment of an international interest conforming to the provisions of Article 30 may be registered by the assignee;

    [(f)] the registration of a registered interest may, prior to the expiry of the registration period, be extended by the holder of such interest;

    [(g)] a subordination of a registered interest may be registered by the person in whose favour the subordination was made;

    [(h)] a discharge of a registered interest, a registered prospective international interest or a registered prospective assignment of an international interest may be registered by the holder thereof.

2 The holder of a registered interest may at any time discharge the registration.

ARTICLE 22

Registration of an international interest remains effective for the period of time specified in the Protocol or the Regulations as extended in conformity with Article 21(1)(f).

ARTICLE 23

1 A person may, in the manner prescribed by the Protocol and Regulations, make or request a search of the International Registry concerning interests registered therein.

2 Upon receipt of a request therefor, the Registrar, in the manner prescribed by the Protocol and Regulations, shall issue a registry search certificate with respect to any object:

    (a)stating all registered information relating thereto, together with a statement indicating the date and time of registration of such information; or

    (b)stating that there is no information in the International Registry relating thereto.

The Registrar shall maintain a list of the categories of non-consensual right or interest declared by Contracting States in conformity with Article 38(2) and the date of each such declaration. Such information shall be made available as provided in the Protocol and Regulations to any person requesting it.]

ARTICLE 25

A document in the form prescribed by the Regulations which purports to be a certificate issued by the International Registry is *prima facie* proof:
(a) that it has been so issued; and
(b) of the facts recited in it, including the date and time of registration of the information referred to in Article 21(1).

[ARTICLE 26

The liability rules for errors and omissions in the operation and administration of the International Registry, and the procedures for dealing with claims against the International Registry, shall be set forth in the Protocol.]

ARTICLE 27

1 When the obligations secured by a security interest [or the obligations giving rise to a registrable non-consensual right or interest] have been discharged, or the conditions of transfer of title under a title reservation agreement have been fulfilled, the obligor may, by written demand delivered to the holder of such a registered interest, require the holder to remove the registration relating to the interest.
2 Where a prospective international interest or a prospective assignment of an international interest has been registered, the intending grantor or assignor may by notice in writing, delivered to the intended grantee or assignee at any time before the latter has given value or incurred a commitment to give value, require the relevant registration to be removed.

Chapter VI – Effects of an international interest as against third parties

ARTICLE 28

1 A registered interest has priority over any other interest subsequently registered and over an unregistered interest.
2 The priority of the first-mentioned interest under the preceding paragraph applies:
(a)even if the first-mentioned interest was acquired or registered with actual knowledge of the other interest; and
(b)even as regards value given by the holder of the first-mentioned interest with such knowledge.
3 The buyer of an object acquires its interest in it:
(a)subject to an interest registered at the time of its acquisition of that interest; and
(b)free from an unregistered interest even if it has actual knowledge of such an interest.
4 The priority of competing interests under this Article may be varied by agreement between the holders of those interests, but an assignee of a subordinated interest is not bound by an agreement to subordinate that interest unless at the time of the assignment a subordination had been registered relating to that agreement.
5 Any priority given by this Article to an interest in an object extends to insurance proceeds payable in respect of the loss or physical destruction of that object.

ARTICLE 29

1 An international interest is valid against the trustee in bankruptcy of the obligor if prior to the commencement of the bankruptcy that interest was registered in conformity with this Convention.
2 For the purposes of this Article 'trustee in bankruptcy' includes a liquidator, administrator or other person appointed to administer the estate of the obligor for the benefit of the general body of creditors.
3 Nothing in this Article affects the validity of an international or other interest against the trustee in bankruptcy where that interest is valid against the trustee in bankruptcy under the applicable law.

Chapter VII – Assignments of international interests

ARTICLE 30

1 The holder of an international interest ('the assignor') may make an assignment of it to another person ('the assignee') wholly or in part.
2 An assignment of an international interest shall be valid only if it:
(a)is in writing;
(b)enables the international interest and the object to which it relates to be identified;
(c)in the case of an assignment by way of security, enables the obligations secured by the assignment to be identified.

3 For the purposes of this Convention 'assignment' means an outright transfer or any other kind of transfer or agreement, whether by way of security or otherwise, which confers on the assignee rights in or over the international interest.

ARTICLE 31

1 An assignment of an international interest in an object made in conformity with the preceding Article transfers to the assignee, to the extent agreed by the parties to the assignment:
    (a) all the interests and priorities of the assignor under this Convention; and
    (b) all associated rights [so far as such rights are assignable under the applicable law].
2 Except as otherwise agreed by the obligor, an assignment made in conformity with the preceding paragraph shall take effect subject to:
    (a) all defences of which the obligor could have availed itself against the assignor; and
    (b) any rights of set-off in respect of claims existing against the assignor and available to the obligor at the time of receipt of a notice of the assignment under Article 33.
3 In the case of an assignment by way of security, the assigned rights revest in the assignor, to the extent that they are still subsisting, when the security interest has been discharged.

ARTICLE 32

The provisions of Chapter V (other than Article 21(1)(a)) shall apply to the registration of an assignment or prospective assignment of an international interest as if the assignment or prospective assignment were the international interest or prospective international interest and as if the assignor were the grantor of the interest.

ARTICLE 33

1 To the extent that an international interest has been assigned in accordance with the provisions of this Chapter, the obligor in relation to that interest is bound by the assignment, and, in the case of an assignment within Article 31(1)(b), has a duty to make payment or give other performance to the assignee, if but only if:
    (a) the obligor has been given notice of the assignment in writing by or with the authority of the assignor;
    (b) the notice identifies the international interest; and
    (c) the obligor does not have [actual] knowledge of any other person's superior right to payment or other performance.
2 Irrespective of any other ground on which payment or performance by the obligor discharges the latter from liability, payment or performance shall be effective for this purpose if made in accordance with the preceding paragraph.
3 Nothing in the preceding paragraph shall affect the priority of competing assignments.

ARTICLE 34

1 In the event of default by the assignor under the assignment of an international interest made by way of security, Articles 9, 10 and 12 to 15, in so far as they are capable of application to intangible property, apply as if references:
    (a) to the secured obligation and the security interest were references to the obligation secured by the assignment of the international interest and the security interest created by that assignment;
    (b) to the chargee and chargor were references to the assignee and assignor of the international interest; and
    (c) to the object included references to the assigned rights relating to the object.
2 Where, in the case of an assignment by way of security, the sums collected or received by the assignee of the international interest as the result of the exercise of any remedy provided by virtue of the preceding paragraph exceed the amount secured and any reasonable costs incurred in the exercise of any such remedy, then unless otherwise ordered by the court the assignee shall pay the excess to the holder of the assignment registered immediately after its own or, if there is none, to the assignor of the international interest.

ARTICLE 35

Where there are competing assignments of international interests and at least one of the assignments is registered, the provisions of Articles 2–3 apply as if the references to an international interest were references to an assignment of an international interest.

ARTICLE 36

Where the assignment of an international interest has been registered, the assignee shall, in relation to the associated rights transferred by virtue of the assignment, have priority over the holder of associated rights not held with an international interest to the extent that the first-mentioned associated rights relate to:

(a)   a sum advanced and utilised for the purchase of the object;
(b)   the price payable for the object; or
(c)   the rentals payable in respect of the object; and
(d)   the reasonable costs referred to in Article 9(5).

ARTICLE 37

An assignment of an international interest is valid against the trustee in bankruptcy of the assignor if prior to the commencement of the bankruptcy that assignment was registered in conformity with this Convention.

Chapter VIII – Non-consensual rights and interests

ARTICLE 38

1 A Contracting State may at any time in an instrument deposited with the depositary list the categories of non-consensual right or interest which shall be registrable under this Convention as regards any category of object as if the right or interest were an international interest and be regulated accordingly.

2 In proceedings before the courts of a Contracting State a non-consensual right or interest (other than a registrable non-consensual right or interest) which under the law of that State would have priority over an interest in the object equivalent to that held by the holder of the international interest (whether in or outside the insolvency of the obligor) has priority over the international interest to the extent, and only to the extent:

(a) set out by that State in any instrument deposited with the depositary prior to the time when the registration of the international interest takes effect; and

(b) that, without any act of publication, the non-consensual right or interest would under the national law of that State have priority over a registered interest of the same type as the international interest.

[Chapter IX – Relationship with other conventions]

Chapter [X] – [Other] Final provisions

ARTICLE U

A Protocol to this Convention may provide for the application of the Convention, with such modifications as may be necessary, to a transfer (otherwise than under a title reservation agreement) of an interest in an object of a category listed in Article 3.

ARTICLE V

[Insert provision by given minimum number or proportion of Contracting States to request convening of a Conference to consider further initial Protocols in accordance with specified procedure, including requisite majority of those present and voting.]

ARTICLE W

A Contracting State may declare at the time of signature, ratification, acceptance, approval of, or accession to the Protocol that it will not apply this Convention in relation to [a purely domestic transaction] [4].. Such a declaration shall be respected by the courts of all other Contracting States.

ARTICLE X

This Convention shall enter into force as regards a category of object:

(a) at the time of entry into force of the Protocol;
(b) subject to the terms of that Protocol; and
(c)   as between Contracting States Parties to that Protocol.

ARTICLE Y

1 A Contracting State may declare at the time of signature, ratification, acceptance, approval of, or accession to this Convention or the Protocol that while the charged object is situated within or controlled from its territory the chargee shall not grant a lease of the object in that territory.

2 A Contracting State may declare at the time of signature, ratification, acceptance, approval of, or accession to this Convention or the Protocol that any remedy available to the obligee under Articles 9 to 11 which is not there expressed to require application to the court may only be exercised with leave of the court.

ARTICLE Z

A Contracting State may declare at the time of signature, ratification, acceptance, approval of, or accession to this Convention or the Protocol that it will not apply the provisions of Article 15, wholly or in part.

Notes

1 This draft was prepared by a Unidroit Study group at the conclusion of its fourth session, held in Rome from 3 to 7 November 1997. It is subject to the approval of the Governing Council of Unidroit before submission to governmental experts in preparation for a diplomatic conference.

2 It was agreed that it will be necessary in due course to prepare a Preamble to the Convention.

3 It was noted by the Aircraft Protocol Group that Article 17(3) is an example of the type of provision which was envisaged as being subject to Article X(b) and which may therefore find itself modified by the terms of a Protocol.

4 To be defined by taking account of the location of the object and the location of the parties.

Appendix E

Annex IV to the arrangement on guidelines for officially supported export credits

Sector understanding on export credits for civil aircraft

Chapter I. – New Large Commercial Aircraft

1 Form and Scope

This chapter complements the Arrangement on guidelines for officially supported export credits. It sets out the particular complementary guidelines that are applicable to officially supported export credits for financing sales or leases of large civil aircraft listed in the appendix and supersedes the terms of the OECD 'Standstill' (TC/ECG/M/75.1, Item 6 and Annex III-A) with respect to such aircraft.

2 Objective of this chapter

The objective of this chapter is to establish a balanced equilibrium that, on all markets:

- equalises competitive financial conditions between participants;
- neutralises finance among participants as a factor in the choice among competing aircraft; and
- avoids distortions of competition.

3 Credit terms and conditions

(a) Cash payments

The minimum cash payment is 15% of the aircraft's total price (the price of the airframe and any installed engines plus the spare engines and spare parts described in paragraph 28). Participants shall not provide official support for such cash payments other than insurance and guarantees against the usual pre-credit risks.

(b) Maximum repayment term

The maximum repayment term of an officially supported credit is 12 years.

4 Interest rates

(a) Minimum interest rates

Notwithstanding the provisions of paragraph 5, the following minimum interest rates, inclusive of credit insurance premia and guarantees, apply where participants are providing official financing support by way of direct credit, refinancing or interest rate subsidy:

1 Financing in US dollars:

Number of years in maximum repayment term

Up to 10 years	From 10 to 12 years
TB 10 + 120 basis points	TB 10 + 175 basis points

where TB 10 means 10-year Treasury bond yields at constant maturity, averaged over the previous two calendar weeks.
2 Financing in the currencies of the currency cocktail (German mark, French franc, pound sterling, ecu)[1]
A currency cocktail package, based on 10-year government bond yields for the German mark, French franc and the pound sterling[2] plus a margin applies. This margin, calculated as a weighted average of the margins applicable to each currency, is equal to the margin applicable in the case of financing in US dollars.
In the case of financing in ecus the minimum rate applicable is the long-term ecu bond yield[3] less 20 basis points plus a margin equal to the margin applicable in the case of financing in US dollars.

(b) Interest rate adjustments

An adjustment is made to the minimum rates of interest set out in (a) if the two-weekly average of the 10-year government bond yields at constant maturity at the end of each two-week period differs by 10 basis points or more from the average of the 10-year government bond yield at constant maturity at the end of the last two calendar weeks of June 1985. When such a change occurs, the levels of the minimum rates of interest set out above are adjusted by the same number of basis points and the recalculated minimum rates are rounded off to the nearest five basis points. Subsequently, minimum rates of interest are adjusted on a two-weekly basis according to the aforementioned method if there is a change of 10 basis points or more in the interest rate underlying the preceding change in minimum rates of interest. Similar provisions apply to the ecus in the case of changes in the ecu bond yield.

(c) Special adjustments

1 If a participant believes that at least two significant sales in any six-month period:
(i) for which participants are direct competitors; and
(ii) on which offers have been made with official financial support (see paragraphs 5(a) and (b)) have been concluded on a pure cover basis, other than Pefco, at a fixed interest rate below the applicable minimum interest rates specified in this chapter,
the participants shall consult immediately in order to determine the interest rates on the basis of which the sales have been concluded and, if necessary, to find a permanent solution that ensures that the objectives of paragraph 2 are fully met.

2 If during these consultations:
(i) it cannot be determined whether the interest rates for the sales in question were at, above, or equivalent to the applicable minimum interest rates specified in this chapter, and
(ii) if a solution cannot be found within 30 days from the start of the consultations,
then the minimum interest rates specified in paragraph 4(a)(1) are reduced by 15 basis points, unless the participants agree that the sales concerned are not significant. In no case is the interest rate for the 10-year option reduced below TB 10 plus 105 basis points. Such adjustments are made without prejudice to continuing consultations to find a solution, including the possibility of a recoupment in the event that additional cases do not occur.

3 If, in any six-month period, two or more sales for which participants are direct competitors are concluded on a floating-rate pure cover basis, consultations to ensure that the objectives of paragraph 2 are fully met shall be held at the request of any participant.

(d) Differential between 10- and 12-year financing options[4]

1 If, subject to the conditions outlined below, at the end of the period between 1 July 1985 and 1 July 1986, 66% or more of all sales of aircraft, financed either by means of official support or by Pefco, have been concluded on a 10-year term, then the minimum interest rate on the 10-year financing option shall be increased by 15 basis points.
If, during the following year, 66% or more of all sales of aircraft, financed either by means of official support or by Pefco, have been concluded on a 10-year term, then the participants shall review the differential between 10- and 12-year financing options with a view to finding a permanent solution to the problem of equating the differential between the two options. If, on the other hand 66% or more of the above sales have been concluded under the 10- to 12-year financing option, then the minimum interest rate on the 10-year financing option shall be decreased by 10 basis points.

2 If, subject to the conditions outlined below, at the end of the period 1 July 1985 and 1 July 1986, 66% or more of all sales have been concluded on a 10- to 12-year term then the minimum interest rate on the 10-year financing option shall be decreased by 15 basis points.
If, during the following year, 66% or more of all sales of aircraft have been concluded under the 10- to 12-year term, then the participants shall review the differential between 10- and 12-year financing options with a view to finding a permanent solution to the problem of equating the differential between the two options. If, on the other hand, 66% or more of the above sales have been concluded under the 10-year option, then the 10-year minimum interest rate shall be increased by 10 basis points.

(e) Date of determination of interest rate offer

A participant may offer the borrower a choice of one of the two following methods for selecting the date on which the minimum interest rate (as defined in paragraph 4 (a) *et seq.*) on official fixed interest rate financing (see paragraph 5(a)) and on Pefco financing (see paragraph 5 (b)) is determined. The selection by the borrower is irrevocable. The minimum rate is:
(i) the minimum rate prevailing on the date of the offer by the lender; or
(ii) the minimum rate prevailing on whichever one of a series of dates may be selected by the borrower.
The date selected shall in no event be later than the date of delivery of the aircraft.

5 Amount of financing

(a) Official fixed interest rate financing

1 The maximum percentage of the aircraft total price (as that term is defined in paragraph 3(a)) that may be financed at the fixed minimum rates specified in paragraph 4(a) by means of official financing support is 62.5% when repayment of the loan is spread over the entire life of the financing and 42.5% when repayment of the loan is spread over the later maturities. Participants are free to use either repayment approach, subject to the ceiling applicable to that pattern. A participant offering such a tranche shall notify the other participants of the amount, the interest rate, the date on which the interest rate is set, the validity period for the interest rate and the pattern of repayment.

2 The participants will review the two ceilings at the time of each review pursuant to paragraph 14, to examine whether one ceiling provides more advantages than the other with a view to adjusting the more advantageous so that a balance is more evenly struck.

(b) Pefco financing

1 Fixed-rate funds may be officially financed in a manner comparable to that provided by the Private Export Funding Corporation (Pefco). Weekly information on Pefco's borrowing costs and applicable lending rates, exclusive of official guarantee fees on fixed-rate finance for immediate disbursement and for disbursements over a series of dates, for contract offers and for bid offers, shall be communicated to the other participants on a regular basis. A participant offering such a tranche shall notify the other participants of the amount, interest rate, date on which interest rate is set, validity period for the interest rate and pattern of repayments. Any participant matching such financing offered by another participant shall match it in all of its terms and conditions other than the validity period of offers of commitment (see paragraph 6).

2 These rates as notified shall be applicable by all participants as long as the 24-month disbursement interest rate does not exceed 225 basis points above TB 10 (see paragraph 4). In the event the 24-month rate exceeds 225 basis points, participants are free to apply the rate of 225 basis points for 24 months disbursement and all the corresponding rates and shall consult immediately with a view to finding a permanent solution.

(c) 'Pure cover' tranche

Official support by means of guarantees only ('pure cover') is permitted subject to the ceiling specified in (d). However, a participant offering such a tranche shall notify the other participants of the amount, term, pattern of repayments, and, where possible, interest rates.

(d) Total official support

The total amount of funds benefiting from official support pursuant to paragraph 5(a), (b) and (c) shall not exceed 85% of the total price as defined in paragraph 3(a).

6 Validity period of commitments

The duration of fixed interest rate offers of commitment on the tranches of financing defined in paragraphs 5(a) and (b) shall not exceed three months.

7 Fees

Commitment and management fees are not included in the interest rate.

8 Security

Participants retain the right to decide on security acceptable to themselves autonomously and will communicate fully to other participants on this point, as requested or when deemed appropriate.

9 Aid credits

There shall be no tied or partially untied aid credits (including tied and partially untied grants) for any item covered by the Sector Understanding. Participants shall not provide any other kind of financing on credit conditions that are more favourable than those set out in this Sector Understanding[5]. However, participants shall consider sympathetically any requests for a common line for tied or partially untied aid for humanitarian purposes.

10 Model changes

It is understood that when a loan contract has been concluded on one type of aircraft, the terms contained therein cannot be transferred to another type bearing a different model designation.

11 Leases

It is also understood that a participant may match a 12-year officially supported lease transaction with a 12-year repayment term and 85% credit financing support, subject to the other terms and conditions of this chapter.

12 Competition reference point

In the event of officially supported competition, aircraft that are in the list of large civil aircraft in the Appendix and that compete with other aircraft may benefit from the same export credit terms and conditions.

13 Procedures

The procedures outlined in the Arrangement on guidelines for officially supported export credits apply to this chapter. In addition, should any participant believe that another participant is offering an officially supported export credit that is not in conformity with the Guidelines without giving advance notice, consultations shall be held within 10 days on request.

14 Review

The information procedures and conditions outlined in this chapter are subject, in principle, to an annual review. However, the participants shall review the provisions of this chapter whenever requested, notably in relation to the possible development of certain financing and interest rate trends (see paragraph 4(c) and (d)).

Chapter II – All new aircraft except large commercial aircraft

15 Form and scope

This chapter complements the Arrangement on guidelines for officially supported export credits. It sets out the particular complementing Guidelines that are applicable to officially supported export credits financing contracts for the international sale or lease of new (not used) aircraft not covered by chapter I of this Sector Understanding. It does not apply to hovercraft.

16 Participation

The rules on participation of the Arrangement shall apply.

17 Best endeavours

The provisions of this chapter represent the most generous terms that participants are allowed to offer when giving official support. Participants shall however continue to respect customary market terms for different types of aircraft and shall do everything in their power to prevent these terms from being eroded[6].

18 Categories of aircraft

The following categories have been agreed on in view of the competitive situation:
A Turbine-powered aircraft - including helicopters - (e.g. turbo jet, turbo-prop, and turbo-fan aircraft), with generally between 30 to 70 seats. In case a new large turbine-powered aircraft with over 70 seats is being developed, immediate consultations shall be held on request with a view to agree on the classification of such an aircraft in this category or in chapter I of this Sector Understanding in view of the competitive situation.
B Other turbine-powered aircraft, including helicopters.
C Other aircraft, including helicopters.
An illustrative list of aircraft in categories A and B is in the Appendix.

19 Credit terms and conditions

Participants undertake not to support credit terms more favourable than those set out in this paragraph.
Category A: 10 years at SDR-based rate for recipient countries classified in category III or respective CIRRs.
Category B: seven years at SDR-based rate for recipient countries classified in category III or respective CIRRs.
Category C: five years at SDR-based rate for recipient countries classified in category III or respective CIRRs.

20 Sales or leases to third countries (relay countries)

In cases where the aircraft are to be on-sold or on-leased to an end-buyer or end-user in a third country, the interest rate shall be that applicable to the country of final destination.

21 Matching provisions

In the event of officially supported competition, aircraft competing with those from another category or chapter shall, for a specific sale, be able to benefit from matching of the same export credit terms and conditions. Before making the matching offer, the matching authority shall make reasonable efforts to determine the export credit terms and conditions the competing aircraft benefits from. The matching authority will be considered to have made such reasonable efforts if it has informed, by means of instant communication, the authority assumed to offer the terms it intends to match of its intention to do so but has not been informed within three working days that the terms it intends to match will not be used to support the transaction in question.

22 Insurance premiums and guarantee fees

Participants shall not waive in part or in total insurance premiums or guarantee fees.

23 Aid credits

There shall be no tied or partially untied aid credits (including tied and partially untied grants) for any item covered by the Sector Understanding. Participants shall not provide any other kind of financing on credit conditions that are more favourable than those set out in this Sector Understanding[5]. However, participants shall consider sympathetically any requests for a common line for tied or partially untied aid for humanitarian purposes.

24 Consultation and notification procedures

The procedures of the Arrangement shall apply to officially supported export credits not in conformity with the terms of this Sector Understanding. In addition, should any participant believe that another participant may be offering an officially supported export credit not in conformity with this chapter without giving advance notice, consultations shall be held within 10 days on request.

25 Review

The provisions of this Chapter are subject to review annually, normally during the spring meeting of the participants of the Arrangement. In the review, the participants will examine possible modifications of the provisions, notably in order to bring them closer to market conditions. In addition, if market conditions or customary financing practices change considerably, any participant is entitled to ask for a special review of the provisions.

Chapter III – Used Aircraft, Spare Engines, Spare Parts, Maintenance and Service Contracts

26 Form and scope

This chapter complements the Arrangement on guidelines for officially supported export credits. It sets out the particular complementing Guidelines that are applicable to officially supported export credits financing contracts for the international sale or lease of used aircraft, and of spare engines, spare parts, maintenance and service in conjunction with both new and used aircraft. It does not apply to hovercraft.

Provisions in Chapters I and II apply, except the following:

27 Used aircraft

Participants shall not support credit terms more favourable that those set out in this Sector Understanding for transactions concerning new aircraft. Notwithstanding these rules, the following applies to used aircraft:

- when official financing support is to be given, the minimum interest rate shall not be less than the relevant CIRR and
- the participants agree that the normal repayment terms for used aircraft are:

Normal maximum repayment term (in years)

Age (years)	Large Aircraft	Category A	Category B	Category C
1	10	8	6	5
2	9	7	6	5
3	8	6	5	4
4	7	6	5	4
5 to 10	6	6	5	4
>10	5	5	4	3

These terms should be reviewed if the maximum lengths of credit for new aircraft are changed.

28 Spare engines and spare parts

The financing of these items when contemplated as part of the original aircraft order may be on the same terms as for the aircraft, but in that case will be provided as a function of the size of the fleet of each specific aircraft type, including aircraft being acquired, aircraft already on firm orders or aircraft already owned, on the following basis:

- for the first five aircraft of the type in the fleet: 15% of the aircraft price (airframe and installed engines);
- for the sixth and subsequent aircraft of that type in the fleet: 10% of the aircraft price (airframe and installed engines).

When these items are not ordered with the aircraft, participants may offer official support for up to five years for new spare engines and up to two years for other spare parts.

For new spare engines for large aircraft, participants may exceed the standard maximum repayment term of five years up to three years where the transaction:

(a) has a minimum contract value exceeding US $20 million; or

(b) includes a minimum of four new spare engines.

The contract value should be reviewed every two years and adjusted for price escalation accordingly.

Participants reserve the right to change their practice and match the practices of competing participants in matters of detail relating to the timing of the first repayment with respect to spare engines and spare parts.

29 Maintenance and service contracts

Participants may offer official financing support with a repayment term of up to two years for maintenance and service contracts.

30 Consultation and notification procedures

Transactions for used aircraft exceeding the normal repayment terms set out in paragraph 27, and up to the maximum allowable terms specified in paragraphs 3(b) and 19, as the case may be, of the Sector Understanding, shall be subject to prior notification according to paragraph 15(a) of the Arrangement. Paragraphs 10(a) and 12(a) of the Arrangement shall apply to these repayments terms.

31 Review

The provisions of this chapter are subject to review annually, normally during the spring meeting of the participants of the Arrangement. In the review, the participants will examine possible modifications of the provisions, notably in order to bring them closer to market conditions. In addition, if market conditions or customary financing practices change considerably, any participant is entitled to ask for a special review of the provisions.

Notes

1 The 'currency cocktai' financing for the A300 and A310 consists of the following percentages of the following currencies:

- German marrk or ecu   40 per cent
- French franc or ecu   40 per cent
- Pound sterling, US dollar or ecu   20 per cent

For the A320, the 'currency cocktail' consists of the following percentages of the following currencies:

- German mark or ecu   33.7 per cent (provisional)
- French franc or ecu   40.0 per cent (provisional)
- Pound sterling, US dollar or ecu   26.3 per cent (provisional)

2 At constant maturity, averaged over the previous two calendar weeks.

3 As published by the Luxembourg Stock Exchange – long-term bond series, averaged over the previous two calendar weeks.

4 For the operational purposes of this paragraph, it is understood that: the test sample will include only those cases in which the two financing options have been offered by at least one participant, the activation of an interest rate adjustment may take place only if 66% of sales of aircraft according to one option have been concluded under two or more separate transactions, the term 'sales of aircraft' signifies that each separate aircraft sold is included in the sample.

5 Only untied grants are excluded from the ban on aid.

6 Best endeavours shall be made, *inter alia*, with respect to the willingness to respond favourably to the invitation by another participant to consult on possibilities of achieving conditions as close to the market as possible, for example in matching.

APPENDIX

ILLUSTRATIVE LISTS

All other similar aircraft that may be introduced in the future shall be covered by this Sector Understanding and shall be added to the appropriate list in due course. These lists are not exhaustive and serve only to indicate the type of aircraft to be included in the different categories where doubts could arise.

Large civil aircraft

Manufacturer	Designation
Airbus	A 300
Airbus	A 310
Airbus	A 320
Airbus	A 321
Airbus	A 330

Airbus	A 340
Boeing	B 737
Boeing	B 747
Boeing	B 757
Boeing	B 767
Boeing	B 777
Boeing	707, 727
British Aerospace	RJ 70
British Aerospace	RJ 85
British Aerospace	RJ 100
British Aerospace	RJ 115
British Aerospace	BAe 146
Fokker	F 70
Fokker	F 100
Lockheed	L 100
McDonnell Douglas	MD-80 series
McDonnell Douglas	MD-11
McDonnell Douglas	DC-10
McDonnell Douglas	DC-9
Lockheed	L-1011

Category A aircraft

Turbine-powered aircraft - including helicopters - (e.g. turbo jet, turbo-prop and turbo-fan aircraft), with generally between 30 and 70 seats. In case a new large turbine-powered aircraft with over 70 seats is being developed, immediate consultations shall be held upon request with a view to agree on the classification of such an aircraft in this category or in chapter I of this Understanding in view of the competitive situation.

Manufacturer	Designation
Aeritalia	G 222
Aeritalia/Aérospatiale	ATR 42
Aeritalia/Aérospatiale	ATR 72
Aérospatiale/MBB	C 160 Transall
De Havilland	Dash 8
De Havilland	Dash 7
De Havilland	Dash 5
Boeing Vertol	234 Chinook
Broman (US)	BR 2000
British Aerospace	BAe ATP
British Aerospace	BAe 748
British Aerospace	BAe Jetstream 41
Canadair	CL 215T
Canadair	RJ
Casa	CN 235
Dornier	DO 328
EH Industries	EH-101
Embraer	EMB 120 Brasilia
Fokker	F 50
Fokker	F 27
Fokker	F 28
Gulfstream America	Gulfstream I-4
Saab	SF 340
Saab	2000
Short	SD 3-30
Short	SD 3-60
Short	Sherpa
etc.	

Category B aircraft

Other turbine-powered aircraft, including helicopters.

Manufacturer	Designation
Aérospatiale	AS 332
Beech	1900
Beech	Super King Air 300
Beech	Starship 1
Bell Helicopter	206B
Bell Helicopter	206L
Bell Helicopter	212
Bell Helicopter	412
Bell Helicopter	214
British Aerospace	BAe Jetstream 31
British Aerospace	BAe 125
British Aerospace	BAe 1000
Raytheon Co. Jets Inc.	Hawker 1000
British Aerospace	BAe Jetstream Super 31
Canadair	Challenger 601
Canadair	CL 215 (water bomber)
Casa	C 212-200
Casa	C 212-300
Cessna	Citation
Cessna	441 Conquest III
Claudius Dornier	CD2
Dassault Breguet	Falcon
Dornier	Do 228-200
Embraer	EMB 110 P2
Embraer/FAMA	CBA 123
Fairchild	Merlin/300
Fairchild	Metro 25
Fairchild	Metro III V
Fairchild	Metro III
Fairchild	Metro III A
Fairchild	Merlin IVC-41
Gates Learjet	20, 30 and 55 series
Gulfstream America	Gulfstream III and IV
IAI	Arava 101B
Mitsubishi	Mu2 Marquise
Piaggio	P 180
Pilatus Britten-Norman	BN2T Islander
Piper	400 LS
Piper	T 1040
Piper	PA-42-100 (Cheyenne 400)
Piper	PA-42-720 (Cheyenne III A)
Piper	Cheyenne II
Reims	Cessna-Caravan II
SIAI-Marchetti	SF 600 Canguro
Westland	W30
etc.	

Glossary

A-Check the least extensive periodic check for an aircraft.

A Advanced; a common description applied by manufacturers to describe a line of aircraft with advanced characteristics, eg, the Boeing 737-200A.

Accelerated depreciation a rate of depreciation higher than the normal rate, generally for tax purposes.

Accrual method an accounting term that describes a method of keeping accounts whereby expenses incurred and income earned for a given fiscal year are shown in the books even though they may not have actually been paid or received in that period.

ACRS Accelerated Cost Recovery System in the US under the 1981 Tax Act.

Actuarial rate of return the rate at which profit could be withdrawn from a lease. It is calculated as a constant rate of return on the net cash investment in the lease over the period in which there is a positive net cash investment in the lease.

AD Airworthiness Directive.

ADR asset depreciation range; refers to US regulations under the Internal Revenue Code (Section 167(m)) which permits shorter or longer than usual relief to be used for tax depreciation. Rules now largely superseded by ACRS depreciation (see above).

ALPS Aircraft Lease Portfolio Securitisation, a bankruptcy-remote company which issues rated debt securities, and uses the proceeds to acquire a large pool of aircraft leased to a number of geographically diversified lessees.

Alternative minimum tax (AMT) US tax legislation provides that no US corporate taxpayer with substantial economic income can avoid tax liability, and sets a minimum tax rate of 20 per cent. The AMT mechanism particularly affects industries with low marginal profitability and high employment of capital, and the US airline industry is a prime example. An obvious effect of AMT is that as accelerated depreciation and R&Ds are 'preferences' which must be used to calculate AMT liability, investment in capital equipment is effectively penalised by taxation.

Amortisation the retirement of debt through repayment.

AOG Aircraft on Ground; reference to the status of a grounded aircraft.

APU Auxiliary Power Unit; fitted usually in the rear of the aircraft, this provides stand-by power supply in flight and power and air conditioning when the aircraft is on the ground.

ASK/APK available seat-kilometres; or available passenger-kilometres; number of passenger seats available multiplied by the flight stage distance.

ASM Available Seat Miles. Total seats of a carrier available, multiplied by miles actually flown.

Asset value guarantee (AVG); a form of guarantee issued by one or more financial institutions and/or manufacturers guaranteeing the residual value of an aircraft, usually found in option finance. The risk is often 'sliced' at different levels.

ATC Air Traffic Control.

ATK available tonne-kilometres; number of tonnes available for the carriage of revenue load (either passenger, baggage, freight or mail) on each sector of the flight multiplied by the flight stage distance.

Avionics Suites The aircraft instrumentation which ultimately monitors and directs the navigation and movement of an aircraft.

B-Check the second least extensive periodic check for an aircraft, more extensive than an A-check but less extensive than a C-check.

Back-to-back lease leasing structure where equipment is leased to an intermediate lessor and then sub-leased to the actual user.

Balloon payment rentals are paid over the term of the lease with a larger rental known as a 'balloon payment' paid at the end of the lease period. This results in lower periodic rentals and can aid cash flow for the lessee.

Bargain purchase option a provision allowing the lessee, at his option, to purchase the leased asset for a price which is sufficiently lower than the expected fair market value (at the date such option becomes exercisable) that exercise of the option appears, at the inception of the lease, to be reasonably assured.

BFE buyer furnished equipment. BFE is the equipment which is on the aircraft at delivery but which is purchased separately by the buyer in addition to the aircraft price. Examples of BFE are lifejackets and galley equipment.

Blind pool a type of lease financing in the US, whereby funds are raised from individual investors by a leasing intermediary acting as a 'general partner' with no predetermined particular asset. The instrument offers advantages of diversification and time, flowing from the latitude allowed to the general partner.

Bonds certificates evidencing indebtedness.

Broker a company or person who arranges the sale or lease of an aircraft for a fee.

Burdensome buyout a provision in a lease allowing the lessee to purchase the leased equipment at a predetermined value in excess of termination value or at a value to be determined in some fashion when the buyout is exercised, in the event that payments under the tax or general indemnity clauses are deemed by the lessee to be unduly burdensome.

C-Check a relatively major overhaul of an aircraft, typically carried out at annual intervals. An operating lease will typically require the aircraft to have undergone a C-check immediately prior to redelivery to the lessor.

CAA Civil Aviation Authority, the UK regulatory body responsible for, *inter alia,* certifying the airworthiness of UK registered aircraft. The CAA may also issue ADs.

Cabotage also known as the 'eighth freedom of the air' in which an airline picks up passengers, cargo and mail at one point in a state, other than the state of its own registry, and discharges same at another point in the grantor's state.

Call option an option to purchase an asset at a set price at some particular time in the future.

Capacity tonne-kilometres (CTK) another measurement of aircraft and airline productivity. The payload capacity of an aircraft or a fleet multiplied by the distance flown.

Capital allowances the amount of depreciation allowed by the UK Inland Revenue to be offset against taxable profits.

Capital lease a lease in the US is classified and accounted for by a lessee as a capital lease under FAS13 if it meets any of the following criteria: (a) the lease transfers ownership to the lessee at the end of the lease term; (b) the lease contains an option to purchase property at a bargain price; (c) the lease term is equal to 75 per cent or more of the estimated economic life of the property (exceptions for used property leased towards the end of its useful life); or (d) the present value of minimum lease rental payments is equal to 90 per cent or more of the fair market value of the leased property less related ITC retained by the lessor. There are corresponding rules in the UK under SSAP21, as modified by FRS5.

Casualty value see Insured value. Also used to mean the stipulated loss value payable on a total loss.

Certificate of acceptance a document whereby the lessee acknowledges that the equipment to be leased has been delivered to him and is acceptable to him.

Certification engines and airframes have to be certified by the various regulatory authorities before use.

Code sharing see Dual designator agreement.

Collateral security for a financial obligation: under a loan, this might be the asset itself.

Combi Combination; an aircraft in which the proportion of space accommodating passengers and cargo can be varied quickly in order to achieve the most economic proportion of passengers to cargo. Visibly, these aircraft can be identified by their larger doors needed for cargo.

Combustor the part of the engine in which fuel combustion takes place.

Compressor compresses air before its passage through the engine.

Conditional sale a transaction for the purchase of an asset under which legal title passes on fulfilment of the final condition in which the user may for tax purposes be treated as the owner of the equipment at the outset of the transaction.

Consortium lease a lease in which a number of lessors participate. The usual reason for this is that the cost or the potential risk is too high to be borne by one lessor, or to introduce additional tax shelter.

Conv Convertible; an aircraft which can be converted quickly from carrying passengers to one carrying cargo and vice versa.

Cowl the outer casing of the engine, which covers the fan.

Crédit-bail a form of lease used in France under which the lessor retains the tax benefits. The purchase option is fixed usually at 5-10 per cent of cost.

Cross-border leasing where the lessor and lessee are in different countries and/or the transaction involves two or more legal systems.

Cross-collateralisation a structure where each aircraft in a pool stands as collateral for the debt relating to the whole pool, as in a typical fleet financing by a syndicate of banks. It is also a feature of some Enhanced ETC's, enabling recovery of principal to be a function of the proceeds received under all the obligations. Excess proceeds received from the sale of some aircraft would be available to offset shortfalls that occur when other aircraft in the pool are sold.

CRS computer reservation system.

CSR cold section refurbishment of an engine.

Currency swap a technique of trading currency exchange risks with a counterparty (or a bank acting as intermediary between two counterparties).

Current Fair Market Value (CFMV) or Appraisal Value a valuation conducted by an International Society of Transport Aircraft Traders (ISTAT) entity that is considered to have an expert opinion. The valuation must be conducted in accordance with the Principles of Appraisal Practice and Code of Ethics of ISTAT. The quoted CFMV is the appraiser's opinion of the most likely trading price that would be generated for an aircraft under market circumstances that are perceived to exist at the time in question.

The valuation is conducted on a 'desk-top' basis and does not involve a physical inspection of the aircraft or their records. The valuation is based upon the current secondary market for the subject aircraft. Assumptions are made that the parties to the transaction are willing, able and knowledgeable, free from duress to complete the transaction, the transaction is for cash and involves only one aircraft, the aircraft is valued for its highest and best use, and that the transaction would be negotiated in an open and unrestricted market on an arm's length basis, and sufficient time is allowed for an effective international marketing effort over a period of 12 to 18 months. It is further assumed that the aircraft is not encumbered by any attached lease, tax benefit, or other extraneous considerations. Typically, appraisals are determined based upon one of three methods: comparable recent sales, replacement cost, or rate of return to investor. The valuation includes the general assumptions that the aircraft is in average condition, is currently flying, and that the aircraft has half-time remaining to its next major overhauls or scheduled shop visit.

Cycle a complete flight by an aircraft, measured from the time when the wheels leave the ground to touchdown. Contrast with flight hour.

D-Check the most extensive periodic major overhaul to an aircraft.

Declining balance method a method of depreciation of assets under which the rate of depreciation is applied in one depreciation period to the balance of undepreciated cost at the end of the previous depreciation period. In some jurisdictions an optimal switch to the straight line method is permitted at the appropriate time.

Deductibles a stipulated amount of loss (normally a fixed percentage of the aircraft's worth) which an airline's insurance policy does not cover.

Defeasance the prepayment of financial obligations, through a third party usually, in circumstances where the third party assumes the responsibility to discharge such financial obligations, and the lessor/lender has no recourse to the original obligor therefor (legal defeasance) or retains recourse to the original obligor (economic defeasance).

Deficit Reduction Tax Act introduced in the US in 1984, the Act reduced the tax benefits for property used by tax-exempt entities is generally ineligible for ITC and depreciation benefits are limited to straight line deductions over the longer of 125 per cent of the lease term or the mid-point Asset Depreciation Range in effect in January 1981. However there are certain exceptions pertaining to aircraft financing: (1) for certain widebody aircraft and (2) for property subject to short-term leases.

Deregulation generally refers to the US Deregulation Act of 1978 which introduced the US airline industry to a free-market environment as opposed to a sheltered market where pricing was approved by the authorities and based on costs and where routes were allocated according to a formula (trunk, regional, or commuter). Other notable features of the Act were: (a) the withdrawal of government subsidies to airlines (although the federal guarantee of air service to small communities was maintained) and (b) the elimination of the Civil Aeronautics Board (CAB). The CAB's functions concerning international air transportation, anti-trust agreements, essential air service and postal rates were assigned to other agencies.

Derivatives the latest generation of an airframe or engine family, whose technology is derived from an earlier generation. All modern jet engines are derivative by definition.

Direct financing lease under US accounting rules, a non-leveraged lease by a lessor (not a manufacturer or dealer) where the lease meets the criterion of a capital lease (see above), plus the extra requirement that the collectability of lease payments is reasonably predictable, and that no uncertainties surround the amount of reimbursable costs to be incurred by the lessor under the lease.

Direct investor the lessor in a direct financing lease.

Direct lease same as a direct financing lease.

Discounted cash flow a technique for assessing the present value of future income and payments which takes account of the time value of money.

Double-dipping the structuring of leases to utilise tax benefits in more than one country.

Dry lease a lease of an aircraft which is operated and staffed entirely by the lessee: crew and back-up are not included in the lease package. Most aircraft leases are dry leases.

Dual designator agreement also called code-sharing, an agreement whereby one airline's services are linked in a CRS under the flight prefix of a major airline. Dual designator refers to flights that are listed, for example, under both a major airline's and a regional's flight prefix (some are thus listed twice). However, many such flights are only listed under the major's prefix.

Dual rate of return an internal rate of return measure. An arbitrary reinvestment rate is applied to periods in which cash surpluses arise under the lease. The appropriate pre-tax borrowing rate at which the lease breaks even is then determined by iterative procedures.

Economic life of leased property the estimated remaining period during which the property is expected to be economically usable by one or more users, with normal repairs and maintenance, for the purpose for which it was intended at the inception of the lease.

ECU European Currency Unit.

EGT Engine Gas Temperature.

Ejector suppressor aerodynamic intake that brings in external air and mixes it with exhaust gas.

Enhanced ETC an ETC security that has been enhanced through the addition of collateral and structuring techniques such as a liquidity facility, tranching, and special purpose vehicles providing superior credit protection over a company's unsecured and secured creditors due to the differing payment priorities and asset claims.

EPNdB (Effective Perceived Noise Decibels): noise measurement used by FAA to determine restrictions on engine use.

EPR Engine Pressure Ratio.

ETC or Equipment Trust Certificate securities representing the debt portion of an aircraft financing, usually representing 80 per cent of the acquisition cost of an aircraft. The airline may retain the 20 per cent equity portion of the aircraft through its own funds, as in a secured financing or capital lease or, more commonly, may lease the aircraft from a third party owner participant via a leveraged lease.

Equity participants investors in a lease seeking the tax benefits resulting from ownership as distinct from the debt participants.

ER Extended Range; a version of a model with, inter alia, larger fuel tanks, eg, the Boeing 767-300ER.

EROPS UK terminology for Extended Range Operations for twin-engined aircraft.

ERTA the US Economic Recovery Tax Act, 1981, which introduced the 'safe harbour lease'.

Estimated residual value of leased property the estimated fair value of the property at the end of the lease term.

ETOPS Extended Twin-Engined Overwater Operations, a term used to indicate that an aircraft has been approved by the FAA to operate with two engines over oceans at such a distance that it would take either 120 or 180 minutes to return to land. This approval is granted for a specific aircraft fitted with a specific engine model. ETOPS capability is a valuable feature and would enhance the value of an aircraft in the secondary market. ETOPS certified aircraft are referred to as 'Extended Range' or 'ER' aircraft (eg, Boeing 767-300ER).

EU European Union.

Eurocontrol European Organisation for the Safety of Air Navigation; the centralised European agency established in 1960 pursuant to an international convention relating to the cooperation for the safety of air navigation.

Eurocontrol States parties to the Eurocontrol Convention which currently comprise Belgium, Cyprus, France, Germany, Greece, Ireland, Luxembourg, Malta, Netherlands, Portugal, Turkey and the United Kingdom.

Evergreen renewal option a pre-Reagan Tax Act proposal to help leases of equipment with high residual values (like aircraft) both to be attractive and to remain within the true lease guidelines of the IRS. Each 'renewal' was an alternative to purchasing at fair market value.

Exhaust mixer combines fan and core air in the tailpipe and reduces the velocity of hot core exhaust air.

Exhaust nozzle the rear end of the engine.

F Freighter; an aircraft configured for cargo transportation.

FAA Federal Aviation Administration, the US regulatory body responsible for, inter alia, certifying the airworthiness of US registered aircraft. The FAA also issues ADs.

FADEC Full Authority Digital Electronic Control: fly-by-wire control for engines. The systems give fuel economy, ease of starting, and optimum fuel scheduling.

FAR 36 Federal Aviation Regulations Part 36: regulation setting down Stage III noise limits for commercial aircraft.

FAS13 Statement of Financial Accounting Standards No. 13, Accounting for Leases; issued by the Financial Accounting Standards Board, Stamford, Connecticut, November 1976. Sets forth financial accounting standards on accounting for leases.

FASB Financial Accounting Standards Board.

FFG Fuel Flow Governor.

Finance lease a financing device whereby a user can acquire use of an asset for most of its useful life. Rentals are net to the lessor, and the user is responsible for maintenance, taxes and insurance. Rent payments over the life of the lease are sufficient to enable the lessor to recover the cost of the equipment plus a return on its investment. The reversionary interest in the aircraft vests with the lessee, however, a lessor may in certain circumstances be entitled to recover the aircraft in the event of default under the lease by the lessee. The risks and rewards of operating the aircraft generally remain with the lessee. Distinguished, for accounting purposes, from an operating lease.

Financing Statement in the US, a notice of a security interest filed under the Uniform Commercial Code.

FIR Flight Information Region; these are regions in which countries divide their airspace, eg, in the Netherlands there is one FIR; in the case of France there are five: Paris FIR, Brest FIR, Bordeaux FIR, Marseille FIR and France Upper FIR.

First lien the first security interest against an asset.

First loss deficiency guarantee a type of guarantee normally issued by airframe and aircraft engine manufacturers. This provides that the manufacturer is willing to guarantee up to a limited amount the resale value of the product in the event of the borrower's default.

Five freedoms of the air (1) the right to fly over the territory of a foreign nation without landing; (2) the right to land on the territory of a foreign nation for non-traffic purposes (ie, refuelling, emergency repairs); (3) the right to put down in a foreign country passengers, mail and cargo taken on in the state whose nationality the aircraft possesses; (4) the right to take on passengers, mail and cargo in a foreign country for the state whose nationality the aircraft possesses; and (5) the right to put down or take on, in a foreign country, passengers, mail and cargo from (or for) the territory of a foreign country.

Fixed price purchase option a purchase option where the price which the lessee would have to pay to become the equipment owner on lease termination is established at the start of the lease, and may be nominal.

Flight hour a single hour in flight.

Floating rate rental rental which is subject to upward or downward adjustments during the lease term, by reference to floating interest rates (eg, Libor).

Floating to drawdown in the UK, when leases have been negotiated some time before the primary period begins, the rate may be fixed according to a formula which allows for changes in funding cost occurring before the drawdown. Thereafter, rates remain fixed for the life of the lease.

FMV Fair Market Value.

Forward sale selling an aircraft or other asset for a fixed price with delivery at an agreed future date.

Fuel burn the fuel consumption - depends upon engine efficiency, weight, pilot handling, and wind-speed.

Fuel transference balance control system for transferring fuel to the engines from tanks, usually located in the wings.

Full payout lease see Finance lease.

GIE Groupement d'Intérêt Economique: a French corporate entity which is a grouping of mutual economic interests, transparent for tax purposes, commonly used for syndicated tax based lease transactions.

Grantor trust a trust used as the owner trust in US leveraged lease transactions, usually with only one equity participant. The Internal Revenue Code refers to such a trust as a grantor trust.

Grossing up the requirement to increase payments under leases which are subject to deduction of tax at source so that the net amount received by the payee is equal to the amount expressed to be payable.

Half Life a component is in half life condition when it is exactly mid-way between scheduled overhaul/replacement.

Hell-or-high-water clause a clause in a lease which states the unconditional obligation of the lessee to pay rent for the entire term of the lease, regardless of any event affecting the equipment or any change in the circumstances of the lessee.

Hire purchase agreement English terminology for a lease with a purchase option.

HP high pressure (for turbines).

HSI hot section inspection of an engine.

HSR hot section refurbishment of an engine.

Hub-and-spoke a synchronised wave of arrivals followed by a wave of departures from a 'hub' airport. This maximises the number of one-stop connecting flights between 'spoke' cities.

Hushkit noise-reduction system that deadens the engine by enclosing it in insulating material, so that it becomes Stage 3 qualified.

IAS 17 the international accounting standard on treatment of leases, published by the International Accounting Standards Committee in 1982. The standard is not binding on individual lease transactions but is expected to serve as a model for mandatory rules adopted by national organisations in future.

IATA International Air Transport Association; economic association of commercial airlines offering scheduled air services.

ICAO International Civil Aviation Organisation; a specialised agency of the UN with responsibility for the development of a standardised system for such matters as air navigation, licensing, safety and landing procedures. It also has an advisory capacity in economic affairs.

IFR Instrument Flight Rules.

Indemnity a provision whereby a lessee or other person holds the lessor or another person harmless against any cost or loss arising by reason of the occurrence of certain events or circumstances, eg, the non-achievement of the desired tax treatment of the transaction.

Indenture Trust an agreement between the owner trustee and the indenture trustee whereby the owner trustee mortgages the equipment and assigns the lease and rental payments under the lease as security for amounts due to the lenders. The same as a security agreement or mortgage.

Indenture trustee in a US leveraged lease, the indenture trustee holds the security interest in the leased equipment for the benefit of the lenders. In the event of a default, the indenture trustee exercises the rights of a mortgagee. The indenture trustee also is responsible for receiving rent payments from the lessee and using such funds to pay the amounts due the lenders, with the balance being paid to the owner trustee.

Inlet inlet guide vanes in an engine.

Institutional investors investors such as banks, insurance companies, trusts, pension funds, foundations, and educational, charitable and religious institutions.

Insured value the agreed value of equipment for insurance purposes at various times during the term of the financing.

Interest rate implicit in a lease the discount rate which, when applied to minimum lease payments, causes the aggregate present value of such lease payments to equal the cost of the leased property at the inception of the lease.

Interest rate swap technique of trading interest risks with a counterparty (or a bank acting as intermediary between two counterparties).

Interim rent daily rental accruing from delivery, acceptance and/or funding until a later date for a basic lease term. Often used when equipment delivers over a period of time.

Internal rate of return investment appraisal method which establishes the discount rate which would be necessary to make present and future costs and returns balance out, using discounted cash-flow techniques.

Investment period method a lessor accounting method in the UK which apportions profit earned on a lease to those periods where lessor has an after tax net cash investment in the lease.

IP intermediate pressure (for compressors).

ITC investment tax credit.

JAA Europe's Joint Aviation Administration.

Japanese leveraged lease a technique which came to maturity in 1986 and has been used primarily for the cross-border financing of large commercial aircraft. In a Japanese leveraged lease, a pool of investors provides equity for the lease and non-recourse debt is provided by financial institutions.

LATCC London Air Traffic Control Centre.

LDC lesser developed country.

Lease a contract between a lessor and lessee for the hire of a specific asset. The ownership of the asset is retained by the lessor but the right to the use of the asset is given to the lessee for an agreed period of time in return for a series of rentals paid by the lessee to the lessor.

Lease line a lease line of credit similar to a bank line of credit which allows a lessee to add equipment, as needed, under the same basic terms and conditions without negotiating a new lease contract.

Lease rate the equivalent simple annual interest rate implicit in minimum lease rentals. Not necessarily the same as the interest rate implicit in a lease.

Lease term the fixed term of the lease. Includes, for accounting purposes, all periods covered by fixed rate renewal options which for economic reasons appear likely to be exercised at the inception of the lease.

Lease underwriting an agreement whereby a packager or bank commits to enter into a lease on certain terms and assumes the risk of arranging any financing.

Lessee the user of the equipment being leased.

Lessee's incremental borrowing rate the interest rate which the lessee, at the inception of the lease, would have incurred to borrow over a similar term the funds necessary to purchase the leased assets. In a leveraged lease the rate on the bonds is normally used.

Lessor the owner of the equipment which is being leased to a lessee or user. The equity investor, also referred to as the owner participant. The lessor is the entity in a leveraged lease transaction who takes the depreciation expense.

Level payments equal payments over the term of the lease.

Leverage an amount borrowed. In a leveraged lease, the debt portion of the funds used to purchase the asset represents leverage to the equity holder.

Leveraged lease a long term lease for an aircraft involving three parties (a lessee, a lessor, and a long-term creditor) in which the lessor borrows most of the funds needed to acquire the asset financed from a third party. The lessor, which is both the equity participant and borrower, puts up the balance of the cost and acquires the asset. The financing is generally without recourse to the lessor. In return for the loan, the lessor gives the lender a mortgage in the asset and assigns the lease and lease payments. As owner of the asset, the lessor is entitled to tax deductions for depreciation on the asset and interest on the loan.

LIBOR London Interbank Offered Rate.

Lien the right to keep possession of another person's property until a debt owed in respect of it is paid (a possessory lien). Alternatively used to mean any form of security interest.

Life limited a component is life-limited if the manufacturer recommends that it be replaced after a specified number of hours use.

Limited partnership constituting a general partner and numerous limited partners, this instrument is frequently utilised to enable individuals to invest collectively in lease transactions. The general partner, usually a leasing company, will manage the investment which is put up by the individual or limited partners.

Limited use property plant or equipment which would not have any identifiable market value because of its specialised purpose for the lessee. Ineligible for depreciation benefits in some jurisdictions.

Liquidity Facility in securitisations, ETC's and other highly structured financings, a dedicated source of liquidity sufficient to cover, say, three interest payments (one and a half years) in the event of default. This facility is typically provided by an A1/P1 entity. The rating agencies require an 18 month source of liquidity, as this is the length of time the agencies consider it will take to effectively market and resell an aircraft in order to maximise value. Most Enhanced ETC transactions have no liquidity facility on the lowest rated tranche, and therefore do not garner the 'enhanced' qualification for that tranche.

Load Factor Calculated by dividing ASM into RPM; broadly speaking this represents the proportion of aircraft seating capacity sold.

Loan certificates debt certificates or bonds issued to lenders.

Loan participant a lender in a leveraged lease; a holder of debt in a leveraged lease evidenced by loan certificates or bonds issued by the owner trustee.

Loan to Value Ratio (LTV) the ratio reflecting the percentage of an aircraft's appraised market value that the loan represents. The inverse of LTV is the collateral coverage ratio, or number of times that an aircraft's market value covers the loan. For example, an LTV of 40 per cent implies a loan coverage ratio of 2.5 times. This number is valuable as a security measure, especially in light of US Section 1110 protection that allows Enhanced ETC holders to take possession an aircraft in a default event. The effect on LTV of a theoretical reduction in underlying aircraft value can be analysed.

Long-range those aircraft capable of operating unrestricted over water and on flights of over 2,000 statute miles (or over 3,200 km).

LP low pressure (for turbines).

Master lease a lease line of credit which allows a lessee to add equipment under the same basic terms and conditions without negotiating a new lease contract.

Medium-range applies to those aircraft operating on ranges between 1,000 and 2,000 statute miles (or 1,600-3,200 km) or used on routes with block times of two to four hours.

MEW Operating Empty Weight.

Minimum lease payments all payments which the lessee is obliged to make or can be required to make in connection with leased property, including residual value guaranteed the lessor and bargain renewal rents or purchase options, but excluding guarantees of lessor's debt (seldom encountered) and executory costs such as insurance, maintenance and taxes.

MLW Maximum Landing Weight.

MTGW Maximum Taxi Gross Weight.

MTOGW Maximum Take Off Gross Weight.

MTOW Maximum Take-off Weight.

MZFW Maximum Zero Fuel Weight.

Narrowbody a jet aircraft with a single aisle and five or six abreast seating.

Nacelles the cladding round an aircraft engine.

Net lease in a net lease, the rentals are payable net to the lessor. All costs in connection with the use of the equipment are to be paid by the lessee and are not a part of the rental. For example, taxes, insurance and maintenance are paid directly by the lessee. Most aircraft leases are net leases.

Net present value the discounted value of a future rental stream, allowing for the time value of money. Also, investment appraisal method taking the opposite approach to internal rate of return. This method starts by choosing an appropriate discount rate, uses the discount to apply to future payments and income, and compares this with the present cost for each alternative form of finance.

NMI Nautical Miles.

Noise footprint pattern of noise emissions of an engine/airframe combination.

Noise regulations under the US Airport Noise and Capacity Act, 1990, no Stage 2 aircraft may operate to or from any US airport after 1999.

Non-recourse finance debt funding where the creditor's rights, either expressly or in practice, do not extend to all of the borrower's assets; or those assets comprise only the relevant equipment.

Novation the substitution of one party for another in a contract. Where the lessee has already placed an order for the equipment when the leasing facility is agreed, the lessor may acquire title by having the existing contractual arrangement cancelled and replaced by new arrangements between the lessor and the supplier. The lessee is thereby released from the obligation to pay the supplier.

Off-shore registration the registration of an aircraft without requiring that the aircraft or operator have any formal connection with the country of registry.

Oil price swap a technique which, acting in similar fashion to an interest rate swap, aims to provide a long-term cash-flow stability for oil producers and volume consumers, such as airlines. The producer and consumer act as counterparties in the swap, probably with an investment bank arranging the swap and mediating difference settlements.

Open-ended lease a lease which contains a provision for the extension of the lease on predetermined terms after the end of the fixed period.

Operating lease for financial accounting purposes, a lease which does not meet the criteria of a capital lease or finance lease, so is off the lessee's balance sheet. Also used generally to describe a short-term lease whereby a user can acquire use of an asset for a fraction of the useful life of the asset, and where the lessor does not recover its full investment. The reversionary interest in the aircraft vests with the lessor, ie, at the end of the lease, the aircraft will be returned to the lessor. Otherwise, the risks and rewards of operating the aircraft generally pass to the lessee. Operating leases are typically arranged by aircraft manufacturers or specialist lessors who are obliged to take back the aircraft at the end of the lease term. Operating leases provide airlines with enhanced flexibility but are usually more expensive than alternatives.

Option finance a financing structure which, in the case of an aircraft transaction, allows an airline either to return an aircraft at a certain date or dates without penalty or to continue with the aircraft for the remainder of its useful life, thus providing operating lease balance sheet treatment with the option of a finance lease.

Owner trustee the entity acting as trustee for the owner/equity participants in a transaction.

Participation agreement an agreement between the owner trustee, the lenders, the equity participants and the lessee which specifies the obligations of the parties and procedures for closing a transaction; typically found in US leveraged leases.

Pass Through Certificate securities representing ownership of two or more ETCs, created by pooling or bundling ETC's, in which payment of principal and interest payments on the ETC's are passed through to the Pass Through Certificate holders via a trust structure. The Pass Through structure is created as a means of diversifying the aircraft pool and/or increasing the size of the total offering.

Peppercorn rental the nominal rental paid during the secondary period of a lease.

Performance usually measured in terms of fuel burn and MTOGW.

PNdB Perceived Noise Decibel; a unit a noise that takes account of the discomfort caused by sounds at certain frequencies.

Pooling an arrangement between airlines, and sometimes with manufacturers, under which engines and parts can be swapped, either on a title retention or a title exchange basis.

Present value the current equivalent value of cash available immediately for a future payment or a stream of payments to be received at various times in the future. The present value will vary with the discount (interest) factor applied to the future payments.

PRI Political risks insurance.

Primary period the period, in a finance lease, during which the lessor expects to recover the full capital cost of the asset, his money costs and his profit. However, sometimes used simply to distinguish the agreed loan terms from the renewals.

Purchase option an option to purchase leased property at the end of the lease term.

Put an option for one person to sell an asset to another person, usually at a set price at some established point in time in the future. In lease agreements, a lessor sometimes negotiates an option to sell leased equipment to the lessee or to some third party at an established price at the end of the lease term.

Re-engining replacement of an aircraft's engines to prolong its working life. First developed by CFM in the 1970s for DC-8s, but commercially dominated by Rolls-Royce.

Rear-end loading the practice of constructing a rental schedule where the larger payments are made towards the end of the lease.

Reinvestment rate the interest rate a lessor earns on lease cash surpluses during the period following the investment period of a lease.

Related parties in leasing transactions under FAS 13, a parent and its subsidiaries, an owner and its joint ventures, an investor and its investees, provided the parent, owner, or investor has the ability to exercise significant influence over the financial and operating policies of the related party. Under the Internal Revenue Code, 50 per cent. of ownership is a general test for a related party.

Renewal option an option to renew the lease at the end of the initial lease term.

Rental rebate a refund of rentals to a lessee commonly found in UK finance leases where it is used to pass back the residual to a lessee by reference to the proceeds of the sale of the leased asset at the end of a lease.

Residual or residual value the value of equipment at the conclusion of the lease term.

Residual sharing an agreement between the lessor and another party providing for a division of the residual value between them.

Residual value insurance a policy that insures a specific value on a specific piece of equipment, at some specified future date. If the equipment was sold for a lower price than that stipulated on the policy at the future date, the insurer would pay the difference. Also known as asset value insurance or equipment value insurance.

Retrofitting generic term for hushkitting, re-engining or any type of upgrading.

Return on investment the yield. The interest rate earned by the lessor in a lease which is measured by the rate at which excess cash flows permit recovery of investment. The rate at which the cash flows not needed for debt service or payment of taxes amortise the investment of the equity participant.

Revenue procedures commonly used in US leasing to refer to the IRS Revenue Procedures 75-21 and 75-28, which set forth requirements for obtaining a favourable revenue ruling on a leveraged lease.

Route Charge States Countries which use Eurocontrol to administer en route flight charges and which currently comprise the Eurocontrol States, Austria, Spain and Switzerland.

RPK revenue passenger-kilometres; equals the number of revenue passengers carried on a flight stage multiplied by the flight stage distance.

RPM Revenue Seat Miles. Total seats sold by a carrier multiplied by the average revenue received for each seat flown. See also ASM and Load Factor.

RTK revenue tonne-kilometres performed; number of tonnes of revenue load carried on each flight stage multiplied by the flight stage distance.

Safe harbour provisions the provisions in the US Economic Recovery Tax Act (1981) defining the basic criteria under which a financing transaction could meet the definition of a lease for tax purposes. The rules represented a considerable liberalisation of former IRS guidelines on true leases, and allowed pure tax benefit transfers.

Sale-leaseback a transaction which involves the sale of property by the owner and a lease of the property back to the seller.

Salvage value the minimum value for a depreciable asset. After sufficient depreciation is taken, such that cost less accumulated depreciation equals salvage value, no more depreciation may be taken. Not the same as residual value.

Samurai lease jargon for Japanese-source dollar-denominated leases designed to fund foreign assets intended to reduce the Japanese balance of payments.

SB Service Bulletin.

Secondary period the period in a finance lease which follows the full pay-out of the lessor's investment plus profit or, alternatively, the period following the committed primary period.

Section 1110 of the US Bankruptcy Code. Section 1110 generally allows lenders under certain circumstances to repossess aircraft from a bankrupt airline. 1110 is a right of protection granted to a secured party with a security interest in an aircraft or of a lessor or conditional vendor of such equipment to take possession of such equipment from an airline operating under bankruptcy court protection within 60 days after such filing unless the airline cures all defaults and agrees to continue to perform under such security agreement, lease, or conditional sale contract. The code was amended on October 22, 1994 in order to strengthen the rights of the creditors by more clearly defining the terms of Section 1110.

Section 41 Reference to the front section of, for instance a Boeing 747, of which the cockpit forms part.

Security agreement in a US leveraged lease an agreement between the owner trustee and the indenture trustee whereby the owner trustee and the indenture trustee assign title to the equipment, the lease, and rental payments under the lease as security for amounts due the lenders. The same as an indenture trust.

Shogun lease yen-denominated lease introduced in 1981 to take advantage of interest differentials between Japan and advanced Western countries. In contrast to Samurai leases, the Shogun lease was not subsidised by the government but promoted by Japanese leasing companies using funds on a commercial basis.

Short-haul applies to those aircraft operating on routes up to 1,000 statute miles (about 1,600 km) or used on routes with block times less than two hours.

Short-term lease generally refers to an operating lease.

Single investor lease a lease structure that only involves a lessor and a lessee. The lessor provides all the capital necessary to purchase an asset from its own funds.

Sinking fund a reserve or a sinking fund established or set aside for the purpose of payment due at a later date. (Generally applicable in lessor cash flows for leveraged leases.)

Sinking rate fund the rate of interest allocated to a sinking fund set aside for future repayment of taxes. (Generally applicable in lessor cash flows for leveraged leases).

SR Short Range; a short range version of an aircraft, eg, Boeing 747-300SR.

SSAP 21 the UK Accounting Standard, 'Accounting for leases and hire-purchase transactions', issued by the Accounting Standards Committee. Under the standard, finance leases should be capitalised by the lessee. It has detailed provisions for lessor accounting. It now has to be interpreted in conjunction with FRS5.

Stage 3 the regulations that stipulate maximum noise levels for aircraft. The Stage 3 regulations stipulate that an airline's fleet must be:

- 55 per cent Stage 3 by the end of 1994;
- 65 per cent Stage 3 by the end of 1996;
- 75 per cent Stage 3 by the end of 1998;
- 100 per cent Stage 3 by the end of 1999;

or, if an airline is phasing out Stage 2 aircraft, its fleet must be:

- no more than 75 per cent Stage 2 by the end of 1994;
- no more than 50 per cent Stage 2 by the end of 1996;
- no more than 25 per cent Stage 2 by the end of 1998.

In order for an aircraft to be financed by an Enhanced ETC, it must be Stage 3.

STC Supplementary Type Certificate - issued by authorities for engine use.

Stepped rentals rental payments which vary from one another in a structured lease. Usually done for specific cash-flow and/or tax reasons.

Stipulated loss value (SLV) the sum payable on an early termination of a lease, for default, voluntary termination and, typically, on a total loss.

Stolport short take-off and landing airport.

Straight-line method an accounting method for depreciating assets which spreads the depreciation equally over the estimated useful life of the asset.

Stretched aircraft are typically 'stretched' once prototypes and initial versions are shown to offer performance beyond the design parameters, or are improved. A stretched aircraft typically offers substantial economies of scale.

Strip debt debt in connection with a leveraged lease, arranged in tiers with different maturities and amortisation to improve the lessor's cash flow and reduce the lessee's costs.

Strip guarantee a term which has evolved in the context of Japanese leveraged leases, normally used to mean a guarantee of a limited portion of a termination sum on an early termination of the lease.

Sub-lease a transaction in which leased property is leased by the original lessee to a third party, where the lease agreement between the two original parties remains in effect.

SUD stretched-upper-deck; refers to the Boeing 747-300.

Sum of the digits method an accounting method for depreciating assets providing for the largest depreciation to be taken at the beginning of the asset's life, and the smallest depreciation to be taken in the later years.

Tax indemnity clause clause in a tax-based lease providing for increases in rentals in the event of circumstances which adversely affect the lessor's ability to claim the anticipated tax benefits on the equipment or interest deductions.

Tax variation clause a clause in tax-based lease agreements in the UK which allows the lessor to vary the rentals if either the rate of tax or the tax basis changes.

Tax written down value the value of an asset after deducting the total depreciation allowances claimed from the cost of the asset.

TGT Turbine Gas Temperature.

Thrust reverser system the engine's brakes - uses thrust to decelerate. May be bucket type, in which the 'bucket' deflects thrust upwards or downwards as opposed to backwards, or cascade type, in which thrust is deflected in several directions at once.

Thrust division of engines according to thrust broadly follows the following lines: up to 18,000lbs thrust, executive jets; 19-35,000lbs thrust, short-medium range airliner; over 35,000lbs thrust, medium-long range airliner.

Title exchange a principle which means that if an aircraft engine or part substitution takes place the owner/financier will acquire title to the substituted engine while it is on his airframe.

Title preservation a principle which means that if an aircraft engine or part is removed it will remain subject to the original owner's ownership (and any financier's security), regardless of its location.

TOGW Take Off Gross Weight.

Total loss the actual or agreed total loss of an aircraft or circumstances such that it is lost, destroyed, damaged beyond repair or rendered permanently unfit for use.

Transition rules refers to provisions in the US Deficit Reduction Act of 1986 under which large commercial aircraft ordered before 31 December 1985 and delivered before 1 January 1989 are eligible for investment tax credit and ACRS allowances. However, the amount of ITC which can be offset against tax is gradually reduced in the interim period. The transition rules also provide for a gradual reduction in corporate tax levels from 46 per cent. to 34 per cent. through the interim period.

True lease a true lease in the US is a transaction which qualifies as a lease under the Internal Revenue Code so the lessee can claim rental payments as tax deductions and the lessor can claim tax benefits of ownership such as depreciation and ITC.

Trust certificate document evidencing the beneficial ownership of a trust estate of an equity participant (or owner participant, trust or owner or grantor owner) in an owner trust

Turbofan the modern jet engine - an unducted jet.

UHB Ultra high bypass engine, also known as propfan.

Unguaranteed residual value the portion of residual value 'at risk' for a lessor in his yield computation, ie, for which there is no party obligated to pay.

Uprating usually denotes increase in engine thrust capacity.

Useful life the period of time during which an asset will have economic value and be usable. Useful life of an asset is sometimes called the economic life of the asset.

Walkaway lease a lease permitting the lessee to walk away, ie, terminate the lease and hand back the aircraft, at agreed times on notice without cost.

Wet Lease a lease, typically between two airlines, under which the aircraft is crewed by the lessor. The classic wet lease is known as 'ACMI' which stands for Aircraft, Crew, Maintenance and Insurance, with the lessor providing all four.

Whitetail an unsold aircraft: 'whitetail' refers to the absence of an airline's livery on the tail plane.

Wide Chord Fan offers greater thrust for a given fan diameter.

Withholding tax this may be payable on the rentals received from cross-border leases or interest payable, usually depending on the double taxation arrangements between the countries involved.

Writing down allowance a depreciation allowance in the UK where each year's allowance is based on a percentage of the written-down value at the end of the previous year.

Yield the interest rate earned by the lessor or equity participant in a lease, which is measured by the rate at which the excess cash flows permit recovery of investment.

Authors' biographies

Dr Ken Holden is a Fellow of the Royal Aeronautical Society. At Aer Lingus he was responsible for planning the introduction of the B747. He has been involved in the aircraft leasing and finance business since the mid-1980s, first with GPA Group plc as Chief Strategist and then with General Electric Capital Aviation Services (GECAS) as Senior Vice President, Business Development and Strategy.

Van DuBose has responsibility for Goldman Sachs' transportation sector practice in Europe.

Stephen Gee, Director of Syndications, Greenwich NatWest, has over 15 years experience in structured and limited recourse financing and currently has responsibility for the placement and distribution of all such transactions at Greenwich. He was a leading member of the team that won *Project Finance International's* 'Arranger of the Year' award for 1996.

Stephan Sayre is Head of Global Transportation Group, Structured Finance at Greenwich NatWest responsible both for the firm's strategy to the sector and for a team of professionals located in London, New York, Hong Kong and Tokyo. He has been responsible for and involved in numerous equity, debt, advisory and structured financing assignments for Airlines and Manufacturers throughout the world.

Robert Murphy was educated at Trinity College and University College Dublin. He is a qualified Irish and English solicitor and joined Freshfields in 1993 having worked with GPA from 1989 to 1993 as director of Legal Training. He is a partner in Freshfields' Asset Finance Group.

Colm Barrington is a partner with Babcock & Brown in Dublin, from where he specialises in the arrangement and management of aircraft operating lease transactions. Prior to joining Babcock & Brown, he was president of GE Capital Aviation Services Limited and was Chief Operating Officer of GPA Group plc. He was the founder and Chief Executive of GPA Capital.

Arthur J Bernstein is the founder of AMBER International (Boca Raton, Florida) which provides corporate finance transaction advice to its clients. He has negotiated tax-based aerospace financings aggregating more than three billion dollars, holds a BA in Economics and Mathematics from Cornell University and an MBA in Finance from the University of Rochester Graduate School of Management.

James V Babcock is President of Babcock & Brown. Founded in 1977, it operates in domestic and crossborder finance and operating leasing (leveraged and non-leveraged), project finance and tax-advantaged equity and product design execution through 15 offices worldwide. Mr Babcock is a graduate of Harvard College and Harvard Law School, where he was an officer of the law review. He sits on the Committee on University Resources for Harvard University and the Dean's Advisory Council for Harvard Law School.

Mark Bewsher has headed the financial analysis and systems development group at Babcock & Brown since its inception in 1977. He has degrees in physics, mathematics and engineering from the University of Tasmania, Australia, and Balliol College, Oxford.

Chris Boobyer is director of Structured Leasing & European Operations for Barclays Mercantile Business Finance. He has specialised in big ticket leasing since 1988 and has been responsible for international leasing activities since January 1998. He is a regular chairman and speaker at conferences on leasing, accounting and taxation, and a member of various committees and working parties. He is editor and co-author of *Leasing Finance 3rd edition*, published by Euromoney Books.

Simon A D Hall joined Freshfields, London in February 1977. In 1983 he was seconded to the Wall Street law firm of Cravath, Swaine & Moore and in autumn 1984 joined Freshfields New York office. He returned to the London office in September 1985. He is now head of Freshfields' Finance Department. He is a co-author of *Leasing Finance 3rd edition*, published by Euromoney Books.

Paul Ibbotson joined the London-based Project Finance advisory team at Babcock & Brown in 1992. From 1993 to 1997 he was General Manager of Nomura Babcock & Brown in Tokyo, where he concentrated on cross-border Japanese Leveraged Leases and operating leases. Prior to 1992 he worked for Freshfields where he specialised in banking and asset-based and project financing.

Ian F Reid is a managing director of Chase Manhattan Asia Limited in their Hong Kong-based Global Aerospace Group covering the Asia Pacific region. He joined Chase in 1983 and in 1990 he moved to Hong Kong as a principal with the Transportation Group before rejoining Chase in Hong Kong. He now covers Asian airlines from an overall banking perspective.

Stephen McGairl is a partner of Freshfields with over 20 years experience of international aircraft transactions. He has worked in the London, Paris and Moscow offices of the firm. He is a member of the Study Group of Unidroit which has developed the draft Convention on International Interests in Mobile Equipment.

Richard Bouma is Executive Director at HSBC Equator Bank plc. He has 19 years experience working in sub-Saharan Africa He has held a number of positions since joining Equator, initially being responsible for the bank's West Africa Region. In 1994 he established Equator's Johannesburg office which is now the base for a major component of the bank's investment banking team.

Philip A Baggaley analyses airlines and aircraft leasing companies, and manages Standard & Poor's transportation, aerospace and defence rating team. He joined the company in 1985, took over direction of the transportation group in 1990, and of defence ratings in 1993. He has a PhD in History and a BA in History and International Relations.

Klaus Heinemann has global management responsibility for The Long-Term Credit Bank of Japan's Aviation and Shipping Department. Concurrent with his management functions there, he is an executive director of Persson & Partners, the Aviation Corporate Finance Advisory firm. He holds appointments as advisor and lecturer on Aviation Industry matters with the Department of Trade and Industry (UK), IATA and Unidroit.

Edward Hansom is General Manager, Treasury of GPA Group plc which he joined in 1988 from Schroders. Prior to taking up his current position in 1994, he was General Manager of GPA Capital, working on sales of aircraft on lease to Asian investors and the ALPS92-1 portfolio aircraft sale. He is a graduate of Magdalen College, Oxford and Manchester Business School.

Colin Thaine is head partner of the aviation group at Wilde Sapte. He has worked with the airline industry for 24 years and has been involved in tax-driven cross-border structured financings and a variety of operating lease transactions coupled with manufacturer support. He is a former chairman of the Aeronautical Committee of the Business Section of the International Bar Association and an Associate of the Royal Aeronautical Society.

Andrew Littlejohns is a partner in Freshfields' Asset Finance Group in London. He joined Freshfields in 1983, and has specialised since then in aircraft finance. He became a partner in 1987.

Peter Viccars has been involved in the insurance industry for over 30 years, specialising since 1970 in aviation matters and, particularly, insurance considerations of contracts and agreements. He is Chairman of Lloyds Insurance Brokers Aviation Technical Sub Committee. In 1997 he was elected a fellow of the Royal Aeronautical Society.

David Maule is a director at Investment Insurance International, which he first joined in 1977. Between 1979 and 1990 he worked as a political risk broker in France and Germany before returning to III. He now has principal responsibility for business emanating from France, Germany, Scandinavia and South Africa and lectures frequently on political risk insurance.

Neil Lewis qualified as a solicitor in Scotland in 1987 and in England in 1992. He joined Freshfields Finance Department in London in 1990 specialising in aircraft finance and aviation regulation and has advised manufacturers, airlines, arrangers and lenders. Neil is currently on secondment to Nomura Babcock & Brown in Tokyo.